CONCEPTS AND CHALLENGES IN
Life Science

Annotated Teacher's Edition
Revised Third Edition

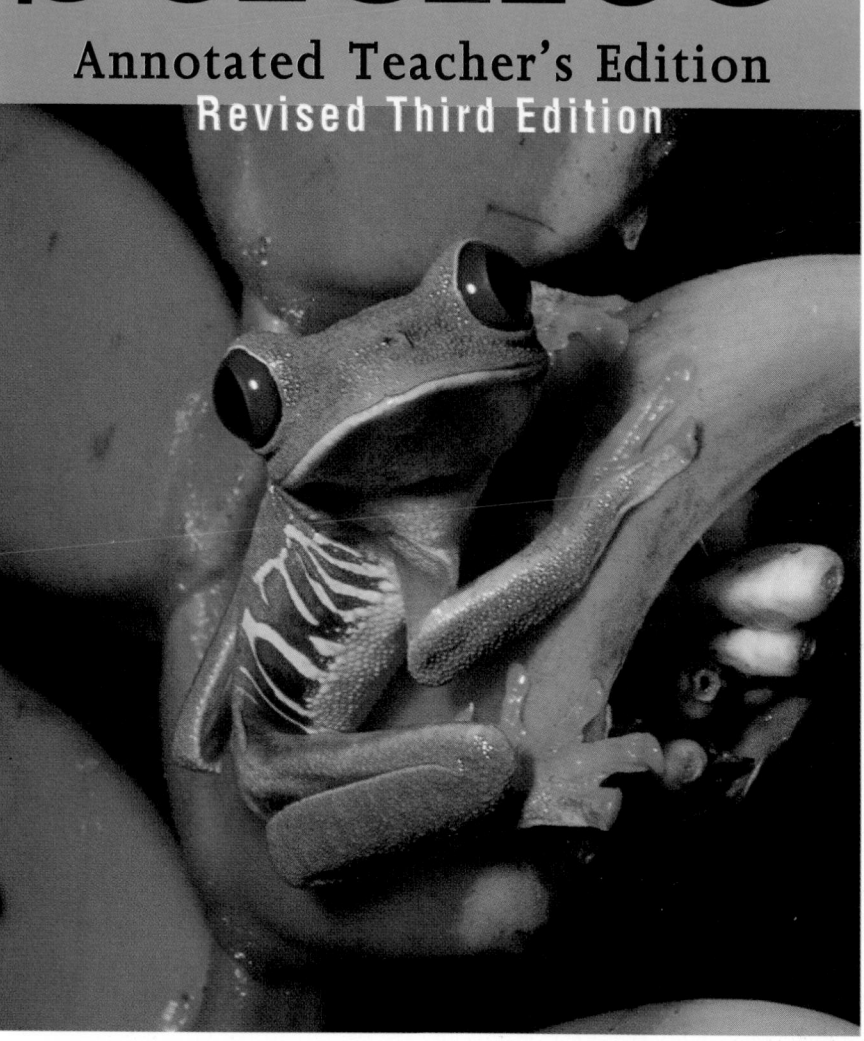

Leonard Bernstein • Martin Schachter • Alan Winkler • Stanley Wolfe

STANLEY WOLFE
Project Coordinator

 Globe Fearon Educational Publisher
A Division of Simon & Schuster
Upper Saddle River, New Jersey

AUTHORS

Leonard Bernstein

Martin Schachter

Alan Winkler

Stanley Wolfe
Project Coordinator

TEACHING THE COVER

Background: Avocado leaf *(Eduardo Garcia, FPG)*
The leaf is a food-making factory. Leaf structure is adapted for transportation of raw materials needed for and products produced by photosynthesis. A network of veins in the leaf surface conduct the exchange of oxygen and carbon dioxide with the surrounding air. Cells in the leaf interior are loaded with chloroplasts. The chloroplasts contain the pigment chlorophyll, which imparts the green color to the leaf. To help your students learn more about leaves, see pages 150–153. For more information, visit this web site on the internet:
http://www.mbgnet.mobot.org/MBGnet

Inset: Red-eyed tree frog *(G. Bradley and J. Ireland)*
This nocturnal amphibian lives in trees in moist tropical forests of Central and South America. The tips of its toes are enlarged to form adhesive pads, which help it climb on and cling to the moist surfaces of leaves and twigs. To help your students learn more about amphibians, see page 198. For information about this frog, visit this web site on the internet:
http://eagle.online.discovery.com/DCO/doc/1012/world/nature/ frog/treefrogs1.html

Printed in the United States of America
   2 3 4 5 6 7 8 9 10   01 00 99 98

ISBN 0-835-92244-8

Globe Fearon Educational Publisher
A Division of Simon & Schuster
Upper Saddle River, New Jersey

Contents

CONCEPTS AND CHALLENGES IN LIFE SCIENCE PROGRAM

Student's Edition

Annotated Teacher's Edition

Teacher's Resource Book including

Lesson Review Worksheets

TechTerm Review Worksheets

Enrichment Worksheets

Evaluation Package

Foreign Language Supplement—Spanish

Laboratory Program, Student Edition

Laboratory Program, Annotated Teacher's Edition

CONCEPTS AND CHALLENGES

In Life, Earth, and Physical Science

Revised Third Edition

As we move into the 21st century, educators agree that teaching science successfully requires special tools. The essentials include a strategy for teaching that maximizes the potential for learning success and maintains a high level of interest and motivation in the classroom.

Concepts and Challenges in Life, Earth, and Physical Science translates this strategy into a practical teaching and learning tool. Students often wonder how science relates to their daily lives. *Concepts and Challenges* addresses this issue by emphasizing everyday experiences to show students that science is all around them.

Over the past decade, almost one million *Concepts and Challenges* textbooks have been used in classrooms throughout the nation. The Revised Third Edition continues to maximize your students' potential for learning success. Experience *Concepts and Challenges* and help your students relate to science while they develop their problem-solving skills, expand their vocabulary, and strengthen their critical-thinking skills.

A wealth of resources to introduce your students to a wide range of science topics.

Life Science

Covering a broad spectrum of topics, this text provides a fascinating introduction to the myriad life forms that inhabit our world. Students will also learn about the many variables that affect life: The diseases that afflict different organisms... the effect of ecology on plants and animals... how various life forms adapt to changes.

Unit Topics: Scientific Methods and Skills • Needs of Living Things • Ecology • Cells, Tissues and Organs • Classification • Simple Organisms • Plants • Plant Structure and Function • Animals Without Backbones • Animals With Backbones • Nutrition and Digestion • Support and Movement • Transport • Respiration and Excretion • Regulation and Behavior • Health and Disease • Reproduction and Development • Heredity and Genetics • Change Through Time

Earth Science

From our own world to the outer reaches of space, the text teaches all about the earth, and also explores other heavenly bodies of the universe. Students will gain insights into the various characteristics that make the earth unique in the solar system, and learn how the objects and phenomena of the universe that they study affect the way we live on our planet.

Unit Topics: Scientific Skills and Methods • Studying the Earth • Minerals • Rocks and How They Form • Wearing Down the Earth • Agents of Erosion • Building up the Earth • Plate Tectonics • The Rock Record • The Hydrosphere • The Atmosphere • Weather • Climate • Natural Resources • Exploring Space • The Solar System • Motions of the Earth • Stars

Physical Science

The principles, theories, and assumptions that guide our understanding of the world and universe are explored in this text. Physics, chemistry, and mathematics are just some of the major topics that help students comprehend the processes that shape every aspect of the universe. They'll learn what causes reflections in a mirror... the nature of matter... how machines work... and more.

Unit Topics: Scientific Methods and Skills • Force • Energy and Work • Motion • Machines • Heat • Waves • Sound • Light • Electricity • Magnetism • Matter • Density • Atoms • Compounds and Mixtures • Chemical Formulas • Chemical Reactions • Metals • Solutions • Suspensions • Acids, Bases, and Salts

THE STUDENT EDITION

*T*his, the Revised Third Edition of a time-tested classroom favorite, continues the features that have made the *Concepts and Challenges in Science* approach to science instruction successful.

The key to the *Concepts and Challenges* approach is student books designed to help students who are reading below grade level to grasp science concepts. Manageable two-page lessons present each topic with a "concept" and a "challenge." The concept, on the left-hand page, is presented in short, manageable paragraphs. The challenge, on the right-hand page, measures understanding with comprehension checks, applications, and engaging activities.

Other features include:

- Learning objectives to define the goal of the lesson
- TechTerms vocabulary to enhance understanding of scientific terminology
- Gradual introduction of new concepts to build understanding
- Frequent questions to reinforce understanding
- Engaging activities to develop interdisciplinary, critical-thinking, problem-solving, and collaborative-learning skills
- Colorful illustrations and photographs to bring concepts to life
- Unit Reviews to provide additional avenues for assessment and application

The real-world emphasis of this program helps students connect content to their daily life as they learn about scientists, science careers, and the practical applications of science.

6-4 What are algae?

Flagellum
Eyespot
Vacuole
Chloroplast with chlorophyll
Nucleus

Objective ▶ Identify and describe different kinds of algae.

TechTerms

- ▶ **chlorophyll** (KLAWR-uh-fil): green pigment used by some organisms to make food
- ▶ **plankton** (PLANK-tun): organisms that float at the water's surface

Algae Algae are classified in the protist kingdom. All algae contain **chlorophyll** (KLAWR-uh-fil). Chlorophyll is a green pigment found in plant cells and algae. Plants and algae use chlorophyll to make food. The food-making process is called photosynthesis (foht-uh-SIN-thuh-sis).

▶ **Compare:** How are algae and plants alike?

One-Celled Algae Some kinds of algae are made up of only one cell. Most one-celled algae live in a watery environment. They float on the surface of the water. Algae make up **plankton** (PLANK-tun). Plankton are all the tiny plants and animals that float on the surface of the oceans and lakes.

Although all algae have chlorophyll, all kinds of algae are not green. Fire algae are one-celled algae that are red in color. Golden-brown algae can have a color ranging from yellowish-green to golden-brown. These differences in color are due to other pigments, or colorings, in the algae.

▶ **Identify:** What is plankton?

Euglena The euglena is a unicellular, or one-celled, algae. It is both plantlike and animallike. Like all algae, the euglena contains chlorophyll. It uses the chlorophyll to make food from sunlight. When light is not available, the euglena also can take in food. A structure in the euglena called the eyespot can detect light. The euglena uses its eyespot to find light in the water. The euglena moves to the light by beating the flagellum that extends from its body.

▶ **Explain:** How is the euglena animal

Many-Celled Algae Some kinds of al made up of many cells. These are the multi algae. Pigments in multicellular algae m them a green, red, or brown coloring. Mo algae live in fresh water.

Red and brown algae live in the ocean. algae often are called seaweed or kelp. algae are the largest and most complex algae. If you have visited a beach, you ma seen brown algae washed up along the sh

▶ **Infer:** Why are all types of algae not

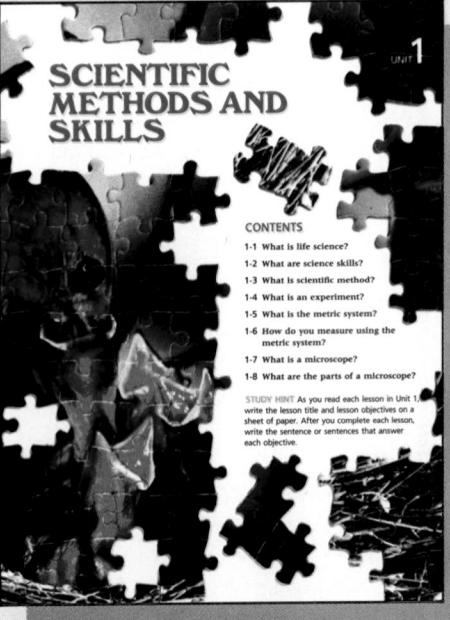

SCIENTIFIC METHODS AND SKILLS

Unit 1

CONTENTS

1-1 What is life science?
1-2 What are science skills?
1-3 What is scientific method?
1-4 What is an experiment?
1-5 What is the metric system?
1-6 How do you measure using the metric system?
1-7 What is a microscope?
1-8 What are the parts of a microscope?

STUDY HINT As you read each lesson in Unit 1, write the lesson title and lesson objectives on a sheet of paper. After you complete each lesson, write the sentence or sentences that answer each objective.

The convenient Unit Opener page gives students a quick preview of concepts to be covered. The Study Hint provides helpful tips for more effective learning.

---

used b▷

▶ **plankton** (PLANK-tun): organisms that float at the water's surface

Algae Algae are classified in the protist kingdom. All algae contain **chlorophyll** (KLAWR-uh-fil). Chlorophyll is a green pigment found in plant cells and algae. Plants and algae use chlorophyll to make food. The food-making process is called photosynthesis (foht-uh-SIN-thuh-sis).

▶ **Compare:** How are algae and plants alike?

One-Celled Algae Some kinds of algae are made up of only one cell. Most one-celled algae live in a watery environment. They float on the surface of the water. Algae make up **plankton** (PLANK-tun). Plankton are all the tiny plants and animals that float on the surface of the oceans and lakes.

Although all algae have chlorophyll, all kinds

Only one idea is introduced in each short paragraph, an effective learning approach for the reluctant reader plus phonetic spellings of new or complex terms to aid in pronunciation.

LESSON SUMMARY

- ▶ All algae contain chloroph own food by photosynthes
- ▶ Some kinds of algae are o
- ▶ All algae are not green, b phyll.
- ▶ The euglena is a single-c both plantlike and animal
- ▶ Some algae are multicellu
- ▶ Red and brown algae are

CHECK *Complete the following.*

make the

Lesson Summaries, at the beginning of each "challenges" page reinforce concepts learned by providing an encapsulated review of key ideas.

ON SUMMARY

l algae contain chlorophyll and make their
wn food by photosynthesis.

me kinds of algae are one-celled.

l algae are not green, but still have chloro-
yll.

he euglena is a single-celled algae that is
oth plantlike and animallike.

me algae are multicellular.

d and brown algae are multicellular algae.

K *Complete the following.*

lgae _____ make their own food.

ants and algae both contain the green
gment _____ .

he euglena uses its _____ to detect light.

re algae are _____ in color.

he largest kind of algae is _____ .

Y *Complete the following.*

ompare: How is the Euglena similar to the
rypanosome?

7. Suppose you needed to obtain a water sample
that contained both algae and protozoans.
Where would you go to obtain the sample?

Skill Builder

▲ *Organizing* When you organize information,
you put the information into some kind of order.
A table is one way to organize information. Make
a table with the following headings: "Type of
Algae" and "Product." Use library references to
determine the kinds of algae used to make the
following products: toothpaste, marshmallows,
ice cream, detergent, cheese, and silver polish.

ENCE CONNECTION

AL BLOOMS

e make their own food by photosynthesis. For
osynthesis to occur, three things must be present --
ophyll, sunlight, and carbon dioxide. However, algae also
have water and other nutrients, such as nitrogen and
phorous, to carry out their life processes. When all of these
ents are present, algae can reproduce quickly and in large
ers. A sudden, large growth of algae is called an algal
.

lgal blooms often occur when wastes containing
hates are dumped into ponds or lakes. Phosphates are
nonly found in detergents. When an algal bloom occurs,
can be seen living at the surface of a lake or pond in
numbers. However, an algal bloom can be a problem for
isms that live in the lake or pond. As the algae die, they
roken down by bacteria. The bacteria use oxygen from the
r when they break down the algae. If the bacteria use too
oxygen, fishes and other organisms living in the water do
ave enough oxygen to carry out their life processes. As a
, the organisms may die.

123

Skill Builder

▲ *Organizing* When you organize information,
you put the information into some kind of order.
A table is one way to organize information. Make
a table with the following headings: "Type of
Algae" and "Product." Use library references to
determine the kinds of algae used to make the
following products: toothpaste, marshmallows,
ice cream, detergent, cheese, and silver polish.

*A wide variety of Challenge Fea-
tures provide exercises designed
to help students develop thinking
and learning skills and helps to
relate science to their daily lives:
Skill Builders, Ideas in Action,
Designing an Experiment, Infosearch, Health and Safety Tip,
and State the Problem.*

SCIENCE CONNECTION ◆○◆○◆○◆○◆○◆○◆○◆○◆○◆○◆○◆○◆○◆○◆○◆○◆

ALGAL BLOOMS

Algae make their own food by photosynthesis. For
photosynthesis to occur, three things must be present --
chlorophyll, sunlight, and carbon dioxide. However, algae also
must have water and other nutrients, such as nitrogen and
phosphorous, to carry out their life processes. When all of these
elements are present, algae can reproduce quickly and in large
numbers. A sudden, large growth of algae is called an algal
bloom.

Algal blooms often occur when wastes containing
phosphates are dumped into ponds or lakes. Phosphates are
commonly found in detergents. When an algal bloom occurs,
algae can be seen living at the surface of a lake or pond in
great numbers. However, an algal bloom can be a problem for
organisms that live in the lake or pond. As the algae die, they
are broken down by bacteria. The bacteria use oxygen from the
water when they break down the algae. If the bacteria use too
much oxygen, fishes and other organisms living in the water do
not have enough oxygen to carry out their life processes. As a
result, the organisms may die.

Lesson Features include:
- *Science Connection Activities*
- *People in Science*
- *Leisure Activities*
- *Technology and Society*
- *Looking Back in Science*
- *Careers in Science*

*Designed to motivate students to
learn with thought-provoking
facts, interesting insights and
exercises that make science fun.*

golden-br... ...hese differences in color are
to other pigments, or colorings, in the algae.

▶ *Identify:* What is plankton?

Euglena The euglena is a unicellular, or one-
celled, algae. It is both plantlike and animallike.
Like all algae, the euglena contains chlorophyll. It
uses the chlorophyll to make food from sunlight.
When light is not available, the euglena also can
take in food. A structure in the euglena called the
eyespot can detect light. The euglena uses its
eyespot to find light in the water. The euglena
moves to the light by beating the flagellum that
extends from its body.

Red and brown algae live in the ocean. Brown
algae often are called seaweed or kelp. Brown
algae are the largest and most complex kind of
algae. If you have visited a beach, you may have
seen brown algae washed up along the shoreline.

▶ *Infer:* Why are all types of algae not green?

122

*Frequent questions, interwoven throughout the lesson reinforce
understanding and give students immediate insights into the
relationship of scientific principles.*

▶ Red and brown algae are multicellular algae.

CHECK *Complete the following.*

1. Algae _____ make their own food.
2. Plants and algae both contain the green
pigment _____ .
3. The euglena uses its _____ to detect light.
4. Fire algae are _____ in color.
5. The largest kind of algae is _____ .

APPLY *Complete the following.*

6. **Compare:** How is the Euglena similar to the
trypanosome?

*The two-part lesson review en-
courages students to think about
what they've learned, and helps
them grasp abstract concepts by
having them apply what they
know to hypothetical situations.*

STUDENT BOOK UNIT REVIEW

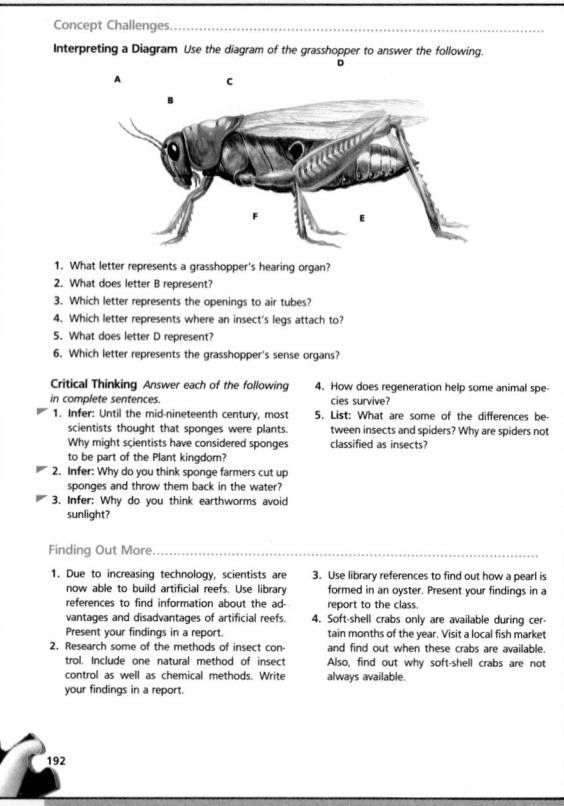

Concept Challenges

Interpreting a Diagram *Use the diagram of the grasshopper to answer the following.*

1. What letter represents a grasshopper's hearing organ?
2. What does letter B represent?
3. Which letter represents the openings to air tubes?
4. Which letter represents where an insect's legs attach to?
5. What does letter D represent?
6. Which letter represents the grasshopper's sense organs?

Critical Thinking *Answer each of the following in complete sentences.*
1. **Infer:** Until the mid-nineteenth century, most scientists thought that sponges were plants. Why might scientists have considered sponges to be part of the Plant kingdom?
2. **Infer:** Why do you think sponge farmers cut up sponges and throw them back in the water?
3. **Infer:** Why do you think earthworms avoid sunlight?

4. How does regeneration help some animal species survive?
5. **List:** What are some of the differences between insects and spiders? Why are spiders not classified as insects?

Finding Out More
1. Due to increasing technology, scientists are now able to build artificial reefs. Use library references to find information about the advantages and disadvantages of artificial reefs. Present your findings in a report.
2. Research some of the methods of insect control. Include one natural method of insect control as well as chemical methods. Write your findings in a report.
3. Use library references to find out how a pearl is formed in an oyster. Present your findings in a report to the class.
4. Soft-shell crabs only are available during certain months of the year. Visit a local fish market and find out when these crabs are available. Also, find out why soft-shell crabs are not always available.

192

At the end of every unit, a comprehensive Unit Review provides complete reinforcement of all key concepts learned in the lessons that made up that unit. Students will find a wealth of valuable resources to help them retain the information they've studied. These include tips to help students sharpen their study skills…a review of the "Tech Terms" learned in each lesson…additional questions to measure concept and content knowledge and retention…and numerous activities that promote independent learning and critical thinking. In addition, these exercises build confidence by letting students see for themselves how well they're progressing.

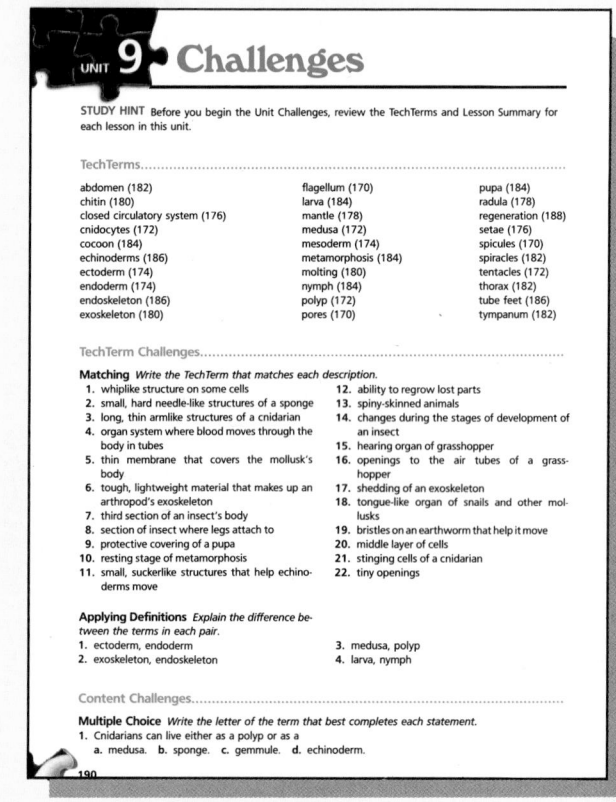

UNIT 9 Challenges

STUDY HINT Before you begin the Unit Challenges, review the TechTerms and Lesson Summary for each lesson in this unit.

TechTerms

abdomen (182)	flagellum (170)	pupa (184)
chitin (180)	larva (184)	radula (178)
closed circulatory system (176)	mantle (178)	regeneration (188)
cnidocytes (172)	medusa (172)	setae (176)
cocoon (184)	mesoderm (174)	spicules (170)
echinoderms (186)	metamorphosis (184)	spiracles (182)
ectoderm (174)	molting (180)	tentacles (172)
endoderm (174)	nymph (184)	thorax (182)
endoskeleton (186)	polyp (172)	tube feet (186)
exoskeleton (180)	pores (170)	tympanum (182)

TechTerm Challenges

Matching *Write the TechTerm that matches each description.*
1. whiplike structure on some cells
2. small, hard needle-like structures of a sponge
3. long, thin armlike structures of a cnidarian
4. organ system where blood moves through the body in tubes
5. thin membrane that covers the mollusk's body
6. tough, lightweight material that makes up an arthropod's exoskeleton
7. third section of an insect's body
8. section of insect where legs attach to
9. protective covering of a pupa
10. resting stage of metamorphosis
11. small, suckerlike structures that help echinoderms move
12. ability to regrow lost parts
13. spiny-skinned animals
14. changes during the stages of development of an insect
15. hearing organ of grasshopper
16. openings to the air tubes of a grasshopper
17. shedding of an exoskeleton
18. tongue-like organ of snails and other mollusks
19. bristles on an earthworm that help it move
20. middle layer of cells
21. stinging cells of a cnidarian
22. tiny openings

Applying Definitions *Explain the difference between the terms in each pair.*
1. ectoderm, endoderm
2. exoskeleton, endoskeleton
3. medusa, polyp
4. larva, nymph

Content Challenges

Multiple Choice *Write the letter of the term that best completes each statement.*
1. Cnidarians can live either as a polyp or as a
   a. medusa. b. sponge. c. gemmule. d. echinoderm.

190

Concept Challenges develop critical thinking skills. Additional activities motivate students to use visuals and conduct research in learning activities outside of the classroom.

Content Challenges reinforce concepts and help students practice science skills. A wide range and variety of questions hold student interest.

Reading Critically encourages the practice of interdisciplinary skills and measures concept understanding. Page numbers in parentheses help students find sections they may want to re-read.

TEACHER'S ANCILLARY MATERIALS

The **Teacher's Resource Book** is a complete package of teaching aids, conveniently organized in an easy-to-use binder. If you have ESL students, you'll appreciate the Spanish supplement. And all worksheets, reviews and testing material—more than 300 pages—are cross-referenced to Student Book lessons. All teaching aids are in reproducible Blackline Master format.

Vocabulary Practice activities designed to make learning more fun.

The Enrichment Worksheet to help develop critical thinking skills, while motivating them to explore concepts further.

A Lesson Review Worksheet provides a variety of review exercises and reinforces key concepts.

The Annotated Teacher's Edition provides complete Student Book text along with on-page annotations. It also contains other vaulable information, including:

- A correlation chart
- Teaching Tips
- Suggestions for cooperative learning activities
- A Materials List
- Supplies and address lists for equipment and materials

LABORATORY PROGRAM

*H*ands-on activities and experiments for students are central to the *Concepts and Challenges in Science* Laboratory Program. Fun and interesting, these formal laboratories enable students to see a wide range of basic scientific processes firsthand. Each Laboratory Program:

- Correlates to activities in the Student Edition to synthesize the lesson concept and help students see it in action.
- Gives students an opportunity to practice the Scientific Method and enhance their critical thinking skills.
- Encourages the use of science process skills as an aid to comprehension.
- Enhances comprehension with numerous drawings, tables, charts, and graphs.

With every experiment students perform, they'll gain not only understanding, but the *confidence* that builds learning success.

Name _____ Class _____ Date _____

Laboratory Challenge 25

How do insects develop?

Insects go through several stages of development as they mature. The changes that take place are called metamorphosis. Metamorphosis may be complete or incomplete. In incomplete metamorphosis, the insect that comes out of a hatched egg looks like a small version of the adult. It is called a nymph. Grasshoppers and roaches are insects that undergo incomplete metamorphosis.

In complete metamorphosis, the insect that comes out of the hatched egg is a larva. The larva usually does not look anything like the adult. For example, a caterpillar is the larva of the butterfly. A larva grows rapidly for a while, and then begins a resting stage in which it is called a pupa. Following this resting stage, the adult insect emerges. In this Challenge, you will observe the metamorphosis of the mealworm, which is the larva of the tenebrio beetle.

Skills: *observing, identifying*

Materials

| magnifying lens | petri dish |
| mealworm culture | forceps |

Procedure

1. **OBSERVE:** Examine a mealworm culture in a petri dish. Use the magnifying lens to get a better look. Do you see any eggs? What do they look like? Write your observations in Table 1.
2. Examine some of the larvae. Use forceps to handle them. What do they look like? Write your observations in Table 1.
3. As mealworms grow, they shed their old skins. Can you find any empty skins in the culture? Record your observations in Table 1.
4. Find a mealworm in the pupal stage. Does the pupa seem active or inactive? How does it look compared to the larvae? Write your observations in Table 1.
5. Examine an adult tenebrio beetle with your magnifying lens. Look for ways in which it is different from its larva. Notice its color, number of legs, level of activity, and other features. Write your observations in Table 1.

Copyright ©1991 by Globe Book Company   71

A question identifies the problem that's being explored.

Easily obtainable materials used in the experiment are clearly listed. The skills that students will use are also listed.

Step-by-step procedures, and diagrams are provided as a learning aid.

Ample space is provided for recording observations.

A series of simple questions to strengthen observation skills, and the ability to reach logical conclusions are included.

Name _____ Class _____ Date _____

Observations

Table 1   Observing a Mealworm Culture

Item	Present? (Y or N)	Observations
eggs		
larvae		
skins		
pupa		
adult beetles		

Conclusions

1. What is metamorphosis? _____

2. What happens during incomplete metamorphosis? _____

3. What happens during complete metamorphosis? _____

4. **IDENTIFY:** Does the tenebrio beetle undergo complete or incomplete metamorphosis? _____

72   Copyright ©1991 by Globe Book Company

The Annotated Teacher's Edition of the Laboratory Program provides an overview of the laboratory activities and advice on teaching students reading below grade-level. Features include:

- A section on Reading Skills and laboratory procedures
- Using Laboratory Skills Worksheets
- Teaching Tips
- Suggestions for cooperative learning
- activities
- Guidelines for Safety
- Materials List
- A comprehensive Skills Matrix
- Supplies and address lists for equipment and materials

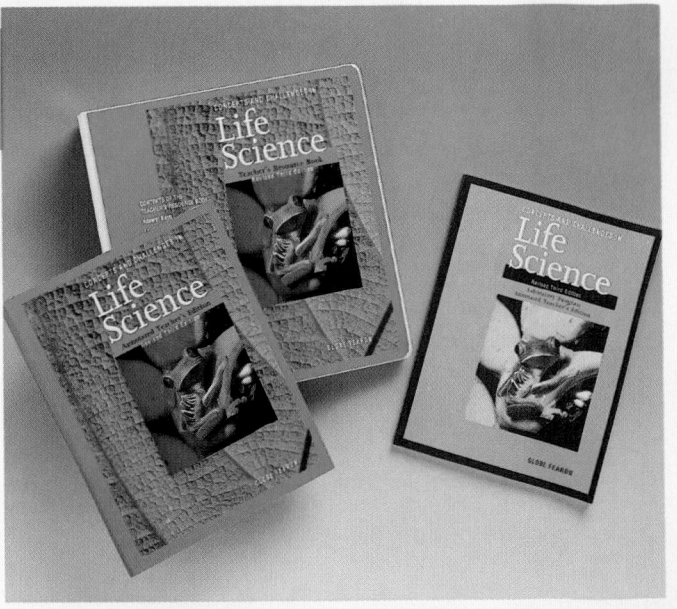

SKILLS DEVELOPMENT IN LIFE SCIENCE

In recent years, science curricula and pedagogy have shifted in order to make science more immediate and relevant for students. Prior to the late 1980s, science teaching was based largely on memorization of vocabulary terms, facts, concepts, and principles. Mastery was evaluated on a student's ability to recall isolated facts. Today, science curricula stress relationships among the facts, concepts, and principles within each branch of science and among the different branches of science. Students are encouraged to apply reading, writing, and study skills to the study of science. Instruction focuses on teaching the methods, processes, and skills of science and on promoting cooperative learning and critical thinking.

Concepts and Challenges has been developed with these new directions in mind. The Revised Third Edition is a readable, relevant, lively textbook. The writing style is highly motivating, interesting, and challenging without being overwhelming.

Science Process Skills and Methods

The implementation of science process skills and methods is a unique and important feature of *Concepts and Challenges*.

- Nine key process skills—organizing, classifying, measuring, observing, inferring, predicting, analyzing, modeling, and hypothesizing—are highlighted and integrated with the presentation of content and with assessments. Process skills are identified with a label, a symbol, and a definition as they appear throughout the text.

- Lesson 1–2 is devoted to explaining the nine highlighted skills in the text in an interesting, readable format. Two additional skills—communicating and researching—are introduced.

- Lesson 1–3 is devoted to explaining scientific methods.

- Lesson 1–4 is devoted to experimental design such as recognizing variables, using controls, and communicating information via a written laboratory report.

- Lessons 1–5 through 1–6 stress measuring while using several other skills throughout each lesson.

Study Skills

To help students study science more successfully, effective study skills are introduced and modeled throughout the text.

- Study Hints on each unit opener page present six important study strategies for approaching the unit content.

- Students are given a study reminder before each Unit Review.

- Lesson Summary statements help students recap important information in each lesson.

- To help students develop good study skills, you may want to suggest that they follow one or more of these procedures:

  1. **Previewing** Ask students to read the title and objective of each lesson and to review the TechTerms, their phonetic respellings, where applicable, and their definitions.

  2. **Note Taking** Each lesson is divided into several short sections made up of one or two paragraphs. Each paragraph has a topic sentence. Encourage students to write the topic sentences for each paragraph.

  3. **Rereading** Encourage students to reread short sections if they cannot answer the question at the end of the section.

  4. **Observing and Analyzing** Encourage students to make use of the graphics on each page to help them understand a concept.

  5. **Questioning** Encourage students to write questions about the content as they read the lesson.

  6. **Answering Questions** Writing often reinforces learning. Have students write answers to in-text questions and assessment questions. Have students discuss their written responses in small groups or as a class.

Comprehension and Reading Skills

The presentation of content, the writing style, and the overall format of a text play a major role in reading comprehension. *Concepts and Challenges* has been developed with student comprehension in mind.

- Two-page, self-contained lessons allow students to concentrate on a complete concept in a manageable amount of text.

- Illustrations support content and help build understanding.

- Each lesson has a consistent design.

  1. Each **lesson title**, presented as a question, provides a clear aim for the day's lesson.

  2. Clearly stated **objectives** provide students with learning goals.

  3. The new vocabulary, **TechTerms**, is introduced prior to reading the lesson.

  4. Paragraphs that support **one main idea** help students focus and build to the overall lesson concept.

  5. Follow-up **questions** after each short section of text reinforce learning. Students can find the answers by rereading a short passage.

Frequent Review

Each short section in a lesson is followed by a question. Questions stress reading comprehension and skills development. Reading comprehension questions have answers explicitly stated in the reading. If students are unable to answer the question, they should be able to find the answer by rereading the passage.

Skills questions are more challenging but can be answered by rereading a passage or by using the graphics on the page. The gratification of answering these questions successfully reinforces learning and acts as motivation to read each short section carefully.

Vocabulary

The study of science requires a working knowledge of words and terms that may be unfamiliar to students. *Concepts and Challenges* introduces vocabulary terms only when they are essential to the key concept or principle in each lesson. Lessons generally have between one and four new terms. In this way, students are introduced to important terms and develop a working science vocabulary without the burden of memorizing too many new terms.

Each term is introduced before the lesson under the heading TechTerms. The terms are phonetically respelled and defined. Within the lesson, the science terms are boldfaced, phonetically respelled, and defined in context. Students are thus provided with a preview of terms and a reinforcement of the same terms.

Recognizing that vocabulary skills development is important, vocabulary skills such as using prefixes, suffixes, and root words and identifying word origins are further highlighted and developed in many Skill Builder features. Vocabulary development also is reinforced in the Unit Challenge exercises. Besides evaluating knowledge of vocabulary, these exercises stress word relationships and apply definitions.

Writing Skills

Writing is important to all academic disciplines. The process of writing involves a number of skills, including the ability to collect, analyze, and organize information. *Concepts and Challenges* enhances writing competence by correlating writing activities directly to the text. Students are encouraged to collect, analyze, and organize information. Writing activities are found in the Challenge features: Skill Builder, InfoSearch, Ideas in Action, Health & Safety, State the Problem, and Design an Experiment.

Mathematics Skills

The language of scientists includes mathematics. The program also illustrates the close relationship between science and mathematics. Throughout *Concepts and Challenges*, students are encouraged to apply basic arithmetic skills.

- Opportunities are provided to add, subtract, multiply, and divide with whole numbers and decimals.
- Students are encouraged to use mathematical formulas to solve problems.
- Measurement skills are developed through opportunities for students to use metric rules, calibrated tubes and beakers, and balances.

Critical Thinking Skills

Students are encouraged to use critical thinking skills in the Apply section of each Challenge page. Here students are asked to observe, identify, classify, analyze, infer, model, hypothesize, interpret, explain, sequence, compare, and contrast. Questions are labeled to help students make connections to the skill they will apply. Each Unit Review includes a critical thinking section.

Skills Matrix

A comprehensive matrix of skills and lesson features is provided on pages T-xii–T-xiii. The scope and sequence of the skills used throughout the program can be used as a teaching tool to help to develop and reinforce student application skills.

Additional Classroom Support

To reinforce science learning, consider these other science products from Globe Fearon.

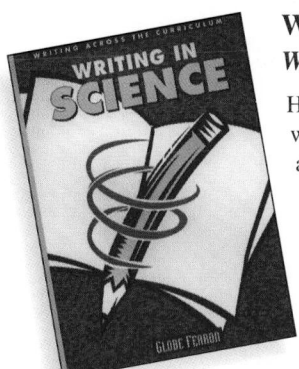

Writing Across The Curriculum:
Writing in Science

Helpful hints for students on mastering writing skills needed in science: Keeping a science journal, taking notes, conducting and recording experiments, writing science reports, and more.

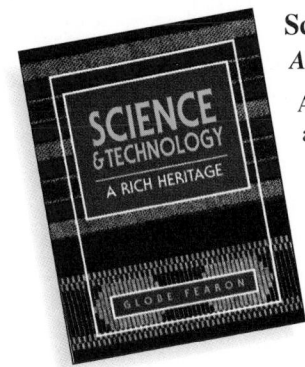

Science & Technology:
A Rich Heritage

An inspirational introduction to the achievements of African American men and women in the fields of science and technology.

Janus:
Life, Earth and Physical Science

These three hardcover texts parallel the topics and instruction found in *Concepts and Challenges* at a lower reading level. Key features found in *Concepts and Challenges*, such as pre-teaching vocabulary, stating lesson objectives, making real-life connections, and providing frequent opportunities for review and reinforcement, are also found in *Janus Life, Earth & Physical*.

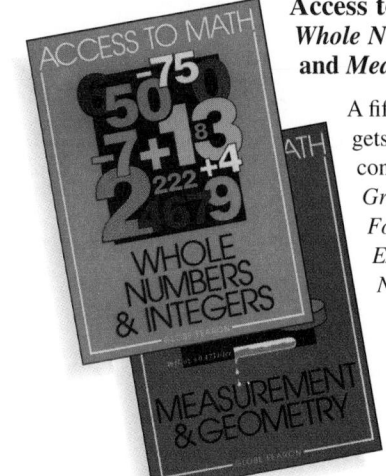

Access to Math:
Whole Numbers & Integers and *Measurement & Geometry*

A fifteen-volume series that targets specific math skills and concepts. Other titles include *Graphing & Interpreting Data, Formulas, Decimals* and *Exponents & Scientific Notation*.

COMPREHENSIVE SKILLS AND FEATURES MATRIX BY LESSON

Category		1-1	1-2	1-3	1-4	1-5	1-6	1-7	1-8	2-1	2-2	2-3	2-4	2-5	2-6	2-7	3-1	3-2	3-3	3-4	3-5	3-6	3-7	3-8	3-9	3-10	3-11	4-1	4-2
SCIENCE SKILLS	Observe		●			●	●	●				●		●				●				●	●	●					
	Measure		●															●											
	Infer	●	●				●			●	●	●		●	●	●		●	●			●	●	●	●			●	●
	Organize		●		●																								
	Classify	●	●								●		●					●		●		●	●			●			
	Predict		●										●	●						●					●		●		
	Hypothesize		●								●		●			●						●							
	Model		●											●									●						●
	Analyze	●	●		●	●	●				●		●	●								●	●		●				
	Research		●												●	●												●	
	Communicate		●															●											
INTERDISCIPLINARY SKILLS	Define			●	●		●			●		●		●			●	●	●	●		●	●		●	●	●	●	
	Build Vocabulary	●																				●							●
	Finding Main Ideas																												
	Identify		●							●	●	●	●	●				●	●		●		●		●				
	Locate																												
	Compare				●		●																						
	Contrast													●											●				
	Sequence				●									●									●			●			
	Calculate							●	●																				
CHALLENGE FEATURES	Skill Builder	●		●		●		●	●			●	●				●		●			●	●		●			●	
	InfoSearch											●						●		●	●				●				●
	Ideas in Action		●							●					●										●	●	●		
	Health & Safety														●									●					
	State the Problem								●																	●			
	Design an Experiment				●								●																
LESSON FEATURES	Activity		●			●	●				●			●										●					●
	Career	●								●								●											
	Technology							●					●								●					●			
	Science Connection			●						●									●		●	●		●					
	Leisure Activity													●						●					●				
	People in Science			●									●													●	●		
	Looking Back in Science							●						●															

	9-7	9-8	9-9	9-10	10-1	10-2	10-3	10-4	10-5	10-6	10-7	10-8	11-1	11-2	11-3	11-4	11-5	11-6	11-7	11-8	11-9	11-10	11-11	12-1	12-2	12-3	12-4	12-5
SCIENCE SKILLS																												
Observe			●			●		●		●			●													●		●
Measure																												
Infer		●	●	●	●	●	●	●	●	●	●		●	●	●			●	●	●	●		●	●	●	●		●
Organize												●			●	●												
Classify	●	●				●				●	●													●				●
Predict						●	●																					
Hypothesize								●		●			●				●	●						●		●		
Model								●		●			●															
Analyze						●		●			●		●	●	●					●		●						
Research												●		●						●							●	
Communicate																												
INTERDISCIPLINARY SKILLS																												
Define		●		●	●								●		●	●		●	●	●	●	●		●		●	●	
Build Vocabulary			●																									
Finding Main Ideas																												
Identify				●	●									●			●	●	●	●	●	●						●
Locate																												
Compare		●							●	●								●				●						
Contrast			●	●		●		●		●	●																●	
Sequence		●						●			●								●	●								
Calculate																	●											
CHALLENGE FEATURES																												
Skill Builder		●			●	●				●	●		●	●	●		●			●				●			●	●
InfoSearch	●					●		●				●			●		●		●			●			●			
Ideas in Action																							●					
Health & Safety								●		●				●				●				●						
State the Problem			●																									
Design an Experiment																												
LESSON FEATURES																												
Activity								●		●			●	●		●					●	●			●			
Career		●		●											●				●									●
Technology			●			●																●	●					
Science Connection	●			●													●	●									●	
Leisure Activity		●								●																		
People in Science																												
Looking Back in Science								●						●						●								

12-6	13-1	13-2	13-3	13-4	13-5	14-1	14-2	14-3	14-4	14-5	14-6	14-7	15-1	15-2	15-3	15-4	15-5	15-6	15-7	15-8	15-9	15-10	16-1	16-2	16-3	16-4	16-5	16-6	16-7	16-8	16-9	16-10	17-1	17-2	17-3	17-4	17-5	17-6	17-7
●						●			●					●	●		●		●											●	●								
		●					●																																
●	●	●	●	●	●			●	●		●	●	●	●							●		●	●	●	●	●		●		●	●		●					
																																		●		●			●
							●							●	●					●										●									
		●									●		●									●																	
●	●										●												●			●	●		●							●			
								●	●	●																													
	●		●	●			●				●									●				●		●		●		●	●	●					●	●	
																															●								
	●		●	●			●				●	●																							●				
			●							●													●		●														
	●	●					●					●	●	●	●					●	●	●		●	●	●	●		●		●	●	●	●	●	●	●	●	●
													●																										
	●						●	●															●										●	●	●	●	●		
																													●							●		
●			●	●							●			●				●											●							●		
																												●										
		●		●			●		●		●		●						●		●		●			●	●		●	●	●	●				●		
	●		●		●				●								●		●		●	●	●	●		●		●					●						
	●						●		●		●		●												●											●		●	
●			●					●												●			●			●		●		●	●					●			
												●																											
●	●	●	●				●		●		●			●		●	●						●					●	●	●	●						●		
			●																																				●
							●			●	●		●				●	●	●						●										●			
			●																						●			●					●	●	●	●	●		
			●																																				
		●	●																							●													
																										●	●												

Txv

Category		18-1	18-2	18-3	18-4	18-5	18-6	18-7	18-8	18-9	18-10	18-11	18-12	19-1	19-2	19-3	19-4	19-5	19-6
SCIENCE SKILLS	Observe			●		●								●				●	
	Measure																	●	
	Infer	●	●		●		●		●		●	●	●					●	●
	Organize																		
	Classify																		
	Predict			●	●		●												
	Hypothesize			●			●	●		●	●			●		●	●		●
	Model												●						
	Analyze	●	●						●					●	●				
	Research			●													●		
	Communicate																		
INTERDISCIPLINARY SKILLS	Define	●	●	●	●		●		●	●		●	●	●	●	●			
	Build Vocabulary																		●
	Finding Main Ideas																		
	Identify		●		●			●			●		●						
	Locate																		
	Compare				●					●		●							
	Contrast				●														●
	Sequence														●		●		
	Calculate							●										●	
CHALLENGE FEATURES	Skill Builder			●		●						●		●	●	●		●	
	InfoSearch	●		●		●		●		●		●	●						
	Ideas in Action		●																●
	Health & Safety																		
	State the Problem							●											
	Design an Experiment									●						●			
LESSON FEATURES	Activity				●	●			●						●		●		
	Career										●								
	Technology						●	●				●							
	Science Connection									●						●			
	Leisure Activity																		
	People in Science	●	●																●
	Looking Back in Science			●					●							●		●	

MATERIALS LIST
(per 30 students)

Item	Quantity	Lesson	Item	Quantity	Lesson
Acorn nuts, to fit			Nickles	30	18-5
¼″ × 1½″ screws	30	5-4	Oil	1 bottle	4-5
Alcohol, Isopropyl	1 bottle	8-4	Oil, cooking	1 bottle	11-10
Bags, brown paper	30	11-1	Onions	30	8-9
Baking soda	1 box	11-10	Oranges	15	6-6
Balloons	30	9-5	Over-the-counter		
Boxes	30 of each		drugs or		
3 different sizes	size	1-6	medicine labels,	30 of each	
Bread	1 loaf	6-6	3 different kinds	kind	16-8
Calculators	30	16-7	Paper clips	30	12-6
Cardboard	30 pieces	15-2	Paper towels	2 rolls	6-6, 8-4
Celery stalks	30	8-2	Paper, construction		
Clay	1 box	19-1	black	30 sheets	18-4
Clay,	1 box of		blue	60 sheets	11-2, 18-4
3 colors	each color	15-2	brown,		
Clock or watch			11″ × 17″	30 sheets	19-4
with second hand	1	13-2, 15-10	green	30 sheets	18-4
Containers, plastic			green,		
small	30	4-2	11″ × 17″	30 sheets	19-4
with lids	90	6-6	red	60 sheets	11-2, 18-4
Cotton swabs	1 box	15-4	white	30 sheets	18-4
Cups, large plastic	30	4-5	yellow	30 sheets	18-4
Cups, paper			Paper, graph	120 sheets	1-2, 10-8,
large	90	19-1			16-9, 17-6
small	30	8-9	Paper, tracing	30 sheets	18-4
Dishes, small	30	8-8, 10-6	Pennies	30	18-5, 19-1
Drawing compasses	30	4-6	Pens, black felt	30	8-4
Eggs	120	4-5, 10-6	Petroleum jelly	1 jar	19-1
Field guides			Pine cones	30 of each	
plants	30	8-3	3 different types	type	7-4
trees	30	7-4	Pipe cleaners	270	4-6
Flashlights	15	2-3	Plaster of Paris	5 pounds	19-1
Food samples,	30 of each		Plastic bags, small	30	4-2
5 different kinds	kind	11-1	Plastic wrap	1 roll	4-5
Gelatin	30 packages	4-2	Pliers	30	5-4
Glasses, drinking	30	8-2, 8-9,	Potatoes	6	6-6
		15-4	with eyes	15	8-9
Grapes	30	4-2	Scissors	30	8-4, 9-5, 11-1,
Index cards	570	3-7, 15-10			11-2, 11-11,
Ink	1 bottle	8-2			18-4, 19-4
Iodine	1 bottle	8-8	Seeds,	30 of each	
Knives	30	8-2, 8-8, 8-9	5 different kinds	kind	8-8
Leaves,	60 of each		Soil	15 cups	8-9
10 different types	type	7-5, 8-3	Straws, plastic	30	9-5
Lemon juice	1 bottle	15-4	String	3 balls	4-5, 9-5, 11-11
Machine screws,			Table salt	1 container	15-4
¼″ × 1½″	30	5-4	Tape		

Item	Quantity	Lesson	Item	Quantity	Lesson
Magazines and newspapers	30	16-10	cellophane	3 rolls	7-5, 9-5, 15-2
Magnifying glass	30	6-6	masking	2 rolls	11-11, 1
Markers	30	4-6, 18-5	Test tubes, with stoppers	60	11-10
Markers or pencils, 4 colors	30 of each color	15-4	Tonic water	1 bottle	15-4
Measuring spoons	30	11-10	Toothpicks	2 boxes	8-9, 15-2
Medicine droppers	30	8-8, 11-10	Vinegar	1 bottle	4-5
Metric rulers	30	1-5, 1-6, 4-5, 7-4, 8-2, 8-4, 11-11, 15-5	Wire, floral	90 pieces	5-4

UNIT AND LESSON TEACHING STRATEGIES

UNIT 1
SCIENTIFIC METHODS AND SKILLS (p. 13)

Previewing the Unit

Read the titles of the lessons in this unit aloud. Identify terms in the titles with which students are unfamiliar. Write these terms on the chalkboard. Use the Glossary of the text or a dictionary to define the terms as a class. Then have students carry out the task in the Study Hint as they read each lesson.

Bulletin Board Suggestions

1. Assemble a bulletin board entitled *Branches of Life Science.* Have students look for photographs and articles illustrating the main branches of life science. Students can use Table 1 on page 14 as a guide. Discuss with students what each branch of life science entails. If a second bulletin board panel is available, have students devote the bulletin board to the topic of *Biotechnology.* Have students attach articles and photographs that exemplify biotechnology. Discuss with students the branch of life science to which each article or photograph relates.
2. Create a bulletin board entitled *Tools of the Life Scientist.* Cut out photographs and drawings of the tools to which students will be introduced during their study of life science such as meterstick or metric ruler, a balance, a thermometer, a graduated cylinder, a simple microscope, and a compound microscope. Attach the pictures to the bulletin board. Label each tool with its name and its use. You also may wish to label the measuring tools with their metric units.

LESSON 1-1
What is life science? (p. 14)

Teaching Strategies

PREVIEW Before students begin this lesson, have them copy the information in Table 1 into their notebooks. Tell students to leave plenty of space between each entry so that they can add information to their tables. As students read the lesson, have them add careers to their tables. Encourage students to add additional careers to their tables as they continue their study of life science.

DISCUSSION Ask students what they think *science* is. Discuss all student responses. Tell students that people use science to try to understand the world in which they live. Explain that scientists observe what is going on in the world and try to figure out why and how things happen. Point out that because there are so many things to study, many scientists specialize in a particular area of study.

CLASS ACTIVITY Write the term *specialist* on the chalkboard. Elicit from students that a specialist is a person who studies, or works, in only one part of a subject. Ask students to name specialists with which they are familiar. If students have difficulty with this concept, point out a few of the medical specialists with which they are likely to have dealt, such as pediatricians, or dermatologists. Then ask students to name specialists who work in areas other than medicine.

DISCUSSION Ask students how life science affects their lives. Review the topics covered in the text. Use these topics as a springboard to other examples, such as the kinds of clothing people wear and the ways in which food is prepared and stored.

RETEACHING OPTION Bring pieces of a jigsaw puzzle to class. Label each piece with the name of a branch of life science. As you describe each branch of life science, join the pieces of the puzzle together. Emphasize that together the branches make up the field of life science.

Answers to Challenges (p. 15)

Apply

9. ecologist

Skill Builder: Building Vocabulary

doctor: diagnoses and treats illnesses; **physical therapist:** works with patients to strengthen damaged body parts; **physiologist:** studies how the parts of a living thing work; **chiropractor:** works with patients to relieve pain, especially pain related to the spinal column; **horticulturist:** specializes in gardening; **florist:** specializes in the growing and arranging of flowers; **veterinarian:** specializes in the medical care of animals; **marine biologist:** studies or works with living things that live in the ocean; **microbiologist:** studies microscopic living things and their effects on other organisms; **pathologist:** studies the tissues of living things; **ecologist:** studies the interaction between living things and their environments

Teaching Tips for Career in Life Science
Wildlife Biologist

EXTENSION If possible, arrange for a park or forest ranger or an animal conservationist to speak with your class. Ask the person to describe what his or her career entails and the training that is involved within the profession.

COOPERATIVE/COLLABORATIVE LEARNING Have interested students write to the Fish and Wildlife Service of the Department of the Interior to find out about careers in wildlife biology. Have students present their findings to the class.

Questions

1. INFER Why is it important to have laws that regulate hunting and fishing? (Answers will vary. Accept all logical responses.)
2. DEFINE What is "wildlife?" (the natural plants and animals that live in an area)

LESSON 1-2
What are science skills? (p. 16)

Teaching Strategies

PREVIEW Before beginning this lesson, write the title of each section on the chalkboard. Have students copy these titles in their notebooks using an outline format. As students read each section, they should write the topic sentence for each paragraph in the section in their outlines.

DISCUSSION As students read the description of each science skill, ask them to identify examples of how they use the skill in their daily life. Emphasize that these skills are used in all disciplines, not only in science.

CLASS ACTIVITY Have students collect articles from newspapers and magazines about topics related to life science issues. Point out to students that the information in the articles is based upon the research of scientists.

REINFORCEMENT Emphasize to students that observations are made using all of the senses, not just the sense of sight, and that measurements are a way of making observations more exact.

RETEACHING OPTION Students may be able to remember the science process skills more easily if you point out relationships among the skills. For example, classifying is one way to organize information; measurements make observations more concrete by quantifying observations; modeling combines methods of organizing and analyzing information.

COOPERATIVE/COLLABORATIVE LEARNING Have students work in pairs or small groups to answer the Check and Apply Questions.

Answers to Challenges (p. 17)

Ideas in Action

Answers will vary. Accept all logical responses. Likely responses include using a clock or watch to tell time, setting the temperature of an oven or thermostat, measuring the number

of pounds of air pressure in a bicycle tire, using a scale to measure body weight, or using a measuring cup or spoon while cooking a meal.

Teaching Tip for Activity
Organizing Data

Skills: *analyzing, organizing, comparing*

COOPERATIVE/COLLABORATIVE LEARNING Students must work individually at the beginning of this activity and then work in groups of three to carry the activity to completion. Encourage students to carefully analyze the variety of methods used to organize similar sets of data.

Questions

1. Answers will vary. Accept all logical responses.
2. Students should compare their methods of organization.

LESSON 1-3
What is scientific method? (p. 18)

Teaching Strategies

PREVIEW Before beginning this lesson, read the list of TechTerms aloud so students can hear their pronunciations.

DISCUSSION Present scientific method as a step-by-step approach to solving a problem. Have students note that many people use the scientific method in everyday life to help solve problems.

DISCUSSION List the steps of scientific method on the chalkboard. As you describe each step, emphasize that because each problem is different, scientists may use all or part of scientific method in a way that is best suited to a particular problem.

REINFORCEMENT To help reinforce the many skills used in science, have students match the skills and symbols introduced in Lesson 1-2 to the step of scientific method to which each skill relates. Students should recognize that some skills will be used more than once, and that some steps will involve more than one skill.

Answers to Challenges (p. 19)
Skill Builder: Writing a Laboratory Report

Check students' reports for a logical use of the steps of scientific method.

Teaching Tips for Science Connection
Pure and Applied Science

DISCUSSION Be sure students recognize the difference between pure and applied science. You can help to clarify the difference by pointing out the effects of applied science (technology) on students' everyday lives.

INTRASCIENCE CONNECTION Point out to students that technology involves all of the sciences and is not limited to biology. As an example, discuss X-rays. Explain that using X-rays requires knowledge of physical science principles. Then point out how these principles are applied to fields such as medicine and earth science.

Questions

1. APPLY How is technology a part of your everyday life? (Answers will vary. Accept all logical responses.)
2. RELATE Television, computers, and medicines all are examples of technological advances. How have these products changed peoples' lives? (Answers will vary. Accept all logical responses.)

LESSON 1-4
What is an experiment? (p. 20)

Teaching Strategies

PREVIEW Before beginning this lesson, write the title of each section in the lesson on the chalkboard. Have students copy these titles in their notebooks using an outline format. As students read each section, they should write the topic sentence for each paragraph in their notebooks.

DISCUSSION Explain how to conduct a controlled experiment. Use the figure on page 20, investigating the effect of fertilizer on the growth of a plant, to describe a controlled experiment. Ask the class to explain why the plant on the left is the control.

DISCUSSION When designing an experiment, scientists look at variables. A variable is anything that can effect the results of an experiment. Have students reread the passage titled *Analyzing an Experiment.* Then have students list all of the variables in this experiment. Elicit from students that a well-designed experiment tests only one variable at a time.

CLASS ACTIVITY Have students work in small groups to carry out the experiment described on page 20. When each group has concluded the experiment, have students compare their results. Discuss reasons for variations in results as a class.

Answers to Challenges (p. 21)
Apply

6. A control allows scientists to determine how a variable affects the results of an experiment.
7. By changing only one variable, scientists can be sure that any differences between the control and the experimental setup were caused by the variable being tested.
8. Answers will vary. Accept all logical responses.

Designing an Experiment

Check students' experimental designs for logic and accuracy. Be sure students have included a control and are testing only one variable (sunlight) in their experiments. You may wish to have volunteers describe their experiments to the rest of the class.

Teaching Tips for People in Science
Jane Goodall

EXTENSION Have interested students research the life and work of Jane Goodall. Tell students to present their findings in an oral report. Students will be able to find many interesting articles by Jane Goodall in issues of *National Geographic.*

Questions

1. DEFINE What is a zoologist? (scientist who studies animals)
2. EXPLAIN Was the work done by Dr. Leakey and Jane Goodall conducted as a field study or in the laboratory? (as a field study)

LESSON 1-5
What is the metric system? (p. 22)

Teaching Strategies

PREVIEW Before beginning this lesson, have students review the TechTerms and read the Lesson Summary.

ITERDISCIPLINARY CONNECTION Discuss some of the units of measurements people used in the past. Tell students that at one time the distance from a king's nose to his hand equaled 1 yard and the length of a king's foot equaled 1 foot. Elicit from students why this system of measurement created problems. (The measuring system changed each time a new king took the throne.) Use this discussion to emphasize the importance of having a standard system of measurement.

CLASS ACTIVITY Ask students to define an inch, foot, yard, ounce, and pound. Write student responses on the chalkboard. Point out that no simple relationship exists between these units. Perform a sample calculation on the chalkboard, such as changing 1.5 miles into feet. (1 mile = 5280 feet) Then, write the number 1500 mm on the chalkboard. Show students how this number can be changed to centimeters (150) or meters (1.5) simply by moving the decimal point to the left.

REINFORCEMENT Review the rules for multiplying and dividing by 10,100 and 1000. This will help students convert from one metric unit to another.

EXTENSION The second is the universal unit of time. The only units common to the metric and English systems are the second and its multiples (minute, hour, day, and so on).

Answers to Challenges (p. 23)
Apply

8. 15000
9. 400

Skill Builder: Sequencing

6 millimeters, 3 centimeters, 40 millimeters, 50 centimeters, 2 hectometers, 6 hectometers, 3 kilometers, 10 kilometers

Teaching Tips for Activity
Measuring Length

Skills: *observing, organizing, sequencing*

COOPERATIVE/COLLABORATIVE LEARNING Answer the questions as a class.

DEMONSTRATION Show students a metric ruler. Point out centimeter and millimeter divisions. Demonstrate the proper way to measure using a metric ruler.

Questions

1. 30 cm.
2. 300 mm.
3. the desk
4. the fingernail

How do you measure using the metric system? (p. 24)

Teaching Strategies

CLASS ACTIVITY Introduce the square centimeter and square meter as units of area. Using a meterstick, measure the length and width of your classroom. Then have students calculate the area of the classroom.

DISCUSSION Display a one-liter flask and explain that its volume is equal to 1000 cubic centimeters. Remind students that 1/1000 of a liter is equal to a milliliter and, therefore, 1 milliliter is equal to 1 cubic centimeter.

DEMONSTRATION Show students how to measure the volume of a liquid using a graduated cylinder and the volume of a rectangular solid using the formula: volume = length × width × height.

CLASS ACTIVITY Using Table 1, read out the temperatures of things listed on one of the scales. Have students identify the temperature readings on the other two scales.

CLASS ACTIVITY Distribute one-gram masses to the class. Have students heft these masses. Using only the heft of these masses for comparison, challenge students to estimate the mass (in grams) of books, pencils, and other common objects. Then have students check their estimates using a balance.

Answers to Challenges (p. 25)
Health and Safety Tip

Mercury should be disposed of properly. Because mercury can be absorbed through the skin, a person should wear protective gloves to clean up spilled mercury. The mercury can be cleaned up with paper towels.

Teaching Tips for Activity
Calculating Area and Volume

Skills: *calculating, measuring, organizing*

COOPERATIVE/COLLABORATIVE LEARNING Have students work in pairs.

REINFORCEMENT Review the formulas for calculating area and volume before students begin this activity.

RETEACHING OPTION Tell students that area is recorded in square units because it involves two dimensions (length and width) and volume is recorded in cubic units because it involves three dimensions (length, width, and height).

What is a microscope? (p. 26)

Teaching Strategies

CLASS ACTIVITY Hand out magnifying lenses to students. Have students look at various objects through the lenses and describe what they see. Point out that a lens is a curved piece of glass and that a magnifying lens makes objects look larger.

DISCUSSION Discuss the application of lenses in a microscope. Tell students that a compound microscope has two or more lenses.

INTRASCIENCE CONNECTION Before describing an electron microscope, draw a model of an atom on the chalkboard. Point out the electrons, protons, and neutrons. Identify these different particles as the three main parts of an atom.

ITERDISCIPLINARY CONNECTION After discussing the use of lenses in microscopes, ask students for other examples of tools and instruments that use lenses (eyeglasses, telescopes, cameras, and so on) Discuss with students the functions of the lenses in each of these objects. If possible, display each object in front of the classroom.

EXTENSION You may wish to introduce students to the terms *concave lens* and *convex lens.* If possible, bring examples of each kind of lens to class. Allow students to view objects through the lenses to see how each lens changes the appearance of an object.

Answers to Challenges (p. 27)
Check

1. simple microscope has one lens; compound microscope has two or more lenses
2. curved piece of glass that bends light rays
3. electron microscope
4. television

Apply

5. A compound microscope has a greater magnifying power than a simple microscope.
6. sight

Skill Builder: Making a Simple Microscope

Students should observe that as they move the key, the water acts as a lens and magnifies objects beneath it. Moving the key serves the function of focusing the object being magnified. The drop of water is the lens.

Teaching Tips for Looking Back in Science
Development of the Microscope

RETEACHING OPTION On the chalkboard draw a time line summarizing the information in this feature.

Questions

1. APPLY   What kind of microscope was used by the ancient Greeks? (simple microscope)
2. IDENTIFY   Who developed the first compound microscope? (Hans and Zacharias Janssen)

What are the parts of the microscope? (p. 28)

Teaching Strategies

PREVIEW Have students read the Lesson Summary before beginning this lesson.

DISCUSSION Display a compound microscope in front of the classroom. As students read about the parts of the compound microscope, point out each part of the microscope. As you point out each part, review its function.

DEMONSTRATION Demonstrate the proper procedures for the care and handling of a compound microscope. Establish a procedure for the distribution, handling, and storage of microscopes. Stress the importance of caring for a microscope. You may wish to distribute a sheet listing rules for working with a microscope. Discuss why only lens tissue should be used to clean microscope lenses. If microscopes are distributed for class use, demonstrate the proper procedure for carrying the microscope.

EXTENSION Have students view prepared slides using a compound microscope. Discuss with the class the use of stains in prepared microscope slides. Point out that stains make microscopic organisms, cells, and so on, easier to see. Identify iodine and methylene blue as two common laboratory stains.

REINFORCEMENT Distribute outline drawings of the microscope and have the students label the parts. You also may wish to have students describe the function of each part of the microscope.

Answers to Challenges (p. 29)

Apply

7. A compound microscope uses light to produce an image.
8. A fuzzy image leads to inaccurate observations. Answers will vary. Accept all logical responses.
9. Changing the objective lenses makes an image larger or smaller.

Skill Builder: Calculating

a. 50 x   **b.** 215 x   **c.** 100 x   **d.** 200 x   **e.** 100 x

Teaching Tips for Technology and Society

Microsurgery

DISCUSSION Discuss how microsurgery benefits society. Relate the development of improved microscopes to improved medical techniques.

Questions

1. RELATE   How do you think the ability to perform microsurgery has benefited accident victims? (Accident victims are more likely to survive or retain lost limbs due to microsurgery.)
2. PREDICT   How might improved microscopes affect health care in the future. (Answers will vary. Accept all logical responses.)

Answers to Unit Challenges (pp. 30-32)

Understanding the Features: Reading Critically

1. as field studies
2. application of science to everyday situations
3. chimpanzees
4. an anthropologist; fossil-hunter
5. rock crystals, water in glass balls, glass lenses
6. Improved microscopes have led to the ability to perform techniques such as microsurgery.

Critical Thinking

1. An electron microscope uses electrons instead of light to view specimens; electron microscopes have a much greater magnification ability than do light microscopes. Accept all logical responses.
2. Microscopes allow microbiologists to study living things that are too small to see with the unaided eye.
3. The Kelvin scale would be most useful since it begins at absolute zero.
4. Microscopes of today have higher magnifications and better resolution than those of two hundred years ago.

Interpreting a Diagram

1. compound microscope
2. to magnify objects
3. mirror (light)
4. 2
5. 100 X
6. One hand should be under the base the other hand should grasp the arm.
7. stage clips
8. greater than
9. A compound microscope has two lenses; a simple microscope has only one lens.
10. curved piece of glass that bends light and makes an object look either larger or smaller

UNIT 2
NEEDS OF LIVING THINGS (p. 33)

Previewing the Unit

Read the titles of the lessons in this unit aloud. Identify terms in the titles with which students are unfamiliar. Write these terms on the chalkboard. Use the Glossary of the text or a dictionary to define the terms as a class. Have students write the terms in their notebooks. Then have students carry out the task in the Study Hint.

Bulletin Board Suggestion

Assemble a bulletin board showing the six characteristics common to all forms of life. Cut out pictures that illustrate cells, adaptations, reproduction, growth, response, and energy use. Attach the pictures to the bulletin board. As you discuss the characteristics of life, have students point to the pictures that illustrate each characteristic.

LESSON 2-1
What are living things? (p. 34)

Teaching Strategies

PREVIEW Have students write the lesson title and objective in their notebooks. As students read the lesson, have them write the sentences from the lesson that meet the objective.

DISCUSSION Write the following heads on the chalkboard: *Living Things* and *Nonliving Things.* Ask students to take turns listing examples of things that belong under each head. Write students' responses on the chalkboard beneath the correct heads. Ask students what all the living things have in common. Discuss student responses. Then list and describe the six characteristics of living things.

DEMONSTRATION Bring a flashlight, a book of matches, and a wind-up or battery-driven toy to class. Demonstrate how each of these objects uses energy. Identify the energy source for each object. Lead students to recognize that nonliving things may have some of the characteristics of living things, but in order to be classified as a living thing, something must have all of the six characteristics of living things.

RETEACHING OPTION Write a list of several different organisms on the chalkboard. Ask students to explain how each organism meets the six characteristics of life.

Answers to Challenges (p. 35)

Apply

8. Grass uses energy from sunlight to make food. The energy is transferred to the cow when it eats the grass.

9. No; living things produce more living things like themselves.

10. Cars and flashlights do not have all of the characteristics of living things. For example, cars and flashlights do not have cells, do not respond to changes in their surroundings, and do not produce more organisms like themselves.

Ideas in Action

Answers will vary. Accept all logical responses.

Teaching Tips for Science Connection
Matter

DISCUSSION Define matter as anything that has mass and volume. Emphasize that everything that exists is either matter or energy.

DISCUSSION On the chalkboard, list the four kinds of organic compounds that are important in the body (carbohydrates, lipids, proteins, nucleic acids). Then discuss the roles of these compounds in the body.

Questions

1. CONTRAST How do elements differ from compounds? (Elements are made up entirely of atoms of the same kind. Compounds are made up of two or more elements that combine chemically).
2. DEFINE What is mass? (the amount of matter an object contains)

LESSON 2-2
What are adaptations? (p. 36)

Teaching Strategies

PREVIEW Before beginning this lesson, have students scan the lesson looking for words with which they are unfamiliar. Have students work in pairs or small groups to define each of the words on their lists.

DISCUSSION Define the environment as everything that surrounds a living thing. Ask students to describe their environment. Be sure students understand that both living and nonliving things make up their environment.

CLASS ACTIVITY Bring in pictures of animals in their natural habitats. Hold up each picture in front of the class. Have students try to identify the features that make each kind of animal adapted to its environment.

DEMONSTRATION If possible, show students an actual cactus plant. Point out the thick stem and the spines. Identify these structures as adaptations that help a cactus survive in the desert.

DEMONSTRATION To demonstrate the importance of a human's thumb, tape the thumbs of two volunteers to the palm of their hands. Ask the students to try to write their names on the chalkboard using the hands with the taped thumbs. Then, provide the students with a shirt that is buttoned down the front. Ask the students to try to unbutton the shirt. Student will observe how the thumb serves as an adaptation for humans.

Answers to Challenges (p. 37)

Check

1. everything that surrounds a living thing
2. air, water, sunlight, rocks, soil
3. any trait of an organism that helps the organism live in its environment
4. dry, desert environment
5. It allows people to use their hands to do many things.
6. air conditioning and heating systems

Apply

7. Answers will vary. Accept all logical responses.

8. Answers will vary. Accept all logical responses.
9. c **10.** d **11.** b **12.** a **13.** e

State the Problem

Students should recognize that a polar bear and a penguin could not survive in a desert environment. These two animals are adapted to cold, snowy environments.

Teaching Tips for Career in Life Science
Ecologist

DISCUSSION Direct students' attention to the photograph illustrating this feature. Ask students what the ecologist in the photograph is doing. (measuring the length of an alligator) Ask students why the ecologist might be interested in finding the length of the alligator. Discuss all student responses.

EXTENSION If possible, arrange for an ecologist from a local university to visit your class. Tell students to prepare questions they would like to ask the ecologist beforehand.

Questions

1. INFER Is the work of an ecologist more likely to involve work in the laboratory or work in the field? (in the field; however, ecologists also may work in laboratories)

LESSON 2-3
What are responses? (p. 38)

Teaching Strategies

PREVIEW Before beginning this lesson, read the list of TechTerms aloud so students can hear their pronunciations.

DISCUSSION Introduce the concept of stimulus and response relationships. Provide students with several examples of how they respond to stimuli in their daily lives. Common examples of stimulus-response relationships include watering of the mouth at the smell of food, answering a ringing telephone, and answering the door when a knock is heard. Have students identify the stimulus and the response in each example. Then tell students plants and other animals also respond to changes in their environments.

CLASS ACTIVITY Place a plant in the classroom with its leaves facing away from the sun. Have students observe the plant for the next week. Students will observe that the leaves of the plant will grow back toward the sun.

EXTENSION You may wish to tell students that plant responses are called tropisms. Some of the stimuli to which plants respond are gravity, light, water, and chemicals.

DISCUSSION Discuss various types of simple responses. Be sure students understand that different organisms may respond in different ways to the same environmental change.

COOPERATIVE/COLLABORATIVE LEARNING Have a volunteer explain the difference between innate and learned behaviors to the rest of the class.

Answers to Challenges (p. 39)
InfoSearch

You may wish to discuss students' questions and answers as a class.

Teaching Tips for Activity
Pupil Responses to Light

Skills: *observing, inferring, hypothesizing, predicting*

COOPERATIVE/COLLABORATIVE LEARNING Students must work in pairs.

Questions

1. The pupil got smaller in size. Increased light caused the pupil to get smaller.
2. a. the light **b.** The pupil gets smaller.
3. a. It got larger. **b.** The pupil got larger to allow more light into the eye.
4. Answers will vary. Accept all logical responses.
5. in total darkness

LESSON 2-4
Where do living things come from? (p. 40)

Teaching Strategies

PREVIEW Before students begin this lesson have them review the objective and read the Lesson Summary.

REINFORCEMENT To help students understand the theory of spontaneous generation, have students look up the definitions of "spontaneous" and "generation" in a dictionary. Tell students to write the definitions. Then tell students to use the meanings of the two words to write the definition of "spontaneous generation" in their own words.

EXTENSION Have interested students research the life of Francesco Redi and write a brief biography of his life.

REINFORCEMENT Review the experiment performed by Redi to disprove spontaneous generation. As you review the experiment, have students identify the variables and the control for the experiment.

Answers to Challenges (p. 41)
Check

1. idea that living things can come from nonliving matter
2. Redi
3. a stage in the life cycle of a fly
4. the meat serves as a food source for the developing offspring
5. the sealed jar

Apply

6. to make sure that any changes that occur during the experiment are caused by the variable being tested
7. that flies do not develop from rotting meat
8. Answers will vary. Accept all logical responses.

Designing an Experiment

Have volunteers describe their experiments to the rest of the class.

Teaching Tips for People in Science

Louis Pasteur

EXTENSION Have interested students research the process of pasteurization. Tell students to present their findings in an oral report.

DEMONSTRATION To help students better understand Pasteur's experiment, demonstrate a similar experiment. Prepare a broth by boiling water with the contents of an instant bouillon packet. Pour the broth into two flasks. Seal one flask immediately and leave the other flask exposed to the air. After a few days, have students observe the broths under a microscope. Students will observe microorganisms growing in the broth that was exposed to air.

Questions

1. APPLY What kinds of products do you think are pasteurized? (Pasteurization is most often used for dairy products.)

2. APPLY How did Pasteur's experiment help to disprove the theory of spontaneous generation? (Pasteur showed that microorganisms carried in the air were responsible for the production of new microorganisms.)

LESSON 2-5

How does life continue on the earth? (p. 42)

Teaching Strategies

PREVIEW Have students scan the lesson for the science process skills symbols. Encourage students to review the definition given on page 16 of their texts for each skill listed.

CLASS ACTIVITY To introduce this lesson, write the following head on the chalkboard: *Reproduction.* From this head, draw arrows to each of the following heads: *Asexual Reproduction, Sexual Reproduction.* From the head *Asexual Reproduction,* draw arrows to each of the following: *Fission, Budding.* Have students copy the chart in their notebooks. Then describe the differences between asexual reproduction and sexual reproduction. Tell students to copy the information in their notebooks under the proper heads.

DEMONSTRATION Demonstrate the difference between fission and budding using a ball of clay. First, roll a ball of clay in your hands. Then, break the ball of clay into two pieces of equal sizes. Tell students that during fission, the parent organism splits in two to produce two offspring (daughter cells) of equal size. Then, put the two pieces of clay together. Again, form a ball with the clay. Gently squeeze a small piece of the clay so a small ball of clay is formed on the side of the large ball. Break the small piece of clay free from the larger ball. Tell students that this demonstration models budding, the process in which a small piece of the parent organism breaks off to form a new organism. Have students observe that the new organism is smaller than the original parent organism.

EXTENSION You may wish to tell students that budding and fission are the most common methods of reproduction for single-celled organisms such as bacteria and yeast. Complex multicellular organisms usually reproduce sexually.

Answers to Challenges (p. 43)

Apply

6. The kind of organism may become extinct.
7. Check students' diagrams. Diagrams should resemble Figure 1 on page 42.
8. fission
9. asexual reproduction

Skill Builder: Researching

Check students' tables. goats: kids; pigs: piglets; giraffes: calves; gorillas: babies; tigers: cubs; deer: fawns; bears: cubs; cows: calves; ducks: ducklings

Teaching Tips for Technology and Society

Cloning

DISCUSSION Tell students that because cloning involves reproduction of an organism from a single cell, it is a form of asexual reproduction.

ENRICHMENT Have interested students research some of the bioethical concern's regarding cloning. Encourage students to present their findings in oral reports.

Questions

1. DESCRIBE Why would people want to clone animals? (to produce organisms with specific traits)

2. DEFINE What is insulin? (a drug used to treat people who can't keep the right amount of sugar in their blood)

LESSON 2-6

What are life processes? (p. 44)

Teaching Strategies

PREVIEW Before students begin the lesson have them review the TechTerms and read the Lesson Summary.

RETEACHING OPTION To introduce this lesson, write the following head on the chalkboard: *Life Processes.* From this head, draw arrows to each of the following heads: *Nutrition, Respiration, Excretion, Transport.* Then point to each heading and describe the life process. Have students copy the information in their notebooks.

REINFORCEMENT Be sure students understand the difference between ingestion and digestion. Emphasize that nutrition is a combination of ingestion and digestion.

DISCUSSION Be sure students understand that plants carry out life processes. Point out that although plants can make their own food, they must take in nutrients in order to carry out their food-making process. Also, stress that plants carry on respiration. Students may tend to think that only animals carry on respiration.

COOPERATIVE/COLLABORATIVE LEARNING Have students quiz each other on the material in this lesson.

Answers to Challenges (p. 45)

Apply

7. If any of the life processes are not carried out, an organism will die.

8. Food is taken into the organism (ingestion) and then broken down into usable forms (digestion). The usable food is transported to cells, where it is combined with oxygen to produce energy (respiration). Waste products formed by respiration and digestion are transported to parts of the organism where they are removed (excretion).

Health and Safety Tip

Check students' charts.

Skill Builder: Researching

$6H_2O + 6CO_2 \rightarrow C_6H_{12}O_6 + 6O_2$
Water plus carbon dioxide yields glucose plus oxygen; photosynthesis is the reverse reaction of respiration.

Teaching Tips for Looking Back in Science

Transport in Humans

EXTENSION   Have interested students find out more about the work of William Harvey. Tell students to write their findings in a report.

Question

What tiny blood vessels connect large blood vessels? (capillaries)

LESSON 2-7
What are the needs of organisms? (p. 46)

Teaching Strategies

PREVIEW   Before students begin this lesson, have them review the objective and read the Lesson Summary.

DISCUSSION   To begin this lesson, ask students what they need to survive. Responses will most likely include food, water, and oxygen. Use students' knowledge as a springboard for a discussion of the needs of all living things.

REINFORCEMENT   As students read about each of the needs of organisms, relate each need to the life process to which it is related. For example, food and water are needed for respiration and nutrition. Air is needed for respiration and photosynthesis. A proper temperature is needed for most chemical reactions (respiration, digestion) to occur. Living space provides organisms with the materials they need from their environment as well as shelter and a place to reproduce.

DISCUSSION   The concept of homeostasis may be difficult for students to grasp. Tell students that homeostasis is an automatic response of the body that enables organisms to maintain constant internal conditions. Discuss how shivering and perspiring help humans maintain a body temperature of 37 °C.

RETEACHING OPTION   Ask students what needs of living things are shown in the picture on page 46. Write student responses on the chalkboard. Then review why each of these things is needed by living things.

Answers to Challenges (p. 47)

Apply

6. Shivering and perspiring are ways that the body maintains a constant temperature.
7. Answers may vary. Accept all logical responses.
8. Students may suggest that some organisms die because they cannot meet their needs, while others move to other living spaces. Accept all logical responses.

Ideas in Action

Responses may include drinking, cooking, washing dishes, bathing, swimming, and recreation. Accept all logical responses.

Health and Safety Tip

Botulism bacteria are most commonly found in foods such as canned green beans, peas, and tomatoes.

Teaching Tips For Leisure Activity

Cooking

COOPERATIVE/COLLABORATIVE LEARNING   Some of your students may already enjoy cooking as a hobby. Encourage students to bring in their favorite recipes. The recipes can be placed together and photocopied to make a class cookbook.

ENRICHMENT   You may wish to have a professional chef speak to the class about a career as a cook. Have the chef discuss the credentials needed to become a chef.

Questions

1. APPLY   How is cooking related to life science? (Answers will vary. Accept all logical responses.)
2. LIST   What materials do you think you need to begin cooking as a hobby? (Responses may include a stove, pots, pans, food, and utensils. Accept all logical responses.)

Answers to Unit Challenges (pp. 48-50)

Understanding The Features: Reading Critically

1. scientist who studies the relationships between living things and their environments
2. to produce animals with specific traits
3. carbohydrates, lipids, proteins, nucleic acids
4. how transport occurs in the body
5. by performing an experiment with broth, flasks, air, and microorganisms
6. according to similar foods

Interpreting a Diagram

1. the uncovered jars and the jars with the veils
2. jar B
3. jar A
4. the flies could not get into the jar with the lid or the jar with the veil.
5. eggs laid by the flies
6. The experiment showed that flies did not develop from rotting meat.

Critical Thinking

1. A robot does not have all the characteristics of organisms and does not carry out the life processes.
2. Growth is one way in which organisms develop.
3. energy, carbon dioxide, and water
4. Living things compete with each other for living space, food, water, and other needs provided by the environment.
5. because the offspring are made up of cells from both parents

Previewing the Unit

Read the titles of the lessons in this unit aloud. Identify terms in the titles with which students are unfamiliar. Write these terms on the chalkboard. Using the Glossary of the text of a dictionary, define the terms as a class. Have students write the terms and their definitions in their notebooks. Then, have students work in small groups to carry out the task in the Study Hint.

Bulletin Board Suggestions

1. Assemble a bulletin board that shows the six major land biomes. List the names of the land biomes on the bulletin board. Have students find and collect pictures of the plants and animals that inhabit each biome. Attach the pictures under the correct heads.

2. Assemble a bulletin board showing a complex food web. Attach pictures of producers, and first-, second-, and third-level consumers to the bulletin board to make a food web. Add arrows to show the relationships among the organisms.

LESSON 3-1
What is ecology? (p. 52)

Teaching Strategies

PREVIEW Before beginning this lesson, have students review the TechTerms and their definitions and read the Lesson Summary.

REINFORCEMENT Remind students that everything that surrounds a living thing makes up its environment. Then introduce the definition of ecology.

EXTENSION You may wish to introduce the terms *biotic* and *abiotic*. The biotic factors in an environment are the living things. Biotic factors include plants, animals, protists, bacteria, and fungi. Abiotic factors are the nonliving parts of the environment. Ask students to list as many abiotic factors as they can for their classroom environment. Write student responses on the chalkboard.

CLASS ACTIVITY If possible, set up an aquarium in the classroom. Have students identify the living and nonliving things in the aquarium environment. List student responses on the chalkboard under the heads *Living* and *Nonliving*. Be sure that things students cannot see, such as dissolved gases and microorganisms, are included.

DISCUSSION Ask students to list the titles of at least 10 people they interact with in their community. (Responses may include teacher, doctor, cashier, and so on.) Point out that human society has many interactions. Then discuss the interactions that occur in nature. Have students observe Figure 1 on p. 52 and use the interactions on an African plain as an example.

Answers to Challenges (p. 53)
Skill Builder: Classifying

1. lion: predator; zebra: prey
2. fly: prey; frog: predator

3. snake: predator; rabbit: prey
4. robin: predator; worm: prey
5. mouse: prey; cat: predator
6. cheetah: predator; antelope: prey

Teaching Tips for Career in Life Science
Air Pollution Technician

DISCUSSION Be sure students understand the meaning of the term *pollutants*. Point out that pollutants are harmful substances that enter the environment. Describe some of the substances that cause air pollution such as chemicals and dust and soot. Explain to students that people are the cause of pollution and therefore must be the solution to the problem. Discuss with students methods for reducing the amounts of pollutants in the air.

EXTENSION If possible, arrange for an air pollution technician to speak to your class. Ask the technician to describe a typical working day.

Question

DEFINE What are pollutants? (harmful substances that enter the environment)

LESSON 3-2
What is an ecosystem? (p. 54)

Teaching Strategies

PREVIEW Have students write the lesson title and objective in their notebooks. As students read the lesson, tell them to write down the sentence or sentences that provide the information needed in the objective.

DISCUSSION This lesson introduces three key terms of ecology: *population, community,* and *ecosystem.* Define each of these terms for the class. Be sure students understand that a community is all the populations living in a region, and not the region itself. Point out that there usually are many complex relationships among the populations of a community. Most of these are feeding patterns, but others may involve protection and reproduction. You may wish to describe the pollination of plants by insects as an example of a relationship that is not a feeding relationship in itself, but an outcome of one.

RETEACHING OPTION Hold up a nature scene showing a variety of different kinds of animals. Ask students how many different animal populations are shown. Tell students that all the populations together make up a community. Then point out some of the nonliving parts of the environment in the picture. Ask students what the living and nonliving parts of the environment make up. (ecosystem)

COOPERATIVE/COLLABORATIVE LEARNING Ask a volunteer to describe the four processes that occur in an ecosystem to make it self-supporting.

Answers to Challenges (p. 55)
Apply

6. 2
7. 2
8. The pond is made up of both living and nonliving parts. The organisms in the pond interact with the nonliving parts of the environment and with each other.

InfoSearch

You may wish to discuss students' questions and answers as a class.

Teaching Tips for Science Connection
The *Gaia* Hypothesis

REINFORCEMENT   This feature provides a perfect opportunity to review the meanings of the terms *hypothesis* and *theory*.

DISCUSSION   Not all scientists agree with the *Gaia* Hypothesis. After students read the feature, ask them if they agree or disagree with Lovelock's ideas. Use the question for an open ended discussion of the *Gaia* hypothesis.

Questions

1. HYPOTHESIZE   Why might a small change in the Earth's environment be harmful to living things? (Answers will vary. Accept all logical responses.)
2. IDENTIFY   Who formulated the *Gaia* Hypothesis? (James Lovelock)

LESSON 3-3
What are habitats and niches? (p. 56)

Teaching Strategies

PREVIEW   Before beginning this lesson, read the list of TechTerms aloud so students can hear their pronunciations.

DISCUSSION   To provide motivation for this lesson, ask students what their roles, or jobs, in life are. (They will most likely respond that they are students.) Use the question as a springboard for a discussion of a niche. Point out that all organisms have a role in their communities. Define niche as an organism's role in its habitat.

REINFORCEMENT   Be sure students understand why organisms may have the same habitat but not the same niche. Emphasize that competition among species living in the same place is the reason organisms cannot share the same niche.

Answers to Challenges (p. 57)
Apply

6. The population most suited to the environment will survive and reproduce. The other population will decrease in size.
7. No; a rattlesnake is not adapted for life in a cold, Arctic habitat.
8. air and land
9. salt water
10. land
11. fresh water
12. salt water, fresh water
13. fresh water
14. air and land
15. land

Skill Builder: Communicating

Answers will vary. Accept all logical responses.

Teaching Tips for Leisure Activity
Nature Photography

DISCUSSION   Have students bring in some of their own nature photographs to display and discuss.

CLASS ACTIVITY   Have students flip through their textbooks to observe some photographs taken by nature photographers. Ask students to choose their favorite photographs in the book.

Questions

1. EXPLAIN   Why should nature photographers learn about the animals they wish to photograph? (Answers will vary. Accept all logical responses.)
2. LIST   What are three great places for photographing plants and animals? (state and national parks, recreation areas, seashores, wildlife preserves)

LESSON 3-4
What are limiting factors? (p. 58)

PREVIEW   Before beginning this lesson, write the title of each section in the lesson on the chalkboard in an outline format. Have students copy these titles in their notebooks. As students read each section, have them write the topic sentence of each paragraph beneath each section title.

DISCUSSION   Introduce this lesson with a discussion of the childhood game *Musical Chairs.* Make an analogy between the number of chairs and limiting factors. Relate the number of people who can sit to an area's carrying capacity.

CLASS ACTIVITY   Have students work in small groups to make graphs showing the relationship between the sizes of animal populations and the sizes of plant populations. Students' graphs should show that as plant populations decrease, animal populations decrease.

INTRASCIENCE CONNECTION   Have students collect soil samples from around their neighborhoods. Have students examine the soil and make a chart listing the following information: overall appearance, kind and size of soil particles, shape of rock particles, presence of organic material. Use the information students organize to determine the type of soil in your area. Point out that type of soil is a limiting factor for plants.

RETEACHING OPTION   Write the following head on the chalkboard: *Limiting Factors.* From this head, draw arrows to each of the following heads: *Plants, Animals.* From the head *Plants,* draw arrows to the following: *Amount of Sunlight, Type of Soil, Temperature, Amount of Water.* From the head *Animals,* draw arrows to the following: *Temperature, Water, Food Supply, Shelter.* Have students copy the charts in their notebooks.

Answers to Challenges (p. 59)
Apply

5. Humans can eat many different kinds of food, can make their own shelters, and can make clothing that helps them to live in different climates.
6. Yes, because humans rely on plant and animal populations to meet their need for food.

InfoSearch

You may wish to discuss students' questions and answers as a class.

Teaching Tips for Science Connection
World Population Growth

EXTENSION   Have students research world population growth for the past 300 years. Tell students to organize their findings in a graph.

Questions

1. What is the total world population today? (about 5 billion)
2. Why can the earth carry a population that is so much larger than it was 20,000 years ago? (improved methods of food production, medical advances)

LESSON 3-5
What cycles take place in nature? (p. 60)

Teaching Strategies

PREVIEW Before beginning this section, have students scan the lesson looking for words with which they are unfamiliar. Have students work in pairs or small groups to define each of the words on their lists.

DISCUSSION Describe the water cycle, the oxygen-carbon dioxide cycle, and the nitrogen cycle. Use the pictures on p. 60 to illustrate your descriptions.

CLASS ACTIVITY Divide the class into small groups. Have students in each group draw pictures of plants, animals, soil, the sun, clouds, and so on. Have students cut out the pictures and assemble them in ways that illustrate the water cycle, the oxygen-carbon dioxide cycle, and the nitrogen cycle. Have students paste the pictures on a posterboard and then add arrows to show the flow of water, oxygen and carbon dioxide, and nitrogen through the environment.

Answers to Challenges (p. 61)

Apply

7. Answers will vary. Accept all logical responses.
8. They supply each other with the gases needed for the life processes.
9. Nitrogen given off by animals is changed into a useable form by nitrogen-fixing bacteria and is then used by other living things. Thus, the nitrogen is recycled through the environment.

InfoSearch

You may wish to discuss students' questions and answers as a class.

Teaching Tips for Science Connection
The Rock Cycle

DEMONSTRATION Bring in examples of an igneous rock, a sedimentary rock, and a metamorphic rock. Display the rocks in front of the classroom. List the three main types of rocks on the chalkboard. Then pass around a sample of each type of rock for students to examine.

Questions

1. CLASSIFY What kind of rock is rock that forms when liquid volcanic rock cooled? (igneous rock)
2. DEFINE What is the rock cycle? (process by which rocks change form)

LESSON 3-6
What are producers and consumers? (p. 62)

Teaching Strategies

PREVIEW Before beginning this lesson, have students scan

the lesson for the science process skill symbols. Have students identify each skill used in the lesson. Students should then review the definition given for each skill on page 16 of their text.

DISCUSSION Introduce students to the four major groups of organisms, as classified by the way they get food. Have students provide familiar examples of producers, consumers, scavengers, and decomposers to illustrate these groups.

EXTENSION You may wish to tell students that animals that eat only plants are called herbivores, animals that eat only meat are called carnivores, and animals that eat both plants and animals are called omnivores.

REINFORCEMENT Remind students that algae are plantlike protists. If possible, display a wall chart showing various types of algae. Emphasize the importance of algae as the main producers in lakes and oceans.

Answers to Challenges (p. 63)

Apply

6. Organisms depend upon each other for food.
7. A human is a primary consumer when eating plant products, such as fruits and vegetables. A human is a secondary consumer when eating animal products such as eggs, milk, poultry, and lamb that come from plant-eating animals. A human is a tertiary consumer when eating meats that come from animal-eating animals.
8. consumers

Skill Builder: Building Vocabulary

1. omnivore	5. omnivore
2. carnivore	6. herbivore
3. herbivore	7. carnivore
4. carnivore	8. herbivore

Teaching Tips for Technology and Society
Hydroponics

CLASS ACTIVITY If possible, arrange for your class to visit a place where plants are grown using hydroponics. Possible places include a local university's research laboratory or a botanical garden.

Questions

1. What are the advantages of growing plants using hydroponics? (Plants are protected from harsh weather and from insect and animal pests.)
2. INFER What are two minerals that are put in the special liquid used for hydroponics? (nitrogen, calcium)

LESSON 3-7
What are food chains, webs, and energy pyramids? (p. 64)

Teaching Strategies

PREVIEW Before beginning this lesson, write the title of each section in the lesson on the chalkboard. Have students copy these titles in their notebooks using an outline format. As students read each section, they should write the topic sentence for each paragraph in the section in their notebooks.

DISCUSSION Refer students to the pictures on p. 64 showing a food chain and a food web. Tell students that the major difference between the two models is that the food web shows how a number of food chains are related. Be sure students understand that a food web is a more accurate account of what happens in nature.

CLASS ACTIVITY Have students work in small groups to construct various food chains and food webs. Tell students to label the producers, the primary consumers, the secondary consumers, and the tertiary consumers on their models. Have students illustrate their models with pictures. When all groups are finished, have a representative from each group display and describe the group's models for the rest of the class.

DEMONSTRATION Make a model of an energy pyramid using four different sized boxes, the largest on the bottom and the smallest on the top. Label each of the pyramid levels with appropriate examples. Use the model the explain how energy moves through a food chain.

REINFORCEMENT Be sure students understand that energy is not recycled through the environment. Emphasize that at each level of the energy pyramid, energy is lost. Ask students why they think energy is lost at each level. (Elicit from students that energy is lost as heat during growth, respiration, and other life processes.)

Answers to Challenges (p. 65)

Apply

6. There would be more minnows in the pond because they are at a lower level in the food chain.
7. flower
8. primary consumer
9. Check students' models to make sure that the arrows are pointing in the correct direction.
10. Students' models will vary. Accept all logical organisms. Check students' models for logic and accuracy.

Skill Builder: Modeling

The grass should be at the bottom of the pyramid; the rabbit at the primary consumer level; the snake at the secondary consumer level; and the wolf at the tertiary consumer level.

Teaching Tips for Activity
Modeling Food Chains

Skills: *analyzing, relating concepts, organizing, modeling*

COOPERATIVE/COLLABORATIVE LEARNING Have students compare their food chains with a partner.

Questions

1. Answers will vary. Accept all logical responses.
2. Answers will vary.
3. a. tree, grass, shrub **b.** rabbit, field mouse, snake, owl, elk, cricket, mountain lion, hawk, frog
4. Check students' food webs for logic and accuracy.

LESSON 3-8
What is succession? (p. 66)

Teaching Strategies

PREVIEW Have students read the lesson feature before beginning the lesson. Discuss the concepts presented in the

feature. Ask students how they think this information relates to topics they have already studied or to the lesson they are about to study.

DISCUSSION Introduce students to the process of ecological succession. Explain that environments go through a series of changes in their populations and communities, until a climax community forms.

CLASS ACTIVITY Divide the class into four groups. Have each group draw one of the following communities on a posterboard: open field, shrub land, pine forest, hardwood forest. Then display the students' artwork in sequence to illustrate succession.

EXTENSION Succession can occur when an ecosystem is changed due to fire, wind, farming, and so on. An ecosystem also can change when a new habitat, such as an island is created. Ecological succession also can start in areas that did not previously support live. Have students research how lichens can start ecological succession. Tell students to write their findings in a report.

Answers to Challenges (p. 67)

Apply

5. No, because different organisms live in different places.
6. Faster-growing plants that can live in the burnt soil grow first.
7. A bog is an area with plants and very wet land.
8. pond, bog, meadow, shrub land, pine forest, hardwood forest

Health and Safety Tip

Student responses will vary but may include that matches should be completely extinguished before being disposed of, campfires should be confined to a small area, and a campfire should never be left unattended. Accept all logical responses.

Teaching Tips for Science Connection
Seed Dispersal

CLASS ACTIVITY Bring in an assortment of fruits. Cut the fruits open to expose their seeds, and pass the fruits around the class.

DISCUSSION Discuss how wind, water, and animals play a role in the dispersal of seeds.

Questions

1. ANALYZE Why do you think a fruit does not ripen until its seeds are mature? (to insure survival of the plant; Animals will not eat the fruit until the seeds are ready for dispersal.)
2. DEFINE What is seed dispersal? (movement of seeds away from the parent plant)

LESSON 3-9
What are biomes? (p. 68)

Teaching Strategies

PREVIEW Have students write the lesson title and objective in their notebooks. As students read the lesson, tell them to write down the sentence or sentences that provide the information needed in the objective.

DISCUSSION Refer students to the biome map on p. 68. Have students locate the six major biomes as you describe the plants and animals that are characteristic of each biome.

EXTENSION You may wish to tell students that the tropical rain forests of the world are being cut down at an alarming rate. Point out that the destruction of tropical rain forests leads to the extinction of many species and the loss of valuable resources.

INTRASCIENCE CONNECTION Be sure students understand the difference between weather conditions and climate. Explain that weather is the day-to-day conditions of the atmosphere, such as wind conditions, humidity, and temperature. Climate is the overall weather in an area over a long period of time.

EXTENSION Have interested students research the marine biome which is the largest biome of Earth. Tell students to find out the characteristics of the ocean, estuary, and intertidal zone. Tell students to write their findings in a report.

Answers to Challenges (p. 69)

Apply

5. More kinds of plants are suited to life in the deciduous forest than in the tundra. Therefore, a larger and more diversified animal population can be supported. Accept all logical responses.
6. Deserts receive far less rainfall than tropical rain forests.

InfoSearch

You may wish to discuss students' questions and answers as a class.

Teaching Tips for Leisure Activity

Leaf Peeping

CLASS ACTIVITY If possible, take students on a leaf peeping class trip.

EXTENSION You may wish to identify the New England states on a map of the United States. The New England states are Maine, New Hampshire, Vermont, Massachusetts, Rhode Island, and Connecticut.

Questions

1. Would you like to go leaf peeping? Why or why not? (Answers will vary. Accept all logical responses.)
2. IDENTIFY What are some great places for leaf peeping in the United States? (the New England states)

LESSON 3-10
What are natural resources?
(p. 70)

Teaching Strategies

PREVIEW Before beginning this lesson, have students review the TechTerms and their definitions and read the Lesson Summary.

RETEACHING OPTION Write the following head on the chalkboard: *Natural Resources*. From this head, draw arrows to each of the following heads: *Renewable Resources, Nonrenewable Resources*. Under *Renewable Resources* list air, water, soil, and living things. Under *Nonrenewable Resources* list oil, coal, natural gas, and minerals. Have students copy the charts in their notebooks.

DISCUSSION Discuss conservation. Be sure students understand the necessity of conserving renewable resources, as well as nonrenewable resources.

COOPERATIVE/COLLABORATIVE LEARNING Have one student explain and give examples of renewable resources. Have another student explain and give examples of nonrenewable resources.

Answers to Challenges (p. 71)

Apply

6. Answers will vary. Accept all logical responses.
7. because they take millions of years to form
8. renewable resources: plants, soil, elephant, flies, water, sun; nonrenewable resources: coal, motor oil

Ideas in Action

Answers will vary. Accept all logical responses.

Skill Builder: Classifying

Renewable resources include nutrients, food, oxygen, wood, and fish. Nonrenewable resources include marble, gasoline, charcoal, methane gas, kerosene, and propane gas.

Teaching Tips for Technology and Society

Nuclear Energy

CLASS ACTIVITY Have a class debate about the pros and cons of nuclear energy.

CLASS ACTIVITY Have students collect articles pertaining to nuclear energy from magazines, newspapers, and so on. Read and discuss the articles as a class.

Questions

1. DEFINE What is nuclear energy? (energy released when atoms are split)
2. What is the most common fuel for nuclear energy? (uranium)

LESSON 3-11
What is balance in an ecosystem? (p. 72)

Teaching Strategies

PREVIEW Before beginning this lesson, read the TechTerms aloud so students can hear their pronunciations.

DISCUSSION Write the term *Pollution* on the chalkboard. Discuss what students think of when they hear the word *pollution*. Emphasize that pollution is upsetting the balance of the environment.

EXTENSION Have students find out what measures are being taken to prevent endangered animals from becoming extinct. Tell students to present their findings in an oral report.

Answers to Challenges (p. 73)

State the Problem

Polluted water is flowing into the lake.

Teaching Tips for People in Science

Rachel Carson

EXTENSION Have students read *Silent Spring* and write a book report.

Question

What were Rachel Carson's two main occupations? (biologist, writer)

Answers to Unit Challenges (pp. 74-76)

Understanding the Features: Reading Critically

1. harmful substances that enter the environment
2. 3.5%
3. Learning the habits of the animals makes it easier to obtain photographs of the animals in their natural habitats. Accept all logical responses.
4. It is getting larger.
5. igneous, sedimentary, metamorphic
6. growing of plants in water instead of soil
7. Seeds are carried to new places where they are more likely to germinate. An area undergoing succession has more space for the seed to grow and develop. Accept all logical responses.

8. the fall
9. energy released when atoms split
10. marine science; Accept all logical answers.

Interpreting a Diagram

1. food web
2. grass
3. rabbit, mice, grasshoppers
4. wolves, owls, snakes, frogs, hawks
5. hawks and snakes
6. the food relationships among organisms
7. Check students' drawings for logic and accuracy.
8. Answers will vary. Accept all logical responses.

Critical Thinking

1. Check students' energy pyramids for logic and accuracy.
2. Both show the movement of energy through an ecosystem.
3. Because the bacteria can make their own food, they are producers.
4. Scavengers feed upon the remains of organisms without breaking down the remains.
5. The remains of dead organisms would pile up.

CELLS, TISSUES, AND ORGANS (p. 77)

Previewing the Unit

Have students work in small groups to carry out the task in the Study Hint. Have students record the words on their lists in a Unit Glossary. Students should include a definition for each word in their glossaries.

Bulletin Board Suggestions

1. Create a bulletin board display entitled *Cells.* Divide the bulletin board into two sections, labeled *Plant Cells* and *Animal Cells.* Beneath each section include a large labeled drawing of each kind of cell. Be sure the drawing illustrates each of the cell parts discussed in Lessons 1 through 4 of this unit. Refer to the bulletin board as you discuss each cell part.
2. Create a Bulletin board display entitled *Human Organ Systems.* Down the left side of the bulletin board, list each of the ten organ systems of the human body. Place cards listing the major organs of each system next to the name of each organ system.

LESSON 4-1
What are cells? (p. 78)

Teaching Strategies

PREVIEW Before students begin this lesson, have them read the objective and review the Lesson Summary.

DISCUSSION To introduce this lesson, build a small house of cards in front of the classroom. Ask students to identify the basic unit of structure of a card house. (a card) Then tell students that the basic unit of structure in living things is the cell. Point out that all living things are made up of one or more cells.

CLASS ACTIVITY Have students observe cork slices with a compound microscope. Tell students to sketch what they see. Then have students compare their drawings with the picture of cork cells on p. 78.

DISCUSSION Write the three parts of the cell theory on the chalkboard and discuss each part. Explain to students that scientists consider these ideas to be a theory because the ideas have been supported by data over time. Be sure students understand each of the ideas that make up the cell theory.

EXTENSION Have interested student find out more about the work of Hooke or van Leeuwenhoek. Tell students to write their findings in a report. Students should recognize that these men were pioneers in scientific studies.

Answers to Challenges (p. 79)
Check

1. an idea that explains something; A theory is supported by data over and over.
2. cell
3. Robert Hooke
4. single-celled organisms
5. other living cells

Apply

6. As microscopes improve, scientists are better able to see the parts of a cell and how they function.
7. Yes; respiration is a life process and cells carry on all life processes.
8. No; cork is made up of dead plant cells. Only living cells can produce new cells.

Ideas in Action

Answers will vary. Accept all logical responses.

Skill Builder: Researching

The organisms seen by van Leeuwenhoek were protozoans. Because protozoans are able to move, van Leeuwenhoek likened them to animals.

Teaching Tips for People in Science
Schleiden and Schwann

DISCUSSION Stress to students that although both Schleiden and Schwann contributed to the cell theory, the two scientists did not work together. Point out the importance of communication among scientists and of how scientific research builds upon past discoveries.

EXTENSION Have interested students research Schwann cells. Tell students to draw and label a Schwann cell and to briefly describe its function.

Questions

1. IDENTIFY In what branch of life science did Matthias Schleiden work? (botany)
2. RELATE How did the studies of Schleiden and Schwann contribute to the development of the cell theory? (Both Scientists observed that living things were made up of cells.)

LESSON 4-2
What are the main cell parts? (p. 80)

Teaching Strategies

PREVIEW Before students begin this lesson, read the list of TechTerms aloud so students can hear their correct pronunciations.

DISCUSSION Draw and label the three main parts of the cell on the chalkboard. Tell students that although the size, shape, and function of cells may differ, almost all cells have a nucleus, cytoplasm, and a cell membrane. Then describe the functions of these three cell parts.

REINFORCEMENT The functions of the nucleus of a cell often are compared to the functions of the brain. Explain to students that the brain controls all of the activities of their bodies. The nucleus controls all of the functions in a cell.

EXTENSION You may wish to tell students that most of the cytoplasm of a cell is made up of water. This is important because most of a cell's activities take place in the cytoplasm and most chemical reactions take place in water.

CLASS ACTIVITY Divide the class into small groups. Distribute three different colors of clay to each group. Have students use the clay to make models showing the three main parts of a cell.

RETEACHING OPTION Have students begin a table in their notebooks listing cell parts and their functions. Tell students to add to their tables as they learn about other cell parts.

Answers to Challenges (p. 81)

Apply

6. nucleus
7. The functions of the nuclear membrane are the same as those for the cell membrane: support, shape, and the control of materials into and out of the nucleus.
8. Check students' models for logic and accuracy.

Skill Builder: Building Vocabulary

The prefix *cyto-* means ''cell.'' Answers will vary, but definitions should include the term cell.

Teaching Tips for Activity

Modeling a Cell

Skills: *modeling, comparing*

COOPERATIVE/COLLABORATIVE LEARNING Have students work in pairs. Encourage students to compare their models with those of their classmates.

DISCUSSION Place a completed model at the front of the class. Discuss which cell part is represented by each part of the model.

Questions

1. Check students' diagrams.
2. a. cell membrane **b.** cytoplasm **c.** nucleus
3. a. gelatin **b.** Most of a real cell is made up of cytoplasm, which is represented by the gelatin.

LESSON 4-3
What are other cell parts?
(p. 82)

Teaching Strategies

PREVIEW Before beginning this lesson, have students read the Lesson feature.

DISCUSSION Compare a cell to a factory. Relate the machines in a factory to the ''machines'' in a cell. Point out that each organelle has a special job to do. Then describe the functions of mitochondria, vacuoles, ribosomes, and transport tubes.

DISCUSSION Tell students that the singular form of mitochondria is mitochondrion.

DEMONSTRATION Show students photomicrographs of actual cells. Point out the different organelles in the pictures.

Answers to Challenges (p. 83)

Apply

6. railroad: transport tubes; cabinets: vacuoles; battery: mitochondria; electric company: mitochondria
7. There are more mitochondria in muscle cells. Extra mitochondria are needed to provide the energy muscle cells need to carry out their functions.
8. Check students' diagrams.

InfoSearch

You may wish to discuss students' questions and answers as a class.

Teaching Tips for Technology and Society

Electron Microscopes

DEMONSTRATION To help students understand the differences between SEMs and TEMs, bring in photomicrographs of images produced by each kind of microscope. Challenge students to identify the kind of microscope that produced each image and to explain their choices.

INTRASCIENCE CONNECTION Images produced by a SEM are black and white. Discuss with students the use of computers to colorize these images. Ask students why scientists might want to colorize the images. Discuss all student responses.

Questions

1. ANALYZE Which kind of electron microscope would be more useful for studying a living cell, an SEM or a TEM? Explain. (a SEM; A TEM kills cells.)
2. CONTRAST How does an electron microscope differ from a compound microscope? (An electron microscope is larger, more costly, and has a higher magnification than a compound microscope. An electron microscope uses electrons instead of light to form images.)

LESSON 4-4
How do plant and animal cells differ? (p. 84)

Teaching Strategies

PREVIEW Before students begin this lesson, have them review the TechTerms and their definitions and read the Lesson Summary.

REINFORCEMENT Before beginning this lesson, review the basic structure of an animal cell.

DISCUSSION Have students study the diagram of a plant cell shown on p. 84. Ask students how plant and animal cells differ. Encourage students to use their own observations to state the similarities and differences of plant and animal cells.

CLASS ACTIVITY Have students view prepared slides of plant and animal cells under a microscope. Tell students to sketch and label the parts of the cells they observe.

RETEACHING OPTION Prepare a table that lists each of the cell structures students have studied down the left-hand column. Across the top of the table list the following heads: *Plant Cell, Animal Cell.* Have students place a plus sign (+) below the appropriate head if the structure listed is found in a plant cell or an animal cell. If the structure is not found in the cell have students place a minus sign (−) in the column. Tell students to use their tables as study guides.

COOPERATIVE/COLLABORATIVE LEARNING Have students work in pairs to answer the Check and Apply questions.

Answers to Challenges (p. 85)

Check

1. Plants do not need a skeleton because their cell walls provide them with support.
2. The cell wall gives a plant cell shape and support. It also protects the inside of the cell.

3. structures within a plant cell that contain chlorophyll
4. a nonliving material that makes up plant cell walls
5. They are smaller and more numerous.
6. Chlorophyll is used by plants to trap the energy in sunlight to make food.

Apply

7. **a.** Plant cells and animal cells have a cell membrane, a nucleus, ribosomes, mitochondria, transport tubes, and cytoplasm. **b.** Plant cells have a cell wall and chloroplasts. Plant cells also have fewer and larger vacuoles than do animal cells.
8. a, d, and e
9. Nonliving; wood is made up mostly of cellulose, which is a nonliving material.

InfoSearch

You may wish to discuss students' questions and answers as a class.

Teaching Tips for Activity
Analyzing Cells

Skills: *measuring, analyzing, inferring*

COOPERATIVE/COLLABORATIVE LEARNING Answer the questions as a class.

Questions

1. nucleus, cell membrane, ribosomes.
2. **a.** A **b.** B **c.** Plant cells have a cell wall.
3. **b.** Yes. **c.** It contains chlorophyll.

which direction the Os will move. (The Os will move into the cell until an equal number of Os are inside and outside the cell.)

REINFORCEMENT Be sure students understand the difference between diffusion and osmosis. Point out that osmosis is a special kind of diffusion.

Answers to Challenges (p. 87)
Apply

5. in a glass of fresh water; The concentration of existing molecules in the fresh water is less than that of the salt water, thereby allowing the salt to dissolve more rapidly in the less concentrated solution.
6. The carbon dioxide will move into the cells.
7. The molecules given off by the bread will move through the air by diffusion.

State the Problem

Students should recognize that the arrow in this diagram shows the molecules moving in the wrong direction. The model could be fixed by pointing the arrow in the opposite direction.

Teaching Tips for Activity
Measuring Diffusion in Eggs

Skills: *measuring, observing, calculating*

COOPERATIVE/COLLABORATIVE LEARNING Have students work in pairs.

Questions

1. **a.** the vinegar **b.** Answers will vary.
2. The eggs got larger as the volume of the liquid decreased.
3. the vinegar's

LESSON 4-5
What is diffusion? (p. 86)

Teaching Strategies

PREVIEW Before beginning this lesson, have students scan the lesson for the science process skill symbols. Have students identify each skill used in the lesson. Students should then review the definition given for each skill on p.16 of their text.

DEMONSTRATION To demonstrate diffusion, open a bottle of perfume in the classroom. The molecules of perfume will diffuse throughout the room. Have students raise their hands as they observe the scent of the perfume.

DEMONSTRATION Place a few drops of ink in a glass filled with water. Ask students why the ink begins to move through the water. (The molecules of ink are moving.) Have students observe that the ink molecules move from areas where they are crowded to areas where they are less crowded until they are evenly distributed. Identify this process as diffusion.

RETEACHING OPTION Draw an arc representing a cell membrane on the chalkboard. Draw ten Xs and five Os on the inner side of the arc. Draw five Xs and ten Os on the outer side of the arc. Using the idea that a cell membrane will try to keep substances balanced both inside and outside the cell, elicit from students in which direction the Xs will move. (They will move out of the cell until an equal number of Xs appear inside and outside the cell.) Then ask students in

---

LESSON 4-6
How do cells produce new cells? (p. 88)

Teaching Strategies

PREVIEW Before beginning this lesson, read the list of TechTerms aloud so students can hear their pronunciations.

DISCUSSION Provide motivation for this lesson by asking students the questions: ''How much did you weigh when you were born?''; How much do you weigh now? Ask students to account for the differences in their present weights and their weights at birth. Develop the idea that living things grow because cells reproduce and make more cells. Explain that new cells are produced by the process of cell division.

DISCUSSION Refer students to the diagram on p. 88 showing cell division in an animal cell. Use the diagram to introduce and explain the process of mitosis.

DEMONSTRATION Use charts, models, and prepared slides to show students the process of mitosis.

REINFORCEMENT Be sure students understand the difference between cell division and mitosis. Emphasize that mitosis is division of the nucleus. Cell division includes mitosis, as well as the splitting of the parent cell into two daughter cells.

Answers to Challenges (p. 89)

Check

1. process by which cells reproduce
2. division of the nucleus
3. nucleus
4. Their cells can reproduce and make new cells.
5. The two new cells formed by cell division.
6. cell parts that determine what traits a living thing will have

Apply

7. The same number of chromosomes must go to each new daughter cell.
8. asexual reproduction; It involves only one parent cell.
9. c, a, d, b
10. plant cell division

Health and Safety Tip

The seven warning signs for cancer are: a sore that does not heal, unusual bleeding or discharge, thickening or lump in the breast or elsewhere, continued indigestion or difficulty in swallowing, a nagging cough, obvious change in a wart or mole, change in bowel or bladder habits.

Teaching Tips for Activity

Modeling Cell Division in an Animal Cell

Skills: *modeling, relating*

COOPERATIVE/COLLABORATIVE LEARNING Have students work in pairs.

Questions

1. **a.** large circle: cell; smaller circle: nucleus
   b. chromosomes
2. 4
3. by drawing two more separate cells

LESSON 4-7
Why do cells have different shapes? (p. 90)

Teaching Strategies

PREVIEW Before beginning this lesson, write the title of each section in the lesson on the chalkboard. Have students copy these titles in their notebooks using an outline format. As students read each section, they should write the topic sentence for each paragraph in the section in their notebooks.

DISCUSSION Describe the shapes and functions of nerve cells, muscle cells, blood cells, and guard cells. Lead students to conclude that the shape of a cell is related to its function.

DEMONSTRATION Using a bioscope, project as many slides as possible of different cells. Have students note the size and shape of each cell. Review the function of the various types of cells shown.

Answers to Challenges (p. 91)

Apply

7. A nerve cell is long and thin like a telephone wire. The size and shape of a nerve cell allows it to carry messages from one part of the body to another.

8. Red blood cells do not have a nucleus.

InfoSearch

You may wish to discuss students' questions and answers as a class.

Teaching Tips for Career in Life Science

Cytology Lab Technician

REINFORCEMENT Read the term "cytology" aloud so that students can hear its pronunciation.

EXTENSION If possible, arrange for a cytology lab technician to visit your class. Ask the technician to describe a typical workday. Have students prepare questions they would like to ask the technician beforehand.

Questions

1. Where do cytology lab technicians work? (universities and hospitals)
2. DESCRIBE What does a cytology lab technician do on the job? (works with tissue samples, prepares slides of cells, performs tests on cells)

LESSON 4-8
What are tissues? (p. 92)

Teaching Strategies

PREVIEW Before beginning this lesson, read the list of TechTerms aloud so students can hear their pronunciations.

DISCUSSION To provide motivation for this lesson, ask students to name their favorite team sports and their favorite teams. List student responses on the chalkboard. Then hold up action photographs of a baseball or football game. Ask students to point out all the players in the pictures who are on the same team. Ask students how they know which players are on the same team. Elicit the response that players on the same team wear the same uniform. The players work together to try and win the game. Then make an analogy between sports teams and tissues. Point out that a tissue is made up of a group of cells that look alike and work together. Describe the four main kinds of tissue and give students examples of each type.

CLASS ACTIVITY If possible, allow students to examine prepared slides showing the four main kinds of tissues. Tell students to sketch the different tissues in their notebooks. Have students identify individual cells.

RETEACHING OPTION Write the following head on the chalkboard: *Tissues.* From this head, draw arrows to each of the following heads: *Muscle Tissue, Epithelial Tissue, Connective Tissue, Nerve Tissue.* Under *Muscle Tissue* list muscles. Under *Epithelial Tissue* list skin. Under *Connective Tissue* list bone, ligaments, tendons, and blood. Under *Nerve Tissue* list the brain, spinal cord, and nerves. Have students copy the chart in their notebooks.

Answers to Challenges (p. 93)

Apply

7. Muscle tissue makes movement possible; connective tissue holds parts of the body together and supports and protects the body; nerve tissue carries messages.

8. to prevent calcium in the bones from being used by other parts of the body

Health and Safety Tip

Check students' posters. To help prevent brain and spinal cord injuries people should always wear seatbelts, check depths of water before diving, wear helmets when cycling or playing contact sports, and so on.

Teaching Tips for Technology and Society
Cornea Transplants

DEMONSTRATION   If available, point out the cornea and other parts of the eye on a model or wall-sized poster of the eye.

Questions

1. DEFINE   What is the cornea? (clear, outer layer of the eye)
2. Where was the first eye bank formed? (New York City)

LESSON 4-9
What are organs and organ systems? (p. 94)

Teaching Strategies

PREVIEW   Have students write the lesson title and objective in their notebooks. As students read the lesson, tell them to write down the sentence or sentences that provide the information needed in the objective.

DISCUSSION   Review the definition of tissue. Elicit that a tissue is a group of similar cells which work together to do a job. Then list several body organs on the chalkboard. Point out that each organ listed consists of several different tissues. Develop the concept that organs are made of different kinds of tissues which work together to do a job. Be sure students realize that plants also have organs.

REINFORCEMENT   Challenge the class to list a number of animal organs and to identify the kinds of tissues found in each organ.

CLASS ACTIVITY   Refer students to Table 1 on p. 94. Randomly read out the major organs listed. Have students identify the organ systems and their functions.

REINFORCEMENT   You may wish to develop flash cards to help students review organ systems. On the front side of index cards, write the names of each organ system. On the other side of the cards, write the major organs that make up each system. Hold up each card in front of the class. Show students the sides listing the major organs. Have students identify the organ system. To vary this activity, show students the names of the organ systems and have students identify the major organs.

Answers to Challenges (p. 95)

Apply

10. b, d, c, e, a
11. muscles and bone tissue, nerve tissue, epithelial tissue, blood

Skill Builder: Researching

Check students' tables. The main functions: epidermis: pre-vents drying out; ground tissue: stores food and provides support for a plant; vascular tissue: transports food and water throughout a plant; meristem tissue: growth

Teaching Tips for Technology and Society
The Visible Human Project

EXTENSION   Ask interested students to visit the website http://www.nlm.nih.gov/research/visible for the project and download the sample images. Show the images to the class and have them identify any body organs they recognize.

Question

DESCRIBE   What is the Visible Human Project? (a computer program showing the entire male and female body in three-dimensional detail)

Answers to Unit Challenges (pp. 96–98)
Understanding the Features: Reading Critically

1. a kind of nerve cell

2. A TEM cannot be used to study living things. A scanning electron microscope can be used to study living things.

3. Keeping careful records is important in all scientific research. Accept all logical responses.

4. A damaged cornea is removed from the eye during surgery. The cornea from a donor is then used as a replacement for the damaged cornea.

5. An eye bank worker may keep records, be responsible for shipping organs, or assist in the removal and preparation of transplant organs. Accept all logical responses.

6. The Visible Human can be used to practice medical treatments, to test products, or to train Army medics.

Critical Thinking

1. Answers will vary. Suggested response: cells are too small to be seen without the assistance of a microscope.
2. All living things are made up of one or more cells, cells are the basic units of structure and function in living things, and cells come only from other living cells.
3. mitochondria: produce energy for a cell; ribosomes: make protein; vacuoles: store food and waste; transport tubes: move substances in the cell from one organelle to another
4. Plant cells have cell walls; plant cells contain chlorophyll and chloroplasts; animal cells have many small vacuoles; plant cells usually have one or two very large vacuoles.
5. It is the movement of water through a cell membrane.
6. In animal cells, the cell pulls apart and forms two daughter cells. In plant cells, a new cell wall and cell membrane form down the middle of the cell and form a wall between two new nuclei.

Interpreting a Diagram

1. chloroplast; animal cells contain no chloroplasts
2. transport tubes
3. cytoplasm
4. mitochondria
5. cell wall; animal cells have no cell walls
6. vacuoles
7. ribosomes; They make proteins.

CLASSIFICATION (p. 99)

Previewing the Unit

Read the titles of the lessons in this unit aloud. Identify terms in the titles with which students are unfamiliar. Write these terms on the chalkboard. Using the Glossary of the text or a dictionary, define the terms as a class. Have students write the terms and their definitions in their notebooks. Then, have students work in small groups to carry out the task in the Study Hint.

Bulletin Board Suggestions

1. Assemble a bulletin illustrating the five kingdoms. Divide the bulletin board into five sections. Place one of the following heads at the top of each section: *Monerans, Protists, Fungi, Plants, Animals.* Attach pictures showing representative organisms under the appropriate heads. Use the bulletin board when describing the characteristics of organisms in each kingdom.
2. Assemble a bulletin board entitled *Animals.* Have students find and collect pictures of as many different animals as possible. Tell students to look for pictures of both vertebrates and invertebrates. Make a collage with all the students' pictures.

LESSON 5-1
What is classification? (p. 100)

Teaching Strategies

PREVIEW Before beginning this lesson, have students review the TechTerms and their definitions and read the Lesson Summary.

DISCUSSION Display a variety of grocery store products in front of the classroom, such as a can of soup, apples, a bottle of juice, toothpaste, dog food, and so on. Ask students why they can find products in a grocery store with relative ease. Elicit the response that items in a grocery store are classified, or grouped based upon similarities. Point out that if supermarkets shelves were stacked randomly, it would be very difficult to find anything. Then relate classification in a grocery store to taxonomy. Stress that in order to keep track of living things, scientists have established a classification system for them.

REINFORCEMENT Be sure students understand that taxonomists do not classify organisms based solely on physical appearance. Emphasize that scientists also study chromosome structure, blood proteins, and embryology.

Answers to Challenges (p. 101)

Apply

5. New organisms are discovered and new information becomes available.
6. Answers will vary. Accept all logical responses.
7. Some organisms that look alike may not be related.

Skill Builder: Comparing

In libraries that use the Dewey Decimal System, books are divided into ten major categories and each category is numbered with a call number. In libraries that use the Library of Congress Classification System, books are classified by a set of capital letters and numbers. The first letter indicates a major area of study. The second letter stands for a subclassification. The number represents a specific topic.

Teaching Tips for Activity
Classifying Objects

Skills: *classifying, observing*

COOPERATIVE/COLLABORATIVE LEARNING Answer the questions as a class.

Questions

1. Answers will vary. Accept all logical responses.
2. Answers will vary. Accept all logical responses.
3. Answers will vary. Accept all logical responses.
4. Answers will vary. Accept all logical responses.

LESSON 5-2
How are living things classified? (p. 102)

Teaching Strategies

PREVIEW Before beginning this lesson, read the list of TechTerms aloud so students can hear their pronunciations.

DISCUSSION List the seven major classification groups on the chalkboard starting with kingdom and ending with species. Discuss the stepwise progression from the broadest category of kingdom to the narrowest of species. Emphasize the idea that the kingdom has the largest number of different kinds of organisms and the number of different kinds of organisms decreases as you move from the kingdom level to each of the next levels. Be sure students understand that a species is made up of only one kind of organism.

REINFORCEMENT You may wish to tell students that they can remember the order of the classification groups by remembering the sentence: *Kings play cards on fat green stools.* Point out that the first letter of each word is the first letter for each group.

CLASS ACTIVITY Refer students to Table 1 on p. 102 to observe the classification of four organisms. Ask students a variety of questions based on the table, such as: To what class do humans belong? Then have students identify which organisms are the most closely related (dogs and wolves).

EXTENSION When writing a scientific name, tell students that the genus name begins with a capital letter and both the genus and species name are written in italics or underlined.

Answers to Challenges (p. 103)

Apply

4. four
5. *Homo sapiens*
6. dogs and wolves

InfoSearch

You may wish to discuss students' questions and answers as a class.

Teaching Tips for Looking Back in Science
History of Classification

CLASS ACTIVITY Have students make time lines to summarize the information in this feature.

Questions

1. RELATE   How did exploration affect classification? (Many organisms were discovered as a result of exploration. Scientists recognized the need for an improved system of classification.)
2. HYPOTHESIZE   What problems do you think resulted from Aristotle's classification system? (Answers will vary. Accept all logical responses.)

LESSON 5-3
What are the five kingdoms?
(p. 104)

Teaching Strategies

PREVIEW   Have students write the lesson title and objectives in their notebooks. As students read the lesson, tell them to write down the sentence or sentences that provide the information needed in the objective.

RETEACHING OPTION   Write the following head on the chalkboard: *Five Kingdoms.* From this head, draw arrows to each of the following heads: *Monerans, Protist, Fungi, Plants, Animals.* List sample organisms under each head. Have students copy the chart in their notebooks.

REINFORCEMENT   Emphasize the differences between monerans and protists, and fungi and plants. Be sure students understand that monerans do not have a true nucleus.

DEMONSTRATION   Show students as many interesting pictures as possible of members of the five kingdoms. Hold up each picture. Identify the organism and the kingdom to which it belongs. Have students describe some of its characteristics based on the kingdom.

COOPERATIVE/COLLABORATIVE LEARNING   Have students quiz each other on the material in this section.

Answers to Challenges (p. 105)
Apply

7. Monerans do not have a nucleus or other organelles; Protists do.
8. Fungi and plants are not closely related. Fungi do not have chlorophyll and cannot make their own food.
9. As technology improves, the classification of living things has changed.

Skill Builder: Organizing Information

Check students' tables.

Teaching Tips for People in Science
Robert Whittaker

DISCUSSION   Describe Robert Whittaker's contributions to science. Although he is best-known for the five-kingdom classification system, Whittaker made many other contributions to science.

Questions

1. In what two fields of science did Whittaker work? (ecology and botany)
2. What did Whittaker use to learn how substances move in a food chain? (radioactive tracers)

LESSON 5-4
Are viruses living? (p. 106)

Teaching Strategies

PREVIEW   Before beginning this lesson, have students scan the lesson for the science process skill symbols. Have students identify each skill used in the lesson. Students should then review the definition given for each skill on page 16 of their text.

REINFORCEMENT   Before beginning this lesson, review the six characteristics of living things. This review will help students understand why viruses are not classified as living things.

DISCUSSION   To provide motivation for this lesson, ask students what they think of when they hear the word *Virus.* Most students will correctly identify the term with disease. Use students' knowledge as a springboard for a discussion of the characteristics of viruses. Stress that the main activity of viruses is replication.

CLASS ACTIVITY   Have students work in small groups to make models of viruses. Tell students to label the capsids and nucleic acids on the models.

RETEACHING OPTION   List several viral diseases on the chalkboard such as measles, mumps, chicken pox, yellow fever, polio, AIDS, and influenza. Have students read the names of the diseases aloud. Ask students what each of the diseases has in common with the others. Point out that each disease is caused by a virus.

Answers to Challenges (p. 107)
Apply

7. attachment to the surface of a cell; release of enzymes, which make a hole in the surface of the cell; nucleic acid of the virus enter; the cell; virus takes control and causes the cell to make new viruses
8. A virus does not have cytoplasm or cell parts, does not carry on any life processes, and can only reproduce inside a living cell.
9. Answers will vary. Accept all logical responses.

Ideas in Action

Check students' tables. The viruses that cause measles, the flu, and the common cold are spread through the air. The hepatitis virus is spread by contact with an infected person or eating contaminated foods. Chicken pox is spread by contact with an infected person.

InfoSearch

You may wish to discuss students' questions and answers as a class.

Teaching Tips for Activity
Modeling a Bacteriophage

Skills: *modeling, identifying, applying*

COOPERATIVE/COLLABORATIVE LEARNING   Have students work in pairs.

Questions

1. bacteriophage
2. bacteria
3. capsid

How are plants classified? (p. 108)

Teaching Strategies

PREVIEW Have students read the lesson feature before beginning the lesson. Discuss the concepts presented in the feature. Ask students how they think this information relates to topics they have already studied or to the lesson they are about to study.

CLASS ACTIVITY Have students observe prepared slides of plant cells under a microscope. Tell students to look for the cell wall and chloroplasts.

RETEACHING OPTION Write the following head on the chalkboard: *Plant Divisions.* From this head, draw arrows to each of the following heads: *Tracheophytes, Bryophytes.* Describe the characteristics of each plant division. Be sure students understand that bryophytes do not have transport tissue.

EXTENSION In botany, the term *division* is used instead of phylum.

INTRASCIENCE CONNECTION You may wish to compare the transport tissue of tracheophytes to the blood vessels in animals.

DEMONSTRATION If possible, bring a sample bryophyte, such as a moss to class. Have students note how small bryophyte plants are. Allow students to observe the moss specimens with a hand lens.

Answers to Challenges (p. 109)

Apply

6. Bryophytes do not have transport tissue or true roots, stems, or leaves. Tracheophytes have transport tissue and roots, stems, and leaves.
7. Answers will vary. Accept all logical responses.

InfoSearch

You may wish to discuss students' questions and answers as a class.

Teaching Tips for Career in Life Science
Florist

EXTENSION Hobby and craft stores often give classes in flower arranging. Students who are interested in a career as a florist may benefit from taking a flower arranging class. Tell interested students to contact a local craft store for more information.

Question

What is a florist? (a person who arranges and sells fresh flowers and plants)

How are animals classified?
(p. 110)

Teaching Strategies

PREVIEW Before beginning this section, have students scan the lesson looking for words with which they are unfamiliar.

Have students work in pairs or small groups to define each of the words on their lists.

CLASS ACTIVITY To begin this lesson, tell students to run their hands along their backbones. Ask students if they know what the "bumps" they feel are called (vertebrae). Point out that vertebrae are small bones that make up the backbone. Then, tell students that animals that have backbones are called vertebrates. Explain that vertebrates are one of the two large groups of animals. Then introduce some of the characteristics of both vertebrates and invertebrates.

RETEACHING OPTION Bring in a variety of pictures showing vertebrates and invertebrates. Hold up each picture in front of the class and have students classify each organism as a vertebrate or an invertebrate. Point out the exoskeletons of any invertebrates.

Answers to Challenges (p. 111)
Apply

6. a. e **b.** i **c.** i **d.** i **e.** e **f.** i

7. a. invertebrate **b.** invertebrate **c.** vertebrate **d.** vertebrate **e.** invertebrate **f.** invertebrate

Skill Builder: Building Vocabulary

The prefix *endo-* means inside; *exo-* means outside. Answers will vary.

Teaching Tips for Science Connection
Taxonomy Today

DISCUSSION Ask students to compare the way Carolus Linnaeus classified organisms to the way modern-day taxonomists classify organisms. Be sure students understand that modern-day taxonomists still study physical appearances. However, they also study other factors, such as embryology, to establish relationships among organisms.

Questions

1. DEFINE What is embryology? (study of organisms in the early stages of development)
2. LIST What are four things modern-day taxonomists study to classify organisms? (physical appearance, chromosomes, blood proteins, embryology)

Answers to Unit Challenges (pp. 112-114)

Understanding the Features: Reading Critically

1. ecology and botany
2. physical appearance, chromosomes and blood proteins, embryology
3. Carolus Linnaeus
4. Answers will vary. Accept all logical responses.

Critical Thinking

1. Answers will vary. Accept all logical responses.
2. Taxonomy involves studying many aspects of an organism.
3. It is difficult to treat viral infections because they are found inside living cells.
4. multicellular, cells are organized into tissues and organs, cells have cell walls, cells contain chlorophyll
5. Fungi are not green, but were thought to be plants.

Interpreting a Diagram

1. viral reproduction
2. capsid
3. nucleic acid
4. The nucleic acid of the virus is entering a cell.
5. New viruses are leaving the cell.

Previewing the Unit

Read the titles of the lessons in this unit aloud. Identify terms in the titles with which students are unfamiliar. Write these terms on the chalkboard. Using the Glossary of the text or a dictionary, define the terms as a class. Have students write the terms and their definitions in their notebooks. Then, have students work in small groups to carry out the task in the Study Hint.

Bulletin Board Suggestions

1. Assemble a bulletin board showing the importance of bacteria. Attach pictures illustrating bacterial diseases, food spoilage, the nitrogen cycle, products made using bacteria, and so on. Use the bulletin board when teaching Lesson 6-2.
2. Assemble a bulletin board illustrating members of the Kingdoms *Monera, Protista,* and *Fungi.* Divide the bulletin board into three sections. Label each section with one of the following heads: *Monerans, Protists, Fungi.* Attach representative organisms under each head. Be sure to include both a protozoan and algae under protists.

LESSON 6-1
What are bacteria? (p. 116)

Teaching Strategies

PREVIEW Before beginning this lesson, read the list of TechTerms aloud so students can hear their pronunciations.

REINFORCEMENT Remind students that bacteria are members of the Kingdom *Monera.* Have students recall how monerans differ from members of the other four kingdoms. (Monerans do not have a nucleus or cell organelles.)

CLASS ACTIVITY Obtain prepared slides of cocci, spirilla, and bacilli from a biological supply house. Have students view the different types of bacteria under a microscope. Tell students to sketch and label the bacteria they observe.

DISCUSSION Review the process of photosynthesis before describing blue-green bacteria. Then point out that blue-green bacteria are unusual because they carry out photosynthesis.

COOPERATIVE/COLLABORATIVE LEARNING Have volunteers draw the three different shapes of bacteria on the chalkboard. Have other volunteers go to the chalkboard and label the drawings.

Answers to Challenges (p. 117)
Apply

8. No, blue-green bacteria can make their own food.
9. a. cocci **b.** cocci **c.** spirilla **d.** bacilli

Skill Builder: Building Vocabulary

Diplo- means two; *staphylo-* means bunches; *strepto-* means chains. diplococci: cocci that form pairs; staphylococci: cocci that grow in grapelike bunches; streptococci: cocci that form chains. Check students' models.

Teaching Tips for Looking Back in Science
Classification of Bacteria

DISCUSSION Describe the progression of classification from two kingdoms to five kingdoms. Emphasize the relationship between the classification of living things and improved technology.

Questions

1. Why were bacteria once classified with the protists? (Bacteria are simple, one-celled organisms.)
2. CONTRAST How are the cells of bacteria different from those of protists, plants, and animals. (Bacteria do not have a nucleus or cell organelles.)

LESSON 6-2
How are bacteria helpful and harmful? (p. 118)

Teaching Strategies

PREVIEW Before beginning this lesson, have students scan the lesson for the science process skill symbols. Have students identify each skill used in the lesson. Students should then review the definition given for each skill on page 16 of their text.

DISCUSSION Bring in an empty milk bottle or carton and display it in front of the classroom. Point out the term "pasteurized" on the bottle. Ask students if they know what the term means. Discuss all student responses. Point out that pasteurization is a process used to kill bacteria growing in milk. Tell students that the term pasteurization is named for the scientist who developed the process, Louis Pasteur. Identify Louis Pasteur as the scientist who started the science of bacteriology.

CLASS ACTIVITY Display photographs or actual samples of butter, buttermilk, cheese, sauerkraut, coffee, and cocoa. Ask students what all of the foods have in common. Write student responses on the chalkboard. When you are satisfied that students have exhausted possible answers, guide students to an understanding that bacteria are used in the production or preparation of all the foods.

REINFORCEMENT Draw the nitrogen cycle on the chalkboard. Remind students that special bacteria in the soil allow plants to use the nitrogen in the atmosphere.

DISCUSSION Write the names of several bacterial diseases on the chalkboard, such as scarlet fever, strep throat, diphtheria, tetanus, and typhoid fever. Challenge the class to state what all of these human diseases have in common. Elicit the response that each of these diseases is caused by a different type of bacteria. Then point out that people are not the only living things affected by bacteria. Describe some plant diseases caused by bacteria, such as blight and rot. Emphasize the economic loss these diseases cause.

EXTENSION Have interested students research the role of bacteria in sewage treatment plants or in producing antibiotics. Tell students to write their findings in a report.

RETEACHING OPTION Students often have many misconceptions concerning bacteria and view bacteria solely as disease-causing organisms. Tell students that of the thousands of known bacteria, only a small number are harmful. Then, describe how bacteria are helpful to people and other organisms.

Answers to Challenges (p. 119)

Apply

6. Bacteria are growing in the can.
7. They stop bacterial growth.
8. Answers will vary. Accept all logical responses.

InfoSearch

You may wish to discuss students' questions and answers as a class.

Teaching Tips for Technology and Society
M.A.P.: Modified Atmosphere Packaging

DISCUSSION Describe how M.A.P. stops food spoilage. Be sure students understand that canning, pickling, and freezing slow down the action of bacteria by impeding the conditions bacteria need to grow. M.A.P. actually prevents airborne bacteria from reaching food.

Question

COMPARE How are the plastic coverings used in M.A.P. similar to a cell membrane? (The plastic coverings and cell membranes only allow certain substances to pass in and out.)

LESSON 6-3
What are protists? (p. 120)

Teaching Strategies

PREVIEW Have students write the lesson title and objective in their notebooks. As students read the lesson, tell them to write down the sentence or sentences that provide the information needed in the objective.

DISCUSSION Discuss the characteristics of protists. Explain that most protists have only one cell, but that some have many cells. Emphasize that many-celled protists do not have tissues or organs.

DISCUSSION Refer students to the diagrams on p. 120 showing an amoeba, a paramecium, and a trypanosome. Have students locate the pseudopods, cilia, and flagella as you describe these structures and how they are used for movement.

REINFORCEMENT Ask if any students have ever been in a rowboat. If so, have the students describe their experiences to the rest of the class. Compare the movement of cilia to a rowboat's oars.

RETEACHING OPTION Write the following head on the chalkboard: *Protists.* From this head, draw arrows to each of the following heads: *Protozoans, Algae, Slime Molds.* Identify protozoans as the animallike protists and algae as the plantlike protists. Have students copy the chart in their notebooks.

Answers to Challenges (p. 121)

Apply

6. protozoans, algae, slime molds
7. Both are used for movement in protists.

InfoSearch

You may wish to discuss students' questions and answers as a class.

Teaching Tips for Activity
Analyzing Movement in Protists

Skills: *classifying, observing, inferring*

COOPERATIVE/COLLABORATIVE LEARNING Answer the questions as a class.

Questions

1. animallike; the protists move.
2. a. Anarma **b.** 25
3. in water
4. a microscope; Most protists are microscopic.

LESSON 6-4
What are algae? (p. 122)

Teaching Strategies

PREVIEW Before beginning this lesson, write the title of each section in the lesson on the chalkboard. Have students copy these titles in their notebooks using an outline format. As students read each section, they should write the topic sentence for each paragraph in the section in their notebooks.

DISCUSSION Describe the characteristics of algae. Point out how algae are plantlike. Be sure students understand that all algae contain chlorophyll, although not all algae are green.

EXTENSION You may wish to tell students that the microscopic algae and tiny plants that float on the surface of water are called phytoplankton. The tiny animals are called zooplankton. Together, all of the organisms are called plankton.

CLASS ACTIVITY If possible, take the class on a field trip to observe a stagnant pond. Students will see many different types of algae. Collect samples from the surface of the pond. Have students examine the samples under a microscope when they return to the classroom. Tell students to sketch their observations and identify as many algae as they can.

RETEACHING OPTION Ask students who have been to a beach if they noticed any seaweed washed up along the shoreline. Have students describe the seaweed. Point out that seaweed is one type of multicellular algae. Then describe the other types of algae to the class.

Answers to Challenges (p. 123)

Apply

6. Answers will vary. Accept all logical responses.
7. Answers will vary. Accept all logical responses.

Skill Builder: Organizing

Brown algae are used to make toothpaste and ice cream. Golden-brown algae are used to make detergent, silver polish, and toothpaste. Red algae are used to make ice cream, cheese, and marshmallows.

Teaching Tips for Science Connection
Algal Blooms

DISCUSSION Bring in a detergent with a label stating that the detergent does not contain phosphates. Before students read the feature, ask them if they know what the label means and why it is put on the detergent. Discuss student responses. Then have students read the feature to find out how phosphates may cause an algal bloom.

Questions

1. When do algal blooms often occur? (when wastes containing phosphates are dumped into ponds or lakes)
2. RELATE How does an algal bloom affect the oxygen content of a lake or pond? (Oxygen content decreases.)

LESSON 6-5
What are fungi? (p. 124)

Teaching Strategies

PREVIEW Have students read the lesson feature before beginning the lesson. Discuss the concepts presented in the feature. Ask students how they think this information relates to topics they have already studied or to the lesson they are about to study.

DISCUSSION Discuss the similarities and differences between plants and fungi. Emphasize that the differences led scientists to classify fungi in their own kingdom.

CLASS ACTIVITY If possible, take students on a field trip to observe different kinds of fungi. Have students draw the fungi they observe and use a field guide to identify the group to which each fungus belongs.

CLASS ACTIVITY Grow bread mold as a class. Moisten a piece of bread and place it in a dark, warm place. After a few days, have students check the bread for mold growth. Allow students to use a hand lens to examine the mold.

DEMONSTRATION Bring a mushroom to class. Point out the cap, the stalk, and the gills.

RETEACHING OPTION Write a recipe for making bread on the chalkboard that calls for using yeast. Some students may know that yeast is used to make bread rise. Ask students why they think yeast makes bread rise. Discuss all student responses. Point out that yeasts are one-celled fungi. Tell students that as bread dough is baked, yeast in the dough produces carbon dioxide gas. The gas causes bubbles to form in the bread. As the bubbles form in the bread, the bread rises.

Answers to Challenges (p. 125)

Apply

7. Spores from the parent mushroom are carried away by wind, water, or insects.
8. Answers will vary. Accept all logical responses.
9. A mushroom is not green.

Health and Safety Tip

Answers will vary. Accept all logical responses.

Teaching Tips for Science Connection
Fungicides

CLASS ACTIVITY To help students remember that fungicides are used to kill fungi, have them look up the meaning of the suffix -cide in a dictionary. (-cide: relating to killing) Then, ask students how its meaning relates to its use in the term fungicide.

Question

RELATE Why do you think drying the skin between the toes after bathing reduces your chances of getting athlete's foot? (Fungi grow best in moist places.)

LESSON 6-6
How do yeasts and molds reproduce? (p. 126)

Teaching Strategies

PREVIEW Before beginning this lesson, have students review the TechTerms and their definitions and read the Lesson Summary.

CLASS ACTIVITY Mix a pinch of baker's yeast with 100 mL of warm water and 1/2 teaspoon of sugar. Gently swirl the mixture for 15 minutes. Then have students make slides of the yeast solution. Have students add a drop of crystal violet to stain the slides. Tell students to observe the yeast cells under the microscope. Have students sketch the yeast cells and look for budding cells.

DISCUSSION Describe sporulation in bread molds. Use the diagram on p. 126 to illustrate your description.

COOPERATIVE/COLLABORATIVE LEARNING Have one student describe the process of budding to the rest of the class. Have another student describe sporulation.

Answers to Challenges (p. 127)
Check

1. one
2. yeasts
3. thousands
4. attached to the parent cell
5. It produces many more offsprings.

Apply

6. Both mushrooms and molds produce spores.
7. Answers will vary. Accept all logical responses.

InfoSearch

You may wish to discuss students' questions and answers as a class.

Teaching Tips for Activity
Growing Mold

Skills: *observing, inferring, hypothesizing*

COOPERATIVE/COLLABORATIVE LEARNING Have students work in pairs.

Questions

1. Answers will vary. Accept all logical responses.
2. **a.** Answers will vary. Accept all logical responses.
b. Answers will vary. Accept all logical responses.
3. They are different types of molds.
4. moisture, darkness, a food source
5. Answers will vary. Accept all logical responses.

Answers to Unit Challenges (pp. 128-130)

Understanding the Features: Reading Critically

1. ponds and lake into which wastes containing phosphates are dumped
2. chemical preparation used to prevent or cure diseases caused by fungi
3. because they were simple, one-celled organisms
4. a method of keeping fresh foods from spoiling based on controlling the food's environment

Interpreting a Diagram

1. cap
2. gills
3. to produce spores
4. stalk
5. rhizoids
6. anchor the mushroom; absorb nutrients

Critical Thinking

1. They take away one or more of the conditions needed for bacterial growth.
2. They do not have tissues or organs.
3. Fungi grow in soil, have cell walls, and most are multicellular. Fungi do not have chloroplasts or chlorophyll.
4. Nitrogen-fixing bacteria in the soil change nitrogen into compounds that can be used. Animals get nitrogen compounds by eating plants. Animals use the compounds to make proteins.
5. dark, warm, moist places

Previewing the Unit

Read the titles of the lessons in this unit aloud. Identify terms in the titles with which students are unfamiliar. Write these terms on the chalkboard. Using the Glossary of the text or a dictionary, define the terms as a class. Have students write the terms and their definitions in their notebooks. Then, have students carry out the task in the Study Hint.

Bulletin Board Suggestions

1. Assemble a bulletin board illustrating the importance of plants. Attach pictures showing products that are made from or derived from plants, such as food products, medicines, lumber, clothing, and so on.
2. Divide the bulletin board into two sections. Label each section with one of the following heads: *Gymnosperms, Angiosperms.* Have students look for and collect pictures of different seed plants. Tell students to label each picture. Attach all the pictures under the appropriate heads to make a collage.

LESSON 7-1
Why are plants important?
(p. 132)

Teaching Strategies

PREVIEW Before beginning this lesson, have students scan the lesson for the science process skill symbols. Have students identify each skill used in the lesson. Students should then review the definition given for each skill on page 16 of their text.

DISCUSSION Begin this lesson by asking students why plants are important. Discuss all student responses. Elicit from students that plants are used for food and to make many useful products, such as paper. Point out that plants also are used to make drugs and medicines.

RETEACHING OPTION Bring in a variety of products made from plant parts and display them in front of the classroom. Products may include paper, rubber, wood, plastics, string, cotton, and linen. Ask students what all the products have in common. Point out that they are all obtained from plants.

CLASS ACTIVITY If possible, arrange for your class to visit a botanical garden. Ask a tour guide to point out and describe some of the plants commonly used by people to make useful products.

Answers to Challenges (p. 133)
Ideas in Action

You may wish to have students list the plants on the chalkboard.

Teaching Tips for People in Science
George Washington Carver

EXTENSION You may wish to explain how legumes help revive soil from which minerals have been depleted. Nitrogen-fixing bacteria live in nodules on the roots of legumes. The bacteria change nitrogen gas from the atmosphere into nitrogen compounds that plants can use.

Questions

1. INFER What is crop rotation? (planting legumes one season and plants such as cotton in the same field the next year)
2. LIST What are three uses for peanuts? (Answers will vary. Accept all logical responses.)

LESSON 7-2
What are spore plants? (p. 134)

Teaching Strategies

PREVIEW Before beginning this lesson, read the list of TechTerms aloud so students can hear their pronunciations.

REINFORCEMENT Before beginning this lesson, remind students that botanists have divided plants into two main divisions, bryophytes and tracheophytes. Ask students on what the two divisions are based. (how water and dissolved minerals are moved throughout a plant)

CLASS ACTIVITY Bring some samples of moss to class. Have students observe the moss specimens with a hand lens. Tell students to note the short main stalk, the flat, green leaflike structures growing around it, and the rhizoids. Tell students to also look for spore cases.

EXTENSION Have interested students research the use of peat moss in gardens and as a fuel source. Tell students to write their findings in a report.

DEMONSTRATION If possible, bring a liverwort and a hornwort to class and point out the various structures on each plant.

RETEACHING OPTION Write the following head on the chalkboard: *Bryophytes.* From this head, draw arrows to each of the following heads: *Mosses, Liverworts, Hornworts.* Then describe the characteristics of bryophytes. Have students copy the information in their notebooks.

Answers to Challenges (p. 135)
Apply

6. Bryophytes need water for reproduction.
7. Rhizoids grow down into the soil and anchor a plant. They also take in water and dissolved minerals.

Teaching Tips for Looking Back in Science
Scouring Rushes

REINFORCEMENT Be sure students understand that horsetails are spore plants, but not bryophytes. Horsetails were among the first tracheophytes to appear on the earth.

Questions

1. Why would horsetails be good for cleaning pots? (The rough surface of horsetails can remove dirt.)
2. COMPARE How do modern horsetails compare to ancient horsetails? (They are smaller.)

LESSON 7-3
What are ferns? (p. 136)

Teaching Strategies

PREVIEW Have students write the lesson title and objective in their notebooks. As students read the lesson, tell them to write down the sentence or sentences that provide the information needed in the objective.

DEMONSTRATION Hold up a fern in front of the classroom. Point out the fronds, the rhizomes, and the spore cases.

DISCUSSION Discuss the similarities and differences between ferns and bryophytes. Point out that both ferns and bryophytes reproduce by spores. Then, tell students that unlike bryophytes, ferns have true roots, stems, and leaves. Ask students to state in which plant division ferns are classified. (tracheophytes)

EXTENSION Have interested students research the life cycle of a fern, which involves alteration of generations. Tell students to write their findings in a report. Have students include a diagram showing the life cycle of a fern.

COOPERATIVE/COLLABORATIVE LEARNING Have students work in pairs to answer the Check and Apply questions.

Answers to Challenges (p. 137)

Apply

5. Check students' drawings
6. frond; It is the leaf of a fern.

InfoSearch

You may wish to discuss students' questions and answers as a class.

Skill Builder: Researching

Lignite is called brown coal. Bituminous coal is called soft coal. Anthracite is the hardest kind of coal.

Teaching Tips for Leisure Activity
Indoor Gardening

CLASS ACTIVITY Have students set up a terrarium suitable for the growth of ferns in the classroom. Assign two students to take care of the terrarium each week.

Questions

1. Why are ferns common house plants? (Ferns are attractive and easy to take care of.)
2. LIST What are the growth requirements of ferns? (light, peat-filled soil, water, moist air, indirect light)

LESSON 7-4
What are gymnosperms? (p. 138)

Teaching Strategies

PREVIEW Before beginning this lesson, write the title of each section in the lesson on the chalkboard. Have students copy these titles in their notebooks using an outline format. As students read each section, they should write the topic sentence for each paragraph in the section in their notebooks.

DISCUSSION Obtain colorful pictures of gymnosperms, such as sequoias, red woods, spruces, firs, ginkgoes, and cycads. While displaying the pictures to the class, point out that all of the plants produce seeds as opposed to having spores.

CLASS ACTIVITY If possible, have students examine the cones of several different conifers. Tell students to note the size and shape of the cones. Students may be able to shake some pollen from a fresh pollen cone. If so, have students examine the pollen with a hand lens.

DEMONSTRATION Try to obtain mature pinecones. Boil the cones and remove the seeds. Have students examine the seeds.

DISCUSSION Discuss the economic significance of gymnosperms. Point out that they are used as a source of lumber, fuel, and many other products.

Answers to Challenges (p. 139)
Apply

7. Check students' models.
8. A; It has needles.

Ideas in Action

Check students' tables. Answers will vary.

Teaching Tips for Activity
Observing Pine Cones

Skills: *comparing, contrasting, measuring*

COOPERATIVE/COLLABORATIVE LEARNING Answer the questions as a class.

LESSON 7-5
What are angiosperms? (p. 140)

Teaching Strategies

DISCUSSION Provide motivation for this lesson by asking students to name as many flowering plants as they can. List student responses on the chalkboard. Students will most likely name plants with noticeable flowers. Add to the list examples, such as carrots, oak trees, corn, eggplants, palm trees, grass, and so on. Emphasize that all of these plants are angiosperms. Point out that angiosperms are the dominant plants today.

REINFORCEMENT Try to dispel the idea that fruits can be only like apples and oranges. Give the example of an acorn, which is the fruit of an oak tree.

DISCUSSION Distinguish between monocots and dicots, stressing that cotyledons store food for the developing plant in the seed.

CLASS ACTIVITY Have students bring some leaves to class. Have them observe the venation of the leaves to determine if the plants are monocots or dicots.

Answers to Challenges (p. 141)

Apply

7. Check students' models. The monocot should have petals in groups of three and parallel veins. The dicot should have petals in groups of four or five and branched veins.

Skill Builder: Using Prefixes

Mono- means one; *di-* means two. Monocots have one cotyledon. Dicots have two cotyledons. A monorail is a transportation system with one rail. A monosyllable is a one syllable word.

Teaching Tips for Activity

Classifying Monocots and Dicots

Skills: *modeling, classifying*

COOPERATIVE/COLLABORATIVE LEARNING Have students work in pairs.

Answers to Unit Challenges (pp. 142-144)

Understanding the Features: Reading Critically

1. cheese substitutes, paper, face cream, soap, ink, dyes
2. by growing legume plants in the soil
3. silica
4. Answers will vary. Accept all logical responses.
5. A fern grows best in dark, moist places.

Critical Thinking

1. Answers will vary. Accept all logical responses.
2. Both are spore plants.
3. cone
4. A monocot has flowers with petals arranged in groups of three. A dicot has flowers with petals arranged in groups of four or five. The veins in the leaves of monocots are parallel. The veins in the leaves of dicots are branched.
5. Answers will vary. Accept all logical responses.

Interpreting a Diagram

1. cotyledons
2. Corn; it has a single cotyledon.
3. Bean; it has two cotyledons.
4. within the seeds
5. seed coat

PLANT STRUCTURE AND FUNCTION (p. 145)

Previewing the Unit

Before students begin this unit, have them read the objectives and Lesson Summary for each lesson in the unit. Then, have students work in pairs to carry out the task in the Study Hint. As you read each lesson, have student volunteers read their descriptions of how the information in the lesson applies to their daily lives.

Bulletin Board Suggestion

Assemble a working bulletin board on plants to use while teaching this unit. Attach a diagram of a plant with perfect flowers to the bulletin board. Label the structures of a plant as they are introduced to students. Labeled structures should include the roots, the stem, the leaves, and the male and female parts of the flower.

LESSON 8-1
What are roots? (p. 146)

Teaching Strategies

PREVIEW Before you begin the lesson, read the TechTerms aloud so students can hear their pronunciations.

DEMONSTRATION To introduce this lesson, bring a potted plant to class. Pull the plant out of the pot in front of the class. Have students observe the plant's roots. Identify the kind of root system the plant has. Point out the root hairs extending from the root and describe their function. Then repot the plant.

DISCUSSION Refer students to the diagrams on p. 146 showing a cross section and a longitudinal section of roots. Have students locate the three layers of roots as you describe a root's structure. Tell students to observe the root cap as you discuss its protective function.

CLASS ACTIVITY If possible, have students observe prepared slides of root tips under a microscope to see the different cells found in a root.

INTRASCIENCE CONNECTION Ask students if they have ever noticed cracked or uplifted sidewalks in areas near trees. Have students discuss what they think caused the cracking and uplifting. Point out that it was caused by the action of tree roots. Root action is one cause of mechanical weathering.

RETEACHING OPTION Emphasize the fact that plants have organs. Identify roots as a plant organ. List the functions of roots on the chalkboard: **1.** anchorage **2.** absorption **3.** food storage. Point out that roots also conduct absorbed materials up to the stem, which is another plant organ.

Answers to Challenges (p. 147)
Apply

6. 606 km. It is most likely more than the area of the classroom.
7. Difficult; the many roots that make up the root system would tend to hold the plant firmly in the soil.

8. taproot: a, b; fibrous roots: c

Skill Builder: Organizing Information

Check students' tables.

Teaching Tips for Science Connection
Specialized Roots

REINFORCEMENT Write the following head on the chalkboard: *Specialized Roots.* From this head, draw arrows to each of the following heads: *Aerial Roots, Prop Roots, Aquatic Roots.* Then describe the functions of these specialized roots. Have students copy the information in their notebooks under the proper heads.

Questions

1. What are three plants that have aerial roots? (orchids, bald cypress, English ivy)
2. What is the function of prop roots? (They help support a plant.)

LESSON 8-2
What are stems? (p. 148)

Teaching Strategies

PREVIEW Before you begin the lesson, have students read the TechTerms and their definitions and review the Lesson Summary.

DEMONSTRATION A few hours before class begins, obtain two large beakers and two stalks of celery. Cut several centimeters from the bottom of the celery. Fill one beaker halfway with water and place a celery stalk in it. Fill the other beaker halfway with water and add several drops of food coloring to the water. Place the other stalk of celery in the beaker. When class begins, place the two beakers in front of the classroom. Students will observe that water has been conducted through the stalk. Tell students that water is transported up from the roots by tubes called xylem. Identify transport as one function of stems. Then ask students to state another function of stems. (support)

DISCUSSION Describe the two kinds of stems. Note that plants with woody stems usually live for more than two years, whereas plants with herbaceous stems usually live for only one or two years.

COOPERATIVE/COLLABORATIVE LEARNING Have students work in pairs to answer the Check and Apply questions.

Answers to Challenges (p. 149)
Apply

5. roots, xylem, leaves
6. The weight of the plant would cause the stem to bend and break.
7. herbaceous: a, c, e; woody: b, d, f

InfoSearch

You may wish to discuss students' questions and answers as a class.

Teaching Tips for Activity
Transport in Plants

Skills: *measuring, predicting, organizing data*

COOPERATIVE/COLLABORATIVE LEARNING Have students work in pairs.

Questions

1. The ink rose through the celery.
2. Answers will vary.
3. transport

LESSON 8-3
What are leaves? (p. 150)

Teaching Strategies

PREVIEW Before beginning this lesson, read the TechTerms aloud so students can hear their pronunciations.

DEMONSTRATION Bring a leaf to class. Point out the stalk, the blade, and the veins in the leaf as you describe these structures. Be sure students understand that the veins are made up of xylem and phloem.

DISCUSSION Distinguish between simple and compound leaves. If possible, show some examples of each.

DISCUSSION Refer students to the diagram on p. 150 showing the structure of a leaf. Discuss, in turn, the epidermis, the stomates, and the mesophyll.

CLASS ACTIVITY Divide the class into small groups and distribute different colored clay to each group. Have students use the clay to make models of a leaf. Tell students to use the diagram on p. 150 as a guide.

Answers to Challenges (p. 151)

Apply

5. The epidermis of the leaf protects the leaf. The skin protects the parts of the body.
6. The stomata would be closed on a hot day to prevent the plant from losing too much water.
7. because the many plants in the forest are giving off carbon dioxide and water
8. simple leaf
9. compound leaf
10. simple leaf

Health and Safety Tip

All three plants have compound leaves. Check students' drawings for accuracy.

Teaching Tips for Activity
Classifying Leaves

Skills: *modeling, analyzing, measuring, classifying*

SAFETY TIP Caution students not to touch the leaves of poison ivy, poison oak, or poison sumac.

COOPERATIVE/COLLABORATIVE LEARNING Have students work in pairs.

Questions

1. Pictures in a field guide can be compared to the leaf specimens gathered and used as a means of identification.

Answers may vary. Accept all logical responses.
2. Answers will vary depending upon the leaves chosen.
3. Answers will vary depending upon the leaves chosen.
4. Students should see two basic vein patterns, parallel and branched.

Lesson 8-4
What is photosynthesis? (p. 152)

Teaching Strategies

PREVIEW Before students begin this lesson, have them review the TechTerms and read the Lesson Summary.

REINFORCEMENT Review the role of plants as producers. Remind students that plants are able to make their own food by the process of photosynthesis. Point out that the food plants make is sugar.

DISCUSSION Write the chemical equation for photosynthesis on the chalkboard: $CO_2 + H_2O$ —energy→ $C_6H_{12}O_6 + O_2$. Point to and identify each substance involved in the reaction. Develop the concept that carbon dioxide and water are the materials needed for photosynthesis and that oxygen is a waste product of photosynthesis. Explain that the oxygen produced by photosynthesis is used by both plants and animals to carry on respiration. Ask students where plants get the energy to carry on photosynthesis. (sunlight)

EXTENSION Have interested students use library references to find out more about accessory pigments, such as carotenoids and phycobilins. Tell students to write their findings in a report.

Answers to Challenges (p. 153)

Apply

5. B
6. Water enters the leaf through C.
7. No; it does not have chloroplasts.

Skill Builder: Building Vocabulary

Photo- means light; *synthesis* means to put together; *chlor-* means green; *-plast* means structure or body: *-phyll* means leaf. Chlorophyll is a green (chlor-) pigment found in leaves (-phyll); chloroplast is a green (chlor-) structure (-plast) inside plant cells. Photosynthesis is a process in which plants use sunlight (photo-) and other raw materials to put together (synthesis) food.

Teaching Tips for Activity
Separating "Plant Pigments"

Skills: *observing, predicting, modeling*

COOPERATIVE/COLLABORATIVE LEARNING Have students work in pairs.

Questions

1. It began to separate into different colors.
2. Students should detect at least three colors; however depending upon the ink used, more colors may be evident.
3. plant pigments
4. The plant pigment would separate into its component colors.

LESSON 8-5
What are flowers? (p. 154)

Teaching Strategies

PREVIEW Before you begin this lesson, read the TechTerms aloud so students can hear their pronunciations.

DISCUSSION To provide motivation for this lesson, ask students what their favorite flowers are and why. List student responses on the chalkboard. Point out that people appreciate flowers for their beauty and fragrance. Then develop the concept that flowers are the organs of sexual reproduction in plants.

DEMONSTRATION Bring actual flowers to class, including a perfect flower and an imperfect flower. Point out and describe the sepals, the petals, the pistils, and the stamens.

REINFORCEMENT Draw a perfect flower on the chalkboard. Have students come up to the chalkboard and label the parts of the flower.

COOPERATIVE/COLLABORATIVE LEARNING Have a volunteer explain the difference between a perfect flower and an imperfect flower for the rest of the class.

Answers to Challenges (p. 155)
Apply
5. Students' models should resemble the diagram of a flower on p. 154.
6. a. perfect **b.** perfect **c.** imperfect
Skill Builder: Classifying
A pistillate flower has a pistil, but no stamens. A staminate flower has stamens, but no pistil. Pistillate and staminate flowers are imperfect flowers. The flower shown in C is a pistillate.

Teaching Tips for Leisure Activity
Gardening

DISCUSSION Have any students who enjoy gardening describe their hobby to the rest of the class.

CLASS ACTIVITY If possible, have students grow and maintain a garden on the school grounds.

Questions

1. Why do people like to garden? (to beautify their homes; to have fresh cut flowers; to raise their own fruits and vegetables)
2. ANALYZE Why do you think gardening is good exercise? (Answers will vary. Accept all logical responses.)

DISCUSSION To provide motivation for this lesson, ask students if they, their friends, or members of their families suffer from hay fever. Ask students if they know what causes hay fever. As a hint, refer to the pollen count given during certain months of the year. Elicit from students that pollen is responsible for hay fever. Define pollen grains as the male reproductive cells in plants.

REINFORCEMENT Be sure students understand the difference between fertilization and pollination. Students often confuse the two terms.

DISCUSSION Ask students to describe some instances of pollination that they have observed in nature, such as bees pollinating flowers. Guide students to understand that for pollination to take place, pollen must move from the stamen to the pistil. Tell students that wind, birds, and insects are important agents of pollination. Then ask students to suggest the importance of color and odor in flowers. Discuss all student responses. Point out that these features are ways of making flowers attractive to insects.

COOPERATIVE/COLLABORATIVE LEARNING Have a volunteer explain the difference between self-pollination and cross-pollination for the rest of the class.

Answers to Challenges (p. 157)
Apply
6. An insect carries pollen from one flower to another in its mouth or on its body when it feeds upon the flowers.
7. flat open flowers; Flat open flowers would be more easily pollinated than tall closed flowers.

Health and Safety Tip
Check students' posters.

Teaching Tips for Science Connection
Mutualism

EXTENSION Have interested students find out about other relationships among organisms such as commensalism and parasitism. Tell students to define these terms in a report and to give examples of each.

Questions

1. DEFINE What is mutualism? (relationship between two living things that is helpful to both living things)
2. How are bees helpful to plants? (Bees help pollinate plants.)

LESSON 8-6
How do flowering plants reproduce? (p. 156)

Teaching Strategies

PREVIEW Before beginning this lesson, have students scan the lesson for the science process skill symbols. Have students

LESSON 8-7
What are seeds and fruits? (p. 158)

Teaching Strategies

PREVIEW Have students write the lesson title and objectives in their notebooks. As students read the lesson, tell them to write down the sentence or sentences that provide the information needed in the objectives.

DISCUSSION Describe the parts of a pistil and the growth of a pollen tube. Use the diagrams on p. 158 to illustrate your descriptions.

DEMONSTRATION Remove as many pollen grains from a flower as you can. Add the grains to a small test tube filled with water and a little sugar. Allow the test tube to stand overnight. The next day prepare microscope slides of the pollen. Have students observe the slides under a microscope to look for growth of pollen tubes.

CLASS ACTIVITY Bring in an assortment of fruits. Cut the fruits open to expose their seeds. Have students explain how the seeds form and to note whether each fruit has one or many seeds.

RETEACHING OPTION Write the following heads on the chalkboard: *Stamen, Pistil.* From the head *Stamen,* draw arrows to each of the following heads: *Filament, Anther.* From the head *Pistil,* draw arrows to each of the following heads: *Stigma, Style, Ovary.* Have students copy the charts in their notebooks.

Answers to Challenges (p. 159)

Apply

5. Check students' drawings.
6. The stickiness of the stigma helps to attract and keep pollen grains on the flower.

Skill Builder: Organizing Information

Students' tables will vary depending upon the fruits selected. Check students' table for logic and accuracy.

Skill Builder: Classifying

a. tomato: fruit; vegetable **b.** beets: vegetable; vegetable **c.** cucumber: fruit; vegetable **d.** carrot: vegetable; vegetable **e.** peach: fruit; fruit **f.** celery: vegetable; vegetable **g.** lettuce: vegetable; vegetable **h.** papaya: fruit; fruit **i.** green pepper: fruit; vegetable

Teaching Tips for Career in Life Science

Greengrocer

EXTENSION Arrange for a greengrocer to visit your class. Ask the greengrocer to describe a typical work day.

Questions

1. What are two things a greengrocer does on the job? (Students should restate two things listed in the feature.)
2. Why should you take science and mathematic courses in high school if you want to become a greengrocer? (Caring for fruits and vegetables requires some knowledge of science. Running a business requires mathematical skills.)

LESSON 8-8
What are the parts of a seed?

(p. 160)

Teaching Strategies

PREVIEW Before beginning this lesson, have students scan the lesson looking for words with which they are unfamiliar. Have students work in pairs or small groups to define each of the words on their lists.

CLASS ACTIVITY Provide motivation for this lesson by distributing dry lima beans to the class. Tell students to note the hard, outer covering of the seed. Discuss the protective function of the seed coat.

CLASS ACTIVITY Distribute lima beans that have been soaked in water overnight to the class. Have students locate the hilum and the small opening near it. Point out that the opening is where the pollen tube entered the ovule.

RETEACHING OPTION If possible, show students time-lapsed pictures of plant germination. Have students describe what is happening in each picture.

Answers to Challenges (p. 161)

Apply

7. sunlight

Ideas in Action

Answers will vary. Accept all logical responses.

Skill Builder: Inferring

a. wind **b.** attachment to animals
c. wind **d.** water **e.** animals

Teaching Tips for Activity

Testing Seeds for Starch

Skills: *observing, measuring, analyzing*

SAFETY TIP Caution students to be careful when using a knife.

COOPERATIVE/COLLABORATIVE LEARNING Have students work in pairs.

Questions

1. a. black **b.** Answers will vary depending upon the kinds of seeds chosen.
2. a. food **b.** energy
3. All of the seeds have seed coats.

LESSON 8-9
How do plants reproduce asexually? (p. 162)

Teaching Strategies

PREVIEW Before beginning this lesson, write the title of each section in the lesson on the chalkboard. Have students copy these titles in their notebooks using an outline format. As students read each section, they should write the topic sentence for each paragraph in the section in their notebooks.

DISCUSSION To begin this lesson, ask students if they think it is possible to grow a plant without seeds. Discuss student responses. Develop the concept that some plants can reproduce by asexual reproduction.

DEMONSTRATION Bring in a potato. Identify the potato as an underground stem called a tuber. Point out the buds, or eyes, of the potato. Tell students that when planted, each eye may grow into a new potato plant.

CLASS ACTIVITY Have students plant the eyes of white potatoes. Tell students to check their potatoes for growth and to report on their results.

DISCUSSION Bring in an onion and display it in front of the classroom. Point out that an onion is a bulb. Define a bulb as an underground stem covered with fleshy leaves. Tell students that a bulb is another organ of vegetative propagation. Then ask students if they know of any other plants that grow from bulbs. (Some students may be familiar with the bulbs of plants such as tulips and daffodils.)

CLASS ACTIVITY Have students use cuttings of plants, such as carrots, turnips, beets, or sweet potatoes, to grow new plants.

Answers to Challenges (p. 163)

Apply

6. a. root **b.** stem **c.** stem

InfoSearch

You may wish to discuss students' questions and answers as a class.

Teaching Tips for Activity

Growing Plants Asexually

Skills: *observing, comparing*

SAFETY TIP Caution students to be careful when using a knife.

COOPERATIVE/COLLABORATIVE LEARNING Have students work in pairs.

EXTENSION You may wish to have students grow plants using other methods of vegetative propagation such as leaf cuttings and stem grafting.

Questions

1. Both the onion and the potato can reproduce through vegetative propagation.
2. Answers may vary, but the onion is more likely to develop roots first.

LESSON 8-10
What are tropisms? (p. 164)

Teaching Strategies

PREVIEW Before you begin this lesson, have students read the TechTerms and review the Lesson Summary.

REINFORCEMENT Review the concept of stimuli and responses. Ask students to give some examples of animals responding to stimuli. Then remind students that response is one of the six characteristics used to classify something as living. Emphasize that plants respond to changes in their environment too. Define tropism as the reaction of a plant to a stimulus.

DEMONSTRATION You can demonstrate the response of a plant toward light by placing a plant near a window that receives sunlight. Place the plant so its leaves and/or flowers are facing in a direction away from the light. Have students observe the plant for the next week. In a few days, students should observe that the plant has changed position so that its leaves and/or flowers are facing toward the sun.

EXTENSION You may wish to introduce the concept of positive and negative tropisms. In a positive tropism, a plant part grows in a direction *toward* the stimulus. In a negative tropism, a plant part grows *away* from the stimulus.

EXTENSION You may wish to introduce the term *auxins*. Auxins are plant hormones. Auxins are responsible for the growth of plants toward or away from stimuli.

Answers to Challenges (p. 165)

Apply

6. For a short time, the plant stems would grow up, away from the pull of gravity. However, the plant would quickly die if not exposed to light because it would be unable to carry on photosynthesis.
7. The roots of the willow tree have grown into the drain causing the clog.

Skill Builder: Building Vocabulary

The prefix *geo-* means earth; *hydro-* means water; and *photo-* means light. When added to the word *tropism*, each of these prefixes identifies the stimulus to which a plant is responding.

Teaching Tips for Science Connection

Carnivorous Plants

DEMONSTRATION Bring in a Venus' flytrap to show the class.

Question

How does a Venus' flytrap digest an insect? (Special chemicals that digest the soft parts of an insect are given off by the leaf.)

Answers to Unit Challenges (pp. 166-168)

Understanding the Features: Reading Critically

1. a relationship between two living things that is helpful to both living things
2. sells fresh fruit and vegetables; buys fruit and vegetables from growers; arranges fruit and vegetables; answers customers' questions
3. Answers will vary. Accept all logical responses.
4. Special chemicals are given off by the leaf.
5. aerial roots, prop roots, aquatic roots

Interpreting a Diagram

1. e
2. b
3. c
4. d
5. c and d
6. perfect; It has both male and female reproductive structures.
7. a
8. f

Critical Thinking

1. It would grow up.
2. The stem would bend and break.
3. Pollination is the transfer of pollen from the stamen to the pistil. Fertilization is the union of male and female reproductive cells.
4. The fruit will normally not be eaten until the seeds are ready for distribution. This helps ensure survival of the species.
5. It helps the root tip move easily through the soil.

Previewing the Unit

Read the titles of the lessons in this unit aloud. Identify terms in the titles with which students are unfamiliar. Write these terms on the chalkboard. Using the Glossary of the text or a dictionary, define the terms as a class. Have students write the terms and their definitions in their notebooks. Then, have students work in small groups to carry out the task in the Study Hint.

Bulletin Board Suggestions

1. Assemble a bulletin board illustrating the animal phyla introduced in this unit. At the top of the bulletin board write the following head: *Animals Without Backbones.* Underneath the head attach pictures of representative sponges, cnidarians, flatworms, segmented worms, mollusks, echinoderms, and arthropods. Label each picture with the name of the organism and its phylum. Use the bulletin board to show students the wide variety of invertebrates.

2. Assemble a bulletin board illustrating the importance of invertebrates to people. Attach pictures to the bulletin board showing the ways invertebrates are both harmful and helpful to humans. You may wish to include pictures showing natural sponges, pearl jewelry, seafoods. coral reefs, honey, insects pollinating flowers, crop destruction by insects, diseases caused by parasitic invertebrates, and so on.

LESSON 9-1
What are sponges? (p. 170)

Teaching Strategies

PREVIEW Before students read this lesson, have them scan through the lesson looking for the science process skill symbols. Have students identify each skill used in the lesson. Students should then review the definition given for each skill on page 16 of their text.

REINFORCEMENT Before beginning this lesson, remind students that taxonomists divide animals into two large groups, invertebrates and vertebrates. Have students recall that invertebrates are animals without backbones.

DISCUSSION To introduce this lesson, ask students what they think of when they hear the term *sponge.* (Most students probably will think of the synthetic sponges used for cleaning.) Point out that there also are natural sponges and they are the simplest animals in the animal kingdom. Then tell students that sponges were once classified as plants. Ask students if they can figure out why. Discuss all student responses. Point out that unlike most animals, sponges do not move from place to place.

DISCUSSION Describe the structure of the sponge. Refer students to the diagram of a sponge on p. 170. Have students locate the two cell layers, the collar cells and their flagella, the wandering cells, and the spicules as you describe the function of each of these structures.

DISCUSSION Bring a natural sponge to class. Show students the many pores of the sponge.

CLASS ACTIVITY Obtain natural sponges and a variety of synthetic sponges made out of different materials. Divide the class into small groups. Distribute a natural sponge and synthetic sponge to each group. Have students in each group work together to design experiments testing the absorbance capabilities of each kind of sponge. Tell students to present their results in laboratory reports. (Students should observe that a natural sponge absorbs more water than a synthetic sponge.)

DISCUSSION Using the diagram of the sponge on p. 170, trace the path of water into and out of a sponge. Be sure students recognize that water moves through the sponge in only one direction.

Answers to Challenges (p. 171)
Apply

6. As its name implies, a sponge contains many pores.
7. A sponge filters the materials it needs from water to survive.
8. No; the job of the flagella is to keep water moving through the sponge. If no water moves through the sponge, the sponge cannot take in the materials it needs for its life processes.

Ideas In Action

Most synthetic sponges are made from rubber products. The prices for synthetic sponges usually are much less than the prices of natural sponges.

Teaching Tips for Leisure Activity
Snorkeling

COOPERATIVE/COLLABORATIVE LEARNING Have any students who have been snorkeling describe their experiences to the rest of the class.

Questions

1. Would you like to go snorkeling? Why or why not? (Answers will vary.)
2. LIST What equipment do you need to go snorkeling? (fins, a face mask, a snorkel)

LESSON 9-2
What are cnidarians? (p. 172)

Teaching Strategies

PREVIEW Before students begin this lesson, have them read the objective and review the Lesson Summary.

REINFORCEMENT Before beginning this lesson, review the definition of tissues. Ask students what a tissue is. (group of cells that look alike and work together) This review will help students understand the structure of cnidarians because the cells of these animals are organized into tissues.

DISCUSSION Provide motivation for this lesson by asking students to describe any personal experiences they may have had with jellyfish. Students who have spent time at the seashore may already be familiar with the appearance of jellyfish. Point out that jellyfish are one kind of cnidarian.

CLASS ACTIVITY If possible, obtain some hydra from a biological supply company. Place a few hydra in a petri dish and allow students to observe the hydra under a binocular microscope. Tell students to describe their observations of movement and response by the hydra.

EXTENSION Have interested students find out about the Portuguese man-of-war. Tell students to present their findings in an oral report.

REINFORCEMENT Students may be better able to remember the body forms of cnidarians if you tell them that the mouth of a medusa always faces downward and is on the bottom of the cnidarian. In contrast, the mouth of a polyp always faces upward and is at the top of the cnidarian.

RETEACHING OPTION Show students pictures of sea anemones and coral polyps. Ask students if they think the organisms in the pictures are plants or animals. After discussing student responses, point out that the organisms are animals called cnidarians. Then identify jellyfish as cnidarians with which students probably are more familiar.

Answers to Challenges (p. 173)

Check

1. The phylum gets its name from the cnidocytes.
2. All cnidarians live in water.
3. medusa
4. digestive, muscle, nerve, and sensory tissues

Apply

5. a jellyfish
6. Both medusas and polyps have one opening (a mouth), two cell layers, a jellylike layer between the cell layers, and tissues.
7. Cnidarians have cells organized into tissues.

Health and Safety Tip

When a person is stung by a jellyfish, it is important to keep the victim calm and to seek medical attention as soon as possible.

Teaching Tips for Science Connection

Coral Reefs

EXTENSION You may wish to tell students that in the United States, coral reefs are located off the coasts of Florida, Texas, and California.

EXTENSION Have interested students research artificial reefs and their uses. Tell students to write their findings in a report.

Questions

1. LIST What are the three kinds of coral reefs? fringing reef, barrier reef, atoll)
2. Why are coral reefs valuable to marine organisms? (They are important sources of food and shelter.)

LESSON 9-3
What are flatworms and roundworms? (p. 174)

Teaching Strategies

PREVIEW Have students read the lesson feature before beginning the lesson. Discuss the concepts presented in the feature. Ask students how they think this information relates to topics they have already studied or to the lesson they are about to study.

DISCUSSION Write the term worms on the chalkboard. Ask students what they think of when they hear the word worm. (Most students probably will think of the earthworm.) Point out that there are many other kinds of worms too. Then describe the characteristics of flatworms and roundworms. Stress that flatworms are the simplest animals with bilateral symmetry and roundworms are one of the simplest animals to have a complete digestive system.

CLASS ACTIVITY To help students remember the three cell layers of worms, have students look up the meanings of the prefixes ecto-, endo-, and meso- in a dictionary. (ecto-: outer; endo-: inner; meso-: middle)

DEMONSTRATION If possible, obtain planaria from a biological supply company. Place the worms in petri dishes filled with spring water or distilled water. Have students observe the planaria and note their eyespots.

DISCUSSION Discuss the meaning of the term parasite. Point out that both flukes and tapeworms are parasites. Have students locate the hooks and suckers on the diagram of a tapeworm on p. 174. Identify these structures as adaptations for life as a parasite.

RETEACHING OPTION Write the following head on the chalkboard: Worms. From this head, draw arrows to each of the following heads: Flatworms, Roundworms, Segmented Worms. Under flatworms list planaria, flukes, and tapeworms. Have students copy the chart in their notebooks. Tell students they will learn more about segmented worms in the next lesson.

Answers to Challenges (p. 175)

Apply

6. The flatworms have long, flat, ribbonlike bodies.
7. The parasite takes in nutrients that the host organism needs for growth.

Health and Safety Tip

Pork must be cooked thoroughly to avoid contamination by the trichina worm.

Teaching Tips for Science Connection

Pets and Worms

EXTENSION If possible, have a veterinarian visit your class to discuss how pets are treated for worms.

Questions

1. IDENTIFY What are the most dangerous parasites of dogs? (heartworms)
2. How can you help prevent your pet from getting worms? (keep pets on a leash or in a yard; clean its area regularly; feed it a balanced diet; have it checked by a veterinarian)

LESSON 9-4
What are segmented worms? (p. 176)

Teaching Strategies

PREVIEW Before beginning this lesson, have students scan the lesson for the science process skill symbols. Have students identify each skill used in the lesson. Students should then review the definition given for each skill on page 16 of their text.

DISCUSSION Tell students that the third phylum of worms, *Annelida,* includes the worms most familiar to students--earthworms. Ask students to describe an earthworm. Try to elicit that an earthworms' most striking characteristic is its segmentation.

CLASS ACTIVITY Set up a terrarium for earthworms in the classroom. Have students observe the external structure of an earthworm and the way an earthworm burrows in soil.

DISCUSSION Refer students to the diagram of an earthworm on p. 176. Have students observe the diagram as you describe the features and organ systems of an earthworm. Emphasize that earthworms are the simplest animals to have a closed circulatory system.

REINFORCEMENT Have students draw a diagram of an earthworm. Tell students to label its external and internal structures.

RETEACHING OPTION Ask students what happens to earthworms during a heavy rain. Challenge students to explain why so many earthworms can be found on the streets and sidewalks after a heavy rain. List student responses on the chalkboard. Point out that during a heavy rain, earthworms begin to drown as the soil becomes saturated with water. The water prevents earthworms from obtaining enough gases through their skin.

Answers to Challenges (p. 177)

Apply

6. The bodies of annelids are made up of many ringlike sections, or segments.
7. If exposed to direct sunlight, the earthworm would dry out and be unable to carry on respiration through its moist skin. As a result, the earthworm would die.

InfoSearch

You may wish to discuss students' questions and answers as a class.

Teaching Tips for Looking Back in Science
Medical Uses of Leeches

ITERDISCIPLINARY CONNECTION You may wish to tell students that George Washington's death is attributed to the practice of ''bloodletting'' using leeches.

EXTENSION If possible, show students a preserved specimen of a leech.

Question

How are leeches being used in medicine today? (The chemicals given off by leeches are being used to keep blood from clotting, dilate blood vessels, heal damaged tissues, and prevent infection.)

LESSON 9-5
What are mollusks? (p. 178)

Teaching Strategies

PREVIEW Before beginning this section, have students scan the lesson looking for words with which they are unfamiliar. Have students work in pairs or small groups to define each of the words on their lists.

DISCUSSION Provide motivation for this lesson by asking

students if they have ever eaten clams, scallops, oysters, mussels, escargots, or squid. Point out that all of these seafood are animals that belong to the phylum *Mollusca.* Then describe the three major classes of mollusks and the characteristics of each.

EXTENSION You may wish to tell students that mollusks with one shell are called univalves, mollusks with two shells are called bivalves, and mollusks with no shell are called cephalopods.

DISCUSSION Describe the three body parts of mollusks and their organ systems using the clam as an example. Refer students to the diagram of a clam on p. 178 to illustrate your description.

CLASS ACTIVITY If possible, obtain a variety of different kinds of mollusk shells. Allow students to examine the shells closely to see how the shells differ.

CLASS ACTIVITY If your school is located near a shoreline, you may wish to arrange a class trip to the ocean to provide students with an opportunity to collect and observe mollusk shells first-hand.

INTRASCIENCE CONNECTION Describe Newton's third law of motion and relate it to the way cephalopods move. Newton's third law of motion states that for every action there is an equal and opposite reaction.

ITERDISCIPLINARY CONNECTION Have interested students read Jules Verne's *Twenty Thousand Leagues Under the Sea* and write a book report.

Answers to Challenges (p. 179)

Apply

5. The movement of squid and octopuses is an example of an action-reaction relationship. These animals shoot out a stream of water from their bodies. The force of the water causes the body to move in a direction opposite the stream of water.

InfoSearch

You may wish to discuss students' questions and answers as a class.

Teaching Tips for Activity
Modeling Squid Jet Propulsion

Skills: *analyzing, modeling*

SAFETY TIP Caution students to be careful when using scissors.

COOPERATIVE/COLLABORATIVE LEARNING Have students work in pairs.

Questions

1. opposite the direction of its neck
2. The movement caused by the balloon releasing air is the same as the movement that would be caused by the squid releasing water.
3. The squid would move farther and faster.

LESSON 9-6
What are arthropods? (p. 180)

Teaching Strategies

PREVIEW Read the TechTerms aloud so that students can hear their pronunciations.

DISCUSSION Describe the main characteristics of arthropods. Point out that arthropods have a segmented body, jointed legs, an exoskeleton, an open circulatory system, and undergo the process of molting.

REINFORCEMENT To help students visualize an arthropod's exoskeleton, you may wish to compare it to a knight's suit of armor.

EXTENSION The two other classes of arthropods are centipedes and millipedes. Have interested students research the characteristics of these organisms. Tell students to write their findings in a report.

REINFORCEMENT Students often mistakenly refer to spiders, ticks, and scorpions as insects. Be sure students understand that these organisms are arachnids.

RETEACHING OPTION Show students many interesting pictures of arthropods to illustrate the great diversity of this largest group of animals. Try to include pictures which show the many different specialized body parts of arthropods. Have students try to identify the organisms shown and classify them into their proper classes.

Answers to Challenges (p. 181)

Check

1. Chitin is the material that makes up the exoskeleton of arthropods.
2. Arachnids are one class of arthropods.
3. *Arthropoda*
4. Accept any three of the following: exoskeleton, segmented body, jointed legs, open circulatory system, molting.
5. When an arthropod molts, it sheds its exoskeleton and grows a new one.
6. Claws are used for defense and capturing food.

Apply

7. The ants and flies are insects, the lobster is a crustacean, and the spider is an arachnid.
8. Arthropods with wings are able to fly.
9. A grasshopper moves by jumping and flying. Large back legs enable a grasshopper to jump large distances.

Health and Safety Tip

The rash that results from Lyme disease usually forms in the shape of a bull's eye target. Other symptoms of the disease include fever and pain in the joints. The white-tail deer often serves as a carrier for the deer tick that causes Lyme disease.

Teaching Tips for Technology and Society

Uses of Chitin

CLASS ACTIVITY After students read this feature, have them work in pairs to construct charts summarizing the uses of chitin.

Questions

1. Why is chitin especially good as a material for medical uses? (It does not cause allergic reactions in most people.)
2. INFER Why do you think chitin can be used in water filters? (It is waterproof.)

LESSON 9-7
What are insects? (p. 182)

Teaching Strategies

PREVIEW Before beginning this lesson, read the list of TechTerms aloud so students can hear their pronunciations.

DISCUSSION Ask students what they think of when they hear the word *insect*. Discuss all student responses. Many students probably will think of insects solely in negative terms. Point out that many insects are helpful to people and the environment. Cite pollination by bees as an example. Emphasize that insects are incredibly successful organisms in terms of their number of species and distribution.

RETEACHING OPTION Obtain a wall-sized poster of a grasshopper. Have volunteers locate the grasshopper's three body segments, three pairs of legs, and antennae. Stress that these structures are characteristic of all insects.

EXTENSION Have interested students research beekeeping as a career. Tell students to present their findings in an oral report. Students may obtain information by writing to the New Jersey Beekeepers Association, 157 Five Point Road, Colts Neck, NJ 07722.

Answers to Challenges (p. 183)

Apply

7. There are more insect species than there are other animal species.
8. The fly is larger to show that the number of insect species is greater than the number of all other animal species.

InfoSearch

You may wish to discuss students' questions and answers as a class.

Teaching Tips for Science Connection

Camouflage and Mimicry

CLASS ACTIVITY Before students read this feature, refer them to the photograph on p. 183. Ask students to find the walking stick in the photograph. This activity will demonstrate the adaptation of camouflage.

ITERDISCIPLINARY CONNECTION You may wish to discuss the use of camouflage by people. Many students probably are familiar with *camouflage* as the uniform worn by members of the military. Ask students why they think members of the armed forces wear green and brown uniforms. (to blend into the surroundings)

Question

1. EXPLAIN Why do birds avoid eating the viceroy butterfly? (It looks like the monarch butterfly, which tastes bad to birds.)
2. DEFINE What is camouflage? (ability of an organism to blend in with its surroundings)

LESSON 9-8
How do insects develop? (p. 184)

Teaching Strategies

PREVIEW Before beginning this lesson, have students review the TechTerms and their definitions and read the Lesson Summary.

DISCUSSION Describe the differences between complete and incomplete metamorphosis. Guide students to understand that in complete metamorphosis, an insect undergoes a *complete* change in form. In *incomplete* metamorphosis, the young insect (nymph) closely resembles the adult. A complete change in form does not take place.

CLASS ACTIVITY If possible, show students a sequence of time-lapsed photographs showing the metamorphosis of a butterfly. Arrange the photographs in front of the classroom in random order. Have students put the pictures in the proper sequence and identify each stage of development.

COOPERATIVE/COLLABORATIVE LEARNING Have students quiz each other on the TechTerms for this lesson.

Answers to Challenges (p. 185)

Apply

6. The eggs of insects, like the eggs of birds, contain yolk that the developing embryo uses for food. Accept all logical responses.
7. During the pupa stage the insect does not eat.
8. a, e, d, b, c

Teaching Tips for Career in Life Science
Exterminator

REINFORCEMENT Be sure students understand that an exterminator may kill mice and rats as well as insect pests.

Questions

1. RELATE Why should a person interested in becoming an exterminator take biology and chemistry courses in high school? (Extermination involves living things and often the use of chemicals to destroy them.)
2. INFER Why are termites harmful to people? (Termites destroy property.)

LESSON 9-9
What are echinoderms? (p. 186)

Teaching Strategies

PREVIEW Have students write the lesson title and objectives in their notebooks. As students read the lesson, tell them to write down the sentence or sentences that provide the information needed in the objectives.

DEMONSTRATION If possible, obtain a preserved specimen of a seastar to show to the class. As you discuss each echinoderm characteristic, point to the part of the seastar that exemplifies the characteristic.

DEMONSTRATION Demonstrate the action of tube feet with a medicine dropper. Place the tip of a medicine dropper against the tip of your finger. Squeeze the bulb of the medicine dropper to force all air out of the tube. When you release the bulb, the vacuum formed by the lack of air inside the dropper should cause the dropper to remain attached to your finger. Relate this to the action of a seastar's tube feet.

Answers to Challenges (p. 187)

Apply

7. The sand or mud would not allow the tube feet to form the vacuum needed to grasp a surface.
8. The animals who fed on sea stars would decrease.

Skill Builder: Building Vocabulary

Check students' diagrams.

Teaching Tips for Leisure Activity
Seashore Collections

DISCUSSION Point out to students that seashore collections usually are made up of shells from mollusks, crustaceans, and echinoderms.

CLASS ACTIVITY If possible, arrange for a class trip to a shoreline or an aquarium for students to observe different seashells.

Question

Why should a person avoid collecting live animals on a beach? (Answers will vary. Accept all logical responses.)

LESSON 9-10
What is regeneration? (p. 188)

Teaching Strategies

PREVIEW Before beginning this lesson, write the title of each section in the lesson on the chalkboard. Have students copy these titles in their notebooks using an outline format. As students read each section, they should write the topic sentence for each paragraph in the section in their notebooks.

DEMONSTRATION Obtain a planarian from a biological supply company. Cut the planarian in half using a scalpel. Have students observe that each half eventually regenerates into a new planarian.

REINFORCEMENT Be sure students understand that regeneration of a whole organism is a form of asexual reproduction.

COOPERATIVE/COLLABORATIVE LEARNING Have a volunteer compare the regeneration abilities of a planaria and a human for the rest of the class.

Answers to Challenges (p. 189)

Apply

6. Both methods of asexual reproduction allow a new organism to grow from a part of the parent organism.
7. because a whole new organism is not produced
8. A crab can regrow a lost claw. A seastar can regrow an entire organism.

State the Problem

Students should recognize that new seastars would grow from the parts, and the population of seastars would increase.

Teaching Tips for Technology and Society
Organ Transplants

CLASS ACTIVITY Have students find and collect recent newspaper and magazine articles pertaining to organ transplants. Read and discuss the articles as a class.

Questions

1. What are some organs that can be transplanted? (liver, kidneys, heart, pancreas, lungs)
2. Why is cyclosporine important in organ transplants? (It helps keep the body of the person receiving the organ from rejecting the transplanted organ.)

Answers to Unit Challenges (pp. 190-192)

Understanding the Features: Reading Critically

1. for safety reasons
2. fringing reef, barrier reef, atoll
3. Answers will vary. Accept all logical responses.
4. Chemicals given off by leeches are being used to keep blood from clotting, dilate blood vessels, heal damaged tissue, and prevent infection.
5. A type of thread made from chitin is used for sewing up wounds and incisions.
6. It looks like a monarch butterfly, which birds do not like to eat. Thus, birds also avoid eating the viceroy butterfly.
7. Answers will vary. Accept all logical responses.
8. Answers will vary. Accept all logical responses.
9. liver, kidneys, heart, pancreas, lungs

Interpreting a Diagram

1. F
2. head
3. E
4. C
5. abdomen
6. A

Critical Thinking

1. They do not move.
2. They will regenerate and their population will increase.
3. Sunlight would dry out an earthworm. An earthworm must be moist in order to breathe.
4. Answers will vary. Accept all logical responses.
5. Answers will vary. Accept all logical responses.

ANIMALS WITH BACKBONES (p. 193)

Previewing the Unit

Before beginning this unit, read the titles of the lessons in the unit aloud. Then, have students work in pairs to carry out the task in the Study Hint.

Bulletin Board Suggestions

1. Create a bulletin board display entitled *Vertebrates.* Tell students to find and collect as many photographs of each vertebrate class discussed in this unit as possible. Attach each photograph to the bulletin board under a heading that identifies the class name. Refer to the bulletin board as you discuss characteristics and examples of the animals in each class.

2. Prepare a bulletin board display entitled *Kinds of Birds.* Divide the bulletin board into five sections. Label each section with one of the following heads: *Swimming Birds, Birds of Prey, Perching Birds, Wading Birds, Nonperching Land Birds.* Attach pictures of representative birds under each head. Have students choose one of the birds included in the bulletin board display on which they would like to do further research. When you are discussing Lesson 10-6, have each student point out the bird they chose on the bulletin board and present the class with information about their bird such as where it lives, what it eats, and any unique nesting or mating habits it has.

LESSON 10-1
What are chordates? (p. 194)

Teaching Strategies

PREVIEW Before beginning this lesson, have students copy the section titles into their notebooks using an outline format. As students read each section, have them write the topic sentence for each paragraph in the section into their notebooks beneath the appropriate section head. Encourage students to use their outlines as study guides.

DISCUSSION Describe the phylum *Chordata,* which includes the animals students are most familiar with. Emphasize that all chordates have three features at some time during their development: a notochord, a hollow nerve cord, and gill slits. Point out that these features distinguish chordates from all other animals.

REINFORCEMENT Be sure students understand that two subphyla of chordates do not have backbones.

CLASS ACTIVITY List the names of the five classes of vertebrates on the chalkboard. Ask students to provide you with the names of several animals that are included in each class. Write the names of each animal on the chalkboard under the appropriate head. Tell students to copy the lists into their notebooks.

REINFORCEMENT Direct students' attention to the picture of the lancelet on p. 194. As you review the characteristics of chordates, have students locate each characteristic on the diagram.

Answers to Challenges (p. 195)

Apply

8. Gills; the flexible backbone of a fish also is an adaptation for life in water.

9. the backbone

10. Answers may include any two of the following: a notochord or a backbone, gill slits, and a hollow nerve cord at some stage of development.

Skill Builder: Applying Definitions

Endo- means inner or inside; *meso-* means middle; *ecto-* means outer or outside. Students should identify the inner layer (B) as the endoderm, the outer layer (C) as the ectoderm, and the middle layer (A) as the mesoderm.

Teaching Tips for Career in Life Service
Animal Technician

EXTENSION You may wish to tell students about other careers that involve working with animals, such as animal center management and animal husbandry. Information about these careers also can be obtained by writing to the American Veterinary Medical Association.

Questions

1. INFER What kinds of science courses might be helpful to an animal technician? (Answers will vary. Accept all logical responses.)

2. APPLY A parasite is an organism that lives on or inside another organism and causes it harm. Many worms are parasites of dogs and cats. Why would an animal technician need to know about these parasites? (Answers will vary. Accept all logical responses.)

LESSON 10-2
What are fishes? (p. 196)

Teaching Strategies

PREVIEW Before students begin this lesson, have them scan the lesson for the science process skill symbols. Have students identify each skill used in the lesson. Students should then review the definition given for each skill on page 16 of their text.

DISCUSSION Describe the characteristics of fishes. Emphasize to students that in most vertebrates the gill slits disappear at some stage of development, but that in fishes, these structures become gills.

CLASS ACTIVITY If possible, set up an aquarium in the classroom and have students observe different examples of bony fishes. Tell students to note the scales, which cover and protect the skin, and the fins, which are used for steering and balance.

RETEACHING OPTION Write the following head on the chalkboard: *Fishes.* From this head, draw arrows to each of the following heads: *Jawless Fishes, Cartilaginous Fishes, Bony Fishes.* Under *Jawless Fishes,* list lampreys and hagfish. Under *Cartilaginous Fishes* list sharks, rays, and skates. Under *Bony Fishes* list tuna, salmon, bass, and flounder. Have students copy the chart in their notebooks.

CLASS ACTIVITY Have students touch the tips of their noses and their outer ears to feel cartilage. Point out that cartilage is a tough, flexible tissue which makes up some parts of the human body, and the entire skeletons of cartilaginous fishes.

REINFORCEMENT Be sure students recognize that only a few kinds of fishes are classified as either jawless fishes or cartilaginous fishes. Stress that most fishes with which students are familiar are bony fishes.

Answers to Challenges (p. 197)

Check

1. animal whose body temperature changes with the temperature of its surroundings
2. organs that absorb dissolved oxygen from water
3. 2
4. lampreys and hagfish
5. skeleton made up of cartilage
6. for steering and balance

Apply

7. 5
8. **a.** bony fish **b.** bony fish **c.** jawless fish **d.** cartilaginous fish **e.** jawless fish **f.** cartilaginous fish **g.** bony fish **h.** cartilaginous fish

Skill Builder: Inferring

The coloring of a flounder helps it blend in with its surroundings so that it can remain unseen by both its predators and prey. Having both eyes on top of its head allows a flounder to see fishes and other organisms that swim above it.

Teaching Tips for Science Connection

Unusual Fishes

EXTENSION Have interested students research other unusual fishes such as the lantern fish, the walking catfish, the halibut, and the blowfish. Tell students to write their findings in a report. Tell students to be sure to discuss how each fish's unusual adaptation helps it survive.

LESSON 10-3
What are amphibians? (p. 198)

Teaching Strategies

PREVIEW Before students begin this lesson, have them read the TechTerm and its definition and review the Lesson Summary.

DISCUSSION Write the term *Amphibian* on the chalkboard. Tell students that the word *amphibian* comes from the Greek word meaning double life. Then ask the students how they think double life applies to amphibians. Discuss all student responses. Elicit from students that most amphibians spend part of their life in water and part of their life on land.

REINFORCEMENT Be sure students understand that although adult amphibians live on land, all amphibians must reproduce in water.

DISCUSSION Refer students to the photographs of amphibians on p. 198. Describe the three different orders of amphibians. Have students identify the representative organism shown.

EXTENSION Have interested students research the estivation behavior of toads and frogs. Tell students to present their findings in oral reports.

COOPERATIVE/COLLABORATIVE LEARNING Have a volunteer describe the main characteristics of amphibians.

Answers to Challenges (p. 199)

Check

1. double life
2. fishes
3. moist, bumpy skin
4. tailless amphibian
5. so that oxygen and carbon dioxide can be exchanged through the skin

Apply

6. A salamander has a tail at all stages of development; a frog does not have a tail at all stages of development.
7. Amphibians have webbed feet to help them move quickly through water.
8. Accept any six of the following: amphibians spend part of their lives in water and part on land; have smooth, moist skin; are coldblooded; have webbed feet; breathe through gills, lungs, and their skin; do not lay eggs with shells; lay their eggs in water; have a closed circulatory system; have a three-chambered heart.

InfoSearch

You may wish to review students' questions and answers as a class.

Teaching Tips for Technology and Society

Computer Dissections

DEMONSTRATION If possible, run a frog dissection simulation disk. Show students the different organs and organ systems of a frog on the computer screen.

Questions

1. What do you think about live dissection? (Answers will vary. Accept all logical responses.)
2. DEFINE What is a simulation? (a moving model)

LESSON 10-4
How do frogs develop? (p. 200)

Teaching Strategies

PREVIEW Before students begin this lesson, have them copy the lesson objective into their notebooks. As students read the lesson, have them write the sentences that meet the objective.

REINFORCEMENT Before beginning this lesson, students may benefit from a review of insect metamorphosis. Remind students that there are two kinds of metamorphosis, complete and incomplete. Point out that the development of the frog is an example of complete metamorphosis.

DISCUSSION Trace the development of a frog from egg to adult. Refer students to the diagram showing metamorphosis on p. 200 to illustrate your description.

CLASS ACTIVITY Divide the class into small groups. Tell students in each group to draw pictures of frog eggs, tadpoles, young frogs, and adult frogs. Have students cut out their pictures and arrange them in sequence to show metamorphosis. Tell students to use the diagram or p. 200 as a guide.

COOPERATIVE/COLLABORATIVE LEARNING Have students work in pairs to answer the Check and Apply questions.

Apply

7. b, d, c, e, a

8. Check students' flow charts for logic and accuracy. Students' flow charts should indicate the following stages: Eggs are laid, tadpoles hatch from the eggs, legs begin to develop, the tail grows shorter and then disappears, lungs develop and gills disappear, a young frog suited to life on land has developed.

9. Students should recognize that laying a large number of eggs helps to ensure that some amphibians will develop into adults. Accept all logical responses.

10. Amphibian eggs are not protected by a shell. Laying eggs in water helps to prevent the eggs from drying out.

Health and Safety Tip

Warts are caused by viruses. The appearance of a wart in some ways resembles the bumps on a toad's skin. This similarity in appearance is responsible for the misconception that toads cause warts.

Teaching Tips for Activity
Sequencing Tadpole Development

Skills: *sequencing, analyzing*

COOPERATIVE/COLLABORATIVE LEARNING Answer the questions as a class.

Questions

1. The tadpole develops gills and a tail. The young frog has a tail, four legs, gills, and lungs. The frog loses its tail and gills.

2. The tadpole lives in water. It has a tail to help it swim and gills.

3. The frog lives on land. It has four feet and lungs.

LESSON 10-5
What are reptiles? (p. 202)

Teaching Strategies

PREVIEW Before students begin this lesson, have them read the objectives and review the Lesson Summary.

DISCUSSION You may wish to introduce this lesson by having students read the feature about dinosaurs on p. 203. Students often are very interested in dinosaurs, so this feature can serve as a motivational exercise. After students read the feature, discuss the many characteristics of dinosaurs and why some scientists think dinosaurs became extinct.

DISCUSSION Describe the characteristics of reptiles. Present the reptiles as animals that are well adapted to living on land. Point out that reptiles lay eggs with a tough leathery shell. Then compare the skin of reptiles and amphibians. Elicit from students the advantages of a hard, dry, scaly skin.

REINFORCEMENT Students often confuse amphibians and reptiles. As you discuss reptiles, you may wish to create a table that compares the major characteristics of amphibians and reptiles. Tell students to copy the table in their notebooks. Have students use their tables to identify characteristics that the two groups of animals share and to identify differences between amphibians and reptiles.

EXTENSION Tell students that in many areas, alligators are a protected species. Have interested students research why alligators are in danger of becoming extinct and what efforts

are being made to save alligators. Have students present their findings in oral reports.

CLASS ACTIVITY If possible, take your class to the reptile house of the local zoo to observe the different orders of reptiles.

Check

1. in eggs
2. They have many features of ancient reptiles.
3. Snakes do not have legs.
4. on land
5. by looking at their heads

Apply

6. Snakes do not have legs.
7. Answers may include that the dinosaurs shown have two pairs of legs and clawed feet; the dinosaurs have skin covered with scales. Accept all logical responses.

InfoSearch

You may wish to discuss students' questions and answers as a class.

Teaching Tips for Looking Back in Science
The Age of Dinosaurs

EXTENSION If possible, take students to a museum of natural history where models of dinosaurs are on display.

Questions

1. Why is the Mesozoic Era sometimes called the Age of Reptiles? (Dinosaurs were the dominant animals during the Mesozoic Era.)

2. HYPOTHESIZE Why do you think dinosaurs became extinct? (Answers will vary. Accept all logical responses)

LESSON 10-6
What are birds? (p. 204)

Teaching Strategies

PREVIEW Before students begin this lesson, have them review the TechTerm and its definition and read the Lesson Summary.

DISCUSSION List the features of birds on the chalkboard in an outline format. Discuss each feature. Emphasize that birds are the only animals with feathers.

DISCUSSION Describe the five groups of birds: birds of prey, perching birds, wading birds, swimming birds, and nonperching land birds. Discuss how the birds are classified by the shapes of their beaks and feet. Refer students to Figure 1 on p. 204 to illustrate your descriptions.

CLASS ACTIVITY Take the class on a field trip to observe birds. Bring along a field guide on birds and ask students to try to identify some of the birds they observe.

ITERDISCIPLINARY CONNECTION Have interested students research the life and work of Audubon. Encourage students to study some of the artwork produced by Audubon and to write a brief biography of his life. As an extension to this activity you may wish to have students research the role of the Audubon Society. Encourage interested students to write to the Audubon Society to find out what the goals of this organization are. Have students share their findings with the class.

To introduce this lesson, ask if any students have down jackets or coats. Point out that down clothing is lightweight and very warm. Tell students that down feathers are small fluffy feathers that are close to a bird's skin. Elicit from students that down feathers help to keep a bird warm.

Answers to Challenges (p. 205)

Apply

7. a. bird of prey **b.** swimming bird **c.** perching bird
d. nonperching land bird **e.** wading bird **f.** bird of prey
8. Sea gulls have webbed feet and beaks suited to capturing and eating small sea animals such as fish.
9. The upper chambers of the human heart are the atria. The lower chambers are the ventricles.
10. the presence of feathers

Health and Safety Tip

Symptoms of *salmonella* poisoning include stomach cramps, fever, diarrhea, and vomiting. One way to avoid *salmonella* poisoning is to not eat raw eggs or undercooked poultry products. Another way to avoid *salmonella* poisoning is to not use the same cooking utensils and cutting boards for raw poultry as are used for other foods.

Teaching Tips for Activity

Observing a Bird Egg

Skills: *observing, modeling, hypothesizing*

COOPERATIVE/COLLABORATIVE LEARNING Have students work in pairs.

DISCUSSION You may wish to tell students that the chicken eggs they purchase at supermarkets are unfertilized eggs. Farmers are able to determine which eggs have been fertilized and which eggs have not been fertilized by holding the eggs up to light.

Questions

1. a. white or brown **b.** slightly bumpy
2. a. colorless **b.** yellow
3. the egg white and the yolk
4. a. to protect the developing embryo **b.** to provide food for the developing embryo
5. to help protect the eggs from damage by the environment or predators; Accept all logical responses.

LESSON 10-7
What are mammals? (p. 206)

Teaching Strategies

PREVIEW Before students begin this lesson, have them write the lesson objective in their notebooks. As students read the lesson, have them write the sentences from the lesson that provide the information needed in the objective.

DISCUSSION On the chalkboard, outline the main characteristics of mammals: body hair, a four-chambered heart, warmblooded, highly developed brain and nervous system, nursing of young from mammary glands. Tell students how each of these characteristics has helped mammals become one of the most successful groups of animals on the earth.

CLASS ACTIVITY Take the class on a field trip to a local zoo or natural history museum to observe different kinds of mammals.

RETEACHING OPTION Write the following head on the chalkboard: *Mammals.* From this head, draw arrows to each of the following heads: *Egg Laying, Pouched, Placental.* Under *Egg Laying,* list the duckbill platypus and the spiny anteater. Under *Pouched,* list kangaroos, opossums, and koala bears. Under *Placental,* list dogs, cats, cattle, seals, whales, bats, and humans. Tell students to copy the chart in their notebooks. Point out that the largest group of mammals is the placentals.

EXTENSION You may wish to tell students that egg-laying mammal are called monotremes and pouched mammals are called marsupials.

REINFORCEMENT Be sure students understand that seals, whales, and bats are mammals. Students often confuse the classification of these animals. They tend to classify seals and whales as fishes and bats as birds.

Answers to Challenges (p. 207)

Apply

8. Spiny anteaters and duckbill platypuses are warmblooded, have a body covering of hair, and other mammalian characteristics. Accept all logical responses.
9. The way in which their young develop.

Skill Builder: Classifying

Check students' posters for logic and accuracy.

Teaching Tips for Leisure Activity

Pets

DISCUSSION Ask students to describe their pets. Discuss the kinds of animals people keep as pets and the care and handling that are required for each kind of animal.

Question

What is a pet's main role? (to be its owner's friend)

LESSON 10-8
How do animal embryos develop? (p. 208)

Teaching Strategies

PREVIEW Before students begin this lesson, have them read the TechTerms and their definitions and review the Lesson Summary.

DISCUSSION Provide motivation for this lesson by displaying a variety of animal eggs. Depending upon availability, frog, fish, snake, turtle, or bird eggs could be displayed. Then develop the concepts of internal and external fertilization. Guide students to understand that internal fertilization takes place in most land animals. Refer to the fertilization of reptiles, birds, and mammals as internal fertilization. Point out that fish and amphibians have external fertilization.

REINFORCEMENT Be sure students understand that some organisms have internal fertilization, but external embryonic development. Emphasize that mammals are the only organisms in which embryos develop within the mother's body.

COOPERATIVE/COLLABORATIVE LEARNING Have students work in pairs to answer the Check and Apply questions.

Answers to Challenges (p. 209)

Check

1. female sex cell

2. male sex cell
3. union of a male sex cell and a female sex cell
4. a developing organism
5. the yolk
6. from the mother
7. inside the mother's body
8. in a hard shell

Apply

9. The development of the embryo of most animals takes place outside the body of the mother. The development of most mammal embryos takes place inside the mother's body.
10. the placenta

Skill Builder: Researching

The gestation periods for the mammals listed are elephant: 20-22 months; mouse: 20 days; dog: 63 days; cat: about 9 weeks; humans: 9 months; guinea pigs: about 28 days; horse: 11 months; cow: 40 weeks. Check students' graphs for logic and accuracy.

Teaching Tips for Activity

Comparing Gestation Time and Animal Size

Skills: *calculating, sequencing, graphing*

COOPERATIVE/COLLABORATIVE LEARNING   Answer the questions as a class.

Questions

1. hamster, rabbit, dog, sheep, human, gorilla, cow, elephant.

2. Check students' tables for logic and accuracy.
3. As a rule, larger animals take longer to develop and have longer gestation periods than do smaller animals.

Answers to Unit Challenges (pp. 210-212)

Understanding the Features: Reading Critically

1. high school diploma; two-year animal technology program
2. to protect it from other animals
3. Answers will vary. Accept all logical responses.
4. Mesozoic Era
5. Answers will vary. Accept all logical responses.

Critical Thinking

1. The body temperature of a coldblooded animal changes with the temperature of its environment. A warmblooded animal's body temperature remains the same. Humans are warmblooded.
2. coldblooded; moist skin; webbed feet; use gills, lungs, and their skin to exchange oxygen and carbon dioxide; eggs do not have shells; live part of their life on land and part in water
3. Answers will vary. Accept all logical responses.
4. to crack the seeds without breaking their beaks
5. Answers will vary. Accept all logical responses.

Interpreting a Diagram

1. eye
2. gill cover
3. the gills
4. A and F
5. mouth
6. to take in food and water

NUTRITION AND DIGESTION (p. 213)

Previewing the Unit

Read the titles of the lessons in this unit aloud. Identify terms in the titles with which students are unfamiliar. Write these terms on the chalkboard. Using the Glossary of the text or a dictionary, define the terms as a class. Have students write the terms and their definitions in their notebooks.

Bulletin Board Suggestions

1. Assemble a bulletin board illustrating the four basic food groups. Divide the bulletin board into four sections. Label each section with one of the following heads: *Dairy Group, Meat Group, Vegetable-Fruit Group, Bread-Cereal Group.* Attach pictures of representative foods under each heading.
2. Assemble a bulletin board showing the human digestive system. Attach a large picture of the digestive system to the bulletin board. Label each organ and gland. Add arrows to show the path of food through the digestive tract.

LESSON 11-1
What are nutrients? (p. 214)

Teaching Strategies

PREVIEW Have students write the lesson title and objective in their notebooks. As students read the lesson, tell them to write down the sentence or sentences that provide the information needed in the objective.

DISCUSSION To introduce this lesson, ask students what fuel provides the energy a car needs to run. (gasoline) Then compare the human body to a car. Point out that the body also needs fuel to run. Elicit from students that food is the body's fuel. Define nutrients as the chemical substances in food that are needed for growth and energy.

CLASS ACTIVITY Randomly read out the names of the foods shown on p. 214. Have students identify the nutrients each food supplies the body with.

CLASS ACTIVITY Have each student bring in three food labels from different foods. Tell students to circle all the nutrients on the labels and their amounts. Then review the labels as a class. Have students determine which foods are high in nutrients and which foods are low in nutrients.

RETEACHING OPTION Write the following head on the chalkboard: *Nutrients.* From this head, draw arrows to each of the following heads: *Carbohydrates, Fats, Proteins, Vitamins, Minerals.* From *Carbohydrates,* draw arrows to each of the following heads: *Simple, Complex.* Under *Simple,* list sugars. Under *Complex,* list starches. Have students copy the chart in their notebooks.

Answers to Challenges (p. 215)

Apply

6. Starches give the body energy over long periods of time.
7. Simple carbohydrates only give the body short, quick bursts of energy.

InfoSearch

You may wish to discuss students' questions and answers as a class.

Teaching Tips for Activity

Testing For Fats

Skills: *observing, summarizing*

COOPERATIVE/COLLABORATIVE LEARNING Answer the questions as a class.

Questions

1. by rubbing the foods on paper
2. Answers will vary.
3. Answers will vary. Accept all logical responses.
4. Answers will vary. Accept all logical responses.

LESSON 11-2
Why are proteins important?
(p. 216)

Teaching Strategies

PREVIEW Before beginning this lesson, have students scan the lesson for the science process skill symbols. Have students identify each skill used in the lesson. Students should then review the definition given for each skill on page 16 of their text.

DISCUSSION Discuss the structure and importance of proteins. As the building blocks of living material, the importance of proteins cannot be overemphasized. When discussing the structure of proteins, be sure students understand that although there are only 20 amino acids, they can be put together in many different ways to form thousands of proteins. Make an analogy between amino acids and proteins and the 26 letters of the alphabet and words.

EXTENSION You may wish to point out that under normal circumstances the body does not use proteins as a source of energy. However, if deprived of other nutrients, the body will break down proteins for energy. Point out that the breakdown of proteins is one reason starvation diets are unhealthy and cause the loss of muscle tissue.

CLASS ACTIVITY Cut out twenty different shapes from sheets of construction paper. Label each shape with the name of a different amino acid. To illustrate that amino acids can be combined to form thousands of proteins, have students take turns putting the shapes in different sequences.

REINFORCEMENT Be sure students understand that proteins are broken down into amino acids in the body. The amino acids are then used by body cells to make new proteins. Many students have difficulty understanding this concept.

Answers to Challenges (p. 217)

Apply

6. Proteins are needed for growth and repair.
7. To ensure that they take in all eight of the amino acids needed by the body.
8. Check students' models.

Skill Builder: Researching

A low-protein diet is characterized by a swollen stomach and thin limbs.

Teaching Tips for Activity
Modeling Protein Molecules

Skill: *modeling*

SAFETY TIP Caution students to be careful when using sharp objects.

COOPERATIVE/COLLABORATIVE LEARNING Have students compare their models.

Questions

1. amino acids
2. **a.** Answers will vary. **b.** Answers will vary.
3. **a.** 20 **b.** It combines the amino acids in different ways.
4. The number of possible proteins increases.

LESSON 11-3
Why are vitamins important?
(p. 218)

Teaching Strategies

PREVIEW Have students read the lesson feature before beginning the lesson. Discuss the concepts presented in the feature. Ask students how they think this information relates to topics they have already studied or to the lesson they are about to study.

DISCUSSION Bring in a bottle of vitamins and display it in front of the classroom. Point to the bottle and ask students if they know why vitamins are important. Discuss all student responses. Point out that vitamins are needed for the body to function properly. Then outline some of the specific functions of vitamins on the chalkboard.

REINFORCEMENT Be sure students understand that vitamins do not supply the body with energy. Students often mistakenly think of vitamins as energy sources.

CLASS ACTIVITY Randomly read out the names of the vitamins listed in Table 1 on p. 218. Have students state each vitamin's use in the body and the good sources of each vitamin. Then read out the deficiency diseases listed in Table 1 and have students state the vitamin that is lacking.

EXTENSION You may wish to tell students that the body uses ultraviolet rays from the sun to make vitamin D. Vitamin K is made in the large intestine with the help of bacteria that inhabit the intestine.

COOPERATIVE/COLLABORATIVE LEARNING Have students quiz each other on the material in this lesson.

Answers to Challenges (p. 219)
Apply

4. K
5. B_1, B_2, B_3
6. C
7. riboflavin
8. night blindness

Skill Builder: Organizing

Check students' tables. The signs and symptoms of each deficiency disease are: night blindness: difficulty seeing in dark; beriberi: tiredness, loss of appetite, muscle cramps, paralysis; pellagra: rough skin, diarrhea; scurvy: sore gums; rickets: soft bones and teeth.

Health and Safety Tip

To make the skin and peels of fruits and vegetables safe to eat, they should be scrubbed in water.

Teaching Tips for Looking Back in Science
Scurvy

DISCUSSION You may wish to use this feature to point out that cures for certain disorders and diseases have been discovered before their causes.

Questions

1. **RELATE** Why did many sailors at sea get scurvy? (They did not eat foods containing vitamin C.)
2. What are the symptoms of scurvy? (sore, bleeding gums; fatigue; slow healing)

LESSON 11-4
Why are minerals important?
(p. 220)

Teaching Strategies

PREVIEW Before beginning this lesson, have students scan the lesson looking for words with which they are unfamiliar. Have students work in pairs to define each of the words on their lists.

INTRASCIENCE CONNECTION Point out that the minerals organisms need to grow come from the earth. Minerals are natural solids formed from elements or compounds in the earth's crust.

DEMONSTRATION To provide motivation for this lesson, bring in specimens of some of the minerals needed by living things, such as iron, calcium, sodium, and phosphorus. Show each mineral sample to the class. Have students describe each mineral's properties. Then describe the importance and use of each mineral in the human body.

REINFORCEMENT Bring in a variety of pictures showing the foods listed in Table 1 on p. 220. Point to each food in the pictures. Have students use Table 1 to identify the mineral or minerals each food supplies.

EXTENSION You may wish to point out that iron-deficiency anemia is very common in teen-age girls because of poor eating habits and the loss of some iron during menstruation. Emphasize the importance of eating foods with a lot of iron.

Answers to Challenges (p. 221)
Skill Builder: Organizing

Check students' tables. Answers will vary.

Teaching Tips for Career in Life Science
Nutritionist

EXTENSION If possible, have a nutritionist or the school dietician visit your class. Ask the nutritionist to discuss the relationship between diet and health with your students.

Questions

1. **DESCRIBE** What do nutritionists do in industry? (help to research, develop, and test new food products)
2. What is the educational requirement for a nutritionist? (college degree with a major in nutrition)

LESSON 11-5
What is a balanced diet? (p. 222)

Teaching Strategies

PREVIEW Before beginning this lesson, write the title of each section in the lesson on the chalkboard. Have students copy these titles in their notebooks using an outline format. As students read each section, they should write the topic sentence for each paragraph in the section in their notebooks.

DISCUSSION Discuss the meaning of a balanced diet. Point out that a balanced diet contains the proper amounts of nutrients. Emphasize that a balanced diet is essential for good health. Tell students that they should use the Food Guide Pyramid as a guide to good eating.

CLASS ACTIVITY Distribute an index card to each student. Tell students to write down the name of one food on the index card. Then collect all the cards and have students classify all the foods into the proper food groups as a class.

EXTENSION Have students plan a balanced diet for a whole day.

Answers to Challenges (p. 223)
InfoSearch

You may wish to discuss students' questions and answers as a class.

Teaching Tips for Activity
Planning a Balanced Diet

Skills: *classifying, analyzing*

COOPERATIVE/COLLABORATIVE LEARNING Have volunteers show their menus to the rest of the class.

Questions

1. bran flakes, bread
2. margarine
3. Answers will vary. Accept all logical responses.
4. Answers will vary. Accept all logical responses.

LESSON 11-6
How do living things get energy? (p. 224)

Teaching strategies

PREVIEW Before beginning this lesson, have students review the TechTerms and their definitions and read the Lesson Summary.

DISCUSSION Introduce this lesson by reviewing the things organisms need to live. Ask students to name the things they need to survive. (Answers will most likely include food, water, oxygen, and shelter.) Then develop an understanding of why people need food and oxygen. Discuss the term *oxidation.* Point out that oxidation is the process by which sugar is broken down and energy released.

CLASS ACTIVITY Bring a hand mirror to class. Ask a volunteer to breathe on the mirror. Have students observe that water collects on the mirror. Use this activity to show students that water is a waste product of oxidation.

REINFORCEMENT You may wish to tell students that the oxidation of foods in the body is cellular respiration. Write the chemical and word equations for cellular respiration on the chalkboard to help students identify the reactants and products of this process:
$$C_6H_{12}O_6 + O_2 \rightarrow H_2O + CO_2 + \text{energy}$$
glucose + oxygen → water + carbon dioxide + energy

DISCUSSION All students probably are familiar with the term *Calorie.* Many students probably associate the term solely with dieting. Point out that a Calorie is a unit used to measure the amount of energy given off by food.

EXTENSION Some students may wonder why the term *Calorie* is capitalized. You may wish to tell them that a *calorie* (small letter) is equal to the amount of energy needed to raise the temperature of one gram of water 1 °C. A *Calorie* is equal to a kilocalorie, or 1000 calories. Be sure that students understand that on food labels the number of Calories is listed.

Answers to Challenges (p. 225)
Check

1. oxidation
2. water, carbon dioxide
3. no
4. Calorie
5. from food
6. fat

Apply

7. 45 Calories
8. Fats give off more energy than carbohydrates.
9. You would gain weight.

Skill Builder: Calculating

A: 85; **B:** 128; **C:** 49; **D:** 99; **E:** 102

Skill Builder: Comparing

Answers will vary. Accept all logical responses.

Teaching Tips for Science Connection
Chemosynthesis

REINFORCEMENT Before students read this feature, read the term *chemosynthesis* aloud so students can hear its pronunciation.

Questions

1. RELATE Why is photosynthesis not possible on the ocean floor? (No sunlight can reach the ocean floor.)
2. DEFINE What is chemosynthesis? (process of making food from chemicals)

LESSON 11-7
What is the digestive system? (p. 226)

Teaching Strategies

PREVIEW Before beginning this lesson, read the list of TechTerms aloud so students can hear their pronunciations.

DISCUSSION   Refer students to Figure 1 on p. 226. Have students locate each organ of the digestive system as you describe the path of food through the digestive tract. Be sure students understand the difference between the digestive tract and the digestive system. Point out that the liver, pancreas, and gall bladder are part of the digestive system but not of the digestive tract.

DEMONSTRATION   Demonstrate peristalsis with a piece of rubber tubing and a marble. (The rubber tubing should not be wider than the marble.) Place the marble in the rubber tubing. Then move the marble through the tubing by squeezing behind it.

Answers to Challenges (p. 227)

Apply

6. Check students' flowcharts. Their charts should show the following sequence: mouth, esophagus, stomach, small intestine, large intestine.
7. in order to be swallowed without harming the body or choking

Health and Safety Tip

A person who is choking, but is able to cough should not be interfered with. However, if a person's windpipe is completely obstructed, the Heimlich maneuver should be performed.

Teaching Tips for Science Connection

Vestigial Organs

EXTENSION   Have interested students research the symptoms of appendicitis. Tell students to present their findings in an oral report.

Questions

1. DEFINE   What is a vestigial organ? (small part of the body that seems to have no use)
2. Why do scientists think some snakes evolved from animals with hips? (The snakes have vestigial hip bones.)

LESSON 11-8
What is digestion? (p. 228)

Teaching Strategies

PREVIEW   Have students read the lesson feature before beginning the lesson. Discuss the concepts presented in the feature. Ask students how they think this information relates to topics they have already studied or to the lesson that they are about to study.

DEMONSTRATION   Show students simple examples of physical and chemical changes. To demonstrate a physical change, tear up a piece of paper or break up a cracker. To show students a chemical change, burn a match. Then describe mechanical and chemical digestion. Ask students whether mechanical digestion is a physical or chemical change. (physical)

DISCUSSION   Describe the parts of the mouth that are involved in the breakdown of foods. Be sure students understand that the teeth and tongue aid in mechanical digestion, and saliva begins the chemical digestion of foods.

REINFORCEMENT   Be sure students understand that enzymes control chemical reactions in all parts of the body, not just in

the digestive system. Remind students that enzymes are proteins.

DEMONSTRATION   To demonstrate how mechanical digestion increases surface area, hold two sugar cubes together. Ask students how many sides are exposed. (6) Then pull the sugar cubes apart. Again, ask how many sides are exposed. (12)

RETEACHING OPTION   Write the following head on the chalkboard: Digestion. From this head, draw arrows to each of the following heads: Mechanical Digestion, Chemical Digestion. Define these two types of digestion. Have students copy the charts and definitions in their notebooks.

Answers to Challenges (p. 229)

Apply

6. to avoid choking
7. starches and sugars

InfoSearch

You may wish to discuss students' questions and answers as a class.

Teaching Tips for Career in Life Science

Dental Hygienist

EXTENSION   Invite a dental hygienist to talk to your classroom about the proper care of teeth. Have students prepare questions they would like to ask beforehand.

Questions

1. INFER   Why must dental hygienists be skillful in working with their hands? (Answers will vary. Accept all logical responses.)
2. What are two things a dental hygienist may do on the job? (Students should restate two of the things given in the feature.)

LESSON 11-9
What happens to food in the stomach? (p. 230)

Teaching Strategies

PREVIEW   Have students write the lesson title and objective in their notebooks. As students read the lesson, tell them to write down the sentence or sentences that provide the information needed in the objective.

DISCUSSION   Introduce this lesson by asking students if they know what causes their stomachs to "growl." Discuss all student responses. Point out that stomach growling is the result of contractions of stomach muscles. Then discuss the mechanical and chemical digestion that occurs in the stomach. Guide students to understand that contractions of stomach muscles aid in mechanical digestion.

RETEACHING OPTION   Hold up an antacid in front of the class. Ask students what antacids are used to treat. (Many students will know that antacids are used to treat an upset stomach caused by excess stomach acids.) Use students' knowledge of antacids as a springboard for a discussion of chemical digestion in the stomach. Tell students that hydrochloric acid is the acid found in the stomach and that pepsin can only work in an acidic environment.

COOPERATIVE/COLLABORATIVE LEARNING Have one student describe mechanical digestion in the stomach. Have another student describe chemical digestion in the stomach.

Answers to Challenges (p. 231)

Check

1. protects the stomach lining from hydrochloric acid and pepsin.
2. Stomach muscles tighten and squeeze the food.
3. pepsin
4. thick liquid
5. The stomach is a J-shaped, baglike organ.

Apply

6. It carries out both mechanical and chemical digestion.
7. Pepsin could not work.
8. The protein was digested.
9. Food is broken down mechanically and chemically. It enters the small intestine as a thick liquid. The digestion of starches and proteins has started.

Skill Builder: Researching

Check students' tables. How and why ulcers occur is not completely understood. However, stress is known to be a contributing factor. Symptoms include pain in the stomach, especially after eating. Most ulcers are treated with medication.

Teaching Tips for Looking Back in Science

William Beaumont

EXTENSION Dr. William Beaumont experimented with gastric juice and its effect on various foods. Thus, he was able to demonstrate and explain how gastric juice changes foods.

Question

Why was the ability to view a functioning body system extraordinary in the early 1800s? (The use of X rays had not yet been discovered. Most information about body systems was obtained by examining the remains of the deceased.)

LESSON 11-10
What happens to food in the small intestine? (p. 232)

Teaching Strategies

PREVIEW Before beginning this lesson, read the list of TechTerms aloud so students can hear their pronunciations.

DISCUSSION Copy Table 1 on p. 232 onto the chalkboard. Have students note where the digestion of different nutrients begins and ends. Emphasize that all digestion is completed in the small intestine.

DEMONSTRATION Using a meterstick, measure off 6.5 m in the classroom. Tell students that this is the length of the small intestine.

REINFORCEMENT Display a wall chart showing the liver, gall bladder, stomach, pancreas, and small intestine. Point to each accessory organ and describe its digestive function. Point out that the liver is the largest and one of the most important organs in the body.

DEMONSTRATION Place some water and vegetable oil in a jar. Students will observe that the substances do not mix. Then add a detergent to the jar and shake the jar. Ask students to describe what happens. (The detergent causes the oil layer to break up.) Relate this demonstration to the action of bile on fats.

Answers to Challenges (p. 233)

Apply

7. mouth
8. stomach
9. fat

InfoSearch

You may wish to discuss students' questions and answers as a class.

Teaching Tips for Activity

Investigating Fat Digestion

Skills: *observing, comparing*

COOPERATIVE/COLLABORATIVE LEARNING Have students work in pairs.

Questions

1. The oil and water did not mix.
2. The oil layer was broken up.
3. test tube without baking soda
4. test tube with baking soda
5. Baking soda breaks down fats.

LESSON 11-11
How is food absorbed by the body? (p. 234)

Teaching Strategies

PREVIEW Before beginning this section, have students scan the lesson looking for words with which they are unfamiliar. Have students work in pairs or small groups to define each of the words on their list.

DISCUSSION Remind students that organisms need food for growth, repair, and energy. Have students recall that nutrients are needed by body cells. Elicit from students that if nutrients remained in the small intestine, they would do the body no good. Emphasize the importance of absorption.

REINFORCEMENT After students have completed this lesson, review the digestive system and the entire digestive process. Refer students back to the diagram of the digestive system on p. 226. Trace the path of food through the digestive tract. Describe the digestive processes that occur in each organ. Stress the roles of the pancreas, liver, and gall bladder in digestion. Describe absorption in the small intestine. Finally, discuss what occurs in the large intestine.

COOPERATIVE/COLLABORATIVE LEARNING Have students quiz each other on the material in this lesson.

Answers to Challenges (p. 235)

Apply

7. so it can be carried to all body cells

8. Curved lines have a greater surface area than straight lines.

9. It may burst.

Ideas in Action

Answers will vary. Accept all logical responses.

Health and Safety Tips

Check students' reports. Bran foods and vegetables are high in fiber.

Teaching Tips for Activity

Calculating Surface Area

Skills: *measuring, analyzing, calculating*

COOPERATIVE/COLLABORATIVE LEARNING   Answer the questions as a class.

Questions

1. 8 cm
2. about 18 cm
3. curved string
4. They increase the surface area.

Answers to Unit Challenges (pp. 236-238)

Understanding the Feature: Reading Critically

1. sore, bleeding gums; fatigue; slow healing
2. hospital, industry, private practice
3. process of using chemicals to make food
4. appendix, third eyelid, muscles in the outer ear, tailbone
5. Answers will vary. Accept all logical responses.
6. his studies of the stomach
7. Answers will vary. Accept all logical responses.

Critical Thinking

1. mechanical; Bile breaks fats into small droplets.
2. The large surface area increases the amount of absorption that takes place.
3. Nutrients must be carried by the blood to all body cells.
4. Answers will vary. Accept all logical responses.
5. Answers will vary. Accept all logical responses.

Interpreting the Diagram

1. to carry food from the throat to the stomach
2. E
3. I
4. to produce digestive enzymes, which are released into the small intestine
5. C
6. small intestine

Previewing the Unit

Read the titles of the lessons in this unit aloud. Identify terms in the titles with which students are unfamiliar. Write these terms on the chalkboard. Using the Glossary of the text or a dictionary, define the terms as a class. Have students write the terms and their definitions in their notebooks. Then, have students work in small groups to carry out the task in the Study Hint.

Bulletin Board Suggestions

1. Assemble a bulletin board that highlights the skeletal system. Attach a diagram of the skeleton to the bulletin board. Label some of the major bones with both their scientific and common names. Use the diagram on p. 240 as a guide. Circle the different types of joints on the skeleton and label each type. Use the bulletin board to help students identify different bones and the places where different types of joints are found.
2. Assemble a bulletin board illustrating the different kinds of muscle tissue in the body. Attach pictures of skeletal muscle, smooth muscle, and cardiac muscle to the bulletin board. Label each different kind of muscle tissue. Use the bulletin board when teaching Lesson 12-5.

LESSON 12-1
What is the skeletal system?
(p. 240)

Teaching Strategies

PREVIEW Have students read the lesson feature before beginning the lesson. Discuss the concepts presented in the feature. Ask students how they think this information relates to topics they have already studied or to the lesson they are about to study.

DISCUSSION To introduce this lesson, ask students if they have ever seen a house or skyscraper being built. Point out that a house has a wooden framework and a skyscraper has an iron girder frame. Ask students what the frame of a building does. (Many students probably will know that the frame supports a building.) Then introduce the skeletal system as the frame of the body. Ask students what they think is one job of the skeletal system. (support)

REINFORCEMENT Remind students that animals are divided into two large groups, vertebrates and invertebrates. Explain that some invertebrates have soft bodies and others have exoskeletons. Have students recall that vertebrates have an endoskeleton.

CLASS ACTIVITY Tell students to feel and describe their knee bones and the bridges of their noses. Elicit the response that bones are very hard. Then, tell students to touch the tips of their noses and their outer ears. Ask students to describe these structures. Explain that the tip of the nose and the outer ear are made up of cartilage. Define cartilage as a tough, flexible connective tissue.

Answers to Challenges (p. 241)

CLASS ACTIVITY Divide the class into small groups. Challenge each group to construct a model of the arm muscles using cardboard, rubber bands, and balloons. When all groups are finished, display the models in the classroom.

REINFORCEMENT Muscle action is a difficult concept for students to understand. Use as many models and diagrams as possible to demonstrate how muscles move bones.

Apply

5. endoskeleton: fish; exoskeleton: grasshopper

Skill Builder: Relating Roots and Word Parts

Answers will vary. Accept all logical responses.

Teaching Tips for Technology and Society
Arthroscopic Surgery

CLASS ACTIVITY Have students look up the meaning of the prefix *arthro-* in a dictionary. (*arthro-:* of the joints) Tell students to write in their own words how the meaning of *arthro-* is related to its use in the term arthroscopic surgery.

Questions

1. IDENTIFY   On what body part is arthroscopic surgery most often performed? (knee)
2. LIST   What are the advantages of arthroscopic surgery? (a person stays awake and thus recovers faster; less tissue is damaged; only a very small scar is left)

LESSON 12-2
What are bones? (p. 242)

Teaching Strategies

PREVIEW Before beginning this lesson, have students review the TechTerms and their definitions and read the Lesson Summary.

DEMONSTRATION If possible, point out the bones of the body on a skeleton. Point out some small bones, such as the finger bones, and some large bones, such as the femur. Have students note that bones come in all shapes and sizes.

REINFORCEMENT Stress that although bones have many different shapes and sizes, all bones have a similar structure.

DISCUSSION Describe the structure of bones. Refer students to the diagram of a bone on p. 242 to illustrate your description. Be sure students understand that bones are made up of both living and nonliving material. To help students remember that calcium is the nonliving material that makes bones hard, discuss the relationship between ''drinking milk and healthy bones.'' Point out that milk and other diary products are good sources of calcium.

CLASS ACTIVITY Obtain prepared slides showing a cross section of bone from a biological supply company. Have students view the slides under a microscope and identify as many parts of bone as they can.

DEMONSTRATION Obtain a bone from a butcher shop. Cut the bone lengthwise. Point out the different parts of the bone.

EXTENSION Have interested students find out about osteoporosis. Tell students to write their findings in a report.

Answers to Challenges (p. 243)

InfoSearch

You may wish to discuss students' questions and answers as a class.

Teaching Tips for Technology and Society
Bone Marrow Transplants

EXTENSION Before students read this feature, you may wish to tell them that leukemia is a disease in which the body produces millions of abnormal immature white blood cells and anemia is a blood disorder in which the blood cannot carry normal amounts of oxygen to body cells.

Questions

1. What are two disorders treated with bone marrow transplants? (anemia, leukemia)
2. HYPOTHESIZE Why do you think a patient's body may reject new bone marrow? (The new marrow is a foreign substance to the body.)

LESSON 12-3
How do joints work? (p. 244)

Teaching Strategies

PREVIEW Before beginning this section, have students scan the lesson looking for words with which they are unfamiliar. Have students work in pairs or small groups to define each of the words on their lists.

DISCUSSION To introduce this lesson, ask students if they have ever broken a bone. Have any students who have broken bones describe how the bones were treated and set for the rest of the class. Then point out that broken bones illustrate that bones do not bend. Explain that movement only can occur where bones meet. Define a joint as the place where two or more bones meet. Describe the three main kinds of joints and give students examples of each.

CLASS ACTIVITY As students read about the four kinds of movable joints on p. 244, have them locate the joints on their bodies.

RETEACHING OPTION Write the following head on the chalkboard: *Joints.* From this head, draw arrows to each of the following heads: *Fixed, Partly Moveable, Movable.* From the head *Movable,* draw arrows to each of the following heads: *Ball-and-socket joints, Gliding joints, Hinge joints, Pivotal joints.* Have students copy the chart in their notebooks. Then give students examples of each type of joint. Tell students to list the examples under the proper heads.

EXTENSION Have interested students find out the differences among compound, simple, and greenstick fractures. Tell students to share their findings in an oral report.

COOPERATIVE/COLLABORATIVE LEARNING Have students quiz each other on the material in this lesson.

Answers to Challenges (p. 245)

Apply

5. Answers may vary, but should include that movement in the shoulder and arm would be limited.
6. to allow the rib cage to move during breathing

InfoSearch

You may wish to discuss students' questions and answers as a class.

Teaching Tips for Activity
Observing Joint Movements

Skill: *observing*

SAFETY TIP Caution students that they should not force movements at their joints.

COOPERATIVE/COLLABORATIVE LEARNING Answer the questions as a class.

LESSON 12-4
What is the muscular system?
(p. 246)

Teaching Strategies

PREVIEW Before beginning this lesson, write the title of each section in the lesson on the chalkboard. Have students copy these titles in their notebooks using an outline format. As students read each section, they should write the topic sentence for each paragraph in the section in their notebooks.

DISCUSSION Tell students to "flex their arm muscles." Most students will know that you are asking them to bend their arms. Use students' knowledge as a springboard for a discussion of the muscular system. Point out that muscles that bend joints are called flexors and muscles that straighten joints are called extensors. Describe how flexors and extensors work together to move the body. Emphasize that muscles can only pull bones.

DEMONSTRATION Show students the cartilage on the end of a chicken bone.

RETEACHING OPTION Write the functions of the skeletal system on the chalkboard in an outline format. Then refer students to the diagram of the skeleton on p. 240. Read out the names of some of the major bones of the body. Have students locate each bone on the diagram.

Answers to Challenges (p. 247)

Check

1. A tendon is a strong elastic band of tissue.
2. contracted

Skill Builder: Researching

You may wish to discuss students' exercise programs as a class. Mode refers to the kind of exercise, duration refers to how long an exercise lasts, intensity refers to the level of exercise, and frequency refers to how often an exercise is performed.

Skill Builder: Researching

Sprains and strains are caused by small tears in muscles. Charley horses are caused by bruises and tears in muscle. A muscle cramp occurs when a muscle contracts suddenly and strongly. Tendonitis is caused by an inflammation of tendons.

Teaching Tips for Science Connection
Anabolic Steroids

REINFORCEMENT Taking steroids to increase the size of muscles has become increasingly popular among teenage boys. Emphasize the dangerous side effects of taking steroids.

Questions

1. DEFINE What are hormones? (chemicals that regulate body functions)
2. What is the only way to increase muscle mass and strength? (weight training exercise)

LESSON 12-5
What are the kinds of muscles? (p. 248)

Teaching Strategies

PREVIEW Before beginning this lesson, read the list of TechTerms aloud so students can hear their pronunciations.

DISCUSSION Describe the three kinds of muscle tissue. Emphasize that many internal organs are made up of muscle. Students may tend to think of muscle tissue only in terms of skeletal muscle.

CLASS ACTIVITY Have students observe prepared slides under a microscope showing the three kinds of muscle tissue in the body. Tell students to sketch and label each kind of muscle in their notebooks. Have students note that both skeletal muscle and cardiac muscle are striated.

RETEACHING OPTION To introduce this lesson, tell students to move their feet and to open and close their fingers. Then tell students to stop their stomach muscles from contracting and to stop their hearts from beating for the next few seconds. Obviously, students will be able to carry out your first two directives and not the last two. Use this activity to point out the difference between voluntary muscles and involuntary muscles. Identify smooth muscle and cardiac muscle as involuntary muscles. Then ask students what kind of muscle they think skeletal muscles are. (voluntary)

Answers to Challenges (p. 249)
Skill Builder: Classifying

voluntary: c, f, g; involuntary: a, b, d, e

Teaching Tips for Career in Life Science
Exercise Specialist

EXTENSION If possible, invite an exercise specialist to give a lecture to your class about the benefits of regular exercise.

Questions

1. INFER Why must an exercise specialist enjoy working with people? (The job of an exercise specialist requires a lot of contact with people.)
2. Why do hospitals employ exercise specialists? (to develop exercise programs for patients)

LESSON 12-6
What is skin? (p. 250)

Teaching Strategies

PREVIEW Before beginning this lesson, have students re-view the TechTerms and their definitions and read the Lesson Summary.

DISCUSSION Discuss the structure and function of the skin. Refer students to the diagram of the skin on p. 250. Have students locate the epidermis, dermis, pores, sweat glands, oil glands, and hair follicles on the diagram as you describe each of these structures.

CLASS ACTIVITY Have students work in small groups to make models of the skin. Tell students to use the diagram on p. 250 as a guide. Allow students to use common materials such as buttons, clay, string, and pipe cleaners to make their models.

REINFORCEMENT To help students remember the definitions of the terms epidermis and dermis, tell students that the terms *derm* and *derma* are from the Greek word for skin. Then ask students to list products whose names contain the terms *derm* or *derma*. (Many face creams, make-ups, and skin moisturizers contain the terms *derm* or *derma*.) Have students note that all of these products are used on the skin.

Answers to Challenges (p. 251)
Check/Apply

6. epidermis is the outer layer; dermis is the inner layer of skin
7. oil gland softens and moistens skin; sweat gland removes liquids from the body in the form of sweat
8. The skin covers and protects the body.
9. to replace cells that have been worn away
10. dermis; tiny blood vessels have been cut
11. wrist; skin is a sense organ for touch

Teaching Tips for Activity
Touch Receptors

Skills: *observing, inferring*

COOPERATIVE/COLLABORATIVE LEARNING Students must work with a partner.

Questions

1. Answers will vary. Accept all logical responses.
2. **a.** Answers will vary. Accept all logical responses. **b.** It is depended upon for touch.

Answers to Unit Challenges (pp. 252-254)
Understanding the Features: Reading Critically

1. People are awake during arthroscopic surgery. The cut made is small.
2. whether the healthy bone marrow produces more healthy bone marrow; rejection of the new marrow
3. an increase in the number of muscles fibers
4. Answers will vary. Accept all logical responses.

Critical Thinking

1. When a skeletal muscle contracts, it pulls on a bone.
2. They keep the vertebrae from rubbing against each other.
3. It stretches.
4. injury
5. Answers will vary. Accept all logical responses.

Interpreting a Diagram

1. ilium, ischium, sacrum
2. two
3. cranium
4. knee
5. phalanges
6. collar bone

UNIT 13
TRANSPORT (p. 255)

Previewing the Unit

Read the titles of the lessons in this unit aloud. Identify terms in the titles with which students are unfamiliar. Write these terms on the chalkboard. Using the Glossary of the text or a dictionary, define the terms as a class. Have students write the terms and their definitions in their notebooks.

Bulletin Board Suggestion

Assemble a bulletin board illustrating the heart and the path of blood through the body. Use the diagram on p. 264 as a guide. Use the bulletin board to show students how blood travels from the heart to the lungs, back to the heart, to all other parts of the body, and then back to the heart.

LESSON 13-1
What are the parts of the heart? (p. 256)

Teaching Strategies

PREVIEW Before beginning this lesson, read the list of TechTerms aloud so students can hear their pronunciations.

DISCUSSION Tell students to make a fist and to place it in the center of their chest. Explain to students that the heart is a muscular organ, about the size of a fist, which is found in the center of the chest. Describe the structure of the heart. Compare the atria to receiving rooms and the ventricles to shipping rooms.

REINFORCEMENT Have students study the diagram of the heart on p. 256. Tell students to locate the right and left atria and ventricles. Be sure students understand that as they look at the diagram, the heart's left side is on their right and vice versa. Have students turn their textbooks around and place the books against their chests. Students will then observe that the left side of the diagram is on the left side of their bodies.

CLASS ACTIVITY Divide the class into small groups. Distribute different colors of clay to each group. Have students work together to make models of the heart using the clay. Tell students to label the different parts of the heart. When all groups have completed their models, display the models in the classroom.

DISCUSSION Describe the function of heart valves. Compare the action of a heart valve to a one-way door.

CLASS ACTIVITY If possible, bring a stethoscope to class so that students can listen to their heartbeats.

RETEACHING OPTION Draw a large square on the chalkboard and divide it into four equal parts. Compare the square to the heart. Identify and label the upper and lower chambers of the heart. Emphasize that blood enters the heart through the atria and leaves the heart by way of the ventricles.

Answers to Challenges (p. 257)

Ideas in Action

Check students' tables.

Teaching Tips for Activity
Comparing Animal Heart Rates

Skills: *analyzing, hypothesizing*

COOPERATIVE/COLLABORATIVE LEARNING Answer the questions as a class.

Questions

1. **a.** mouse **b.** small
2. **a.** elephant **b.** large
3. As size decreases, heart rate increases.
4. **a.** Answers will vary. Accept all logical responses. **b.** by finding out the heart rates of people of varying sizes

LESSON 13-2
What are blood vessels? (p. 258)

Teaching Strategies

PREVIEW Have students write the lesson title and objective in their notebooks. As students read the lesson, tell them to write down the sentence or sentences that provide the information needed in the objective.

DISCUSSION Describe the characteristics of arteries, veins, and capillaries. Emphasize that capillaries are the blood vessels through which the exchange of materials takes place.

REINFORCEMENT To help students remember that arteries carry blood away from the heart, tell them to associate the two words beginning with the letter *a, artery* and *away.*

DEMONSTRATION Demonstrate the flow of blood through arteries. Insert a one-hole stopper in a plastic bottle filled with water. Insert a glass tube through the stopper. Squeeze the bottle. Students will observe that water squirts out of the tube. Compare the heart's pumping action on blood in the arteries to your squeezing of the water in the bottle.

CLASS ACTIVITY Have students take their own pulses. Tell students to place their index and middle fingers on the thumb side of their wrist. Tell students to take readings for one minute. Have students record their pulse rates in their notebooks. Be sure students understand that their pulse rates and heartbeat rates are the same.

COOPERATIVE/COLLABORATIVE LEARNING Have students work in pairs to answer the Check and Apply questions.

Answers to Challenges (p. 259)
Apply

7. Arteries carry blood away from the heart. They have thick muscular walls. Veins carry blood back to the heart. Veins have thinner walls than arteries.
8. Blood travels through the veins under low pressure.

InfoSearch

You may wish to discuss students' questions and answers as a class.

Teaching Tips for Activity
Measuring Pulse Rate

Skills: *measuring, analyzing*

COOPERATIVE/COLLABORATIVE LEARNING Have a volunteer demonstrate this activity for the rest of the class.

Questions

1. The pulse rate increased.
2. It increased.
3. Exercise increases heart rate.

LESSON 13-3
What is blood? (p. 260)

Teaching Strategies

PREVIEW Have students read the lesson feature before beginning the lesson. Discuss the concepts presented in the feature. Ask students how they think this information relates to topics they have already studied or to the lesson they are about to study.

DISCUSSION Discuss the functions of blood. Emphasize that blood is a tissue which is part solid and part liquid. Describe the liquid and solid parts of blood. As you describe each part, list it on the chalkboard.

CLASS ACTIVITY If possible, have students observe prepared slides of blood. Tell students to sketch and label in their notebooks the blood cells they observe.

EXTENSION You may wish to tell students that plasma from which clotting factors have been removed is called serum.

RETEACHING OPTION To introduce this lesson, ask students why they think their blood is red. List student responses on the chalkboard. Point out that blood gets its color from the red blood cells in it. Describe the job of red blood cells. Then discuss the other parts of blood and their functions.

Answers to Challenges (p. 261)
Health and Safety Tip

Emphasize the importance of knowing your blood type.

Teaching Tips for People in Science
Charles Drew

EXTENSION Have interested students find out more about the Red Cross and write their findings in a report. Tell students to include an outline of the organization's functions and goals.

Questions

1. LIST What are two advantages of using plasma in blood transfusions rather than whole blood? (Plasma lasts longer than whole blood. Plasma can be used in a transfusion for any blood type.)
2. Why were Charles Drew's research findings timely? (The blood plasma that was collected by blood banks saved many lives during World War II.)

LESSON 13-4
What is circulation? (p. 262)

Teaching Strategies

PREVIEW Before beginning this lesson, have students scan the lesson for the science process skill symbols. Have students identify each skill used in the lesson. Students should then review the definition given for each skill on page 16 of their text.

DISCUSSION To introduce this lesson, show students pictures of different roads and railroad tracks. Point out that these pathways make up the transport system of the United States. Elicit from students that trucks and trains carry materials along these pathways. Then point out that the circulatory system is the transport system of the body. Make an analogy between the trucks and trains and blood. Compare the goods carried by trucks and trains to the materials carried by the blood, such as oxygen, carbon dioxide, glucose, and wastes. Emphasize that transport is the main function of the circulatory system.

DISCUSSION Many students probably are familiar with the sight of a person's face turning red when the person is hot. Use students' knowledge as a springboard for a discussion of how the circulatory system helps regulate body temperature. Point out that when a person is hot there is an increase in blood flow to the surface of the skin. This allows heat loss from the body.

EXTENSION Problems of the circulatory system are the leading causes of death in the United States. Have interested students write to the American Heart Association to find out the risk factors associated with cardiovascular disease. Tell students to organize the information in a chart.

RETEACHING OPTION Write the functions of the circulatory system on the chalkboard in an outline format. Describe each function. Have students copy the information in their notebooks. When describing the transport of hormones, you may wish to tell students that they will learn more about hormones in Unit 15.

Answers to Challenges (p. 263)
Apply

6. Blood is a liquid tissue that carries the materials that are essential for life.

InfoSearch

You may wish to discuss students' questions and answers as a class.

Teaching Tips for People in Science
William Harvey

EXTENSION In addition to studying the circulation of blood in animals, William Harvey also measured the amount of blood pumped by the heart each day. Based on his measurements, Harvey concluded that it would be impossible for the body to replenish the amount of blood pumped by the heart each day. He concluded that blood must be recycled in the body.

Questions

1. On what did William Harvey base his conclusion about circulation? (careful observations and experiments)
2. What was Harvey's profession? (Harvey was a physician.)

LESSON 13-5
What happens to blood as it circulates? (p. 264)

Teaching Strategies

PREVIEW Before beginning this lesson, write the title of each section in the lesson on the chalkboard. Have students copy these titles in their notebooks using an outline format. As students read each section, they should write the topic sentence for each paragraph in the section in their notebooks.

DISCUSSION Refer students to the diagrams on p. 264. Have students trace the path of blood on the diagrams as you describe systemic and pulmonary circulation. When describing the circulation of blood, tell students to think of the heart as a two-sided pump. Point out that the right side of the heart sends blood to the lungs and the left side of the heart pumps blood to all other parts of the body.

REINFORCEMENT Some students may have the misconception that blood returning to the heart is blue. Emphasize that blood returning to the heart is red. It is never blue. You may wish to tell students that veins appear blue because of the way light passes through the skin.

RETEACHING OPTION Using a wall chart of the circulatory system, trace the flow of blood throughout the body. Distinguish between the aorta and pulmonary arteries, and between arteries and veins in general. Make sure students understand that gases and other materials are exchanged between the blood and the body cells across the capillaries.

Answers to Challenges (p. 265)

Apply

8. Check students' flowcharts.

9. The content of blood changes as blood circulates. Blood returning to the right atrium contains more carbon dioxide and wastes. Blood returning from the lungs to the left side of the heart contains a fresh supply of oxygen.

Skill Builder: Building Vocabulary

carotid artery: neck and head; femoral artery: leg; bronchial artery: arm; renal artery: kidney; coronary artery: heart

Teaching Tips for Leisure Activity

Aerobic Exercise

CLASS ACTIVITY Before students read this feature, ask students to name their favorite sports or types of exercise. List student responses on the chalkboard. Circle any activities that are aerobic exercises.

Question

RELATE How can aerobic exercise lower the risk of heart disease? (Regular exercise lowers the amount of fatty materials in the blood, which keeps them from building up on the walls of the blood vessels.)

Answers to Unit Challenges (pp. 266-268)

Understanding the Features: Reading Critically

1. Plasma lasts longer than whole blood. Plasma can be used in a transfusion for any blood type.

2. research in blood plasma; setting up blood banks

3. that blood moved in a circular path

4. Answers will vary. Accept all logical responses.

5. It strengthens the heart, makes a person feel better, gives a person a better physical shape, and lowers the risk of heart disease.

Critical Thinking

1. Blood leaves the heart from the left ventricle and travels to all parts of the body, except the lungs. Blood returns to the heart via the right atrium. From the right atrium, blood flows into the right ventricle. Blood is pumped from the right ventricle to the lungs. Blood returns from the lungs to the heart through the left atrium. Blood flows from the left atrium to the left ventricle and the cycle begins again.

2. When tissues are injured, chemicals are given off by the blood. These chemicals form tiny, sticky threads. The threads stick together and form a clot.

3. The number of white blood cells increases because it is the job of white blood cells to destroy germs.

4. White blood cells in the blood fight disease and harmful chemicals.

Interpreting a Diagram

1. atria
2. ventricles
3. between the left and right sides of the heart
4. It connects to the left ventricle.
5. to carry blood from the heart to the body
6. left atrium
7. from the atria to the ventricles
8. pulmonary veins
9. more carbon dioxide
10. artery

RESPIRATION AND EXCRETION (p. 269)

Previewing the Unit

Read the titles of the lessons in this unit aloud. Identify terms in the titles with which students are unfamiliar. Write these terms on the chalkboard. Using the Glossary of the text or a dictionary, define the terms as a class. Have students write the terms and their definitions in their notebooks. Then, have the students work in small groups to carry out the task in the Study Hint.

Bulletin Board Suggestions

1. Assemble a bulletin board illustrating the respiratory system. Attach a large picture of the respiratory system to the bulletin board. Use the diagram on p. 270 as a guide. Add arrows to the picture to show the flow of air through the respiratory system.
2. Assemble a bulletin board illustrating the excretory system. Attach pictures of the lungs, the skin, the kidneys, and the large intestine to the bulletin board. Next to each excretory·organ, attach labels of the waste products, each organ excretes from the body.

LESSON 14-1
What is the respiratory system? (p. 270)

Teaching Strategies

PREVIEW Before beginning this lesson, read the list of TechTerms aloud so students can hear their pronunciations.

DISCUSSION Refer students to the diagram of the respiratory system on p. 270. Have students trace the flow of air through the respiratory system as you describe what happens to air in each part.

EXTENSION You may wish to tell students that the bronchi divide into many small tubes called bronchioles.

CLASS ACTIVITY Tell students to place their hands on the front of their necks to feel their windpipes. Point out that the bulge near the top of the trachea is the larynx. Tell students that the larynx contains the vocal cords. Students will be able to feel their vocal cords vibrate if they place their hands on their larynxes while speaking.

RETEACHING OPTION Ask students to name the parts of the body that help them to breathe. Write all correct answers on the chalkboard. Fill in any parts of the respiratory system that students omit. Then describe the path air takes on its journey through the respiratory system.

COOPERATIVE/COLLABORATIVE LEARNING Answer the Check and Apply questions as a class.

Answers to Challenges (p. 271)

Apply

6. b, d, a, c, e, f

7. The bronchi and branches of the bronchi are like the branches of a tree. The windpipe is like a tree's trunk.

InfoSearch

You may wish to discuss students' questions and answers as a class.

Teaching Tips for Career in Life Science
Respiratory Therapist

EXTENSION Have students look in the classified sections of different newspapers to find jobs offered in respiratory therapy. Have students describe the information listed in the classifieds.

Questions

1. DESCRIBE What does a respiratory therapist do on the job? (helps patients with breathing problems)
2. How does a person become a respiratory therapist? (A person must complete a one- or two-year training program and then pass an examination.)

LESSON 14-2
What are breathing and respiration? (p. 272)

Teaching Strategies

PREVIEW Have students write the lesson title and objectives in their notebooks. As students read the lesson, tell them to write down the sentence or sentences that provide the information needed in the objectives.

CLASS ACTIVITY To introduce this lesson, tell students to place their hands on their ribs while breathing. Ask students what happens to their ribs when they breathe in, or inhale (The ribs move out.) and what happens when they breathe out, or exhale. (The ribs move in.) Then describe the process of breathing in terms of movement of the ribs and the diaphragm.

DEMONSTRATION Show students a bell-jar lung model. Tell students that when the volume inside the jar increases, air rushes in and inflates the balloons. When the volume inside the jar decreases, air is forced out of the balloons. Relate this model to what happens to the lungs in the chest cavity during breathing.

INTRASCIENCE CONNECTION The amount of force on a unit of area is called pressure. Air pressure is the force air exerts on the earth's surface. People do not feel air pressing down on them because air pressure is equal in all directions. The air inside the body presses outward in all directions.

REINFORCEMENT Emphasize the interaction of the circulatory system and respiratory system. Remind students of the importance of pulmonary circulation.

RETEACHING OPTION Write the following head on the chalkboard: *Respiration.* From this head, draw arrows to each of the following heads: *External, Internal, Cellular.* Have students copy the chart in their notebooks. Then describe each of the three parts of respiration. Emphasize that respiration is a chemical process. Have students copy the information in their notebooks under the proper heads.

COOPERATIVE/COLLABORATIVE LEARNING Have a volunteer

explain the difference between respiration and breathing to the rest of the class.

Answers to Challenges (p. 273)

Check

1. It moves up.
2. Breathing is the process by which air is taken into the body.
3. no
4. carbon dioxide and water
5. It becomes larger.
6. to breathe in
7. to breathe out

Apply

8. **a.** B **b.** A
9. the lungs
10. the diaphragm
11. the chest cavity

Ideas in Action

Answers will vary. Accept all logical responses.

Teaching Tips for Activity
Exercise and Breathing Rate

Skills: *comparing, analyzing, measuring*

COOPERATIVE/COLLABORATIVE LEARNING Students must work in pairs.

Questions

1. **a.** Answers will vary. **b.** Answers will vary.
c. Answers will vary.
2. Answers will vary.
3. Exercise increases breathing rate.

LESSON 14-3
What happens to air before it reaches the lungs? (p. 274)

Teaching Strategies

PREVIEW Have students read the lesson feature before beginning the lesson. Discuss the concepts presented in the feature. Ask the students how they think this information relates to the topics they have already studied or to the lesson they are about to study.

DISCUSSION Describe what happens to air before it reaches the lungs. Discuss the functions of nasal hairs, mucus, and cilia. Point out that in addition to being filtered before it reaches the lungs, air also is warmed and moistened.

RETEACHING OPTION Introduce this lesson by describing two occurrences that are familiar to everyone, sneezing and coughing. Lead students to understand that sneezing and coughing are ways of removing dirt, dust, and germs from the body. Describe the roles of mucus and cilia in protecting the respiratory system. Relate their actions to sneezing and coughing.

COOPERATIVE/COLLABORATIVE LEARNING Have students work in pairs to answer the Check and Apply questions.

Answers to Challenges (p. 275)

Apply

7. a, b
8. Check students' flow charts.

Health and Safety Tip

Check students' lists. Be sure they include the four different Surgeon General's warnings.

Teaching Tips for Science Connection
Respiratory Diseases

REINFORCEMENT Emphasize the health hazards of smoking. Have students make posters encouraging people not to smoke.

EXTENSION Have interested students research other respiratory diseases such as pneumonia, bronchitis, pleurisy, and tuberculosis. Tell students to write their findings in a report.

Questions

1. **RELATE** Why is asbestos being removed from buildings? (to eliminate the risk of getting lung disease from asbestos)
2. Why is secondhand smoke dangerous? (It can cause health problems in nonsmokers.)

LESSON 14-4
How does oxygen get into the blood? (p. 276)

Teaching Strategies

PREVIEW Before beginning this lesson, have students scan the lesson for the science process skill symbols. Have students identify each skill used in the lesson. Students should then review the definition given for each skill on p. 16 of their text.

DISCUSSION To introduce this lesson, bring a bunch of grapes to class. Compare the grapes to alveoli. Emphasize that the alveoli are the units of structure and function in the lungs.

CLASS ACTIVITY Divide the classroom into small groups. Distribute small balloons and markers to each group. Tell students to use the balloons and markers to make models showing gas exchange in the alveoli. Have students use the diagram on p. 276 as a guide. When all groups have completed their models, have a representative of each group display and describe the group's model to the rest of the class.

DEMONSTRATION To show students that exhaled air contains water, ask a volunteer to breathe on a hand mirror. Students will observe that water vapor forms on the mirror.

COOPERATIVE/COLLABORATIVE LEARNING Have a volunteer explain the content differences between inhaled air and exhaled air.

Answers to Challenges (p. 277)

Check

1. mixture of gases
2. alveoli
3. very tiny blood vessels
4. exhalation
5. oxygen
6. carbon dioxide

Apply

7. 78%
8. a
9. b; Exhaled air has a lower concentration of oxygen and a higher concentration of carbon dioxide.

Skill Builder: Graphing

Check students' graphs.

Teaching Tips for Activity
Analyzing Exhaled Air

Skills: *observing, inferring*

COOPERATIVE/COLLABORATIVE LEARNING   Have a volunteer perform this activity in front of the class.

Questions

1. a. water vapor   **b.** exhaled air
2. It becomes cloudy because exhaled air contains carbon dioxide.
3. It contains carbon dioxide.

LESSON 14-5
What is excretion? (p. 278)

Teaching Strategies

PREVIEW   Before beginning this lesson, write the titles of each section in the lesson on the chalkboard. Have students copy these titles in their notebooks using an outline format. As students read each section, they should write the topic sentence for each paragraph in the section in their notebooks.

DISCUSSION   Describe the parts of the excretory system. Some students may tend to think of only the kidneys and urinary system as excretory organs. Emphasize that the skin, the lungs, and the large intestine also get rid of body wastes.

REINFORCEMENT   Relate the burning of fuel in a furnace to the ''burning,'' or oxidation, of food by the body. Point out that in a furnace, waste materials are formed and must be removed. Tell students that this also is true of the materials taken into the body. Explain that during cellular respiration, waste products, which must be removed from the body, are formed.

Answers to Challenges (p. 279)
Check

1. carbon dioxide, water
2. process of removing waste products from the body
3. remove waste products from the body
4. It gets rid of liquid wastes and helps you get rid of extra heat.
5. Water is removed from wastes in the large intestine.
6. They are excreted through the anus.

Apply

7. c
8. a
9. g
10. respiratory, excretory

Ideas in Action

Answers will vary. Accept all logical responses.

Teaching Tips for Technology and Society
Using Sound to Break Apart Kidney Stones

DISCUSSION   To help students understand this feature, compare the breaking up of kidney stones by sound waves to the breaking of glass by a soprano hitting a high note.

Questions

1. LIST   What are three ways that kidney stones are treated? (medication, surgery, sound waves)
2. How do sound waves break apart kidney stones? (Sound waves cause particles in kidney stones to vibrate. The motion of the particles makes the stones break apart.)

LESSON 14-6
How does the skin remove wastes? (p. 280)

Teaching Strategies

PREVIEW   Before beginning this lesson, have students review the TechTerms and their definitions and read the Lesson Summary.

DISCUSSION   To provide motivation for this lesson, ask students when people tend to perspire a lot. Elicit the response that people perspire when they are hot. Then describe how perspiring helps the body to keep cool, in addition to ridding the body of waste water and salts.

CLASS ACTIVITY   Have students work in small groups to make models showing the structure of the skin. Tell students to use common objects such as clay, string, and pipe cleaners. Have students use the diagram on p. 280 as a guide.

INTRASCIENCE CONNECTION   Students may wonder why they feel ''sticky'' on hot, humid days. Humidity is the amount of water vapor in the air. High humidity means there is a lot of water vapor in the air. The air is almost full of water vapor. Therefore, perspiration does not evaporate from the skin.

Answers to Challenges (p. 281)
Apply

6. Shivering warms the body.
7. Salts are lost in perspiration.

Designing an Experiment

You may wish to have volunteers describe their experiments to the rest of the class.

Skill Builder: Building Vocabulary

A deodorant is a substance that prevents or destroys undesired odors. An antiperspirant prevents perspiration.

Teaching Tips for Activity
Evaporation and Cooling

Skills: *observing, comparing*

COOPERATIVE/COLLABORATIVE LEARNING   Answer the questions as a class.

Questions

1. The wet finger feels cooler.

2. The finger with alcohol feels cooler.
3. a. step 1 **b.** It compares how the fingers feel without any substance on them to how they feel with a substance on them.

LESSON 14-7
How do the kidneys work?
(p. 282)

Teaching Strategies

PREVIEW Before beginning this lesson, have the students scan the lesson for words with which they are unfamiliar. Have students work in pairs or small groups to define each of the words on their lists.

DISCUSSION Compare the kidneys to an aquarium filter. Tell students that an aquarium filter removes waste products and contaminates from an aquarium. Point out that the kidneys remove liquid wastes from the body. The main job of the kidneys is to filter out wastes from the blood.

REINFORCEMENT Be sure students understand the difference between urea and urine. Point out that urea is a waste product formed by the breakdown of proteins. Urine is made up of water, salts, and urea.

EXTENSION You may wish to tell students that the tiny tubes inside the kidneys are called nephrons. Emphasize that the nephrons are the functional units of the kidneys.

DISCUSSION Refer students to the diagram of the urinary system on p. 282. Have students trace the movement of urine through the urinary system from the kidneys to the outside of the body.

RETEACHING OPTION Filter some clay out of a water suspension. Then describe the kidneys as blood filters and explain how the kidneys work.

Answers to Challenges (p. 283)
Apply
7. kidneys, ureters, urinary bladder, urethra
8. Check students' flow charts.
9. nitrogen

10. They are used by the body.
Ideas in Action
Answers will vary. Accept all logical responses.

Teaching Tips for Technology and Society
Dialysis

EXTENSION If possible, arrange for a trip to a local hospital to have students observe a kidney dialysis machine.

Questions
1. DEFINE · What is biomedical engineering? (a field of study that uses engineering ideas to help design machines the help or replace diseased organs)
2. What does a dialysis machine do? (filters a patient's blood and removes waste materials)

Answers to Unit Challenges (pp. 284-286)
Understanding the Features: Reading Critically
1. to prevent lung diseases
2. a field of study that uses engineering ideas to help design machines that help or replace diseased organs
3. medication, surgery, sound waves
4. asthma, pneumonia

Critical Thinking
1. nose or mouth, throat, windpipe, bronchi, small tubes, lungs
2. Dirt, dust, and germs are trapped by mucus. Cilia push the mucus toward the nose.
3. Breathing is the mechanical process by which air is taken into the body. Respiration is the chemical process by which energy is released.
4. Materials are exchanged between the alveoli and the blood.
5. The evaporation of perspiration from the skin helps keep the body cool.

Interpreting a Diagram
1. windpipe
2. bronchi
3. nose and mouth
4. It has nasal hairs that filter the air and mucus that traps dirt and germs.
5. windpipe

UNIT 15
REGULATION AND BEHAVIOR (p. 287)

Previewing the Unit

Read the titles of the lessons in this unit aloud. Identify terms in the titles with which students are unfamiliar. Write these terms on the chalkboard. Using the Glossary of the text or a dictionary, define the terms as a class. Have students write the terms and their definitions in their notebooks. Then, have students carry out the task in the Study Hint.

Bulletin Board Suggestion

Assemble a bulletin board highlighting the nervous and endocrine systems. Divide the bulletin board in half vertically. Draw an outline of the body on both sides of the bulletin board. In one outline, illustrate the nervous system. Use the diagram on p. 288 as a guide. Label the brain, the spinal cord, and the nerves. In the other outline, draw in the endocrine glands at their approximate locations in the body. Label each gland. Use the bulletin board to emphasize how the nervous and endocrine systems work together to regulate body functions.

LESSON 15-1
What is the nervous system? (p. 288)

Teaching Strategies

PREVIEW Before beginning this lesson, read the list of TechTerms aloud so students can hear their pronunciations.

DISCUSSION Introduce this lesson with a discussion of a sports team's captain. Ask students what the captain of the team does. Elicit the response that the captain of the team gathers information, makes important decisions, and so on. Then make an analogy between the captain of a sports team and the nervous system. Point out that the nervous system is the captain of the body. Identify the brain and spinal cord as the central nervous system. Have students locate the brain and spinal cord in the diagram on p. 288. Then tell the students to locate the nerves. Point out that the nerves carry information to and from the central nervous system.

DISCUSSION Draw and label a neuron on the chalkboard. Point out the parts of a neuron and describe the function of each part. Emphasize that the neuron is the unit of structure and function in the nervous system.

REINFORCEMENT To help students remember the function of the axon, tell them to associate the words beginning with the letter *a*, *axon*, and *away*.

Answers to Challenges (p. 289)
InfoSearch

You may wish to discuss students' questions and answers as a class.

Teaching Tips for Technology and Society
Seeing Soft Tissues

EXTENSION Have interested students find out more about MRI. Tell students to research the specific use of magnets and sound waves in MRI. Have students write their findings in a report.

Question

EXPLAIN Why is MRI valuable in detecting cancer? (MRI can detect some tumors of organs such as the kidneys, liver, and brain.)

LESSON 15-2
What are the parts of the brain? (p. 290)

Teaching Strategies

PREVIEW Have students write the lesson title and objective in their notebooks. As students read the lesson, tell them to write down the sentence or sentences that provide the information needed in the objective.

DEMONSTRATION If possible, show students a model of the brain. Point out the cerebrum, the cerebellum, and the medulla on the model.

RETEACHING OPTION Write the following head on the chalkboard: *The Brain*. From this head, draw arrows to each of the following heads: *Cerebrum, Cerebellum, Medulla*. Have students copy the chart in their notebooks. Then describe the functions of each part of the brain. Tell students to copy the information under the proper heads.

EXTENSION You may wish to tell students that the cerebrum is divided into two halves and that each half controls the opposite side of the body. The left half of the cerebrum is usually dominant over the right, which explains why most people are right-handed. Ask students which half of the cerebrum they think is dominant in people who are left-handed. (right side)

Answers to Challenges (p. 291)
Check

1. cerebrum, cerebellum, medulla

2. cerebrum

3. at the back of the brain

4. at the base of the skull

5. to receive and interpret messages

6. eyes, ears, nose, tongue, and skin

Skill Builder: Inferring

Answers will vary. Accept all logical responses. Students should recognize that damage to the medulla would affect digestion, breathing, heartbeat rate, and the activities of many glands and muscles.

Teaching Tips for Activity
Modeling the Brain

Skills: *modeling, observing, relating*

COOPERATIVE/COLLABORATIVE LEARNING After students complete this activity, have them display their models in the classroom.

Questions

1. **a.** cerebrum **b.** It is the largest part of the brain.

2. spinal cord

3. spinal cord

LESSON 15-3
What are reflexes? (p. 292)

Teaching Strategies

PREVIEW Have students read the lesson feature before beginning this lesson. Discuss the concepts presented in the feature. Ask the students how they think this information relates to topics they have already studied or to the lesson they are about to study.

DISCUSSION Describe reflexes and give students some examples of reflexes, such as sneezing and blinking. Emphasize the protective nature of reflexes. Guide students to understand that reflexes allow the body to react quickly to painful or dangerous situations.

DEMONSTRATION Demonstrate the knee-jerk reflex by tapping a volunteer's knee with a little rubber mallet.

CLASS ACTIVITY Refer students to the diagram on p. 292. Have students trace the path of a reflex as you describe a reflex arc.

REINFORCEMENT Have students draw a reflex arc showing what would happen if a person stuck his or her finger with a pin. Tell students to use the diagram of a reflex arc on p. 292 as a guide. Be sure students understand that the spinal cord, not the brain, controls reflexes.

Answers to Challenges (p. 293)
Apply

7. **a.** stimulus: stepping on a tack; response: pulling your foot away **b.** stimulus: knock; response: opening the door **c.** stimulus: bright light; response: blinking **d.** stimulus: food; response: coughing

Designing an Experiment

Have volunteers describe their experiments to the rest of the class.

Teaching Tips for Technology and Society
Treating Spinal Injuries with Bionics

EXTENSION Have students find magazine and newspaper articles about current research in the treatment of spinal injuries. Have students report their findings to the class.

Questions

1. **DEFINE** What is bionics? (computerized replacements for injured body parts)

2. How are computers used in bionics work? (Nerve signals go through the computer rather than through the spinal cord. The computer signals nerves to move.)

LESSON 15-4
What are sense organs? (p. 294)

Teaching Strategies

PREVIEW Before beginning this lesson, write the title of each section on the chalkboard. Have students copy these titles in their notebooks using an outline format. As students read each section, they should write the topic sentence for each paragraph in the section in their notebooks.

CLASS ACTIVITY Have students observe their surroundings. Tell students to describe what they see, what they hear, what they smell, what they feel, and what they taste. List students responses on the chalkboard. Then ask students what organs they used to observe their surrounding. (eyes, ears, nose, skin, tongue) Point out that the eyes, ears, nose, skin, and tongue are sense organs. Explain that sense organs help people gather information about their surroundings. Emphasize that the sense organs do not work alone, but rather as an integrated unit.

CLASS ACTIVITY Divide the class into small groups. Tell students in each group to work together to draw pictures illustrating the sense organs and their functions. Tell students to use the pictures on p. 294 as a guide. When all groups are finished, have a representative from each group display and describe the group's pictures.

Answers to Challenges (p. 295)
InfoSearch

You may wish to discuss students' questions and answers as a class.

Teaching Tips for Activity
Locating Taste Receptors

Skills: *modeling, observing, comparing*

COOPERATIVE/COLLABORATIVE LEARNING Have students compare their models with two of their classmates.

Questions

1. sugar-sweet; lemon juice-sour; table salt-salty; tonic water-bitter

2. **a.** Answers will vary. Accept all logical responses. **b.** Answers will vary. Accept all logical responses.

LESSON 15-5
How do you see? (p. 296)

Teaching Strategies

PREVIEW Before beginning the lesson, have students scan the lesson for the science process skill symbols. Have students identify each skill used in the lesson. Students should then review the definition given for each skill on p. 16 of their text.

RETEACHING OPTION This lesson can be most effectively taught with the aid of a wall chart or model showing the parts of the eye. Using the wall chart or model, point out the various parts of the eye and discuss the functions of each part.

INTRASCIENCE CONNECTION The eyes work by sensing light. Light is a form of electromagnetic energy that can be changed into heat, electricity, and other forms of energy. The images formed by the lens of the eye are converted into electrical impulses and carried from the optic nerve to the brain.

CLASS ACTIVITY Have students work in small groups to make models of the eye. Have different colors of clay available for student use. Tell students to label each part of the eye on their models.

CLASS ACTIVITY Have students work in pairs to observe how the pupils respond to light. Tell students to observe their partners' pupils after their eyes have been shut for one minute. Students will observe that the pupils become larger to allow in more light.

Answers to Challenges (p. 297)

Skill Builder: Applying Definitions

lens: a curved material that bends light. The lens of the eye bends light to form an image on the retina.

Skill Builder: Applying Concepts

myopia: eye condition in which light rays from distant objects are focused in front of the retina; astigmatism: an irregularity in the curvature of the lens so that light rays from an object do not meet at a single focal point

Teaching Tips for Activity

Investigating Optical Illusions

Skill: *observing*

COOPERATIVE/COLLABORATIVE LEARNING Answer the questions as a class.

Questions

1. **a.** The line on the right. **b.** both lines are the same length

2. Answers will vary.

3. **a.** The closest post **b.** the farthest post **c.** each post is the same height

4. Answers will vary. Accept all logical responses.

LESSON 15-6
How do you hear? (p. 298)

Teaching Strategies

PREVIEW Before beginning the lesson, have students review the TechTerms and their definitions and read the Lesson Summary.

DISCUSSION Refer students to the diagram of the ear on p. 298. Have students trace the path of sound waves from the outer ear to the cochlea.

DEMONSTRATION If possible, show the students a model of the ear.

EXTENSION You may wish to point out that the ears also function in maintaining balance. Point out that there are three looped tubes in the inner ear called semicircular canals. The tubes are filled with a liquid. Balance is affected by the movement of the liquid in the tubes.

Answers to Challenges (p. 299)

Apply

5. The large outer ears gather sounds.

6. Some sounds are too soft to hear. Others are too high-pitched.

7. The brain interprets signals from the cochlea so a person can understand what the signals mean.

InfoSearch

You may wish to discuss students' questions and answers as a class.

Health and Safety Tip

You may wish to discuss students findings as a class.

Teaching Tips for Technology and Society

Hearing Aids

DISCUSSION You may wish to discuss the two kinds of hearing aids. One kind sends amplified sounds into the ear canal. The other kind sends sound vibrations into the bones of the skull. Discuss with students when they think each kind of hearing aid is used. (The hearing aid that sends amplified sounds into the ear canal is used for people who are hard of hearing. The hearing aid that sends sound vibrations into the bones of the skull is used for people who are partially deaf, or have nerve deafness.)

EXTENSION You may wish to have an otologist visit your classroom. Have the otologist bring in different kinds of hearing aids and describe how they work.

Question

ANALYZE How does a hearing aid work? (makes sounds louder so the damaged part of the ear can vibrate)

LESSON 15-7
What is the endocrine system? (p. 300)

Teaching Strategies

PREVIEW Before beginning this section, have students scan the lesson looking for words with which they are unfamiliar. Have students work in pairs or small groups to define each of the words on their lists

DISCUSSION Introduce this lesson by having students recall what they learned about saliva and perspiration in Units 11 and 14, respectively. Remind students that saliva is produced by salivary glands and perspiration is produced by sweat glands. Define glands as organs that make chemical substances used or released by the body. Point out that sweat glands and salivary glands have ducts. Compare glands with ducts to endocrine glands. Explain that together the endocrine glands make up the endocrine system. Then have students locate the glands that make up the endocrine system in Figure 1 on p. 300.

EXTENSION You may wish to tell students that glands with ducts also are called exocrine glands.

REINFORCEMENT Draw a diagram on the chalkboard illustrating the feedback mechanism of a thermostat and a furnace. Guide students to understand how the endocrine system is regulated by making an analogy between a thermostat and the hypothalamus.

Answers to Challenges (p. 301)

Apply

6. testes

7. at the base of the brain.

8. parathyroid, adrenal, ovaries, testes

Skill Builder: Using Prefixes

Endo- means inner; *exo-* means outer.

Teaching Tips for Technology and Society
Human Growth Hormone

REINFORCEMENT You may wish to tell students that they will learn more about genetic engineering in Unit 18.

Questions

1. What organisms do scientists use to produce large amounts of human growth hormone? (bacteria)

2. What does the amount of human growth hormone released determine? (how tall a child will grow)

LESSON 15-8
What are hormones? (p. 302)

Teaching Strategies

PREVIEW Have students write the lesson title and objectives in their notebooks. As students read the lesson, tell them to write down the sentence or sentences that provide the information needed in the objectives.

DISCUSSION Introduce this lesson by asking students what they think people mean when they say someone's ''adrenalin is pumping.'' (Some students probably will know that adrenalin is related to the body's response to stressful situations.) Use students' knowledge as a springboard for a discussion of hormones. Define hormones as chemical substances that regulate body functions. Then describe the specific functions of some hormones, such as growth hormone, insulin, and adrenalin.

CLASS ACTIVITY Randomly read out the names of the hormones listed in Table 1 on p. 302. Have students identify the endocrine gland that secretes each hormone and each hormone's functions.

RETEACHING OPTION Draw an outline of the human body on the chalkboard. Draw in the endocrine glands at their approximate locations in the body. Next to each organ, write the names of the hormones it produces. Describe the functions of the various hormones.

Answers to Challenges (p. 303)

Check

6. Insulin controls blood sugar levels.

7. Growth hormone controls the growth of bones.

Apply

8. Melatonin, growth hormone, ACTH, thyroxin, parathyroid hormone, thymosin, adrenalin, and insulin are found in both females and males. Testosterone is produced by the

testes, which are found in men. Estrogen and progesterone are produced by the ovaries, which are found in women.

9. abnormal bone growth

10. ACTH

11. the thymus

InfoSearch

You may wish to discuss students' questions and answers as a class.

Teaching Tips for Technology and Society
Insulin Pumps and Pens

DISCUSSION Discuss with students the advantages of an insulin pump. One advantage of an insulin pump is that it is more like the pancreas than are the daily injections of insulin. Another advantage is that the insulin pump releases insulin into the body only when the body needs it. This helps make the diet and exercise program of the diabetic less restrictive.

EXTENSION Have any students who have diabetes describe how they are being treated—by diet, medication, or daily injections of insulin.

Questions

1. **IDENTIFY** What is the purpose of the insulin pump? (It puts insulin into the bloodstream; this is a treatment for diabetes.)

2. **INFER** What is the advantage of the insulin pen? (It is easy to carry with you.)

LESSON 15-9
What is behavior? (p. 304)

Teaching Strategies

PREVIEW Before beginning this lesson, have students review the TechTerms and read the Lesson Summary.

DISCUSSION Write the following actions on the chalkboard: coughing, swallowing, sneezing, blinking, reading, talking, playing baseball, writing. Ask students which of the actions involve learning and thought and which of the actions cannot be controlled. Discuss student responses. Guide students to understand that coughing, swallowing, sneezing, and blinking are automatic responses, or reflexes. Point out that reflexes also are called innate behaviors. Explain that behaviors such as reading, talking, playing baseball, and writing require learning and are called learned behaviors.

DEMONSTRATION Bring a tape recorder to class. Insert a tape and play a short song. Then rewind the tape and play the song again. Repeat this procedure a few times. Make an analogy between innate behavior and running the same tape over and over in a tape recorder.

DISCUSSION Ask students how they learned to read, tie their shoes, ride a bicycle, and so on. Discuss all student responses. Guide students to understand that learned behaviors must be practiced.

COOPERATIVE/COLLABORATIVE LEARNING Have a volunteer explain the difference between innate behavior and learned behavior for the rest of the class.

Answers to Challenges (p. 305)

Apply

6. innate

7. Classmates would start being late.

Health and Safety Tip

Emphasize the importance of knowing what to do in case of a fire. Point out that schools have fire drills so that students will know what to do in case of fire in the schools.

Ideas in Action

Answers will vary. Accept all logical responses.

Teaching Tips for People in Science

B. F. Skinner

REINFORCEMENT Be sure students understand that many things besides food can serve as reinforcements. Ask students what other things they think serve as reinforcements. (water, approval, and so on)

Questions

1. In what field did B.F. Skinner specialize? (psychology)

2. How does a teaching machine present difficult material? (in a series of small steps)

LESSON 15-10
How do you learn? (p. 306)

Teaching Strategies

PREVIEW Before beginning this lesson, have students scan the lesson for science process skill symbols. Have students identify each skill used in the lesson. Students should then review the definition given for each skill on p.16 of their text.

DISCUSSION Describe the ways in which people learn. Have students relate examples of how they have learned by trial and error, memorizing, reasoning, and reward and punishment.

DEMONSTRATION Bring a lock and a variety of keys to class, including the key that fits the lock. Try the keys until you find the right one to demonstrate trial and error learning.

COOPERATIVE/COLLABORATIVE LEARNING Have any students who have taught their pets ''tricks'' describe how they trained the animals. (Students will most likely have used rewards.)

DISCUSSION Ask students what rewards and punishments affect their behavior. Discuss all student responses.

Answers to Challenges (p. 307)

Check

1. kind of learning in which each time a person makes a mistake, the person tries something else

2. Answers will vary. Accept all logical responses.

3. reasoning

Apply

8. Answers will vary. Accept all logical responses.

9. Answers will vary. Accept all logical responses.

Ideas in Action

Answers will vary. Accept all logical responses.

Teaching Tips for Activity

Remembering Information

Skill: *observing*

COOPERATIVE/COLLABORATIVE LEARNING Have a student demonstrate this activity for the rest of the class.

Questions

1. Answers will vary.

2. Answers will vary.

3. Answers will vary.

Answers to Unit Challenges (pp. 308-310)

Understanding the Features: Reading Critically

1. the growth of bones

2. a field of science that uses biological principles in engineering

3. psychology

4. It can be used to detect tumors of soft organs.

5. auxins

6. Answers will vary. Accept all logical responses.

Interpreting a Table

1. the rate of body growth

2. growth hormone, ACTH

3. melatonin

4. pancreas

5. calcium and phosphorus

6. problems related to protection against disease

7. muscle reaction, blood clotting, blood pressure

Critical Thinking

1. They allow organisms to respond quickly to dangerous situations.

2. Both the eye and a camera use light to create images; both have lenses to focus light.

3. Trial and error learning involves trying something new each time you make an error. Reasoning is a way to solve problems by thinking about past experiences.

4. Thirty-one nerves branch out from the spinal cord.

5. They regulate body functions. Answers will vary. Accept all logical responses.

Previewing the Unit

Read the titles of the lessons in this unit aloud. Identify terms in the titles with which the students are unfamiliar. Write these terms on the chalkboard. Using the Glossary of the text or a dictionary, define the terms as a class. Have students write the terms and their definitions in their notebooks. Then, have students work in small groups to carry out the task in the Study Hint.

Bulletin Board Suggestions

1. Assemble a bulletin board highlighting some bacterial and viral diseases. List the names of different bacterial and viral diseases down the left side of the bulletin board. (You may wish to use Table 1 and Table 2 on p.316 as guides.) Across the top of the bulletin board, write the following heads: *Cause, Transmission, Symptoms, Treatment.* Fill in the information for each disease. Use the bulletin board when teaching Lesson 16-3.

2. Assemble a bulletin board showing how alcohol affects the body. Construct a chart on the bulletin board showing blood alcohol concentration and its effects. Use the table on p.329 as a guide. Use the bulletin board to emphasize that alcohol is a depressant. Ask students a variety of questions based on the chart.

LESSON 16-1
How does the body fight disease? (p. 312)

Teaching Strategies

PREVIEW Before beginning this lesson, have students scan the lesson for the science process skill symbols. Have students identify each skill used in the lesson. Students should then review the definition given for each skill on p.16 of their text.

DISCUSSION To introduce this lesson, ask students to describe the function of a country's military. (defense) Have students name different branches of the military. (army, navy, air force, marines, and so on) Explain that the human body is constantly waging a battle against germs. Just as most countries have different military branches for defense, the body has different lines of defense to fight germs. Then describe the defenses of the human body.

REINFORCEMENT Have students recall what they learned about the digestive, circulatory, and respiratory systems in Units 11, 13, and 14, respectively. Remind students that hydrochloric acid in the stomach destroys germs that enter the stomach. Review the function of white blood cells. Have students describe the roles of nasal hairs, cilia, and mucus found in the respiratory system.

EXTENSION When describing antibodies, you may wish to tell students that antibodies are produced when antigens, or foreign substances, are in the body. Each antibody fights off a specific antigen. You can demonstrate the antibody - antigen reaction with two interlocking pieces of a jigsaw puzzle.

RETEACHING OPTION Display a wall chart or model of the skin that details the several layers and structures within the skin. Have students note the arrangement of the epidermal cells to form a protective layer. Point out that healthy, unbroken skin acts like a barrier to prevent organisms and foreign substances from entering the body. Then describe the other defenses of the human body.

Answers to Challenges (p. 313)
Apply

7. to prevent germs from being spread through the air

8. The bandage acts as a barrier to prevent germs from entering the body.

9. People would be prone to many infections.

Health and Safety Tip

Check students' reports. Answers will vary. Accept all logical responses.

Teaching Tips for Science Connection
Preventive Medicine

REINFORCEMENT Emphasize the importance of preventive medicine. Stress that decisions students make today relative to a healthy life-style will affect their futures.

Questions

1. STATE What are two ways you can help prevent disease? (Students should state two of the ways given in the feature.)

2. Why is it important to have regular yearly checkups by a doctor and dentist? (Regular checkups can help detect any health problems early and the earlier a health problem is caught, the easier it is to treat.)

LESSON 16-2
What is immunity? (p. 314)

Teaching Strategies

PREVIEW Have students write the lesson title and objectives in their notebooks. As students read the lesson, tell them to write down the sentence or sentences that provide the information needed in the objectives.

DISCUSSION To introduce this lesson, discuss an occurrence with which all students should be familiar, receiving a vaccine. Ask students how they think vaccines are helpful to people. Discuss all student responses. Point out that vaccines are one way of getting active acquired immunity. Describe immunity as resistance to a specific disease. Then explain the differences among natural immunity and active and passive acquired immunity.

RETEACHING OPTION Write the following heads on the chalkboard: *Natural Immunity, Acquired Immunity.* From the head *Acquired Immunity,* draw arrows to each of the following heads: *Active Immunity, Passive Immunity.* Describe each kind of immunity and give students examples of each. Have students copy the information in their notebooks under the proper heads.

REINFORCEMENT Be sure students understand that natural immunity is an immunity that people are born with, but that a developing baby receiving antibodies from its mother is an example of passive acquired immunity.

COOPERATIVE/COLLABORATIVE LEARNING Have students work in pairs to answer the Check and Apply questions.

Answers to Challenges (p. 315)

Apply

7. They all provide the body with resistance to disease.

8. Acquired; the antibodies were not produced by the baby.

InfoSearch

You may wish to discuss students' questions and answers as a class.

Teaching Tips for Looking Back in Science
Edward Jenner's Discovery of Vaccinations

EXTENSION Have students find out the recommended schedule for immunizations. Tell students to organize their findings in a chart.

Questions

1. NAME Who developed the first vaccine? (Edward Jenner)

2. RELATE Why did Edward Jenner inject material from cowpox sores into people? (so they would produce antibodies to destroy the smallpox virus)

LESSON 16-3
What are some bacterial and viral diseases? (p. 316)

Teaching Strategies

PREVIEW Have students read the lesson feature before beginning the lesson. Discuss the concepts presented in the feature. Ask students how they think this information relates to topics they have already studied or to the lesson they are about to study.

REINFORCEMENT Before beginning this lesson, you may wish to review the characteristics of bacteria and viruses, which were covered in Units 5 and 6.

DISCUSSION To provide motivation for this lesson, list the names of the following diseases on the chalkboard: diphtheria, meningitis, strep throat, tetanus, toxic shock syndrome, pneumonia, and scarlet fever. Challenge students to state what all of these diseases have in common. Point out that they are all caused by bacteria. Then discuss the germ theory of disease.

CLASS ACTIVITY Randomly read out the names of the diseases listed in Table 1 and Table 2 on p. 316. Have students state whether each disease is caused by a bacterium or a virus and describe the symptoms of each disease.

EXTENSION You may wish to tell the students that most disease-causing bacteria are harmful to the body because they produce toxins, or poisons. The poisons damage a cell's life processes.

EXTENSION Have interested students find out how each disease listed in Tables 1 and 2 on p. 316 is spread and how it is treated. Tell students to organize their findings in a table.

Answers to Challenges (p. 317)

Apply

6. Viruses can be seen only with an electron microscope.

7. diphtheria, strep throat

8. mumps

9. fever, low blood pressure

InfoSearch

You may wish to discuss students' questions and answers as a class.

Teaching Tips for Looking Back in Science
Koch's Postulates

REINFORCEMENT After students read this feature, write the four steps of Koch's postulates on the chalkboard. Have students copy the steps in their notebooks.

Questions

1. DEFINE What is a bacteriologist? (a scientist who studies bacteria)

2. What is the first step of Koch's postulates? (to remove disease-causing bacteria from a diseased animal)

LESSON 16-4
What are antibiotics? (p. 318)

Teaching Strategies

PREVIEW Before beginning this lesson, have students scan the lesson looking for words with which they are unfamiliar. Have students work in pairs or small groups to define each of the words on their lists.

CLASS ACTIVITY Have students look up the meanings of the prefix *anti-* and the term *biotic* in a dictionary. (*anti-*: against; *biotic*: pertaining to life) Then relate the meanings of these words to the definition of antibiotic. Point out that antibiotics are substances that destroy bacteria.

DEMONSTRATION If possible, show students a sample of *Penicillium notatum*, which is the mold most commonly used in penicillin production.

REINFORCEMENT Be sure students understand that some antibiotics are produced by some types of bacteria and used to destroy other bacteria, and that antibiotics do not work against viruses.

RETEACHING OPTION Ask students if they have ever taken penicillin, streptomycin, or tetracyclene. Point out that these three widely used medicines are antibiotics. Define an antibiotic as a chemical substance that kills bacteria. Identify molds as the major sources of antibiotics, but tell students that some bacteria, plants, and animals also produce antibiotics. Then describe the selectivity of antibiotics. Explain that each antibiotic can be used against only certain kinds of organisms.

Answers to Challenges (p. 319)

Check

1. in a part of the dish where some mold had formed

2. penicillin

3. chemical substances that kill bacteria

4. No.

5. They make people sick.

6. molds

7. Alexander Fleming

Apply

8. Yes; the person could become infected with a virus or bacteria against which penicillin has no effect.

9. No.

Skill Builder: Building Vocabulary

Check students' definitions.

Health and Safety Tip

Emphasize the importance of medical ID bracelets.

Teaching Tips for People in Science

Joseph Lister

EXTENSION You may wish to tell students that the development of sterilization techniques also greatly reduced the mortality rate of women after childbirth. Joseph Lister discovered that mortality rates of women could be reduced almost tenfold if midwives washed their hands between patients.

Questions

1. What did Joseph Lister hypothesize about the infections patients got after surgery? (that they were caused by bacteria)

2. INFER Why do you think surgeons wear masks over their noses and mouths during surgery? (to prevent germs they may breathe out from infecting patients)

LESSON 16-5
What is heart disease? (p. 320)

Teaching Strategies

PREVIEW Before beginning the lesson, read the list of TechTerms aloud so that students can hear their pronunciations.

CLASS ACTIVITY To introduce this lesson, write the factors contributing to heart disease on the chalkboard: age, family history, gender, smoking, high blood pressure, obesity, physical inactivity, and high cholesterol levels. Then ask a volunteer to go up to the chalkboard and circle any of the risk factors that can be controlled. Discuss the student's selections. Guide students to understand that there are ways they can prevent heart disease. Point out that age, family history,

and gender are the only risk factors for heart disease that cannot be controlled.

DISCUSSION Describe atherosclerosis. Refer students to the picture on p. 320 to illustrate your description.

REINFORCEMENT Be sure that students understand the relationship among high cholesterol levels, atherosclerosis, and heart attacks. Stress that the heart has its own system of blood vessels.

REINFORCEMENT Be sure students understand that the term *heart disease* does not only refer to actual diseases of the heart, but of the blood vessels as well.

Answers to Challenges (p. 321)

Apply

6. The width of the artery stays the same but the size of the opening inside the artery generally decreases with age due to fat buildup.

7. reduce the amount of fatty substances in the diet

8. smoking, high blood pressure, obesity, physical inactivity, high cholesterol levels

9. Answers will vary. Accept all logical responses.

InfoSearch

You may wish to discuss students' questions and answers as a class.

Teaching Tips for Science Connection

Cholesterol

DISCUSSION Ask student what they know about cholesterol. Have students describe advertisements that mention this term. Then discuss the importance of a low cholesterol diet.

Questions

1. How can a person cut back on cholesterol? (by limiting the amount of red meat, eggs, and whole milk dairy products in the diet)

2. COMPARE What is the incidence of heart disease in people who eat more fish than red meat compared with people who eat red meat more often? (It is lower.)

LESSON 16-6
What is cancer? (p. 322)

Teaching Strategies

PREVIEW Before beginning this lesson, write the title of each section in the lesson on the chalkboard. Have students copy these titles in their notebooks using an outline format. As students read each section, they should write the topic sentence for each paragraph in the section in their notebooks.

DISCUSSION It is unlikely that any of your students have not heard or used the term *cancer*. Ask students what they think when they hear the word *cancer*. Discuss student responses. Emphasize that cancer is a group of diseases, not a single disorder.

REINFORCEMENT Review the process of mitosis, which is covered in Unit 4. Point out that normal cells usually divide in an orderly manner, while cancerous cells divide in a rapid, uncontrolled way.

DISCUSSION Describe how cancer spreads and some of its causes. Then refer students to Table 1 on p. 322 and discuss the warning signs of cancer.

COOPERATIVE/COLLABORATIVE LEARNING Have a volunteer explain the difference between a benign tumor and a malignant tumor for the rest of the class.

Answers to Challenges (p. 323)

Apply

8. More women are smoking.

Skill Builder: Building Vocabulary

Benign and malignant are antonyms. Answers will vary. Accept all logical responses.

Health and Safety Tip

Emphasize the importance of practicing self-examination on a monthly basis.

Teaching Tips for Technology and Society

Cancer Detection and Treatment

DISCUSSION Describe the various methods used to treat cancer. Some students may be confused by the use of radiation to treat cancer since radiation also can cause cancer. Point out that carefully controlled dosages are used in radiation therapy.

Questions

1. LIST What are four ways to treat cancer? (surgery, radiation, lasers, drugs)

2. What is a problem of using drugs to fight cancer? (The drugs affect normal cells as well as cancerous cells.)

LESSON 16-7
What is AIDS? (p. 324)

Teaching Strategies

PREVIEW Before beginning the lesson, have students review the TechTerms and their definitions and read the Lesson Summary.

CLASS ACTIVITY Have students look up the meaning of each word of the acronym AIDS: acquired; immune; deficiency; syndrome. Tell students to use the meanings of each word to write a brief description of AIDS in their own words.

DISCUSSION Write the term *AIDS* on the chalkboard. Explain the cause, symptoms, and transmission of this fatal disease. Point out that, at this time, there is neither a cure nor a vaccine for AIDS.

CLASS ACTIVITY Have students find and collect recent newspaper and magazine articles about AIDS. Read and discuss the articles as a class.

Answers to Challenges (p. 325)

Check

5. No.

6. No.

Apply

9. to slow down the spread of AIDS among intravenous drug users

10. It prevents infections from overtaking the body.

InfoSearch

You may wish to discuss students' questions and answers as a class.

Teaching Tips for Activity
Investigating the Spread of AIDS

Skills: *calculating, analyzing*

COOPERATIVE/COLLABORATIVE LEARNING Answer the questions as a class.

Questions

1. a. New York **b.** Maryland

2. 394,021

3. Answers will vary. Accept all logical responses.

LESSON 16-8
How do some drugs affect the body? (p. 326)

Teaching Strategies

PREVIEW Before beginning this lesson, read the list of TechTerms aloud so students can hear their pronunciation.

DISCUSSION Most students are aware that drug abuse is a major problem in the United States. Ask students what they think of when they hear the word *drug*. Elicit from students whether they think drugs are "good" or "bad." Then discuss some of the beneficial uses of drugs, as well as the problem of drug abuse. Emphasize the devastating effect drug abuse has on a person's life.

CLASS ACTIVITY Explain the difference between over-the-counter drugs and prescription drugs. Have students name as many over-the-counter drugs as they can. List student responses on the chalkboard. Then classify each drug named as a painkiller, decongestant, antacid, and so on.

EXTENSION Arrange for a speaker from a drug rehabilitation program to talk to your class. An ex-abuser's discussion of his or her own personal experience may have a dramatic effect on young people's attitudes toward drugs.

RETEACHING OPTION Write the following head on the chalkboard: *Commonly Used Drugs.* From this head, draw arrows to each of the following heads: *Depressants, Stimulants, Hallucinogens.* Under *Depressants,* list barbiturates and narcotics. Under *Stimulants,* list cocaine and crack. Under *Hallucinogens,* list LSD and marijuana. Have students copy the chart in their notebooks. Be sure students recognize that crack is a form of cocaine.

Apply

7. Coffee speeds up the action of the central nervous system.

Health and Safety Tip

Emphasize that a person should work with certain products, such as paint thinners, only in well-ventilated areas.

Skill Builder: Classifying

stimulants: amphetamines, nicotine; depressants: heroin, morphine, tranquilizers; hallucinogens: PCP

Teaching Tips for Activity

Reading Drug Labels

Skills: *observing, hypothesizing*

COOPERATIVE/COLLABORATIVE LEARNING Have students work in pairs.

Questions

1. when the drug should no longer be used because it is ineffective

2. how much and how often the drugs should be taken

3. A child weighs less than an adult.

4. Keep this and all drugs out of the reach of children.

3. They think and react more slowly.

4. It harms the body.

5. an alcoholic

Apply

6. Answers will vary. Accept all logical responses.

Health and Safety Tip

Emphasize the danger of mixing alcohol and other drugs.

Skill Builder: Researching

Check students' reports.

Teaching Tips for Activity

Comparing Blood Alcohol Concentration

Skills: *observing, analyzing*

COOPERATIVE/COLLABORATIVE LEARNING Answer the questions as a class.

Questions

1. 0.08–0.09

2. 0.05–0.06

3. Yes; if a person drinks too much too quickly, unconsciousness, coma, and death may occur.

LESSON 16-9

How does alcohol affect the body? (p. 328)

Teaching Strategies

PREVIEW Before beginning this lesson, have students review the TechTerms and read the Lesson Summary.

DISCUSSION Remind students that alcohol is a depressant. Point out that although many people think alcohol is a stimulant, it actually slows down the action of the central nervous system. Ask students to recall the name of the control center of the brain. (the cerebrum) Explain to students that alcohol greatly affects the cerebrum. When alcohol enters the cerebrum, coordination and judgement are impaired and reaction time is slowed.

REINFORCEMENT Emphasize the dangers of drinking and driving. Alcohol-related car accidents are the leading cause of death of young people.

EXTENSION You may wish to tell students that in addition to harming the liver, heavy drinking also can damage the linings of the esophagus, stomach, and small intestine, as well as the heart and the kidneys.

COOPERATIVE/COLLABORATIVE LEARNING Have students quiz each other on the materials in this lesson.

Answers to Challenges (p. 329)

Check

1. ethyl alcohol

2. It slows them down.

LESSON 16-10

How does tobacco affect the body? (p. 330)

Teaching Strategies

PREVIEW Have students write the lesson title and objective in their notebooks. As students read the lesson, tell them to write down the sentence or sentences that provide the information needed in the objective.

REINFORCEMENT Before beginning this lesson, review the functions of the cilia and air sacs found in the respiratory system.

DISCUSSION Bring in a tube of toothpaste specifically made for smokers. Ask students why there is a need for a special toothpaste for smokers. (Tobacco stains the teeth.) Then describe how substances in tobacco also "stain" the lungs. Point out that smokers have a higher death rate from lung diseases than do nonsmokers. Refer students to the picture on 330 showing a healthy lung and a smoker's lung. Tell students to note the destruction of lung tissue in the smoker's lung. Point out that smokers also have a higher risk of heart disease.

DISCUSSION Discuss the reasons people smoke. Ask students how they think peer pressure is involved in the decisions of young people to start smoking. Encourage students to respond to each other's comments.

CLASS ACTIVITY Have students work in groups to create anti-smoking commercials. Then have each group perform its commercial for the rest of the class.

Answers to Challenges (p. 331)

Apply

5. It would reduce a person's ability to exercise.

6. The body is dependent on nicotine.

InfoSearch

You may wish to discuss students' questions and answers as a class.

Teaching Tips for Activity

Classifying Cigarette Advertisements

Skill: *analyzing*

COOPERATIVE/COLLABORATIVE LEARNING Have students work in pairs.

Questions

1. Answers will vary.

2. Answers will vary.

3. a. tobacco companies **b.** American Lung Association; American Heart Association

Answers to Unit Challenges (pp. 332-334)

Understanding the Features: Reading Critically

1. eat a balanced diet, get the proper amount of rest, exercise regularly, keep clean

2. Vaccines enable people to produce antibodies against certain diseases.

3. remove disease-causing bacteria from a diseased animal; isolate and grow the bacteria; inject the bacteria into a healthy animal; remove and compare bacteria when the animal gets sick

4. The use of antiseptics and sterilization reduces the number of post-operative infections.

5. chicken and fish; Accept all logical responses.

6. surgery, radiation, lasers, drugs

Interpreting a Table

1. 0.08–0.09

2. feeling of relaxation

3. 0.50

4. 28 ounces

5. reaction time is slowed; lack of judgement

6. slight loss of coordination

7. 0.40

8. blood alcohol concentration

Critical Thinking

1. They can get AIDS and hepatitis.

2. Answers will vary. Accept all logical responses.

3. Answers will vary. Accept all logical responses.

4. to prevent their germs from spreading

5. Answers will vary. Accept all logical responses.

Previewing the Unit

Before beginning this unit, read the titles of the lessons in this unit aloud. As a class, define any terms in the titles with which students are unfamiliar. Then, have students write the lesson titles in their notebooks. As you proceed through the unit, remind students to carry out the task in the Study Hint.

Bulletin Board Suggestions

1. Assemble a bulletin board illustrating human embryonic development. Attach pictures to the bulletin board showing development during each trimester. Label each picture and attach the pictures to the bulletin board in sequence.

2. Assemble a bulletin board illustrating the five stages of the human life cycle. Have students find and collect pictures representing infancy, childhood, adolescence, adulthood, and old age. Attach all the pictures to the bulletin board to make a collage.

LESSON 17-1
What is meiosis? (p. 336)

Teaching Strategies

PREVIEW Before beginning this lesson, have students scan through the lesson looking for words with which they are unfamiliar. Have students use the Glossary of the text or a dictionary to define each of the terms they have identified.

DISCUSSION Introduce the term *gametes*. Define gametes as reproductive cells. Tell students that during the formation of gametes, the number of chromosomes is cut in half. Identify this process as meiosis. Guide students to understand that meiosis is a special kind of cell division that takes place only in the formation of gametes. Develop the idea that during fertilization gametes combine. Point out that since each gamete contains half the number of chromosomes present in body cells, the original number of chromosomes is restored in the zygote.

DEMONSTRATION Using common objects such as pennies, model meiosis for the class.

RETEACHING OPTION Draw the stages of meiosis on the chalkboard. Use the diagram on p. 336 as a guide. Review each stage of meiosis to help students understand this complex process. Be sure students understand that the diagram begins with a cell that has already undergone chromosome replication.

Answers to Challenges (p. 337)

State the Problem

Students should recognize that the gamete has an extra chromosome.

Skill Builder: Organizing Information

Check students' lists for logic and accuracy.

Teaching Tips for Science Connection
Nondisjunction

CLASS ACTIVITY After students finish reading this feature have them study the photograph on p. 337 and locate the extra chromosome in the 21st pair.

REINFORCEMENT Refer students back to the State the Problem exercise. Elicit from students that the gamete shows evidence of nondisjunction.

Questions

1. In what field did B.F. Skinner specialize? (psychology)

2. How does a teaching machine present difficult material? (in a series of small steps)

LESSON 17-2
What are the parts of the female reproductive system?

(p. 338)

Teaching Strategies

PREVIEW Before beginning this lesson, read the list of TechTerms aloud so students can hear their pronunciations.

DISCUSSION Refer students to the diagram of the female reproductive system on p. 338. Have students locate each part of the female reproductive system on the diagram as you describe their structures and functions.

REINFORCEMENT Emphasize that the ovaries are the main organs of the female reproductive system. Point out that the ovaries produce both hormones and egg cells. Remind students that estrogen and progesterone are the two hormones produced by the ovaries.

CLASS ACTIVITY If possible, have students observe prepared slides of an egg cell under a microscope. Tell students to sketch their observations.

COOPERATIVE/COLLABORATIVE LEARNING Have students work in pairs to answer the Check and Apply questions.

Answers to Challenges (p. 339)
Skill Builder: Making a Diagram

Check students' diagrams for logic and accuracy.

Teaching Tips for Science Connection
Ectopic Pregnancy

REINFORCEMENT Before students read this feature, briefly review the function of the uterus. Remind students that an embryo normally develops inside the uterus.

EXTENSION You may wish to point out that the possibility of an ectopic pregnancy is one reason a woman should see a doctor as soon as she thinks she might be pregnant.

Questions

1. DEFINE What is fertilization? (the joining together of a sperm cell and an egg cell)

2. IDENTIFY What are two possible causes of a tubule ectopic pregnancy? (swelling of the oviducts; scar tissue)

LESSON 17-3
What are the parts of the male reproductive system? (p. 340)

Teaching Strategies

PREVIEW Before you begin this lesson, have students read the TechTerms and review the Lesson Summary.

DISCUSSION Point out the structures of the male reproductive system in Figure 1 on p.340. Explain the function of each structure. Point out that the testes are contained in a pocket of skin (the scrotum) that lies outside the body cavity.

EXTENSION As you discuss the role of testosterone in the development of secondary sex characteristics in males, you may wish to point out that in females, secondary sex characteristics are caused by the production of the hormones estrogen and progesterone.

CLASS ACTIVITY If possible, have students observe prepared slides of a sperm cell under a microscope. Tell student to sketch their observations. Have students look for the head and tail of a sperm cell.

REINFORCEMENT Emphasize that in males, the urethra is part of the excretory system and the reproductive system. Point out that both urine and sperm exit the body through the urethra in males. Be sure students understand that in females the urinary and reproductive systems are completely separate.

Answers to Challenges (p. 341)
Skill Builder: Organizing Information

Review students' tables for logic and accuracy.

Teaching Tips for Science Connection
Sexually Transmitted Diseases

EXTENSION Have interested students research the complications that arise if sexually transmitted diseases, such as gonorrhea, syphilis, or chlamydia are left untreated. Tell students to present their findings in an oral report. Have students include a discussion of how sexually transmitted diseases can affect the babies of pregnant women.

Questions

1. LIST What are two sexually transmitted diseases? (gonorrhea and syphilis)

2. HYPOTHESIZE Why is it not possible to get a sexually transmitted disease through casual contact with an infected person? (The pathogens that cause sexually transmitted diseases cannot live outside the body.)

LESSON 17-4
What is menstruation? (p. 342)

Teaching Strategies

PREVIEW Have students write the lesson title and objective in their notebooks. As students read the lesson, tell them to write down the sentence or sentences that provide the information needed in the objective.

DISCUSSION Describe the menstrual cycle. Point out that ovulation and menstruation are the main occurrences of the menstrual cycle.

EXTENSION In order to emphasize the interaction of the endocrine and reproductive systems, you may wish to identify and describe the hormones that regulate the menstrual cycle. A more detailed description also may help students understand the menstrual cycle, although it is not necessary for students to remember the names of the various hormones. At the beginning of the menstrual cycle, the pituitary gland releases follicle stimulating hormone, or FSH. FSH causes an egg to mature. After about 14 days, another hormone produced by the pituitary, luteinizing hormone, or LH, causes ovulation. The ruptured egg follicle forms a corpus luteum, which secretes estrogen and progesterone. These hormones cause the lining of the uterus to thicken. They also stop the release of FSH and LH. After about 10 days, the corpus luteum begins to break apart. Thus, the amount of estrogen and progesterone in the blood decreases. This causes the lining of the uterus to break apart and menstruation to occur. The inhibition of LH and FSH release also stops and the cycle begins again.

REINFORCEMENT Be sure students understand the difference between the menstrual cycle and menstruation. Emphasize that the menstrual cycle is a monthly cycle of change and that menstruation is only one part of the menstrual cycle.

Answers to Challenges (p. 343)
Apply

6. Yes. A female will continue to have a menstrual cycle, regardless of her age, as long as mature eggs are released from her ovaries.

7. In both reproductive systems, hormones trigger the production of sex cells.

8. d, c, b, a

Skill Builder: Diagramming

Check students' diagrams for logic and accuracy.

Teaching Tips for Science Connection
Hormone Therapy

REINFORCEMENT Have students reread the feature on p. 301 about human growth hormone to illustrate how technology has affected hormone therapy.

Questions

1. DEFINE What is a hormone deficiency? (condition in which a person's body does not produce enough of one or more hormones)

2. DEFINE What is hormone therapy? (a way of treating people suffering from a hormone deficiency disease)

LESSON 17-5
How does fertilization take place? (p. 344)

Teaching Strategies

PREVIEW Before beginning this lesson, write the title of each section in the lesson on the chalkboard. Have students copy these titles in their notebooks using an outline format. As students read each section, they should write the topic sentence for each paragraph in the section in their notebooks.

DISCUSSION To provide motivation for this lesson, refer students to the photograph on p. 344 and ask students to describe what they think is shown in the picture. Discuss all student responses. Point out that the photograph shows an egg cell covered with sperm cells. Describe fertilization. Emphasize that only one sperm cell fertilizes an egg cell.

CLASS ACTIVITY Using the diagrams on p. 344 as guides, draw an egg cell and a sperm cell on the chalkboard. Have volunteers come up to the chalkboard and label the parts of each reproductive cell.

COOPERATIVE/COLLABORATIVE LEARNING Have a volunteer explain the difference between ovulation and fertilization for the rest of the class.

Answers to Challenges (p. 345)

Apply

6. Fertilization can occur only during ovulation. Ovulation is the stage of a menstrual cycle during which a mature egg is present in an oviduct.

7. Sperm cells move using their whiplike tails. Egg cells move when the hairs lining the oviduct move them.

8. 23

9. 23

Health and Safety Tip

Answers will vary. Accept all logical responses.

Teaching Tips for Technology and Society
Reproductive Technologies

CLASS ACTIVITY Have students find and collect newspaper and magazine articles pertaining to infertility and methods used by infertile couples, including *in vitro* fertilization. Read and discuss the articles as a class.

Questions

1. Why do you think that babies produced by *in vitro* fertilization sometimes are called "test tube babies"? (Fertilization of these babies occurs in the laboratory.)

2. HYPOTHESIZE Why do you think some women are unable to become pregnant? (Answers will vary. Accept all logical responses.)

LESSON 17-6
How does a human embryo develop? (p. 346)

Teaching Strategies

PREVIEW Before beginning this section, have students scan the lesson looking for words with which they are unfamiliar. Have students work in pairs or small groups to define each of the words on their lists.

DISCUSSION Write the following heads on the chalkboard: *Zygote, Embryo, Fetus.* Distinguish between these three stages of embryonic development. Have students copy the information in their notebooks under the appropriate heads.

REINFORCEMENT Emphasize that the blood of a mother and a developing embryo do not mix. Nutrients and wastes are exchanged by the process of diffusion.

ITERDISCIPLINARY CONNECTION Bring a pack of cigarettes to class and read aloud the Surgeon General's warning that smoking by pregnant women may result in fetal injury, premature birth, and low birth weight. Emphasize that everything that enters a pregnant woman, including harmful substances such as drugs, alcohol, and tobacco, cross the placenta and affect the developing embryo.

RETEACHING OPTION Display a variety of pictures showing different stages in an unborn baby's development in front of the classroom. Arrange the pictures in sequence. Have students identify the placenta, the umbilical cord, and the amnion in any pictures in which these structures are evident.

Answers to Challenges (p. 347)

Ideas in Action

You may wish to discuss students' answers.

Teaching Tips for Activity
Graphing Changes in Fetal Development

Skills: *graphing, analyzing*

COOPERATIVE/COLLABORATIVE LEARNING Answer the questions as a class.

LESSON 17-7
What are the stages of human development? (p. 348)

Teaching Strategies

PREVIEW Have students read the lesson feature before beginning the lesson. Discuss the concepts presented in the feature. Ask students how they think this information relates to topics they have already studied or to the lesson they are about to study.

DISCUSSION To introduce the lesson, define the development of an organism as its life cycle. Then ask students to name the stages of the human life cycle. List students' responses on the chalkboard. (Students probably will mention the stages discussed in their textbooks.) Add to the list any of the five stages that students do not mention. Then describe the events that characterize each stage.

REINFORCEMENT Emphasize that many of the traits characterizing old age are lessened by maintaining a healthful lifestyle throughout a person's entire life. Stress to students that decisions they make today will influence their future health. Encourage students to avoid tobacco and alcohol, and to exercise on a regular basis.

COOPERATIVE/COLLABORATIVE LEARNING Have any students with infant siblings describe the learning processes they have observed in their baby brothers and sisters for the rest of the class.

Answers to Challenges (p. 349)

Apply

6. A very young infant does not identify the new person as a stranger. The 9-month old can relate to its environment, and knows the difference between a stranger and his or her parents.

7. During infancy, muscle development is increasing while during old age, it is declining.

8. childhood

Skill Builder: Organizing Information

Check students' labels for logic and accuracy.

Teaching Tips for Career in Life Science
Day Care Worker

EXTENSION Arrange for a day care worker to visit your class. Have the day care worker describe a typical work day. Tell students to prepare beforehand questions they would like to ask.

Questions

1. What are the educational requirements for a day care worker? (a high school diploma)

2. Why must day care workers be patient and understanding? (They work with young children who are just learning many new skills.)

Answers to Unit Challenges (pp. 350-352)
Understanding the Features: Reading Critically

1. a condition in which chromosome pairs do not separate correctly

2. It can harm the mother if an embryo grows outside the uterus.

3. gonorrhea, syphilis, AIDS

4. Through hormone therapy, a person suffering from Addison's disease can lead a normal life.

5. They might have blocked or missing oviducts.

6. They work with young children.

Interpreting a Diagram

1. 4

2. 2

3. beginning of meiosis

4. One chromosome from each pair is going to the end of the cell.

Critical Thinking

1. They both produce reproductive cells and hormones.

2. These substances will cross the placenta and harm a developing fetus.

3. Answers will vary. Accept all logical responses.

4. The fetus would not be able to get food or oxygen and would die.

5. It happens over and over.

6. Answers will vary. Accept all logical responses.

UNIT 18
HEREDITY AND GENETICS (p. 353)

Previewing the Unit

Read the titles of the lessons in this unit aloud. Identify terms in the titles with which students are unfamiliar. Write these terms on the chalkboard. Using the Glossary of the text or a dictionary, define the terms as a class. Have students write the terms and their definitions in their notebooks.

Bulletin Board Suggestions

1. Assemble a bulletin board showing the use of Punnett squares to predict the inheritance of traits. Draw Punnett squares on the bulletin board and diagram a variety of different crosses. Include at least one cross to show blending, the determination of sex, and the inheritance of sex-linked traits.

2. Assemble a bulletin board illustrating controlled breeding. Divide the bulletin board into three sections. Label each section with one of the following heads: *Mass Selection, Inbreeding, Hybridization.* Have students find and collect pictures of organisms produced by these methods of controlled breeding. Group and attach the pictures under the appropriate heads.

LESSON 18-1
What is heredity? (p. 354)

Teaching Strategies

PREVIEW Have students read the lesson feature before beginning the lesson. Discuss the concepts presented in the feature. Ask students how they think this information relates to topics they have already studied or to the lesson they are about to study.

DISCUSSION Provide motivation for this lesson by asking students if they look like other members of their families. Challenge students to explain their answers. Students probably will refer to characteristics such as eye color, hair color, skin color, and height. List these characteristics on the chalkboard and identify them as inherited traits. Define inherited traits as characteristics that are passed from parents to their offspring.

REINFORCEMENT Have students recall that during fertilization, male and female sex cells join together. Point out that each of the sex cells contains material that determines the inherited traits of the offspring.

COOPERATIVE/COLLABORATIVE LEARNING Have a student explain the difference between heredity and genetics for the rest of the class.

Answers to Challenges (p. 355)
Apply

6. They inherit the traits from the same parents.

7. They are identical twins.

8. Answers will vary. Accept all logical responses.

InfoSearch

You may wish to discuss students' questions and answers as a class.

Teaching Tips for People in Science
Gregor Mendel

CLASS ACTIVITY Bring a variety of pea pods to class to demonstrate some of the traits studied by Mendel. For example, bring in smooth and wrinkled seeds, and green and yellow pods. Have students observe each seed and pod and record their observations.

Questions

1. Why was Mendel able to observe many generations of pea plants? (Pea plants grow and reproduce quickly.)

2. IDENTIFY What was Mendel's original hypothesis? (Traits are passed from parents to offspring.)

LESSON 18-2
What are genes and chromosomes? (p. 356)

Teaching Strategies

PREVIEW Before beginning this lesson, have students review the TechTerms and their definitions and read the Lesson Summary.

REINFORCEMENT Before beginning this lesson, review the processes of cell division and meiosis. Remind students that during cell division, each chromosome makes a copy of itself. Have students recall that meiosis is the special process by which gametes are formed. Ask students to compare the number of chromosomes in gametes and in body cells. (Gametes have only half the number of chromosomes as body cells.) Point out that during fertilization, two gametes combine and the original number of chromosomes is restored in the zygote. Emphasize that since chromosomes control heredity, the zygote receives traits from both parents.

CLASS ACTIVITY Have students look up the meanings of the word parts *chromo-* and *-some* in a dictionary. (*chromo-:* colored; *-some:* body) Ask students how the meanings of these word parts are related to the term *chromosomes*. (Chromosomes are dark-colored structures, or bodies, in the nucleus.)

EXTENSION You may wish to tell students that the German biologist Walther Fleming coined the term *chromosomes* to describe the dark, threadlike particles he observed in the nucleus using a microscope. Fleming made his observations in 1882.

Answers to Challenges (p. 357)
Check

1. in the nucleus of cells

2. its parents

3. along each chromosome

4. genes

5. inherited

Apply

6. One produced by asexual reproduction because it would receive all its chromosomes from one parent cell.

7. Daughter cells would have only half the number of chromosomes as their parent cells.

Ideas in Action

Answers will vary. Accept all logical responses.

Teaching Tips for People in Science

Barbara McClintock

EXTENSION The term "jumping" genes actually refers to the ability of chromosomes to break apart and join together differently during the formation of eggs or sperm. This process allows each egg and sperm cell to contain a different combination of genes.

Questions

1. INFER How could Barbara McClintock tell where "jumping" genes occurred? (A "jumping" gene caused changes in the traits controlled by the genes next to the place where it landed.)

2. Why do you think most scientists did not take Barbara McClintock's work seriously in 1951? (Answers will vary. Accept all logical responses.)

LESSON 18-3
How do chromosomes carry traits? (p. 358)

Teaching Strategies

PREVIEW Before reading this lesson, write the title of each section in the lesson on the chalkboard. Have students copy these titles in their notebooks using an outline format. As students read each section, they should write the topic sentence for each paragraph in the section in their notebooks.

DISCUSSION Refer students to the diagram on p. 358 showing the structure of a DNA molecule. Compare a DNA molecule to a twisted ladder. Have students locate the sugar molecules and the phosphate groups that make up the sides of the DNA ladder and the nitrogen bases that make up the steps of the ladder. Tell students to note that adenine and thymine, and cytosine and guanine always occur in pairs. Emphasize that the arrangement of nitrogen bases in a DNA molecule determines inherited traits.

CLASS ACTIVITY Using commercial kits or common items such as styrofoam, toothpicks, pipe cleaners, and so on, have students build models of DNA molecules. Tell students to identify and label each part of a DNA molecule. Display students' models in the classroom.

DEMONSTRATION Show students a model of DNA replication using a zipper.

REINFORCEMENT Students may have difficulty understanding the meaning and roles of genes, chromosomes, and DNA. Stress that chromosomes are long strands of DNA. Genes are particular sequences of nitrogen bases in the DNA.

EXTENSION Students may wonder how the genetic code in DNA controls an organisms traits. You may wish to point out that the traits of all organisms depend on the proteins in their cells. DNA controls the making of proteins. Each particular sequence of nitrogen bases, or gene, codes for a particular amino acid.

Answers to Challenges (p. 359)

Check

1. DNA

2. nitrogen bases

3. cytosine

4. inherited traits

5. by replication

Apply

6. Answers will vary. Accept all logical responses.

7. They will be identical twins.

8. sugar molecules and phosphates

9. No; base C pairs only with base G.

InfoSearch

You may wish to discuss students' questions and answers as a class.

Teaching Tips for Looking Back in Science

Discovering the Structure of DNA

EXTENSION Have interested students find out about the work of the American biologist Walter Sutton. He developed the chromosome theory, which states that genes are sections of chromosomes. Tell students to write their findings in a report.

Questions

1. LIST What three scientists discovered the structure of DNA. (Watson, Crick, and Franklin)

2. On what did Rosalind Franklin base her prediction of the shape and composition of a DNA molecule? (X-ray photographs of DNA crystals)

LESSON 18-4
Why can offspring differ from their parents? (p. 360)

Teaching Strategies

PREVIEW Before beginning this lesson, read the list of TechTerms aloud so students can hear their pronunciations.

DISCUSSION Provide motivation for this lesson by asking students if they have the same eye color as both of their parents. From the class response, it should become apparent that offspring can have different inherited traits from their parents. Explain how pairs of genes determine an organism's traits.

RETEACHING OPTION Describe Mendel's work with pea plants. Draw diagrams on the chalkboard to illustrate Mendel's crosses. Introduce and define the terms *pure* and *hybrid*. Follow this with a development of the terms *dominant* and *recessive*.

Answers to Challenges (p. 361)

Apply

6. two tall genes; one tall gene and one short gene

7. No; because the short gene in pea plants is recessive.

8. brown

9. Answers will vary. Accept all logical responses.

Skill Builder: Researching

Check students' posters.

Skill Builder: Defining

The Principle of Dominance: One factor, or gene, for a trait may hide the other gene and prevent it from being expressed in an organism. The Principle of Separation: The two factors for a trait separate, or segregate, during the formation of gametes. The Principle of Independent Assortment: Factors for different traits separate independently of one another during the formation of gametes.

Teaching Tips for Activity

Modeling the Structure of DNA

Skills: *modeling, inferring*

SAFETY TIP Caution students to be careful when using scissors.

COOPERATIVE/COLLABORATIVE LEARNING Have students work in pairs.

Questions

1. a. guanine **b.** adenine

2. a. sugars, phosphates **b.** nitrogen bases

3. No; the sequence of nitrogen bases is not the same in all DNA molecules.

LESSON 18-5
How do genes combine in offspring? (p. 362)

Teaching Strategies

PREVIEW Before beginning the lesson, have students scan the lesson looking for words with which they are unfamiliar. Have students work in pairs or small groups to define each of the words on their lists.

REINFORCEMENT Be sure students understand that the lower case letter of the dominant trait is used to represent a recessive trait. Some students may be tempted to write the first letter of the recessive trait.

DISCUSSION Describe how Punnett squares are used to predict traits. Guide students through the examples shown on p. 362.

CLASS ACTIVITY Have students practice monohybrid crosses using Punnett squares. Have students work in pairs or small groups. Place more able students with students of lesser ability to allow for peer tutoring.

RETEACHING OPTION Draw Punnett squares on the chalkboard and diagram various monohybrid crosses. Identify the dominant trait and the recessive trait for each cross. Have students describe the genetic makeup and appearance of the offspring for each cross.

Answers to Challenges (p. 363)

Apply

6. 2

7. 2

8. Two of the four offspring are hybrids.

InfoSearch

You may wish to discuss students' questions and answers as a class.

Teaching Tips for Activity

Investigating the Effects of Chance on Heredity

Skills: *analyzing, measuring*

COOPERATIVE/COLLABORATIVE LEARNING Answer the questions as a class.

Questions

1. a. unattached ear lobes **b.** attached ear lobes

2. Answers will vary.

LESSON 18-6
How are traits blended? (p. 364)

Teaching Strategies

PREVIEW Before beginning this lesson, have students scan the lesson for the science process skill symbols. Have students identify each skill used in the lesson. Students should then review the definition given for each skill on p.16 of their text.

DEMONSTRATION Put blue food coloring in one cup of water and red food coloring in another. Mix the two cups of water together. The water will turn purple. Relate this activity to blending.

EXTENSION You may wish to tell students that other terms for blending are incomplete dominance and codominance.

REINFORCEMENT Emphasize that blended genes do not disappear. Draw a Punnett square on the chalkboard. Use the Punnett square to show students that blending occurs only in hybrids and that when hybrids are crossed, the pure traits appear again in their offspring.

DEMONSTRATION If possible, bring a white, a red, and a pink four-o'clock flower to class to show students an organism that exhibits blending.

Answers to Challenges (p. 365)

Apply

8. Neither gene is dominant.

9. No blending can occur in organisms that are pure for a certain trait. They have two of the same genes.

Skill Builder: Predicting

Two kittens will have short tails. One kitten will have a long tail and one kitten will not have a tail.

Teaching Tips for Technology and Society
The Human Genome Project

EXTENSION Have interested students contact the National Insititutes of Health (NIH) or the Ethical, Legal, and Social Issues (ELSI) Working Group for more information on social issues concerning the project. Tell students to share their findings with the class.

Questions

1. What are some benefits to mapping the human genome? (treating genetic disorders, preventing genetic disease)

2. What are some ethical issues that a genome map might raise? (random genetic testing and possible discrimination)

LESSON 18-7
How is sex determined? (p. 366)

Teaching Strategies

PREVIEW Have students write the lesson title and objective in their notebooks. As students read the lesson, tell them to write down the sentence or sentences that provide the information needed in the objective.

DISCUSSION Refer students to the photograph of human chromosomes on p. 366. Remind students that humans have 23 pairs of chromosomes. Have students observe pair 23 and describe the difference between the two chromosomes in the pair. Elicit the response that the two chromosomes are not identical. Point out that the chromosome map shown is that of a male. Explain that in humans males have different sex chromosomes called Y. Then describe how chromosomes in a sperm cell determine the sex of offspring. Be sure students understand that the sex chromosomes in females are identical.

REINFORCEMENT Draw a Punnett square on the chalkboard showing the inheritance of sex. Ask students what ratio of offspring will be male (1/2) and what ratio will be female. (1/2)

REINFORCEMENT Be sure students understand that all body cells contain chromosome pair 23. Stress that sex chromosomes are not found only in gametes. Students often have this misconception.

ITERDISCIPLINARY CONNECTION King Henry VIII of England (1491-1541) had some of his wives put to death for failing to bear him sons. His actions had important political and religious ramifications. Point out the irony of Henry VIII blaming his wives for failure to produce sons.

Answers to Challenges (p. 367)
Apply

6. Egg cells, because they all have an X chromosome.

7. 125; The ratio of males produced during fertilization is 1/2.

InfoSearch

You may wish to discuss students' questions and answers as a class.

Teaching Tips for Technology and Society
Amniocentesis

REINFORCEMENT Before students read this feature, read the term *amniocentesis* aloud so that students can hear its pronunciation.

Question

What is amniocentesis? (a test performed during a woman's pregnancy that involves removing amniotic fluid surrounding the fetus to learn about fetal chromosomes and enzyme levels)

LESSON 18-8
What are sex-linked traits?
(p. 368)

Teaching Strategies

PREVIEW Have students read the lesson feature before beginning the lesson. Discuss how they think this information relates to topics they have already studied or to the lesson they are about to study.

DISCUSSION Briefly review the inheritance of sex. Then point out that certain other traits are inherited along with sex. Identify these traits as sex-linked traits. Emphasize that most of the genes for sex-linked traits are found on the X chromosomes.

REINFORCEMENT Using the Punnett square on p. 368, show students how sex-linked disorders are inherited. Stress that because most genes for sex-linked disorders are carried on the X chromosome and are recessive, a woman must be pure recessive to show the trait.

EXTENSION People with normal color vision can sense the three basic colors of red, green, and blue. Colorblind people have reduced ability to see red or green, or both.

COOPERATIVE/COLLABORATIVE LEARNING Have a volunteer show a cross involving a sex-linked disorder to the rest of the class.

Answers to Challenges (p. 369)
Apply

6. by inheriting two X chromosomes carrying the recessive gene for hemophilia

7. One gene is normal and one gene is for the sex-linked disorder.

State the Problem

Acquired characteristics are not passed from parents to offspring.

Teaching Tips for Looking Back in Science
Hemophilia in the Royal Family

CLASS ACTIVITY Show students a pedigree chart for the British royal family. Ask students to name the members of the royal family who were carriers for hemophilia, who suffered from the disorder, and who were normal. Write student responses on the chalkboard.

Question

How many of Queen Victoria's offspring inherited the gene for hemophilia? (three)

LESSON 18-9
What are some inherited diseases? (p. 370)

Teaching Strategies

PREVIEW Before beginning the lesson, write the title of each section on the chalkboard. Have students copy these titles in their notebooks using an outline format. As students read each section, they should write the topic sentence for each paragraph in the section in their notebooks.

DISCUSSION Introduce this lesson by having students recall what they learned about diseases in Unit 16. Remind students that some diseases are caused by bacteria and viruses that enter the body. Then compare infectious diseases and inherited diseases. Point out that an inherited disease is caused by an inherited gene. Stress that people are born with inherited diseases. Identify sickle-cell anemia, Tay-Sachs disease, and PKU as three inherited diseases.

REINFORCEMENT Review the normal structure of red blood cells and the size of capillaries. This review will help students understand the effects of sickle-cell anemia.

DEMONSTRATION If possible, show students slides of sickle cells and normal red blood cells.

EXTENSION People who have PKU lack an enzyme that breaks down phenylalanine to thyroxine. Instead, phenylalanine is converted to phenylpyruvic acid. If left untreated, phenylpyruvic acid damages various organs, especially the brain. A baby who tests positive for PKU is fed a diet lacking phenylalanine, which prevents all symptoms of the disease. You may wish to show students the actual warnings for people with PKU that are on some food labels. The warning states that the food contains phenylalanine.

RETEACHING OPTION Write the following head on the chalkboard: *Inherited Diseases*. From this head, draw arrows to each of the following heads: *Sickle-Cell Anemia, Tay-Sachs Disease, PKU.* Describe the symptoms of each inherited disease. Have students copy the information in their notebooks under the proper heads.

Answers to Challenges (p. 371)

Check

1. an inherited gene

2. They are shaped like a sickle or crescent.

3. a person who inherits one recessive gene and one dominant gene

4. Phenylketonuria is an inherited disease.

Apply

9. Both diseases stop an enzyme from being produced.

10. No; neither parent carries a gene for sickle-cell anemia.

InfoSearch

You may wish to discuss students' questions and answers as a class.

Teaching Tips for Activity
Predicting Tay-Sachs Disease

Skills: *analyzing, predicting*

COOPERATIVE/COLLABORATIVE LEARNING Answer the questions as a class.

Questions

1. hybrid

2. Tt

3. one

4. TT

5. 1 out of 4

LESSON 18-10
Can the environment affect inherited traits? (p. 372)

Teaching Strategies

PREVIEW Before beginning this section, have students scan the lesson looking for words with which they are unfamiliar. Have students work in pairs or small groups to define each of the words on their lists.

DEMONSTRATION Provide motivation for this lesson by demonstrating how the environment might affect inherited traits. Show students two plants, one having received the proper amount of sunlight and one that was kept in a darkened place. Encourage students to describe the plants and to suggest how the unhealthy plant may be helped. Elicit the response that the plant should be put in sunlight. Point out that when the environment of a plant is not right, it will not grow and develop properly.

REINFORCEMENT Emphasize that the genes for traits are not affected by the environment. Only the development of the trait is affected.

EXTENSION Have interested students use library references to research the studies that have been done on identical twins to determine how the environment affects inherited traits. Have students present their findings in an oral report.

Answers to Challenges (p. 373)

Apply

7. lack of sunlight; lack of water

8. No.

9. They would not be able to make vitamin D.

Designing an Experiment

Have volunteers describe their experiments to the rest of the class.

Teaching Tips for Science Connection
Plant Fertilizers

DISCUSSION Bring a bottle of plant food to class. Read out the names of the minerals contained in the plant food. Then discuss why plant food is used.

Questions

1. LIST What nutrients do the most widely used chemical fertilizers contain? (nitrogen, phosphorus, potassium)

2. Why do plants need nutrients from the soil? (to carry on their food making processes)

LESSON 18-11

How is genetics used to improve living things? (p. 374)

Teaching Strategies

PREVIEW Before beginning this lesson, read the list of TechTerms aloud so students can hear their pronunciations.

DISCUSSION Provide motivation for this lesson by asking students to imagine that they are corn farmers. Tell them that as they walk through their corn fields, they notice some corn plants that are taller and look healthier than the others. Ask students to explain what they might do to grow more of these tall, healthier-looking plants. Discuss all student responses. Then describe the different methods of controlled breeding, and in particular mass selection.

CLASS ACTIVITY Bring in pictures showing the many different breeds of dogs. Hold up each picture in front of the class. Have students identify as many breeds as they can. Point out that purebred animals are produced by inbreeding. Define inbreeding as the mating of closely related organisms.

REINFORCEMENT When explaining hybridization, be sure students do not confuse organisms that are produced by hybridization, such as mules, with organisms that are hybrid for certain traits.

RETEACHING OPTION Write the following head on the chalkboard: *Controlled Breeding.* From this head, draw arrows to each of the following heads: *Mass Selection, Inbreeding, Hybridization.* Have students copy this chart in their notebooks. As you describe each method of controlled breeding, have students copy the information under the appropriate head.

Answers to Challenges (p. 375)

Check

1. to produce offspring with certain traits

2. mass selection

3. inbreeding

4. the mating of two different kinds of organisms

5. They are very similar.

Apply

6. They are used to produce organisms with certain traits.

7. Yes; inbreeding involves mating closely related organisms. Hybridization involves mating two different species.

8. Undesirable traits also are passed to offspring.

9. Answers will vary. Accept all logical responses.

InfoSearch

You may wish to discuss students' questions and answers as a class.

Teaching Tips for Career in Life Science
Animal Breeder

EXTENSION If possible, arrange for a professional animal breeder to talk to your class about his or her work.

Questions

1. RELATE Why should you enjoy working outdoors if you would like to become an animal breeder? (Most animal breeders work directly with animals outdoors.)

2. IDENTIFY For what trait is a workhorse bred? (strength)

LESSON 18-12

What is genetic engineering?
(p. 376)

Teaching Strategies

PREVIEW Before beginning this lesson, have students review the TechTerms and their definitions and read the Lesson Summary.

DEMONSTRATION Show students a model of gene splicing. Cut out a strip of construction paper. Bend the strip into a circle and staple the ends together to make a DNA chain. Then cut the chain open and insert a strip of different colored construction paper by stapling it to the original strip.

REINFORCEMENT Be sure students understand that gene splicing is carried out by chemical means on large numbers of bacteria. Some students may envision a scientist snipping open a DNA chain and manually inserting genes.

EXTENSION You may wish to tell students that pieces of DNA that contain DNA from a different organism are called recombinant DNA.

REINFORCEMENT Be sure students understand the point of genetic engineering. Remind students that genes control inherited traits. Point out that by inserting human genes into bacteria scientists get bacteria to produce human proteins such as insulin.

COOPERATIVE/COLLABORATIVE LEARNING Have a volunteer describe the three steps of gene splicing for the rest of the class.

Answers to Challenges (p. 377)

Apply

6. Scientists may use bacteria to produce the enzyme that is lacking by inserting the human gene that codes for the enzyme into the DNA of bacteria.

7. Answers will vary. Accept all logical responses.

Skill Builder: Modeling

Check students' models.

Teaching Tips for Technology and Society
Genetic Engineering

EXTENSION Have students interview an agricultural extension agent or plant scientist to find out about other foods that are genetically engineered. Have students find newspaper articles reporting the information.

Question

What are three proteins that genetically-engineered farm animals can produce in their milk? (an enzyme that fights emphysema, an enzyme that dissolves blood clots, and lactoferin, which fights bacteria)

Answers to Unit Challenges

Understanding the Features: Reading Critically

1. Mendel's hypothesis about inherited traits forms the basis of modern genetics

2. She discovered jumping genes.

3. The two scientists who discoverd the structure of DNA.

4. map all of the human genes; sequence all the base pairs

5. Amniocentesis is performed to obtain fetal cells for doctors to study

6. Queen Victoria's grandchildren married members of other royal families.

7. fertilizer

8. Answers will vary. Accept all logical responses.

9. Genetic engineering can produce tomatoes that taste better.

Critical Thinking

1. Answers will vary. Accept all logical responses.

2. Answers will vary. Accept all logical responses.

3. Sequences of DNA, or genes, code for specific proteins.

4. They show the expected results of various crosses.

5. Answers will vary. Accept all logical responses.

Interpreting a Diagram

1. adenine

2. cytosine

3. thymine

4. guanine

5. Adenine pairs with thymine. Guanine pairs with cytosine.

6. Chromosomes make copies of themselves.

Previewing the Unit

Read the titles of the lessons in this unit aloud. Identify terms in the titles with which the students are unfamiliar. Write these terms on the chalkboard. Using the Glossary of the text or a dictionary, define the terms as a class. Have students write the terms and their definitions in their notebooks.

Bulletin Board Suggestions

1. Assemble a bulletin board illustrating the different kinds of fossils that scientists study to learn about evolution. Attach pictures showing imprints, bones, shells, animals preserved in ice, and so on. Use the bulletin board to point out each type of fossil.

2. Assemble a bulletin board showing the geologic time scale. Draw the geologic time scale on the bulletin board. Fill in the dates for each era, period, and epoch. Attach pictures showing the dominant life forms of each time span.

LESSON 19-1
How are fossils formed? (p. 382)

Teaching Strategies

PREVIEW Have students write the lesson title and objective in their notebooks. As students read the lesson, tell them to write down the sentence or sentences that provide the information needed in the objective.

DISCUSSION Show students pictures or actual samples of fossils. Point out that fossils are the remains, or traces, of organisms that lived long ago. Identify each type of fossil you display and describe how it was formed.

CLASS ACTIVITY If possible, arrange for your class to visit a natural history museum. Have students observe the different types of fossils on display in the museum.

DEMONSTRATION Bring in an ice cube in which you have frozen a small leaf. Point out that freezing is one way extinct organisms have been preserved.

DEMONSTRATION Demonstrate sedimentation. Mix some mud and sand in a jar of water. Allow the jar to stand. Have students observe and describe what happens. (The mud and sand settle in layers.) Point out that the sand and mud are sediments. Relate this demonstration to the formation of sedimentary rocks.

INTRASCIENCE CONNECTION Obtain samples of the sedimentary rocks coquina and shell limestone. Allow students to examine the two types of sedimentary rock. Have students look for shells and fossils in the coquina.

Answers to Challenges (p. 383)
Apply

5. The fossils were buried under sediments before they turned to rock.

6. Answers will vary. Accept all logical responses.

InfoSearch

You may wish to discuss students' questions and answers as a class.

Teaching Tips for Activity
Making Fossils

Skills: *modeling, observing*

COOPERATIVE/COLLABORATIVE LEARNING Have students work in pairs.

Questions

1. Answers will vary. Accept all logical responses.

2. The fossil made with petroleum jelly is the mold. The fossil made without petroleum jelly is the cast.

LESSON 19-2
What is geologic time? (p. 384)

Teaching Strategies

PREVIEW Before beginning the lesson, write the title of each section in the lesson on the chalkboard. Have students copy these titles in their notebooks using an outline format. As students read each section, they should write the topic sentence for each paragraph in the section in their notebooks.

CLASS ACTIVITY To help students understand what is meant by the relative age of rocks, find out the relative height of students. Have all of the students stand. Have one student state how tall he or she is. Then have each student state whether he or she is taller or shorter than the previous student. Point out that students are not stating their exact heights. They are describing their heights relative to other students.

CLASS ACTIVITY Have students work in small groups to make models of sedimentary rock beds. Tell students to use different colors of clay to represent each rock layer. After all groups are finished making their models, have a representative from each group describe the relative ages of the rock layers. Have the student point out which layer is the oldest, which is the youngest, and so on.

DISCUSSION Have students observe the geologic time scale on p. 384. Point out the major divisions on the scale. Read out the names of the eras, periods, and epochs so students can hear their pronunciations. Tell students to note the dominant life forms of each era.

Answers to Challenges (p. 385)
Apply

6. Sediments build up layer by layer.

7. Mesozoic

8. Cenozoic

Skill Builder: Sequencing

F, E, D, C, B, A; Fossil B is younger than fossil D.

Teaching Tips for Science Connection
Radioactive Dating

EXTENSION You may wish to point out that the carbon-14 radioactive dating method is used only for fossils less than 50,000 years old. Other radioactive dating methods are used for older fossils.

Questions

1. CALCULATE If you had a 20-gram sample of C-14 today, how much would be left in 5730 years? (10 grams)

2. DEFINE What is a half-life? (the unit used to measure the rate of decay of a radioactive element)

LESSON 19-3
What is evolution? (p. 386)

Teaching Strategies

PREVIEW Have students read the lesson feature before beginning the lesson. Discuss the concepts presented in the feature. Ask students how they think this information relates to topics they have already studied or to the lesson they are about to study.

DISCUSSION Define evolution as the process by which organisms change over time. Be sure students understand that evolution can occur only when there is a change in the gene pool of the population. Remind students that genes control inherited traits. Identify mutation as one way the gene pool of a population can change.

CLASS ACTIVITY Tell each student to carefully observe four different organisms and list as many different adaptations as they can for each of the organisms they observe. Review students' lists as a class. Have students explain how each organism's adaptations enable the organism to survive in its environment.

COOPERATIVE/COLLABORATIVE LEARNING Have students work in pairs to answer the Check and Apply questions.

Answers to Challenges (p. 387)
Apply

6. Some mutations cause organisms to die before they reproduce.

Skill Builder: Designing an Experiment

Have volunteers describe their experiments to the rest of the class.

Teaching Tips for Looking Back in Science
The Voyage of the *Beagle*

REINFORCEMENT Have students trace the path of the *HMS Beagle's* voyage and locate the Galapagos Islands on a world map.

INTRASCIENCE CONNECTION During his voyage on the *Beagle,* Darwin also observed how earthquakes and other geologic processes could change the land. These observations influenced Darwin's ideas about evolution. He began to think that organisms would have to adapt to such changes in their environment.

Questions

1. What was the purpose of the voyage of the *HMS Beagle?* (to prepare maps and to observe and collect specimens of various plants and animals)

2. What did Darwin infer about the 13 species of finches in the Galapagos Islands? (They had evolved from a common ancestor.)

LESSON 19-4
What is natural selection? (p. 388)

Teaching Strategies

PREVIEW Before beginning this lesson, have students scan the lesson for the science process skill symbols. Have students identify each skill used in the lesson. Students should then review the definition given for each skill on p.16 of their text.

DISCUSSION Describe the four main ideas of Darwin's theory of evolution: overproduction, competition, variation, and survival of the fittest. Be sure students understand the evolution of a new species occurs over a long period of time.

CLASS ACTIVITY Bring in a variety of pictures showing members of the same species. Hold up each picture in front of the class. Tell students to observe how variations occur among members of the same species. Ask students to describe how the organisms shown in each picture are alike and how they are different.

REINFORCEMENT Darwin's theory of evolution is often difficult for students to understand. Be sure students understand that the environment does not cause evolution. The environment only determines which variations will be selected.

EXTENSION Have students research the work of Alfred Russell Wallace. Wallace was a British scientist who influenced Darwin's theory of evolution. Tell students to write their findings in a report.

Answers to Challenges (p. 389)
Apply

4. a. Variation **b.** Struggle **c.** Survival

Skill Builder: Researching

Check students' reports. Lamarck's theory of evolution was based upon acquired characteristics being passed on from parents to offspring.

Teaching Tips for Activity
Modeling Natural Selection

Skills: *modeling, hypothesizing*

SAFETY TIP Caution students to be careful when using scissors.

COOPERATIVE/COLLABORATIVE LEARNING Have students work in pairs.

LESSON 19-5
What evidence supports evolution? (p. 390)

Teaching Strategies

PREVIEW Before beginning this lesson, have students scan the lesson looking for words with which they are unfamiliar. Have students work in pairs or small groups to define each of the words on their lists.

DISCUSSION Have students study the diagrams on p. 390 showing the evolutionary history of the horse. Emphasize that the fossil record of the horse is very complete. Compare the earliest horse to the modern horse. Point out the ways horses have changed over time. Tell students to note that the size of horses has changed. Ask students to describe other ways horses have changed. (The number of toes and the structure of the legs have changed.)

EXTENSION You may wish to tell students that in addition to the fossil record, the study of living things also has revealed important evidence of evolution. There is evidence of evolution from anatomy, embryology, and biochemistry.

EXTENSION Have each student research one species of dinosaurs. Tell students to write their findings in reports. Encourage students to include pictures in their reports.

Answers to Challenges (p. 391)

Check

1. The most complete fossil record of evolutionary change is that of the horse.

2. that changes have taken place throughout the earth's history

3. Nobody knows for sure.

4. about 400 different species

5. about the size of a small dog

Apply

6. Answers will vary. Accept all logical responses.

7. It has become bigger.

Skill Builder: Measuring and Calculating

1 mm = 100 mm

Teaching Tips for Looking Back in Science

The Moths of Manchester

REINFORCEMENT Be sure students understand that the example of the moths of Manchester illustrates natural selection, not evolution.

Question

EXPLAIN Why did the population of the black moths increase after coal-burning factories were built? (Soot given off by the factories changed the color of the tree trunks from gray to black. This enabled the black moths to blend in with the tree trunks, and thus, fewer black moths were eaten by birds.)

LESSON 19-6
How have humans changed through time? (p. 392)

Teaching Strategies

PREVIEW Before beginning this lesson, have students review the TechTerm and its definition and read the Lesson Summary.

DISCUSSION Refer students to the pictures of hominid skulls on p. 392. Have students compare the size of the skulls as you describe human evolution. Emphasize the trend toward increasing brain size.

REINFORCEMENT Draw a time line on the chalkboard highlighting human evolution.

EXTENSION Have interested students find out about one of the following hominid species: *Australopithecus afarensis, Australopithecus africanus, Homo habilis, Homo erectus.* Tell students to describe the characteristics of the species they choose in oral reports. Be sure students identify where, when, and by whom the species was discovered.

INTRASCIENCE CONNECTION Neanderthals lived during the Ice Age in Europe. They lived in caves and used fire to keep warm.

COOPERATIVE/COLLABORATIVE LEARNING Have one student describe the characteristics of Neanderthals for the rest of the class. Have another student describe Cro-magnons.

Answers to Challenges (p. 393)

Check/Apply

6–7. Answers will vary. Accept all logical responses.

Skill Builder: Building Vocabulary

Anthropo- means human. It comes from the Greek word *anthropos* meaning man. *-Logy* means study of. It comes from the Greek word *logia*.

Ideas in Action

Answers will vary. Accept all logical responses.

Teaching Tips for People in Science

The Leakeys

CLASS ACTIVITY Have students find and collect articles written by the Leakeys in *National Geographic.* Read and discuss the articles as a class.

Questions

1. IDENTIFY What is the goal of most anthropologists? (to trace the evolutionary development of humans.)

2. Where was "Upright Human" discovered? (Kenya, Africa)

Answers to Unit Challenges (p. 394-396)

Understanding the Features: Reading Critically

1. to prepare maps and observe and collect specimens of various plants and animals

2. Answers will vary. Accept all logical responses.

3. Anthropologists use carbon-14 to date fossils.

4. Mary Leakey and Richard Leakey both discovered "Handy Man." Richard Leakey also discovered "Upright Human."

Critical Thinking

1. All the carbon-14 would be changed to nitrogen.

2. A variation is a difference in a trait among individuals of the same species. A mutation is a change in a gene.

3. The long-necked giraffes were able to reach the leaves of trees. They were better able to compete and survive in the environment. Thus, they reproduced and passed on the trait of being long-necked to their offspring.

4. Answers will vary. Accept all logical responses.

5. Answers will vary. Accept all logical responses.

Interpreting a Table

1. eras, periods, epochs

2. Cenozoic

3. 225 million years

4. a scale showing the living things dominating each era in the earth's history

5. Paleocene

6. Cretaceous

7. primitive apes
8. Cenozoic, Mesozoic, Paleozoic, Precambrian

9. 0.025 million years ago

Internet Addresses and Other Resources for
CAREERS IN LIFE SCIENCE

The Student Edition of *Concepts and Challenges* introduces students to many exciting careers in life science. Following are both street and Internet addresses of organizations to which your students can write for more information on the careers highlighted in this book. Encourage students to pursue information about careers that interest them.

UNIT 1
Lesson 1-1
Career in Life Science: Wildlife Biologist (p. 15)

CONTACT
U.S. Department of the Interior
Fish and Wildlife Service
18th and C Street, NW
Washington, DC 20210

ON THE INTERNET
http://www.fws.gov/

UNIT 3
Lesson 3-1
Career in Life Science: Air Pollution Technician (p. 53)

CONTACT
Air and Waste Management Association
1 Gateway Center, Third Floor
Pittsburgh, PA 15222

ON THE INTERNET
http://www.awma.org/

UNIT 4
Lesson 4-8
Technology and Society: Cornea Transplants (p. 93)

CONTACT
Eye-Bank for Sight Restoration, Inc.
210 East 64th Street
New York, NY 10021

UNIT 5
Lesson 5-5
Career in Life Science: Florist (p. 109)

CONTACT
Society of American Florists
1601 Duke Street
Alexandria, VA 22314

ON THE INTERNET
http://www.safnow.org/

UNIT 10
Lesson 10-1
Career in Life Science: Animal Technician (p. 195)

CONTACT
American Veterinary Medical Association
1931 North Meacham Road
Schaumburg, IL 60173

ON THE INTERNET
http://www.avma.org/

UNIT 11
Lesson 11-4
Career in Life Science: Nutritionist (p. 221)

CONTACT
American Dietetic Association
216 W. Jackson Boulevard, Suite 800
Chicago, IL 60606-6995

ON THE INTERNET
http://www.eatright.org/

UNIT 12
Lesson 12-5
Career in Life Science: Exercise Specialist (p. 249)

CONTACT
The American Alliance for Health,
Physical Education, Recreation and Dance
1900 Association Drive
Reston, VA 20191

ON THE INTERNET
http://www.aahperd.org/

UNIT 18
Lesson 18-6
Technology and Society: Human Genome Project (p. 365)

CONTACT
National Human Genome Research Institute (NHGRI)
9000 Rockville, 31 Center Drive
Bethesda, MD 20892

ON THE INTERNET
http://www.nhgri.nih.gov/

TEACHER NOTES

CONCEPTS AND CHALLENGES IN

Life Science

Revised Third Edition

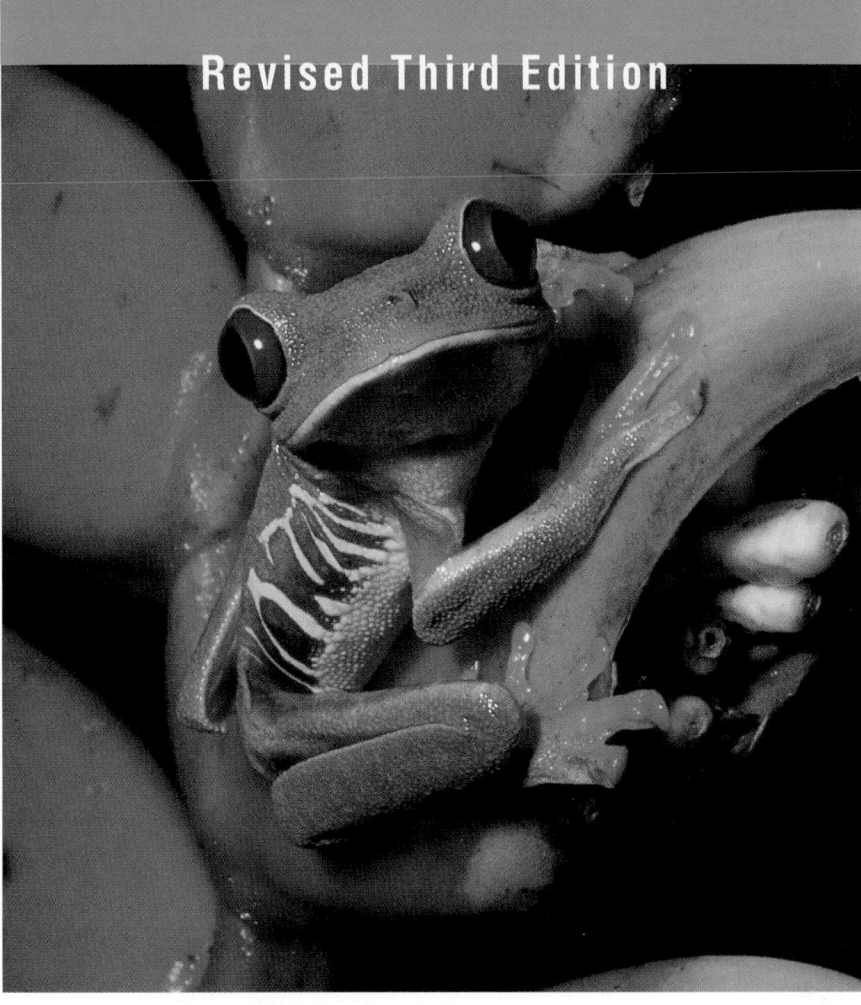

Leonard Bernstein • Martin Schachter • Alan Winkler • Stanley Wolfe

STANLEY WOLFE
Project Coordinator

Globe Fearon Educational Publisher
A Division of Simon & Schuster
Upper Saddle River, New Jersey

AUTHORS

Leonard Bernstein

Martin Schachter

Alan Winkler

Stanley Wolfe
Project Coordinator

ABOUT THE COVER

Background: Avocado leaf *(Eduardo Garcia, FPG)*
A network of veins in the leaf supply water and minerals
to the cells that make food for the plant.

Inset: Red-eyed tree frog *(G. Bradley and J. Ireland)*
This frog lives in trees in the forests of Central and
South America.

Printed in the United States of America
2 3 4 5 6 7 8 9 10   01 00 99 98

ISBN 0-835-92240-5

 Globe Fearon Educational Publisher
A Division of Simon & Schuster
Upper Saddle River, New Jersey

Contents

UNIT 4
CELLS, TISSUES, AND ORGANS *77-98*

UNIT 5
CLASSIFICATION
99-114

UNIT 18

HEREDITY AND GENETICS *353-380*

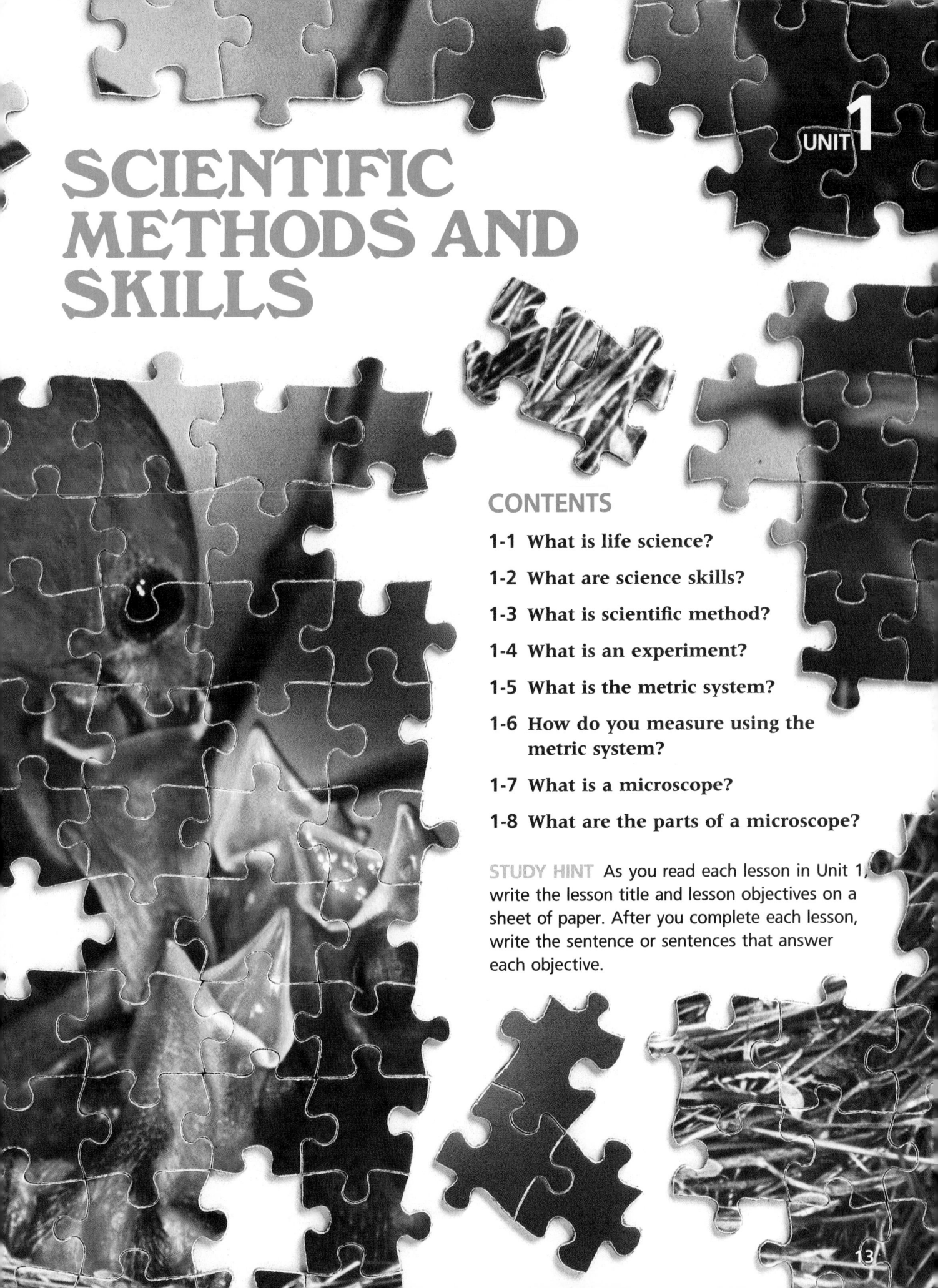

SCIENTIFIC METHODS AND SKILLS

CONTENTS

STUDY HINT As you read each lesson in Unit 1, write the lesson title and lesson objectives on a sheet of paper. After you complete each lesson, write the sentence or sentences that answer each objective.

1-1 What is life science?

Objective ▶ Identify and describe what is studied in some of the branches of life science.

TechTerms

▶ **specialization** (SPESH-uh-lih-zay-shun): studying or working in only one part of a subject

Studying Life Science Science is an organized collection of knowledge about the world. It also is a way of finding out why things happen as they do. It is a way of solving problems by testing possible answers to see if they work. The knowledge of science is based on observations.

The study of the areas of science that deal with living things is called life science. Life science is like a tree. It is made up of many different branches. One branch is biology (by-AHL-uh-jee). Biology is the study of living things. Table 1 lists some of the life sciences. Two—botany and zoology—are part of biology.

◣ *Analyze:* What are four branches of life science? Answers will vary.

Specialization As more and more is learned about the world, people must choose specific subjects to study. This is called **specialization** (SPESH-uh-lih-zay-shun). A person who studies or works in one part of a subject is called a specialist (SPESH-ul-ist). There are many life science specialists. For example, some zoologists (zoh-AHL-uh-jists) study only one group of animals. Some scientists study diseases that affect only animals. Other scientists study diseases in plants.

▧▶ *Describe:* What is meant by specialization? studying or working in only one part of a subject.

Importance of Life Science Life science is part of your everyday life. The study of living things affects your life in many ways. The medicine you take for a cold was developed based on scientific study. The causes and warning signs of cancer were learned from scientific research. Operations can be done because doctors know about the parts of the human body and how they work.

The kinds of foods you eat were grown by using information about plants. The making of some foods also uses knowledge of life science. Many cheeses could not be made without molds. Pickles could not be made without bacteria. People had to learn about bacteria and molds to use them to make these foods.

▧▶ *Explain:* How was life science part of your life today? Answers will vary.

Table 1 Branches of Life Science		
BRANCH	**WHAT IS STUDIED**	**CAREERS**
Anatomy (uh-NAT-uh-mee)	parts that make up living things	Doctor Physical therapist
Physiology (fiz-ee-AHL-uh-jee)	how the parts of living things work	Physiologist Chiropractor
Botany (BAHT-un-ee)	plants	Horticulturist Florist
Zoology (zoh-AHL-uh-jee)	animals	Veterinarian Marine biologist
Microbiology (my-kroh-by-AHL-uh-jee)	microscopic living things	Microbiologist Pathologist
Ecology (ee-KAHL-uh-jee)	interaction of living things and their surroundings	Ecologist

LESSON SUMMARY

▶ Science is an organized collection of knowledge about the world.

▶ The study of the areas of science that deal with living things is called life science.

▶ Specialization is the study of only one part of a subject.

▶ People are affected everyday by the discoveries of life scientists.

▶ Growing and making food use information about living things.

CHECK *Complete the following.*

1. Botany and _____ are part of biology. zoology

2. The knowledge of science is based on _____ . observation

3. Life science is made up of many different _____ . branches

4. Any life scientist who studies only one small branch of life science is a _____ . specialist

APPLY *Use the table on page 14 to complete the following.*

5. Ecology is the study of living things and their _____ . surroundings

6. The study of how a living thing is put together is _____ . anatomy

7. The study of how the parts of a living thing work is _____ . physiology

8. **Classify:** In which branch of life science would you study each of the following?
   a. whales and birds **b.** corn and barley
   c. the heart and lungs **d.** bacteria and microorganisms. **a.** zoology, **b.** botany, **c.** physiology or anatomy, **d.** microbiology

9. **Infer:** What area of life science would you need to know about to study the problem shown in the drawing?

CAREER IN LIFE SCIENCE

WILDLIFE BIOLOGIST

Do you like working with animals? Do you enjoy working outdoors? If so, you may enjoy working as a wildlife biologist. Wildlife biologists work to protect the natural environments of animals. They also help to save animals from becoming extinct.

There are many jobs in wildlife biology. Some wildlife biologists work as game wardens. They help to enforce hunting and fishing laws. You need a high school diploma to become a game warden. Other wildlife biologists work in wildlife management and research. They may work on a game preserve or in a national park or forest. These jobs usually require a college degree.

1-2 What are science skills?

Objective ▶ Identify and use science skills to solve problems and answer questions.

TechTerm

▶ **hypothesis** (hy-PAHTH-uh-sis): suggested solution to a problem

Science Skills Scientists use many skills to gather information. These skills are sometimes called science skills. You use science skills, too. You probably used some science skills today. When you use most science skills, you use your five senses. The five senses are seeing, hearing, touching, smelling, and tasting.

Eleven science skills are used in this book. You will even see skill symbols for nine skills. These symbols are shown below. They will let you know when you are using a skill. Researching and communicating also are important skills. You will use these skills, too. Soon, you will be thinking like a scientist.

Analyze: Which science skill makes observations more exact? measuring

Researching Have you ever done research for a science project? When you do research, you look for something again. You study or investigate. You can do research by reading books, magazines, and newspapers. You can also perform experiments to do research. Experimenting is a kind of research.

Identify: What are two ways to do research? reading and experimenting

Communicating When you talk to someone, you are communicating, or sharing ideas and information. If you write a letter, you are communicating. Scientists communicate all the time. They write books and magazine or newspaper articles about their work. If you read about a scientist and a new discovery, the scientist has communicated with you. Sharing information is very important to scientists.

Describe: What are you doing when you communicate with someone? sharing ideas and information

Think Scientifically

Observing When you observe, you use your senses. You must pay close attention to everything that happens.

Measuring When you measure, you compare an unknown value to a known value. Measuring makes observations more exact.

Inferring When you infer, you form a conclusion based upon what you think explains an observation.

Classifying When you classify, you group things based upon how they are alike.

Organizing When you organize, you work in an orderly way. You put your information in order.

Predicting When you predict, you state ahead of time what will happen based upon what you already know.

Hypothesizing When you hypothesize, you state or suggest a solution to a problem. A **hypothesis** (hy-PAHTH-uh-sis) is a suggested solution to a problem based upon what is already known or observed.

Modeling When you model, you use a copy of what you are studying to help explain it. A model can be a three-dimensional copy, a drawing, or a diagram.

Analyzing When you analyze, you study information carefully.

LESSON SUMMARY

▶ Scientists use many skills to gather information.

▶ Eleven science skills are used in this book.

▶ Researching includes talking, reading, and experimenting.

▶ Communicating means sharing information.

▶ Other science skills are observing, measuring, inferring, classifying, organizing, predicting, hypothesizing, modeling, and analyzing.

CHECK *Answer the following.*

1. What are your five senses? seeing, hearing, touching, smelling, and tasting

2. Name two ways a scientist can communicate a new discovery to people. Answers will vary.

Complete the following.

3. When you group things based upon how they are alike, you are _____ them. classifying

4. A suggested solution to a problem is a _____ . hypothesis

5. If you put information into a table, you are _____ the information. organizing

APPLY *Complete the following.*

6. **Describe:** Describe two ways in which you used science skills today. What skills did you use? How did they help you to solve a problem? Answers will vary. Accept all logical responses.

Match each skill to its symbol.

7. ▲ b
8. 📁 c
9. ◭ a
10. ❱ d

    a. organizing
    b. modeling
    c. classifying
    d. predicting

11. Which skill do you think is the most important? Give reasons for your choice. Accept all logical answers.

Ideas in Action

IDEA: You make or use many different measurements every day.

ACTION: Describe five situations in which you use measurements during a day.

ACTIVITY

ORGANIZING DATA

You will need a sheet of graph paper, lined paper, and a pencil.

1. Study each set of data.

2. Decide the best way to organize each set of data. You may want to use a table, some kind of graph, a diagram, or another way you think will work.

3. Be sure to give each table, graph, or diagram a title. Tables should have headings for each column.

Questions

1. How did you organize each set of data?

2. Compare the way you organized the data with the ways two classmates organized the data.

Data 1: Animals
fishes; snakes; coral snake; tuna; trout; boa constrictor; birds; robin; rattlesnake; blue jay; bass; sparrow; duck; swordfish

Data 2: Blood Types in a Given Population	
O	45%
A	40%
B	10%
AB	05%

Data 3: Uses of the Peanut
livestock food; peanut butter; salad oil; machine oil; glue; textile fiber; soap; face powder; shaving cream; shampoo; margarine; packing oil for fish; explosives; medicines; insulation; candy; plastic filler.

1-3 What is scientific method?

Objective ▶ Describe how to use scientific method to solve a problem.

TechTerms

▶ **data** (DAY-tuh): information

▶ **hypothesis** (hy-PAHTH-uh-sis): suggested answer to a problem

▶ **scientific method:** model, or guide, used to solve problems and to get information

Scientific Method Scientists solve problems like you do. Suppose a house plant on a window sill looked like it was dying. What would you do? You might check the soil to see if it was dry or maybe had too much water. You might see if a cold draft was coming from the window. You could check to see if too much heat was coming from a radiator. If you did one of these things, you started to use **scientific method.** Scientific method is a model, or guide, used to solve problems.

Scientists do not have one scientific method. They combine some or all of the science skills to solve different problems. Scientists also follow certain steps. Because each problem is different, the steps may be used in any order. You can write a laboratory report using these steps.

▶ *Define:* What is scientific method? model, or guide, used to solve problems

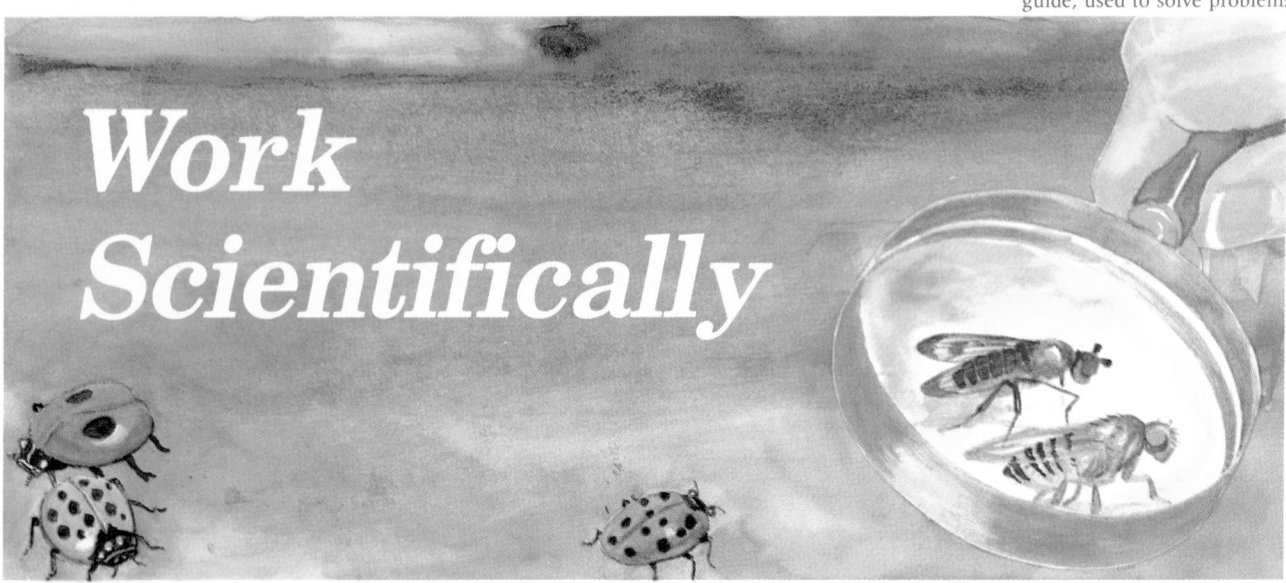

Work Scientifically

▶ **Identify and State the Problem** Scientists often state a problem as a question.

▶ **Gather Information** Scientists read and communicate with one another. In this way, they can learn about work that has already been done.

▶ **State a Hypothesis** Scientists state clearly what they expect to find out. They state a **hypothesis** (hy-PAHTH-uh-sis), or a suggested answer to a problem.

▶ **Design an Experiment** To test a hypothesis, scientists design an experiment.

▶ **Make Observations and Record Data** During an experiment, scientists make careful observations. The information that they get is their **data** (DAY-tuh).

▶ **Organize and Analyze Data** Scientists organize their data. Graphs, tables, charts, and diagrams are ways to organize data. Then the data can be analyzed, or studied.

▶ **State a Conclusion** A conclusion is a summary that explains the data. It states whether or not the data support the hypothesis. The conclusion answers the question stated in the problem.

LESSON SUMMARY

▶ Scientists use a model, or guide, called scientific method to solve problems.

▶ Scientists use different science skills, and different steps of scientific method, to solve different problems.

▶ The steps of scientific method are: Identify and state the problem; Gather information; State a hypothesis; Design an experiment; Make observations and record data; Organize and analyze data; State a conclusion.

CHECK *Complete the following.*

1. A model used to solve problems is called _____ . scientific method

2. Scientists often state a problem as a _____ . question

3. When scientists state what they expect to find out, they are stating a _____ . hypothesis

4. Scientists design experiments to test _____ . hypotheses

5. Data must be organized and _____, or studied. analyzed

6. A _____ is a summary that explains the data. conclusion

7. Another word for information is _____ . data

8. Tables, _____, diagrams, and charts are ways to organize data. graphs

APPLY *Complete the following.*

9. **Explain:** How are a hypothesis and a conclusion related? A conclusion states whether or not the data support the hypothesis.

10. List the steps in scientific method. Students should list the seven steps discussed.

11. Why do you think it is important for scientists to gather information before they begin work on a problem? Answers will vary.

Skill Builder

Writing a Laboratory Report Write a laboratory report describing the following experiment. Be sure to include the steps of scientific method in your report.

Place a few drops of iodine on a piece of bread, a rubber ball, a slice of orange, a piece of potato, a piece of lettuce, a few drops of milk, and piece of paper. Note the color changes that occur. If any substance contains starch, it will turn black. The iodine turns black on the bread and potato. There is no color change on the other things.

SCIENCE CONNECTION

PURE AND APPLIED SCIENCE

At times, science can be thought of as two sciences. In one, the scientist is interested mainly in research. This is pure science. In the other, the science is used to solve everyday problems. This is applied science. Applied science often is called technology. When the life science of biology is used to solve everyday problems, it is called biotechnology (by-oh-teck-NAHL-uh-jee).

Biotechnology is used in industry, medicine, and agriculture. Bacteria are used to tan leather. The leather is used to make clothing and shoes, belts, and jackets. Bacteria also are used to make cheeses, yogurt, pickles, and sauerkraut.

How would you like to eat tomatoes as big as grapefruits and grapefruits as big as watermelons? Biologists are working on it. Turkeys with only white meat and others with only dark meat also are being developed using biotechnology.

Biotechnology also is used in the medical field. Hospitals use machines to keep people alive. A respirator helps a person to breathe. A heart-lung machine takes over the jobs of the heart and lungs. Can you think of any other ways biotechnology is being used to make our lives better?

1-4 What is an experiment?

Fertilizer

After 4 weeks

Objective ▶ Explain why a controlled experiment is important.

TechTerms

- ▶ **control:** part of the experiment in which no change is made
- ▶ **controlled experiment:** two experiments exactly alike except for one change in one of them
- ▶ **experiment** (ik-SPER-uh-munt): something that is done to test a hypothesis or prediction
- ▶ **variable:** anything that can be changed in an experiment

Experimenting Scientists often do **experiments** (ik-SPER-uh-munts). An experiment is something that is done to find out why things happen. Experiments are used to test hypotheses. Experiments are done in laboratories or outdoors. If an experiment is conducted outdoors, it is called a field study. Field studies are done in many areas of the world.

▷ *Explain:* What is the purpose of an experiment? to test a hypothesis

Controlled Experiment Most experiments in biology are **controlled experiments.** In a controlled experiment, two setups are used. Everything about the two setups is exactly the same. One setup is left alone. This experiment is called the **control.** In the other setup, one thing is changed. The thing that is changed is called the **variable.** This part of the controlled experiment is the test, or experimental setup. Both experiments are then observed. Any differences in the results of the two setups would be due to the one thing that was changed.

▷ *Define:* What is a control? The setup in which no changes are made.

Analyzing an Experiment Look at the experiment in the figure. The problem for this experiment is: How does fertilizer affect plant growth?

In the experiment, two plants of the same kind and size are placed in identical pots. Both plants are given the same amount of water. Both plants get the same amount of light. The control plant is left alone. Fertilizer is added to the soil of the test plant. At the end of the experiment, the plants are measured. The number of leaves on each plant are counted. The test plant is larger than the control plant. It also has many more leaves.

◢ *Analyze:* What is the variable in this experiment? the fertilizer

LESSON SUMMARY

▶ Scientists do experiments to test hypotheses.

▶ Experiments are done in laboratories and outdoors.

▶ In a controlled experiment, there are two setups—one called the control and one called the test, or experimental, setup.

▶ Analyzing the results of an experiment helps answer the problem.

CHECK *Complete the following.*

1. A _____ is an experiment that is done outdoors. field study

2. In a controlled experiment, nothing is done to the _____ . control

3. An experiment is performed to test a _____ . hypothesis

4. In a controlled experiment, the outcome of an experiment is affected by the _____ . variables

5. An experiment that involves the observation of mountain lions in the hills of the western United States is an example of a _____ . field study

APPLY *Complete the following.*

6. What is the purpose of a control?

7. **Explain:** Why is it important to change only one variable during an experiment?

8. **Compare:** When would a field study be better than a laboratory experiment?

Designing an Experiment................

Design an experiment to solve the following problem.

PROBLEM: Can healthy plants be grown without sunlight?

Your experiment should:

1. List the materials you need.

2. Identify any safety precautions that should be followed.

3. List a step-by-step procedure.

4. Include a control.

5. Describe how you would record your data.

◆▸▰◀ PEOPLE IN SCIENCE ▸▰◀◆▸▰◀◆▸▰◀◆▸▰◀◆▸▰◀

JANE GOODALL (1934–present)

Jane Goodall is a British zoologist. Jane was interested in animals at an early age. She did field studies on chimpanzees in Africa. She worked with a famous fossil hunter, Dr. Louis Leakey. Leakey convinced Goodall to set up a camp in the Gombe National Park in northwest Tanzania. She observed the behavior of chimpanzees in the park. Through daily contacts with the chimpanzees, she gained their trust. She studied them at close range. She kept detailed reports on their behavior. Her field studies showed that some earlier information on these animals was incorrect.

Scientists thought that chimpanzees ate mostly fruit and vegetables. Sometimes they ate insects and small rodents. Dr. Goodall discovered that chimpanzees often hunted and ate large animals. She also observed the chimpanzees using crude tools. She watched them using tree stems to catch termites. Dr. Goodall pointed out that chimpanzees use tools more than any other animal except humans. She wrote many books on her field studies of chimpanzees. She also did field work on the behavior of African hyenas, jackals and wild dogs.

1-5 What is the metric system?

Objective ► Identify various metric units used to make measurements.

TechTerms

- ► **gram:** basic metric unit of mass
- ► **liter:** basic metric unit of volume
- ► **mass:** amount of matter in an object
- ► **meter** (MEE-tur): basic metric unit of length

Scientific Measurements The metric system is an international system of measurement. It is used in most countries. Everyday measurements are given in metric units (YOU-nits). A unit is an amount used to measure something. In the United States, the English system and the metric system are used.

Since 1960, scientists have used a more modern form of the metric system. This measurement system is called SI. The letters "SI" stand for Systems International. Many of the units in SI are the same as in the metric system.

||||► *Name:* What are two internationally used measurement systems? metric and SI

Metric Units In the metric system, length and distance are measured by a unit called the **meter** (MEE-tur). The meter (m) is the basic unit of length. The basic unit of **mass** in the metric system is the **gram** (g). Mass is the amount of matter in an object. There is more matter in a nail than a tack. The nail has more mass than the tack. The **liter** (L) is the basic unit of volume in the metric system. The amount of space something takes up is its volume.

||||► *Name:* What is basic unit of mass in the metric system? gram

Changing Size The metric system is based on units of 10. This makes it easy to use. Each unit in the metric system is ten times greater or smaller than the next unit. To change the size of a unit, you add a prefix to the unit. The prefix makes the unit larger or smaller. Table 1 shows prefixes and their meanings. Table 2 compares some metric units. It also shows the symbols of the units.

Table 1 Prefixes and Meanings	
PREFIX	MEANING
kilo- (KILL-uh)	one thousand (1000)
hecto- (HEC-tuh)	one hundred (100)
deca- (DEC-uh)	ten (10)
deci- (DESS-ih)	one tenth (1/10)
centi- (SEN-tih)	one hundredth (1/100)
milli- (MILL-ih)	one thousandth (1/1000)

Table 2 Metric Units
1000 millimeters (mm) = 1 meter (m)
100 centimeters (cm) = 1 meter (m)
1000 grams (g) = 1 kilogram (kg)
1 liter (L) = 1000 milliliters (mL)

||||► *Describe:* How do you change the size of a metric unit? Add a prefix to the unit.

Measuring Length A meter stick is used to measure length. A meter stick is divided into 100 equal parts by numbered lines. The distance between two numbered lines is equal to one centimeter (cm). Each centimeter is divided into 10 equal parts. Each of these parts is one millimeter (mm). One millimeter is 1/1000 of a meter.

◢ *Analyze:* How many millimeters are in 1 meter? 1000

LESSON SUMMARY

▶ The metric system is an international system of measurement.

▶ Scientists use a more modern form of the metric system called SI.

▶ Prefixes are used to change the size of a metric or an SI unit.

▶ The meter, gram, and liter are basic metric units.

▶ A meter stick is used to measure length.

CHECK *Answer the following.*

1. Name three systems of measurement. metric, SI, English

2. Which systems of measurement are used by scientists? SI and metric

3. What is the prefix meaning 1000? kilo-

Complete the following.

4. The metric system is based on units of _____ . 10

5. A _____ added to a unit changes the size of the unit. prefix

6. One centimeter is _____ of a meter. 1/100

7. The _____ is the basic metric unit of length. meter

APPLY *Complete the following.*

8. Two towns are 15 km apart. What is the distance in meters?

9. A rug is 4 m wide. How much is this in centimeters?

Calculate: Complete the following equations.

10. 1000 g = _____ kg 1

11. _____ m = 100 cm 1

12. 1 L = _____ mL 1000

13. 1 cm = _____ mm 10

Skill Builder..

Sequencing Arrange the following lengths in order from shortest to longest: 40 millimeters, 10 kilometers, 6 hectometers, 50 centimeters, 6 millimeters, 3 centimeters, 3 kilometers, 2 hectometers.

ACTIVITY

MEASURING LENGTH

You will need a metric ruler.

1. **Observe:** Study your metric ruler carefully.

2. Use the metric ruler to find the width and length of your desk, your textbook, your fingernail, and a sheet of notebook paper. Measure to the nearest millimeter.

3. Use the metric ruler to find the lengths of the objects shown in this activity. Measure to the nearest millimeter.

4. **Organize:** Put your data in a table.

5. **Sequence:** Arrange all the objects in order from smallest to largest.

Questions

1. How long is your metric ruler?

2. How many millimeters are shown on the ruler?

3. Which object is the longest?

4. Which object is the shortest?

1-6 How do you measure using the metric system?

Objective ▶ Understand how to measure different things using the metric system.

TechTerms

- ▶ **degree Celsius:** metric unit of temperature
- ▶ **temperature:** measure of how hot or cold something is

Measuring Area Do you know how people find the area of the floor of a room? They measure the length and width of the room. Then, they multiply the two numbers. You can find the area of any rectangle by multiplying its length by its width. Area is expressed in square units, such as square meters (m^2) or square centimeters (cm^2).

▶ **Calculate:** What is the area of a rectangle 2 cm × 3 cm? 6 cm²

Measuring Volume A graduated cylinder can be used to measure the volume of a liquid in milliliters. Volume can also be measured in cubic centimeters. Imagine a small box shaped like a cube. Each side is 1 cm long. The volume of the cube is 1 cubic centimeter (cm^3). One cubic centimeter is the same as 1 milliliter. The volume of any box can be found by multiplying its length by its width by its height.

If you have a box that is 10 cm on each side, its volume would be 1000 cm^3. A liter is the same as 1000 cm^3. One liter of liquid will fill the box exactly.

▬ **Analyze:** How many milliliters of water would fill a 12-cm^3 box? 12 mL

Measuring Mass Mass is measured with an instrument called a balance. A balance works like a seesaw. It compares an unknown mass with a known mass. Known masses are used on one side. The object is placed on the other side. The mass of the object is equal to the total of the known masses.

▶ **Name:** What instrument is used to measure mass? balance

Measuring Temperature The **temperature** of anything is a measure of how hot or cold it is. You also can say it is the amount of heat energy something contains. Temperature is measured with a thermometer. Temperature can be measured on one of three scales. They are the Fahrenheit (FAHR-uhn-hyt) scale, the Celsius (SEL-see-us) scale, and the Kelvin (K) scale. The Fahrenheit scale is part of the English system of measurement. The Celsius scale is usually used in science. Each unit on the Celsius scale is a **degree Celsius** (°C). The degree Celsius is a metric unit. The Kelvin scale is a part of SI. The Kelvin scale begins at absolute zero, or 0 K. There is no heat energy at absolute zero.

Table 1 Comparing Temperatures			
	°C	K	°F
Absolute zero	−273	0	−459
Freezing Point (Water)	0	273	32
Room Temperature	22	295	72
Human Body Temperature	37	310	98.6
Boiling Point (Water)	100	373	212

👁 **Observe:** What is the freezing point of water on the Celsius scale? 0 °C

LESSON SUMMARY

▶ The area of a rectangle is found by multiplying its length by its width.

▶ Volume can be measured in cubic centimeters.

▶ A balance is used to measure mass.

▶ Temperature is a measure of how hot or cold something is.

▶ Temperature is measured with a thermometer.

▶ Three temperature scales are the Fahrenheit scale, the Celsius scale, and the Kelvin scale.

CHECK *Complete the following.*

1. The area of a rectangle is found by multiplying its length by its _____ . width

2. One liter of liquid is equal to _____ cubic centimeters. 1000

3. The symbol for cubic centimeters is _____ . cm³

4. An instrument used to measure mass is a _____ . balance

5. An instrument used to measure temperature is a _____ . thermometer

6. Three temperature scales are the _____ scale, the Celsius scale, and the Kelvin scale. Fahrenheit

7. The _____ scale begins at absolute zero. Kelvin

APPLY *Use Table 1 on page 24 to complete the following.*

8. **Analyze:** What is the boiling point of water on the Celsius temperature scale? 100 °C

9. **Compare:** What is absolute zero on the Fahrenheit scale? On the Celsius scale? −459°; −273°

10. **Analyze:** What symbol is used for each temperature scale? °C = Celsius; K = Kelvin; °F = Fahrenheit

Health & Safety Tip..........................

Mercury is poisonous if you inhale it. It also can be absorbed through the skin. If you break a thermometer, tell your teacher or your parents immediately. Never clean up a broken thermometer with your hands. Contact your local poison control center. Find out how to clean up mercury properly.

ACTIVITY

CALCULATING AREA AND VOLUME

You will need 3 boxes of different sizes, paper, and a metric ruler.

1. Copy Table 1 on a sheet of paper.

2. Measure the length, width, and height of each box in centimeters. Record each measurement in your table.

3. Calculate the volume of each box. Record each volume in the table.

4. Find the area of every rectangle shown in the diagram. Organize the data in a table.

Questions

1. Which of your three boxes has the largest volume?

2. How many milliliters of liquid would fill each box? Answers will vary. Numbers should be the same as cubic centimeters.

3. How many rectangles are in the diagram? 5; Rectangles are 35 cm², 6 cm², 10 cm², 12.8 cm², and 2.8 cm².

4. What is the area of the largest rectangle? 35 cm²

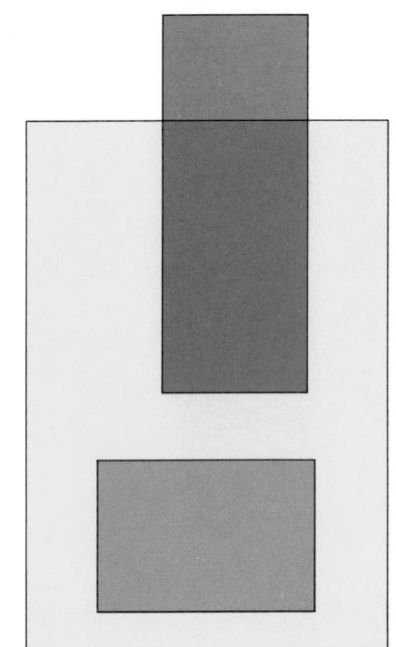

Table 1	Box Measurements			
BOX	LENGTH	WIDTH	HEIGHT	VOLUME
1				
2				
3				

1-7 What is a microscope?

Objective ▶ Identify and describe different kinds of microscopes.

TechTerms

- ▶ **lens** (LENZ): piece of curved glass that causes light rays to come together or spread apart as they pass through
- ▶ **magnify:** to make something look larger than it is
- ▶ **microscope** (MIKE-roh-scope): tool that makes things look larger than they really are

Microscopes One of the most important tools used to study living things is the **microscope** (MIKE-roh-scope). "Micro" means very small. "Scope" means to look at. A microscope is a tool used to make things look larger than they really are. There are different kinds of microscopes.

▶ *Define:* What is a microscope? tool used to make things look larger than they really are

Lenses A **lens** (LENZ) is a curved piece of glass. Some lenses have one curved surface and one flat surface. Others have two curved surfaces.

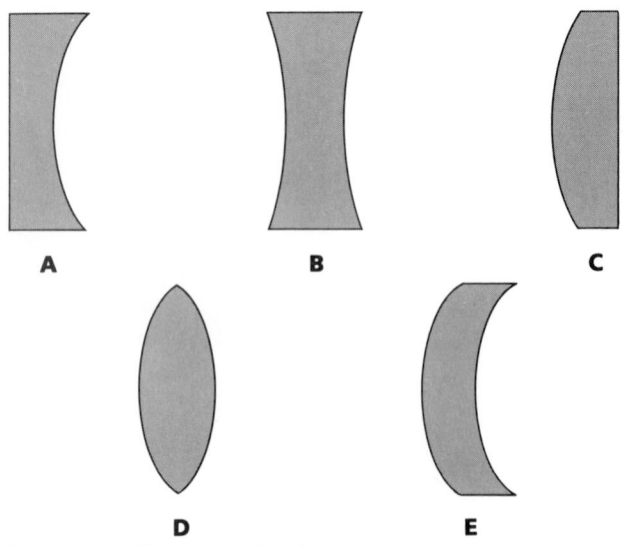

A   **B**   **C**

D   **E**

Figure 1 Different Kinds of Lenses

A lens brings light rays together or spreads them apart. Light that passes through a lens is bent. The bending of the light rays causes the object to look either larger or smaller. If the object looks larger, the lens has **magnified** (MAG-ni-fyd) the object.

👁 *Observe:* Look at Figure 1. Which lenses have two curved surfaces? B, D, E

Light Microscopes The microscopes you use in the classroom are light microscopes. Light microscopes have one or more lenses in them. These microscopes use light and lenses to magnify things.

Have you ever used a magnifying glass? If you have, you have used a simple microscope. A simple microscope has only one lens. Other microscopes have two or more lenses. A compound microscope has two or more lenses. The two lenses make things look larger than does one lens.

▶ *Describe:* How many lenses does a compound microscope have? 2

Electron Microscope An electron microscope uses electrons to magnify objects. It does not use light. Electrons are the particles that light up your television screen. A standard microscope can make an object appear 50 to 400 times larger. An electron microscope can magnify objects up to 300,000X their normal size. One type of electron microscope, scans the object and produces a three-dimensional image. Electron microscopes are very useful but they are very expensive.

▶ *Identify:* What kind of microscope can magnify an object up to 300,000X? electron microscope

- ▶ A microscope makes objects appear larger.
- ▶ A lens is a curved piece of glass that bends light.
- ▶ A magnifying glass is a simple microscope.
- ▶ A compound microscope uses two or more lenses to magnify objects.
- ▶ An electron microscope uses electrons which magnify objects up to 300,000X.

CHECK *Answer the following.*

1. What is the difference between a compound microscope and a simple microscope?

2. What is a lens?

3. What kind of microscope can magnify things up to 300,000 X?

4. What household appliance uses electrons?

APPLY *Answer the following.*

▶ 5. **Infer:** Why do you think a compound microscope is better than a simple microscope?

▶ 6. **Infer:** Which of your senses is aided by using a microscope?

Skill Builder ....

Making a Simple Microscope Dip the part of a key with a hole into a glass of water. Make sure that a drop of water stays in the hole. Look through the drop of water to read the small print in a book. Move the key up and down very slowly. What happens? Which part of the microscope is the drop of water?

⌄⌄⌄ LOOKING BACK IN SCIENCE ⌄⌄⌄⌄⌄⌄⌄⌄⌄⌄⌄⌄⌄⌄⌄⌄⌄⌄⌄⌄⌄

DEVELOPMENT OF THE MICROSCOPE

The ancient Greeks used magnifying glasses in the 2nd century BC. They used them as "burning glasses". The ancient Romans made simple microscopes out of rock crystals. Over 3000 years ago, glass balls filled with water were used as magnifying glasses. In 1590, two Dutch eyeglass makers, Hans and Zacharias Janssen developed the first compound microscope. Their microscope had two lenses, one at each end of a tube. The microscope made objects appear larger, but the image was fuzzy and distorted. Poor lenses caused this problem. Robert Hooke, an English scientist made and used a compound microscope in 1665. He looked at thin slices of cork.

About 1670, a Dutch merchant, Anton van Leeuwenhoek made a lens of fine quality. The lens produced a clear image. Leeuwenhoek made more than 500 lenses. They were used as simple microscopes. Some lenses could magnify objects 250X.

In 1931, two German scientists developed the first electron microscope. Today, electron microscopes are used in many science laboratories. Electron microscopes have a major drawback. They cannot be used to look at living things.

Eyepiece (Ocular lens)

Robert Hook's Microscope

Objective lens

1-8 What are the parts of a microscope?

Objective ▶ Identify and describe the functions of the parts of a compound microscope.

The Compound Microscope The first compound microscope was invented about 1590 by two Dutch lens makers, Hans and Zacharias Janssen. Many scientists made and used them. Much of what is known about living things would not be possible without the microscope.

All compound microscopes have the same basic parts. Using a microscope can be a lot of fun. It is easy to use if you know its parts and what they do.

▶ *Identify:* Who invented the first compound microscope? Hans and Zacharias Janssen

Parts of the Compound Microscope As you read about each part of the compound microscope, find the part on the drawing.

- ▶ **Eyepiece** The eyepiece is located at the top of the microscope. It holds the ocular lens.
- ▶ **Body tube** The body tube is a hollow tube through which light passes. It holds the lenses apart.
- ▶ **Nosepiece** The nosepiece holds the objective lenses.
- ▶ **Objective lens** There are several objective lenses. Each lens has a different magnification power.
- ▶ **Arm** The arm supports the body tube, and is used to carry the microscope.
- ▶ **Coarse-adjustment knob** This knob turns and is used to raise or lower the body tube to focus the microscope.
- ▶ **Fine-adjustment knob** The knob also raises or lowers the body tube. It is used to bring objects into sharp focus.
- ▶ **Stage** The stage is the place where the object you are looking at is put.

- ▶ **Stage clips** The stage clips hold down the slide on the stage.
- ▶ **Diaphragm** The diaphragm (DY-uh-fram) changes the amount of light entering the body tube.
- ▶ **Light source** The light source is located beneath the diaphragm. It sends light toward the hole in the stage. A light source can be an electric light built into the microscope or a mirror that reflects light into the microscope.
- ▶ **Base** The base is the bottom part of the microscope. It often is shaped like a horseshoe. With the one hand holding the arm and one hand under the base, you carry a microscope properly.

▶ *Describe:* How do you carry a microscope properly? One hand holding the arm; other hand under the base

Compound microscope

28

► The first compound microscope was invented by Hans and Zacharias Janssen.

► All compound microscopes have the same basic parts.

CHECK *Complete the following.*

1. The lens at the top of the microscope is found in the _____ . eyepiece

2. When looking through a microscope the _____ lens is closest to your eye. ocular

3. The nosepiece holds the _____ lenses. objective

4. The coarse- and fine- adjustment knobs help _____ the microscope. focus

5. The object to be viewed is placed on the _____ of the microscope. stage

6. The amount of light entering the microscope is controlled by the _____ . diaphragm

APPLY *Answer the following.*

7. **Explain:** Why is a compound microscope called a light microscope?

8. **Infer:** Why do you think it is more important to get a clearer image than one that is fuzzy but greatly magnified?

9. **Infer:** How does changing the objective lenses affect what is seen through the microscope?

Use the microscope shown on page 28 to answer the following.

10. How many objective lenses are on the microscope? 2

11. What is the light source? mirror; sunlight or room light

Skill Builder

Calculating To find the magnification of a microscope multiply the number found on the ocular lens by the number found on the objective lens. Find the magnification of the microscopes listed below.

	Ocular	Objective
a.	5X	10X
b.	5X	43X
c.	10X	10X
d.	10X	20X
e.	5X	20X

TECHNOLOGY AND SOCIETY

MICROSURGERY

An ambulance races across town to a hospital. Inside there is an accident victim. The victim has had a finger severed in a machine. A team of microsurgeons will work to reattach the finger. The surgeons will use microsurgery.

In microsurgery, special microscopes are used by the surgeons to look at the very small parts of the body as they operate. The parts would be too small to operate on with their unaided eyes. With these microscopes, the surgeons can even attach tiny nerve fibers and small blood vessels. They use tiny instruments developed by medical engineers. Some of these instruments are so small the surgeons can stick a needle into a blood cell that is only 0.008 millimeters across.

The special microscope used in microsurgery was developed in the mid-1950s. It was used for ear and eye operations. Today, microsurgery is used in many delicate operations. Some brain surgery is done using microsurgery techniques.

UNIT 1 Challenges

STUDY HINT Before you begin the Unit Challenges, review the TechTerms and Lesson Summary for each lesson in this unit.

TechTerms

control (20)
controlled experiment (20)
data (18)
degree Celsius (24)
experiment (20)
gram (22)

hypothesis (16)
lens (26)
liter (22)
magnify (26)
mass (22)
meter (22)

microscope (26)
scientific method (18)
specialization (14)
temperature (24)
variable (20)

TechTerm Challenges

Matching *Write the TechTerm that best matches each description.*

1. studying or working in only one field specialization
2. suggested solution to a problem hypothesis
3. model or guide used to solve problems scientific method
4. information data
5. test of a hypothesis experiment
6. anything that can change the results of an experiment variable
7. to make something larger magnify
8. tool that makes things appear larger microscope

Identifying Word Relationships *Explain how the terms in each pair are related.* Write your answers in complete sentences. Answers will vary. Accept all logical responses.

1. degree Celsius, thermometer
2. matter, mass
3. lens, microscope
4. gram, balance
5. liter, volume
6. control, controlled experiment
7. meter, length
8. experiment, hypothesis
9. data, research

Content Challenges

Multiple Choice *Write the letter of the term or phrase that best completes each statement.*

1. A florist specializes in the branch of biology called
   a. botany. **b.** zoology. **c.** anatomy. **d.** physiology. a

2. The interaction of living things and their surroundings is studied in the branch of life science called
   a. botany. **b.** zoology. **c.** anatomy. **d.** ecology. d

3. The knowledge of science is based upon
   a. medicine. **b.** plants. **c.** observations. **d.** experimentation. c

4. In the metric system, volume is measured in
   a. centimeters. **b.** square units. **c.** liters. **d.** grams. c

5. When you use a copy of something to help explain it, you are using
   a. a model. **b.** an observation. **c.** a table. **d.** a prediction. a

6. When you share information with someone, you are
   a. modeling. **b.** communicating. **c.** predicting. **d.** hypothesizing. b

7. When you state ahead of time how or when something will happen, you are
   a. inferring. **b.** modeling. **c.** predicting. **d.** hypothesizing. c

8. The first step in scientific method is to
   a. identify and state the problem.   **b.** record data.   **c.** gather information.   **d.** state a conclusion. a

9. An experiment that is performed outdoors is
   a. an observation.   **b.** a field study.   **c.** a laboratory.   **d.** a controlled experiment. b

10. The prefix kilo- means
    a. 10.   **b.** 100.   **c.** 1000.   **d.** 10,000. c

11. A meter is equal to
    a. 1 kilometer.   **b.** 10 kilometers.   **c.** 1000 millimeters.   **d.** 10 millimeters. c

12. A centiliter is equal to
    a. 10 liters.   **b.** 1/100 L.   **c.** 1/100 km.   **d.** 1 liter.   b

Completion *Write the term that best completes each statement.*

1. Plants are studied in the branch of biology called _____ . botany
2. When you classify, you group things based upon how they are _____ . alike
3. Graphs, tables, charts, and diagrams are ways to _____ information. organize
4. An experiment that is done outdoors is called a _____ . field study
5. The prefix deca- means _____ . ten
6. Length is measured with a _____ . meter stick
7. A graduated cylinder is used to measure the volume of a _____ . liquid
8. Mass is measured with an instrument called a _____ . balance
9. The SI unit of temperature is the _____ . Kelvin
10. The Kelvin temperature scale begins at _____ . absolute zero
11. The formula for calculating area is _____ . area = length × width
12. A magnifying lens is an example of a _____ . simple microscope
13. A microscope with two lenses is a _____ microscope. compound
14. The amount of light that passes through a microscope is controlled by the _____ . diaphragm

Understanding the Features..

Reading Critically *Use the feature reading selections to answer the following. Page numbers for the features are shown in parentheses.*

1. **Apply:** Do wildlife biologists do most of their work in a laboratory or as field studies? (15)
2. **Define:** What is technology? (19)
3. What kind of animals has Jane Goodall worked with most? (21)
4. Who was Dr. Louis Leakey? (21)
5. **List:** Identify three things that have been used to make microscopes. (27)
6. **Relate:** How have improved microscopes been helpful in the field of medicine? (29)

Concept Challenges..

Critical Thinking *Answer each of the following in complete sentences.*

1. **Contrast:** What are two differences between an electron microscope and a compound microscope?
2. **Infer:** How are microscopes useful to microbiologists?
3. **Apply:** What temperature scale would you use to measure very cold temperatures? Why?
4. **Relate:** How are the microscopes that are used today better than those that were used two hundred years ago?

Interpreting a Diagram *Answer the questions about the diagram.*

1. **Identify:** What is shown in the diagram?
2. What is the instrument shown used for?
3. What is the light source for the instrument shown?
4. **Observe:** How many objective lenses does this instrument have?
5. **Calculate:** If the magnifying power of the eyepiece lens is 10x and the magnifying power of the low-power objective is 10x, what is the total magnification of the microscope using the low-power lens?
6. **Describe:** How should a microscope be carried?
7. What part of a microscope holds the slide in place?
8. **Infer:** Is the magnification of this microscope greater than or less than the magnification of a hand lens?
9. **Contrast:** How does a compound microscope differ from a simple microscope?
10. **Define:** What is a lens?

Finding Out More

1. **Organize:** Make a poster that shows the tools used to measure length, mass, volume, and temperature. Label each tool on your poster and identify how it is used.
2. **Research:** Use library references to find out about the work done by Dian Fosse. How is the work done by Dian Fosse similar to the work done by Jane Goodall? Write your findings in a report.
3. **Communicate:** Research the work of Louis and Mary Leakey. What kind of fossils were these scientists most interested in? How have the discoveries of the Leakey's helped scientists learn more about humans who lived long ago? Present your findings in an oral report to the class.
4. Find ten products that use metric or SI units on their labels. Combine your labels with those of five of your classmates. Use your labels to make a bulletin board display for your classroom.
5. **Organize:** Create a table that shows and compares the basic units of mass, volume, temperature, length, and weight in the English, metric, and SI systems.

NEEDS OF LIVING THINGS

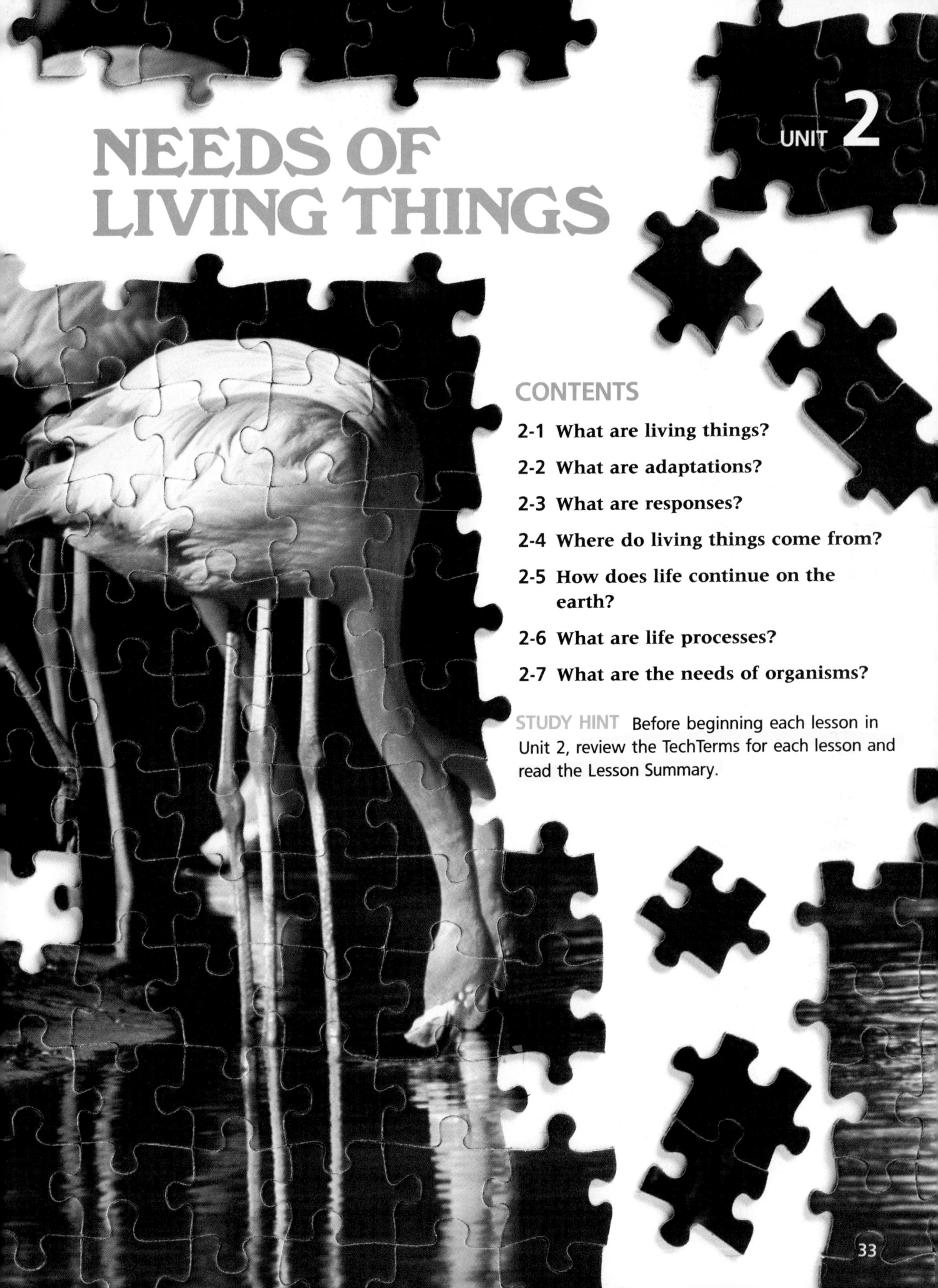

CONTENTS

STUDY HINT Before beginning each lesson in Unit 2, review the TechTerms for each lesson and read the Lesson Summary.

2-1 What are living things?

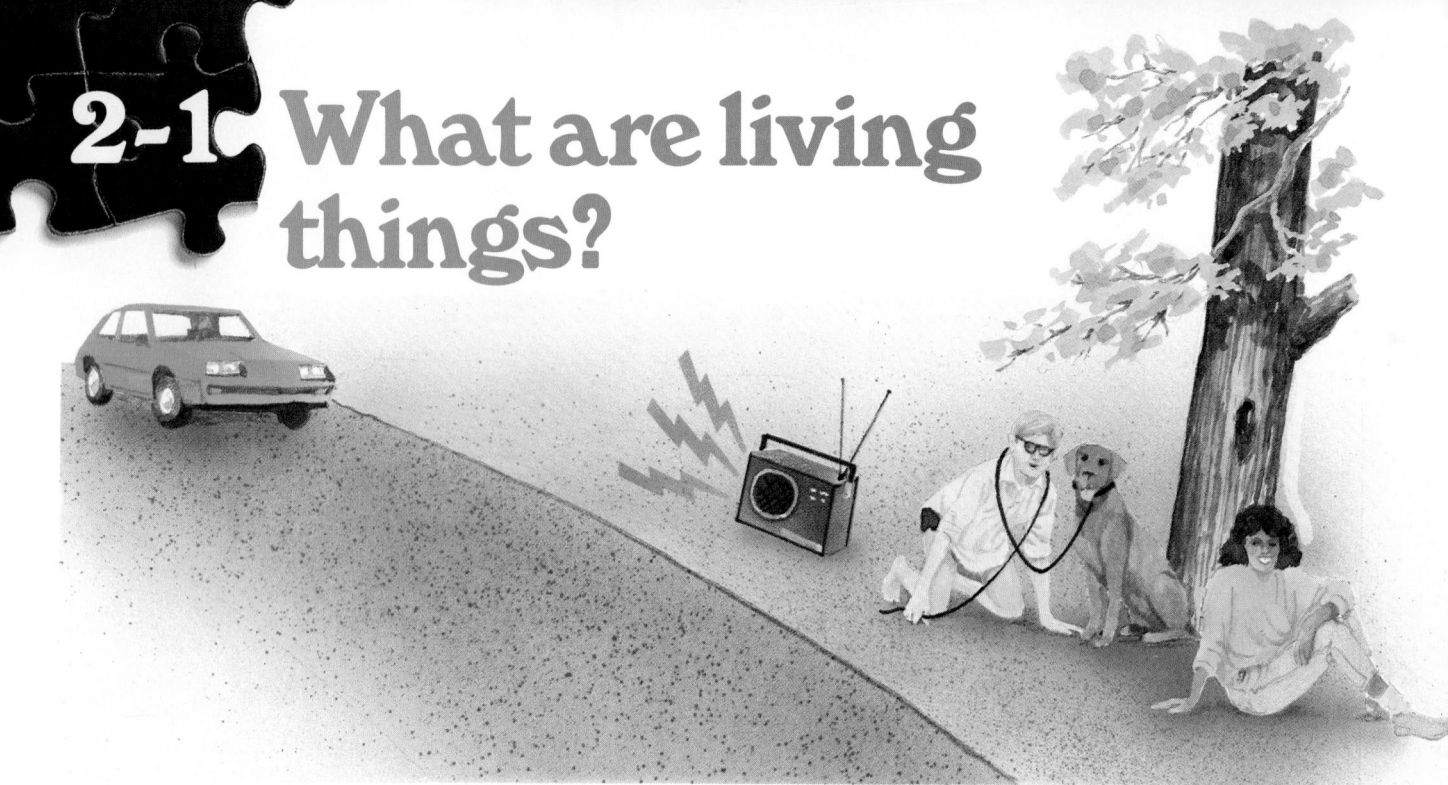

Objective ▶ List and describe the six characteristics of living things.

TechTerms

- ▶ **cell:** basic unit of structure and function in living things
- ▶ **organism** (AWR-guh-niz-um): any living thing
- ▶ **response** (ri-SPAHNS): reaction to a change

Organisms The world around you is made up of many different things. Some things, such as dogs and trees, are living. Living things are called **organisms** (AWR-guh-niz-ums). Other things, such as cars and radios, are nonliving.

▓▶ **Define:** What is an organism? any living thing

Characteristics of Organisms It is not always easy to decide if something is living or nonliving. Nonliving things may do some of the same things as organisms. For example, a robot may move and speak like a person. A robot, however, is not living. Plants and animals grow, or get larger. Icicles also may seem to grow, but icicles are not living.

Biologists use six characteristics to classify something as a living thing. All living things have these six characteristics.

- ▶ Organisms are made up of one or more **cells.** A cell is the basic unit of structure and func-

tion in living things. In fact, cells often are called the "building blocks of life."

- ▶ Energy is the ability to do work. Organisms use energy. Sunlight is the source of energy for most living things. Plants use the energy in sunlight to make food. Animals get energy from the sun by eating plants or animals that have eaten plants.
- ▶ Organisms are adapted (uh-DAP-tud), or suited, to their surroundings. All organisms have features that help them survive in their surroundings. For example, fishes have gills. Gills are organs that allow fishes to breathe in water.
- ▶ Organisms react to changes in their surroundings. Any reaction to a change is called a **response** (ri-SPAHNS). You might respond to the honking of a car's horn by jumping. A bright light may cause you to close your eyes.
- ▶ Organisms produce more organisms of their own kind. Dogs produce more dogs. Pine trees produce more pine trees. The production of new organisms allows each kind of organism to continue living on the earth.
- ▶ Organisms grow and develop. Living things change, or develop during their lifetimes. One way organisms change is by growing. Living things also may change in appearance.

▓▶ **Identify:** What is the source of energy for most living things? sun

LESSON SUMMARY

▶ Living things are called organisms.

▶ It is not always easy to tell living things from nonliving things.

▶ All living things have six characteristics. Living things are made up of cells, use energy, are adapted to their surroundings, produce more of their own kind, grow, and develop.

CHECK *Complete the following.*

1. Organisms are made up of one or more _____ . cells

2. Energy is the ability to do _____ . work

3. Organisms _____ to changes in their surroundings. respond

4. Plants use the energy in _____ to make food. sunlight

5. Organisms are suited, or _____ , to their surroundings. adapted

6. Organisms get larger, or _____ . grow

7. Growth is one of the ways that organisms _____ . change or develop

APPLY *Complete the following.*

8. **Apply:** How does a cow get energy from sunlight?

9. **Hypothesize:** Could an ant be the offspring of a fly? Explain your answer.

10. **Classify:** Flashlights and cars both use energy to work. Use the characteristics of living things to explain why cars and flashlights are not classified as living things.

Ideas in Action

IDEA: All living things respond to changes in their surroundings.

ACTION: Describe three examples of responses you have to changes in your surroundings. Identify the change that causes each response.

SCIENCE CONNECTION

MATTER

Do you know what everything around you has in common? Everything around you is made up of matter. Matter is anything that has a mass and takes up space. *volume*

Matter is made up of tiny particles called atoms. Some substances are made up entirely of atoms of the same kind. These substances are called elements. Most living things are made up mainly of the elements carbon, hydrogen, oxygen, nitrogen, sulfur, and phosphorous.

When two or more elements combine chemically, they form a compound. Four kinds of compounds are important to living things. These compounds are carbohydrates, lipids, proteins, and nucleic acids. Carbohydrates are made up of carbon, hydrogen, and oxygen. They are important energy sources. Lipids are made up mostly of carbon and hydrogen. Lipids store energy. Proteins are the basic building blocks of all living things. Proteins are made up of carbon, hydrogen, oxygen, and nitrogen. Nucleic acids control cell activities. Nucleic acids also control the making of proteins.

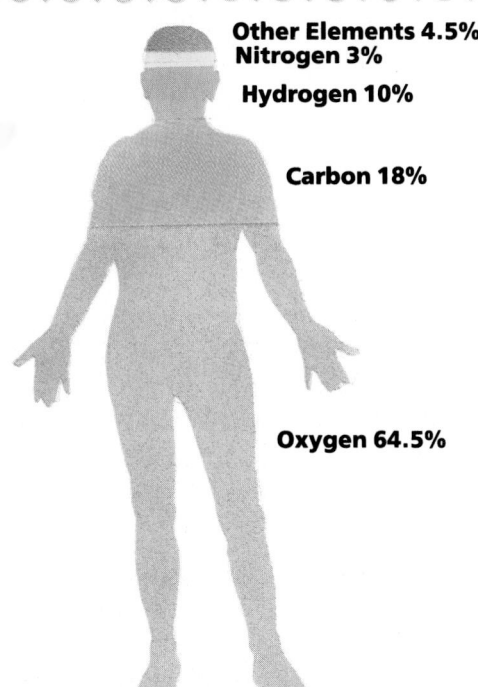

Other Elements 4.5%
Nitrogen 3%

Hydrogen 10%

Carbon 18%

Oxygen 64.5%

2-2 What are adaptations?

Objective ▶ Identify and describe some adaptations of organisms.

TechTerms

▶ **adaptation** (ad-up-TAY-shun): trait of a living thing that helps it live in its environment

▶ **environment** (in-VY-run-munt): everything that surrounds a living thing

Environment All organisms live in an **environment** (in-VY-run-munt). The environment is everything that surrounds a living thing. All the living things that surround you are part of your environment. Your environment also is made up of nonliving things. Some of the nonliving things in the environment are air, water, sunlight, rocks, and soil.

▶ *Name:* What are some nonliving parts of the environment? Accept all logical responses.

Adaptations Any trait of an organism that helps the organism live in its environment is called an **adaptation** (ad-up-TAY-shun). Adaptations make each kind of organism suited to life in its environment. Adaptations allow one kind of organism to live where other kinds of organisms cannot live. A cactus has adaptations that allow it to live in a dry, desert environment. A cactus has a thick, leathery stem that stores water. It also has spines. Spines are special leaves that keep a cactus from losing too much water.

Some living things are adapted to cold environments. Polar bears live in very cold environments. The thick fur and fat layers of a polar bear keep it warm. A polar bear would not be able to survive in a hot, humid jungle.

▶ *Infer:* How are fishes adapted to their environments? Accept all logical responses.

People and Adaptations People have adaptations too. You have a thumb that can touch all of your other fingers. Your thumb allows you to use your hands to do many things. You can write, build things, draw, and so on. Your flexible thumb is an adaptation.

Unlike most organisms, people often adapt their environments to meet their needs. People build shelters to protect themselves from the weather. People control their indoor environments by using air conditioners and heating systems. People also wear different kinds of clothing depending on the weather.

▶ *Describe:* What are two ways that you adapt to a rainy day? Accept all logical responses.

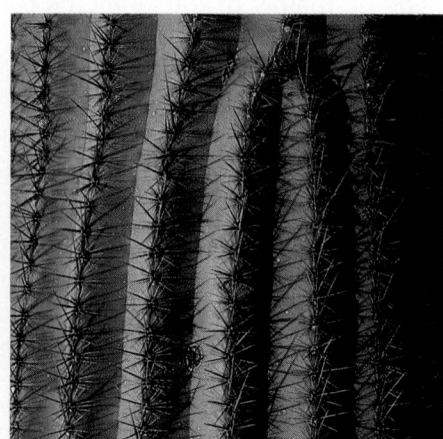

36

LESSON SUMMARY

▶ All organisms live in an environment.

▶ An adaptation is any trait of an organism that helps it live in its environment.

▶ People have adaptations.

▶ People often adapt their environments to meet their needs.

CHECK *Find the sentence in the lesson that answers each question. Then, write the sentence.*

1. What is the environment?

2. What nonliving things are part of the environment?

3. What is an adaptation?

4. To what kind of environment is a cactus adapted?

5. Why is your thumb an adaptation?

6. How do people adapt their indoor environments to meet their needs?

APPLY *Complete the following.*

7. **Identify:** Name two living and nonliving parts of your environment.

8. **Explain:** Give two examples of how you adapt to warm weather.

Match each organism with the environment to which it is most suited.

9. cold, snowy climate   **a.** frog

10. hot, dry desert   **b.** octopus

11. the ocean   **c.** polar bear

12. a pond   **d.** cactus

13. a heavily, wooded forest   **e.** raccoon

State the Problem

Study the illustration. Then, state the problem.

CAREER IN LIFE SCIENCE

ECOLOGIST

Do you enjoy studying plants and animals? Would you like to study how conditions in the environment affect living things? If so, you may enjoy a career as an ecologist (ee-KAHL-uh-jee). Ecologists are scientists who study the relationship between living things and their environments.

Ecologists study many different problems. Some ecologists study only one kind of plant or animal. Most ecologists, however, study entire communities. Some study land communities. Others specialize in water environments. An ecologist may manage forest land and wildlife refuges, evaluate the effects of pollution and mining on living things, study soil composition, or help control insect pests.

An ecologist may work in the field or in a research laboratory. Ecologists are employed by the government, industries, and universities. If you are interested in becoming an ecologist, you should have a good background in the sciences. A college degree is required for most jobs in ecology.

2-3 What are responses?

▸ Explain how stimuli and responses are related. ▸ Identify some kinds of behaviors.

TechTerms

- **behavior** (bi-HAYV-yur): ways in which living things respond to stimuli
- **hibernation** (HY-bur-nay-shun): inactive state of some animals during winter months
- **migration** (my-GRAY-shun): movement of animals from one living place to another
- **stimulus** (STIM-yuh-lus): change that causes a response

Stimulus and Response Living things respond to their environments. In the morning, your alarm clock rings. You respond by waking. The ringing alarm clock is a **stimulus** (STIM-yuh-lus). A stimulus is a change that causes a response. The plural of stimulus is stimuli (STIM-yuh-ly).

Living things respond to stimuli in different ways. Turn a plant so that its leaves face away from the sun. In a few days, the leaves of the plant will turn back toward the sun. The movement of the plant's leaves is a response. Plant responses usually are slower than animal responses.

▌▌▌▶ *Identify:* A flower slowly turns to face the sun. What is the stimulus and response for this action? stimulus: sun; response: turning of flowers

Behavior The way in which an organism responds to stimuli is called **behavior** (bi-HAYV-yur). A behavior that an organism is born with is called an instinct (IN-stinkt). Nest-building is an instinct in some kinds of birds. Birds do not have to be shown how to build nests. Other behaviors have to be learned. Tying your shoelaces is a learned behavior. You have many learned behaviors.

◢ *Analyze:* Foxes are taught how to hunt by other foxes. Is hunting a learned behavior or an instinct in these animals? learned

Animal Behaviors The movement of animals from one living space to another is called **migration** (my-GRAY-shun). Animals often migrate to warmer places during the cold months to find food. Animals also migrate to find a safe place to reproduce and raise their young.

Some animals spend the winter months in a sleeplike state called **hibernation** (HY-bur-nay-shun). During hibernation, an animal is not active. The body temperature of the animal lowers. The heartbeat of the animal slows. The animal does not need as much energy. As a result, the animal can live off the fat stored in its body. Chipmunks and squirrels are two kinds of animals that hibernate.

▌▌▌▶ *Define:* What is hibernation? sleeplike state of some animals in winter months

38

LESSON SUMMARY

- All living things respond to stimuli.
- Living things respond to stimuli in different ways.
- The ways in which living things respond to stimuli is called behavior.
- Migration and hibernation are two behaviors of animals.

CHECK *Write true if the statement is true. If the statement is false, change the underlined term to make the statement true.*

1. Behaviors that an animal is born with are <u>learned behaviors</u>. instincts
2. The movement of animals from one living area to another is <u>hibernation</u>. migration
3. A change that causes a response is a <u>stimulus</u>. true
4. The inactive state of some animals during the winter months is called <u>hibernation</u>. true
5. The ways in which living things respond to stimuli is called <u>migration</u>. behavior
6. During hibernation, an animal's activities <u>speed up</u>. slow down

APPLY *Complete the following.*

7. **Infer:** What happens to a squirrel's breathing rate during hibernation? it slows down

Classify each action described as a learned behavior or an instinct.

8. reading a book
   learned
9. blinking
   instinct
10. a newborn crying
    instinct
11. going to school
    learned

InfoSearch

Read the passage. Ask two questions about the topic that you cannot answer from the information in the passage.

Bird Migration Many kinds of birds migrate during the winter and summer months. Year after year, birds migrate over the same paths, or migration routes. Scientists are not completely sure how birds are able to follow the same route during their round-trip migrations. Some scientists think the birds use the sun as a landmark. Other scientists think birds use wind currents.

SEARCH: *Use library references to find answers to your questions.*

ACTIVITY

PUPIL RESPONSES TO LIGHT

You will need a penlight or flashlight.

1. Work with a partner. Look at the pupil of your partner's eye. The pupil is the dark circle in the middle of the colored part of the eye. Note the size of the pupil.
2. **Observe:** Quickly shine the penlight in your partner's eye. Observe what happens to the size of the pupil.
3. **Observe:** Take the light away. Observe what happens to the size of the pupil.

Pupil

Questions

1. **Observe:** What happened to the size of the pupil when the light was shined on it? When did the pupil get smaller?
2. **a.** What is the stimulus?   **b.** What is the response?
3. **a. Infer:** What happened to the size of the pupil when you took the light away?   **b.** Why do you think this happens?
4. **Hypothesize:** What would happen if the pupil did not change size?
5. **Predict:** When would the size of the pupil be the largest?

2-4 Where do living things come from?

Objective ▶ Recognize that all life comes from existing life.

TechTerm

▶ **spontaneous generation** (spahn-TAY-nee-us jen-uh-RAY-shun): idea that living things come from nonliving things

Spontaneous Generation Do you believe that living things can grow from straw? Hundreds of years ago, people believed that mice came from straw. They also believed that worms and flies grew from rotting meat. The idea that living things came from nonliving things is called **spontaneous generation** (spahn-TAY-nee-us jen-uh-RAY-shun). Until the 1600s, many people believed in spontaneous generation.

▶ *Infer:* Why do you think people who lived hundreds of years ago believed that frogs came from rotting wood and water? Accept all logical responses.

Francesco Redi Francesco Redi was an Italian doctor. He lived during the seventeenth century. Redi did not think that living things came from nonliving things. He thought that living things could come only from other living things. To test his hypothesis, Redi performed an experiment.

▶ *Identify:* What did Redi do to test his hypothesis about spontaneous generation? performed an experiment

Redi's Experiment Redi put some spoiled meat into several jars. Some jars he left uncovered. Some jars he covered with a thin veil. Other jars were sealed tightly with lids. The jars with the lids were Redi's control. The setup for Redi's experiment is shown below.

After a few days, Redi observed wormlike animals on the meat in the uncovered jars. He also observed the wormlike animals on the veil covering some of the jars. There were no wormlike animals in the jars with lids.

The wormlike animals that Redi observed were maggots (MAG-uts). Maggots are a stage in the life cycle of a fly. The maggots hatched from eggs that flies had laid on the meat and veil. Redi showed that maggots did not come from the meat. Today, scientists know that flies often lay eggs on spoiled meat. The meat is food for the maggots. Scientists know that all living things come from other living things of the same kind.

▶ *Infer:* Why did maggots not appear in the covered jars? Flies could not enter the jar to lay their eggs.

EXPERIMENTAL SETUP

LESSON SUMMARY

▶ The idea that living things come from nonliving things is called spontaneous generation.

▶ Francesco Redi was a seventeenth century doctor who believed that living things could not come from nonliving things.

▶ Redi performed an experiment using flies and spoiled meat to disprove the idea of spontaneous generation.

▶ Redi's experiment showed that flies do not come from spoiled meat.

CHECK *Complete the following.*

1. What is spontaneous generation?
2. Who was one of the first people to disprove the idea of spontaneous generation?
3. What are maggots?
4. Why do flies often lay eggs on spoiled meat?
5. What was the control for Redi's experiment?

APPLY *Complete the following.*

6. Why is it important to use a control in an experiment?
7. What did Redi's experiment show?

Look at the illustration. Why do you think people from Redi's time believed that mice came from straw?

Designing an Experiment

Design an experiment to solve the problem.

PROBLEM: Do flies develop from garbage?

Your experiment should:

1. List the materials you need.
2. Identify safety precautions that should be followed.
3. List a step-by-step procedure.
4. Describe how you would record your data.

PEOPLE IN SCIENCE

LOUIS PASTEUR (1822-1895)

Did you have a glass of milk this morning? If so, you may have noticed the term "pasteurized" on the container. Pasteurization is a process by which germs growing in certain food products are killed. The process is named after the scientist who developed it, Louis Pasteur.

Louis Pasteur is one of the great scientists in the history of science. He was a French chemist and microbiologist. Among his many contributions to science, Pasteur performed a simple experiment that disproved spontaneous generation.

In his experiment, Pasteur poured a nutrient broth into swan-necked flasks. The swan-necks prevented dust particles and microorganisms from entering the flasks. He boiled the flasks to kill any microorganisms in the broth. After several days, Pasteur saw no microorganisms growing in the flasks. He then tipped the flasks, allowing dust and microorganisms living in the air to enter the broth. In a few days, microorganisms were growing in the flasks. Pasteur demonstrated that living things did not arise spontaneously from the broth or from the air. They grew from microorganisms carried in the air.

2-5 How does life continue on the earth?

Objective ▶ Describe the two kinds of reproduction.

TechTerms

- **asexual reproduction** (ay-SEK-shoo-wul ree-pruh-DUK-shun): reproduction needing only one parent
- **offspring:** new organisms produced by a living thing
- **reproduction:** process by which living things produce new organisms like themselves
- **sexual** (SEK-shoo-wul) **reproduction:** reproduction needing two parents

Reproduction Every day millions of living things die. Organisms do not live forever. Why is there still life on the earth? Before most organisms die, they produce new organisms like themselves. The process by which organisms produce new organisms is called **reproduction** (ree-pruh-DUK-shun). Reproduction does not keep individual organisms alive. Reproduction only continues each kind of living thing by producing new individuals.

▶ **Define:** What is reproduction? process by which organisms produce like organisms

Offspring All living things reproduce their own kind. The new living things that organisms produce are called **offspring.** The offspring of horses are horses. They are called foals. The offspring of oak trees are seeds called acorns. The acorns grow into oak trees.

▶ **Define:** What are offspring? new living things that result from reproduction

Asexual Reproduction Simple organisms and some plants produce offspring by **asexual** (ay-SEK-shoo-wul) **reproduction.** Asexual reproduction is reproduction that requires only one parent. The simplest form of asexual reproduction is called fission (FISH-un). In fission, new organisms are produced when the parent organism splits in

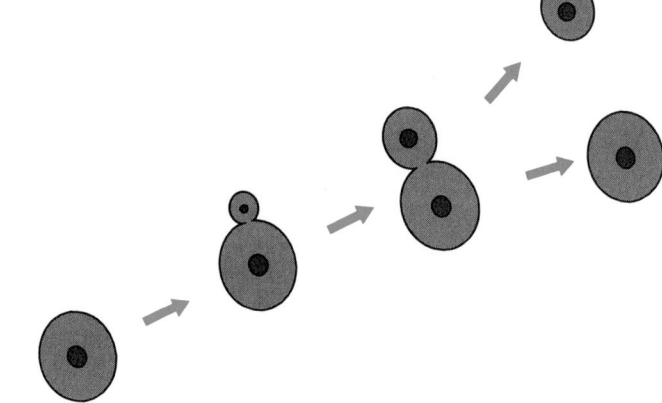

Figure 1 Budding

two. Another kind of asexual reproduction is budding. Budding is the growth of a new organism from the parent organism. In asexual reproduction, each new offspring is an exact copy of its parent.

▶ **Name:** What is the simplest form of asexual reproduction? fission

Sexual Reproduction Most living things reproduce by **sexual** (SEK-shoo-wul) **reproduction.** Sexual reproduction is reproduction needing two parents. During sexual reproduction, cells from two parents join. A new organism develops from the joined cells. This new organism is not exactly like either of its parents. Instead, the offspring has some features of each parent.

▶ **Contrast:** How are sexual and asexual reproduction different? sexual reproduction needs two parents. Asexual reproduction involves one parent.

Figure 2 Cat and offspring

▶ Reproduction is the process through which living things produce new organisms like themselves.

▶ Living things reproduce their own kind.

▶ Reproduction that needs only one parent is called asexual reproduction.

▶ Most living things reproduce by sexual reproduction.

CHECK *Complete the following.*

1. Asexual reproduction involves only-_____ parent. one

2. The simplest form of asexual reproduction is _____ . fission

3. New living things produced by organisms are called _____ . offspring

4. Sexual reproduction needs two _____ . parents

5. During fission, the parent organism _____ in two. splits

APPLY *Complete the following.*

▶ 6. **Predict:** What might happen to a kind of organism that produces few offspring?

▲ 7. **Model:** Draw a diagram showing the process of budding. Label your drawing.

Use the diagram to answer the following.

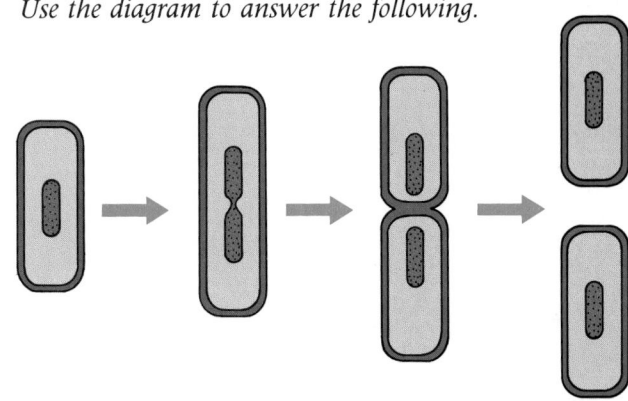

👁 8. **Observe:** What process is being shown?

🔹 9. **Analyze:** Is this a type of asexual or sexual reproduction?

Skill Builder..

Researching The offspring of many animals have specific names. Using library references, find out what the offspring of each of the following animals are called: goats, pigs, giraffes, gorillas, tigers, deer, bears, cows, and ducks. Organize your findings in a table.

⋮⋮⋮ TECHNOLOGY AND SOCIETY ⋮⋮⋮ ⋮⋮⋮ ⋮⋮⋮ ⋮⋮⋮ ⋮⋮⋮ ⋮⋮⋮ ⋮⋮⋮

CLONING

Cloning is the production of cells or organisms with identical traits. Cloning animals is done by first taking the nucleus out of a cell from a donor animal. This nucleus is placed into an egg cell whose own nucleus has been removed. Then the egg cell is placed into the uterus of an adult animal and allowed to develop. When the baby animal is born, it is identical to the donor animal. In 1997, ''Dolly,'' the first sheep cloned from an adult cell, was born.

People can benefit from the cloning of large numbers of organisms that make desired products. For example, scientists often clone bacteria to make drugs. One type of bacteria is cloned because it makes insulin. Insulin is a drug used by people with diabetes. Cloning might be a way to produce animals with desired traits, such as cows that produce more milk or chickens that resist disease.

Scientists also clone organisms to study diseases. Mice that are likely to get cancer can be cloned. Scientists use these mice to study the causes and treament of this disease.

2-6 What are life processes?

▶ Name and describe the life processes.

TechTerms

▶ **digestion** (di-JES-chun): process of breaking down food so that it can be used by living things

▶ **excretion** (iks-KREE-shun): process of getting rid of wastes

▶ **ingestion** (in-JEST-shun): process of taking in food

▶ **respiration** (res-puh-RAY-shun): process of getting energy from food

▶ **transport:** process of moving nutrients and wastes in a living thing

Life Processes All living things carry out life processes. Life processes are the things an organism must do to stay alive. The life processes also are features of living things. Being alive means carrying out all the life processes.

▶ *Define:* What are life processes? all the things an organism must do to stay alive

Nutrition Living things need food because it provides them with nutrients. Nutrients are materials needed for growth and energy. Animals take food into their bodies. Taking in food is called **ingestion** (in-JEST-shun). Plants make their own food. Plants also take in some nutrients from the soil.

Food needs to be changed before an organism can use the nutrients in food. The process of changing food into a useable form is **digestion** (di-JES-chun). You have an organ system that digests your food. It is your digestive system.

$$\frac{\text{ingestion} + \text{digestion}}{\text{nutrition}}$$

▶ *Define:* What is digestion? process of changing food to a usable form

Respiration Living things get energy from food by a process called **respiration** (res-puh-RAY-shun). During respiration, oxygen is used to break food apart. This process produces energy. Carbon dioxide and water also are produced. These are waste products of respiration.

▶ *Name:* What are the waste products of respiration? carbon dioxide and water

Excretion Your body makes many waste products. Some waste products are formed during digestion. Others are formed during respiration. All organisms must get rid of waste products formed by the life processes. Getting rid of waste products is called **excretion** (iks-KREE-shun).

▶ *Name:* Name two life processes that produce waste products. nutrition, respiration

Transport Once food is digested, nutrients must be carried to all parts of a living thing. Waste products must be carried away. The moving of nutrients and waste products is called **transport.**

▶ *Infer:* What materials are transported inside a living thing? nutrients and waste products

LESSON SUMMARY

► All living things carry out life processes.

► Taking in food is called ingestion.

► The process of changing food so it can be used is digestion.

► Living things get energy from food by respiration.

► Living things get rid of waste products by the process of excretion.

► The moving of nutrients and waste products is called transport.

CHECK *Write true if the statement is true. If the statement is false, change the underlined term to make the statement true.*

1. Taking in food is called <u>digestion.</u> ingestion

2. Two waste products of respiration are carbon dioxide and <u>water.</u> true

3. The moving of waste products and nutrients is called <u>excretion.</u> transport

4. <u>Nutrients</u> are needed for growth and energy.
true

5. During respiration, <u>nitrogen</u> is used to break food apart. oxygen

6. <u>Animals</u> take in some nutrients from the soil.
Plants

APPLY *Complete the following.*

7. Why does being alive mean carrying out all the life processes?

8. **Sequence:** Describe what happens to food after it is ingested by an animal. Include a discussion of digestion, respiration, excretion, and transport in your description.

Health & Safety Tip

Food provides you with the nutrients you need for energy, growth, and repair of body tissues. Proper nutrition is important for staying healthy. Find out which nutrients you need. The Food and Drug Administration (FDA) has made a list of the U.S. Recommended Daily Allowance (U.S. RDA) for each nutrient. Find out how much of each nutrient you need. Organize your findings in a chart.

Skill Builder

Researching The process by which plants use the sun's energy to make food is called photosynthesis. Find out the chemical equation for photosynthesis. Write the equation using both symbols and words. Then explain the relationship between photosynthesis and respiration.

LOOKING BACK IN SCIENCE

TRANSPORT IN HUMANS

Today, scientists know that blood is transported through blood vessels. The blood vessels are connected and form a circular path. In the fourth century BC, people believed that the blood vessels carried both air and blood. In the second century, a Greek physician named Galen proved that arteries carried only blood. He still believed that air entered the body from the right side of the heart. Galen did not know the blood moved in a circular path. Galen and others thought that blood mixed with air in the lower parts of the heart. They thought there were holes in the dividing walls of the heart.

In the 16th century, scientists began to think that blood was transported through the heart and lungs in a circular path. In the 17th century, William Harvey, an English physician, explained how blood was transported in the human body. He proved that the heart did not have a wall with holes in it. Harvey could not show that the large blood vessels were connected by smaller blood vessels called capillaries. He did not have a microscope that was powerful enough to see capillaries.

2-7. What are the needs of organisms?

Objective ▶ Identify and describe the needs of living things.

TechTerm

▶ **homeostasis** (hoh-mee-oh-STAY-sis): ability of a living thing to keep conditions inside its body constant

Food and Water All organisms need food for growth and energy. Organisms also need water. Without water, all plants and animals would die. Plants use water to make food. About two-thirds of your body is water.

Most substances dissolve in water. These dissolved substances can then be transported throughout a living thing. Most chemical changes in living things cannot take place without water.

◾ *Analyze:* What is the most common substance in your body? water

Air Without air, most living things would die in minutes. Air is a mixture of gases. Oxygen is one of the gases in air. Oxygen is needed by most living things to change food into energy. Land organisms get oxygen from the air. Water organisms get oxygen from water. The oxygen is dissolved in the water.

◾ *Analyze:* How does a fish get oxygen? from water

Temperature The temperature of the environment is important to living things. Living things need a proper temperature to carry out their life processes. Most living things could live only within a small temperature range if it were not for **homeostasis** (hoh-mee-oh-STAY-sis). Homeostasis is the ability of a living thing to keep conditions inside its body constant. When changes in temperature or other parts of the environment occur, homeostasis keeps things working properly inside a living thing.

�I▶ *Define:* What is homeostasis? ability of an organism to keep conditions inside its body constant

Living Space All organisms need living space. An organism's living space must provide enough air, water, sunlight, food, and shelter. In any environment, living space is limited. All the organisms in the environment compete for living space. They compete for food, water, sunlight, and so on. living space, air, water, sunlight, food, shelter

▮I▶ *Name:* List five needs of living things.

LESSON SUMMARY

- ▶ Organisms need food and water.
- ▶ Most chemical changes in living things cannot take place without water.
- ▶ Oxygen is needed by most living things.
- ▶ Living things need a proper temperature to carry out life processes.
- ▶ All organisms need living space.

CHECK *Write true if the statement is true. If the statement is false, change the underlined term to make the statement true.*

1. Most chemical changes in living things <u>cannot</u> take place without water. true

2. In any environment, living space is <u>limited</u>. true

3. <u>Animals</u> can make their own food. plants

4. Fishes get oxygen from the <u>air</u>. water

5. <u>Homeostasis</u> keeps things working properly inside a living thing. true

APPLY *Complete the following.*

▶ 6. **Infer:** How do you think shivering and perspiring are related to homeostasis?

7. What are the nonliving parts of the environment?

8. **Hypothesize:** What do you think happens to organisms when their living space is destroyed?

Ideas in Action

IDEA: You use water every day.
ACTION: Identify ways in which you use water each day.

Health & Safety Tip

Most living things need oxygen to live. These living things are aerobic (er-OH-bik) organisms. Some kinds of organisms grow only in places without oxygen. These living things are called anaerobic (an-er-OH-bik) organisms.

The organism that causes a deadly food poisoning called botulism is anaerobic. It can grow in improperly canned foods. Cans containing the botulism organism often bulge. Use library references to find out what kinds of foods are most likely to contain the botulism organism. Write your findings in a brief report.

LEISURE ACTIVITY

COOKING

Do you enjoy working in the kitchen? Would you like to prepare a meal that appeals to both the eyes and to the taste? If so, you may enjoy learning how to cook. For many people, cooking is an enjoyable, relaxing activity.

You can learn how to cook by observing an experienced cook at work. You can also try recipes from a cookbook. A good cookbook is an important tool for new cooks. Cookbooks usually have similar foods grouped together. Many have pictures showing the way to prepare foods and the finished recipe.

When you first start cooking, try making simple foods. Make sure you have all the ingredients you will need beforehand. As you become more experienced, try more difficult dishes. Ask your friends and relatives for their special recipes. Soon you may be developing "secret recipes" of your own.

UNIT 2 Challenges

STUDY HINT Before you begin the Unit Challenges, review the TechTerms and Lesson Summary for each lesson in this unit.

TechTerms

adaptation (36)
asexual reproduction (42)
behavior (38)
cell (34)
digestion (44)
environment (36)
excretion (44)

hibernation (38)
homeostasis (46)
ingestion (44)
migration (38)
offspring (42)
organism (34)
reproduction (42)

respiration (44)
response (34)
sexual reproduction (42)
spontaneous generation (40)
stimulus (38)
transport (44)

TechTerm Challenges

Matching *Write the TechTerm that best matches each description.*

1. ability of a living thing to keep conditions inside its body constant homeostastis
2. inactive state of some animals during winter months hibernation
3. idea that living things come from nonliving things spontaneous generation
4. process of getting energy from food respiration
5. reproduction needing two parents sexual reproduction
6. new organisms produced by living things offspring

Identifying Word Relationships *Explain how the words in each pair are related. Write your answers in complete sentences.* Answers will vary. Accept all logical responses.

1. ingestion, digestion
2. environment, adaptation
3. reproduction, asexual reproduction
4. behavior, migration
5. cell, organism
6. excretion, transport
7. stimulus, response

Content Challenges

Multiple Choice *Write the letter of the term that best completes each statement.*

1. Oxygen is used to break food apart during
   a digestion.   **b.** ingestion.   **c.** nutrition.   **d.** respiration. d

2. Two kinds of animals that hibernate are
   a. chipmunks and squirrels.   **b.** birds and chipmunks.   **c.** bears and birds.   **d.** birds and squirrels. a

3. Offspring that are not exactly like either parent are produced by
   a. budding.   **b.** sexual reproduction.   **c.** asexual reproduction.   **d.** fission. b

4. All of the following are nonliving parts of the environment *except*
   a. soil.   **b.** sunlight.   **c.** trees.   **d.** water. c

5. The source of energy for most living things is
   a. oxygen.   **b.** sunlight.   **c.** water.   **d.** soil. b

6. All living things
   a. make their own food.   **b.** hibernate.   **c.** migrate.   **d.** are made up of cells. d

7. The simplest form of asexual reproduction is
   a. spontaneous generation.   **b.** budding.   **c.** fission.   **d.** respiration. c
8. Getting rid of waste products is called
   a. transport.   **b.** excretion.   **c.** response.   **d.** ingestion. b
9. A change that causes a response is
   a. a stimulus.   **b.** behavior.   **c.** an adaptation.   **d.** a reaction. a
10. Behaviors that organisms are born with are called
    a. learned behaviors.   **b.** instincts.   **c.** stimuli.   **d.** adaptations. b
11. The ability of an organism to keep conditions inside its body constant is called
    a. homeostasis.   **b.** hibernation.   **c.** migration.   **d.** reproduction. a
12. The idea that living things could be produced from nonliving things is called
    a. asexual reproduction.   **b.** Redi's theory.   **c.** spontaneous generation.   **d.** Pasteur's theory. c

True/False *Write true if the statement is true. If the statement is false, change the underlined term to make the statement true.*

1. Energy is the ability to do <u>work</u>. true
2. Animals often <u>hibernate</u> to find a safe place to reproduce. migrate
3. In <u>budding</u>, new organisms are produced when the parent organism splits in two. fission
4. The waste products of respiration are carbon dioxide and <u>oxygen</u>. water
5. When changes in temperature occur, <u>homeostasis</u> keeps things working properly inside a living thing. true
6. Biologists use <u>six</u> characteristics to classify something as a living thing. true
7. In any environment, living space is <u>unlimited</u>. limited
8. Plant responses usually are <u>faster</u> than animal responses. slower
9. During hibernation, animals live off <u>fat</u> stored in their bodies. true
10. The <u>environment</u> is everything that surrounds a living thing. true
11. Polar bears are <u>adapted</u> to a cold environment. true
12. During hibernation, the body temperature of an animal <u>raises</u>. lowers
13. Budding and fission are two types of <u>sexual</u> reproduction. asexual
14. New living things produced by organisms are called <u>cells</u>. offspring
15. <u>Animals</u> take in some nutrients from the soil. plants

Understanding the Features...

Reading Critically *Use the feature reading selections to answer the following. Page numbers for the features are shown in parentheses.*

1. **Define:** What is an ecologist? (37)
2. **Infer:** Why might people want to clone animals? (43)
3. **List:** What four kinds of compounds are important to living things? (35)
4. What did William Harvey explain? (45)
5. How did Pasteur disprove spontaneous generation? (41)
6. How are cookbooks usually organized? (47)

Interpreting a Diagram *Use the diagram to complete the following.*

👁 **1. Observe:** Which jars attracted flies?

🪓 **2. Analyze:** Which jar is the control?

3. In which jar did maggots grow?

4. Why did maggots not grow in all the jars?

5. Where did the maggots come from?

6. How did the results of this experiment disprove spontaneous generation?

Critical Thinking *Answer each of the following in complete sentences.*

1. Explain: Why is a robot not an organism?

2. How are growing and developing related?

3. What are three products of respiration?

4. Why must living things compete with each other?

5. Infer: Why does sexual reproduction produce offspring that are not exactly like either of their parents?

Finding Out More..

🔺 **1. Organize:** Using library references, find out how animals are adapted to living in the desert and how plants are adapted to living in very cold environments. Write your findings in a report. Include pictures in your report.

2. Experiment: Design an experiment to show how plants respond to light. Place a plant in sunlight with its leaves facing away from the sun. Observe the plant for the next week. Write a laboratory report describing your observations.

👁 **3. Observe:** Choose five kinds of organisms that live in your neighborhood. Construct a chart explaining two ways that each organism is adapted to its environment.

4. Communicate: Using library references, research the work of the Italian scientist Lazzaro Spallanzani. Find out about his experiment to test spontaneous generation. Explain Spallanzani's experiment in an oral report.

ECOLOGY

CONTENTS

STUDY HINT Before beginning Unit 3, write the title of each lesson on a sheet of paper. Below each title, write a short paragraph explaining what you think each lesson is about.

3-1 What is ecology?

TechTerms

- **ecology** (ee-KAHL-uh-jee): study of living things and their environments
- **environment** (in-VY-run-munt): everything that surrounds an organism
- **interact:** to act upon each other

Ecology Everything that surrounds a living thing makes up its **environment** (in-VY-run-munt). Living things are affected by their environments. Living things also have an effect on their environments.

The study of living things and their environments is **ecology** (ee-KAHL-uh-jee). Scientists who study ecology are ecologists. Ecologists study the relationships between living things and their environments. They also study how living things are adapted, or suited, to their environments.

▶ **Define:** What is ecology? study of living things and their environments

Importance of the Environment All living things need materials to carry out their life processes. Organisms get all the materials they need from their environments. Some materials, called nutrients (NOO-tree-unts), are used by living things for growth and energy. Green plants get nutrients and water from soil. They take carbon dioxide from the air. They use sunlight and carbon dioxide to grow and make food for energy. Plants also need oxygen. Some animals get nutrients and energy by eating plants. Some animals eat other animals. Most animals get oxygen from the air. Fish get oxygen that is dissolved in water.

▶ **List:** What are some materials that organisms get from their environment? nutrients, water, oxygen, energy

Interactions Look at Figure 1. It shows a plain in Africa. There are many different kinds of organisms that live on the plain. The plain is the environment for these organisms. The organisms on the plain **interact,** or act upon each other. The organisms also interact with the nonliving parts of the environment. The gnus (NOOS) eat grasses growing in soil. The wastes produced by the gnus enrich the soil. The enriched soil makes the grasses grow better. The grasses, soil, and gnus each have an effect on each other. An interaction also takes place between the lions and the gnus. Lions eat gnus. If there are many lions hunting gnus, the number of gnus will go down. With fewer gnus, some lions will die from a lack of food. As a result, the number of lions will go down.

▶ **Infer:** What will happen to the number of gnus if the number of lions goes down? The number of gnus will go up again.

Figure 1 African plain

LESSON SUMMARY

- Everything that surrounds a living thing makes up its environment.
- Ecology is the study of the relationships between living things and their environments.
- Living things get all the materials that they need from their environments.
- Organisms interact with each other and with the nonliving parts of their environments.

CHECK *Answer the following.*

1. What is the study of living things and their environments? ecology

2. What materials do living things use for growth and energy? nutrients

3. What specialists study the relationships between living things and their environments? ecologists

Complete the following.

4. Plants use sunlight and _____ to grow and make food. carbon dioxide

5. All the organisms in an environment _____ with each other. interact

APPLY *Complete the following.*

6. What materials do you get from your environment? oxygen, food, water; accept all logical answers

7. **Infer:** What need would a green plant not be able to get growing in a dark cellar? sunlight

Skill Builder

Classifying One interaction in an environment is predator and prey. Use a dictionary to find out what the terms "predator" and "prey" mean. Use this information to classify the organisms in each pair as either the predator or the prey.

1. lion, zebra
2. fly, frog
3. snake, rabbit
4. robin, worm
5. mouse, cat
6. cheetah, antelope

CAREER IN LIFE SCIENCE

AIR POLLUTION TECHNICIAN

Do you enjoy being outdoors? Are you good at putting things together? Can you think like a detective to solve problems? If you answered yes to these questions, you might enjoy a career as an air pollution technician. Air pollution technicians study the chemical make up of air samples. They perform tests on the air samples to identify the kinds of pollutants (puh-LOOT-unts) in the air. Pollutants are harmful substances that enter the environment. Air pollution technicians keep careful records of the test results. They also analyze the test data. They write reports that summarize their findings. Sometimes, they suggest ways to remove a pollutant from the air.

Air pollution technicians work outdoors when collecting air samples. They work in a laboratory to test the samples. The technicians must have good mathematics and science skills. They also must be able to communicate their findings in written reports. Most air pollution technicians have a two-year degree from a technical school.

3-2 What is an ecosystem?

▶ Describe the parts of an ecosystem.

TechTerms

- **community:** all the populations that live in a certain place
- **ecosystem** (EE-koh-sis-tum): living and non-living things in an environment, together with their interactions
- **population:** group of the same kind of organism living in a certain place

Populations A **population** is all of the same kind of organism living in a certain place. Different populations may live in the same environment. Look at the rotting log. There are five mushrooms growing on the log. These five mushrooms make up one population of the log. Count the number of mice living in the log. There are four. The mouse population is four.

👁 **Observe:** What is the fern population on the rotting log? 6

Communities All the populations living on the rotting log make up a **community.** A community is all the populations that live in a certain place. It includes all the different kinds of living things that live together.

▶ **Define:** What is a community? all the populations that live in a certain place

Ecosystem The organisms in a community interact with the nonliving parts of the environment. The organisms in the community also inter-

act with each other. The living and nonliving things in an environment, together with their interactions, make up an **ecosystem** (EE-koh-sis-tum).

There are many kinds of ecosystems. They are different sizes and have different makeups. An ecosystem can be as large as a desert or as small as a rotting log. Ecosystems can be rivers, lakes, or ponds. Even a puddle of water can be an ecosystem.

▶ **Identify:** What is an ecosystem? living and nonliving things in an environment together with their interactions

A Self-Supporting Unit An ecosystem is a self-supporting unit. Four processes occur in an ecosystem to make it self-supporting.

- **Production of Energy** The sun is the source of energy in most ecosystems.
- **Transfer of Energy** Energy is transferred from the sun to plants that make their own food. The stored energy in plants is transferred to animals that eat the plants. Energy is transferred to other animals when they eat the plant-eating animals.
- **Breaking Down of Materials** When organisms die, their bodies decompose, or break down. The chemicals are reused by other living things.
- **Recycling** The materials needed by organisms in an ecosystem are recycled, or used over and over.

▶ **List:** What are the four processes that make an ecosystem self-supporting? production of energy, transfer of energy, breaking down of materials, recycling

► A population is made up of all organisms of the same kind that live in a certain place.

► All the populations that live in a certain place make up a community.

► An ecosystem is made up of the living and nonliving parts of an environment together with their interactions.

► Ecosystems have different sizes and makeups.

► An ecosystem is a self-supporting unit.

CHECK *Complete the following.*

1. All the different kinds of organisms that live in a pond make up a _____ . community

2. All the living and nonliving things in an environment together with their interactions make up _____ . an ecosystem

3. In most ecosystems, the major source of energy is the _____ . sun

4. When organisms die, their bodies _____ . decompose

5. When animals eat green plants, the stored _____ in the plants is transferred. energy

APPLY *Answer the questions about the pond shown.*

6. **Measure:** How many different populations live in the pond?

7. **Observe:** What is the turtle population?

8. Explain why the pond is an ecosystem.

InfoSearch ....

Read the passage. Ask two questions that you cannot answer from the information in the passage.

Commensalism Different kinds of relationships exist between organisms in an ecosystem. Any relationship between two different organisms in which one organism is helped and the other organism is unaffected is called commensalism (kuh-MEN-sul-izm). Orchids growing on trees is an example of commensalism. The orchids have a place to grow with lots of sunlight. The trees are neither harmed nor helped.

SEARCH: Use library resources to find answers to your questions.

SCIENCE CONNECTION ◆○◆○◆○◆○◆○◆○◆○◆○◆○◆○◆○◆○◆○◆○◆

THE GAIA HYPOTHESIS

About 3.5 percent of Earth's oceans is made up of salt. Oceans get salt from rainwater. The rainwater picks up salt from soil and carries it into the oceans. This process has been going on for millions of years. Yet, the oceans do not get saltier. Keeping the salt content at 3.5 percent is good for organisms that live in the oceans. Even a small increase in salt content would be deadly to most kinds of ocean life.

The British scientist James Lovelock has a theory to explain why the salt content of the oceans does not change. He thinks the earth acts like a living organism. He named this organism *Gaia*. The name comes from the Greek goddess *Gaia* or Mother Earth. Lovelock's ideas are called the Gaia Hypothesis.

According to the Gaia Hypothesis, living things on Earth interact with nonliving things. These interactions have kept Earth's environment almost the same for millions of years. According to Lovelock, this interaction has made Earth suitable for life for almost 4 billion years.

3-3 What are habitats and niches?

Objective ▶ Explain how organisms may have the same habitat but not the same niche.

TechTerms

- ▶ **habitat** (HAB-i-tat): place where an organism lives
- ▶ **niche** (NICH): organism's role, or job, in its habitat

Habitat The place where an organism lives is its **habitat** (HAB-i-tat). The habitat of an organism has the food and water the organism needs to live. An organism's habitat also provides shelter and a place to reproduce.

There are many different kinds of habitats. Habitats can be very large or very small. There are land habitats and water habitats. An entire ocean is the habitat of a whale. The habitat of a woodpecker is the trees in a forest. An anthill also is a habitat.

▶ *Infer:* **What is your habitat?** home

Niche What is your role or job in life? Did you answer that you are a student? Student is the job or role that you do where you live. Organisms also have jobs or roles in their communities. The job or role of each organism is its **niche** (NICH). It includes everything an organism does and everything it needs.

▶ *Identify:* **What is a niche?** job or role an organism has in its community

Different Niches Many kinds of organisms share the same habitat. Tigers and deer both live in the same habitats in Asia. Each kind of organism has different needs and roles in the habitat. Tigers hunt deer and other animals. Deer eat grasses. Tigers have one kind of shelter. Deer have another. The activities of these two kinds of organisms are different. They have the same habitat, but they do not have the same niche.

Two populations cannot have the same niche for very long. For example, one animal may be able to hunt better and also find shelter better than another animal. One animal may be able to run away from its enemies faster than another animal. The population of animals that hunt or run better will survive and reproduce. After a while, members of the other populations will be crowded out.

▶ *Infer:* **Do a lobster and a starfish share the same habitat? The same niche?** yes; no

- The place where an organism lives is its habitat.
- There are many different kinds of habitats.
- An organism's niche is its role or job in its habitat.
- Organisms can share the same habitat.
- If two populations share the same niche, the population best-suited to the role will survive and reproduce.

CHECK *Complete the following.*

1. The trees in a forest are the _____ of woodpeckers. habitat

2. An organism's habitat has the food and _____ the organism needs to live. water

3. The role of an organism in its habitat is its _____ . niche

Write true if the statement is true. If the statement is false, change the underlined term to make the statement true.

4. An anthill is an example of a <u>niche</u>. habitat

5. If two populations have the same niche, the population <u>best-suited</u> to the niche will survive and reproduce. true

APPLY *Complete the following.*

6. **Predict:** Two populations of moths live in the same habitat. They will share the same niche. What will happen to these populations?

7. **Infer:** The habitat of a rattlesnake is the hot, dry desert. Could this organism live in a cold, Arctic habitat? Why?

Classify: *In which kind of habitat do each of the organisms listed below live—salt water, fresh water, air, or land?*

8. pigeon	11. water lily	14. bat
9. shark	12. seaweed	15. squirrel
10. garter snake	13. guppy	

Skill Builder

Communicating Construction of a 116 million dollar dam was stopped in the mid-1980s because of a population of tiny fishes called snail darters. The dam was being built on a river in Tennessee. The river was the only habitat for the fish. After several years, it was decided to finish building the dam after all. The dam is expected to change the environmental conditions of the river. What do you think is the fate of the snail darter? Would you have let the dam be built? Write an essay supporting your answers.

LEISURE ACTIVITY

NATURE PHOTOGRAPHY

Do you enjoy taking pictures? Are you interested in plants and animals? Do you like to take hikes and camp outdoors? If you answered yes to these questions, you may enjoy nature photography as a hobby. All you need to begin taking nature photographs is a 35-mm camera. Depending upon the kinds of pictures you want to take, you also may need different kinds of lenses.

You should learn about animals you wish to photograph. You should know where the animal lives, where it sleeps, and what the animal eats. You also should learn how to move quietly so that you do not scare animals away.

State and national parks, recreation areas, seashores, and wildlife preserves all are great places for photographing plants and animals. Nature photographs also can be taken in your own yard. Just put out some food for small animals, such as squirrels and birds. Keep a safe distance from the food. When the animals come to eat, snap away!

Objective ▶ Recognize why organisms live where they do.

TechTerms

▶ **carrying capacity:** largest amount of a population that can be supported by an area

▶ **limiting factors:** conditions in the environment that put limits on where an organism can live

▶ **range** (RAYNJ): area where a type of animal or plant population is found

Limiting Factors Certain conditions in the environment limit where an organism can live. These conditions are called **limiting factors.** Suppose a plant needs warm temperatures and a lot of water. It cannot live where it is cold and dry. Temperature and amount of water are limiting factors for the plant. Other limiting factors for plants are the amount of sunlight and the type of soil. Animals also are limited by conditions in the environment. Limiting factors for animals include temperature, water, food supply, and shelter.

▷ *List:* What are four limiting factors for plants? temperature, moisture, sunlight, soil type

Plants as Limiting Factors The number of green plants in a community is a limiting factor for the animals in the community. Suppose many green plants in a meadow died. Some of the mice that eat the plants would starve. With fewer mice

to eat, some of the owls also would starve. Even though owls do not eat plants, the number of owls is affected by the number of plants. The sizes of animal populations are limited by the sizes of plant populations.

▷ *Predict:* How would the number of mice and owls change if more plants grew than usual? The populations of mice and owls would also grow.

Carrying Capacity The largest amount of a population that can be supported by an area is the area's **carrying capacity.** An area has different carrying capacities for different populations. When a population becomes too large, some of its members must move. They must find a similar habitat with fewer organisms. The spread of organisms from one area to another is called dispersal (dis-PUR-sul). Many animals have no trouble dispersing. They move by walking, running, crawling, swimming, or flying.

▷ *Define:* What is carrying capacity? largest amount of a population that can be supported by an area

Range The area where a kind of population lives is called its **range** (RAYNJ). The size of an organism's range is determined by its limiting factors. For example, black bears can eat a large variety of foods. As a result, the range of black bears is large. Giant pandas eat only bamboo. The range of the giant panda is very small.

▷ *Relate:* What is the relationship between an organism's diet and its range? The more variety in an organism's diet, the greater its range.

► All organisms are limited by conditions in the environment.

► Animal populations are limited by the number of green plants in an area.

► The largest amount of a population that can be supported by an area is the area's carrying capacity.

► The range of a population is determined by its limiting factors.

CHECK *Choose the word that completes each sentence.*

1. Carrying capacity is the (largest/smallest) amount of a population that can be supported by an area. largest

2. The (type/size) of a range is determined by an organism's limiting factors. size

3. The size of all other populations in the area is limited by the (plant/animal) populations. plant

4. A limiting factor for plants is the amount of (sunlight/shelter). sunlight

APPLY *Complete the following.*

5. **Infer:** Why are humans able to live almost anywhere on Earth?

6. **Relate:** Do changes in the size of plant populations have an effect on humans? Explain.

InfoSearch

Read the passage. Ask two questions that you cannot answer from the information in the passage.

Territories A territory (TER-uh-towr-ee) is an area that an animal claims as its own against other animals of the same kind. Having a specific territory gives an animal the space it needs to get food and reproduce. Some kinds of animals claim a territory as a group. Wolves hunt in groups called packs. Each pack claims and protects its own territory.

SEARCH: Use library references to find answers to your questions.

SCIENCE CONNECTION

WORLD POPULATION GROWTH

About 20,000 years ago, almost 3 million people lived on Earth. Today the population of the United States is about 250 million. The total world population is over 5 billion. How can the earth carry a population that is so much larger than it was only 20,000 years ago?

People began to grow crops about 10,000 years ago. The world population increased rapidly after people began to grow crops. The development of agriculture increased the carrying capacity of the land. Land used for growing crops can support more people than land used for hunting.

In modern times, methods of food production have improved. Medical advances have allowed more people to live longer. Increased population has resulted in limited food supplies for some areas on Earth.

No one knows the total carrying capacity of the earth. Some areas may be close to their carrying capacities now. As a result, population growth is a serious problem facing the world today.

5 Billion +

3-5 What cycles take place in nature?

Objective ▶ Explain the oxygen-carbon dioxide cycle and the nitrogen cycle.

TechTerms

- ▶ **cycle** (SY-kul): something that happens over and over in the same way
- ▶ **nitrogen-fixing bacteria:** bacteria that can use nitrogen in soil to make nitrogen compounds

Cycles in Nature There are many cycles (SY-kuls) in nature. A **cycle** is something that happens over and over in the same way. Rocks move through a cycle changing from one kind of rock to another. Water, oxygen, carbon dioxide, and nitrogen also cycle through the environment.

▶ **List:** What are five substances that cycle through the environment? rocks, water, oxygen, carbon dioxide, and nitrogen

The Water Cycle Water falls to the earth as rain, snow, sleet, and hail. Some of this water flows to oceans, lakes, and rivers. Some water evaporates, or changes to a gas. Some water soaks into the ground and is used by plants. All animals drink water. Water is given off by animals and plants during respiration. This water evaporates into the air.

▶ **Identify:** How does water get into the air? It evaporates from bodies of water on the earth, and is given off by plants and animals.

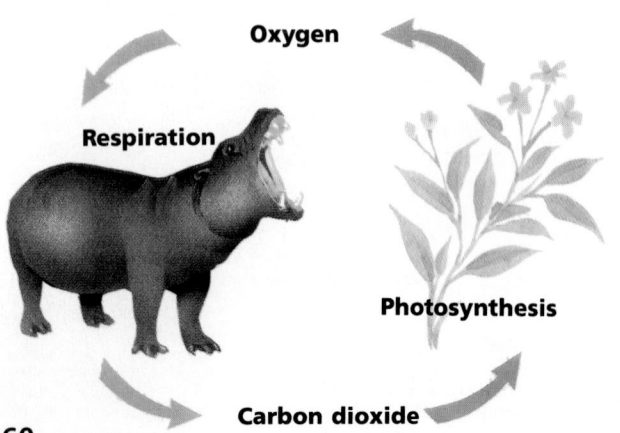

Oxygen-Carbon Dioxide Cycle Oxygen and carbon dioxide cycle through an ecosystem. During photosynthesis, plants take in carbon dioxide and give off oxygen. Animals use oxygen during respiration. They give off carbon dioxide. Respiration and photosynthesis work together to recycle oxygen and carbon dioxide in an ecosystem.

▶ **Name:** What organisms add oxygen to the air? plants

Nitrogen Cycle The using and reusing of nitrogen in an ecosystem is called the nitrogen cycle. Animals and plants need nitrogen to make proteins. However, plants and animals cannot use the nitrogen in the air. Special bacteria called **nitrogen-fixing bacteria** change nitrogen gas into

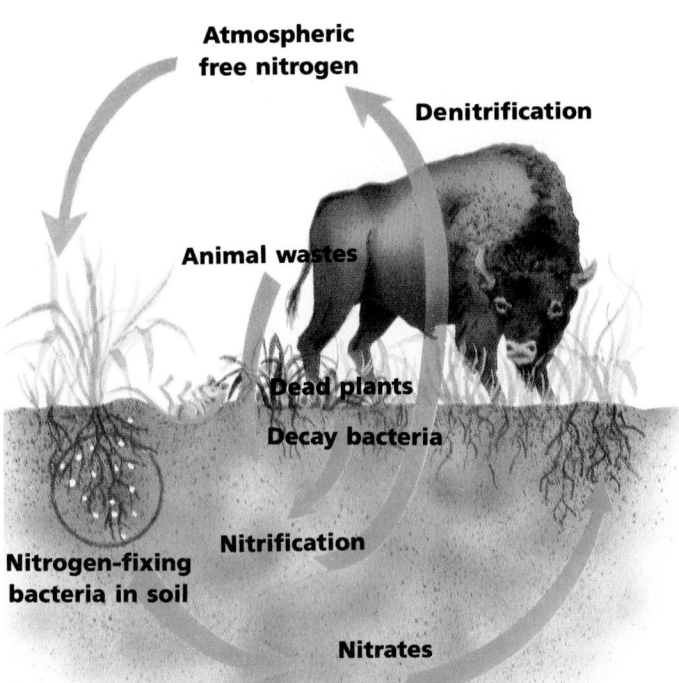

nitrogen compounds. These nitrogen compounds are called nitrites (NY-tryts) and nitrates (NY-trayts). Nitrates and nitrites can be used by living things. When living things die, decay bacteria break down the compounds. Nitrogen gas is given off.

▶ **Define:** What are nitrogen-fixing bacteria? bacteria that change nitrogen gas into nitrogen compounds

LESSON SUMMARY

- ► Rocks, oxygen, carbon dioxide, water, and nitrogen cycle through the environment.
- ► Water is cycled through the environment, falling as a liquid and then evaporating as a gas.
- ► Oxygen and carbon dioxide are cycled through the environment by the processes of photosynthesis and respiration.
- ► Nitrogen-fixing bacteria change nitrogen gas into compounds that can be used by living things.

CHECK *Write true if the statement is true. If the statement is false, change the underlined term to make the statement true.*

1. Something that happens over and over in the same way is called a <u>cycle</u>. true
2. Water is given off by plants and animals during <u>photosynthesis</u>. respiration
3. During photosynthesis, plants take in carbon dioxide and give off <u>oxygen</u>. true
4. Animals take in <u>carbon dioxide</u> during respiration. oxygen
5. Animals and plants need nitrogen to make <u>food</u>. proteins

6. Nitrates and nitrites are two kinds of <u>nitrogen compounds</u>. true

APPLY *Complete the following.*

7. **Hypothesize:** If all the green plants on Earth died, what would happen to the oxygen content of air?
8. **Relate:** How are plants and animals dependent upon each other?
9. Animals give off nitrogen as liquid and solid wastes. What do you think happens to this nitrogen?

InfoSearch...

Read the passage. Ask two questions that you cannot answer from the information in the passage.

Composition of Air Air is a mixture of gases. Gases in the air include nitrogen, oxygen, and carbon dioxide. Nitrogen makes up about 78% of air. Oxygen makes up about 21% of air. Argon, a gas used to make electric light bulbs, makes up a little less than 1% of air. Other gases, including carbon dioxide, make up the remaining 0.03% of air.

SEARCH: Use library references to find answers to your questions.

SCIENCE CONNECTION ◆○◆○◆○◆○◆○◆○◆○◆○◆○◆○◆○◆○◆○◆○◆○◆○◆○◆○◆

THE ROCK CYCLE

Rocks are classified into three groups. Rocks formed when liquid volcanic rock cools are classified as igneous (IG-nee-us) rocks. Rocks formed when rock particles are cemented together are classified as sedimentary rocks. Metamorphic rocks are formed when heat and pressure change igneous or sedimentary rocks.

Rocks can change from one kind to another. The process by which rocks change form is called the rock cycle. For example, a rock can be broken

apart by wind and water. The pieces of rock may then become cemented together. A sedimentary rock is formed. Great heat and pressure can change the sedimentary rock

into metamorphic rock. If the metamorphic rock is forced deep beneath the earth's surface, it may melt into a liquid. If this liquid rock cools, an igneous rock is formed.

3-6 What are producers and consumers?

Objective ▶ Identify producers and different feeding levels of consumers in an ecosystem.

TechTerms

- ▶ **consumer** (kun-SOO-mur): organism that obtains food by eating other organisms
- ▶ **decomposer** (dee-kum-POHZ-er): organism that breaks down the wastes or remains of other organisms
- ▶ **producer** (pruh-DOOS-ur): organism that makes its own food
- ▶ **scavenger** (SKAV-in-jur): animal that eats only dead organisms

Producers Organisms that make their own food are called **producers** (pruh-DOOS-urz). Producers use energy from the sun to make food. On land, the main producers are plants. The main producers in lakes and oceans are algae (AL-jee).

👁 *Observe:* Name all the producers shown on this page. plants: trees, shrubs, grasses

Consumers Most organisms get food by eating other organisms. An organism that eats other organisms is a **consumer** (kun-SOO-mur). Rabbits eat grass and other plants. Rabbits are primary consumers. A primary consumer is an organism that eats producers. Consumers that eat primary consumers are secondary consumers. Weasels eat small plant-eating animals, such as rabbits. Weasels are secondary consumers. Consumers that eat secondary consumers are tertiary consumers. Hawks eat small meat-eating animals, such as weasels. Hawks are tertiary consumers. Some animals, such as hawks, are both secondary and tertiary consumers. Most people are primary, secondary, and tertiary consumers.

📂 *Classify:* Ducks eat plants and small insects or animals. Are ducks primary, secondary, or tertiary consumers? primary and secondary

Scavengers and Decomposers Some animals feed upon dead animals. These animals are **scavengers** (SKAV-in-jurz). Scavengers eat animals that have died or been killed by other animals. Vultures, hyenas, and certain ants, beetles, and worms are scavengers. Scavengers are both secondary and tertiary consumers. Organisms that break down the wastes or remains of organisms are **decomposers** (dee-kum-POHZ-ers). Decay bacteria are decomposers. Decomposers return materials from dead organisms to the soil.

▬▶ *List:* List three organisms that are scavengers. Accept vultures, hyenas, ants, beetles, worms

▶ Producers are organisms that make their own food.

▶ Consumers get food by eating other organisms.

▶ The three types of consumers are primary consumers, secondary consumers, and tertiary consumers.

▶ Scavengers and decomposers eat or break down the remains and wastes of other organisms.

CHECK *Complete the following.*

1. Secondary consumers are eaten by _____ . tertiary consumers

2. Producers use energy from the _____ to make their own food. sun

3. Organisms that eat the remains of dead animals are _____ . scavengers

4. The producers in lakes and oceans are _____ . algae

5. Organisms that eat only producers are _____ consumers. primary

APPLY *Complete the following.*

6. **Analyze:** What is one way in which organisms in an ecosystem depend upon each other?

7. **Explain:** Give an example of when humans are primary, secondary, or tertiary consumers.

8. **Classify:** The organisms shown in the photograph are tube worms. Tube worms live deep in the ocean. They feed upon bacteria that are able to make their own food using chemicals contained in ocean water. Are tube worms producers or consumers?

Skill Builder

Building Vocabulary Three terms used to describe consumers are "herbivore", "carnivore", and "omnivore". Use a dictionary to identify the meaning of each term. Then, classify the organisms listed as herbivores, carnivores, or omnivores.

1. black bear
2. wolf
3. horse
4. hawk
5. human
6. giraffe
7. cat
8. cow

⁘ TECHNOLOGY AND SOCIETY

HYDROPONICS

Plants use energy from the sun to make food. They also use minerals such as nitrogen and calcium. Most plants get these minerals from soil.

A method of growing plants without soil has been developed. This method is called hydroponics (hy-druh-PAHN-iks). The roots of plants are placed in a special liquid. Minerals the plants need are contained in the liquid. Plants grown this way develop as well as plants grown in soil.

Plants grown by hydroponics are protected from harsh weather and from insect and animal pests. The plants can be checked and cared for more easily than if they were outdoors. In addition, the amounts of minerals provided for the plants can be carefully controlled. Hydroponics is a way of growing crops in areas with poor soil. As people look for new and better ways of growing crops, hydroponics is sure to attract more interest.

3-7 What are food chains, webs, and pyramids?

Objective ▶ Explain and construct models to show how organisms are related by how they get their food.

TechTerms

▶ **energy pyramid** (PIR-uh-mid): way of showing how energy moves through a food chain

▶ **food chain:** way of showing the food relationships among a group of organisms

▶ **food web:** way of showing how food chains are related

Food Chains The organisms in an environment are related by how they get their food. A **food chain** is a way of showing these food relationships. Every organism is part of a food chain.

Figure 1

Figure 1 shows a food chain. The arrows in the food chain show the direction that food and energy move along the chain. This food chain starts with grass seeds. A producer, or its seeds and fruit, always is at the start of a food chain.

▸ *Observe:* In the food chain shown, which organism is eaten by the snake? mouse

Food Webs A **food web** is a more complete way of showing food relationships. A food web shows how a number of food chains are related. Figure 2

shows a food web. Notice that the owl can eat either a field mouse or a frog. Many organisms in a food chain eat more than one type of food. Many organisms also are a food source to more than one organism.

▸ *Observe:* In the food web shown, which organisms eat field mice? hawk, snake, and owl

Energy Pyramids An **energy pyramid** (PIR-uh-mid) shows how energy moves through a food chain. Figure 3 shows an energy pyramid. Notice

Figure 3

Tertiary consumers

Energy from the sun

Some energy lost as heat

Secondary consumers

Primary consumers

Producers

that the producers are at the bottom of the pyramid. The producer layer has most of the food and energy in the pyramid. Animals gain only a small amount of energy from the food they eat. So, as you move up the pyramid, the amount of energy decreases. Less energy means fewer organisms can be supported at each level. The tertiary consumers are at the top of the pyramid. They use the least amount of food and energy of all the organisms in the system.

▬ *Analyze:* Which consumers use more food and energy, primary or secondary consumers? primary consumers

Figure 2

LESSON SUMMARY

- ▶ The organisms in an environment are related by how they get their food.

- ▶ Every organism is linked to other organisms in a food chain.

- ▶ Food webs show how a number of food chains are related.

- ▶ An energy pyramid shows that the amount of energy decreases at each level of a food chain.

CHECK *Complete the following.*

1. A food chain always begins with a ___producer___ .

2. The top of an energy pyramid contains _____ . tertiary consumers

3. Arrows show the flow of _____ in a food chain. energy

4. The relationships between food chains are shown in a _____ . food web

5. The layer of an energy pyramid that has the most food and energy contains _____ . producers

APPLY *Complete the following.*

6. **Infer:** Minnows are small fish that eat plant materials. Bass are large fish that feed upon minnows. Would you expect to find more minnows or bass in a pond? Why?

7. **Analyze:** Which organism in the food chain shown is a producer?

8. **Classify:** Is the butterfly a primary, secondary, or tertiary consumer?

9. **Model:** Draw a food chain that shows a butterfly, a bird, and a plant.

10. **Model:** Draw food chains that include you as a primary, secondary, and tertiary consumer.

Skill Builder

▲ **Modeling** Draw an energy pyramid on a sheet of paper. Decide which of these organisms belong at each level: wolf, grass, snake, rabbit. Label each level of the pyramid with the correct organism.

ACTIVITY

MODELING FOOD CHAINS

You will need 12 index cards.

1. Write the names of the organisms listed in the box on 12 separate index cards.

2. Mix up the cards. Choose six cards.

3. Using as many of the six cards as possible, arrange the cards into a food chain. Record the food chain.

4. Return the cards to the pile. Shuffle the cards.

5. Repeat Steps 3 and 4 as many times as you can for 10 minutes.

Questions

1. How many food chains did you complete?

2. How many organisms were in your longest food chain?

3. **a. Classify:** Which organisms on your cards are producers? **b.** Which organisms on your cards are consumers?

▲ 4. **Organize:** Chose several of your food chains and develop a food web.

ORGANISMS
Tree
Grass
Rabbit
Field Mouse
Snake
Owl
Shrub
Elk
Cricket
Mountain Lion
Hawk
Frog

3-8 What is succession?

Objective ▶ Describe how communities of organisms develop.

TechTerms

▶ **climax** (KLY-maks) **community:** last community in a succession

▶ **succession** (suk-SESH-un): gradual change in organisms that occurs when the environment changes

Succession Environments do not always stay the same. When the environment changes, its populations are slowly replaced by new populations. This slow change in organism populations is called **succession** (suk-SESH-un).

A change in one group of organisms causes a change in another group of organisms. The first populations to change are the plant populations. As the plant populations change, different animal populations move in.

▶ **Identify:** What is succession? gradual change in the organisms of an area

Open Field to Forest Suppose a fire burns a forest to the ground. This disaster causes succession to occur in several stages.

▶ **Open Field** The first organisms to grow in the burnt area are grasses and weeds. They grow from roots and seeds left in the soil. As the grasses grow into a thick field, or meadow, small animals move into the area.

▶ **Shrub Land** Shrubs and trees begin to grow. Since these shade the grasses, some of the original grasses die. More shrubs grow and different kinds of animals move in. A new community replaces the community that lived in the grassy field.

▶ **Pine Forest** Pine trees begin to grow in the area. Since the pine trees shade parts of the area, some of the shrubs die. Eventually, a pine forest develops. The community that lives in the pine forest is different from that of the shrub land.

▶ **Hardwood Forest** Soon hardwood trees, such as oak and maple, begin to grow in the area. They grow taller than the pine trees, so the pine trees do not get as much sunlight. Many pine trees die, and the forest becomes a hardwood forest. A different animal community develops.

Once the hardwood forest has formed, succession stops. The hardwood forest is a **climax** (KLY-maks) **community** or last community in a succession. It will remain in the area until the environment changes again.

👁 **Observe:** How many years did the succession process shown take, from weeds to the climax community? 100

OPEN FIELD   SHRUB LAND   PINE FOREST   HARDWOOD FOREST

0 Years   100 Years

LESSON SUMMARY

► As the environment in an area changes, the plant and animal populations also change.

► Populations change in a series of stages, ending with a climax community.

CHECK *Complete the following.*

1. The first stage of forest succession is the _____ . open field

2. The last stage in a succession is the _____ . climax community

3. The first populations to change in succession are the _____ populations. plant

4. Succession begins after the environment has been _____ . changed

APPLY *Complete the following.*

► 5. **Predict:** Is the climax community the same everywhere?

► 6. **Infer:** Suppose a maple-beech forest burns. Why is it that maples and beeches are not the first community in the succession?

Use the diagram of pond succession to answer the following.

► 7. **Infer:** What is a bog?

8. **Sequence:** A pond could develop into a hardwood forest. List the stages in the development of a hardwood forest in the correct order beginning with a pond.

Health & Safety Tip..........................

Lightning causes many forest fires. However, some of the most damaging forest fires are caused by careless people. Find out what safety precautions people should take when camping or cooking outdoors.

SCIENCE CONNECTION

SEED DISPERSAL

After a forest fire, plants may begin to grow from seeds in the ground. What if there were no seeds in the ground? Plants would still grow because seeds can travel.

Seeds often are carried far from their parent plant. The movement of seeds away from the parent plant is called seed dispersal.

The structure of some fruits helps in the dispersal of their seeds. For example, the coconut fruit floats. It can be carried great distances by water currents. The fruit of the maple tree is shaped like a pair of wings. Maple fruits are easily carried by the wind.

Some fruits are sweet and juicy. Birds and other animals eat these fruits as food. However, the seeds are not digested. They pass through the animal's digestive tract. The seeds are carried in the animal's body and then deposited on the ground.

3-9 What are biomes?

Objective ▶ Describe different biomes.

TechTerms

▶ **biome** (BY-ohm): large region of the earth with particular plant and animal communities

▶ **climate:** overall weather in an area over a long period of time

Biomes The overall weather in an area over a long period of time is the area's **climate.** Climate helps determine the kinds of plants and animals that live in an area. A **biome** (BY-ohm) is a large region of the earth that has characteristic plant and animal communities. Each biome has a different climate.

▶ *Define:* What is a biome? a large region of the earth with characteristic plant and animal communities

Six Major Biomes Particular kinds of animals live in different biomes. Biomes often are named for their most common plants. Earth's land areas are divided into six major biomes.

▶ The *tundra* is found in the far north. The ground is permanently frozen. Mosses, grasses, small flowers and shrubs are the only plants that can survive in the tundra. Animals that live in the tundra include birds, wolves, foxes, and reindeer.

▶ South of the tundra lies an area with a cold climate. Enough rainfall falls there for trees to grow. *Coniferous* (kuh-NIF-uhr-us) *forests* made up of evergreens cover the area. Many animals such as moose, squirrels, rabbits, and beavers live in the coniferous forest biome.

▶ South of the coniferous forests is a region with a moderate climate. This area has a long growing season followed by a cold winter. *Deciduous* (di-SIJ-oo-wus) *forests* grow here. Unlike the needles of evergreens, the leaves of deciduous trees fall off in the winter. Many kinds of birds and animals live in the deciduous forest biome.

■ Tundra

■ Taiga

■ Grassland

■ Deciduous forest

■ Desert

■ Tropical rain forest

▶ *Tropical rain forests* occur in areas near the equator. These regions receive large amounts of rainfall and are hot all year. Tall trees and many kinds of plants grow well in tropical rain forests. Many different animals also live in this biome.

▶ Some areas have a moderate climate but not enough rain for tall trees to grow. These areas are *grasslands.* Large herds of animals feed on the many kinds of grasses that grow in this biome.

▶ *Deserts* form where temperatures are moderate or hot, but where there is very little rain. Very few plants can grow in desert biomes. Still, some kinds of animals such as lizards and coyotes find food and shelter there.

◣ *Analyze:* Look at the biome map. In what biome do you live? Answers may vary.

LESSON SUMMARY

▶ The earth can be divided into biomes, large areas with similar plant and animal communities.

▶ There are six major land biomes: tundra, coniferous forest, deciduous forest, tropical rain forest, grassland, and desert.

CHECK *Write the letter of the term that best completes each statement.*

1. The coldest biome is the
   a. tropical rain forest. **b.** grasslands.
   c. tundra. **d.** coniferous forest. c

2. The driest biome is the
   a. deciduous forest. **b.** tundra.
   c. grasslands. **d.** desert. d

3. The biome that is hot and wet is the
   a. tropical rain forest. **b.** coniferous forest. **c.** deciduous forest. **d.** grasslands. a

4. The biome where large herds of animals live is the
   a. deciduous forest. **b.** grasslands. **c.** tundra. **d.** coniferous forest. b

APPLY *Complete the following.*

▶ 5. **Infer:** Why do more kinds of animals live in the deciduous forest than in the tundra?

6. **Contrast:** Deserts and tropical rain forests may both occur in hot areas. How are these biomes different?

InfoSearch

Read the passage. Ask two questions about the topic that you cannot answer from the information in the passage.

Taiga Another name for the coniferous forest biome is the taiga. The taiga has long, snowy winters. Animals that live in the taiga include moose, lynx, porcupines, and red squirrels. Some of these animals hibernate in winter. Many birds spend the summer in the taiga, feeding on the insects that live there.

SEARCH: Use library references to find answers to your questions.

LEISURE ACTIVITY

LEAF PEEPING

Fall is a beautiful time of year in the deciduous forest biome. As the weather gets cool and crisp, the leaves begin to lose their green color. Autumn colors appear. In some areas, the leaves are so bright that people travel there just to see the fall foliage. These tourists sometimes are called "leaf peepers".

Not all parts of the deciduous forest are good for leaf peeping. Some trees, such as oak trees, do not have colorful autumn leaves. Oak leaves simply turn brown in the fall. Some kinds of maple and birch trees turn bright red and gold. Areas where these trees grow are good spots for leaf peeping. It takes the right kind of tree and the right weather conditions to make colorful leaves.

The New England states are a great place for leaf peeping. Many tourists visit these states in the fall. Many parts of Pennsylvania, Delaware and Virginia also are good for leaf peeping.

3-10 What are natural resources?

Objective ▶ Distinguish between renewable and nonrenewable natural resources.

TechTerms

- **conservation** (kon-sur-VAY-shun): wise use of natural resources
- **natural resources** (REE-sowrs-ez): materials found in nature that are used by living things
- **nonrenewable resources:** natural resources that cannot be renewed or replaced
- **renewable resources:** natural resources that can be renewed or replaced

Natural Resources Living things use materials found in nature to survive. These materials are called **natural resources** (REE-sowrs-ez). Air and water are natural resources needed by almost all organisms. People use other natural resources such as oil, coal, and gas as fuels.

Classify: What other natural resources can you name? Answers may include soil, forests, and minerals. Accept all logical responses.

Renewable Resources Some natural resources can be reused or replaced. These resources are called **renewable resources.** Air, water, soil, and living things are renewable resources.

Define: What is a renewable resource? resource that can be reused or replaced

Nonrenewable Resources Some natural resources cannot be reused or replaced. These resources are called **nonrenewable resources.** Oil, coal, natural gas, and minerals are examples of nonrenewable resources. Nonrenewable resources need millions of years to form. Once existing supplies of these resources are used up, they cannot be replaced.

Contrast: What is the difference between renewable and nonrenewable resources? Renewable resources can be replaced while nonrenewable resources cannot be replaced.

Conservation The wise use of natural resources is called **conservation** (kon-sur-VAY-shun). Conservation of all natural resources, including renewable resources, is important. Even though renewable resources are replaced by the environment, the supply of these resources is limited. People must be careful not to use renewable resources faster than they can be replaced.

Since nonrenewable resources cannot be replaced, it is especially important to use them wisely. One way of conserving nonrenewable resources is by using energy-efficient products. Driving cars that get more miles per gallon of gasoline is a way of conserving fuel.

Identify: Why is it necessary to conserve renewable resources? so that their supply is not used faster than they can be replaced

LESSON SUMMARY

▶ Organisms use materials found in nature to survive.

▶ Renewable resources can be reused or replaced.

▶ Nonrenewable resources cannot be reused or replaced.

▶ All natural resources must be used carefully and wisely.

CHECK *Complete the following.*

1. Once they are used up, nonrenewable resources _____ be replaced. cannot

2. All organisms use _____ in order to survive. natural resources

3. Oil and gas are examples of _____ natural resources. nonrenewable

4. Sunlight is considered a _____ natural resource. renewable

5. Using natural resources wisely is called _____ . conservation

APPLY *Complete the following.*

6. **Relate:** What are two ways in which you can conserve natural resources?

7. **Infer:** Fuels such as oil and coal are still forming. Why are these fuels considered nonrenewable resources?

8. **Classify:** Classify each thing shown in the drawings on page 70 as a renewable natural resource or a nonrenewable natural resource.

Ideas in Action.................................

IDEA: You use natural resources every day.
ACTION: List five natural resources that you use daily. Describe how you use each resource. Then, describe one way that you could conserve each resource.

Skill Builder....................................

Classifying Write the headings "Renewable" and "Nonrenewable" on a sheet of paper. Classify each of the following resources as renewable or nonrenewable: copper, nutrients, food, oxygen, wood, fish, marble, gasoline, charcoal, methane gas, kerosene, propane gas. If necessary, use library books for reference.

TECHNOLOGY AND SOCIETY

NUCLEAR ENERGY

Nuclear (new-KLEE-ar) energy is the energy released when atoms of uranium are split. The energy released is in the form of heat, which is used to produce steam. The steam turns large turbines that produce electricity.

Some people think that nuclear energy should be used more. There are large supplies of nuclear energy, and it does not pollute the air.

Other people think that nuclear energy is dangerous. Nuclear fuel is radioactive (ray-dee-oh-AK-tiv). An accident at a nuclear power plant can spread radioactive materials over great distances. These materials can harm the environment and the organisms that live there. Another concern is the wastes that are made at nuclear power plants. These wastes remain dangerous for thousands of years. Storing them safely is a problem.

Nuclear power plants also give off large amounts of heat, often into streams and rivers. Many organisms living in these environments can't survive in the heated water.

3-11 What is balance in an ecosystem?

Objective ▶ Recognize that every organism is part of an ever-changing environment.

TechTerms

- ▶ **endangered species** (in-DAYN-jurd SPEE-sheez): kinds of living things that are in danger of dying out
- ▶ **pollution:** release of harmful materials into the environment

Balance An environment is constantly changing. Sometimes, the changes work together to keep the environment the same. Then the environment is balanced. In a balanced environment, the size of a population may go up and then go down. However, the average size of the population remains the same over time. Sometimes, the balance in an environment is upset. A change in the balance of just one species can be harmful to the other organisms in the environment.

▶ *Define:* What is the balance of nature? changes that work together to keep the environment the same

Natural Disturbances Natural causes such as a volcano or forest fire can upset the balance of an environment. These disturbances destroy organisms and their habitats. There is great loss of

wildlife. It may take many years for the environment to return to its original condition.

▶ *Infer:* What other natural disturbances can upset the balance of nature? floods, earthquakes, severe storms

The Role of People People also can upset the balance of an environment. Often the actions of people destroy the habitats of organisms. They cut down forests to create farms and towns. They build dams and dig mines. Unfortunately, the disturbances caused by people are often permanent. The environment cannot return to normal.

People also damage the environment by causing pollution. **Pollution** is the release of harmful substances into the environment. Harmful gases from cars, power plants, and factories pollute the air. Wastes and chemicals pollute the water. Improper disposal of waste materials pollutes the land. All of these acts upset the balance of nature.

▶ *Explain:* How do people upset the balance of nature? by destroying habitats and polluting the environment

Endangered Species Upsets in the balance of an environment have made it hard for many species to survive. Living things in danger of dying out are called **endangered species** (in-DAYN-jurd SPEE-sheez). The whooping crane, giant panda, elephant, and humpback whale are all endangered species.

▶ *Predict:* What will happen to the number of endangered species if people continue to pollute the environment? It will increase.

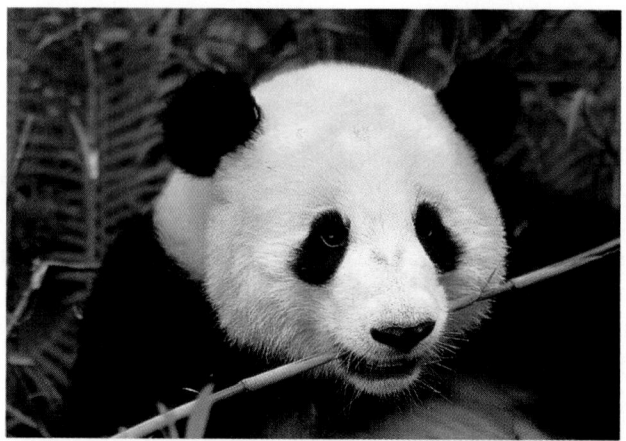

LESSON SUMMARY

- Changes in an ecosystem work to keep it balanced.
- Natural disturbances can upset the balance of an ecosystem.
- People upset the balance of an ecosystem by damaging it or polluting it.
- Endangered species are living things in danger of dying out.

CHECK *Complete the following.*

1. Changes in the balance of an environment can be _____ to organisms that live there. harmful

2. A volcano is an example of a _____ disturbance. natural

3. A species that is in danger of dying out is said to be _____ . endangered

4. Disturbances caused by _____ may be permanent. people

5. The addition of harmful substances to the environment results in _____ . pollution

APPLY *Complete the following.*

6. **Sequence:** Put the following events in the order in which they most likely would occur: species becomes endangered, volcano erupts, species becomes extinct, environment is in balance environment is in balance, volcano erupts, species becomes endangered, species becomes extinct

7. **Relate:** Some states have laws that require deposits on beverage containers. How do these laws help reduce land pollution? People are less likely to throw the containers away and the containers can be recycled.

Ideas in Action

IDEA: Since people cause pollution, everyone must work to reduce or eliminate it.
ACTION: What are some ways that you can help solve the problem of land pollution? proper disposal of waste, return bottles and cans, support recycling efforts

State the Problem

Look closely at the photograph. What problem does the photograph show? How can this problem be corrected?

PEOPLE IN SCIENCE

RACHEL CARSON (1907–1964)

Rachel Carson was a biologist who worked for many years for the United States Fish and Wildlife Service. Her real love, however, was writing. She used her spare time to write about science. In 1952, Rachel Carson received the National Book Award for the best nonfiction book. The book was *The Sea Around Us* which became an international best seller.

Rachel Carson wrote many other books about the sea. She is best remembered for her book *Silent Spring.* This book was published in 1962. In the book, she made people realize that chemical poisons in insect sprays could harm other living things. She made people aware that these poisons could find their way into the plants and animals that people eat.

Rachel Carson was the first person to point out the danger of using pesticides. Pesticides are used to kill unwanted organisms. As a result of her book, chemical insect killers are used more carefully.

Challenges

STUDY HINT Before you begin the Unit Challenges, review the TechTerms and Lesson Summary for each lesson in this unit

TechTerms

biome (68)
carrying capacity (58)
climate (68)
climax community (66)
community (54)
conservation (70)
consumer (62)
cycle (60)
decomposer (62)
ecology (52)

ecosystem (54)
endangered species (72)
energy pyramid (64)
environment (52)
food chain (64)
food web (64)
habitat (56)
interact (52)
limiting factors (58)
natural resources (70)

niche (56)
nitrogen-fixing bacteria (60)
nonrenewable resources (70)
pollution (72)
population (54)
producer (62)
range (58)
renewable resources (70)
scavenger (62)
succession (66)

TechTerm Challenges

Matching *Write the TechTerm that best matches each description.*

1. living and nonliving parts of an environment together with their interactions ecosystem
2. overall weather in an area climate
3. living things in danger of dying out endangered species
4. to act upon each other interact
5. something that happens over and over in the same way cycle
6. bacteria that change nitrogen into nitrogen compounds nitrogen-fixing bacteria
7. materials found in nature that are used by living things natural resources
8. last community in succession climax community

Applying Definitions *Explain the difference between the words in each pair.* Answers will vary. Accept all logical responses.

1. community, population
2. habitat, niche
3. limiting factors, carrying capacity
4. consumer, producer
5. scavenger, decomposer
6. food chain, food web
7. environment, ecology
8. renewable resources, nonrenewable resources
9. range, biome
10. pollution, conservation
11. food chain, energy pyramid
12. succession, balance

Content Challenges

Multiple Choice *Write the letter of the term or phrase that best completes each statement.*

1. In a food chain, plants are classified as
   a. scavengers. **b.** producers. **c.** consumers. **d.** decomposers. b

2. Organisms at the top of an energy pyramid are
   a. producers. **b.** primary consumers. **c.** scavengers. **d.** tertiary consumers. d

3. Of the following, the only organism that can be a primary, secondary, and tertiary consumer is a
   a. tree. **b.** flower. **c.** human. **d.** grasshopper. c

4. Oil and coal are examples of
   a. renewable resources. **b.** endangered species. **c.** nonrenewable resources. **d.** biomes. c

5. Materials used by living things for growth and energy are
   a. nutrients. **b.** pollutants. **c.** scavengers. **d.** bacteria. a

6. The major source of energy for most ecosystems is
   a. plants.　**b.** algae.　**c.** uranium.　**d.** the sun. d

7. An anthill is an example of a
   a. biome.　**b.** habitat.　**c.** niche.　**d.** succession. b

8. The spread of organisms from one area to another is called
   a. succession.　**b.** climate.　**c.** carrying capacity.　**d.** dispersal. d

9. When water evaporates, it changes to
   a. a liquid.　**b.** a solid.　**c.** a gas.　**d.** rain. c

10. Two processes involved in the oxygen-carbon dioxide cycle are respiration and
    a. digestion.　**b.** photosynthesis.　**c.** evaporation.　**d.** excretion. b

11. Algae are classified as
    a. decomposers.　**b.** producers.　**c.** consumers.　**d.** scavengers. b

12. The tundra and deciduous forest are
    a. biomes.　**b.** climax communities.　**c.** climates.　**d.** niches. a

13. The first population to change in succession are the
    a. consumers.　**b.** scavengers.　**c.** producers.　**d.** bacteria. c

14. Tropical rain forests are located
    a. near the equator.　**b.** north of the coniferous forest.　**c.** north of the grasslands.　**d.** in deserts. a

True/False *Write true if the statement is true. If the statement is false, change the underlined term to make the statement true.*

1. An organism that eats grass is a <u>tertiary</u> consumer. primary

2. Vultures, hyenas, and ants are <u>decomposers</u>. scavengers

3. Living things are <u>renewable</u> resources. true

4. The climate of the tundra is <u>cold</u> and dry. true

5. The climate of the desert is warm and <u>wet</u>. dry

6. The number of plants in a community is a <u>limiting factor</u> for the community. true

7. Nitrogen-fixing bacteria are part of the <u>water</u> cycle. nitrogen

8. The organisms at the bottom of an energy pyramid are <u>tertiary consumers</u>. producers

9. The greatest amount of energy is at the <u>top</u> of an energy pyramid. bottom

10. Both renewable and <u>nonrenewable</u> resources should be conserved. true

11. The main producers in the oceans are the <u>fishes</u>. algae

12. During succession an ecosystem <u>is</u> balanced. is not

13. The movement of energy in an ecosystem can be shown by both a <u>food chain</u> and an energy pyramid. true

14. The largest population that can be supported by an area is the area's <u>range</u>. carrying capacity

Understanding the Features..

Reading Critically *Use the feature reading selections to answer the following. Page numbers for the features are shown in parentheses.*

1. **Define:** What are pollutants? (53)
2. What percentage of the earth's oceans is made up of salt? (55)
3. **Infer:** Why is it important for animal photographers to learn about the animals they wish to photograph? (57)

4. **Generalize:** How is the population of the earth changing? (59)
5. **Identify:** What are the three classes of rocks? (61)
6. **Define:** What is hydroponics? (63)
7. **Hypothesize:** How is seed dispersal helpful in succession? (67)
8. **Identify:** In which time of year is leaf peeping done? (69)
9. **Identify:** What fuel is used for nuclear energy? (71)
10. **Infer:** In what branch of science do you think Rachel Carson worked? (73)

Concept Challenges..

Interpreting a Diagram *Use the diagram to complete the following.*

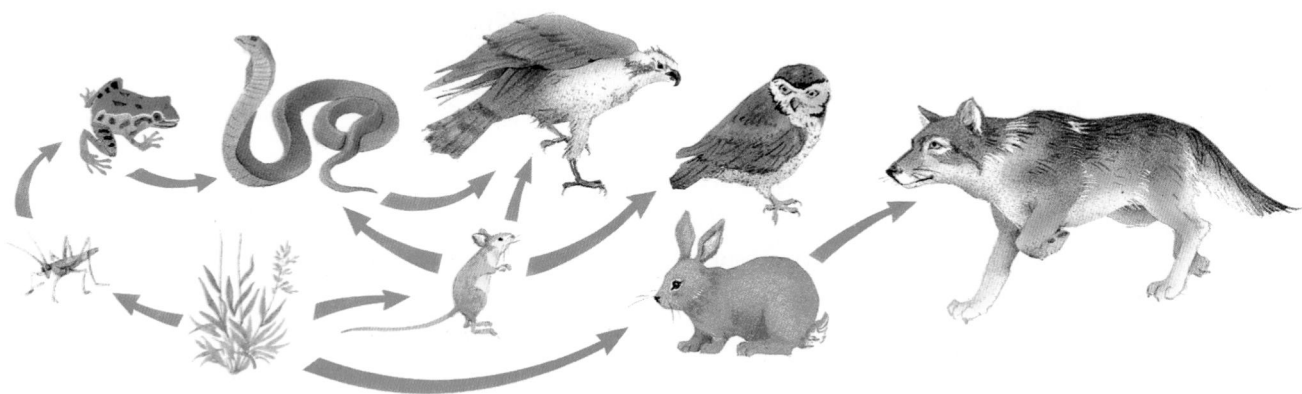

1. What is shown in the diagram?
2. **Classify:** Which organism in the diagram is a producer?
3. **Classify:** Which organisms in the diagram are primary consumers?
4. **Classify:** Which organisms in the diagram are secondary consumers?
5. **Classify:** Which organisms in the diagram are tertiary consumers?
6. What does a food web show?
7. **Model:** Draw one of the food chains shown in the diagram.
8. **List:** Name three organisms that could replace the producer shown in the food chain.

Critical Thinking *Answer each of the following in complete sentences.*

1. **Model:** Make an energy pyramid using one of the food chains shown in the diagram above.
2. **Compare:** How is a food chain similar to an energy pyramid?
3. **Classify:** Some bacteria are able to make their own food using chemicals from their environ- ments. Would you classify these bacteria as producers or consumers? Explain.
4. **Contrast:** How do scavengers differ from decomposers?
5. **Predict:** What would happen if decomposers did not break down the remains of dead organisms?

Finding Out More..

1. **Organize:** Make a list of twenty organisms that live in your community. In a table, classify each organism as a producer or a consumer.
2. **Model:** Cut out pictures of twenty kinds of plants and animals from magazines. Use the pictures to make a food web.
3. **Research:** Find out the names of two animals that are considered endangered. Use library resources to find out what is being done to save these animals.
4. **Organize:** Make a poster that shows how five kinds of natural resources can be conserved.

CELLS, TISSUES, AND ORGANS

CONTENTS

STUDY HINT Before beginning Unit 4, scan through the lessons in the unit looking for words that you do not know. On a sheet of paper, list these words. Work with a classmate to try to define each word on your list.

4-1 What are cells?

Objective ▶ State the cell theory in your own words.

TechTerms

▶ **cell:** basic unit of structure and function in living things

▶ **theory** (THEE-uh-ree): idea that explains something and is supported by data

Cells A brick house is made up of many bricks. A brick is the basic unit of structure of a brick house. The basic unit of structure in living things is a **cell.** All living things are made up of one or more cells. It is also the basic unit of function. Cells carry out all life processes. For example, a cell takes in food and breaks the food down. It breaks down a simple sugar called glucose (GLOO-kohs) to produce energy. This life process is called cellular respiration (res-puh-RAY-shun).

▶ *Define:* **What is a cell?** basic unit of structure and function in living things

Discovery of Cells The first person to observe cells was Robert Hooke. Hooke was an English scientist. He used a compound microscope to look at thin slices of cork. Cork is found in some plants. The cork seemed to be made up of many small boxes. Each box looked like a small room with walls around it. The boxes reminded Hooke of the rooms in which monks slept. These rooms were called cells. Hooke named the structures that made up the cork "cells."

Figure 1 Cork cells

Figure 2 Three kinds of cells

Hooke saw only dead plant cells in cork. Anton van Leeuwenhoek (AN-tun van LAY-vun-hook) was the first person to observe living cells. Van Leeuwenhoek was a Dutch lensmaker. In 1675, he saw single-celled organisms in a drop of pond water. These living things were microscopic. They could not be seen without a microscope.

▶ *Name:* **Who was the first person to see cells?** Robert Hooke

Cell Theory By 1800, better microscopes were being made. Many plants and animals were studied. Scientists had many ideas about cells. In the mid-1800s, these ideas were put together as a **theory** (THEE-uh-REE). A theory is an idea that explains something. The ideas in a theory are supported by data over and over. The theory that was developed is the cell theory. The cell theory states:

▶ All living things are made up of one or more cells.

▶ Cells are the basic units of structure in living things, and cells carry on all life processes.

▶ Cells come only from other living cells.

▶ *Restate:* **What does the cell theory state?** Students should restate the three parts of the theory.

LESSON SUMMARY

▶ Cells are the basic units of structure and function in living things.

▶ The first person to see cells was Robert Hooke.

▶ Anton van Leeuwenhoek was the first person to see living cells.

▶ The cell theory states that all living things are made up of one or more cells, cells are the basic units of structure and function in living things, and cells come only from other living cells.

CHECK *Find the sentence in the lesson that answers each question. Then, write the sentence.*

1. What is a theory?
2. What is the basic unit of structure in living things?
3. Who was the first person to see cells?
4. What did Anton van Leeuwenhoek see in a drop of pond water?
5. Where do cells come from?

APPLY *Complete the following.*

6. **Relate:** What is the relationship between improved microscopes and discoveries about cells?
7. **Apply:** Do cells carry on respiration? Explain.
8. **Apply:** Could new cells be produced by the cork that Hooke observed? Explain.

Ideas in Action

IDEA: Many things have basic units of structure. For example, a brick is the basic unit of structure of a brick house.

ACTION: Name three objects and give the basic units of structure of each object.

Skill Builder

Researching Anton van Leeuwenhoek named the single-celled organisms he observed "animalcules." Using library references, find out what microscopic organisms Leeuwenhoek saw. Why did Leeuwenhoek call these organisms "animalcules?" Write your findings in a report.

PEOPLE IN SCIENCE

SCHLEIDEN (1804–1881) AND SCHWANN (1810–1882)

The cell theory was formed by two scientists—Matthias Schleiden and Theodor Schwann. Schleiden was a German botanist. Schwann was a German zoologist. Although these scientists did not work together, they both contributed to the cell theory.

Matthias Schleiden was a professor of botany from 1839 until 1862. Schleiden studied many plants in order to learn more about living things. In 1838, Schleiden stated that all plants are made up of cells. He also recognized the role of the nucleus in cell division.

Theodor Schwann studied in Berlin. Schwann added to the work of Schleiden. In his work, Schleiden showed that the cell also is the basic unit of structure in animals. Schwann published his ideas in 1839.

Schwann also studied muscle cells and nerve cells in animals. He was the first person to describe the cells that cover and protect nerve cells. These protective cells are called Schwann cells.

4-2 What are the main cell parts?

Objective ▶ Identify the main parts of a cell and describe their functions.

TechTerms

▶ **cell membrane** (MEM-brayn): thin structure that surrounds a cell

▶ **cytoplasm** (SYT-uh-plaz-um): all the living material inside a cell except the nucleus

▶ **nucleus** (NEW-klee-us): control center of a cell

Three Main Parts Most cells have three main parts. The three main parts of the cell are shown in Figure 1. They are the cell membrane (MEM-brayn), the nucleus (NEW-klee-us), and the cytoplasm (SYT-uh-plaz-um).

▶ **Name:** What are the three main parts of a cell? cell membrane, nucleus, cytoplasm

Figure 1 Three main parts of a cell

Nucleus The **nucleus** (NEW-klee-us) of a cell is round or egg-shaped. It usually is near the middle of a cell. The nucleus is darker than the rest of the cell. It is the control center of a cell. It controls all the life processes of a cell. The nucleus also controls cell reproduction.

▶ **Infer:** What would happen to a cell if the nucleus were taken out? The cell would die.

Cytoplasm The **cytoplasm** is all the living material in a cell except the nucleus. The nucleus floats in the cytoplasm. Most of a cell is made up

Figure 2 Nuclei in three cells

of cytoplasm. The cytoplasm looks like the white part of a raw egg. Most of the cell's activities take place in the cytoplasm.

▶ **Describe:** What takes place in the cytoplasm? most of a cell's activities

Cell Membrane The **cell membrane** is a thin structure that surrounds a cell. Sometimes, the cell membrane is called the plasma (PLAZ-muh) membrane. The cell membrane has three important jobs. It protects the inside of a cell. The cell membrane also supports and gives a cell its shape. The cell membrane controls the movement of materials into and out of a cell. Food, water, and oxygen move through the membrane into the cell. Wastes move out of the cell through the cell membrane.

▶ **List:** What are the three jobs of the cell membrane? protection, support, controls the passage of materials in and out of a cell

Figure 3 Skin cell

LESSON SUMMARY

▶ The three main parts of the cell are the cell membrane, the nucleus, and the cytoplasm.

▶ The nucleus is the control center of the cell.

▶ The cytoplasm is all the living material in a cell except the nucleus.

▶ The cell membrane surrounds a cell.

CHECK *Complete the following.*

1. All the life processes of a cell are controlled by the _____ . nucleus

2. The cell membrane also is called the _____ membrane. plasma

3. The three main parts of the cell are the nucleus, the cell membrane, and the _____ . cytoplasm

4. The cell membrane controls the _____ of materials into and out of a cell. movement

5. Most of a cell is made up of _____ . cytoplasm

APPLY *Complete the following.*

6. **Apply:** What part of a cell controls respiration?

7. **Infer:** The nucleus of a cell also is surrounded by a membrane. What do you think the jobs of the nuclear membrane are?

8. **Model:** Label the three main parts of the skin cell in the diagram below.

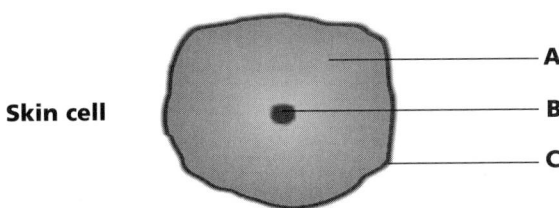

Skin cell — A, B, C

ACTIVITY

MODELING A CELL

You will need a package of gelatin, a grape, a small plastic bag, and a small plastic container.

1. Mix the gelatin by following the directions on the package.
2. Place the bag into the plastic container, so that the open end of the bag extends over the edge of the container.
3. Pour some gelatin into the plastic bag. Let it cool.
4. Before the gelatin hardens, put a grape in the center of the gelatin. Let the gelatin harden.

Questions

1. **Model:** Draw a picture of your cell model. Label the parts.
2. **Relate:** What cell part is represented by the: **a.** plastic bag? **b.** gelatin? **c.** grape?
3. **a. Compare:** What cell part makes up most of your model? **b.** How does this compare to a real cell?

Plastic bag

Grape

Gelatin

Plastic container

4-3 What are other cell parts?

Objective ▶ Name and describe the functions of the parts of a cell.

TechTerms

- ▶ **mitochondria** (myt-uh-KAHN-dree-uh): rice-shaped structures that produce energy for a cell
- ▶ **organelles** (or-guh-NELS): small structures in the cytoplasm that do special jobs
- ▶ **ribosomes** (RY-buh-sohms): small round structures that make proteins
- ▶ **vacuoles** (VAK-yoo-wohls): liquid-filled spaces in the cytoplasm

Organelles You can compare a cell to a factory. There are many machines in a factory. Each machine has a special job. The machines work together to keep the factory working. The "machines" of a cell are its **organelles** (or-guh-NELS). Organelles are small structures that float in the cytoplasm. Each organelle has a special job to do. They keep the cell working properly.

▶ **Define:** What are organelles? small structures in the cytoplasm that have special jobs

Mitochondria One kind of organelle is the **mitochondria** (myt-uh-KAHN-dree-uh). Mitochondria are small, rice-shaped structures. In fact, they are so small they can be seen only with an electron microscope. Mitochondria are the "powerhouses" of the cell. They break down food to make energy for the cell. The energy is used by the cell to carry out its life processes.

▶ **Explain:** Why does a cell need energy? to carry out life processes

Vacuoles The **vacuoles** (VAK-yoo-wohls) of a cell are liquid-filled spaces. The spaces are surrounded by a membrane. Vacuoles are like storage bins. They store food and wastes. Some vacuoles store extra water. They pump extra water out of a cell.

▶ **List:** What are three things that are stored in vacuoles? food, wastes, water

Ribosomes Every cell has many small round structures in its cytoplasm. These structures are **ribosomes** (RY-buh-sohms). Ribosomes make proteins. The proteins are needed for growth.

▶ **Infer:** Why is "protein factory" a good name for a ribosome? Ribosomes make proteins.

Transport Tubes Cells have very small networks of tubes in them. The tubes are like a tiny highway system for the cell. Substances in the cell are moved from one organelle to another in these tubes.

▶ **Describe:** What is the job of the transport tubes? to carry substances from one organelle to another

- Cell membrane
- Transport tubes
- Cytoplasm
- Mitochondrion
- Nucleus
- Vacuole
- Ribosomes

LESSON SUMMARY

▶ Organelles are small structures in the cytoplasm.

▶ Mitochondria break down food to produce energy.

▶ Vacuoles are liquid-filled spaces that store food and wastes.

▶ Ribosomes make proteins.

▶ Cells have small networks of transport tubes.

CHECK *Write true if the statement is true. If the statement is false, change the underlined term to make the statement true.*

1. The "powerhouses" of the cell are <u>ribosomes</u>. mitochondria

2. Small structures in the cytoplasm are <u>organelles</u>. true

3. Ribosomes make <u>proteins</u>. true

4. Liquid-filled spaces are <u>mitochondria</u>. vacuoles

5. Ribosomes are small <u>rice-shaped</u> structures. round

APPLY *Complete the following.*

6. **Compare:** Name the organelle that has a job similar to each of these common objects: railroad, cabinets, battery, electric company.

7. **Infer:** Think about the jobs performed by your muscles and your skin. Do you think there are more mitochondria in muscle cells or in skin cells? Explain.

8. **Model:** Draw a diagram of a cell. Label the parts of your diagram.

TECHNOLOGY AND SOCIETY

ELECTRON MICROSCOPES

Most cells can be seen using a light microscope. However, an electron (ih-LEK-tron) microscope is used to see small cell structures. Electron microscopes use electrons to form images of objects. Electrons are negatively charged parts of atoms.

One kind of electron microscope is the transmission electron microscope, or TEM. A TEM sends beams of electrons through the object that is being viewed. The image that you see is two-dimensional. The TEM can magnify objects up to one million times. It is used to study cell parts, such as mitochondria and nuclei. Unfortunately, the TEM cannot be used to study living specimens. The top picture shows a TEM image.

Another type of electron microscope is the scanning electron microscope, or SEM. This type of microscope sends a beam of electrons over the surface of an object. SEM microscopes produce realistic, three-dimensional images. However, only the surfaces of objects can be viewed. The SEM can be used to study some living things. Single-celled organisms are often studied using SEM images. The bottom picture shows an SEM image.

Objective ▶ Compare plant cells and animal cells.

TechTerms

▶ **cellulose** (SEL-yoo-lohs): hard, nonliving material that makes up the cell wall of a plant cell

▶ **cell wall:** outer, nonliving part of a plant cell

▶ **chlorophyll** (KLOR-uh-fil): green material in chloroplasts that is needed for plants to make food

▶ **chloroplast** (KLOR-uh-plast): green structure in a plant cell that contains chlorophyll

Plant + animal cells are basically the same, except plant cells have cell walls + chloroplasts.

Cell Wall All plant cells have a **cell wall.** Animal cells do not have a cell wall. The cell wall surrounds the cell membrane. The cell wall is nonliving. It is made up of a hard material called **cellulose** (SEL-yoo-lohs). Wood is made up mostly of cellulose.

The cell wall has three jobs. It protects a plant cell and gives the cell its shape. It also gives a plant cell support. Large plants, such as trees and bushes, do not need a skeleton because each cell has support from the cell wall.

▮▮▶ **Name:** What substance makes up most of the cell wall? cellulose

Vacuoles The number and size of vacuoles is different in plant and animal cells. Plant cells have only one or two vacuoles. The vacuoles are usually very large. Animal cells have many small vacuoles.

Vacuoles

👁 **Observe:** How many vacuoles does the plant cell have? 2

Chloroplasts Most plant cells have **chloroplasts** (KLOR-uh-plasts). Chloroplasts are round, green structures. They contain a green material called **chlorophyll** (KLOR-uh-fil). Chlorophyll gives a plant its green color. Chlorophyll is very important to plant cells. Plants need chlorophyll to make food. Animal cells do not have chloroplasts or chlorophyll.

▮▮▶ **Explain:** Why are most plants green? They contain chlorophyll.

Compare

Chloroplast
Cell membrane
Transport tubes
Cytoplasm
Mitochondrion
Nucleus
Cell wall
Vacuole
Ribosomes

endoplasmic reticulum **ANIMAL CELL** *These are the main parts of a cell, but not all of them.* **PLANT CELL**

LESSON SUMMARY

▶ All plants have a cell wall.

▶ The cell wall protects a plant cell, and gives the cell its shape and support.

▶ Plant cells have only one or two large vacuoles.

▶ Most plant cells have chloroplasts.

CHECK *Complete the following.*

1. Why do large plants not need a skeleton?

2. What are the three jobs of the cell wall?

3. What are chloroplasts?

4. What is cellulose?

5. How do the vacuoles in animal cells differ from those in plant cells?

6. Why do plants need chlorophyll?

APPLY *Complete the following.*

7. **a. Compare:** How are plant and animal cells alike? **b.** How do plant and animal cells differ?

8. **Analyze:** Which of the following organisms contain cellulose? **a.** pine tree **b.** cow **c.** rabbit **d.** fern **e.** grass **f.** goldfish

9. **Infer:** Is wood mainly a living or a nonliving material? Explain.

InfoSearch..

Read the passage. Ask two questions about the topic that you cannot answer from the information in the passage.

Pigments When sunlight strikes the leaf of a plant, the sunlight is absorbed by special pigments. Pigments are substances that absorb light. Different pigments absorb different wavelengths of light and reflect others. Chlorophyll is the main pigment needed for photosynthesis. Chlorophyll absorbs large amounts of red, orange, and blue light. It reflects yellow and green light. Because chlorophyll reflects yellow and green light, the leaf looks green.

SEARCH: *Use library references to find answers to your questions.*

ACTIVITY

ANALYZING CELLS

You will need a pencil and a sheet of paper.

1. Study photograph A.

2. **Measure:** Count the number of cells in photograph A.

3. Identify the cell parts and structures that you can see in the cells.

4. Study photograph B.

5. **Measure:** Count the number of cells in photograph B.

6. Identify the cell parts and structures that you can see in the cells.

Questions

1. **Compare:** What cell parts and structures are the same in the cells in both photographs?

2. **a. Analyze:** Which cells are plant cells? **b.** Which are animal cells? **c.** How do you know?

3. **a. Measure:** In one plant cell, count the number of chloroplasts. **b. Infer:** Does this cell make food for the plant? **c. Explain:** How do you know?

Photograph A

Photograph B

4-5 What is diffusion?

TechTerms

▶ **diffusion** (dih-FYOO-shun): movement of material from an area where molecules are crowded to an area where they are less crowded

▶ **osmosis** (ahs-MOH-sis): movement of water through a membrane

Molecules and Diffusion A molecule (mahl-uh-KYOOL) is the smallest part of a substance that is still that substance. Molecules are made up of tiny parts called atoms. Molecules are always moving. Most molecules move from places where they are crowded to places where they are less crowded. The movement of molecules from crowded areas to less crowded areas is called **diffusion** (dih-FYOO-shun). For example, if you open a bottle of perfume in a room, the molecules of perfume will diffuse throughout the room. In the beaker, ink molecules will spread through the water until the molecules of ink are evenly distributed.

▶ **Identify:** What are molecules made up of? atoms

Diffusion in Cells In order for a cell to carry on its life processes, oxygen and other substances must pass through the cell membrane. Wastes must be removed from the cell. The cell membrane has tiny holes in it. Substances can go in and out of a cell by moving through the holes. Some substances move into and out of a cell by diffusion.

Molecules also move in and out to keep the same amount of a substance on both sides of the cell membrane. However, the cell membrane only lets some substances in and out. If a molecule of a substance is too big, it cannot pass through the cell membrane.

▶ **Name:** What cell structure controls the materials that go in and out of a cell? cell membrane

Osmosis The movement of water through a membrane is called **osmosis** (ahs-MOH-sis). Osmosis is a special kind of diffusion. Many substances dissolve in water before they move into a cell. Water moves through a cell membrane by osmosis.

▶ **Predict:** What would happen if water kept entering a cell and no water left the cell? The cell would burst.

Oxygen molecules

Oxygen molecules diffuse into cell

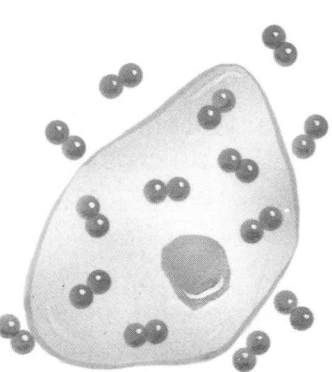

LESSON SUMMARY

▶ The movement of molecules from crowded areas to less crowded areas is called diffusion.

▶ Diffusion in a cell occurs when substances move in and out of a cell.

▶ The cell membrane lets only some substances in and out of a cell.

▶ Osmosis is the movement of water through a membrane.

CHECK *Complete the following.*

1. Movement of molecules from crowded areas to less crowded areas is called _____ . diffusion

2. The movement of water through a membrane is called _____ . osmosis

3. The _____ controls what substances pass in and out of a cell. cell membrane

4. Many substances dissolve in _____ before entering a cell. water

APPLY *Complete the following.*

5. **Hypothesize:** Will a teaspoon of salt dissolve more quickly in a glass of fresh water or a glass of salt water? Explain.

6. **Predict:** In which direction will carbon dioxide move if the amount of carbon dioxide in the fluid outside a cell became greater than the amount of carbon dioxide in the fluid inside the cell?

7. **Explain:** Why would the smell of freshly baked bread eventually fill an entire house?

State the Problem............................

Study the model of diffusion carefully. What is wrong with the model? How could you correct it?

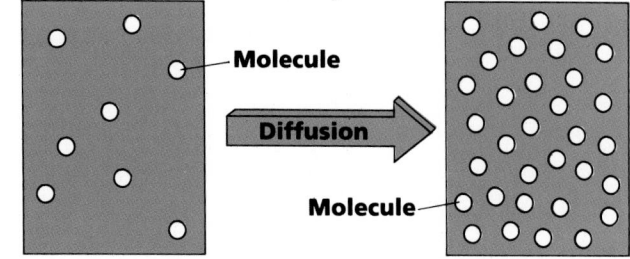

⋅⋅•⋅ ACTIVITY ⋅•⋅⋅•⋅⋅•⋅⋅•⋅⋅•⋅⋅•⋅⋅•⋅⋅•⋅⋅•⋅

MEASURING DIFFUSION IN EGGS

You will need 3 eggs, 3 large plastic cups, vinegar, oil, water, a metric ruler, plastic wrap, a marker, and string.

1. **Measure:** Wrap string around the middle of each egg. Measure the lengths of string. Record the measurements.

2. Repeat step 1 for the lengths of the eggs.

3. Fill a cup half-full with vinegar. Add oil and water to each of the other cups.

4. Mark the liquid level on the outside of each cup.

5. Place an egg in each cup. Cover each cup with plastic wrap.

6. **Measure:** After three days, remove your eggs. Measure and record the size of each egg as you did in steps 1 and 2.

7. Mark the level of the liquid on the side of each cup. Measure and record the height of each of the marks.

Questions

1. **a. Observe:** In which cup did the volume of liquid change? **b. Calculate:** How much did the volume change?

2. **Compare:** How did the size of the egg change as the volume of liquid changed?

3. **Relate:** Which substance's molecules were able to pass through the egg's membrane?

4-6 How do cells produce new cells?

Objective ▶ Describe cell division.

TechTerms

- ▶ **cell division:** process by which cells reproduce
- ▶ **chromosomes** (KROH-muh-sohms): cell parts that determine what traits a living thing will have
- ▶ **daughter cells:** new cells produced by cell division
- ▶ **mitosis** (my-TOH-sis): division of the nucleus

Cell Division Cells can reproduce. They produce new cells. Living things grow because their cells can reproduce and make new cells. The process by which cells reproduce is called **cell division.** The cells of all living things are produced by cell division.

▶ **Define:** What is cell division? process by which cells reproduce

Mitosis The nucleus controls cell division. Inside the nucleus are **chromosomes** (KROH-muh-sohms). Chromosomes are cell parts that determine what traits a living thing will have. During cell division, each chromosome makes an exact copy of itself.

After the chromosomes in the nucleus form twin pairs, the nucleus divides. The division of the nucleus is called **mitosis** (my-TOH-sis). During mitosis, the nuclear membrane disappears. All the pairs of chromosomes line up across the center of the cell. The chromosomes of each pair separate and move to opposite ends of the cell. The cell begins to pull apart. It splits into two new cells.

▶ **Identify:** What controls cell division? nucleus

Daughter Cells The two new cells formed by cell division are called **daughter cells.** The nuclei of the two daughter cells are exactly alike. Each daughter cell is about half the size of the parent cell. In time, each of the daughter cells will divide to form two more daughter cells.

▶ **Name:** What are the two new cells formed by cell division called? daughter cells

Cell Division in Plants Plant cells also reproduce by cell division. Like animal cells, plant cells make copies of their chromosomes and carry out mitosis. In animal cells, the cell pulls apart and forms two daughter cells. This does not happen in plant cells. In plant cells, a new cell wall and new cell membrane form down the middle of the cell. They form a wall between the two new nuclei. Two daughter cells are formed, one on each side of the new cell wall.

▶ **Identify:** What forms down the middle of a dividing plant cell? a new cell wall and new cell membranes

MITOSIS AND CELL DIVISION IN ANIMAL CELLS

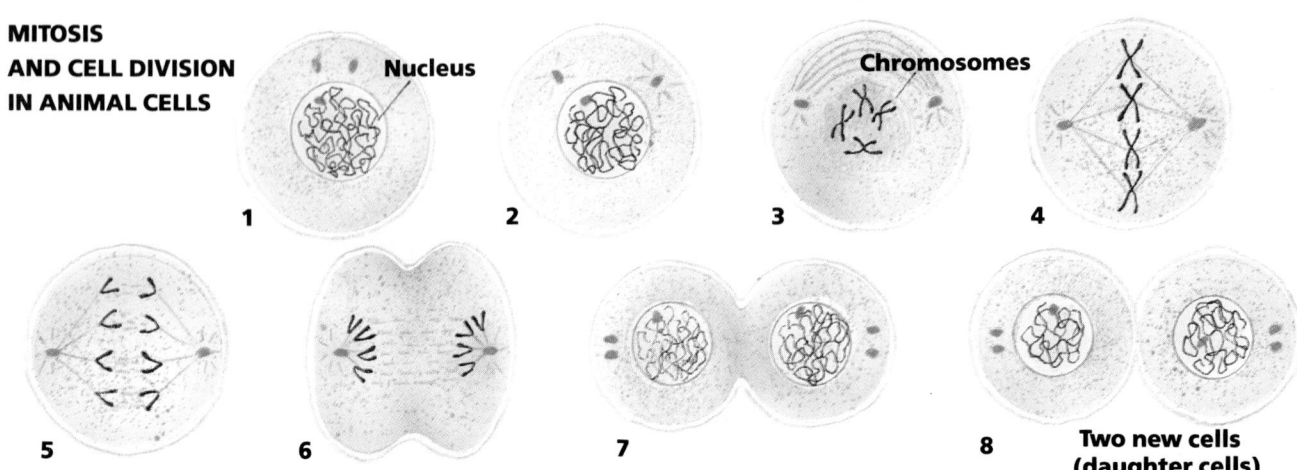

Nucleus

1   2

Chromosomes

3   4

5   6   7   8   Two new cells (daughter cells)

Mitosis and cell division in animals

- ▶ The process by which cells reproduce is called cell division.
- ▶ During cell division, each chromosome makes an exact copy of itself.
- ▶ Division of the nucleus is called mitosis.
- ▶ The two new cells that are formed by cell division are called daughter cells.
- ▶ Plant cells also reproduce by cell division.

CHECK *Answer the following.*

1. What is cell division?
2. What is mitosis?
3. What controls cell division?
4. How can living things grow?
5. What are daughter cells?
6. What are chromosomes?

APPLY *Complete the following.*

7. **Infer:** Why do you think chromosomes are copied during cell division?
8. **Analyze:** Is cell division a form of reproduction? Explain.

9. **Sequence:** Place the descriptions of mitosis in the correct order: **a.** Pairs of chromosomes line up across the center of the cell **b.** chromosomes move to opposite ends of the cell **c.** the nuclear membrane disappears **d.** the chromosomes of each pair separate.

10. **Analyze:** Is plant or animal cell division shown in the diagram? Explain what is happening in each part of the diagram.

Health & Safety Tip...........................

Cells usually divide and grow in an orderly manner. Cancer is a rapid, disorderly growth of cells. A cancerous growth crowds out and destroys healthy tissues. Use library references to find out the seven warning signs for cancer.

ACTIVITY

MODELING CELL DIVISION IN AN ANIMAL CELL

You will need eight pipe cleaners, a sheet of white paper, and a drawing compass.

1. Use the compass to make a large circle on a piece of white paper. Draw a small circle in the middle of the first circle.
2. Place four pipe cleaners in the inner circle.
3. Twist a pipe cleaner around each of the original pipe cleaners. Erase the inner circle.
4. Line up each pair of pipe cleaners in the middle of the large circle.
5. Separate the pipe cleaners. Move each pipe cleaner in a pair to opposite ends of the circle.

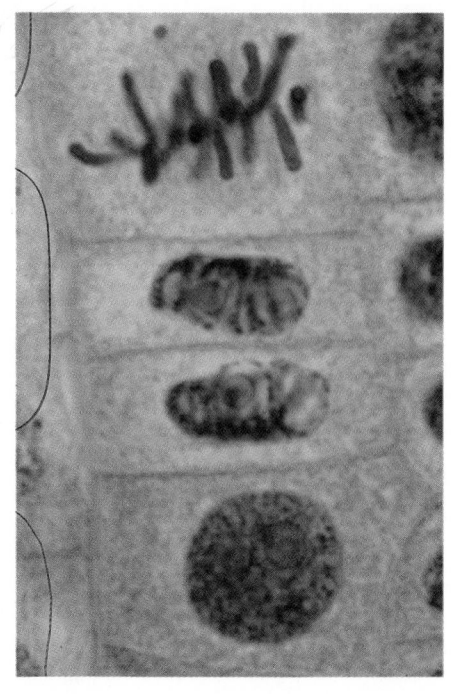

Questions

1. **a. Identify:** In your model, what does each circle represent? **b.** What do the pipe cleaners represent?
2. How many chromosomes does the parent cell have?
3. **Describe:** How could you show the formation of daughter cells on your model?

4-7 Why do cells have different shapes?

Objective ▶ Describe the structures and functions of different kinds of cells.

TechTerms

- **guard cell:** cell in a plant that helps control the passage of materials into and out of the stomates
- **red blood cell:** blood cell that carries oxygen
- **white blood cell:** blood cell that helps destroy germs

Cell Size and Shape In one-celled organisms, the one cell carries on all the life processes. Large animals and plants are made up of many cells. The cells are not all the same. They have different sizes and shapes. Look at the different shapes of the cells shown. Different kinds of cells have different jobs. The shapes of most cells help them to do their jobs.

▎▶ *Explain:* How are cells different? They have different sizes and shapes

Nerve Cells Nerve cells are the "telephone wires" of the body. They carry messages from one part of the body to another. The message carried by a nerve cell is called an impulse. Nerve cells are long and thin. Some nerve cells are the longest cells in your body. The longest cells are the nerve cells in a giraffe's leg. They are 2 m long.

▎▶ *Define:* What is an impulse? message carried by a nerve cell

Muscle Cells Muscle cells are long and thin. The shape of muscle cells can change. Muscle cells can become shorter. Some muscles are attached to bone. When cells in these muscles shorten, they make the bones move.

▎▶ *Explain:* What is the job of some muscles? to make bones move

Blood Cells There are two main kinds of blood cells. **Red blood cells** are round. They do not have a nucleus. The job of a red blood cell is to carry oxygen. **White blood cells** help destroy germs in the body. White blood cells are shapeless, or do not have a definite shape.

▶ *Infer:* Do you think red blood cells reproduce themselves? Why? No. They do not have a nucleus.

Guard Cells A stomate is a tiny opening on the lower surface of a plant leaf. A stomate takes in carbon dioxide from the air and gives off oxygen and water. Two bean-shaped cells called **guard cells** surround each stomate. Guard cells control the size of the stomate. When the guard cells swell, the stomate opens. When the guard cells shrink, the stomate closes.

▶ *Predict:* Does carbon dioxide enter a plant when the guard cells swell or shrink? swell

Guard cells

Stomate

Lower surface of leaf

LESSON SUMMARY

▶ Cells have different sizes and shapes.

▶ Nerve cells carry messages from one part of the body to another.

▶ When muscle cells become shorter, they make bones move.

▶ There are two main kinds of blood cells: red blood cells and white blood cells.

▶ Guard cells surround each stomate.

CHECK *Write true if the statement is true. If the statement is false, change the underlined term to make the statement true.*

1. Germs are destroyed by <u>red</u> blood cells. white

2. Muscle cells can become <u>shorter</u>. true

3. The job of a <u>white blood cell</u> is to carry oxygen. red blood cell

4. The message carried by a nerve cell is called an <u>impulse</u>. true

5. The largest cells in the body are <u>muscle</u> cells. nerve

6. A <u>stomate</u> is a tiny opening on the lower surface of a plant leaf. true

APPLY *Complete the following.*

7. **Relate:** How is the size and shape of a nerve cell related to its function?

8. **Contrast:** How do red blood cells differ from most other kinds of cells?

InfoSearch

Read the passage. Ask two questions about the topic that you cannot answer from the information in the passage.

Body Defenses Some white blood cells protect the body from disease by surrounding and digesting germs. These white blood cells are called phagocytes (FAG-uh-syts). Other white blood cells help destroy germs by making antibodies (AN-ti-bahd-ees). Antibodies are special proteins that destroy bacteria and viruses that invade the body.

SEARCH: Use library references to find answers to your questions.

CAREER IN LIFE SCIENCE

CYTOLOGY LAB TECHNICIAN

Scientists study cells to find answers to questions, such as "Why do some cells become diseased?" Research in cell biology may provide answers to many questions about human health. Cytology (sy-TAHL-uh-jee) lab technicians play an important role in this research.

Cytology lab technicians work with tissue samples. From these samples, the lab technicians prepare slides of cells. The slides are then analyzed under a microscope. Many cytology lab technicians also do tests on cells. They keep careful records of the test results.

Cytology lab technicians are employed by universities or hospitals. Some work in private industry. Most entry-level positions in this field require two years of college with courses in biology, chemistry, or physics. Many cytology lab technicians are hired after completing technical training schools. You can get more information about this career by speaking with your guidance counselor or writing to the personnel director of your local hospital.

4-8 What are tissues?

Objective ▶ Describe the four main kinds of tissues.

TechTerms

- ▶ **connective tissue:** tissue that holds parts of the body together
- ▶ **epithelial** (ep-uh-THEEL-ee-uhl) **tissue:** tissue that covers and protects parts of the body
- ▶ **plasma** (PLAZ-muh): liquid part of blood
- ▶ **tissue:** group of cells that look alike and work together

Tissues On a baseball team, the players work together. They wear uniforms that make them look alike. In many-celled organisms, cells work as teams. A group of cells that look alike and work together make up a **tissue.** Tissues are named for the jobs they do. There are four main kinds of tissue.

▐▌▌▶ *Define:* **What is a tissue?** group of cells that look alike and work together

Muscle Tissue Muscle tissue makes up muscles. Muscle tissue is made up of cells that can become shorter. There are different kinds of muscle tissue. One kind is attached to bones. When these muscles shorten, they pull on the bones and make the bones move.

▐▌▌▶ *Relate:* **How do some muscles and bones work together?** Muscles attached to bones make bones move.

Covering Tissue The skin that covers your body is made up of **epithelial** (ep-uh-THEEL-ee-uhl) **tissue.** Epithelial tissue is made up of cells that join tightly together. Epithelial tissue also covers many parts inside you body. It protects your body. It helps to keep germs out of your body.

▐▌▌▶ *Name:* **What type of tissue is skin?** epithelial tissue

Connective Tissue Tissue that holds parts of the body together is **connective tissue.** It also sup-

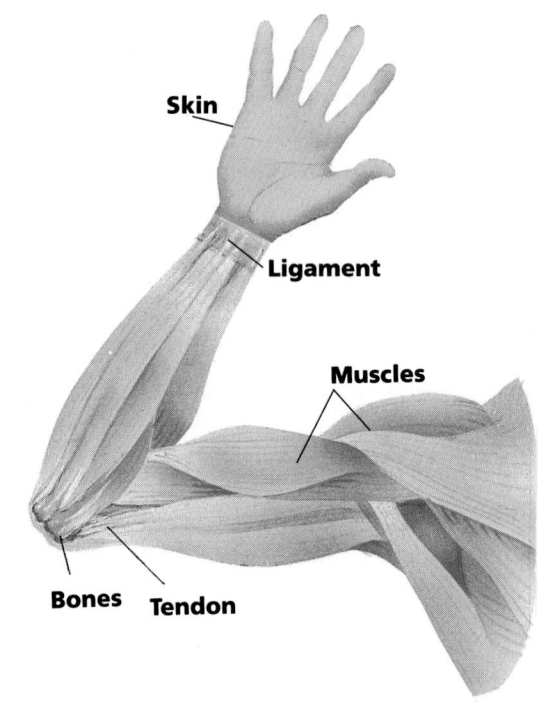

Examples of muscle tissue, covering tissue, and connective tissue

ports and protects the body. Bone is a connective tissue. Other kinds of connective tissue are ligaments (LIG-uh-muhnts) and tendons. Ligaments connect bones to one another. Tendons connect muscles to bones.

Blood is a liquid connective tissue. It has blood cells that float in **plasma** (PLAZ-muh). Plasma is the yellow, liquid part of blood. Plasma carries food, gases, and other important substances to and from all the cells in the body.

▐▌▌▶ *List:* **What are four kinds of connective tissue?** bone, ligaments, tendons, blood

Nerve Tissue Nerve tissue is made up of nerve cells, or neurons. Nerve tissue carries messages. It causes muscles to act. It controls breathing, digestion, and heartbeat. Your brain and spinal cord are made up mostly of nerve tissue.

▶ *Infer:* **What is the function of the brain?** control

LESSON SUMMARY

▶ A group of cells that look alike and work together make up a tissue.

▶ Muscle tissue is made up of cells that can become shorter.

▶ Epithelial tissue protects the body.

▶ Connective tissue holds parts of the body together.

▶ Ligaments and tendons are made up of connective tissue.

▶ Blood is a liquid connective tissue.

▶ Nerve tissue carries messages.

CHECK *Write the letter of the term that best completes each statement.*

1. The brain is made up mostly of
   a. connective tissue. **b.** muscle tissue.
   c. nerve tissue. **d.** epithelial tissue. c

2. Epithelial cells make up
   a. muscles. **b.** skin. **c.** ligaments. **d.** bone. b

3. Bones _____ the body.
   a. support **b.** carry messages in **c.** keep germs out of **d.** cover a

4. Muscles are connected to bones by
   a. plasma. **b.** ligaments. **c.** neurons.
   d. tendons. d

5. Plasma is _____ in color.
   a. red **b.** yellow **c.** colorless **d.** blue b

6. Blood is _____ tissue
   a. a connective **b.** an epithelial **c.** a nervous **d.** a solid a

APPLY *Complete the following.*

7. **Compare:** What are the functions of muscle, connective, and nerve tissue?

▶ 8. **Infer:** Bones have a lot of calcium in them. Why do you think the proper amount of calcium in your diet is important for healthy bones?

Health & Safety Tip

Injuries to the brain and spinal cord often result from sports and automobile accidents. Make a poster showing ways that people can protect their brain and spinal cords from injury in these ways.

TECHNOLOGY AND SOCIETY

CORNEA TRANSPLANTS

Blindness often is caused by scarring of the cornea (KAWR-nee-uh). The cornea is the clear, outer layer of the eye. Light first enters the eye through the cornea. It is now possible to restore lost eyesight in some people with scarred corneas. This can be done through cornea transplant surgery. During a cornea transplant, the scarred cornea is replaced with clear corneal tissue. The healthy tissue comes from an eye donor who has died.

An eye bank is an agency that helps get donated eyes to patients waiting for transplants. An eye bank collects, prepares, and distributes the eyes to specially trained surgeons. Eyes must be removed shortly after a person has died. After removal, they are packed in special containers and put in cold storage. The eyes are examined at an eye bank to see if they can be used for a transplant. If they are useful, the eyes are made available for immediate use in any part of the United States.

The first eye bank was formed in New York City in 1944. Today, many cities and states have eye banks.

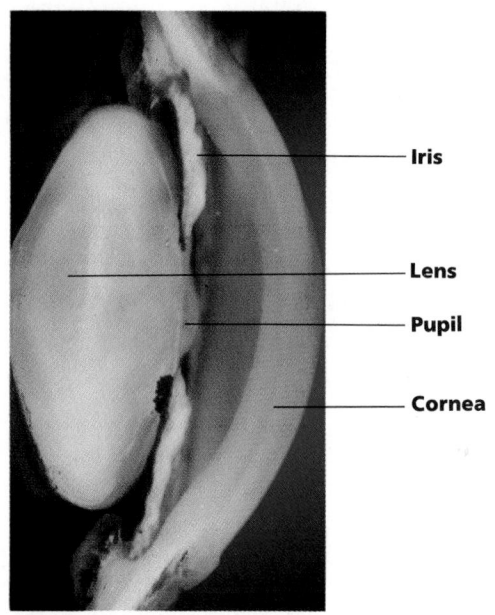

Side view of human eye

4-9 What are organs and organ systems?

Objective ▶ Describe organs and organ systems.

TechTerms

- **organ** (OWR-gun): group of tissues that work together to do a special job
- **organ system:** group of organs that work together

Organs Groups of cells that work together form tissues. Different tissues work together too. A group of tissues that work together to do a special job is called an **organ** (OWR-gun).

Your body has many different organs. Each organ has a special shape and job. Your arm is an organ. It is made up of many different tissues. Muscle and bone tissues work together to move your arm. Nerve tissue carries impulses to the muscles tissue. These impulses make the muscles move your arm. Epithelial tissue forms the skin on your arm. Blood flows through your arm. It supplies all the cells in these different tissues with oxygen and food. Blood also carries wastes away.

▶ *Define:* **What is an organ?** group of tissues that work together to do a job

Organ Systems Organs do not work alone. Groups of organs work together. These groups of organs form **organ systems.** All the organs in an organ system work together to carry on a life process. All the organ systems of a living thing work together to keep the organism alive. The human body has ten organ systems. Each organ system carries out a life process. Some organ systems are listed in Table 1.

◣ *Analyze:* **What is the job of the excretory system?** removal of wastes

Glands Some organs and groups of cells make and give off substances used by the body. These special organs and groups of cells are called glands. Some glands produce chemicals that act as messengers. The blood carries these "messengers" to organs. The organs start to do their work when

Table 1	Organ Systems and Their Jobs	
SYSTEM	MAJOR ORGANS	JOBS
Skeletal	Bone	support and movement
Muscular	Muscles	movement
Digestive	Mouth, Stomach	digestion
Circulatory	Heart, Blood vessels	transport
Respiratory	Lungs	respiration
Excretory	Kidneys, Skin	removal of wastes
Nervous	Brain, Spinal cord	control

the chemical "messengers" arrive. The glands that produce chemical "messengers" make up an organ system. The organ system is the endocrine (EN-duh-krin) system. Many of the chemical "messengers" made by glands control the activities of other tissues and organs.

▶ *Define:* **What is a gland?** special organ or group of cells that makes and gives off substances used by the body.

Plant Organs Plant tissues also form organs. These organs have special jobs. The roots of a plant hold a plant in the soil. Roots also take in water and minerals needed by the plant. The stem of a plant is an organ, too. It carries food and water to other parts of a plant. The leaves of a plant are its food-making organs. A flower is a plant's organ of reproduction.

▶ *Name:* **What are four plant organs?** roots, stems, leaves, flowers

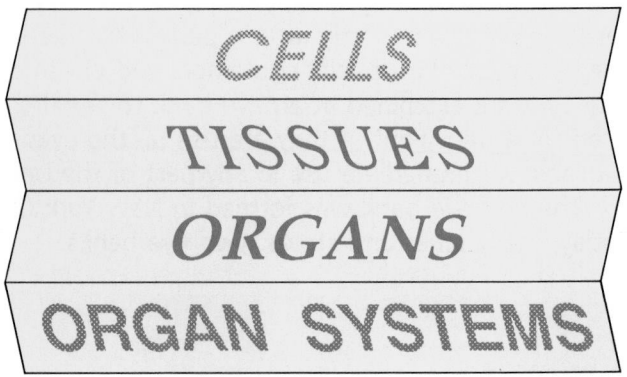

CELLS
TISSUES
ORGANS
ORGAN SYSTEMS

LESSON SUMMARY

- ▶ A group of tissues that work together to do a job is called an organ.
- ▶ Organs are made up of many different tissues.
- ▶ Groups of organs that work together are called organ systems.
- ▶ The human body has ten organ systems.
- ▶ The endocrine system is made up of glands that make and give off substances used by the body.
- ▶ Plant tissues form organs.

CHECK *Complete the following.*

1. The _____ of a plant carries food and water to other parts of the plant. stem

2. Groups of organs form _____ . organ systems

3. Each organ system carries out a life _____ . process

4. A group of tissues that work together is called an _____ . organ

5. The human body has _____ organ systems. ten

6. Glands make and give off _____ "messengers." chemical

APPLY *Use Table 1 on page 94 to complete the following.*

7. The brain and spinal cord make up the _____ system. nervous

8. **Analyze:** The job of the heart and blood vessels is _____ . transport

9. **Analyze:** Bone is part of the _____ system. skeletal

Complete the following.

10. **Sequence:** Place the levels of organization in an organism from smallest to largest. **a.** organism **b.** cells **c.** organ **d.** tissues **e.** organ systems

11. **Apply:** What different kinds of tissues do you think work together in your leg?

Skill Builder

Researching There are four main kinds of plant tissue. They are the epidermis, ground tissue, vascular tissue, and meristem tissue. Use library references to find out the main functions of each of these plant tissues. Organize your findings in a table.

TECHNOLOGY AND SOCIETY

THE VISIBLE HUMAN PROJECT

In 1986, the National Library of Medicine began the Visible Human Project. The goal of the project was to build a three-dimensional computer model of a normal human body. The model is now available on the Internet. Use of the model requires a fee, a license—and two weeks to download.

The model was made by freezing a human body and slicing it into wafer-thin sections. Photographs were taken of each slice. It took nine months to photograph the 1,878 slices that were made. A computer put the photos together to make the model. You can use the model to see single organs or groups of organs.

The computer model can be used for a variety of purposes. Medical students practice operating on the Visible Human before doing actual surgeries. Companies use the model to test products, such as crash helmets. Army medics are learning to treat gunshot wounds using a program developed from the Visible Human. They can use a model wound to stop the bleeding, clean the wound, and apply sutures.

Challenges

STUDY HINT Before you begin the Unit Challenges, review the TechTerms and Lesson Summary for each lesson in this unit.

TechTerms

cell (78)
cell division (88)
cell membrane (80)
cell wall (84)
cellulose (84)
chlorophyll (84)
chloroplast (84)
chromosomes (88)
connective tissue (92)
cytoplasm (80)

daughter cells (88)
diffusion (86)
epithelial tissue (92)
guard cell (90)
mitochondria (82)
mitosis (88)
nucleus (80)
organ (94)
organ system (94)
organelles (82)

osmosis (86)
plasma (92)
red blood cell (90)
ribosomes (82)
theory (78)
tissue (92)
vacuoles (82)
white blood cell (90)

TechTerm Challenges

Matching *Write the TechTerm that best matches each description.*

1. group of organs that work together organ system
2. control center of a cell nucleus
3. basic unit of structure and function in living things cell
4. liquid part of blood plasma
5. outer part of a plant cell cell wall
6. liquid-filled spaces in the cytoplasm vacuoles
7. material that makes up the cell wall cellulose
8. blood cell that helps destroy germs white blood cell
9. controls passage of materials into and out of stomates guard cell
10. group of cells that work together tissue

Identifying Word Relationships *Explain how the words in each pair are related. Write your answers in complete sentences.* Answers will vary. Accept all logical responses.

1. chlorophyll, chloroplast
2. diffusion, osmosis
3. cell division, mitosis
4. organ, organ system
5. red blood cell, connective tissue
6. skin, epithelial tissue
7. organelles, cytoplasm
8. cell membrane, cell wall
9. ribosomes, protein
10. mitochondria, energy
11. chromosomes, daughter cell
12. theory, data

Content Challenges

Multiple Choice *Write the letter of the term or phrase that best completes each statement.*

1. The first person to observe cells was
   a. Theodor Schwann. **b.** Matthais Schleiden. **c.** Anton van Leeuwenhoek. **d.** Robert Hooke. d

2. The main parts of a cell are the cell membrane, the nucleus, and the
   a. plasma. **b.** cytoplasm. **c.** mitochondria. **d.** ribosomes. b

3. The structures that act as "storage bins" for a cell are
   a. mitochondria. **b.** ribosomes. **c.** vacuoles. **d.** organelles. c

4. Organelles float inside a cell's
   a. cytoplasm. **b.** cell membrane. **c.** nucleus. **d.** chromosomes. a

5. One of the functions of the cell wall is to
   a. get rid of oxygen. **b.** give the cell its shape. **c.** give a cell its color. **d.** move water through the cell. b

6. Molecules are made up of
   a. atoms. **b.** water. **c.** oxygen. **d.** cells. a

7. When a cell divides, each chromosome makes a copy that is
   a. identical to the original. **b.** slightly different from the original. **c.** very different from the original. **d.** a mutation of the original. a

8. Cells that carry messages from one part of the body to another are
   a. guard cells. **b.** blood cells. **c.** nerve cells. **d.** muscle cells. c

9. An example of connective tissue is
   a. muscle. **b.** skin. **c.** ligaments. **d.** nerves. c

10. The kind of tissue that keeps germs out of your body is
    a. muscle tissue. **b.** epithelial tissue. **c.** connective tissue. **d.** nerve tissue. b

11. The number of organ systems inside the human body is
    a. 8. **b.** 9. **c.** 10. **d.** 11. c

True/False *Write true if the statement is true. If the statement is false, change the underlined term to make the statement true.*

1. The first person to see living cells was Anton van Leeuwenhoek. true

2. Water, food, and oxygen enter a cell through its nucleus. cell membrane

3. Most of a cell is made up of plasma. cytoplasm

4. The organelles responsible for breaking down food inside a cell are the mitochondria. true

5. The cell wall of a plant is made up of living material. nonliving

6. Chlorophyll is the material that makes food in animal cells. plant

7. The vacuoles in plant cells usually are very large. true

8. The even distribution of ink molecules in a beaker of water is an example of diffusion. true

9. In plant cell reproduction, a new vacuole forms down the middle of the cell. cell wall

10. The messages carried by nerve cells are called stomates. impulses

11. Glands are a part of the nervous system. endocrine

Understanding the Features

Reading Critically *Use the feature reading selections to answer the following. Page numbers for the features follow each question in parentheses.*

1. What are Schwann cells? (79)
2. What is one disadvantage of a transmission electron microscope? What other electron microscope can make up for this disadvantage? (83)
3. **Infer:** Why is it important that cytology lab technicians keep careful records of test results from their work? (91)
4. How is a cornea transplant done? (93)
5. **Describe:** Describe the work done by a worker at an eye bank. (93)
6. **Identify:** What is one way the Visible Human model can be used? (95)

Concept Challenges......

Critical Thinking *Answer each of the following in complete sentences.*

1. **Infer:** Why do you think little was known about cells before the invention of the microscope?
2. What are the three principles that make up the cell theory?
3. Why do you think that organelles can be compared to a factory?
4. **Contrast:** List three differences between plant and animal cells.
5. What makes osmosis a special kind of diffusion?
6. **Contrast:** How does plant cell reproduction differ from animal cell reproduction?

Interpreting a Diagram *Use the diagram to complete the following.*

Figure 1

Figure 2

1. What structure is represented by A: Why is this structure missing from Figure 1?
2. What structures are represented by C?
3. What structure are represented by D?
4. What structure are represented by E?
5. What structure is represented by G? Why is this structure missing from Figure 1?
6. What structure are represented by H?
7. What structures are represented by I? What is their function?

Finding Out More......

1. **Observe:** Find and examine slides or photographs of cells magnified with a compound microscope or an electron microscope. Be sure to use photographs of both plant and animal cells. Identify as many different cell parts as you can in each photograph or slide.

2. **Predict:** Perform a simple experiment on diffusion by spraying some perfume at the front of the classroom. Ask your classmates to raise their hands then they smell the perfume. Predict beforehand how your classmates will respond. Will all students eventually raise their hands? In what order will the hands be raised? Write a summary of the experiment. Tell whether your prediction was correct.

3. **Observe:** Using a compound microscope, examine plant cells from the tip of a leaf. Follow the instructions for mounting the leaf given by your teacher. Make a sketch of one cell and try to identify the location of the vacuoles, the chloroplasts, the nucleus, the cell wall, and the cytoplasm.

4. Using an encyclopedia or other reference book, research organ transplants. Write a report on which organs can be successfully transplanted. Explain briefly how medical experts go about performing one of the transplants you researched.

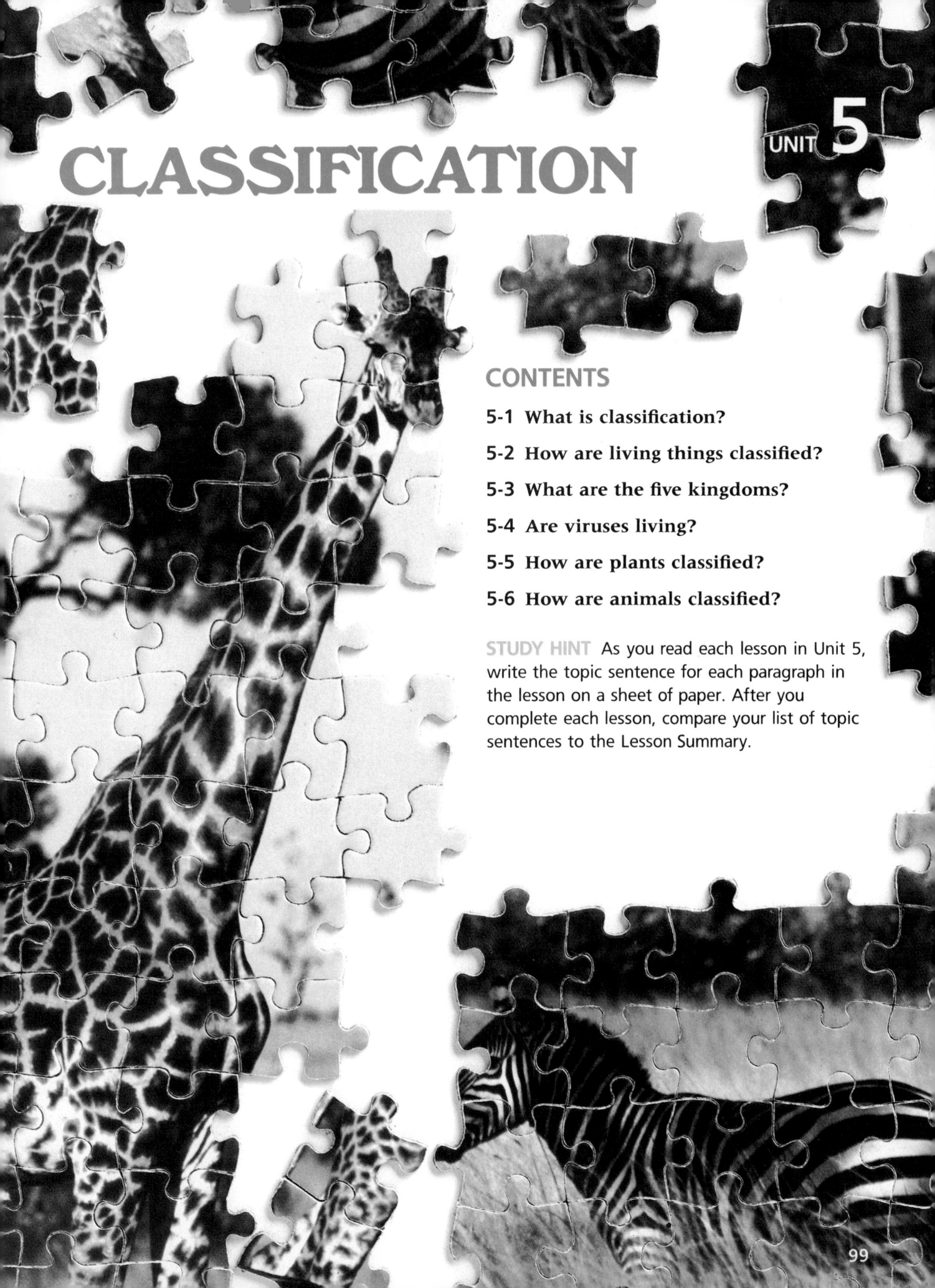

CLASSIFICATION

UNIT **5**

CONTENTS

5-1 What is classification?

5-2 How are living things classified?

5-3 What are the five kingdoms?

5-4 Are viruses living?

5-5 How are plants classified?

5-6 How are animals classified?

STUDY HINT As you read each lesson in Unit 5, write the topic sentence for each paragraph in the lesson on a sheet of paper. After you complete each lesson, compare your list of topic sentences to the Lesson Summary.

5-1 What is classification?

Objective ▶ Explain why it is necessary to classify things.

TechTerms

▶ **classification** (klas-uh-fi-KAY-shun): grouping things according to similarities

▶ **taxonomy** (tak-SAHN-uh-mee): science of classifying living things

Classification Imagine that you are in a bookstore. You are looking for a mystery novel. You look at the signs above each group of books. Each sign names the kinds of books in each area. In no time at all, you find your book and are on your way. In a library you are able to find books quickly because they are classified, or grouped, by subject. Grouping things according to similarities, or how they are alike, is called **classification** (klas-uh-fi-KAY-shun).

📂 *Classify:* Name one other way you could classify books. Answers will vary. Accept all logical responses.

Taxonomy About 1 1/2 million different kinds of organisms have been discovered so far. Each year the list of living things grows longer. Imagine having to keep track of so many living things. To help scientists keep track of living things, scientists use a system of classification. The science of classifying living things is called **taxonomy** (tak-SAHN-uh-mee). Scientists who classify living things are taxonomists.

Why do scientists classify living things? Classification is a way of organizing information about different kinds of living things. Classification also makes it easier for scientists to identify a newly discovered organism.

Name: What is the science of classifying living things called? taxonomy

Classifying Living Things Living things are classified based on how they are alike. Taxonomists do not group organisms together simply because they look alike. Taxonomists use many features to classify organisms. For example, taxonomists study the cells of an organism, and the substances that make up the cell. They study the way the organism grows and develops before it is born. They also study the blood of animals. Taxonomy is a very complex subject.

State: What are two reasons scientists classify organisms? to organize information; to make it easier to identify newly discovered organisms

▶ Grouping things according to how they are alike is called classification.

▶ Taxonomy is the science of classifying living things.

▶ Classification is a way of organizing information about living things.

▶ Taxonomists use many features to classify living things.

CHECK *Complete the following.*

1. When you classify, you put things into _____ according to similarities. groups

2. The science of classifying living things is _____ . taxonomy.

3. Taxonomists study the way organisms grow and develop before they are _____ . born

4. About _____ million different kinds of organisms have been discovered so far. 1 1/2

APPLY *Answer the following.*

▶ 5. **Infer:** Why is taxonomy an ongoing science?

◢ 6. **Analyze:** Food is classified in a supermarket. Books are classified in a library. Name two other classification systems that are used in daily life.

7. Why do you think taxonomists do not classify living things only according to appearance?

Skill Builder

Comparing When you compare things, you look at how the things are alike and how they are different. Libraries classify books using either the Dewey Decimal System or the Library of Congress classification system. Find out how these two classification systems compare. What are some similarities and differences between these two systems?

ACTIVITY

CLASSIFYING OBJECTS

You will need a sheet of paper and a pencil.

1. Carefully examine the vehicles shown in the diagram.
2. On a sheet of paper, list as many features of the vehicles as you can.
3. Classify the vehicles according to one of the features.
4. Repeat Step 3 using another feature.

Questions

1. What feature did you use to classify the vehicles?
2. How many different ways were you able to classify the vehicles?
3. Which classification system had the most groups?
4. Which classification system had the fewest groups?

How are living things classified?

TechTerms

▶ **genus** (JEE-nus): classification group made up of related species

▶ **kingdom:** classification group made up of related phyla

▶ **phylum** (FY-luhm): classification group made up of related classes

▶ **species** (SPEE-sheez): group of organisms that look alike and can reproduce among themselves

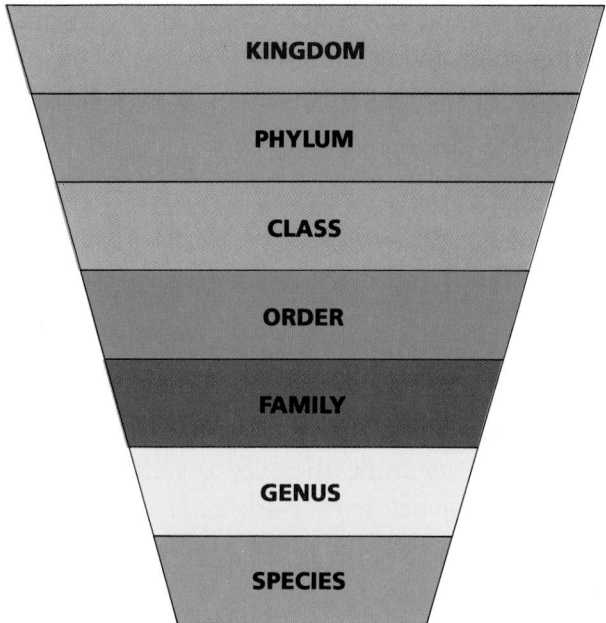

KINGDOM

PHYLUM

CLASS

ORDER

FAMILY

GENUS

SPECIES

Classification Groups Today, organisms are classified into a series of groups. Organisms that are classified in the same group are alike in some ways. The more alike organisms are, the more classification groups they share. The largest classification group is the **kingdom.** Each kingdom is divided into smaller groups called phyla (FY-luh). One group is a **phylum** (FY-luhm). Each phylum is divided into still smaller groups. These groups are called classes.

Altogether, there are seven major classification groups. The number of different kinds of organisms in each group decreases as you move from the kingdom level to each of the next levels. From largest to smallest, the classification groups are: kingdom, phylum, class, order, family, genus, and species.

A **species** (SPEE-sheez) is the smallest classification group. A species is a group of organisms that look alike and can reproduce among themselves. Each species includes only one kind of

organism. All dogs belong to the same species. A **genus** (JEE-nus) is made up of two or more species that are very much alike. For example, dogs and wolves belong to different species, but they belong to the same genus.

▶ *Sequence:* List the seven classification groups from largest to smallest. kingdom, phylum, class, order, family, genus, species

Naming Organisms In the eighteenth century, a Swedish botanist, Carolus Linnaeus (luh-NAY-us), developed a system of naming organisms that is still used today. In this system, each kind of organism is identified by a two-part scientific name. A scientific name is made up of the genus and species names of an organism. For example, the scientific name for pet dogs is *Canis familiaris.*

▶ *Name:* What are the two parts of a scientific name? genus and species names

Table 1	The Classification of Four Organisms						
	KINGDOM	PHYLUM	CLASS	ORDER	FAMILY	GENUS	SPECIES
Dog	Animal	Chordata	Mammalia	Carnivora	Canidae	Canis	familiaris
Wolf	Animal	Chordata	Mammalia	Carnivora	Canidae	Canis	lupus
Human	Animal	Chordata	Mammalia	Primates	Hominidae	Homo	sapiens
Chimpanzee	Animal	Chordata	Mammalia	Primates	Pongidae	Pan	troglodytes

LESSON SUMMARY

▶ Organisms are classified into a series of groups.

▶ The seven classification groups from largest to smallest are: kingdom, phylum, class, order, family, genus, and species.

▶ A species is a group of organisms that look alike and can reproduce among themselves.

▶ The two parts of a scientific name include the genus and species names of an organism.

CHECK *Write the letter of the term that best completes each statement.*

1. The largest classification groups are
   a. species. b. classes. c. orders.
   d. kingdoms. d

2. The classification group that contains only one kind of organism is the
   a. phylum. b. genus. c. species.
   d. order. c

3. A group of organisms that look alike and can reproduce among themselves is a
   a. species. b. class. c. order.
   d. division. a

APPLY *Use Table 1 on page 102 to answer the following questions.*

4. How many classification groups do humans and chimpanzees have in common?

5. What is the scientific name for a human?

6. Which two animals are the most closely related?

InfoSearch...

Read the passage. Ask two questions that you cannot answer from the information in the passage.

John Ray In the seventeenth century, an English botanist named John Ray identified and classified more than 18,000 different kinds of plants. Many of his ideas are used in modern plant taxonomy. Ray also classified animals, and was the first to use the term "species" for each different kind of living thing. Ray defined a species as a group of organisms that looked alike and could reproduce among themselves.

SEARCH: Use library references to find answers to your questions.

LOOKING BACK IN SCIENCE

HISTORY OF CLASSIFICATION

One of the first known classification systems was developed more than 2000 years ago by the Greek philosopher Aristotle (AR-is-taht-ul). Aristotle classified organisms as either plants or animals. Animals were classified into smaller groups based upon where the animals lived. Aristotle had three groups of animals: land animals, water animals, and air animals.

One of Aristotle's students, the Greek philosopher Theophrastus (thee-uh-FRAS-tus) classified plants according to their sizes and kinds of stem. Small plants with soft stems were called herbs. Medium-sized plants with many woody stems were called shrubs. Large plants with one woody stem were called trees.

In the eighteenth century, Carolus Linnaeus developed a new way to classify organisms. Linnaeus classified organisms according to their physical characteristics. Organisms that looked alike were grouped together. Linnaeus is known as the founder of modern taxonomy.

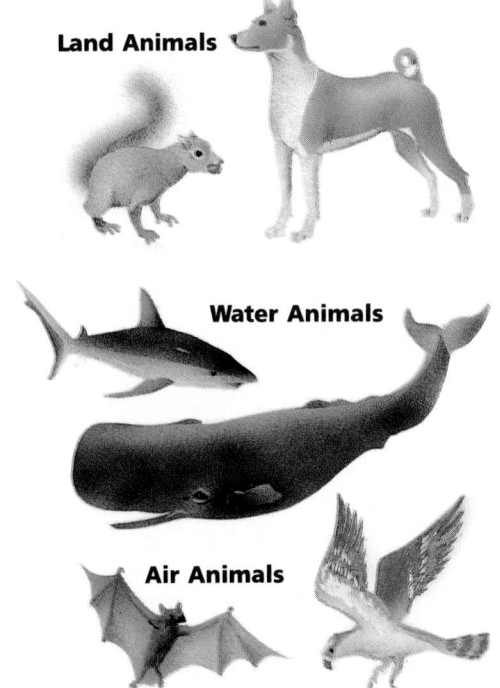

Land Animals

Water Animals

Air Animals

5-3 What are the five kingdoms?

Objective ▶ Name and describe the five kingdoms of living things.

TechTerms

- ▶ **fungi** (FUN-gy): plantlike organisms that lack chlorophyll
- ▶ **monerans** (muh-NER-uns): single-celled organisms that do not have a nucleus
- ▶ **protists** (PROHT-ists): single-celled organisms that have a nucleus

Five Kingdoms At one time, all organisms were classified as either plants or animals. With the development of the microscope, new organisms were discovered. These microscopic organisms were placed into a third kingdom. Using the electron microscope, scientists discovered that microscopic organisms are not all alike. Some microscopic organisms do not have a nucleus or other cell organelles. These organisms were placed into a kingdom of their own. Studies also showed that fungi and plants were not closely related. Scientists placed fungi in a kingdom of their own.

Today, most scientists accept the five kingdom classification system. Some scientists would like to make a sixth kingdom for viruses. As new information becomes available, the five kingdom classification system may change.

Hypothesize: Why may the five kingdom classification system change over time? Answers will vary. Accept all logical responses.

- ▶ **Kingdom** *Monera* The **monerans** (muh-NER-uns) are single-celled organisms. Unlike members of the other four kingdoms, monerans do not have a nucleus. In the monerans, nuclear material is scattered throughout the cell. Monerans also lack most of the organelles found in other kinds of cells. Bacteria are examples of monerans.
- ▶ **Kingdom** *Protista* Most **protists** (PROHT-ists) are single-celled organisms. Some protists are simple, many-celled organisms. Unlike monerans, the cells of protists have a nucleus. Protist cells also have organelles. The protist kingdom includes both plantlike and animal-like organisms. Algae are one example of protists.
- ▶ **Kingdom** *Fungi* Most **fungi** (FUN-gy) are made up of many cells. Some fungi, such as yeast, are made up of only one cell. Like plants, the cells of most fungi have a cell wall. However, fungi do not have chlorophyll. Fungi do not make their own food. They absorb food from their environment.
- ▶ **Kingdom** *Plantae* Plants are many-celled organisms. Plant cells have a cell wall. Plant cells also have rounded structures that contain chlorophyll. Plants use chlorophyll to make food.
- ▶ **Kingdom** *Animalia* Animals are made up of many cells. Most animals have organs that form organ systems. Unlike plants, animal cells do not have a cell wall or chlorophyll. Animals cannot make their own food. Animals obtain food by eating plants and other animals.

KINGDOMS

Monera	Protista	Fungi	Plantae	Animalia

LESSON SUMMARY

▶ There are five kingdoms of classification.

▶ As new information becomes available, the five kingdom classification system may change.

▶ Organisms are classified as either monerans, protists, fungi, plants, or animals.

CHECK *Complete the following.*

1. Today, organisms are classified into _____ kingdoms. five

2. The cell of a _____ does not have a nucleus. moneran

3. Algae are members of the _____ kingdom. protist

4. Some scientists would like to make a sixth kingdom for _____ . viruses

5. The yeasts belong to the _____ kingdom. fungi

6. At one time, all organisms were classified as either plants or _____ . animals

APPLY *Complete the following.*

◢ 7. **Analyze:** Why are protists and monerans placed in separate kingdoms?

◢ 8. **Analyze:** Why are fungi and plants placed in separate kingdoms?

9. How has technology affected classification?

Skill Builder

△ **Organizing Information** When you organize information, you put the information in some kind of order. A table is one way to organize information. Make a table that describes the five kingdoms. Place the names of the kingdoms across the top. For each kingdom, list whether its members are one-celled or many-celled, if they have a nucleus and organelles, and how they get food.

▶◼ PEOPLE IN SCIENCE ▶◼◀◇▶◼◀◇▶◼◀◇▶◼◀◇▶◼◀◇▶◼◀◇▶◼◀◇▶◼◀◇▶◼◀◇▶◼◀◇▶

ROBERT H. WHITTAKER (1924–1980)

The five kingdom classification system that is widely used today was developed by Robert Whittaker. Whittaker was an American ecologist and botanist. In 1969, he presented his ideas for classifying organisms into five kingdoms. In Whittaker's system, organisms are classified according to whether their cells contain a nucleus surrounded by a membrane, whether they are one-celled or many-celled, and how they obtain food.

While Whittaker is best known for his five kingdom classification system, he made many other contributions to science. As a graduate student in botany at the University of Illinois, Whittaker developed a method of recording how moisture, temperature, and altitude affect how and where plants grow. Whittaker also used radioactive tracers to learn how some substances move in a food chain.

Robert Whittaker died of cancer in 1980. In 1984, the Ecological Society of America established the R. H. Whittaker Travel Fellowship in Whittaker's honor. This fellowship enables young ecologists from other countries to study in the United States.

5-4 Are viruses living?

Objectives ▶ Describe the structure of a virus.
▶ Explain why viruses are hard to classify.

TechTerms

▶ **bacteriophage** (bak-TIR-ee-uh-fayj): virus that infects bacteria

▶ **capsid** (KAP-sid): protein covering of a virus

▶ **virus** (VY-rus): piece of nucleic acid covered with a protein

Structure of a Virus The structure of viruses is very different from that of living cells. Viruses do not have any cell parts. A **virus** (VY-rus) is just a piece of nucleic (noo-KLEE-ik) acid covered with an outer coat of protein. This outer coat is called a **capsid** (KAP-sid). The capsid makes up most of the virus.

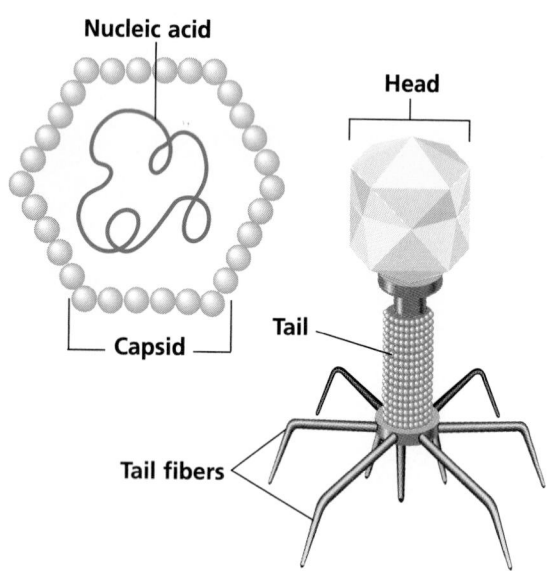

Figure 1

Capsids give viruses their shapes. Some viruses are round. Others look like long rods. The virus shown in Figure 1 attacks and destroys bacteria. A virus that infects bacterial cells is called a **bacteriophage** (bak-TIR-ee-uh-fayj). Notice the unusual shape of a bacteriophage.

▶ **Define:** What is a capsid? protein covering of a virus

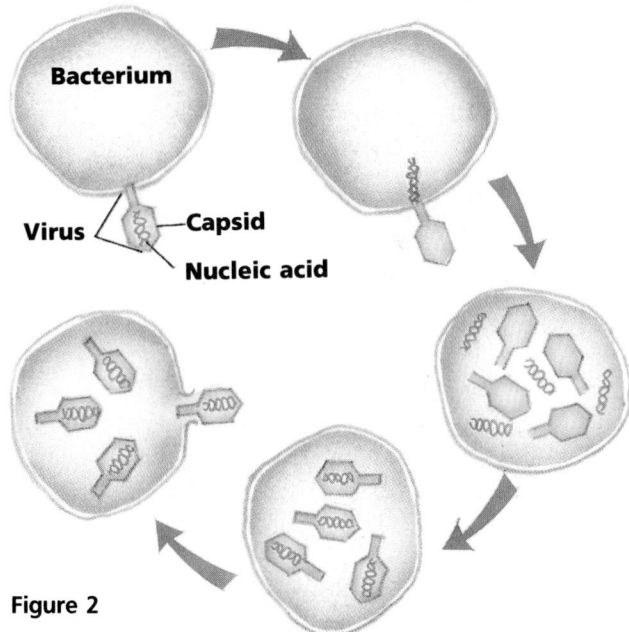

Figure 2

Classifying Viruses Scientists classify viruses according to the living things they infect. The three main groups of viruses are plant viruses, animal viruses, and bacterial viruses.

Viruses are like living cells in one important way. Viruses are able to produce more viruses. However, viruses can produce more viruses only inside a living cell. Outside a cell, viruses appear to be completely nonliving. They have no cytoplasm. They do not carry on life processes.

▶ **Contrast:** How do viruses differ from living cells? Viruses can reproduce only inside living cells; they do not contain cytoplasm, or carry out life processes.

Reproduction in Viruses Scientists first learned about reproduction in viruses by studying bacteriophages. Figure 2 shows that when a bacteriophage attacks a bacterial cell, it first attaches itself to the surface of the cell. The virus then gives off enzymes. The enzymes make a hole in the cell wall of the bacterium. The nucleic acid of the virus enters the cell through this hole. Once inside, the virus takes control of the cell and causes the cell to make new viruses. These new viruses then leave the cell and attack other cells. When viruses leave the cell, it is destroyed.

▶ **Sequence:** What happens once a virus enters a living cell? The virus takes control of the cell and causes the cell to make new viruses.

LESSON SUMMARY

▶ Viruses are made up of a piece of nucleic acid covered by a protein coat.

▶ Capsids give viruses their shape.

▶ Viruses can reproduce only inside a living cell.

▶ Once inside a living cell, viruses take control of the cell.

▶ Viruses are classified according to the living things they infect.

CHECK *Write true if the statement is true. If the statement is false, change the underlined term to make the statement true.*

1. A virus is a piece of <u>cytoplasm</u> covered with a protein coat. nucleic acid

2. A virus that infects a bacterial cell is called a <u>bacteriophage</u>. true

3. Viruses can produce more viruses only inside <u>nonliving</u> cells. living

4. Scientists first learned about reproduction in viruses by studying <u>bacteria</u>. bacteriophages

5. The outer coat of a virus is called a <u>capsid</u>. true

6. The three main groups of viruses are plant, <u>fungal</u>, and animal viruses. bacterial

APPLY *Complete the following.*

7. **Sequence:** List the steps of viral reproduction.

8. **Contrast:** How does a virus differ from a living cell?

9. **Hypothesize:** Why is it difficult to classify viruses?

Ideas in Action

IDEA: Many human diseases are caused by viruses, including chicken pox, measles, hepatitis, the flu, and the common cold.

ACTION: Find out how each of these diseases is spread and what you can do to protect yourself from viral diseases. Organize your findings in a table.

InfoSearch

Read the passage. Ask two questions that you cannot answer from the information in the passage.

Naming Viruses A virus often is named for the disease it causes. For example, the virus that causes polio is called polio virus. Code letters and numbers also are used instead of actual names. T2, T7, and P1 are names given to the viruses that attack bacteria found in the human intestines.

SEARCH: Use library references to find answers to your questions.

ACTIVITY

MODELING A BACTERIOPHAGE

You will need a machine screw, 1/4 inch by 1 and 1/2 inches, 2 acorn nuts that fit the screw, pliers, 3 pieces of floral wire, and a pipe cleaner.

1. Screw the acorn nuts onto the top of the screw.
2. Twist 3 pieces of floral wire around the opposite end of the screw. Use the pliers to bend the ends of the wires down.
3. Wrap the pipe cleaner around the middle of the screw.

Questions

1. **Identify:** What does the model represent?
2. What kinds of organisms can be infected by the virus represented by the model?
3. **Apply:** In which part of your model would the substance that enters living cells be contained?

5-5 How are plants classified?

Objective ▶ Identify the characteristics of plants.

TechTerms

- ▶ **bryophytes** (BRY-uh-fyts): division of plants that has no transport tissue
- ▶ **photosynthesis** (foht-uh-SIN-thuh-sis): food-making process in plants
- ▶ **tracheophytes** (TRAY-kee-uh-fyts): division of plants that has conducting tubes

Characteristics of Plants You probably recognize a plant when you see one. However, some organisms, such as algae, look like plants. How can you tell if an organism is a plant? Plants have many cells. In plants, the cells are organized into tissues and organs. The cells of plants also have cell walls and contain chlorophyll.

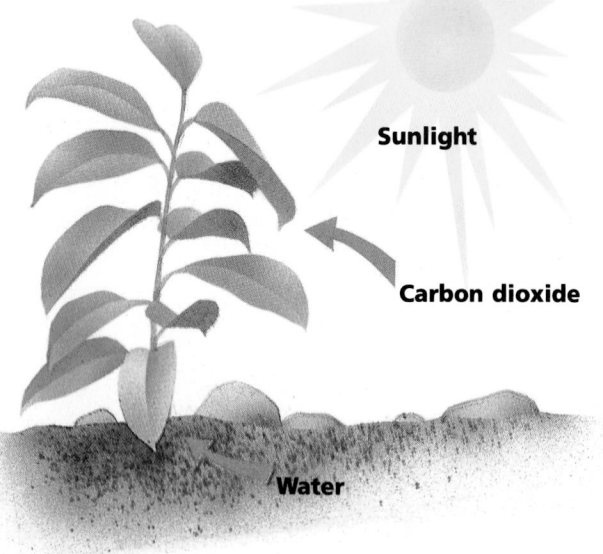

Sunlight

Carbon dioxide

Water

Plants use chlorophyll to trap the energy in sunlight. Plants use the sun's energy to combine carbon dioxide from the air and water from the soil to make food. The food-making process is called **photosynthesis** (foht-uh-SIN-thuh-sis). Photosynthesis provides plants with the food energy they need for growth and development.

� **State:** What are three plant characteristics? Students should restate the three characteristics given above.

Plant Divisions Botanists have classified more than 350,000 organisms in the plant kingdom. They have divided the plant kingdom into two large groups called divisions. The divisions are based on how water and dissolved nutrients (NOO-tree-unts) are moved throughout the plant. The two divisions are the bryophytes (BRY-uh-fyts) and the tracheophytes (TRAY-kee-uh-fyts).

▶ **Identify:** What are the two divisions of the plant kingdom? bryophytes and tracheophytes

Tracheophytes In **tracheophytes,** water and nutrients move through special tubelike cells to all parts of the plant. These tubelike cells make up the transport tissue of the plant. Transport tissue also helps support a plant. The presence of transport tissue allows some tracheophytes to grow to great heights.

Most of the plants you are familiar with probably are tracheophytes. Among tracheophytes, plant tissues are organized into roots, stems, and leaves. The roots of a tracheophyte anchor the plant in the soil. Roots also take in water and dissolved nutrients from the soil.

▶ **Describe:** What are two jobs of roots? to anchor plants in soil; to take in water and nutrients

Bryophytes Unlike tracheophytes, **bryophytes** do not have true roots, stems, or leaves. They have rootlike and leaflike structures. Bryophytes also lack transport tissue. In bryophytes, water and nutrients seep from one cell to another. Bryophytes are small plants. They are usually only a few centimeters high.

Bryophytes are land plants. However, they need water to reproduce. For this reason, botanists believe that bryophytes once lived in water.

▶ **Infer:** Why do you think that bryophytes cannot grow to great heights? They do not have transport tissue.

108

▶ Plant cells have a cell wall and chlorophyll, and are organized into tissues and organs.

▶ Photosynthesis is the food-making process in plants.

▶ The plant kingdom is divided into two divisions: bryophytes and tracheophytes.

▶ Tracheophytes have tubelike cells used to transport materials to all plant parts.

▶ Tracheophytes have roots, stems, and leaves.

▶ Bryophytes are small plants that lack transport tissues.

▶ Bryophytes need water to reproduce.

CHECK *Complete the following.*

1. The two plant divisions are the tracheophytes and the _____ . bryophytes

2. The food-making process in plants is called _____ . photosynthesis

3. Tubelike cells make up the _____ tissue of tracheophytes. transport

4. Among tracheophytes, plant tissues are organized into roots, stems, and _____ . leaves

5. Bryophytes need _____ to reproduce. water

APPLY *Complete the following.*

6. **Contrast:** How do bryophytes differ from tracheophytes?

7. **Hypothesize:** Why do you think tracheophytes are successful land plants?

InfoSearch..

Read the passage. Ask two questions that you cannot answer from the information in the passage.

Pioneer Organisms Bryophytes are called pioneer organisms because they are often among the first plants to grow in bare, rocky places. As bryophytes grow, they help to break down rocks to form soil. When bryophytes die and decay, they add to the richness of the forming soil. As a soil layer builds up, other plants, such as trees and shrubs, may grow. In time, a forest may grow in an area that was once bare.

SEARCH: Use library references to find answers to your questions.

CAREER IN LIFE SCIENCE

FLORIST

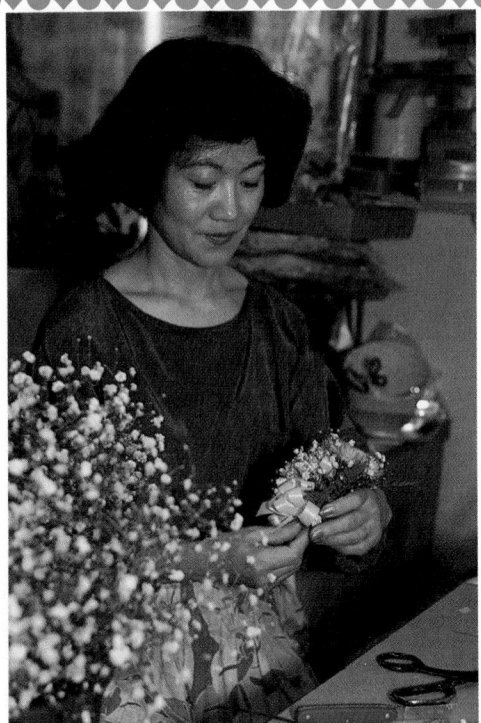

Do you like growing plants at home? Do you enjoy gardening? If so, you may want to become a florist. A florist is a person who arranges and sells fresh flowers and plants. Flower arrangements are often in the form of corsages, bouquets, and table centerpieces.

Customers often ask a florist questions about caring for plants, the best flowers to buy, color schemes, and so on. A good florist is able to answer these questions and provide customers with helpful tips. A florist's success also depends upon ordering enough cut flowers and houseplants for times of heavy demand, such as Valentine's Day and Mother's Day. A successful florist always is well-stocked for special occasions.

If you are interested in becoming a florist, you need a high school diploma. Florists also need training in flower arranging, preserving cut flowers, and caring for houseplants. Courses in small business management also may be helpful.

5-6 How are animals classified?

Objective ▶ Identify characteristics used to classify animals.

TechTerms

- **endoskeleton** (en-doh-SKEL-uh-tun): internal skeleton
- **exoskeleton** (ek-so-SKEL-uh-tun): external skeleton
- **invertebrates** (in-VUR-tuh-brayts): animals without backbones
- **vertebrates** (VUR-tuh-brayts): animals with backbones

Two Large Groups The animal kingdom is made up of more kinds of organisms than the other four kingdoms. Scientists classify animals into two large groups. One group is made up of animals with backbones. The other group is made up of animals without backbones.

� **Name:** What are the two groups into which the animal kingdom is divided? animals with backbones and animals without backbones

Vertebrates Animals that have backbones are called **vertebrates** (VUR-tuh-brayts). Vertebrates live in water as well as on land. They are the most complex organisms in the animal kingdom. They are also the most widely recognized and familiar of all animals. Vertebrates include fishes, frogs, snakes, birds, cats, and many other animals. You are a vertebrate too.

Look at Figure 1. It shows a model of the largest animal on the earth. The largest animals on Earth are vertebrates. Vertebrates may grow very large because they have an **endoskeleton** (en-doh-SKEL-uh-tun), or a skeleton inside their bodies. The endoskeleton does not limit the growth and size of an animal. The endoskeleton covers and protects soft body parts. It also helps give shape and support to an organism.

▶ **Define:** What is an endoskeleton? internal skeleton

Invertebrates Animals without backbones are called **invertebrates** (in-VUR-tuh-brayts). Most animals are invertebrates. In fact, more than 97 percent of all animals are invertebrates. Sponges and jellyfish are invertebrates. Other invertebrates include worms, snails, clams, sea stars, and insects.

Some invertebrates, such as worms, do not have any skeleton at all. They are soft-bodied animals. Other invertebrates have an **exoskeleton** (ek-so-SKEL-uh-tun). An exoskeleton is a skeleton on the outside of the body. It is made up of a hard, waterproof substance. The exoskeleton protects and supports the body. Spiders, lobsters, and insects have an exoskeleton.

▶ **List:** What are three kinds of animals that are invertebrates? sponges, jellyfish, worms, snails, clams, lobsters, insects

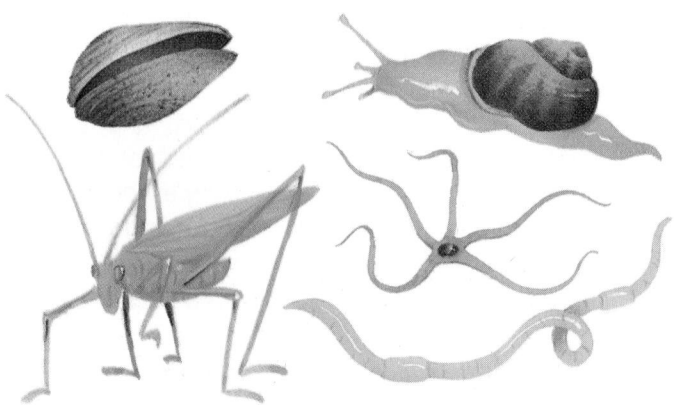

Figure 1

LESSON SUMMARY

► The animal kingdom is divided into two groups, animals with backbones and animals without backbones.

► Vertebrates are animals with backbones.

► Vertebrates have an endoskeleton.

► Invertebrates are animals without backbones.

► Some invertebrates are soft-bodied; others have an exoskeleton.

CHECK *Complete the following.*

1. Animals with backbones are classified as _____ . vertebrates

2. An endoskeleton is a skeleton found _____ the body. inside

3. More than 97 percent of all animals are _____ . invertebrates

4. Invertebrates are animals without _____ . backbones

5. The largest animals on the earth are _____ . vertebrates

APPLY *Complete the following.*

6. **Classify:** Write "I" if the organism has an endoskeleton and "E" if the organism has an exoskeleton.
   a. lobster
   b. rattlesnake
   c. robin
   d. horse
   e. grasshopper
   f. frog

7. **Classify:** Classify each of the following organisms as a vertebrate or an invertebrate.
   a. worm
   b. house fly
   c. robin
   d. squirrel
   e. sea star
   f. clam

SCIENCE CONNECTION

TAXONOMY TODAY

The founder of modern taxonomy, Carolus Linnaeus, classified organisms according to their physical characteristics. In Linnaeus' system, organisms that looked alike were grouped together. Modern-day taxonomists still compare the physical appearances of organisms. Organisms that look the same often are related. However, classification is not based on physical traits alone.

Taxonomists also compare the chromosomes and blood proteins of different kinds of organisms. Scientists have discovered that the chromosomes and proteins in the blood of certain animals are quite similar. If the chromosomes and blood proteins are similar, taxonomists infer that the organisms are related.

Taxonomists also study embryology. Embryology is the study of organisms in the early stages of development. Embryology helps scientists determine how organisms are related. Scientists have found that certain organisms show similarities as embryos. If the embryos develop in the same way, taxonomists infer that the organisms are related.

STUDY HINT Before you begin the Unit Challenges, review the TechTerms and Lesson Summary for each lesson in the unit.

TechTerms

bacteriophage (106)
bryophytes (108)
capsid (106)
classification (100)
endoskeleton (110)
exoskeleton (110)
fungi (104)

genus (102)
invertebrates (110)
kingdom (102)
monerans (104)
photosynthesis (108)
phylum (102)
protists (104)

species (102)
taxonomy (100)
tracheophytes (108)
vertebrates (110)
virus (106)

TechTerm Challenges

Matching *Write the TechTerm that best matches each description.*

1. plantlike organisms that lack chlorophyll fungi
2. virus that infects bacteria bacteriophage
3. internal skeleton endoskeleton
4. single-celled organisms that have a nucleus protists
5. animals with backbones vertebrates
6. food-making process in plants photosynthesis
7. animals without backbones invertebrates
8. external skeleton exoskeleton
9. single-celled organisms that do not have a nucleus monerans

Identifying Word Relationships *Explain how the words in each pair are related. Write your answers in complete sentences.* Answers will vary. Accept all logical responses.

1. genus, species
2. classification, taxonomy
3. capsid, virus
4. kingdom, phylum
5. bryophytes, tracheophytes

Content Challenges

Multiple Choice *Write the letter of the term that best completes each statement.*

1. Tubelike cells make up the transport tissue of
   a. tracheophytes. **b.** bryophytes. **c.** algae. **d.** viruses. a
2. Nuclear material is scattered throughout the cell in
   a. protists. **b.** fungi. **c.** monerans. **d.** yeasts. c
3. Scientists first learned about viral reproduction by studying
   a. fungi. **b.** algae. **c.** bacteriophages. **d.** bacteria. c
4. The largest classification group is the
   a. order. **b.** class. **c.** phylum. **d.** kingdom. d
5. Plants trap the energy in sunlight using
   a. transport tissue. **b.** chlorophyll. **c.** carbon dioxide. **d.** the cell wall b
6. Grouping things according to how they are alike is
   a. taxonomy. **b.** classification. **c.** photosynthesis. **d.** organization. d
7. Two kinds of invertebrates are
   a. frogs and fishes. **b.** snakes and birds. **c.** birds and worms. **d.** worms and insects. d

8. Today, most scientists accept a classification system with
   a. two kingdoms.   **b.** three kingdoms.   **c.** five kingdoms.   **d.** six kingdoms. c
9. Organisms that look alike and can reproduce among themselves make up a
   a. species.   **b.** genus.   **c.** family.   **d.** kingdom. a
10. The kingdom with the most kinds of organisms is the
    a. plant kingdom.   **b.** animal kingdom.   **c.** fungi kingdom.   **d.** protist kingdom. b
11. Botanists have divided plants into two large groups called
    a. kingdoms.   **b.** phyla.   **c.** divisions.   **d.** tracheophytes. c
12. The three main groups of viruses are plant viruses, animal viruses, and
    a. bacterial viruses.   **b.** protist viruses.   **c.** fungal viruses.   **d.** yeast viruses. a
13. Bacteria are
    a. monerans.   **b.** protists.   **c.** fungi.   **d.** animals. a
14. The two parts of a scientific name include the
    a. family and order names.   **b.** genus and species names.   **c.** kingdom and phylum names.
    d. class and order names. b

True/False *Write true if the statement is true. If the statement is false, changes the underlined term to make the statement true.*

1. Some scientists would like to make a sixth kingdom for <u>fungi</u>. viruses
2. <u>Bryophytes</u> need water to reproduce. true
3. Vertebrates have an <u>endoskeleton</u>. true
4. There are <u>ten</u> major classification groups for living things. seven
5. Dogs and wolves belong to the same <u>genus</u>. true
6. Scientists who classify living things are <u>botanists</u>. taxonomists
7. Algae are one example of <u>protists</u>. true
8. The protein covering of a virus is called a <u>capsid</u>. true
9. More than 97 percent of all animals are <u>vertebrates</u>. invertebrates
10. About 1 1/2 <u>billion</u> different kinds of organisms have been discovered so far. million

Understanding the Features..

Reading Critically *Use the feature reading selections to answer the following. Page numbers for the features are in parentheses.*

1. In what branches of biology did Robert Whittaker work? (105)
2. What do modern-day taxonomists study to classify organisms? (111)
3. **Identify:** Who is known as the founder of modern taxonomy? (103)
4. **Hypothesize:** Why might courses in small business management be helpful to a florist? (109)

Concept Challenges..

Critical Thinking *Answer each of the following in complete sentences.*

1. **Analyze:** If you were to discover a new species, how would you determine its classification?
2. Why is taxonomy a complex subject?
3. Do you think it is difficult to treat viral infections? Explain.
4. **List:** What four characteristics are used to classify an organism as a plant?
5. Fungi were once called the nongreen plants. Why do you think fungi were described in this way?

Interpreting a Diagram *Use the diagram to answer the following questions.*

1. What is shown in the diagram?
2. What is the structure labeled A called?
3. What is the structure labeled B called?
👁 4. **Observe:** What is happening in step 2?
👁 5. **Observe:** What is happening in step 5?

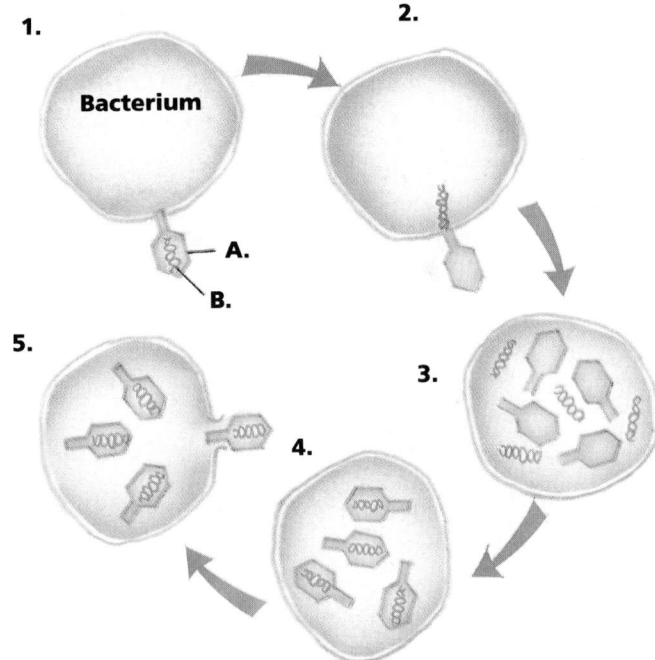

Finding Out More...

1. **Research:** Using library references, find out how the theory of evolution influenced the classification of living things. Write your findings in a report. Include the definition of the term phylogeny in your report.
2. Find and collect pictures of organisms from each of the five kingdoms. Attach the pictures to a posterboard. Label each picture with its proper kingdom.
▲ 3. **Model:** Using common materials, such as clay, styrofoam, and pipe cleaners, make models of

a round virus and a bacteriophage. Label each part of the virus on your model.
4. **Experiment:** Design an experiment to show how liquid is transported in a tracheophyte. Fill a cup halfway with water and add a few drops of food coloring to the water. Cut off about 1 cm of the base of a celery stalk. Place the freshly cut base into the food-coloring solution. Observe the celery for the next 1/2 hour and after 24 hours. Write a laboratory report describing your observations.

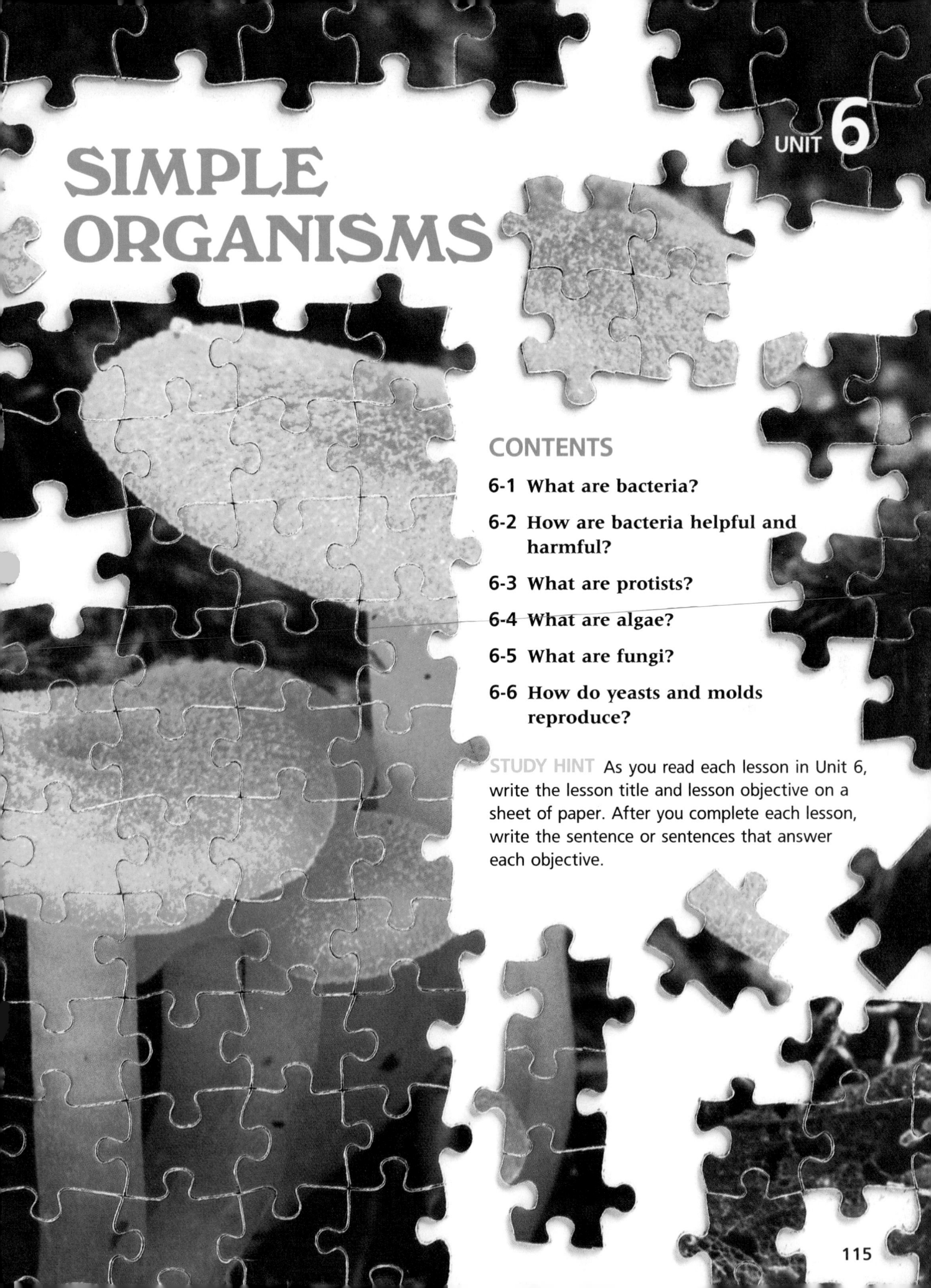

SIMPLE ORGANISMS

CONTENTS

6-1 What are bacteria?

6-2 How are bacteria helpful and harmful?

6-3 What are protists?

6-4 What are algae?

6-5 What are fungi?

6-6 How do yeasts and molds reproduce?

STUDY HINT As you read each lesson in Unit 6, write the lesson title and lesson objective on a sheet of paper. After you complete each lesson, write the sentence or sentences that answer each objective.

6-1 What are bacteria?

Kingdom _Monera_ Bacteria are simple, one-celled living things. They are microscopic. A bacterial cell is made up of cytoplasm, a cell membrane, and a cell wall. Bacteria do not have a nucleus. The material that makes up the nucleus of a bacterial cell is scattered in the cytoplasm of the bacterium. The Kingdom _Monera_ includes all bacteria.

▶ **Compare:** How is a bacterium cell different from an animal cell? Bacteria cells do not contain a nucleus and have a cell wall.

Grouping Bacteria Bacteria are grouped according to their shapes. Some bacteria are round and look like tiny beads. Bacteria with a round, or spherical, shape are called **cocci** (KAK-sy). Some

Cocci

cocci often grow in pairs, chains, or large clusters that look like a bunch of grapes. Other types of bacteria are shaped like a spiral or corkscrew. These bacteria are called **spirilla** (spy-RIL-uh). The most common kind of bacteria are shaped like rods. These bacteria are called **bacilli** (buh-SIL-y). Bacilli often grow in pairs or in chains.

Bacilli

Spirilla

▶ **Identify:** What are the three shapes of bacteria? Round, spiral, and rod-shaped

Blue-green Bacteria Blue-green bacteria are unusual bacteria. They use sunlight to make their own food. Blue-green bacteria also contain the green pigment chlorophyll (KLAWR-uh-fil) in their cytoplasm. Chlorophyll is needed by blue-green bacteria and green plants to make food.

▶ **Explain:** Why can blue-green bacteria make food? The cytoplasm of these cells contains chlorophyll.

Movement in Bacteria Some kinds of bacteria can move on their own. Some bacilli and spirilla have **flagella** (fluh-JEL-uh). Flagella are whiplike structures than enable bacteria to move in liquids. Cocci cannot move on their own because they do not have flagella.

▶ **Describe:** How do some bacteria move? Whiplike structures called flagella push the cell through liquids.

Needs of Bacteria All bacteria need water and a proper temperature. Most live best in darkness. Some bacteria need oxygen. Others can live without oxygen. Some bacteria get their food by living inside plants or animals. Most bacteria feed on the remains of dead plants and animals. The bacteria break down the body of the dead plant or animal. This process is called decay.

Many bacteria can live through periods of extreme heat or cold. When their environments are not right, these bacteria form protective walls around themselves. A bacterium with a protective wall is called an **endospore.** When the environment is favorable, the endospore breaks open. The cell becomes active again.

▶ **Identify:** What is an endospore? bacterium cell enclosed by a protective wall

LESSON SUMMARY

▶ All bacteria are classified in the Kingdom *Monera*.

▶ Bacteria cells have cytoplasm, a cell membrane, and a cell wall. They do not have a nucleus.

▶ Bacteria are grouped according to their shapes.

▶ Blue-green bacteria contain chlorophyll and can make their own food.

▶ Some bacteria have flagella that help them move.

▶ An endospore is a bacterium covered by a protective outer wall.

CHECK *Write true if the statement is true. If the statement is false, change the underlined term to make the statement true.*

1. Bacteria are simple, <u>many-celled</u> organisms.
   one-celled
2. A bacterium cell does not contain a <u>nucleus</u>.
   true
3. Bacteria with a round shape are called <u>bacilli</u>.
   cocci
4. Blue-green bacteria have <u>chlorophyll</u> scattered through their cytoplasm. true
5. The most common bacteria have a <u>spiral</u> shape. rod
6. Whiplike structures that help a bacterium move in liquids are called <u>flagella</u>. true

7. A bacterium with a protective wall is called an <u>endospore</u>. true

APPLY *Complete the following.*

8. **Infer:** A kind of bacteria is discovered feeding on the remains of a dead plant. Are these monerans likely blue-green bacteria? Explain your answer.

9. **Classify:** Classify each of the bacteria shown.

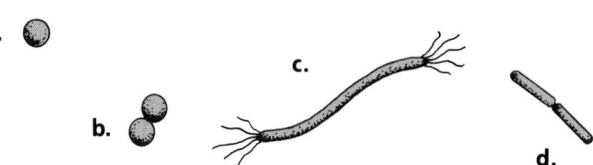

a. b. c. d.

▼.▼.▼. **LOOKING BACK IN SCIENCE** ▼.

CLASSIFICATION OF BACTERIA

At different times during scientific history, bacteria have been classified as plants and protists. Today, bacteria are classified in a separate kingdom. The kingdom is called *Monera.*

When organisms were classified as plants or animals, the bacteria and blue-green bacteria were classified as plants. In fact, blue-green bacteria were called blue-green algae. With the invention of the microscope, scientists discovered a world of microscopic, single-celled organisms. Scientists added the Protist kingdom to the classification system. Bacteria and blue-green bacteria were classified with the protists because they were simple, one-celled organisms.

With the invention of the electron microscope, scientists could see more detailed views of microscopic organisms. They discovered that the cells of bacteria and blue-green bacteria were basically different from those of protists, plants, and animals. So, in recent years, scientists classified bacteria and blue-green bacteria in a separate kingdom of their own.

6-2 How are bacteria helpful and harmful?

Objective ▶ Explain how some bacteria are useful and others are harmful.

TechTerm

▶ **bacteriology** (bak-tir-ee-AHL-uh-jee): study of bacteria

Bacteriology In the mid-1800s the French scientist Louis Pasteur showed how important bacteria are. Pasteur proved that bacteria can cause many diseases. He started the new science of bacteriology (bak-tir-ee-AHL-uh-jee) or the study of bacteria. Pasteur is often called the "father of bacteriology".

▶ *Identify:* Who discovered the importance of bacteria? Louis Pasteur

Bacteria and Foods Many food products are made with the help of bacteria. For example, the action of certain bacteria gives flavor to butter. Other types of bacteria are used to make buttermilk and cheese. Bacteria also are used to make sauerkraut, coffee, and cocoa.

Bacteria play an important part in the digestion of the food you eat. Your digestive tract contains billions of bacteria that help digest proteins. Some digestive bacteria even help form important vitamins.

Figure 1 Digestive bacteria

▶ *List:* Name three foods made by using bacteria. Answers will vary.

Bacteria and Soil Plants need nitrogen to make proteins. Most of the air is nitrogen. However, plants and animals cannot use nitrogen directly

Figure 2 Nodules of nitrogen-fixing bacteria

from the air. Plants can only use nitrogen that has been combined with other elements. Bacteria in soil and in the roots of some plants change nitrogen into compounds plants can use. These bacteria are called nitrogen-fixing bacteria. The "fixed" nitrogen is taken in and used by plants. Animals get the nitrogen they need by eating plants.

▶ *Explain:* Why do living things need nitrogen? to make proteins

Plant Diseases Some types of bacteria can be harmful to plants. Blight is a plant disease caused by bacteria. Blight makes the flowers, young leaves, and stem of a plant die quickly. Rot is another plant disease caused by bacteria. Rot destroys the cell walls of plant tissues. Millions of dollars are lost each year from crop damage caused by these bacterial diseases.

▶ *Explain:* What effect does rot have on a plant? It destroys the cell walls of plant tissues.

Bacteria and Food Decay Bacteria can cause foods to spoil or decay. Some bacteria produce poisons while they are acting on food. It is important that food be protected from the action of bacteria. Cooking foods thoroughly at high temperatures kills harmful bacteria. Canning, pickling, and freezing food are other ways of preventing or slowing down the action of harmful bacteria.

▶ *Infer:* Why are many foods refrigerated? To slow down the action of bacteria on the foods.

LESSON SUMMARY

- ▶ Bacteriology is the study of bacteria.
- ▶ Bacteria are used to make many foods.
- ▶ Bacteria in your digestive tract help you digest foods.
- ▶ Nitrogen-fixing bacteria change nitrogen from the air into nitrogen compounds that can be used by plants to make proteins.
- ▶ Plant diseases, such as blight and rot, are caused by bacteria.
- ▶ Bacteria can cause foods to decay and spoil.

CHECK Complete the following.

1. The study of bacteria is called _____ . bacteriology
2. Bacteria in the digestive tract can help digest _____ . proteins
3. Bacteria that change nitrogen from the air into compounds that plants can use are called _____ . nitrogen-fixing bacteria
4. The plant disease that causes flowers, young leaves, and stems to die quickly is called _____ . blight
5. Some bacteria produce _____ while acting on foods. poisons

APPLY Complete the following.

▶ 6. **Infer:** Why do you think you should not buy canned foods if the can is bulging?

7. Foods that are canned are cooked at a high temperature and then placed in airtight containers. What effect do these actions have on the food?

8. **Apply:** Identify three ways that bacteria affect your life.

InfoSearch

Read the passage. Ask two questions that you cannot answer from the information in the passage.

Pasteurization Pasteurization is a process used to slow down the spoiling of milk and other dairy products. In this process, the milk is quickly heated to kill most of the bacteria. The milk is then quickly cooled. As long as the milk is kept cold, the few living bacteria in it grow very slowly. Pasteurized milk that is kept refrigerated is safe to drink for many days.

SEARCH: Use library references to find answers to your questions.

TECHNOLOGY AND SOCIETY

MAP: MODIFIED ATMOSPHERE PACKAGING

Fruits and vegetables spoil from airborne bacteria. As a result, keeping fruits and vegetables fresh has always been a problem. Chemical sprays have been used on produce to kill bacteria. However, these chemicals remain on the fruit. Some may be harmful to people.

A new method of keeping fresh foods from spoiling is based on controlling the food's environment. The method is called modified atmosphere packaging (MAP). The foodstuff is enclosed by special plastic coverings. This plastic covering only lets in certain gases in the air and lets out other gases. By reducing the amount of oxygen and other gases around the foodstuff, decay is slowed down. The types of packaging used before stopped gases from entering the package. However, they also kept gases from leaving the package. Gases released by the fruits and vegetables were trapped in the package. These gases sped up decay. M.A.P. is unique in that it permits such gases to leave the package. Scientist estimate that the technology of M.A.P. may double the shelf life of fresh produce.

6-3 What are protists?

Objective ▶ Identify some common protists and how they move.

TechTerms

▶ **cilia** (SIL-ee-uh): tiny, hairlike structures

▶ **protozoans** (proh-tuh-ZOH-uns): one-celled, animallike protists

▶ **pseudopod** (SOO-duh-pod): fingerlike projections of cytoplasm used for movement and food-getting

Kingdom *Protista* The protists are a kingdom of very simple organisms. Most protists have only one cell. Some are made up of many cells. All protist cells have a nucleus surrounded by a membrane.

The Protist kingdom is divided into three large groups. The three groups are the **protozoans** (proh-tuh-ZOH-uns), the algae, and the slime molds. The protozoans are one-celled organisms. They often are called the animallike protists because they cannot make their own food. Most protozoans also can move about on their own.

Some algae are one-celled. Others are multicellular (MUL-ti-sel-you-lur), or many-celled. All algae contain chlorophyll. Because they have chlorophyll, algae can make their own food. For this reason, algae are sometimes called plantlike protists.

Classify: Seaweeds are protists that can make their own food. What kind of protist are they? algae

Figure 1 Amoeba

Amoeba The amoeba is a protozoan. Most amoeba live in fresh water. An amoeba uses its pseudopods (SOO-duh-pods) to move through wa-

ter. Pseudopods are fingerlike projections of cytoplasm. The pseudopods of an amoeba also are used to trap and take in food.

Define: What are pseudopods? fingerlike projections of cytoplasm used for movement and food-getting

Paramecium The paramecium is a slipper-shaped protozoan. It is part of a group of protozoans that use **cilia** (SIL-ee-uh) for movement. Cilia are tiny, hairlike structures around the edge of the organism. The cilia move back and forth like tiny oars. The beating of cilia moves a paramecium through water.

Figure 2 Paramecium

Identify: What structure does a paramecium use to move? cilia

Trypanosomes The trypanosome is a disease-causing protozoan. In humans, it causes the disease African sleeping sickness. Trypanosomes are part of a group of protozoans called the flagellates. They have flagella (fluh-JEL-uh). Flagella are whiplike structures used for movement. Some flagellates have one flagellum. Others have two or more.

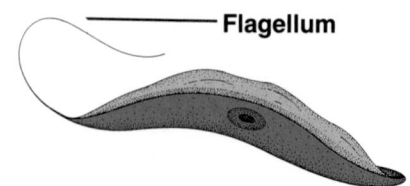

Figure 3 Trypanosomes

Name: How do flagellates move? flagella

- ▶ The protists are a kingdom of very simple animals.

- ▶ Protozoans, algae, and slime molds are classified in the Protist kingdom.

- ▶ Algae are plantlike protists that can make their own food.

- ▶ Pseudopods are used by an amoeba to help it move and get food.

- ▶ A paramecium moves by the beating of cilia.

- ▶ Flagella are whiplike structures that push flagellates through water.

CHECK *Complete the following.*

1. Protozoa, algae, and slime molds all are classified in the _____ kingdom. Protist

2. Amoeba move by using the _____ that extend from their cytoplasm. pseudopods

3. A paramecium moves by beating the _____ that extend from its surface. cilia

4. The whiplike structure that pushes some protozoans through water is called a _____ . flagella

5. African sleeping sickness is caused by a _____ . trypanosome.

APPLY *Complete the following.*

6. **List:** What are the three groups of protists?

7. **Compare:** How are flagella and cilia alike?

InfoSearch....................................

Read the passage. Ask two questions that cannot be answered from the information in the passage.

Slime Molds Slime molds are simple organisms that have two life stages. A slime mold changes as it goes through each of these stages. In its reproductive stage, a slime mold has features similar to a fungus. However, during its feeding stage, a slime mold acts like an amoeba. At one time, scientists classified slime molds as fungi. Today, most scientists classify slime molds with the protists.

SEARCH: Use library references to find answers to your questions.

ACTIVITY

ANALYZING MOVEMENT IN PROTISTS

You will need a pencil and paper.

1. Copy Table 1 on a sheet of paper.

2. Study the protists shown. Complete the table by placing a check mark in the correct column.

3. **Measure:** Count the number of flagella on each flagellate.

Questions

1. **Classify:** Would you classify each of the protists as animallike or plantlike? Explain your answer.

2. **a. Observe:** Which protist has the most flagella? **b.** How many flagella does it have?

3. **Infer:** Where would you most likely find these protists?

4. **Infer:** To study protists, what scientific instrument is most likely to be used? Why?

Anarma

Lacrymaria

Amoeba

Chlamydomonas

Glenodinium

Table 1 Protist Movement			
PROTIST	PSEUDOPOD	FLAGELLA	CILIA
1.			
6.			

Difflugia

6-4 What are algae?

Objective ▶ Identify and describe different kinds of algae.

TechTerms

- ▶ **chlorophyll** (KLAWR-uh-fil): green pigment used by some organisms to make food
- ▶ **plankton** (PLANK-tun): organisms that float at the water's surface

Algae Algae are classified in the protist kingdom. All algae contain **chlorophyll** (KLAWR-uh-fil). Chlorophyll is a green pigment found in plant cells and algae. Plants and algae use chlorophyll to make food. The food-making process is called photosynthesis (foht-uh-SIN-thuh-sis).

▶ **Compare:** How are algae and plants alike? both use chlorophyll to make their own food

One-Celled Algae Some kinds of algae are made up of only one cell. Most one-celled algae live in a watery environment. They float on the surface of the water. Algae are found in **plankton** (PLANK-tun). Plankton are tiny organisms that float on the surface of the oceans.

Although all algae have chlorophyll, all kinds of algae are not green. Fire algae are one-celled algae that are red in color. Golden-brown algae can have a color ranging from yellowish-green to golden-brown. These differences in color are due to other pigments, or colorings, in the algae.

▶ **Identify:** What is plankton? all the tiny plants and animals that float on the surface of lakes and oceans

Euglena The euglena is a unicellular, or one-celled, algae. It is both plantlike and animallike. Like all algae, the euglena contains chlorophyll. It uses the chlorophyll to make food from sunlight. When light is not available, the euglena also can take in food. A structure in the euglena called the eyespot can detect light. The euglena uses its eyespot to find light in the water. The euglena moves to the light by beating the flagellum that extends from its body.

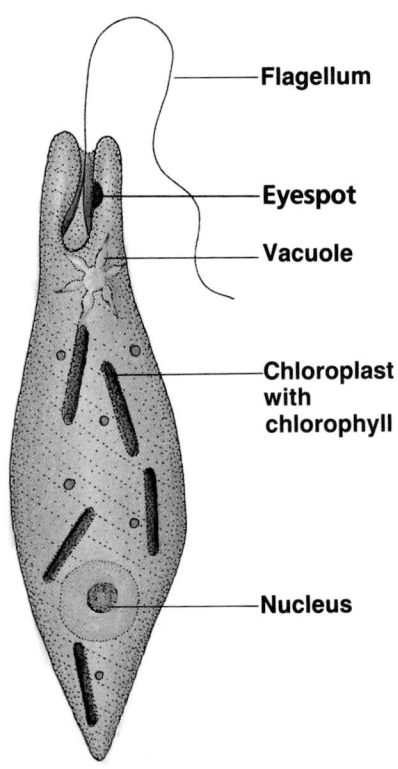

Flagellum
Eyespot
Vacuole
Chloroplast with chlorophyll
Nucleus

▶ **Explain:** How is the euglena animallike? Like animals, it can take in food from the outside and can move.

Many-Celled Algae Some kinds of algae are made up of many cells. These are the multicellular algae. Pigments in multicellular algae may give them a green, red, or brown coloring. Most green algae live in fresh water.

Red and brown algae live in the ocean. Brown algae often are called seaweed or kelp. Brown algae are the largest and most complex kind of algae. If you have visited a beach, you may have seen brown algae washed up along the shoreline.

▶ **Infer:** Why are all types of algae not green? Algae contain pigments of many colors. These pigments sometimes mask the color of chlorophyll.

LESSON SUMMARY

▶ All algae contain chlorophyll and make their own food by photosynthesis.

▶ Some kinds of algae are one-celled.

▶ All algae are not green, but still have chlorophyll.

▶ The euglena is a single-celled algae that is both plantlike and animallike.

▶ Some algae are multicellular.

▶ Red and brown algae are multicellular algae.

CHECK *Complete the following.*

1. Algae _____ make their own food. can

2. Plants and algae both contain the green pigment _____ . chlorophyll

3. The euglena uses its _____ to detect light. eyespot

4. Fire algae are _____ in color. red

5. The largest kind of algae is _____ . brown algae

APPLY *Complete the following.*

6. **Compare:** How is the Euglena similar to the trypanosome?

7. Suppose you needed to obtain a water sample that contained both algae and protozoans. Where would you go to obtain the sample?

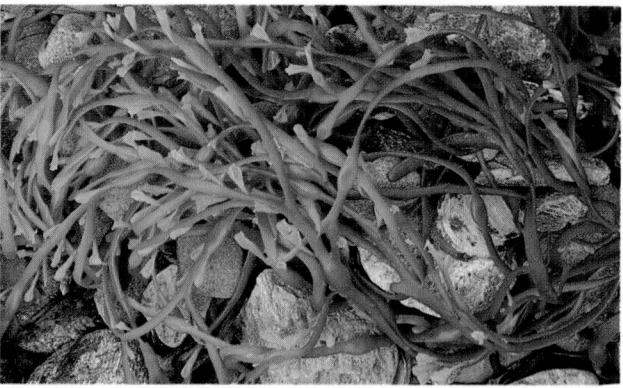

Skill Builder

▲ **Organizing** When you organize information, you put the information into some kind cf order. A table is one way to organize information. Make a table with the following headings: "Type of Algae" and "Product." Use library references to determine the kinds of algae used to make the following products: toothpaste, marshmallows, ice cream, detergent, cheese, and silver polish.

SCIENCE CONNECTION ◆○◆○◆○◆○◆○◆○◆○◆○◆○◆○◆○◆○◆○◆○◆○◆○◆○◆○◆○◆

ALGAL BLOOMS

Algae make their own food by photosynthesis. For photosynthesis to occur, three things must be present -- chlorophyll, sunlight, and carbon dioxide. However, algae also must have water and other nutrients, such as nitrogen and phosphorous, to carry out their life processes. When all of these elements are present, algae can reproduce quickly and in large numbers. A sudden, large growth of algae is called an algal bloom.

Algal blooms often occur when wastes containing phosphates are dumped into ponds or lakes. Phosphates are commonly found in detergents. When an algal bloom occurs, algae can be seen living at the surface of a lake or pond in great numbers. However, an algal bloom can be a problem for organisms that live in the lake or pond. As the algae die, they are broken down by bacteria. The bacteria use oxygen from the water when they break down the algae. If the bacteria use too much oxygen, fishes and other organisms living in the water do not have enough oxygen to carry out their life processes. As a result, the organisms may die.

6-5 What are fungi?

Objective ▶ Describe the different kinds of fungi.

TechTerms

▶ **cap:** umbrella-shaped top of a mushroom

▶ **gills:** structures that produce mushroom spores

▶ **rhizoids** (RY-zoidz): rootlike structures that anchor fungi

Mushroom   **Rhizoids**

Classifying Fungi Fungi are like plants in some ways. The cells of fungi have cell walls. Many fungi also are multicellular, or many-celled, living things. Fungi often grow well in soil like most plants. For these reasons, scientists once classified fungi in the plant kingdom.

Scientists discovered that fungi and plants are not really very much alike. The cells of fungi do not have chloroplasts or chlorophyll. Therefore, fungi cannot make their own food as plants do. Fungi must get food from their surroundings. Fungi get the food they need from other living organisms or from dead organisms. Fungi often have very large cells with many nuclei. They grow well in dark, warm, and wet places. Today, scientists classify fungi in a kingdom of their own. The fungi kingdom includes yeasts, molds, and mushrooms.

▶ **Describe:** Where do fungi usually grow? warm, dark, wet places

Yeasts Yeasts are colorless, one-celled fungi. Yeast cells are surrounded by a cell membrane and a cell wall. Within the cell is cytoplasm and a nucleus. Yeasts grow well where sugar is present. They use the sugar for food.

▶ **Describe:** What structures are found in a yeast cell? cytoplasm, nucleus, cell membrane, and cell wall.

Molds Molds are common kinds of fungi. They grow on bread, fruits, vegetables, and even leath-er. Most molds look like a mass of threads. If you look closely at a bread mold, you will see long threads growing along the surface of the bread. These threads are long, thin strands of cytoplasm. The threads are not divided into separate cells. Instead, each strand has many nuclei.

Some strands produce **spores.** Spores are reproductive cells of fungi. Short threads grow downward into the bread. These rootlike structures are called **rhizoids** (RY-zoidz). The rhizoids anchor the mold to the bread. The rhizoids also release chemicals that break down nutrients in the bread. The nutrients move up through the rhizoids and into the other parts of the mold.

▶ **Identify:** What are rhizoids? Short threads that anchor a mold to its food source.

Mushrooms You probably know a mushroom when you see one because of its shape. The stemlike part of a mushroom is called the **stalk.** At the top of the stalk is an umbrella-shaped top or **cap.** Mushrooms and molds do not look alike, but mushrooms also are made up of threads. In mushrooms, the threads are packed closely together. The underside of the cap is lined with **gills.** The gills produce spores. Spores are the reproductive structures of mushrooms. They are light in weight and easily carried by wind, water, or on the bodies of insects.

▶ **Infer:** What is the job of the stalk of a mushroom? To support the cap.

LESSON SUMMARY

▶ The fungi have cell walls, are usually many-celled, and grow in soil like plants.

▶ Fungi are classified in the kingdom Fungi because they cannot make their own food, have large cells with many nuclei, and grow well in dark, warm, wet places.

▶ Yeasts are one-celled fungi.

Bud forming   **Nucleus dividing**   **Two new cells**

Nucleus

▶ Molds are common fungi that are made up of many threads of cytoplasm.

▶ Mushrooms have a stalk, cap, and gills where spores are produced.

CHECK   *Answer the following.*

1. What are three kinds of fungi? yeasts, molds, and mushrooms
2. Why can fungi not make their own food? They do not have chlorophyll or chloroplasts.
3. Which fungi is colorless and unicellular? yeast
4. What structure anchors a mold to its food source? rhizoids
5. What are the reproductive structures of a mushroom? spores
6. Where are spores produced in mushrooms? the gills

APPLY   *Complete the following.*

7. **Infer:** A mushroom may develop hundreds of kilometers away from the parent mushroom. How might this happen?

8. **Hypothesize:** Mushrooms form a huge number of spores. Why is the ground not covered with mushrooms?

9. **Infer:** Based on the color of a mushroom, how can you tell it does not have chlorophyll?

Health & Safety Tip

Never eat mushrooms that you find growing outdoors. Poisonous mushrooms and edible mushrooms look very similar. Use library references to find out the names of three kinds of poisonous mushrooms. Then draw a picture of each type. Identify any unique trait for each poisonous mushroom you choose.

SCIENCE CONNECTION

FUNGICIDES

Some fungi can cause infections and diseases in people, animals, and plants. Chemical preparations called fungicides are used to prevent or cure diseases caused by fungi. Athlete's foot is a common infection caused by fungi. It is corrected by using a fungicide cream or powder on the infected area. Some nail infections, and scalp diseases in young children are caused by fungi. A mouth infection called thrush is also a fungal infection. Fungal infections are very hard to get rid of. Usually it takes between ten to fourteen days to get ride of a fungal infection. Some infections can take as long as six months to cure. Fungal infections often are treated with medications that can be taken orally. Sulfa drugs and antibiotics are used to treat many fungal infections in people.

Avoiding Athlete's Foot
▶ Wear rubber thongs in public showers.
▶ Always change your socks or stockings each day.
▶ After bathing, be sure to dry the skin between your toes.
▶ Never share socks, shoes, or other footwear.

How do yeasts and molds reproduce?

Objective ▶ Compare and contrast reproduction of yeasts and molds.

TechTerms

- ▶ **asexual** (ay-SEK-shoo-wuhl) **reproduction:** reproduction needing only one parent

- ▶ **budding:** kind of asexual reproduction in which a new organism forms from a bud on a parent

- ▶ **spore cases:** structures that contains spores

- ▶ **sporulation** (spowr-yoo-LAY-shun): kind of asexual reproduction in which a new organism forms from spores released from a parent

Asexual Reproduction In many organisms, only one parent is needed for reproduction. Reproduction that needs only one parent is called **asexual** (ay-SEK-shoo-wuhl) **reproduction.** There are many kinds of asexual reproduction.

▬▶ *Define:* What is asexual reproduction?
Reproduction needing one parent.

Budding One kind of asexual reproduction is **budding.** In budding, a new cell is formed from a tiny bud on a parent cell. Yeast reproduce by budding. During budding, the cell wall of the parent cell pushes outwards. This is the beginning of the bud. The cell nucleus moves toward the bud. The nucleus divides. One nucleus moves into the bud. The other nucleus stays in the parent cell. The bud remains attached to the parent cell and grows larger. In time, a cell wall forms between

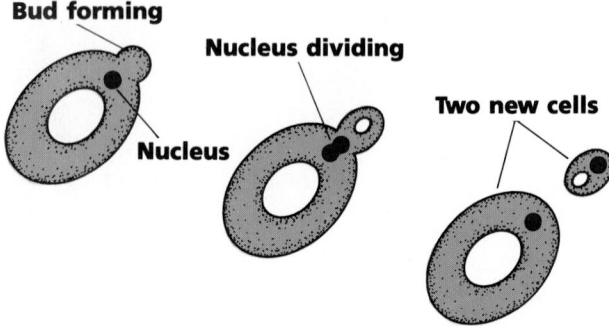

Figure 1 Budding in Yeast

the parent cell and bud. The bud breaks away from the parent cell. It develops into a mature yeast cell.

📁 *Classify:* By what kind of asexual reproduction do yeast cells reproduce? budding

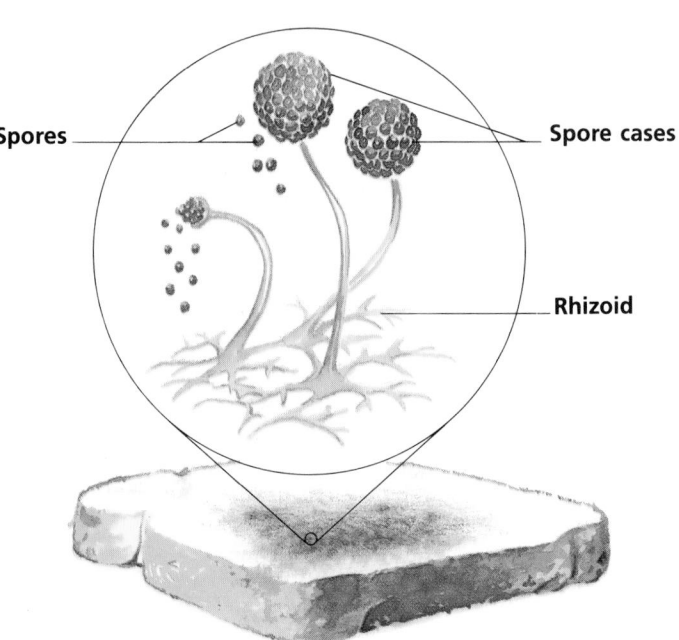

Figure 2 Sporulation in Bread Mold

Sporulation Have you ever seen mold growing on bread? It looks like tangled cotton. Many parts of it are black or gray. Under the low power of a microscope, bread mold looks like many tiny threads. On the top of some of the threads is a ball. This is the **spore case.** Each spore case holds thousands of spores. Spores are the reproductive cells of molds.

When a spore case breaks, thousands of microscopic spores are released. Each spore can grow into a new plant. This kind of reproduction is called **sporulation** (spowr-yoo-LAY-shun). Sporulation is another kind of asexual reproduction. It produces many more offspring than budding.

📁 *Classify:* What kind of reproduction is sporulation? asexual reproduction

▶ Reproduction that needs only one parent is called asexual reproduction.

▶ Budding is a kind of asexual reproduction in which a new organism forms from a bud on a parent organism.

▶ Spore cases contain thousands of spores.

▶ Sporulation is a kind of asexual reproduction.

CHECK *Find the sentence in the lesson that answers each question. Then, write the sentence.*

1. How many parents are needed for asexual reproduction?

2. What fungus reproduces by budding?

3. How many spores are inside a spore case?

4. Where does a bud grow larger?

5. Does sporulation produce more offspring than budding?

APPLY *Complete the following.*

6. **Compare:** How is reproduction of mushrooms similar to that of mold?

7. **Hypothesize:** Why do you think molds are not growing all over everything around you?

InfoSearch

Read the passage. Ask two questions that you cannot answer from the information in the passage.

Alexander Fleming There are many different kinds of molds. Some are harmful. Some types cause disease. Others grow on foods and destroy them. However, there are also molds that are helpful. They are used to make medicines. In 1929, a British scientist named Alexander Fleming was studying bacteria. He discovered that a certain mold could destroy many different kinds of bacteria. This mold is called penicillium. Today penicillin is made from this mold. Penicillin is one of the most important medicines used today.

SEARCH: Use library references to find answers to your questions.

ACTIVITY

GROWING MOLD

You will need three plastic containers with covers, damp paper towels, a magnifying glass, a slice of bread made without preservatives, an orange rind, and a slice of potato.

1. Line the bottom of each container with damp paper towels. Place the bread in one container, the orange in another container, and the potato slice in the third container.

2. Store the containers in a dark place for a few days.

3. Use the magnifying glass to observe the changes in each food sample. Draw a diagram to show the structures you see.

Questions

1. On which food samples did mold grow?

2. **Observe:** Are the molds all the same color? Describe the color.

3. **Infer:** What do the differences in color tell you about the molds?

4. **Infer:** What conditions were needed to grow molds?

5. **Hypothesize:** How could the food samples be protected from mold growth?

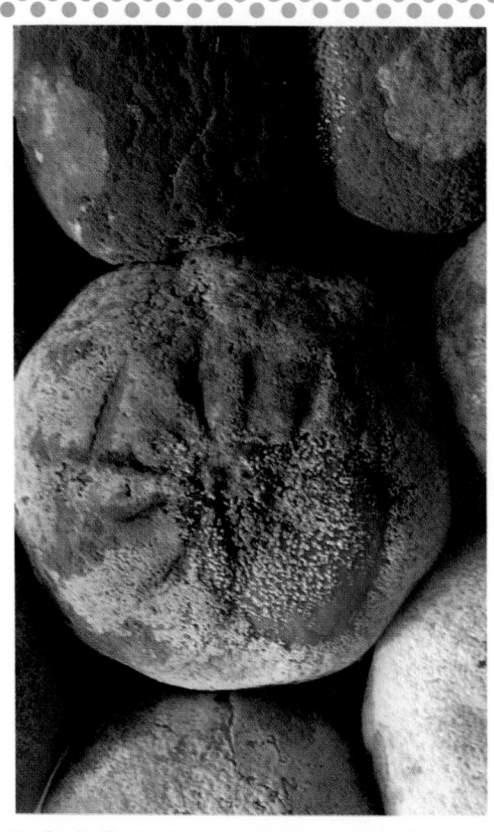

Challenges

STUDY HINT Before you begin the Unit Challenges, review the TechTerms and Lesson Summary for each lesson in this unit.

TechTerms

asexual reproduction (126)
bacilli (116)
bacteriology (118)
budding (126)
cap (124)
chlorophyll (122)

cilia (120)
cocci (116)
endospore (116)
flagella (116)
gills (124)
plankton (122)

protozoans (120)
pseudopod (120)
rhizoids (124)
spirilla (116)
spore cases (126)
sporulation (126)

TechTerm Challenges

Matching *Write the TechTerm that matches each description.*

1. spiral-shaped bacteria spirilla
2. one-celled animallike protists protozoans
3. rootlike structures that anchor fungi rhizoid
4. inactive cell surrounded by a thick wall endospore
5. fingerlike projections of cytoplasm used for movement and food-getting pseudopod
6. spherical bacteria cocci
7. organisms that float at the water's surface plankton
8. material found in chloroplasts that is needed for plants to make food chlorophyll
9. asexual reproduction in which a new organism forms from a bud on a parent budding

Identifying Word Relationships *Explain how the words in each pair are related. Write your answers in complete sentences.* Answers will vary. Accept all logical responses.

1. spore cases, sporulation
2. bacteriology, bacilli
3. cilia, flagella
4. cap, gills
5. asexual reproduction, budding
6. plankton, chlorophyll
7. pseudopod, protozoan

Content Challenges

Multiple Choice *Write the letter of the term that best completes each statement.*

1. Fire algae are
   a. white. **b.** red. **c.** green. **d.** brown. b
2. The *Fungi* kingdom includes yeasts, molds, and
   a. slime molds. **b.** algae. **c.** mushrooms. **d.** protists. c
3. Blight is caused by
   a. bacteria. **b.** fungi. **c.** trypanosomes. **d.** protists. a
4. A paramecium moves by means of
   a. pseudopods. **b.** flagella. **c.** whiplike structures. **d.** cilia. d
5. Yeasts reproduce by
   a. budding. **b.** sporulation. **c.** photosynthesis. **d.** pasteurization. a

6. Bacteria with a round shape are called
   a. cocci.   **b.** spirilla.   **c.** bacilli.   **d.** flagella. a

7. African sleeping sickness is caused by
   a. a paramecium.   **b.** a slime mold.   **c.** an amoeba.   **d.** a trypanosome. d

8. The reproductive cells of fungi are called
   a. rhizoids.   **b.** gills.   **c.** spores.   **d.** threads. c

9. The largest and most complex kind of algae are
   a. red algae.   **b.** brown algae.   **c.** green algae.   **d.** golden-brown algae. b

10. Nitrogen is changed into compounds that plants can use by
    a. fungi.   **b.** bacteria.   **c.** algae.   **d.** protists. b

11. Fungi grow best in places that are
    a. wet.   **b.** dry.   **c.** bright.   **d.** cold. a

12. The eyespot of the *Euglena* can detect
    a. sound.   **b.** water.   **c.** heat.   **d.** light. d

True/False *Write true if the statement is true. If the statement is false, change the underlined term to make the statement true.*

1. Most amoeba live in <u>salt water</u>. fresh
2. The stemlike part of a mushroom is called the <u>cap</u>. stalk
3. All algae contain <u>chlorophyll</u>. true
4. Budding is one kind of <u>asexual</u> reproduction. true
5. Brown algae often are called <u>seaweed</u>. true
6. Bacteria are grouped according to their <u>colors</u>. shapes
7. The study of bacteria was started by <u>Pasteur</u>. true
8. Most protists are <u>many-celled</u> organisms. one-celled
9. A bread mold reproduces by <u>budding</u>. sporulation
10. The <u>paramecium</u> is a slipper-shaped protozoan. true
11. The Kingdom *Monera* includes all bacteria. true
12. Sporulation produces <u>less</u> offspring than budding. more
13. The most common bacteria have a <u>spiral</u> shape. rod
14. Protozoans often are called <u>plantlike</u> protists. animallike
15. Some bacteria can live without <u>oxygen</u>. true

Understanding the Features

Reading Critically *Use the feature reading selections to answer the following. Page numbers for the features follow each question in parentheses.*

1. **Identify:** Where do algal blooms often occur? (123)
2. **Define:** What is a fungicide? (125)
3. Why were bacteria and blue-green bacteria once classified with the protists? (117)
4. **Define:** What is modified atmosphere packaging? (119)

Concept Challenges ....

Interpreting a Diagram *Use the diagram to answer the questions.*

1. What is the part labeled A called?
2. What are the parts labeled B called?
3. What is the function of the parts labeled B?
4. What is the part labeled C called?
5. What are the parts labeled D called?
6. What are the functions of the parts labeled D?

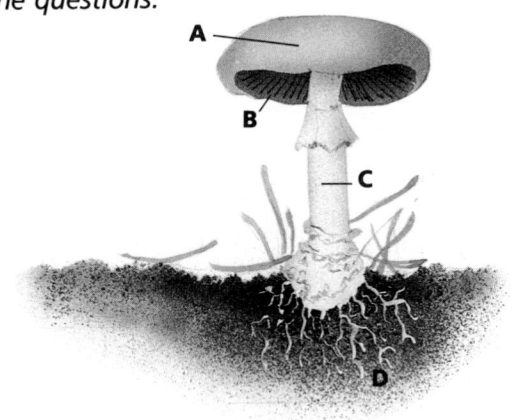

Critical Thinking *Answer each of the following in complete sentences.*

1. How do canning, pickling, and freezing foods prevent the growth of bacteria?
2. **Analyze:** Why do you think many-celled algae are not classified as plants?
3. **Compare:** How are fungi similar to plants? How are they different?

4. How do bacteria help animals in making proteins?
5. **Hypothesize:** If you wanted to find fungi in your area, where would you look?

Finding Out More ....

1. Call the health department in your area and ask about careers in microbiology. Present your findings in an oral report.
2. Chemical preservatives are added to some foods to slow spoilage. Some preservatives are sodium or calcium proprionate, sorbic acid, and sulfur dioxide. Go to the grocery store and find two foods containing each preservative. In a brief report, describe the kinds of foods in which each preservative is used.
3. **Model:** A trypanosome has a complex life cycle that involves two hosts. Using library references, research the life cycle of a trypanosome. Draw a model illustrating the life cycle.

4. **Research:** Agar is a substance used to make foods such as pudding, ice cream, cheese, and marshmallows. Find out how red algae are used to make agar. Write your findings in a report.
5. Examine a mushroom with a hand lens. Identify the cap, the stalk, and the gills. Sketch a diagram of your mushroom.

PLANTS

CONTENTS

STUDY HINT Before beginning Unit 7, review the TechTerms for each lesson and read the Lesson Summary.

7-1 Why are plants important?

Objectives ▶ Identify different plants used for food. ▶ Describe how plants are used in medicine and industry.

TechTerm

▶ **legumes** (LEG-yooms): group of plants that includes beans and peas

Plants for Food Early humans spent much of their time gathering plants to eat. About 10,000 years ago, people began to cultivate, or to plant and grow certain plants just for food. Evidence from prehistoric campsites shows that cereal grains, such as wheat and corn, were the first food crops. Later people began to plant **legumes** (LEG-yooms). Legumes are beans and peas. Fruit crops were cultivated next. The last food crops to be cultivated were roots. Today, about 100 different plants are grown as food crops.

Observe: What are five plants cultivated for food? Answers will vary.

Medicines from Plants Drugs used as medicines are made from many different plants. For instance, the leaves of the foxglove plant contain a

substance that helps people who have had a heart attack. The drug helps the heart pump with more force. The bark of willow trees contains a chemical used to make aspirin. The bark of the cinchona tree is a source of quinine (KWI-nine). Quinine is used against malaria (muh-LER-ee-uh). Malaria is a disease caused by a single-celled organism that destroys red blood cells. When you go to the eye doctor, the doctor uses a drug that comes from the leaves and roots of the belladonna plant. When the drops of the drug are put in your eyes, the drug makes the pupil of your eye open up more. The eye doctor can examine your eyes easier.

Identify: What are three plants that contain medicines? Answers will vary.

Useful Plant Products Plants are used by people in many ways. Trees are used for building materials. Lumber and cork come from trees. Other products that come from trees are turpentine, waxes, and rubber. The oils used to make perfume come from flowers and other plant parts. Some plants provide us with fibers. The fibers can be spun into threads. The threads can be woven into cloth. For example, cotton is made from cotton plants. Linen is made from flax plants. Twine or string is made from linden plants.

The most useful plant product is cellulose (SEL-yoo-lohs). Cellulose is the hard, nonliving material in plant cell walls. It is used to make products you use or see every day. Cellulose is used to make paper. It also is used to make rayon cloth, paints, plastics, sponges, cellophane, camera film, and eyeglass frames.

List: What are five common items obtained from plants? Answers will vary.

LESSON SUMMARY

▶ Many different kinds of plants are grown for food, including cereal grains, legumes, and fruits and vegetables.

▶ Many different kinds of plants are the source of drugs and medicines.

▶ Plants are used for materials, to make perfume oils, and as fibers for cloth.

▶ Cellulose is a plant product that is used to make many different products.

CHECK *Complete the following.*

1. People began to cultivate food crops about _____ years ago. 10,000

2. The _____ plant contains a drug used to help people who have had a heart attack. foxglove

3. Beans and peas are examples of _____ . legumes

4. Corn and wheat are examples of _____ . cereal grains

5. Rayon and plastics can be made from the plant material called _____ . cellulose

APPLY *Complete the following.*

6. **Sequence:** List food plants in the order in which they were first cultivated. cereal grains, legumes, fruits, roots

7. **Infer:** What structure does the cotton plant have that makes it useful in making cloth? It has fibers that can be woven.

Ideas in Action

IDEA: Many different plants are used for food.
ACTION: Work with a partner and list 15 different plants that are eaten by people. As a class, try to list more than 50 plants used for food.

PEOPLE IN SCIENCE

GEORGE WASHINGTON CARVER (1864–1943)

George Washington Carver was a botanist and plant chemist. He was born a slave, but as a young boy he worked hard to get an education. He graduated at the top of his college class.

Carver was invited by Booker T. Washington to join the staff of Tuskegee Institute. There he analyzed soil from local farms. He found that the main crops, cotton and tobacco, had taken most of the minerals from the soil. This poor soil kept the farmers from growing healthy, profitable crops. Carver experimented and found that growing legume crops, such as peanuts and soybeans, in rotation with cotton helped revive the soil.

The farmers soon had more peanuts than they could sell. To solve the problem of all those extra peanuts, Carver developed more than 300 uses for peanuts. These uses included cheese substitutes, paper, face cream, soap, ink, and dyes.

7-2 What are spore plants?

TechTerms

- **bryophyte** (BRY-uh-fyt): plant that reproduces by spores and has no transport tubes
- **rhizoid** (RY-zoid): fine hairlike structure that acts as a root
- **spore:** reproductive cell of bryophytes

Figure 2 Moss plants

Bryophytes Have you ever seen green, velvetlike plants growing on rocks and tree trunks? These plants are mosses. Mosses are classified in the phylum *Bryophyta* (BRY-uh-fuh-tuh). Figure 1 shows two other kinds of plants classified as **bryophytes** (BRY-uh-fyts). They are liverworts and hornworts. The bryophytes are thought to have been the first plants to live on land. Even though they live on land, bryophytes can live only where there is a good supply of water. They need water for reproduction.

Figure 1 (a) Liverworts   **(b)** Hornworts

The bryophytes are spore plants. Spore plants produce spores instead of seeds. A **spore** is a reproductive cell.

◉ *Observe:* What structures of liverworts and hornworts do you think produce spores? Answers will vary. Accept all logical responses.

Structure of Bryophytes Bryophytes are small plants. They are usually only a few centimeters tall. Bryophytes differ from most other plants in a

few ways. Unlike most plants, bryophytes do not have true roots, stems, or leaves. Instead, they have fine hairlike structures called **rhizoids** (RY-zoids). Like roots, rhizoids grow down into the soil and anchor the plant. They also take in water and dissolved minerals.

Most plants have a system of tubes that carry water and dissolved materials throughout the plant. Bryophytes do not have these tubes. Instead, the individual cells get what they need as water and dissolved materials seep from one cell to another. The absence of transport tubes limits the size of these plants.

▶ *Identify:* What are two characteristics of bryophytes? spores and lack of transport tubes

Mosses If you look closely at a moss plant you will see thin stalks with tiny leaflike parts. The leaflike parts make food for the plants. Rhizoids anchor the mosses. You also may see taller stalks. At the top of these stalks, there are spore cases. The spore cases are filled with spores.

▶ *Name:* What structure of a moss holds the spores? spore case

Pioneer Plants Bryophytes are called pioneer plants. Pioneer plants are the first plants to grow in bare or rocky places. As they grow, their rhizoids help break down rocks to form soil. As the plants die and decay, they add richness to the forming soil. As a soil layer builds up, other plants, such as shrubs and trees, may grow. In time, a forest may grow.

▶ *Define:* What are pioneer plants? the first plants to grow in bare or rocky places

LESSON SUMMARY

- The phylum *Bryophyta* includes mosses, liverworts, and hornworts.
- Bryophytes are spore plants.
- Bryophytes are small plants that do not have true roots, stems, or leaves.
- Bryophytes do not have tubes to carry water and dissolved materials throughout the plant.
- Mosses have thin stalks with tiny leaflike parts.
- Pioneer plants are the first plants to grow in bare or rocky places.

CHECK *Complete the following.*

1. What kind of plants are bryophytes? spore plants
2. What are the reproductive structures of bryophytes called? spores
3. Name three kinds of bryophytes. liverworts, mosses, hornworts
4. What are the rootlike structures of bryophytes called? rhizoids
5. In what structure are the spores of mosses produced? spore cases

APPLY *Complete the following.*

▶ 6. **Infer:** In what ways are bryophytes less suited to life on land than other plants?

7. **Compare:** In what ways are rhizoids like roots?

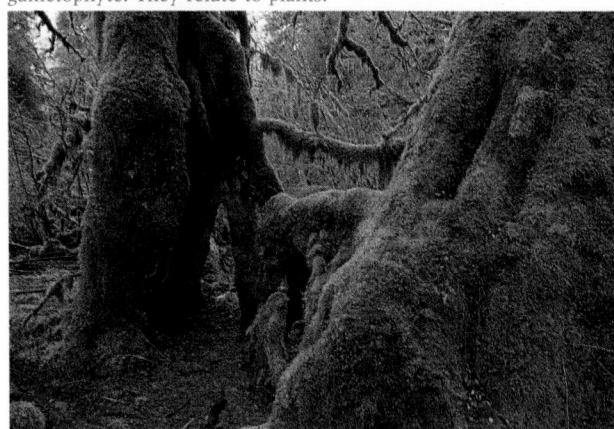

LOOKING BACK IN SCIENCE

SCOURING RUSHES

Horsetails are spore plants that have tubes for transporting materials. They are an ancient plant. Fossil horsetails have been found in rocks nearly 400 million years old. Tree-size horsetails once formed huge forests on the earth. Modern horsetails are smaller than the ancient horsetails. Modern horsetails grow in woodlands and swamps. They have hollow, jointed stems with small leaves around each joint. The stems and leaves look like the tail of a horse. Spores are located in spore cases at the top of some of the stems. The outer layer of the stem is made up of a single layer of cells. The cell walls contain silica (SIL-i-kuh). Silica is a compound in sand. Silica gives horsetails a rough, stiff and gritty texture. American colonists called horsetails "scouring rushes." They used horsetails to clean and scour pots and pans in the days before steel-wool pads and nonstick coatings.

What are ferns?

Blade

Frond

Rhizome

Roots

Objective ▶ Name and describe the structure of a fern.

TechTerms

▶ **frond:** featherlike leaf of a fern

▶ **rhizome** (RY-zohm): underground stem

Ferns Ferns are common spore plants. They grow in great numbers in warm, moist areas, but they also live in cooler, drier areas. Most ferns can be recognized by their featherlike leaves. These leaves are called **fronds.** Each frond is made up of blades. The fronds are the part of the fern that can be seen above ground.

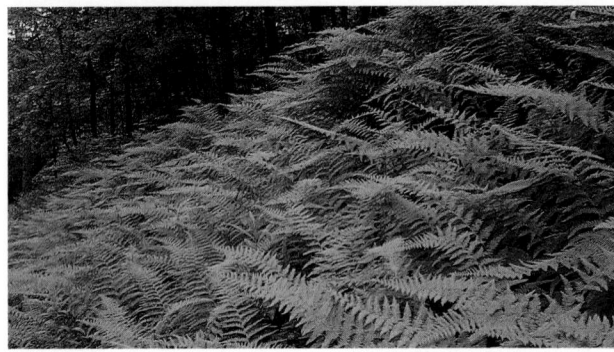

Ferns vary greatly in size and shape. Most ferns are about 1 m tall. Some ferns are only 3 cm tall. Some ferns, however, are giant fern trees of the South Pacific. They grow up to 15 m tall.

▶ *Identify:* What is the most recognizable part of a fern? the featherlike leaves

Prehistoric Ferns About 300 million years ago, giant tree ferns were the most common kind of land plant. They formed huge forests. The remains of these and other plants eventually became buried under thick layers of earth. The pressure of the overlying layers, along with chemical changes, gradually changed this material to coal. Most of the giant tree ferns died out about 225 million years ago.

▶ *Describe:* In what form did prehistoric ferns grow? as giant trees

Structure of a Fern The structure of ferns differs from that of bryophytes. First, most modern ferns are about a meter or so tall. Second, ferns have true roots, stems, and leaves. Fern stems and roots grow underground. The underground stems are called **rhizomes.** They grow parallel to the surface. Roots grow downward from the rhizome, while the fronds grow upward.

Ferns are also similar to bryophytes. They reproduce by spores. If you look underneath a fern frond, you will see tiny brown spots. These are spore cases. Each case is filled with hundreds of spores.

▶ *Name:* What is the underground stem of a fern called? rhizome

LESSON SUMMARY

▶ Ferns are common plants with fronds.

▶ Ferns vary greatly in size and shape.

▶ Prehistoric ferns were giant trees that gradually were changed to coal.

▶ Ferns have true roots, stems, and leaves, and a transporting system of tubes.

▶ Ferns are spore plants.

CHECK *Complete the following.*

1. The featherlike leaves of ferns are the _____ . fronds

2. The rhizome of a fern is an underground _____ . stem

3. Ferns have true stems, _____, and leaves. roots

4. In ferns, spore cases form on the underside of the _____ . fronds

APPLY *Complete the following.*

▲ 5. **Model:** Draw a picture of a fern. Label the frond, rhizome, and blades.

▶ 6. **Infer:** What part of a fern makes food for the fern? How do you know?

InfoSearch

Read the passage. Ask two questions about the topic that you cannot answer from the information in the passage.

Forming Coal Coal is a fossil fuel. It was formed from the remains of giant fern trees and other plants. The plants lived in swamps. When the plants died, they were covered by mud, water, and other sediments. Heat and pressure slowly caused chemical changes to take place. Bacteria also caused chemical changes. After millions of years, most of the compounds in the plants changed so that only carbon was left. The carbon formed coal.

SEARCH: Use library references to find answers to your questions.

Skill Builder

Researching There are four kinds of coal. They are peat, lignite, bituminous coal, and anthracite. Find out about these types of coal. Which kind of coal is called soft coal and brown coal? Which kind of coal is the hardest? Write a report about your findings.

LEISURE ACTIVITY

INDOOR GARDENING

Indoor gardening is a popular activity. Most indoor gardeners like plants that look nice and are easy to take care of. For these reasons, many people grow ferns as house plants. The delicate, feathery fronds of ferns are very attractive. Ferns also grow well in shade. In fact, many kinds of ferns grow well in complete shade. They are perfect for indoor gardening in apartments.

All ferns need a very light, peat-filled soil in order to grow well. The soil should be kept damp at all times. Ferns also like moist air. You should mist ferns with a fine spray of water. It helps them stay healthy. A little liquid plant food during the growing season is useful. Most ferns like a cool place. They should not be put in direct sunlight. A north-facing window is ideal for many ferns.

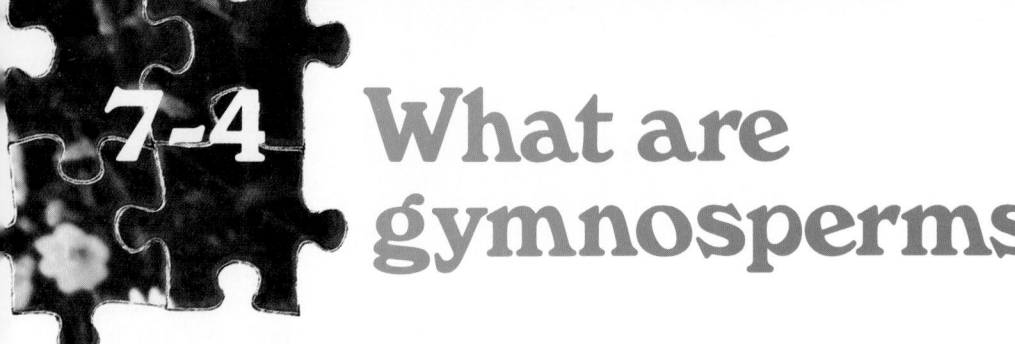

7-4 What are gymnosperms?

Objective ▶ Name and describe three kinds of gymnosperms.

TechTerms

- ▶ **conifer** (KAHN-uh-fur): tree that produces cones and has needlelike leaves
- ▶ **gymnosperms** (JIM-nuh-spurms): group of land plants with uncovered seeds
- ▶ **seed:** structure that contains a tiny living plant and food for its growth

Gymnosperms Millions of years after the appearance of ferns, a group of woody land plants arose. These plants were the **gymnosperms** (JIM-nuh-spurms). The gymnosperms are a large group of land plants that have uncovered seeds. A **seed** is a reproductive structure. The seeds of most plants have a tough outer covering for protection. The seeds of gymnosperms do not have a protective covering. Gymnosperms also have stiff, woody stems. They have a system of tubes for carrying water and dissolved materials. They also have true roots, stems, and leaves.

▌▶ **Define:** What is a gymnosperm? land plant with uncovered seeds

Conifers The most common and best known of the gymnosperms are the evergreens, or **conifers** (KAHN-uh-furs). Conifers are plants that produce cones. The seeds are in the cones. Conifers have special leaves called needles. The needles stay green throughout the year. Pines, cedars, spruces, and hemlock are conifers.

Conifers are grown in all climates and soil types. Many conifers grow in the forests of northern Europe and North America. The giant redwood trees, or sequoias (si-KWOI-uhs), of California also are conifers. Some of these trees are more than 100 m tall and 9 m in diameter. Other gymnosperms are palmlike trees. They grow in tropical areas.

▶ **Infer:** Why are conifers also called evergreens? Their needles stay green throughout the year.

Importance of Conifers The conifers are an important group of plants. They are widely used as a source of lumber and fuel. They also are used in the production of paper. Turpentine, charcoal, tar, and alcohol are made from gymnosperms. Spruces and firs are planted along the edges of farms. The wall of trees slows down the wind, keeping rich soil from blowing away.

▌▶ **List:** What are three uses of gymnosperms? Answers will vary.

Cycads and Ginkgoes Two other kinds of gymnosperms are cycads (SY-kads) and ginkgoes (GIN-kohs). Cycads grow mainly in tropical areas. Most look like small palm trees. They have large, feathery, fernlike leaves. Female trees have a very large conelike structure in the center. The ginkgoes have fan-shaped leaves. Unlike the evergreens, ginkgoes shed their leaves in the fall. Ginkgoes often are grown along city streets because they grow well even in polluted air.

▌▶ **Name:** What are two other groups of gymnosperms? cycads and ginkgoes

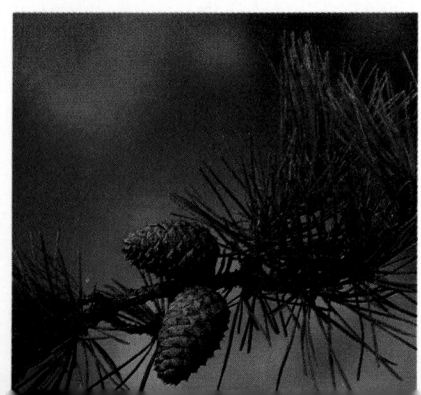

LESSON SUMMARY

▶ Gymnosperms are woody land plants that have true roots, stems, and leaves, transporting tubes, and uncovered seeds.

▶ Conifers are a group of gymnosperms that produce seeds in cones and have needles.

▶ Conifers are used as a source for many different products such as lumber and fuel.

▶ Cycads and ginkgoes are two other groups of gymnosperms.

CHECK *Write true if the statement is true. If the statement is false, change the underlined term to make the statement true.*

1. The most common of the gymnosperms are the <u>ferns</u>. conifers

2. An example of a conifer is a <u>pine</u> tree. true

3. Conifers produce seeds in <u>cones</u>. true

4. The gymnosperms include <u>evergreens</u>. true

5. Turpentine, lumber, and tar are made from <u>cycads</u>. conifers

6. <u>Ginkgoes</u> shed their leaves in autumn. true

APPLY *Complete the following.*

▲ 7. **Model:** A giant redwood tree has a diameter of 9 m. Use the scale 1 mm equals 50 cm. Draw a circle to represent the 9-m diameter of the redwood tree's trunk.

👁 8. **Observe:** Which of the following shows a gymnosperm? How can you tell?

 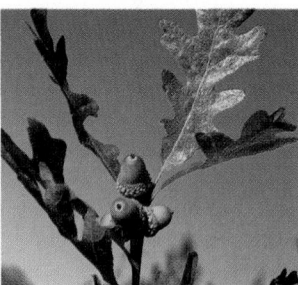

(a)   (b)

Ideas in Action

IDEA: Wood from pine and cedar trees often is used to make furniture, shelving, and doors.
ACTION: Identify objects in your home that are made from wood from these conifers. Organize your information in a table.

ACTIVITY

OBSERVING PINE CONES

You will need several different pine cones, a field guide to trees, and a metric ruler.

1. Collect a pine cone from three different conifers. Take a few cones that have already fallen from each kind of conifer.

2. Use the field guide to help you identify which kind of tree the cones come from. Label the cones.

🧪 3. **Measure:** Look at the cones carefully. Each scale of the cone had a seed. Count the number of seeds that one of the cones could form.

🧪 4. **Measure:** Measure the length of each cone. Organize the data in a table.

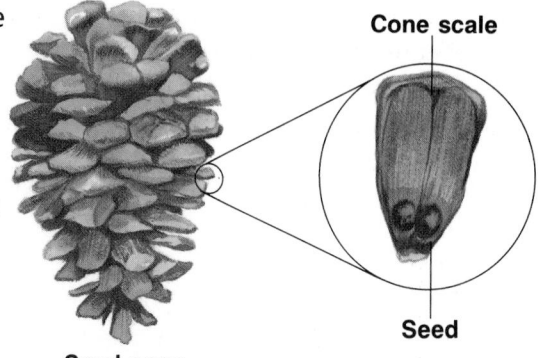

Cone scale

Seed

Seed cone

Questions

1. Are all the cones from the same tree identical? no

2. **Compare and Contrast:** How are the cones from the same tree alike? How are they different? Answers will vary.

3. How many seeds could form in the cone you chose? Answers will vary.

7-5 What are angiosperms?

Objective ▸ Identify monocots and dicots as two kinds of angiosperms.

TechTerms

- **angiosperms** (AN-jee-uh-spurms): flowering plants
- **cotyledon** (kaht-LEED-on): seed structure that contains food for the developing plant
- **dicots:** seed plants with two cotyledons
- **monocots:** seed plants with one cotyledon

Angiosperms The **angiosperms** (AN-jee-uh-spurms) are the flowering plants. Scientists estimate that the angiosperm first appeared about 250 million years ago. They gradually replaced the gymnosperms as the major land plants. Today, scientists have classified about 250,000 kinds of angiosperms. They are the largest plant group.

▸ *Identify:* What is another name for angiosperms? flowering plants

Characteristics of Angiosperms Most of the common plants you see every day are angiosperms. Like gymnosperms, angiosperms have true roots, stems, and leaves. They also have a highly-developed system of transport tubes.

All angiosperms have flowers. No other plant group has flowers. In some angiosperms, the flowers are not very noticeable. You probably have never seen the flowers of grasses, oak trees or corn. They have very small flowers. Other angiosperms have large, colorful flowers.

▸ *Name:* What is the main characteristic of angiosperms? flowers

Seeds and Fruits Like gymnosperms, angiosperms are seed plants. The flowers of angiosperms produce seeds and fruits. The seeds of angiosperms are inside the fruit. Thus, the seeds of angiosperms are covered and protected. The next time you eat a piece of fruit look for the

seeds. You will see one seed or many seeds. Most angiosperms produce a lot of seeds.

▸ *Name:* What do the flowers of angiosperms produce? fruits and seeds

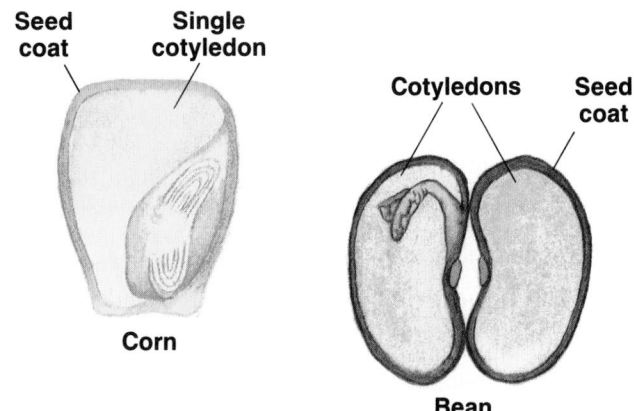

Seed coat — Single cotyledon

Corn

Cotyledons — Seed coat

Bean

Monocots and Dicots Angiosperms are classified into two groups based on their seed structure. Within the seeds of angiosperms are structures that contain food for the developing plant. These structures are called **cotyledons** (kaht-LEED-ons). The seeds of one group contain a single cotyledon. Plants of this group are **monocots.** In plants of the second group, the seeds have two cotyledons. These plants are **dicots.**

▸ *Identify:* What is a cotyledon? seed structure containing food for developing plant

Identifying Monocots and Dicots You can tell if a plant is a monocot or a dicot by looking at its flowers and leaves. Monocots have flowers with petals arranged in groups of three. Petals are the colorful parts of flowers. The veins in the leaves of monocots are parallel. Dicots have flowers with petals arranged in groups of four or five. The veins in the leaves of dicots are branched.

▸ *Contrast:* In what way are monocot flowers and dicot flowers different? number of petals in flowers

LESSON SUMMARY

► Angiosperms are the flowering plants.

► Angiosperms have true leaves, roots, and stems.

► The flowers of angiosperms produce seeds inside fruits.

► Angiosperms are classified as monocots and dicots based upon the number of cotyledons in their seeds.

► Monocots and dicots can be identified by examining their leaf vein pattern and the number of petals that make up the flowers.

CHECK *Complete the following.*

1. Monocots have leaves with _____ veins. parallel

2. The seeds of angiosperms are enclosed in _____ . fruits

3. Angiosperms have a transport system made up of _____ . tubes

4. Fruits are produced by the plant parts called _____ . flowers

5. The number of cotyledons in a dicot seed is _____ . two

6. Monocot flowers have petals in groups of _____ . three

APPLY *Complete the following.*

▲ 7. **Model:** Draw a model of an imaginary monocot and an imaginary dicot. Label the number of petals and the pattern of leaf veins.

Skill Builder

Using Prefixes Use a dictionary to find out the meanings of the prefixes ''mono-'' and ''di-.'' Monocots also are called monocotyledons. Dicots are called dicotyledons. What do the prefixes ''mono-'' and ''di-'' tell you about the difference between monocots and dicots? Use the meaning of the prefix ''mono-'' to define the words *monorail* and *monosyllable*. Check your definitions with a dictionary.

ACTIVITY

CLASSIFYING MONOCOTS AND DICOTS

You will need 10 different leaves, cellophane tape, and 10 sheets of unlined paper.

1. Obtain 10 different leaves.

2. Trace the outline of each leaf on a separate sheet of paper.

▲ 3. **Model:** Draw in the vein patterns of each leaf.

📂 4. **Classify:** Based upon the vein pattern, classify each leaf as a monocot or a dicot. Write a label above each leaf.

Questions

1. **Compare:** How are the monocot leaves alike? All are parallel.

2. **Compare:** How are the dicot leaves alike? All are branching, or net-like.

◢ 3. **Analyze:** What leaf features do not help in classifying them as monocots or dicots? Accept all logical answers, such as color, general shape, shape of the edges, size.

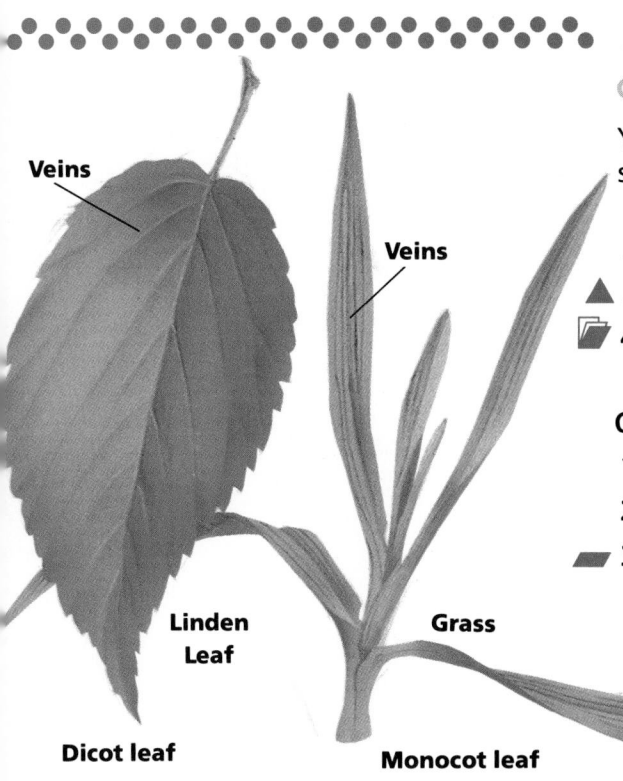

Veins

Veins

Linden Leaf

Grass

Dicot leaf

Monocot leaf

Challenges

STUDY HINT Before you begin the Unit Challenges, review the TechTerms and Lesson Summary for each lesson in this unit.

TechTerms..

angiosperms (140)
bryophyte (134)
conifer (138)
cotyledon (140)
dicots (140)

frond (136)
gymnosperms (138)
legumes (132)
monocots (140)
rhizoid (134)

rhizome (136)
seed (138)
spore (134)

TechTerm Challenges..

Matching *Write the TechTerm that best matches each description.*

1. fine hairlike structure that acts as a root rhizoid
2. tree with cones and needlelike leaves conifer
3. flowering plants angiosperms
4. group of plants that includes beans and peas legumes
5. reproductive cell of bryophytes spore
6. seed plants with two cotyledons dicots
7. plant that reproduces by spores and has no transport tubes bryophyte

Identifying Word Relationships *Explain how the words in each pair are related. Write your answers in complete sentences.* Answers will vary. Accept all logical responses.

1. seed, angiosperm
2. bryophyte, spore
3. conifers, gymnosperms
4. stem, rhizome
5. cotyledons, monocots
6. root, rhizoid
7. frond, leaf

Content Challenges..

Multiple Choice *Write the letter of the term or phrase that best completes each statement.*

1. The most useful plant product is
   a. rubber. **b.** cellulose. **c.** wax. **d.** quinine. b

2. The last food crops to be cultivated were
   a. fruit crops. **b.** cereal grains. **c.** roots. **d.** legumes. c

3. Plants that do not have true roots, stems, or leaves are classified as
   a. bryophytes. **b.** gymnosperms. **c.** ferns. **d.** angiosperms. a

4. Bryophytes can live only where there is a good supply of
   a. minerals. **b.** soil. **c.** water. **d.** unpolluted air. c

5. The underground stem of a fern is a
   a. root. **b.** rhizome. **c.** frond. **d.** rhizoid. b

6. The leaves of conifers are called
   a. needles. **b.** fronds. **c.** cones. **d.** blades. a

7. Plant structures common to all angiosperms are
   a. spore cases. **b.** flowers. **c.** rhizomes. **d.** monocots. b

8. The number of cotyledons in a dicot is
   a. one. **b.** two. **c.** three. **d.** four. a

9. The leaves of a foxglove plant contain a substance used to treat people with
   a. heart problems   b. kidney problems   c. cancer   d. asthma a

10. Linen is made from
    a. cotton plants   b. belladonna plants   c. flax plants   d. cinchona trees c

11. Pioneer plants are
    a. angiosperms   b. gymnosperms   c. bryophytes   d. tracheophytes c

12. Pines, cedars, spruces, and hemlock are
    a. cycads   b. gingkos   c. angiosperms   d. conifers d

13. The largest plant group is made up of
    a. gymnosperms   b. angiosperms   c. bryophytes   d. rhizoids b

True/False *Write true if the statement is true. If the statement is false, change the underlined term to make the statement true.*

1. Plants are used to make many useful products such as <u>turpentine</u>, cork, and lumber. true

2. Legumes are beans and <u>wheat</u>. peas

3. The bark of the <u>cinchona</u> tree is a source of a chemical used to make aspirin. willow

4. Three plants classified as bryophytes are mosses, <u>liverworts</u>, and hornworts. true

5. Spore plants produce <u>flowers</u> instead of seeds. spores

6. Cedars and cycads are classified as <u>gymnosperms</u>. true

7. Conifers are plants that produce <u>cones</u>. true

8. Conifers also are called <u>evergreens</u>. true

9. Flowering plants are classified as <u>gymnosperms</u>. angiosperms

10. Both gymnosperms and <u>bryophytes</u> produce seeds. angiosperms

Understanding the Selections..

Reading Critically *Use the feature reading selections to answer the following. Page number for the features are in parentheses.*

1. **List:** What are some of the products that George Washington Carver made from peanuts? (133)

2. **Explain:** How did George Washington Carver revive soil that had been depleted through cotton and tobacco planting? (133)

3. **Identify:** What compound gives horsetails their rough gritty texture? (135)

4. What are two things the owner of a fern can do to keep the plant healthy? (137)

5. **Infer:** Why might direct sunlight harm a fern? (137)

Concept Challenges..

Critical Thinking *Answer each of the following in complete sentences.*

1. **Contrast:** Explain two ways bryophytes differ from other groups of plants.

2. **Compare:** Identify one way in which ferns are similar to bryophytes.

3. **Identify:** What is the reproductive structure of a gymnosperm?

4. **Contrast:** How does a monocot differ from a dicot?

5. **Predict:** How would your life be different if there were no plants?

Interpreting a Diagram *Answer the questions about the diagram.*

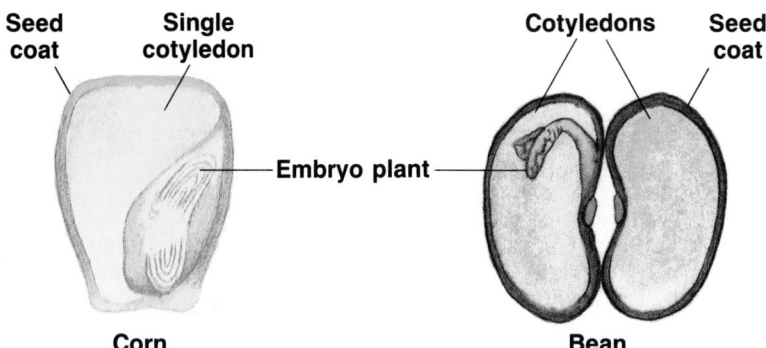

1. **Identify:** Both corn and beans are members of a group of plants called angiosperms. What features of the seeds from these plants identify them as angiosperms?

2. Which seed is a monocot? How do you know?

3. Which seed is a dicot? How do you know?

4. **Describe:** Where is the cotyledon located?

5. **Observe:** What structure encases and protects the cotyledon in both monocots and dicots?

Finding Out More...

1. **Communicate:** Some careers open to plant lovers include working as a florist, a gardener, or a landscape architect. Use library references to find out about the duties and job requirements of one of these careers. Present your findings to the class in an oral report. Be sure to include information about the skills and educational requirements for job as well as information about what the job involves.

2. Make a terrarium in a large bottle using mosses, ferns, and other spore plants. Be sure that your terrarium has the proper growth conditions for each kind of plant. Check your terrarium daily to note any changes in the appearance of your plants. Keep a written record of these changes. Be sure to look for changes in color, size, and growth rate.

3. **Organize:** Make a list of twenty different kinds of plants that are common in your community. Use a field guide to identify each plant. In a table, classify each of the plants you identified as a gymnosperm or an angiosperm.

4. **Classify:** Cut pictures of ten different kinds of flowers from magazines. Make a poster that classifies each kind of flower as a dicot or a monocot.

PLANT STRUCTURE AND FUNCTION

CONTENTS

STUDY HINT After you read each lesson in Unit 8, write a brief summary on a sheet of paper explaining how the information in each lesson applies to your everyday life.

What are roots?

Objectives ▶ Describe the structure of a root. ▶ Explain the jobs of roots.

TechTerms

- **fibrous** (FY-brus) **root system:** root system made up of many thin, branched roots
- **root cap:** cup-shaped mass of cells that covers and protects a root tip
- **root hair:** thin, hairlike structure on the outer layer of the root tip
- **taproot system:** root system made up of one large root and many small, thin roots

Kinds of Roots The two main kinds of root systems are **fibrous** (FY-brus) **root systems** and **taproot systems.** Fibrous root systems are made up of many thin, branched roots. Grass, wheat, and barley have fibrous roots. A taproot system has one large root. Many small, thin roots grow out from the large root. Some taproots can store food. Carrots, radishes, and dandelions have taproots.

▶ *Name:* What are two kinds of root systems? fibrous root system and taproot system

Figure 1 Root systems

Parts of a Root Roots are tubelike structures made up of three layers. The outer part of the root is made up of one layer of cells. This layer mainly absorbs water. Many tiny, hairlike structures called **root hairs** extend from the outer layer. Root hairs increase the surface area of the root,

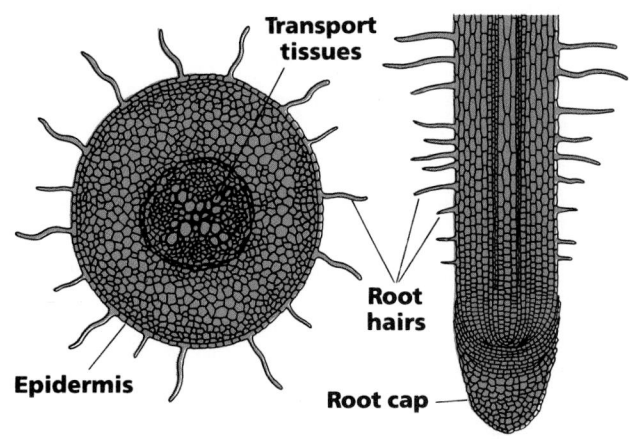

Figure 2 Root structure

allowing the root to absorb more water. The second root layer has soft, loose tissue. Water and food for the root are stored here.

The inner part of a root is made up of the tubes of the transport system. These tubes extend up through the root and into the stems and leaves. Some tubes carry water and dissolved minerals upward. Others carry food made in the leaves to all parts of the plant.

◉ *Observe:* Look at Figure 2. What is the outer part of the root tip called? epidermis

The Root Tip Roots grow from the tip. The tip of a root is covered by a **root cap.** The root cap is a cup-shaped mass of cells. It protects the root tip from damage as the root grows into the soil. As root cap cells are worn off, new cells are produced to take their place. Behind the root cap is an area where new root cells are formed. These new cells gradually change into the different kinds of cells that make up the root.

◀ *Analyze:* Why is the root cap at the end of the root? It protects the root tip as the root grows into the soil.

Functions of Roots Most roots grow underground. Roots anchor, or hold, a plant firmly in the soil. Roots take in water and dissolved minerals from the soil. In some plants, food is stored in the roots.

▶ *List:* What are some functions of roots? hold plant in soil, take in water and minerals, may store food

LESSON SUMMARY

▶ Two kinds of plant root systems are fibrous root systems and taproot systems.

▶ The outer root has root hairs to increase surface area for water absorption.

▶ The inner root contains the transport tubes.

▶ The root tip is protected by a root cap.

▶ Roots hold plants in the soil, absorb water and minerals, and some store food.

CHECK *Complete the following.*

1. Roots take in water and _____ from soil.
   minerals
2. A taproot system has _____ main root. one
3. Structures that increase the surface area of roots are the _____ . root hairs
4. The _____ part of the root contains transport tubes. inner
5. A root cap serves to _____ a root tip. protect

APPLY *Complete the following.*

6. **Calculating and Measuring:** If all the roots and root hairs of a rye plant were laid end to end, the length would be about 606,000 m.

How many kilometers is this? The surface area of the roots and root hairs would total about 210 m². Is this more, less, or about the same as the area of your classroom floor?

▶ 7. **Infer:** Would a plant with a fibrous root system be easy or difficult to pull out of the ground? Explain.

📁 8. **Classify:** Which plants shown have a taproot? Which have fibrous roots?

a.   b.   c.

•••
Skill Builder•••••••••••••••••••••••••••

▲ ***Organizing Information*** A table is one way to organize information. Make a table with these headings: Name of Plant, Type of Root System, Depth of Roots. Use library references to find this information for the following plants: beet, oak tree, alfalfa, turnip, corn.

SCIENCE CONNECTION ◆○◆○◆○◆○◆○◆○◆○◆○◆○◆○◆○◆○◆○◆○◆

SPECIALIZED ROOTS

Some roots have special functions. One kind of root gets water from the air. This is an aerial root. A plant with aerial roots is called an air plant. Orchids and English ivy are examples of plants with aerial roots.

Some roots grow out of other parts of a plant. Roots may grow from the stems above ground. Such roots are called prop roots. They help support a plant. Mangrove trees and corn are two plants that have prop roots. Look at the prop roots of the corn plant. They help keep the corn stem standing up.

Some plants do not grow in soil. For example, water lilies float along the surface of some ponds. These roots can absorb oxygen from water. Water lilies have aquatic (uh-KWAHT-ik) roots.

8-2 What are stems?

Objectives ▶ Distinguish between herbaceous and woody stems. ▶ Explain the jobs of stems.

TechTerms

- **herbaceous** (hur-BAY-shus) **stem:** stem that is soft and green
- **phloem** (FLOH-em): tissue that carries food from the leaves throughout the plant
- **woody stem:** stem that contains wood and is thick and hard
- **xylem** (ZY-lum): tissue that carries water and dissolved minerals upward from the roots

Kinds of Stems There are two kinds of plant stems. They are **herbaceous** (hur-BAY-shus) **stems** and **woody stems.** Herbaceous stems are soft, smooth, and green. Plants with herbaceous stems do not grow taller than 2 m. Plants with these stems grow during spring and summer and then die. Tomato plants and bean plants have herbaceous stems. Woody stems are thick, hard, and rough. The rough outer layer of the stem is the bark. Woody stems are not green. Woody stems may live for many growing seasons. They grow taller and wider each year. All trees, such as oaks and maples, have woody stems.

▶ **Name:** What are two kinds of plant stems?
herbaceous and woody

Figure 1 Herbaceous stems

Functions of Stems Most stems grow above ground. The main job of stems is to support the leaves. Stems also are organs of transport. Special

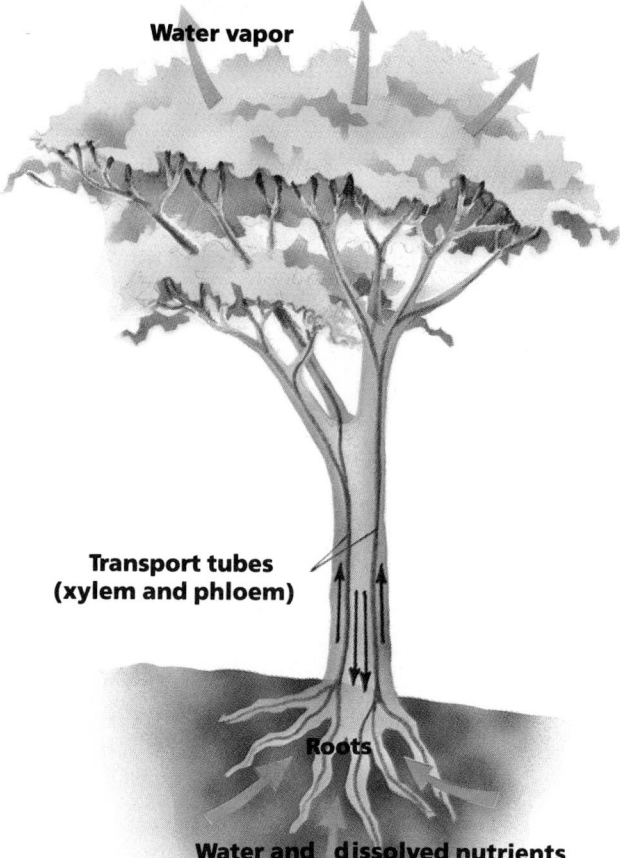

Water vapor

Transport tubes (xylem and phloem)

Roots

Water and dissolved nutrients

Figure 2 Stem structure

tubes within the stems carry materials between the roots and the leaves. In some plants, stems also store food. For example, the stems of sugar cane store large amounts of sugar.

▶ **List:** What are some functions of plant stems? support the leaves, transport of materials, and food storage

Stem Structure Both woody and herbaceous stems have similar tissues. The arrangement of the tissues is different in the two kinds of stems. Stems of both types contain tubes that carry water and dissolved minerals up from the roots. These tubes are called **xylem** (ZY-lum). Xylem carries water into the leaves. Extra water evaporates into the air through the leaves. Tubes that carry dissolved food made in the leaves downward throughout the plant are called **phloem** (FLOH-em). Xylem and phloem make up the conducting, or transport, system of the plant. In monocots and dicots, xylem and phloem are together in bundles.

▶ **Analyze:** Why does a plant need xylem and phloem? to transport both water and food

LESSON SUMMARY

▶ Herbaceous stems are green and soft and live for a short time; woody stems are stiff, rough, not green, and live for many years.

▶ Stems support leaves and transport materials between the roots and the leaves.

▶ Xylem carries water and minerals up from the roots; phloem carries food down from the leaves to the rest of the plant.

CHECK *Write true if the statement is true. If the statement is false, change the underlined term to make the statement true.*

1. Plants with <u>herbaceous</u> stems live for many growing seasons. woody

2. Stems connect the <u>roots</u> and the leaves. true

3. Oak trees have <u>woody</u> stems. true

4. Xylem and phloem are found in <u>bundles</u>. true

APPLY *Complete the following.*

5. **Sequencing:** List the plant structures in order to show how water gets from soil to leaves: leaves, phloem, roots, xylem.

6. **Hypothesize:** What do you think would happen if a herbaceous plant grew taller than 2 m?

7. **Classify:** Which plants listed have herbaceous stems? Which plants have woody stems?
   a. tulip   c. daisy   e. sunflower
   b. oak tree d. apple tree f. willow

InfoSearch

Read the passage. Ask two questions that you cannot answer from the information in the passage.

Tree Rings In woody stems the layers of xylem form a pattern of rings. Xylem formed in spring has larger cells than xylem formed in summer. The pattern of small and large cells forms light and dark bands called annual rings. A tree's age may be determined by counting its rings.

SEARCH: Use library references to find answers to your questions.

ACTIVITY

TRANSPORT IN PLANTS

You will need a glass, water, ink, a celery stalk, a knife, and a metric ruler.

1. Put water in the glass. Add 3 drops of ink.

2. Use the knife to cut a slice off the bottom of the celery stalk. Discard the slice. **Caution: Be careful when using a knife.**

3. Put the cut end of the stalk into the water.

4. Copy the data table.

5. **Measure:** Record the height of the ink in the celery after 5, 10, and 15 minutes.

6. **Predict:** What do you think will happen to the ink in the celery after 24 hours?

7. Keep the celery in the ink for 24 hours. Measure and record the height of ink.

Questions

1. What happened to the ink in the celery?

2. Was your prediction correct? Explain.

3. What life process does this activity show?

Data Table	
TIME	HEIGHT OF INK (mm)
5 minutes	
10 minutes	
15 minutes	
24 hours	

8-3 What are leaves?

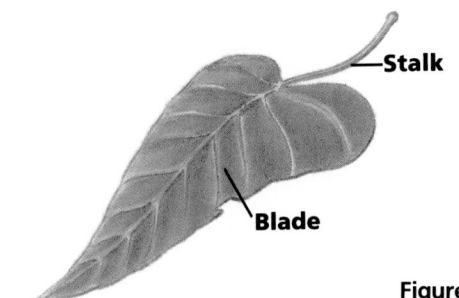

Figure 1 Leaf parts

▶ Describe the structure of leaves. ▶ Classify leaves as simple or compound.

TechTerms

- ▶ **blade:** wide, flat part of a leaf
- ▶ **epidermis** (ep-uh-DUR-mis): outer, protective layer of the leaf
- ▶ **mesophyll** (MES-uh-fil): middle layer of leaf tissue in which food-making occurs
- ▶ **stomata** (STOH-muh-tuh): tiny openings in the upper and lower epidermis of the leaf
- ▶ **vein:** bundle of tubes that contain the xylem and phloem in a leaf

Leaf Structure Most leaves have of a stalk and a wide, flat part called the **blade.** The blade is the most important part of the leaf. Food-making takes place in the blade. The stalk supports the blade and attaches it to the stem of the plant. Throughout the leaf there is a system of tubes called **veins.** They are made up of xylem and phloem. They connect to the xylem and phloem in the stem. The veins carry water and dissolved materials into and out of the leaf. Veins also support the leaf blade.

▶ *Identify:* What are the two main parts of a leaf? blade and stalk

Kinds of Leaves In some plants, the leaf blades are in one piece. This kind of leaf is called a simple leaf. Maple, oak, and elm trees have simple leaves. In other plants, leaf blades are divided into pieces. This kind of leaf is called a compound leaf. The pieces that make up a compound leaf are called leaflets. Each leaflet looks like a small leaf. Poison ivy and roses have compound leaves.

◐ *Observe:* Is the leaf in Figure 1 a simple or a compound leaf? a simple leaf

Leaf Tissues Leaves are covered by a protective layer called the **epidermis** (ep-uh-DUR-mis). This layer prevents the loss of water from the leaf. Scattered throughout the upper and lower epidermis are many tiny openings called **stomata** (STOH-muh-tuh). Two guard cells control the size of each stomate. They open and close the stomate, controlling water loss. They also control the exchange of oxygen and carbon dioxide between the inner tissues of the leaf and the surrounding air.

Beneath the epidermis is a layer of tissue called **mesophyll** (MES-uh-fil). Most of the food-making in the plant occurs in the mesophyll. Veins extend throughout the mesophyll.

▶ *Identify:* In what tissue layer does most food-making take place in a leaf? mesophyll

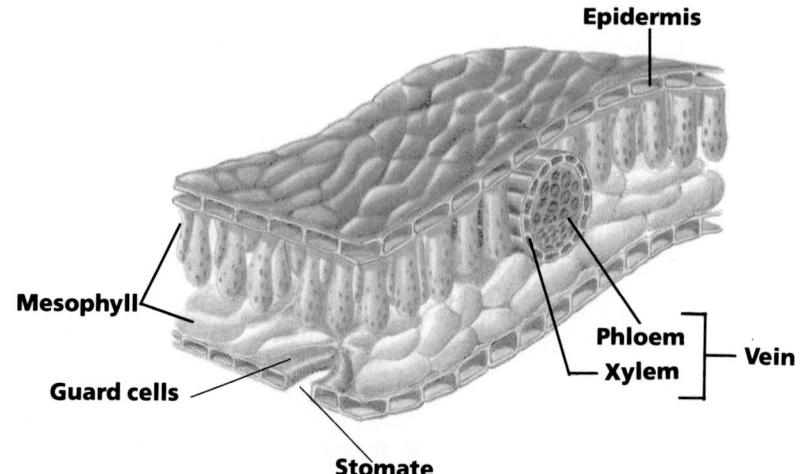

Figure 2 Leaf tissues

LESSON SUMMARY

▶ Most leaves have a blade, a stalk, and veins.

▶ The two kinds of leaves are simple and compound.

▶ The epidermis and the mesophyll are leaf tissues.

▶ Stomates control the gases that go into and out of a leaf and control water loss.

CHECK *Complete the following.*

1. The flat part of a leaf is called a _____ . blade

2. Leaves that are made up of leaflets are _____ leaves. compound

3. The outer, protective layer of a leaf is the _____ . epidermis

4. Water and gases pass into and out of leaves through tiny holes called _____ . stomata

APPLY *Complete the following.*

5. How is the function of leaf epidermis similar to the function of your skin?

6. **Hypothesize:** Would the stomata of a leaf be opened or closed on a hot, dry day? Explain your answer.

7. **Infer:** Why is air in a forest usually humid?

Classify: Classify the leaves as simple or compound.

8.   9.   10.

Health & Safety Tip

Some plants are poisonous to the touch. They contain chemicals that can irritate the skin. Poison ivy, poison oak, and poison sumac are three common examples. Avoid touching any part of these plants. Poison ivy and poison oak have white berries. A useful rhyme to remember is: "Berries white, poisonous sight." Find pictures of poison ivy, oak, and sumac. Make sketches of each plant. How can you identify these plants? Are their leaves simple or compound?

ACTIVITY

CLASSIFYING LEAVES

You will need 10 different leaves and a field guide to plants.

1. Collect 10 different leaves. **CAUTION: Before collecting any leaves, learn how to identify poison ivy, poison oak, and poison sumac. Be sure not to touch the leaves of these plants.** Choose only those that have fallen to the ground.

2. **Model:** Trace an outline of each leaf. Draw in its vein pattern. Describe the vein patterns.

3. Use a field guide to help you identify the plants.

4. **Classify:** Identify each leaf as simple or compound.

Questions

1. **Analyze:** In what way is a field guide helpful in the identification of leaves?

2. **Measure:** Are more of the leaves you collected simple or compound?

3. How many leaflets make up each compound leaf?

4. **Observe:** How many basic vein patterns do you see?

8-4 What is photosynthesis?

Objective ▶ Explain the importance of photosynthesis in plants.

TechTerms

- **chlorophyll** (KLAWR-uh-fil): chemical pigment needed for photosynthesis
- **chloroplast:** organelle of green plant cells where photosynthesis takes place
- **photosynthesis** (foht-uh-SIN-thuh-sis): food-making process that uses sunlight

Food Factories Plants do not have to eat. Green plants can make their own food in their leaves. The leaves are like "food factories." Some green stems also can make food. Food-making in plants is called **photosynthesis** (foht-uh-SIN-thuh-sis). The food that plants make is a sugar called glucose. Plants can change this sugar into starch, fats, and proteins. These nutrients are stored in the plants. They can be used at a later time.

▶ *Name:* What food do green plants make?
sugar or glucose

Photosynthesis In photosynthesis, water and carbon dioxide are used to make sugar. Roots absorb the needed water from the soil. Veins carry the water up into the leaves. Carbon dioxide enters the plant through the stomata. Sunlight supplies the energy the plant needs to make the sugar. During photosynthesis, oxygen and water are given off as waste materials. Look at the word and chemical equation for the process of photosynthesis at the bottom of the page.

▸ *Observe:* On which side of the equation are the waste products shown? right

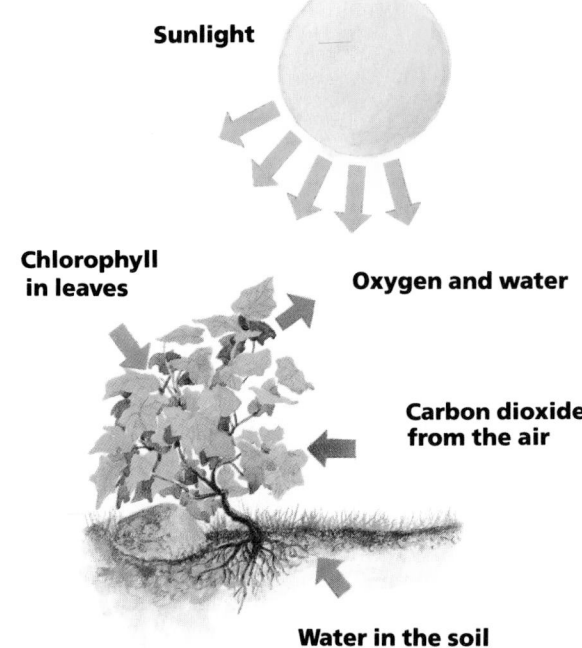

Sunlight

Chlorophyll in leaves

Oxygen and water

Carbon dioxide from the air

Water in the soil

Chlorophyll Photosynthesis cannot occur without chlorophyll (KLAWR-uh-fil). Chlorophyll is a chemical pigment, or coloring, needed for photosynthesis. Other pigments in leaves are masked by chlorophyll. You see the colors of these pigments during the fall. Leaves change color. The different colors are caused by the other pigments.

Wherever there is chlorophyll in a plant, photosynthesis can occur. The chlorophyll is inside special parts of plant cells. The cell parts, or organelles, that contain chlorophyll are called **chloroplasts.** Leaf mesophyll cells contain many chloroplasts. Therefore, most photosynthesis takes place in this layer.

▶ *Name:* In what cell parts of a plant leaf is food made? chloroplasts

$$CO_2 \ + \ H_2O \xrightarrow{\text{Energy}} C_6H_{12}O_6 \ + \ O_2$$

Carbon dioxide + water $\xrightarrow{\text{Sunlight}}$ Glucose + oxygen

LESSON SUMMARY

▶ Green plants can make their own food.

▶ In photosynthesis, carbon dioxide and water react to form sugar, and oxygen and water are given off as wastes.

▶ Chlorophyll is the chemical pigment needed for photosynthesis to take place.

▶ Photosynthesis occurs in the chloroplasts of plant cells.

CHECK *Write the letter of the term that best completes each statement.*

1. The food plants make is
   a. sugar. **b.** chlorophyll. **c.** oxygen.
   d. xylem. a

2. Chloroplasts contain the green material
   a. mesophyll. **b.** chlorophyll. **c.** stomates.
   d. phloem. b

3. Materials a plant uses to make sugar are
   a. oxygen and starch. **b.** carbon dioxide and water. **c.** sugar and protein. **d.** starch and mesophyll. b

4. Water enters the plant through the
   a. roots. **b.** leaves. **c.** stomata. **d.** veins. a

APPLY *Use the diagram to answer the following.*

5. In which layer does photosynthesis occur?

6. Does water for photosynthesis enter or leave the leaf through C?

▶ 7. **Infer:** Does photosynthesis occur in layer A? How do you know?

Skill Builder

Building Vocabulary Look up the meaning of the word parts ''photo-,'' ''synthesis,'' ''chlor-,'' ''-plast,'' and ''-phyll.'' Write their meanings. Explain the relationship of these word parts to the TechTerms.

ACTIVITY

SEPARATING ''PLANT PIGMENTS''

You will need a paper towel, scissors, a metric ruler, a black felt pen, two colored felt pens, isopropyl alcohol, and a glass.

1. Cut a strip of paper towel 3 cm wide and 12 cm long.

2. Use one color felt pen to make a dot about 5 cm from the bottom of the strip. On top of this dot, place a dot of the second color.

3. After the dots dry, use the black felt pen to cover the dots.

4. Pour 1 cm of alcohol into the glass. **Caution: Do not breathe the fumes.** Stand the strip of paper towel in the glass.

▶ 5. **Predict:** What will happen to the dot on the strip?

👁 6. **Observe:** After 5 minutes, look at the strip.

Questions

1. What happened to the dot after 5 minutes?

👁 2. **Observe:** How many colors do you see?

▲ 3. **Model:** What would the ink dot represent in a green plant?

📋 4. **Hypothesize:** What would happen if plant pigment were used instead of ink?

Bend strip over rim of glass

3 cm

12 cm

Isopropyl alcohol

What are flowers?

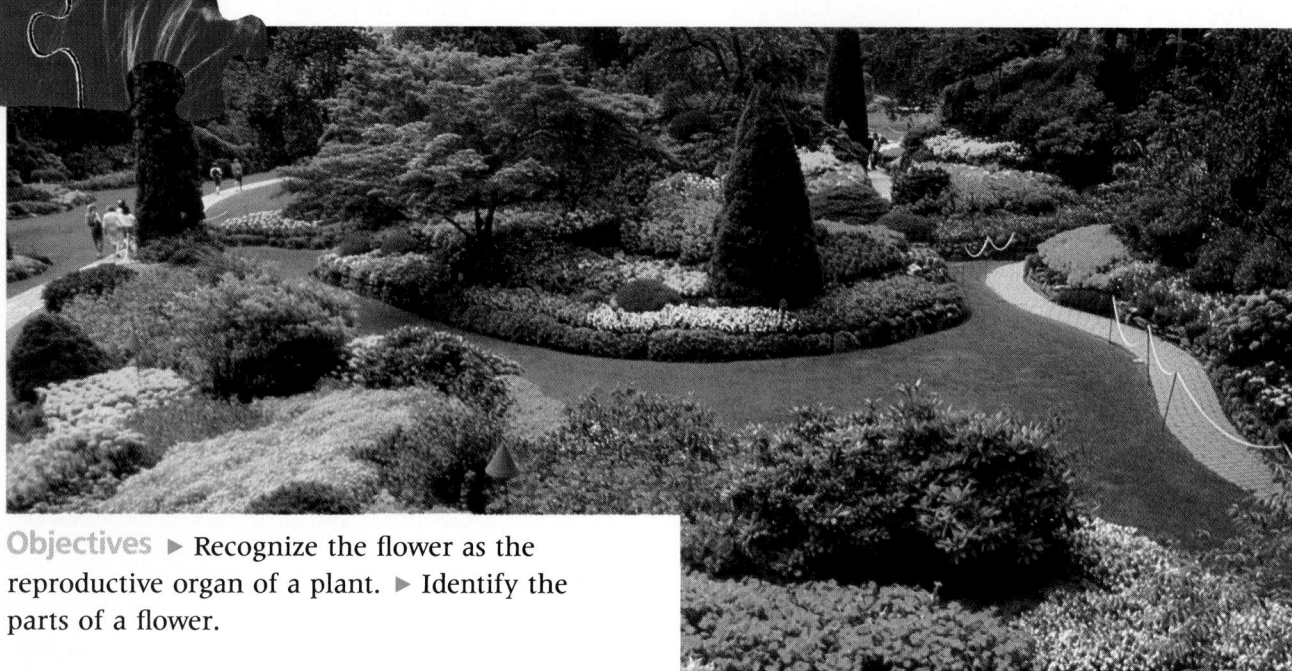

▶ Recognize the flower as the reproductive organ of a plant. ▶ Identify the parts of a flower.

TechTerms

- **petal:** kind of leaf that often is brightly colored
- **pistil:** female reproductive organ in a flower
- **sepal** (SEE-pul): special kind of leaf that protects the flower bud
- **stamen** (STAY-mun): male reproductive organ in a flower

Flowers Not all plants have flowers. However, in plants with flowers, the flower is the organ of sexual reproduction. Flowers contain the male and female parts of a flowering plant.

▶ *Define:* What are flowers? organs of sexual reproduction

Parts of a Flower A flower is made up of several parts. The bottom of a flower is surrounded by **sepals** (SEE-puls). Sepals are a special kind of leaf. They protect the flower bud. In some flowers the sepals look like small green leaves. In others they are large and brightly colored. The **petals** of a flower are just inside the sepals. The petals are another kind of leaf. They may be white or brightly colored. Petals protect the reproductive organs of the plant. Inside the petals are the organs of reproduction for the plant.

▶ *Identify:* What are two special kinds of leaves in a flower? sepals and petals

Reproductive Organs The reproductive organs in a flower are the **pistil** and the **stamen** (STAY-mun). The stamen is the male reproductive organ. The pistil is the female reproductive organ. A flower usually has one pistil, with several stamens around it. These organs are located inside the circle of petals.

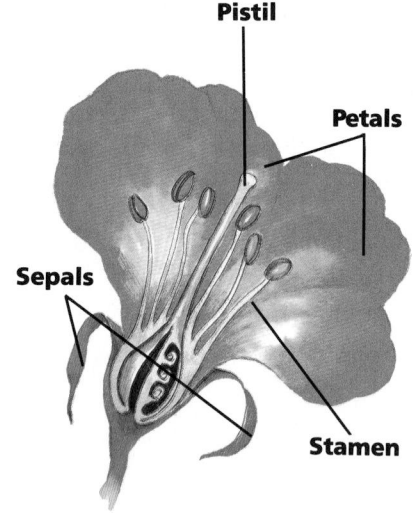

Some flowers have both male and female reproductive organs. These flowers are called perfect flowers. Other flowers may have only male or only female reproductive organs. These flowers are called imperfect flowers.

▶ *Classify:* What system of the plant are the pistil and the stamen part of? reproductive

LESSON SUMMARY

▶ Flowers are organs of sexual reproduction.

▶ The parts of a flower are the sepals, petals, pistil, and stamen.

▶ The reproductive organs in a flower are the stamens and pistils.

▶ Some flowers have male and female reproductive organs. Others have only male or only female reproductive organs.

CHECK *Write the letter of the term that best completes each statement.*

1. The organs of sexual reproduction in plants are the
   a. petals. **b.** flowers. **c.** leaves. **d.** stalks. b

2. Sepals and petals are special kinds of
   a. veins. **b.** flowers. **c.** leaves. **d.** plants. c

3. The _____ is the female reproductive organ in a flower.
   a. stamen **b.** pistil **c.** sepal **d.** vein b

4. The _____ is the male reproductive organ in a flower.
   a. stamen **b.** pistil **c.** sepal **d.** vein a

APPLY *Complete the following.*

▲ 5. **Model:** Draw a model of a flower. Label the petals, sepals, stamen, and pistil.

📁 6. **Classify:** Label each flower as perfect or imperfect.

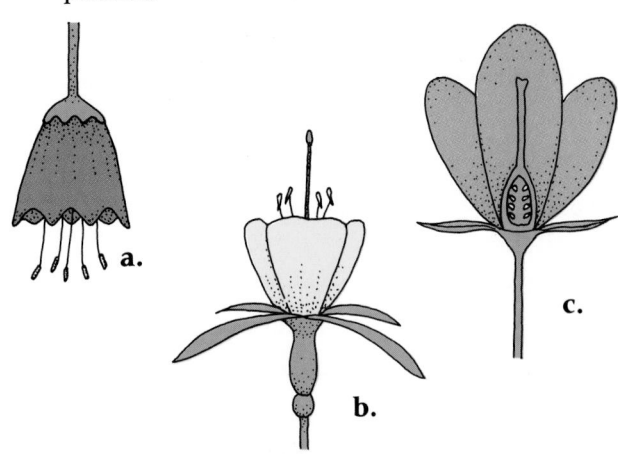

a.

b.

c.

Skill Builder

Classifying When you classify, you group things based upon how they are alike. Use a dictionary or library references to find out the meaning of the terms "pistillate" and "staminate." Classify each of the flowers shown above as perfect and imperfect. Then classify each imperfect flower as pistillate or staminate.

LEISURE ACTIVITY

GARDENING

Gardening is a popular hobby. People who live in the country or who have large back yards often plant gardens. A home garden may be large or small. It may be made up of flowers, herbs, vegetables, or fruits. Even people who live in cities or who have little or no land around their homes plant gardens. Their gardens may be made up of many different pots or other containers. A popular garden used by many people is a window box garden.

People like to garden for many reasons. Some people have gardens to grow flowers and other plants to beautify the grounds of their yards and homes. They cut the flowers to have fresh flowers for inside their homes. Many people like to garden because they enjoy raising their own fruits and vegetables.

No matter what the size or content of your garden, gardening can be fun. It also is good exercise. Gardening also can help lower the food bill. You can find out about amateur gardening by visiting local garden supply centers. Many free gardening booklets are available from companies that sell garden supplies and seeds.

8-6 How do flowering plants reproduce?

Objectives ▶ Describe pollination. ▶ Explain how fertilization and pollination are related.

TechTerms

- **anther:** part of the stamen that produces pollen
- **fertilization:** joining of the nuclei of the male and female reproductive cells
- **filament:** stalk of the anther
- **pollen grains:** male plant reproductive cells
- **pollination** (pahl-uh-NAY-shun): movement of pollen from a stamen to a pistil

Stamens and Pollen Stamens have two main parts. These are the **filament** and the **anther.** The filament is the thin stalk that holds up the anther. The anther is the part that produces **pollen grains.** Pollen grains are the male reproductive cells.

▶ *Define:* What is pollen? male reproductive cell

Fertilization In sexual reproduction, reproductive cells from the male and female must meet. The joining of the nuclei of male and female reproductive cells is called **fertilization** (fur-tul-i-ZAY-shun). In flowering plants, fertilization takes place inside the pistil.

▶ *Define:* What is fertilization? the joining of nuclei of male and female reproductive cells

Pollination For fertilization to take place, pollen grains must first move from a stamen to a pistil. The movement of pollen from a stamen to a pistil is called **pollination** (pahl-uh-NAY-shūn). The pollen often is moved by wind, by insects, and even birds. Sometimes, pollen is carried by water.

▶ *Classify:* What activity of a plant is pollination part of? reproduction

Self-Pollination In many flowers, the stamens are taller than the pistil. Pollen can fall off the anther on top of a stamen and land on the pistil in the same flower. This kind of pollination is called self-pollination. Self-pollination also occurs when pollen from one flower is carried to the pistil of another flower on the same plant.

Self-Pollination

▶ *Explain:* In what two ways may self-pollination occur? Students should state the two ways presented in the text.

Cross-Pollination Sometimes, pollen is carried from a stamen of a flower on one plant to the pistil of a flower on another plant of the same kind. This kind of pollination is called cross-pollination. Some plants have separate male flowers and female flowers. The male flowers have only stamens. The female flowers have only pistils. Usually the male and female flowers are on different plants. These plants have to cross-pollinate. Cross-pollination also can occur between two plants that have flowers with both stamens and pistils.

▶ *Name:* What kind of pollination occurs between flowers on different plants? cross-pollination

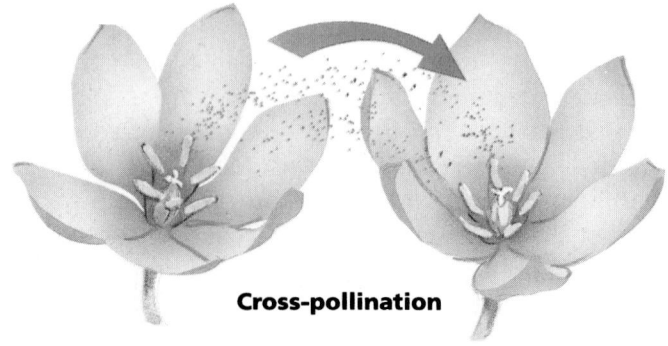

Cross-pollination

- Stamens have a filament and an anther.
- Fertilization occurs when the nuclei of a male and a female reproductive cell join.
- Pollination is the movement of pollen from a stamen to a pistil.
- Self-pollination is pollination of flowers on the same plant.
- Cross-pollination is pollination between flowers on different plants.

CHECK *Complete the following.*

1. Nuclei of male and female reproductive cells join in the process of _____ . fertilization

2. Male reproductive cells are the _____ . pollen grains

3. Movement of pollen from a stamen to a pistil is _____ . pollination

4. Pollination between flowers on different plants is _____ . cross-pollination

5. Pollination between flowers on the same plant is _____ . self-pollination

APPLY *Complete the following.*

6. **Infer:** Would flowers that depend on wind for pollination probably have flat, open flowers or tall, closed flowers? Explain your choice.

7. **Analyze:** How does an insect move pollen from one flower to another?

Health & Safety Tip

Many people suffer from hay fever. Hay fever is an allergic reaction to the pollen of certain plants. Large amounts of pollen in the air cause people with hay fever to sneeze. Their eyes may become red and watery. Prepare a poster that shows what plants cause hay fever, the times of the year that people suffer from hay fever, and what medications can be used to treat hay fever.

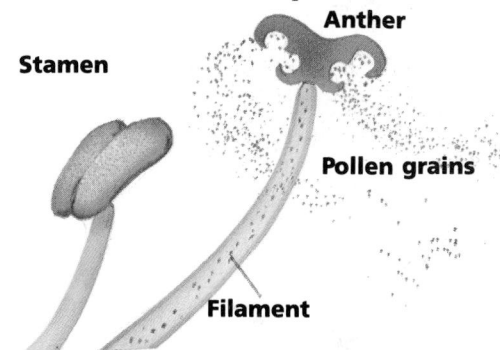

Stamen · Anther · Pollen grains · Filament

SCIENCE CONNECTION

MUTUALISM

Living things interact with each other in many different ways. Some of these interactions are helpful to both living things. These interactions help both living things survive. Other interactions make life more difficult for some living things. An example of a helpful interaction is mutualism (MYOO-choo-wul-izm). Mutualism is a relationship between two living things that is helpful to both living things.

Bees get food from plants. They gather nectar from flowers. When the insects gather the nectar, pollen sticks to their legs. The bees then may fly to the same kind of flower on a different plant. In this way the flowers of the plant are pollinated. The bees get food. Both the bees and flowers are helped by this interaction.

There are many examples of mutualism. Hummingbirds and flowers also are examples of mutualism. A bird called the oxpecker eats pests off rhinoceroses. The oxpecker gets food. The rhinos get rid of pests on their bodies.

8-7

What are seeds and fruits?

Objectives ▶ Identify the parts of the pistil. ▶ Explain how seeds and fruits form.

TechTerms

- ▶ **embryo:** undeveloped plant or animal
- ▶ **ovary** (OH-vuhr-ee): bottom part of the pistil
- ▶ **ovule** (OH-vyool): part of the ovary that develops into a seed after fertilization
- ▶ **stigma** (STIG-muh): top part of the pistil

Parts of a Pistil A pistil is made up of three parts. The top part is the **stigma** (STIG-muh). Below the stigma is a tube called the style. The style connects the stigma to the bottom of the pistil. The bottom of the pistil is called the **ovary** (OH-vuhr-ee). Inside the ovary is the **ovule** (OH-vyool). The ovule contains the female reproductive cells.

Identify: What are the parts of a pistil? stigma, style, ovary

Forming a Seed After a pollen grain lands on the stigma, it begins to change. The pollen cell begins to grow a tube. This tube is called a pollen tube. The pollen tube grows down into the stigma. It continues to grow down through the style and the ovary. Finally, the tip of the pollen tube enters the ovule.

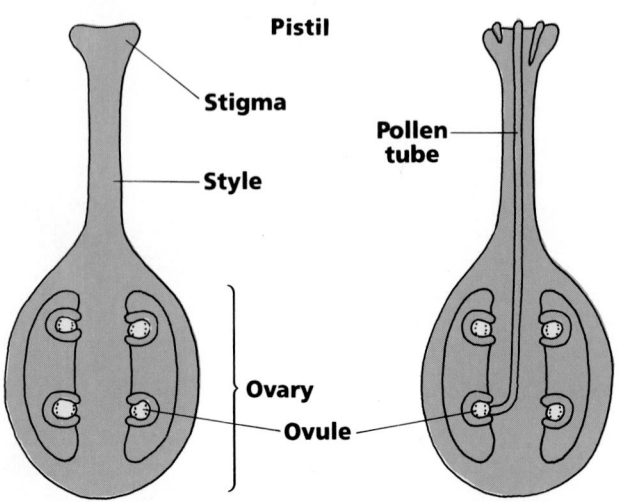

After the pollen tube enters the ovule, the tip of the tube dissolves. The nucleus of the pollen cell moves into the ovule. The nucleus of the pollen cell joins with the nucleus of the reproductive cell in the ovule. The joining of the two nuclei is called fertilization. After fertilization, the ovule develops into a seed. A new plant can grow from a seed.

Analyze: Why does the pollen grain grow a tube after it lands on the stigma? so the nucleus of the pollen cell can enter the ovule

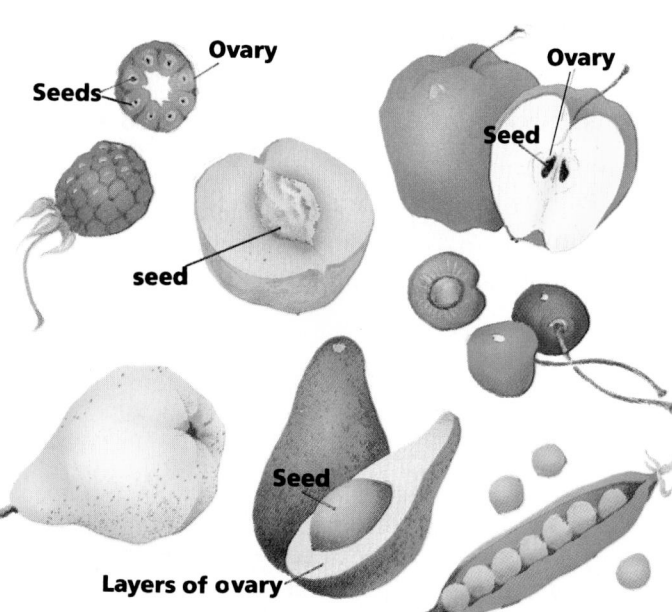

Fruits Ovules are found inside an ovary. An ovary may have only one ovule, or it may have more than one ovule. When the ovules are fertilized, they develop into seeds. Each seed contains a very young, or undeveloped, plant. Scientists call an undeveloped plant or animal an **embryo.** A seed contains a plant embryo.

While the seeds are forming, the ovary is growing. The ovary becomes very large. It surrounds and protects the seeds and the embryos inside the seeds. The large ovary and its seeds is called a fruit.

Distinguish: What is the relationship between the ovary and a seed? seed is inside ovary

LESSON SUMMARY

▶ The parts of a pistil are the stigma, the style, and the ovary.

▶ A pollen grain that lands on a stigma forms a pollen tube that grows down into the ovary.

▶ Fertilization occurs in the ovules.

▶ A fertilized ovule becomes a seed that contains an embryo.

▶ The ovary surrounds and protects the seeds and becomes a fruit.

CHECK *Write true if the statement is true. If the statement is false, changed the underlined term to make the statement true.*

1. The female reproductive cells are in the <u>anther</u>.
   ovules
2. A <u>seed</u> is formed after fertilization. true
3. The undeveloped plant inside a seed is called an <u>ovary</u>. embryo
4. A pollen grain that lands on a stigma grows a <u>pistil</u>. pollen tube

APPLY *Complete the following.*

▲ 5. **Model:** Draw and label the parts of a pistil.

▶ 6. **Infer:** The top of a stigma is usually sticky. What might be an advantage of this stickiness?

Skill Builder

▲ ***Organizing Information*** Make a table showing the number of seeds in different fruits. List the names of 10 fruits in the first column. The relative number of seeds in the second column. Use the terms "one," "a few," and "many." In the third column, classify the seeds as small, medium, or large. What is the relationship between the number of seeds and their sizes?

Skill Builder

Classifying Scientists classify any plant part with seeds as a fruit. Vegetables are the leaves, stems, or roots of plants. People classify fruits and vegetables differently. Classify each of the plant parts listed as if you were a scientist and then as you would everyday.

a. tomato	**d.** carrot	**g.** lettuce
b. beets	**e.** peach	**h.** papaya
c. cucumber	**f.** celery	**i.** green pepper

◆◆◆ CAREER IN LIFE SCIENCE ◆◆◆◆◆◆◆◆◆◆◆◆◆◆◆◆◆◆◆◆◆◆◆◆◆◆◆◆◆◆◆◆◆◆◆◆◆◆◆

GREEN GROCER

Are you interested in food? Are you curious about the wide variety of fruits and vegetables in the world? Would you enjoy putting together attractive displays of fresh fruits and vegetables? If you answered yes to these questions, you may enjoy a career as a green grocer. A green grocer sells fresh fruits and vegetables to the public. They buy fruits and vegetables from growers. They choose items they think are high quality. Green grocers decide on fair prices. They arrange the fruits and vegetables in appealing displays. Green grocers also must be able to answer questions that their customers may have about cooking and storing fresh produce.

Many green grocers own their own stores. Some green grocers work in large supermarkets or in outdoor fresh produce markets. If you would like to work as a green grocer, you should take science and mathematics courses in high school. Courses at technical schools in managing a small business also are helpful.

For more information, you should talk to your guidance counselor. You also may want to talk to a green grocer.

8-8 What are the parts of a seed?

Objective ▶ Identify the parts of a seed.

TechTerms

▶ **hilum** (HY-lum): mark on the seed coat where the seed was attached to the ovary

▶ **seed coat**: outside covering of a seed

Seed Coat All seeds have an outside covering. This outer covering is called the **seed coat.** Most seed coats are hard. The hard coat protects the embryo. Some seeds are protected so well that they can be kept for many years. They will still grow when they are planted.

▶ *Name:* What is the outside covering of a seed called? seed coat

Figure 1 Outer Structure of a Seed

Hilum Look at Figure 1. Find the **hilum** (HY-lum). The hilum is a small mark, or scar on the seed. The hilum is where the seed was attached to the ovary. Near the hilum, there is a small opening. The opening is where the pollen tube entered the ovule.

▶ *Describe:* What is the hilum? mark or scar where the seed was attached to the ovary.

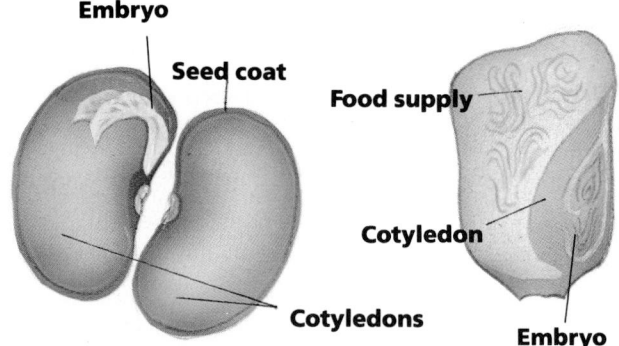

Figure 2 Inside a Seed

Inside a Seed If you soak a bean seed overnight, the seed coat gets soft. You can easily peel it off. Figure 2 shows the insides of two seeds. Notice that the one seed has two large halves, or cotyledons (kaht-ul-EED-uns). These halves store food as starch. Some seeds do not have two halves. Food is stored outside the cotyledon. The food is absorbed through the cotyledon. Food is still stored in the seed. The developing embryo uses this food as it grows.

Look again at Figure 2. You will see that the embryo is attached to one of the seed halves. The embryo has a tiny root, a stem, and leaves. It is only a small part of the seed. If you plant the seed, the embryo will begin to grow, or germinate (JUR-muh-nayt). As the seed germinates, the two halves, or cotyledons, are pushed above ground. When the first leaves unfold and begin to make food, the cotyledons dry up and die. In time, the embryo will develop into an adult plant.

▶ *Infer:* Why would the cotyledons no longer be needed once photosynthesis begins? The plant begins to make its own food.

Figure 3 Seed Germination

LESSON SUMMARY

▶ The outer protective covering of a seed is the seed coat.

▶ The mark or scar on the seed coat where the seed was attached to the ovary is the hilum.

▶ Seeds contain food that the embryo uses as it grows.

▶ The embryo in a seed is a tiny plant that has a tiny root, stem, and leaves.

CHECK *Complete the following.*

1. What is the outside covering of a seed called? seed coat
2. What part of a seed develops into an adult plant? embryo
3. What is the mark on the seed coat where the seed was attached to the ovary called? hilum
4. What makes up most of a seed? food
5. In what form is food stored in a seed? starch
6. What are the three parts of all seeds? seed coat, stored food, embryo

APPLY *Complete the following.*

▶ 7. **Infer:** All plants need water, sunlight, and nutrients to grow. Which of these needs does a seed not need to begin to germinate?

Ideas in Action..................................

IDEA: People use many different kinds of seeds as food.

ACTION: Make a list of the kinds of seeds you eat.

Skill Builder....................................

▶ *Inferring* When you infer, you form a conclusion based upon facts. Seeds are dispersed, or spread, by wind, animals, and water. Study the seeds shown. Decide how each seed is dispersed based upon how it looks. Give reasons for your answers.

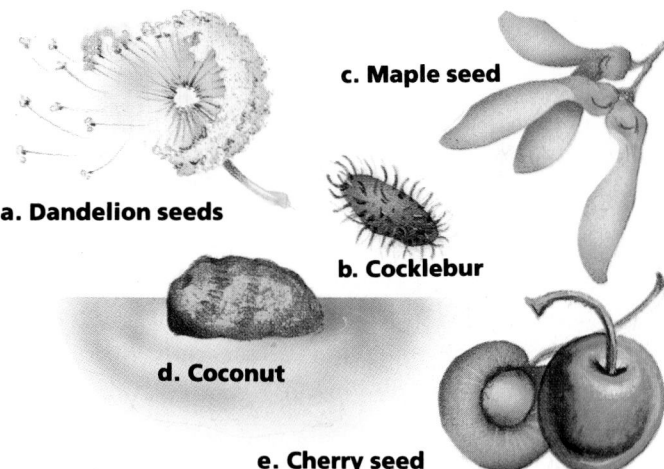

a. Dandelion seeds
b. Cocklebur
c. Maple seed
d. Coconut
e. Cherry seed

ACTIVITY

TESTING SEEDS FOR STARCH

You will need iodine, a medicine dropper, 5 different kinds of seeds, a small dish, water, and a knife.

1. Soak the seeds in a dish of water overnight.
2. The next day, remove the seed coats from the seeds. Observe the seed coats.
3. Break apart the seeds. You may need to cut some of the seeds in half with the knife. **Caution: Be careful when cutting with a knife.**
4. Place a drop of iodine on the side of each seed. Iodine changes color when starch is present.

Questions

👁 1. **a. Observe:** To what color did the iodine change when starch was present? **b.** Which of the seeds contained starch?
2. **a.** What is the starch in the seeds? **b.** What is the starch used for?
3. How many seeds had a seed coat?

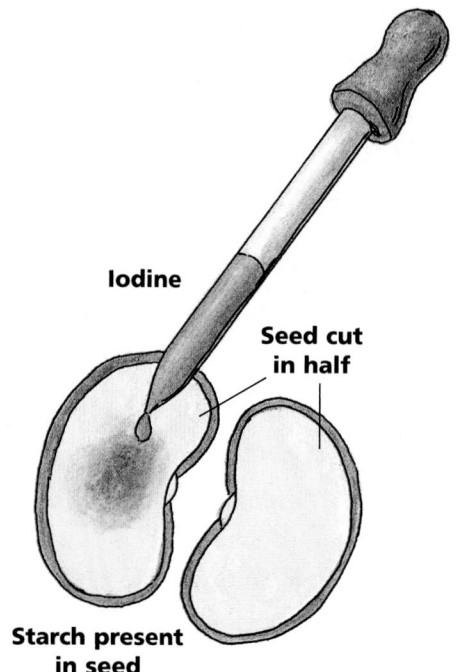

Iodine

Seed cut in half

Starch present in seed

8-9 How do plants reproduce asexually?

Objectives
▶ Recognize that vegetative propagation is a kind of asexual reproduction. ▶ Identify ways that plants reproduce asexually.

TechTerms

- **asexual reproduction:** reproduction needing only one parent
- **bulb:** underground stem covered with fleshy leaves
- **tuber:** underground stem
- **vegetative propagation** (VEJ-uh-tayt-iv prahp-uh-GAY-shun): kind of asexual reproduction that uses parts of plants to grow new plants

Reproduction Without Seeds Some plants can reproduce without male and female cells joining to form seeds. This method of reproduction is called **asexual reproduction.** Asexual reproduction in plants is called **vegetative propagation** (VEJ-uh-tayt-iv prahp-uh-GAY-shun). During vegetative propagation, the growing parts of plants develop into new plants. The growing parts are roots, stems, or leaves.

▶ *Define:* What is vegetative propagation?
asexual reproduction that uses parts of plants to grow new plants

Tubers Some plants, such as white potatoes, have underground stems. An underground stem is called a tuber. A white potato may have many small white buds growing on its skin. These buds are called eyes. The eyes of the potato are the organs of vegetative reproduction. When planted in soil, each eye may grow into a new potato plant. Each new plant is identical to the parent plant.

▶ *Define:* What is a tuber? an underground stem

Bulbs A **bulb** is an organ of vegetative reproduction in some plants. A bulb is an underground stem. It differs from the underground stem called a tuber. A bulb is covered with thick leaves. An

onion is an example of a bulb. Each onion plant produces many bulbs. When planted, each bulb may grow into a new onion plant. Other plants that grow from bulbs are daffodils, lilies, and tulips.

▶ *Name:* What are two plants that grow from bulbs? Answers will vary.

Cuttings Some plants can grow new plants from pieces of themselves. This method of vegetative propagation is called cuttings. Roots make good cuttings. For example, carrots are roots. It also is an organ of vegetative reproduction. A carrot may be cut in two. When the top part is planted, it will begin to grow new roots. In time, a new carrot plant will grow. The new plant will be identical to the parent.

Carrot

New plants may also grow from some leaf and stem cuttings. A leaf is cut off of the plant. The leaf stalk is placed in water. Roots will grow from the stalk, and a new plant will grow. The same thing can be done with the stems of some plants.

▶ *Classify:* What type of reproduction are cuttings? asexual reproduction

LESSON SUMMARY

▶ Plants reproduce asexually by vegetative propagation.

▶ Underground stems called tubers are organs of vegetative propagation in some plants.

▶ Bulbs are organs of vegetative propagation.

▶ Plants may reproduce asexually by using root cuttings.

▶ Leaf and stem cuttings can be used to grow new plants.

CHECK *Write true if the statement is true. If the statement is false, change the underlined term to make the statement true.*

1. White potatoes are examples of <u>bulbs</u>. tubers

2. A bulb of a daffodil is a <u>root</u>. stem

3. A carrot plant may be grown asexually from its <u>seed</u>. root

Answer the following.

4. What kind of reproduction is vegetative reproduction? asexual

5. What kind of organ of reproduction is an onion? bulb

APPLY *Complete the following.*

6. **Classify:** Which part of the plant is used for reproduction in the following diagrams?

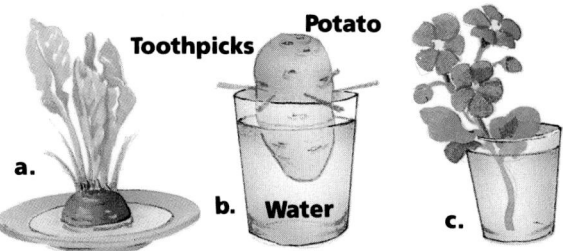

a. b. c.

InfoSearch

Read the passage. Ask two questions that you cannot answer from the information in the passage.

Grafting Grafting is a kind of vegetative propagation. It is used to produce new kinds of plants. Twigs from one tree are attached to another. For example, seedless oranges cannot reproduce by themselves. They can only reproduce by grafting. Twigs from a branch with seedless oranges are grafted onto a regular orange tree. Seedless oranges grow on the grafted branch.

SEARCH: Use library references to find answers to your questions.

ACTIVITY

GROWING PLANTS ASEXUALLY

You will need a paper cup, a glass, soil, water, 4 toothpicks, an onion, potato with eyes, and a knife.

1. Half-fill the cup with soil. Half-fill the glass with water.

2. Equally space 4 toothpicks around the onion. Rest the toothpicks and onion on the glass rim. Add water until the bulb bottom is underwater.

3. Cut a piece of potato that has an eye. **Caution: Be careful when using a knife.** Put it in the cup. Add some soil. Water the soil.

4. **Observe:** Check your plants every day. Keep the bulb bottom wet and the soil moist.

Questions

1. **Compare:** How is the reproduction of the onion and potato similar?

2. Which plant part grew roots first?

8-10 What are tropisms?

Objective ▶ Relate different kinds of stimuli to the tropisms they cause.

TechTerms

- **stimulus** (STIM-yuh-lus): something that causes a reaction to take place
- **tropism:** growth of a plant in response to something in the environment

Plant Responses All plants respond to changes in their environment. They respond to light, gravity, and water. Each response is caused by a **stimulus** (STIM-yuh-lus). A stimulus is a change that causes a response. The reaction of a plant to a stimulus is called a **tropism** (TROH-pizm). A plant responds to each stimulus by growing in a certain direction. Tropisms happen very slowly. You may not notice them.

▶ *Hypothesize:* What stimulus do you think would make a plant part grow downward? gravity

Light Green plants respond to the stimulus of light. Most stems and leaves grow toward light. A plant left near a sunny window will bend toward the light.

Some stems even change their response to light. The flower stem of a peanut plant grows up towards sunlight. After pollination, the flower stem grows away from light. It grows down into the soil, where its peanuts develop in the dark.

▶ *Explain:* How do most plant stems respond to light? They grow toward it.

Gravity Plants respond to the stimulus of gravity. Roots grow down in response to gravity. A plant in a flowerpot could be tilted on its side. The roots will bend and grow down. If the plant is turned upright, the roots will bend again and grow down.

Most stems grow away from the pull of gravity. A plant in a flowerpot could be tilted on its side. The stem will respond by bending and growing up again. Rhizomes (RY-zohms), the underground stems of some plants, grow sideways in response to gravity. They grow horizontally just under the surface of the soil.

▶ *Describe:* How does a plant root respond to gravity? grows downward

Water Plants respond to the stimulus of water. Roots grow toward water. In most plants, this tropism is not very strong. It occurs only when water touches the roots. In some plants, this tropism is very strong. For example, the roots of a willow tree will grow into and clog sewer and water pipes.

▶ *Explain:* How do roots respond to water? grow toward it

LESSON SUMMARY

▶ Tropisms are plant growth responses to stimuli.

▶ Leaves and stems grow toward light.

▶ Some stems change their response to light.

▶ Roots grow down in response to gravity.

▶ Stems grow up in response to gravity.

▶ Roots grow toward water.

CHECK *Write true if the statement is true. If the statement is false, change the underlined term to make the statement true.*

1. Stems grow toward the stimulus of <u>light</u>. true

2. Roots grow <u>against</u> the stimulus of gravity. toward

3. Something in the environment that causes a reaction to occur is a <u>tropism</u>. stimulus

4. Plant responses to most stimuli occur <u>quickly</u>. slowly

5. <u>Roots</u> grow toward water. true

APPLY *Complete the following.*

6. **Analyze:** In what direction would plant stems grow in the dark? Explain your answer.

7. **Infer:** A drain pipe from a house seems to be clogged. A willow tree has been growing near the house for many years. What is one possible reason for the clogged drain?

Skill Builder..............................

Building Vocabulary Each plant tropism has a name based on the stimulus involved. Look up the prefixes "geo-," "hydro-," and "photo-." Use the meanings of these prefixes to help you make new words. Add each prefix to the word "tropism" to make a word that names a plant's response to each stimulus. What are the words? phototropism, geotropism, hydrotropism

◆○◆ SCIENCE CONNECTION ◆○◆○◆○◆○◆○◆○◆○◆○◆○◆○◆○◆○◆○◆○◆○◆

CARNIVOROUS PLANTS

Some plants respond immediately to stimuli. Growth is not involved. The Venus' flytrap is a plant that responds quickly to touch. The Venus' flytrap plant is a carnivorous (kahr-NIV-uh-rus) plant. It ingests small insects.

Each leaf of the Venus' flytrap is hinged so that it can close like a book. Each leaf has stiff spines on its edges. The inner surface of each leaf has six stiff hairs. When an insect walks across a leaf, it may touch the hairs. Touching only one hair causes no reaction. Touching two hairs or jiggling one hair twice makes the leaf snap shut in one second or less. The spines interlock to form a cage. The insect is trapped inside the closed leaf. The leaf stays closed.

Special chemicals are given off by the leaf. The chemicals digest the soft parts of the insect. Digestion may take several weeks. After the insect has been digested, the trap opens again. After a leaf has caught several insects, it dries up and dies.

Challenges

STUDY HINT Before you begin the Unit Challenges, review the TechTerms and Lesson Summary for each lesson in this unit.

TechTerms

anther (156)
asexual reproduction (162)
blade (150)
bulb (162)
chlorophyll (152)
chloroplast (152)
embryo (158)
epidermis (150)
fertilization (156)
fibrous root system (146)
filament (156)
herbaceous stem (148)
hilum (160)

mesophyll (150)
ovary (158)
ovule (158)
petal (152)
phloem (148)
photosynthesis (152)
pistil (152)
pollen grains (156)
pollination (156)
root cap (146)
root hair (146)
seed coat (160)

sepal (152)
stamen (152)
stigma (158)
stimulus (162)
stomata (150)
taproot system (146)
tropism (162)
tuber (162)
vegetative propagation (162)
vein (150)
woody stem (148)
xylem (148)

TechTerm Challenges

Matching *Write the TechTerm that matches each description.*

1. root system made up of large root, and many small, thin roots taproot system
2. stem that contains wood and is thick and hard woody stem
3. kind of leaf that often is brightly colored petal
4. thin, hairlike structure on the outer layer of the root tip root hair
5. stalk of the anther stamen
6. middle layer of leaf tissue in which food-making occurs mesophyll
7. cup-shaped mass of cells that covers and protects a root tip root cap
8. underdeveloped plant or animal embryo
9. top part of the pistil stigma
10. special kind of leaf that protects the flower bud sepal
11. stem that is soft and green herbaceous stem
12. root system made up of many thin, branched roots fibrous root system
13. underground stem tuber
14. asexual reproduction that uses parts of plants to grow new plants vegetative propagation

Identifying Word Relationships *Explain how the words in each pair are related. Write your answer in complete sentences.* Answers will vary. Accept all logical responses.

1. asexual reproduction, vegetative propagation
2. chlorophyll, chloroplast
3. pollen grains, fertilization
4. stimulus, tropism
5. chlorophyll, photosynthesis
6. pistil, pollination
7. stamen, anther
8. ovary, ovule
9. hilum, seed coat
10. vein, blade
11. xylem, phloem
12. epidermis, stomata
13. bulb, tuber

Content Challenges..

Multiple Choice *Write the letter of the term that best completes each statement.*

1. In flowering plants, fertilization takes place inside the
   a. stamen.   **b.** pistil.   **c.** anther.   **d.** sepal. b
2. Most of the food-making in a plant occurs in the
   a. epidermis.   **b.** mesophyll.   **c.** stomata.   **d.** guard cells. b
3. Perfect flowers have
   a. only male reproductive organs.   **b.** only female reproductive organs.   **c.** both male and female reproductive organs.   **d.** neither male nor female reproductive organs. c
4. The rough outer layer of a woody stem is the
   a. root cap.   **b.** xylem.   **c.** mesophyll.   **d.** bark. d
5. The food that plants make is a
   a. starch.   **b.** protein.   **c.** sugar.   **d.** fat. c
6. Fibrous root systems are found in
   a. grass.   **b.** carrots.   **c.** radishes.   **d.** dandelions. a
7. Chloroplasts contain the green material
   a. chlorophyll.   **b.** mesophyll.   **c.** xylem.   **d.** phloem. a
8. The small white buds growing on a potato are called
   a. bulbs.   **b.** eyes.   **c.** tubers.   **d.** cuttings. b
9. A large ovary and its seeds is called
   a. an embryo.   **b.** an ovule.   **c.** a fruit.   **d.** a seed coat. c

True/False *Write true if the statement is true. If the statement is false, change the underlined term to make the statement true.*

1. The two main parts of a <u>pistil</u> are the filament and anther. stamen
2. Asexual reproduction in plants is called vegetative <u>pollination</u>. propagation
3. Most seed coats are <u>soft</u>. hard
4. Tropisms happen very <u>slowly</u>. true
5. Large amounts of sugar are stored in the <u>roots</u> of sugar cane. stems
6. Roots grow from the <u>tip</u>. true
7. An onion is an example of a <u>bulb</u>. true
8. Petals are a kind of <u>leaf</u>. true
9. The pieces that make up a <u>simple</u> leaf are called leaflets. compound

Understanding the Features..

Reading Critically *Use the feature reading selections to answer the following. Page numbers for the features follow each question in parentheses.*

1. **Define:** What is mutualism? (157)
2. What are three things a green grocer does on the job? (159)
3. **Infer:** Why do you think gardening is good exercise? (155)
4. How does a Venus' flytrap digest insects? (165)
5. **List:** What are three kinds of specialized roots? (147)

Content Challenges

Interpreting a Diagram *Use the diagram to complete the following.*

1. Which structure is the male reproductive organ?
2. Which structure is the female reproductive organ?
3. Which structures protect the reproductive organs of a plant?
4. Which structures protect the flower bud?
5. Which structures are specialized leaves?
6. Is the flower a perfect flower or an imperfect flower? Explain.
7. Which structure produces pollen grains?
8. Which structure contains female reproductive cells?

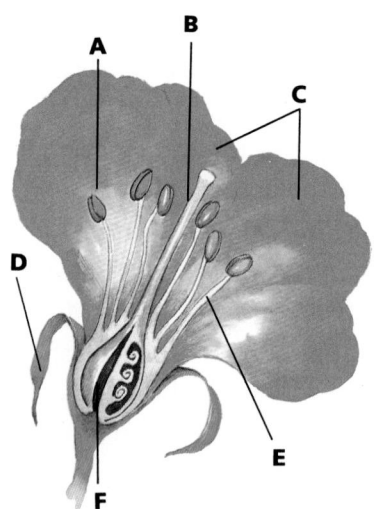

Critical Thinking *Answer each of the following in complete sentences.*

1. **Apply:** What would happen to the stem of a potted plant if you placed the plant on its side?
2. **Hypothesize:** What do you think would happen if a herbaceous plant grew taller than 2 m?
3. **Contrast:** What is the difference between pollination and fertilization?
4. **Analyze:** Fruit does not usually ripen until a seed is mature. Why is this important for the survival of the plant?
5. A slimy substance is produced by the root cap. How do you think this substance helps a plant?

Finding Out More

1. **Research:** The xylem of a tree goes through two growth periods each year, one in the spring and one in the summer. These different growth periods result in annual rings on a tree's woody stem. Using library references, find out about annual rings, why they form, and how they can be used to determine the age of a tree that has been cut down. Write your findings in a report.
2. Collect leaves from a variety of trees. Find the blade and stalk of each leaf. Locate the veins in the blades. Make a sketch of each leaf and label its parts. Classify each leaf as a simple of compound leaf.
3. Obtain a flower. Identify as many parts of the flower as possible. Draw a sketch of your flower and label each part. Next to the label, write the function of each part. Classify your flower as a perfect or an imperfect flower.
4. Grafting and layering are two methods of vegetative propagation. Find out how plants can be grown using these methods. Present your findings in an oral report.

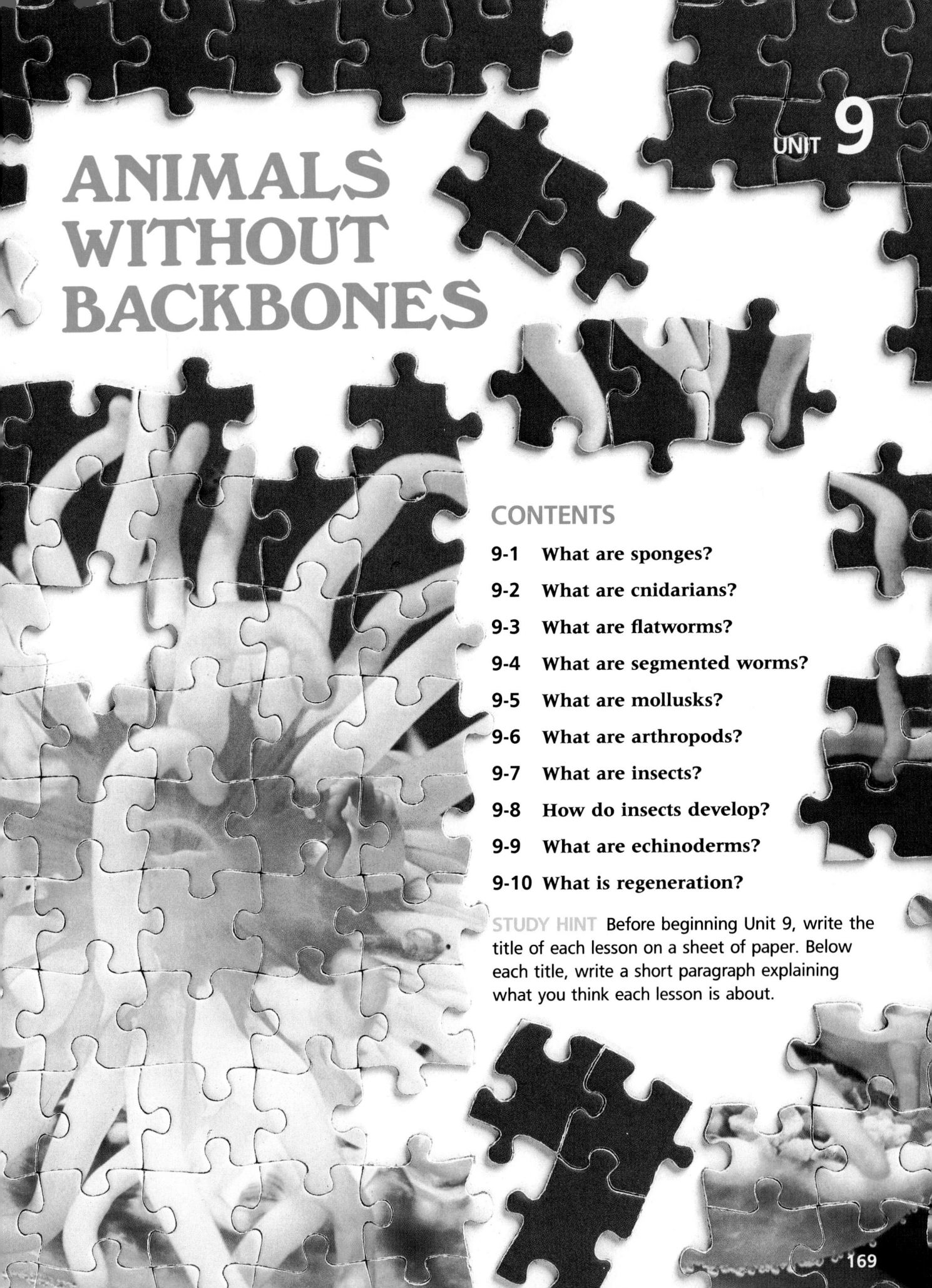

ANIMALS WITHOUT BACKBONES

CONTENTS

STUDY HINT Before beginning Unit 9, write the title of each lesson on a sheet of paper. Below each title, write a short paragraph explaining what you think each lesson is about.

9-1 What are sponges?

Objective ▶ Describe the structure of a sponge.

TechTerms

▶ **flagellum** (fluh-JEL-uhm): whiplike structure on some cells

▶ **pores:** tiny openings

▶ **spicules** (SPIK-yools): small, hard needlelike structures of a sponge

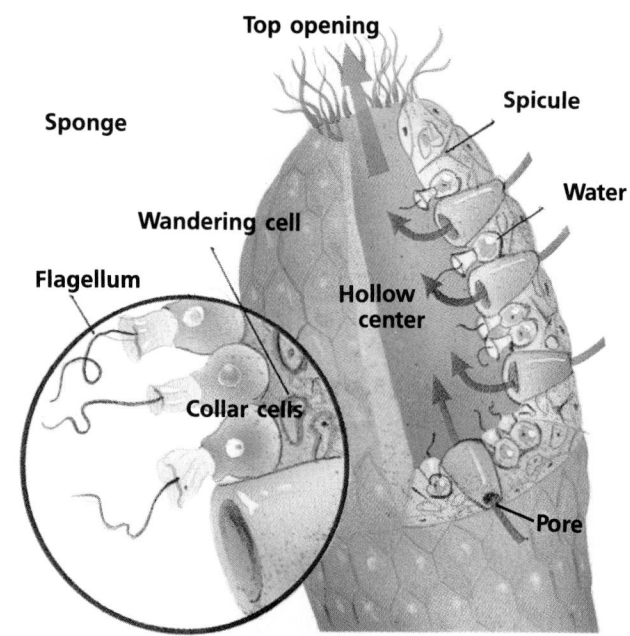

Porifera In the past, people thought that sponges were plants because they do not move from place to place like most other animals do. Sponges live attached to objects on the ocean floor. Today, scientists classify sponges in the Animal Kingdom in the phylum *Porifera* (paw-RIF-uhr-uh). The word *"Porifera"* means "pore-bearer." If you look at a sponge, you will see it has many **pores,** or tiny openings.

▧▶ *Identify:* In what phylum are sponges classified? *Porifera*

Structure of a Sponge Sponges are very simple animals. You can compare the body of a sponge to an empty sack. The sponge is closed at the bottom, and has a large opening at the top. The center of the sponge is hollow. The body of a sponge is made up of only two layers of cells. The outer layer is made up of thin, flat cells. The inner layer is made up of special cells called collar cells. The collar cells line the hollow center of the sponge. Each collar cell has a long whiplike structure called a **flagellum** (fluh-JEL-uhm). A jellylike substance fills the space between the two cell layers. In the jellylike substance, there are special cells that can move around like amoebas (uh-MEE-buhs). These wandering cells carry food to other cells. They also help a sponge to reproduce.

▧▶ *Describe:* What is the shape of a sponge? A sponge is shaped like an empty sack, closed at the bottom and open at the top.

Spicules Small, needlelike structures called **spicules** (SPIK-yools) are in the jellylike layer. They

link together to form a simple skeleton. Spicules support the sponge. Some spicules are chalklike. Others are made up of the mineral that makes up sand. They are glasslike. Still other spicules are made up of a rubbery, flexible material called spongin (SPUN-jin). Spongin skeletons are dried and sold in stores as natural sponges. Most sponges you use are not natural sponges. They are factory-produced.

▧▶ *Define:* What are spicules? small, hard, needlelike structures found between the two cell layers of the sponge

Life Functions Sponges feed by filtering tiny organisms and bits of material from the water that passes through their bodies. Water flows through the pores into the hollow center. Water flows out through the large opening at the top of the sponge. The constant beating of each flagellum keeps the water moving into and out of the sponge. As the water flows by, tiny bits of food are trapped by the collar cells. They also absorb oxygen from the water. The wandering, amoeba-like cells carry food and oxygen to all cells. These cells also pick up wastes. The wastes are given off into the water passing through the sponge. The wastes are then carried out through the large opening.

▧▶ *Observe:* In how many directions does water move in a sponge? one

LESSON SUMMARY

▶ Sponges are classified in the phylum *Porifera*.

▶ Sponges are shaped like empty sacks that are closed at the bottom and open at the top.

▶ The body of a sponge is made up of two cell layers with a jellylike substance between the layers.

▶ Spicules form a simple skeleton and support the sponge.

▶ Sponges feed by filtering food from the water that passes through them.

CHECK *Write true if the statement is true. If the statement is false, change the underlined term to make the statement true.*

1. Sponges have <u>three</u> cell layers. two

2. The <u>collar cells</u> help move water through a sponge. true

3. Water enters a sponge through its large <u>top opening</u>. pores

4. Sponges are classified in the phylum <u>*Animalia*</u>. Porifera

5. The rubbery material that makes up some spicules is called <u>spongin</u>. true

APPLY *Complete the following.*

6. **Explain:** Think about the structure of a sponge. Why is *Porifera* a good name for this phylum?

7. **Infer:** Why can a sponge be considered a living filter?

8. **Hypothesize:** Suppose each flagellum was removed from the collar cells of a sponge. Do you think the sponge would be able to feed? Explain.

Ideas in Action..

IDEA: Most sponges sold in stores are not natural sponges.

ACTION: Find out what types of sponges are sold at a hardware store, drug store, or supermarket near you. Look at the labels on the sponges. What materials are the sponges made of? Try to find natural sponges. How do the prices of the natural sponges and the synthetic sponges compare?

LEISURE ACTIVITY

SNORKELING

Have you ever wondered what kinds of plants and animals live in the ocean? Snorkeling is a good way to find out. You can discover how fish and other water animals live together.

You only need a few pieces of equipment to go snorkeling. Fins, a face mask, and a snorkel, or breathing tube are needed. Fins help you move quickly and easily through the water. The face mask gives you a clear view through the water. The snorkel allows you to swim along the surface of the water without raising your head to breathe.

If you are snorkeling in cool water, you may want to wear a wet suit. A wet suit is a form-fitting covering that helps keep in body heat. It is called a wet suit because the swimmer gets wet while wearing it. Water seeps in between the suit and the body. Once your body warms this layer of water, your body stays warm.

Always snorkel with a buddy and under proper supervision. Be sure you know all the safety rules.

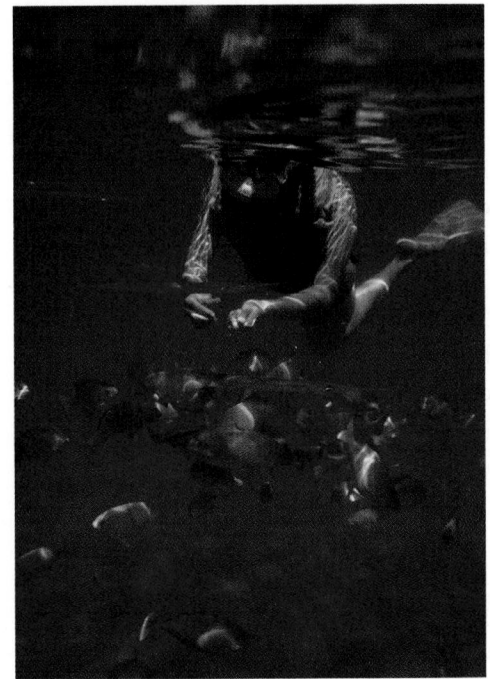

9-2 What are cnidarians?

Objective ▶ Identify and describe the body forms of cnidarians.

TechTerms

- ▶ **cnidocytes** (NY-duh-syts): stinging cells
- ▶ **medusa** (muh-DOO-suh): umbrellalike form of a cnidarian
- ▶ **polyp** (PAL-ip): cuplike form of a cnidarian
- ▶ **tentacles:** long, armlike structures

Cnidarians If you have seen a jellyfish, you have seen a cnidarian (ni-DER-ee-un). Jellyfish are classified in the phylum *Cnidaria*. All cnidarians have **tentacles,** or long, thin armlike structures. The tentacles have special stinging cells, called **cnidocytes** (NY-duh-syts). The phylum gets its name from the cnidocytes.

All cnidarians live in water. Corals, jellyfish, and most other cnidarians live in the ocean. The hydra lives in lakes and ponds.

Classify: Name three cnidarians. jellyfish, coral, hydra

Body Forms Cnidarians have two body forms, or shapes. Some cnidarians have an umbrella shaped body called a **medusa** (muh-DOO-suh). Tentacles hang down from the edge of the umbrella. The mouth is in the center of the bottom surface. The medusa form can float on the surface of the water. It also can swim through the water. Other cnidarians have a tube-shaped body. It is called a **polyp** (PAL-ip). A polyp does not usually move from place to place. It lives attached to a surface in water. The mouth is at the top. It is surrounded by tentacles.

Classify: Is a jellyfish a medusa or a polyp? medusa

Structure of Cnidarians Like sponges, cnidarians have two cell layers. There is a jellylike layer in between the two layers. In cnidarians, however, the cells are organized into tissues. Cnidarians have digestive, muscle, nerve, and sensory tissues. The tissues surround a central cavity (KAV-uh-tee), or hollow space. The mouth opens into the cavity. The mouth is the only body opening.

▶ **Infer:** Why are cnidarians considered more complex than sponges? Cnidarians have cells organized into tissues; sponges do not.

Figure 2 Food-getting in hydra

Food Getting Cnidarians use their tentacles to catch their food. Cnidocytes on the tentacles have coiled stingers inside. When a small animal gets close or touches the tentacles, the stingers shoot out. The poison in the stinger stuns or kills the animal. The tentacles wrap around the animal and pull it into the mouth and body cavity. Here the food is changed into a form that the cells can use.

▶ **Explain:** How do cnidocytes get food? Small animals are stunned by cnidocytes then grabbed by the tentacles and put in the mouth.

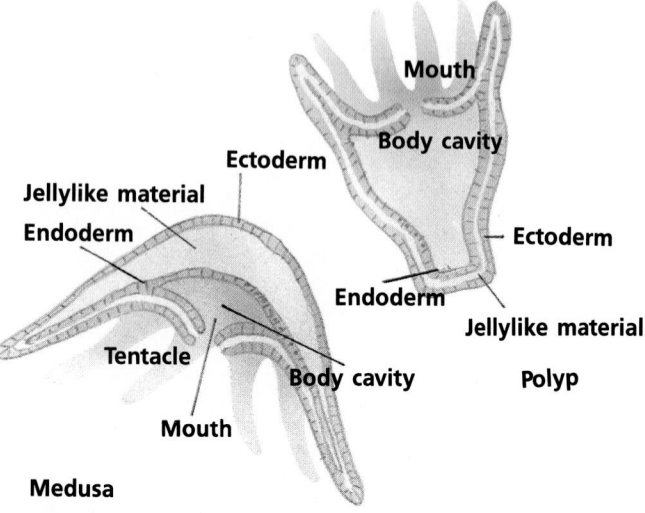

Mouth

Body cavity

Ectoderm

Jellylike material

Endoderm

Ectoderm

Endoderm

Jellylike material

Tentacle

Body cavity

Polyp

Mouth

Medusa

Figure 1 Body forms

LESSON SUMMARY

▶ All cnidarians have tentacles and cnidocytes.

▶ All cnidarians live in water.

▶ The two body forms of cnidarians are polyps and medusas.

▶ Cnidarians have two cell layers and tissues.

▶ Cnidarians use their tentacles to catch their food.

CHECK *Find the sentence in the lesson that answers each question. Then, write the sentence.*

1. How did the phylum *Cnidaria* get its name?

2. Where do cnidarians live?

3. What is the umbrella-shaped body form of a cnidarian called?

4. What types of tissue are found in cnidarians?

APPLY *Use Figure 1 on page 172 to answer the following.*

5. Observe: Does a jellyfish or a hydra have a larger jellylike layer?

6. Compare: How are the two body shapes of cnidarians alike?

7. Analyze: How are cnidarians more complex than sponges?

Health & Safety Tip.........................

Never touch a jellyfish, even if it looks dead. It may still be able to sting you. The poison given off by some cnidarians can be harmful to humans. The sting of a jellyfish is painful. One type of jellyfish, the sea wasp, gives off a deadly poison. Its sting can kill a human in less than 3 minutes. If you do get stung by a jellyfish, get first aid as soon as you can. Use a first aid manual or other reference to find out how to treat a jellyfish sting.

SCIENCE CONNECTION ◆○◆○◆○◆○◆○◆○◆○◆○◆○◆○◆○◆○◆○◆○◆○

CORAL REEFS

Corals live together in colonies. As each coral polyp grows, it forms a hard rocklike external skeleton. When corals die, their skeletons remain in place. Young polyps attach themselves to these skeletons. As new layers of coral form on top of the skeletons, large mounds are built up. Billions of skeletons covered by a layer of living coral make up a coral reef.

A coral reef is one of the busiest places in the ocean. Sponges may live attached to the surface of the reef. Many different types of animals including sea urchins, marine worms, crustaceans, and fish, spend some of their time around the reef. The reef supplies nooks and crannies in which small animals can hide. The small animals serve as food for larger ones.

There are three kinds of coral reefs. A fringing reef forms close to shore. A barrier reef forms farther out in the ocean. One of these reefs is the Great Barrier Reef off the coast of Australia. It is about 6000 km long and 80 km wide. An atoll forms a ring around a lagoon when a fringing reef sinks.

Barrier reef

Fringing reef

Atoll

9-3 What are flatworms?

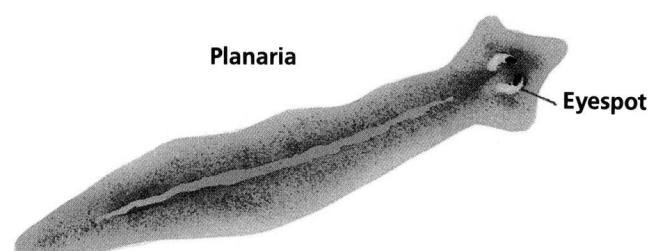

Eyespot

Objective ▶ Discuss the different kinds of worms and their features.

TechTerms

- **ectoderm** (EK-tuh-durm): outer tissue layer
- **endoderm** (EN-duh-durm): inner tissue layer
- **mesoderm** (MES-uh-durm): middle tissue layer

Classification of Worms When you think of worms, you probably think of earthworms. However, there are many other kinds of worms. They are so different from each other that they are classified in three different phyla. These three phyla are flatworms, roundworms, and segmented worms.

All common worms are invertebrates. They have three cell layers. The outer layer is the **ectoderm** (EK-tuh-durm). The inner layer is the **endoderm** (EN-duh-durm). The middle layer is the **mesoderm** (MES-uh-durm). Some organs and organ systems develop from the mesoderm.

All worms also have a top and bottom. They have a head end and a tail end. They also have a left side and a right side.

▶ **Identify:** What are the three cell layers in worms? endoderm, ectoderm, mesoderm

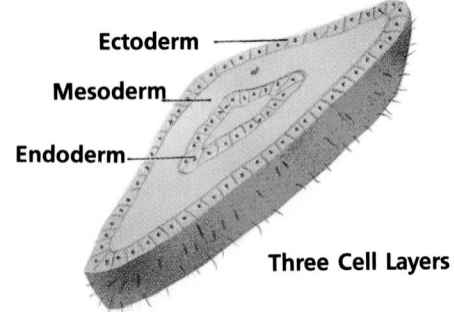

Ectoderm

Mesoderm

Endoderm

Three Cell Layers

Flatworms Flatworms are classified in the phylum *Platyhelminthes* (plat-ee-HEL-minthes). They have flattened, ribbonlike bodies. Flatworms are the simplest worms. There are three groups of flatworms. One group lives in ponds and streams.

The most common flatworm is the planarian (pluh-NER-ee-uhn). Planaria are small flatworms between 5 and 25 mm long. They live attached to underwater twigs and branches. They have two small eyespots that can sense light.

The other two groups of flatworms are parasites (PAR-uh-syts). Parasites live inside or on other organisms. They feed on and harm the organisms they live in. Flukes and tapeworms are parasites. Special body parts help parasites live inside other organisms. Hooks and suckers hold the parasite in place. One kind of fluke lives in the human liver. Flukes range in length from 2 mm to 15 cm. Tapeworms live in the intestines of many kinds of animals, including humans. Tapeworms can grow to several meters in length. In the intestines, tapeworms absorb, or take in food that is already digested.

▶ **Classify:** Name three examples of flatworms. planarian, fluke, tapeworm

Roundworms Roundworms make up the phylum *Nematoda* (NEM-uh-tohd-uh). Roundworms can live almost anywhere. They can live in soil or in water. Some are parasites of plants or animals. Hookworms and *ascaris* worms are two roundworms that live in the intestines of humans.

Roundworms have a threadlike body with pointed ends. It is covered by a smooth, tough skin. Roundworms are one of the simplest animals to have a complete digestive system. Food can pass through in only one direction. There is a mouth at one end and an anus (AY-nus) at the other end. An anus is an opening for getting rid of wastes. Roundworms also have simple excretory and nervous systems. They do not have a circulatory or a respiratory system. However, roundworms have a well-developed reproductive system.

▶ **Identify:** Name two kinds of roundworms. hookworm, *ascaris*

174

LESSON SUMMARY

▶ Worms are classified in three different phyla.

▶ The body of a worm is made up of three tissue layers—the ectoderm, endoderm, and mesoderm.

▶ Flatworms, members of the phylum *Platyhelminthes,* have a flattened body.

▶ Parasites, such as flukes and tapeworms, feed on and harm the organisms they live in.

▶ Roundworms, members of the phylum *Nematoda,* can live almost anywhere.

▶ The body of a roundworm is more complex than that of a flatworm.

CHECK *Complete the following.*

1. There are _____ different phyla of worms.
   three

2. The tissue layer between the ectoderm and the endoderm is the _____ . mesoderm

3. The phylum *Platyhelminthes* is made up of the _____ . flatworms

4. Special body parts, such as hooks and _____, help some parasites live inside other organisms. suckers

5. The phylum *nematoda* is made up of the _____ . roundworms

APPLY *Complete the following.*

▶ 6. **Infer:** The name *Platyhelminthes* is based on the Greek word *"platys"* meaning broad and flat. How does this definition help you remember an important trait of this phylum?

7. **Hypothesize:** A parasite often causes the organism it lives in to lose weight. Why?

Hooks · Suckers · Tapeworm

SCIENCE CONNECTION

PETS AND WORMS

Do you take your dog or cat to the veterinarian for check-ups? One thing that the veterinarian checks for is the presence of worms. Roundworms and hookworms are common parasites of both dogs and cats. Both parasites are found in the dirt. Pets can swallow roundworm eggs by eating scraps of food found in the dirt. Pets can get hookworms by walking on an infected area. Hookworms go through the skin on the animal's feet.

Heartworms are the most dangerous parasite of dogs. Heartworms are carried by mosquitos. Dogs can get heartworms by being bitten by an infected mosquito. Veterinarians supply pills that can prevent infections.

To prevent worms, keep your pet on a leash or in your yard. Clean its area regularly. Feed it a balanced diet. Also, have your pet checked by a veterinarian. If worms are found, the pet can be treated. It is important to start treatment as soon as possible. It can save your pet's life.

Female · Male

9-4 What are segmented worms?

Objective ▶ Describe the features of segmented worms.

TechTerms

- ▶ **closed circulatory system:** an organ system in which blood moves through blood vessels
- ▶ **setae** (SEET-ee): tiny, hairlike bristles

Segmented Worms The most complex worms are the segmented worms. They are classified in the phylum *Annelida* (AN-ul-id-uh). The word "annelid" means "little rings." If you look at the body of a segmented worm, you will see that it is made up of many ringlike sections, or segments.

There are more than 9000 species of segmented worms. Most live in the ocean. Others live in fresh water. The best-known segmented worm is the earthworm. It lives in the soil.

▥▶ *Name:* Where do most segmented worms live? the ocean

Earthworms Earthworms are the most complex worms. Look at Figure 1 as you read about the features of the earthworm.

- ▶ Like all worms, earthworms have a right side and a left side. They have a head end and a tail end. There is a mouth at the head end and an anus at the tail end.
- ▶ Each segment except the first and last has four pairs of small bristles. They are called **setae.**

Earthworms use their setae and tiny sets of muscles to move.

- ▶ Earthworms have a complex digestive system. Food passes into two organs where it is stored, and then ground up. Food is digested and absorbed in the small intestine.
- ▶ Earthworms have a **closed circulatory system.** In a closed circulatory system, blood moves through tubes in the body. In the head end, the two large vessels meet and form five pairs of hearts. The hearts pump blood through the blood vessels.
- ▶ Earthworms have a nervous system. Nerves run along the body and connect to a simple brain at the head end.
- ▶ Earthworms have male and female sex organs. A single worm, however, does not mate with itself. Earthworms reproduce sexually.
- ▶ Earthworms do not have a respiratory system. Gases pass into and out of the earthworm through its moist skin.

👁 *Observe:* What are the two organs that store and grind up food called? crop and gizzard

Leeches The leech is a segmented worm that lives in ponds and streams. Most leeches are parasites. They live on the surface of other animals. The leech uses suckers to attach itself to the animal. The leech feeds on the blood of the animal.

▥▶ *Compare:* How do leeches differ from some other worms that are parasites? They live on the outside of another animal.

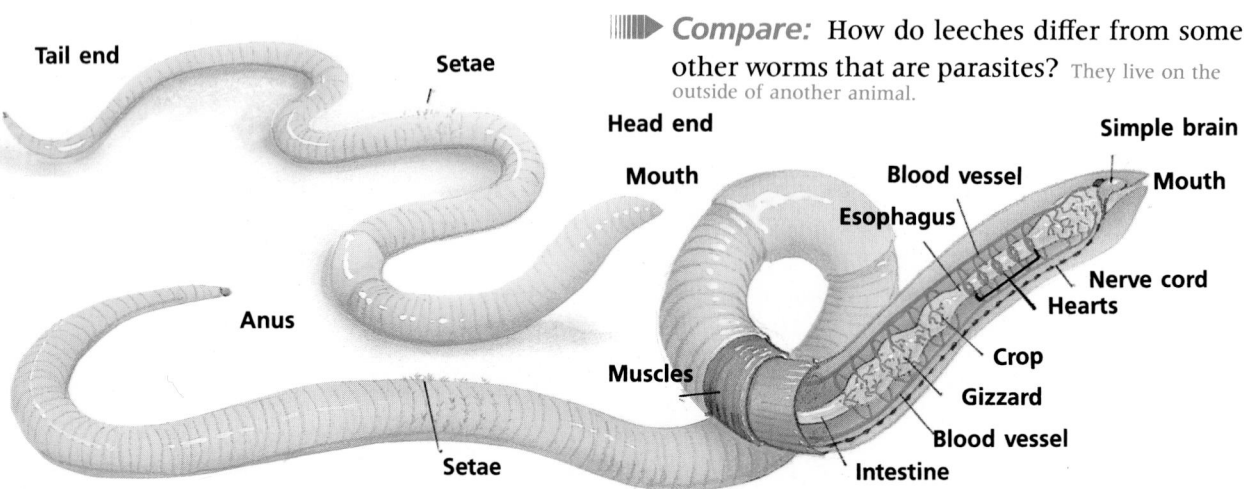

Figure 1 The earthworm

Tail end · Setae · Anus · Setae · Head end · Mouth · Esophagus · Blood vessel · Simple brain · Mouth · Nerve cord · Hearts · Crop · Gizzard · Blood vessel · Intestine · Muscles

LESSON SUMMARY

► Segmented worms belong to the phylum *Annelida*.

► There are more than 9000 species of segmented worms.

► An earthworm is divided into segments and has setae on its bottom surface.

► The earthworm is typical of segmented worms.

► Earthworms have a closed circulatory system.

► Earthworms have a complex digestive system.

► Earthworms have a reproductive system and a nervous system.

► Earthworms lack a respiratory system.

► Most leeches are parasites.

CHECK *Complete the following.*

1. Segmented worms are classified in the phylum _____ . *Annelida*

2. Segmented worms live in the _____, fresh water, and soil. *ocean*

3. The earthworm uses small bristles called _____ for movement. *setae*

4. Gases pass in out of the earthworm through the _____ . *skin*

APPLY *Complete the following.*

6. **Explain:** The dictionary shows that the word *Annelida* means "little ring." Explain why this term is a good description for segmented worms.

► 7. **Infer:** Why do earthworms avoid direct sunlight?

InfoSearch

Read the passage. Ask two questions about the topic that you cannot answer from the information in the passage.

Importance of Earthworms Earthworms help to improve the soil. They make tunnels as they move through the soil. Air and water can then flow through the tunnels and reach the roots of plants. Earthworms get food from soil. Undigested food is passed out through the anus as wastes. These wastes help make rich soil.

SEARCH: Use library references to find answers to your questions.

LOOKING BACK IN SCIENCE

MEDICAL USES OF LEECHES

In the past, "bleeding" was a common medical treatment. Leeches would be placed on a patient's skin. The leeches would attach themselves and suck out blood. In a few cases, bleeding was helpful to the patient. In most cases, however, it was not a good treatment.

Barbers used to use leeches to treat black eyes. The blackness of the eye is caused by blood from broken capillaries. To speed up the healing, barbers would place a leech on the blackened part of the eye. The leech would take in the blood that collected. Today, leeches are again being used in medicine. Scientists have discovered special chemicals given off by leeches. One of these chemicals keeps blood from clotting. Another chemical widens blood vessels. Others help heal damaged tissue. One chemical even helps to prevent infection.

Using chemicals from leeches has important medical uses. In some types of surgery, tiny blood vessels are reconnected. Often the blood stops flowing through the vessels. As a result, tissues around the blood vessels die. Chemicals taken from the leech can keep the blood flowing and keep the tissues healthy.

9-5 What are mollusks?

▶ Describe the features of mollusks. ▶ Give examples of different kinds of mollusks.

TechTerms

▶ **mantle:** thin, membrane that covers a mollusk's organs

▶ **radula** (RAJ-oo-luh): rough, tonguelike organ of a snail

Mollusks The mollusks are the soft-bodied animals. They are classified in the phylum *Mollusca* (muh-LUS-kuh). All mollusks have a soft, fleshy body. Most mollusks are covered by hard shells. Mollusks live in salt water, in fresh water, and on land.

The mollusks are divided into three major classes. One class is made up of mollusks with one-shell. This class includes snails. Another class consists of mollusks made up of two-part shells. Clams, oysters, and mussels are mollusks with two-part shells. The third class of mollusks have a small shell or no shell. Squids and octopuses are classified in this group.

Classify: Name four animals classified as mollusks. Answers will vary.

Three Body Parts Mollusks have three body parts. They have a head, a foot, and a mass of tissue that contains well-developed organ systems, reproductive organs, and a heart. A thin membrane covers the soft fleshy body of a mollusk. The membrane is the **mantle.** In some mollusks, the mantle forms the shell.

Define: What is the mantle? thin membrane that covers the soft body

Organ Systems Mollusks have a digestive system and a reproductive system. Mollusks also have a nervous system. The nervous system has many sense organs. It is well-developed in octopuses and squids.

Mollusks have an open circulatory system. The blood is not always inside blood vessels. Instead, the blood flows out of vessels into open spaces in the body. It bathes the body organs. At another point, the blood flows back into a blood vessel. Blood is moved by the beating of the heart.

Name: What two kinds of mollusks have well-developed nervous systems? squids and octopuses

Special Structures In mollusks with shells, the foot is a muscular organ. It is used for movement. In squids and octopuses, the foot is divided into tentacles. They are used for movement and feeding. Squids and octopuses swim by jet action. They take in water and squirt the water out through a tubelike structure in its head end.

Many mollusks, such as snails, have a **radula** (RAJ-oo-luh). The radula is a tongue-like organ. It is covered with hooked toothlike structures. The radula is used to scrape food, such as algae, from plants and rocks.

Define: What is a radula? tongue-like organ used to get food

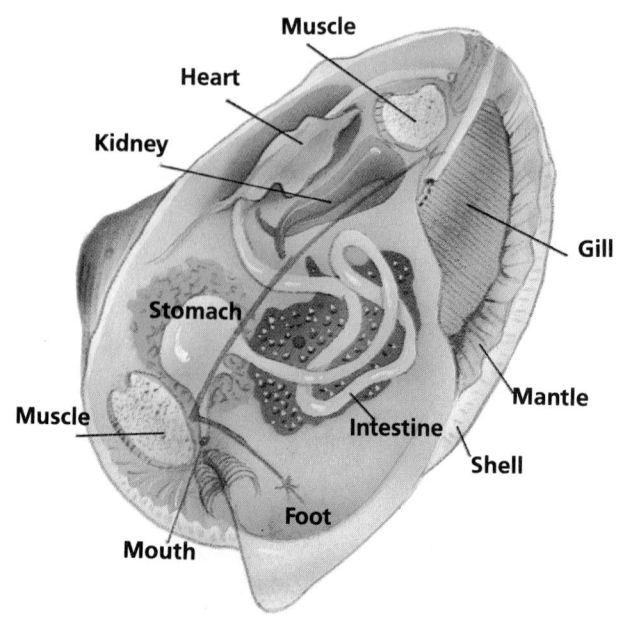

178

▶ Mollusks are soft-bodied animals classified in the phylum *Mollusca*.

▶ Mollusks are classified into three major classes.

▶ Mollusks have a head, a foot, and a fleshy mass of tissue that contains well-developed organs and organ systems.

▶ Mollusks have a digestive system, reproductive system, nervous system, and an open circulatory system.

▶ In mollusks with shells, the foot is muscular; in squids and octopuses, the foot is divided into tentacles.

▶ Many mollusks have a radula used for getting food.

CHECK *Write true if the statement is true. If the statement is false, changed the underlined term to make the statement true.*

1. The <u>foot</u> is a fleshy tissue that covers the internal organs of a mollusk. mantle

2. The <u>radula</u> is a tongue-like organ covered with hooked, toothlike structures. true

3. Snails are <u>one-shelled</u> mollusks. true

4. Octopuses and <u>clams</u> have tentacles. squids

APPLY *Complete the following.*

5. Newton's Third Law of Motion states that for every action there is an equal and opposite reaction. Explain what this means. Compare this law of motion to a squid's movement.

InfoSearch

Read the passage. Ask two questions that you cannot answer from the information in the passage.

Chambered Nautilus The chambered nautilus is classified as a head-foot mollusk. Unlike the octopus and squid, the chambered nautilus forms a shell outside its body. When the nautilus outgrows its shell, it adds on a new chamber, or section. In time, the nautilus shell has many chambers. The nautilus lives in the outer chamber. It can move up and down in the water by filling or emptying its chambers with gases.

SEARCH: Use library references to find answers to your questions.

ACTIVITY

MODELING SQUID JET PROPULSION

You will need a plastic straw, scissors, 4 meters of string, cellophane tape, a balloon, and 2 desk chairs.

1. Use the scissors to cut a 2-cm long piece of the straw. **CAUTION: Be careful when using scissors.**

2. Thread the string through the short piece of straw. Tape the straw to the middle of the uninflated balloon.

3. Tie the string to the backs of two chairs placed about 4 m apart.

4. Blow up the balloon. Hold the end closed with your fingers.

5. Release the balloon. Observe the direction it moves.

Questions

1. In which direction did the balloon move?

2. How does the movement of the balloon compare to the movement of the squid?

3. **Analyze:** How do you think the squid would move if it took in a large amount of water?

9-6 What are arthropods?

Objective ▶ List the main features of arthropods and give examples of some arthropods.

TechTerms

- ▶ **chitin** (KYT-in): hard material that makes up the exoskeleton of arthropods
- ▶ **exoskeleton** (ek-so-SKEL-uh-tun): hard covering that supports and protects the body
- ▶ **molting:** process by which an animal sheds its outer covering

Classifying Arthropods Arthropods (ar-thruh-PODS) are animals that have jointed legs. They are classified in the phylum *Arthropoda* (AHR-thruh-pahd-uh). Arthropods make up the largest group of animals. Scientists think that there are more than one million species.

Arthropods are divided into several classes. The largest classes are the insects, crustaceans (krus-TAY-shuns), and arachnids (uh-RAK-nidz). Insects include flies, butterflies, moths, ants, bees, mosquitoes, cockroaches, and many others. Crustaceans include lobsters, crabs, and shrimp. Arachnids include spiders, ticks, mites, and scorpions.

▶ *Identify:* Name the three largest classes of arthropods. insects, crustaceans, arachnids

Arthropod Features All arthropods have a hard body covering and a segmented body. The hard covering is an **exoskeleton** (ek-so-SKEL-uh-tun). An exoskeleton is an external skeleton. It protects and supports the soft, inner body parts. The exoskeleton is made up of a material called **chitin** (KYT-in). Chitin is tough, but light in weight.

Arthropods have jointed legs. The legs are made up of several pieces. The pieces are connected by joints, which can bend. The legs are moved by muscles attached to the exoskeleton.

Arthropods have an open circulatory system. Blood moves through open spaces in their bodies. It does not flow through tubes.

▶ *Identify:* What material makes up the exoskeleton of an arthropod? chitin

Molting When you grow, your bones grow. Your skeleton grows along with the rest of your body. An exoskeleton, however, cannot grow. It is not made of living material. As an arthropod grows, it becomes too big for its exoskeleton. At this time, the exoskeleton is shed. This process is called **molting.** The exoskeleton splits open and the animal works its way out. Gradually a new, larger exoskeleton grows.

▶ *Define:* What is molting? process by which an animal sheds its outer covering

Special Body Parts Depending upon where they live, what they eat, and how they move, arthropods have different body parts. Insects have special mouth parts that help them get food. These mouth parts are used for biting, chewing, or sucking, depending on how the insect feeds. Most insects also have wings. Some crustaceans, such as lobsters and crabs, have large front claws. They

use the claws to get food and to protect themselves. Spiders have silk glands that make silk for their webs. Many different types of arthropods also have antennae that are used for touch and taste.

▶ *List:* What are some special body parts of arthropods? mouth parts, wings, claws, silk glands, antennae

- ▶ Arthropods are animals with jointed legs.

- ▶ The largest arthropod classes are the insects, crustaceans, and arachnids.

- ▶ Arthropods have jointed legs, an exoskeleton, and a segmented body.

- ▶ Arthropods have an open circulatory system.

- ▶ When an arthropod grows, it molts its old exoskeleton, and grows a new one.

- ▶ Arthropods have special body parts that are suited to the foods they eat, the places they live, and the way they move.

CHECK *Explain the relationship between the words in each pair.*

1. chitin, exoskeleton

2. arthropod, arachnid

Complete the following.

3. What is the name of the largest animal phylum?

4. What are the three arthropod features?

5. Describe molting.

6. How are large claws helpful for a crustacean?

APPLY *Complete the following.*

7. **Classify:** Identify the class of each arthropod shown on page 180.

8. **Analyze:** Can you tell which of these arthropods can fly? How?

9. **Infer:** How are the grasshopper's large back legs suited to how it moves?

Health & Safety Tip

Watch out for ticks in heavily wooded areas. When you walk through the woods, tuck your pants into your socks. Wear long sleeves and a cap. Some ticks are carriers of Lyme disease. Lyme disease is a serious illness with many different symptoms.

Use reference books to find out about the rash that may form from Lyme disease. What are other symptoms of the disease? What is the role of the white-tailed deer in Lyme disease?

TECHNOLOGY AND SOCIETY

USES OF CHITIN

What do crab shells, some contact lenses, and certain types of varnish have in common? They are all made of chitin. Scientists are finding new uses for tough, protective chitin.

Chitin is especially good as a material for medical uses. It does not cause allergic reactions in most people. For this reason, chitin is used to make some kinds of contact lenses. Chitin is also used to make artificial skin. This skin can be used to protect badly burned parts of the body until new skin can form. A type of thread made from chitin is used for sewing up wounds or incisions. This type of thread dissolves in the body. It does not need to be removed.

Researchers have found many other uses for chitin. Varnish made of chitin makes an excellent finish for some musical instruments. Seeds coated with chitin are protected from infection. Chitin has also been used in water filters. Research on the uses of chitin continues. Chitin is now being tested as a coating for fabrics and paper. Who knows? Some day you may be wearing chitin-treated T shirts and reading science lessons printed on chitin-coated paper!

9-7 What are insects?

Objective ▶ Describe the features of insects.

TechTerms

- **abdomen** (AB-duh-mun): third section of an insect's body
- **spiracles** (SPIH-ruh-kuls): openings to air tubes of a grasshopper
- **thorax** (THOR-aks): middle section of an insect's body
- **tympanum** (TIM-puh-num): hearing organ in a grasshopper

Insects Insects are the largest class of arthropods. There are more different kinds of insects than any other kind of animals. In fact, more than 700,000 insects have been identified. Insects live almost everywhere, except the oceans. They live in the air and in the soil. They live inside the walls of buildings and on the leaves of plants. Beetles, fleas, termites, moths, and ants are all insects.

📖 *Classify:* What is the largest class of arthropods? insect

The Grasshopper The grasshopper is a good model to use when you study insects. Like all arthropods, a grasshopper has jointed legs, a segmented body, and an exoskeleton.

Like all insects, a grasshopper has three pairs of legs and antennae (an-TEN-ay). Antennae are sense organs. All insects have three body segments. They are the head, **thorax** (THOR-aks), and **abdomen** (AB-duh-mun). The thorax is the middle section of an insect's body. The three pairs of legs are attached to the thorax. The abdomen is the third section of an insect's body. Like most insects, the grasshopper also has wings.

Find the **spiracles** (SPIH-ruh-kuls). The spiracles are openings to air tubes inside the grasshopper. The grasshopper breathes by moving air in and out through the spiracles. Find the **tympanum** (TIM-puh-num). It is used for hearing.

▕▊▶ *State:* What are three features of all insects? three pairs of legs, three body segments, and wings

Social Insects Most insects live alone. Some live together in colonies. Insects that live in colonies are called social insects. Ants and honeybees are social insects.

In a honeybee hive, there are three kinds of honeybees. They are the queen, the drones, and the workers. Each one has its own job in the beehive. The queen bee lays eggs. The drones fertilize the eggs. The workers take care of the eggs. They feed the queen and the drones. Workers gather honey and pollen. Workers also build and protect the hive.

▕▊▶ *Name:* Name the three kinds of honeybees. queen, drone, worker

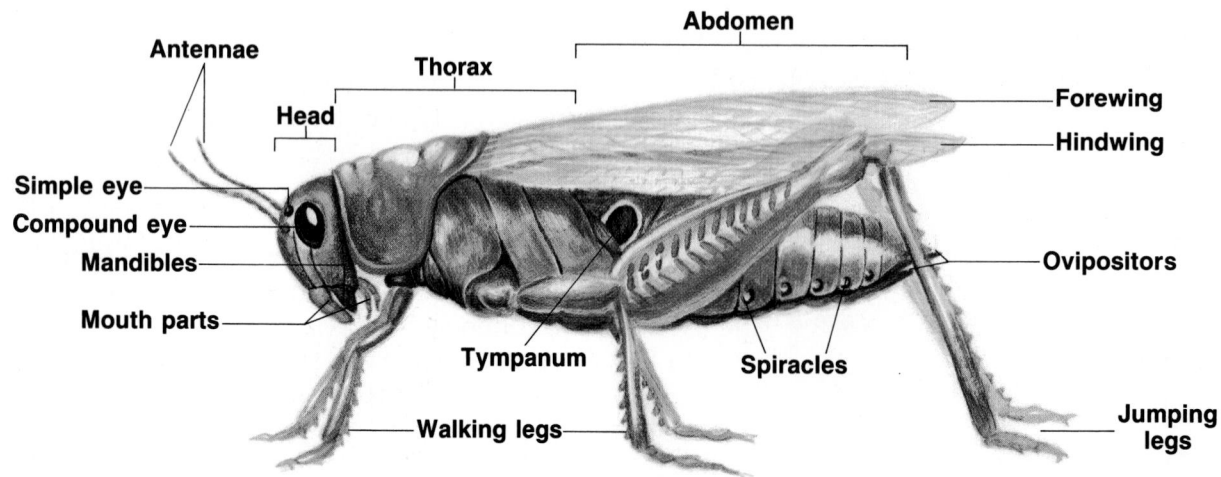

LESSON SUMMARY

- ▶ There are more species of insects than of all other animal species put together.
- ▶ A grasshopper is a good insect model to study.
- ▶ All insects have three pairs of legs, three body segments, and antennae.
- ▶ Spiracles and the tympanum are located on the abdomen of a grasshopper.
- ▶ Social insects, such as honeybees and ants, live together in colonies.
- ▶ In a beehive, each kind of bee has its own job.

CHECK *Answer the following.*

1. What animals make up the largest class of arthropods? insects
2. What are three body parts of an insect? head, thorax, and abdomen
3. How many legs do insects have? 6
4. What are the openings to air tubes on a grasshopper called? spiracles
5. What do grasshoppers use for hearing? tympanum
6. What are insects that live in colonies called? social insects

APPLY *Use the pictograph to answer the following.*

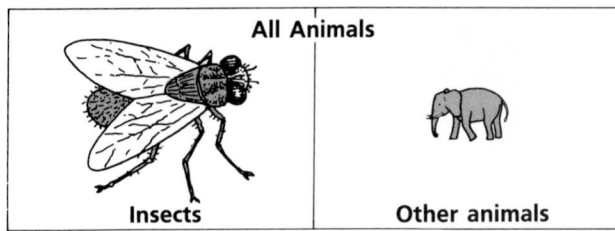

All Animals

Insects — Other animals

7. **Interpret:** How does the number of insect species compare to the number of all other animal species?
8. **Explain:** Why is the drawing of the fly larger than the drawing of the elephant?

InfoSearch

Read the passage. Ask two questions about the topic that you cannot answer from the information in the passage.

Helpful and Harmful Insects Some insects are helpful. Others are harmful. Bees and butterflies help pollinate flowers. Bees produce honey and wax that are used by people. Insects are food for many larger animals. Some insects, such as termites, eat wood and destroy buildings. Weevils ruin food crops. Other insects carry diseases.

SEARCH: Use library references to find answers to your questions.

SCIENCE CONNECTION

CAMOUFLAGE AND MIMICRY

Can you find the walking stick in the photograph? The walking stick looks like a twig. When it stands still, birds cannot see it. The walking stick is camouflaged, or hidden, by its body shape. Many insects and other animals are protected by camouflage. Their body shapes or coloring help them blend into their surroundings.

Some animals do not hide from their predators. They may have bright colors and bold patterns. Often these brightly colored animals mimic, or look like, other animals. The viceroy butterfly looks like a monarch butterfly. Birds avoid eating the monarch butterfly because it tastes bad to birds. Because the harmless viceroy butterfly looks like the monarch butterfly, birds avoid the viceroy butterfly. Mimicry can be found in other insects and in larger animals too. For example, some kinds of fish have a large dark circle on their tails. These circles mimic the eyes of a larger and more dangerous fish.

9-8 How do insects develop?

Objective ▶ Identify and describe the stages of metamorphosis.

TechTerms

- ▶ **cocoon** (kuh-KOON): protective covering around the pupa
- ▶ **larva** (LAHR-vuh): wormlike stage of insect development
- ▶ **metamorphosis** (met-uh-MOR-fuh-sis): changes during the stages of development of an insect
- ▶ **nymph** (NIMF): young insect that looks like the adult
- ▶ **pupa** (PYOU-puh): resting stage during complete metamorphosis

Metamorphosis All insects lay eggs. The developing insect, or embryo (EM-bree-oh), feeds on yolk stored in the egg. The eggs are laid on or near a food supply. After the eggs hatch, the young insect uses this food.

When an insect hatches from its egg, the insect usually does not look at all like the adult insect. For example, a small butterfly does not hatch from a butterfly egg. After the insect hatches from the egg, the insect goes through changes in form and size. The changes during the stages of development of an insect are called **metamorphosis** (met-uh-MOR-fuh-sis).

▶ *Define:* What is metamorphosis? changes during the stages of insect development

Incomplete Metamorphosis Some insects, such as grasshoppers, undergo incomplete meta-

morphosis. Incomplete metamorphosis has three stages. They are the egg, **nymph** (NIMF), and adult. The eggs hatch into nymphs. Nymphs look very much like a small adult. Nymphs have big heads and no wings. They also do not have reproductive organs. Nymphs gradually change and grow into an adult insect.

▶ *List:* What are the three stages of incomplete metamorphosis? egg, nymph, adult

Complete Metamorphosis Some insects, such as butterflies and moths, undergo complete metamorphosis. Complete metamorphosis has four stages. There is a change in body form in each stage of development.

The egg hatches into a **larva** (LAHR-vuh). The larva is a wormlike stage of an insect. A caterpillar is the larva of a butterfly or moth. Larvas eat a lot of food. They grow very quickly. After a time, the larva goes into a resting stage called the **pupa** (PYOU-puh). During this stage, many insects spin a covering around themselves. The covering is a **cocoon** (kuh-KOON). In the pupa stage, the insect does not eat. Many body changes take place inside the cocoon. The organs of the adult form. When the adult has formed, the cocoon opens. An adult insect comes out.

▶ *Sequence:* Place the stages of complete metamorphosis in the correct order. egg, larva, pupa, adult.

Incomplete Metamorphosis

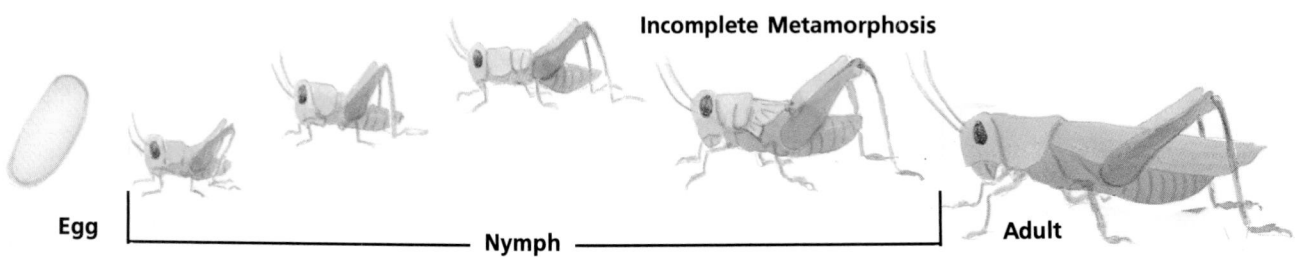

Egg   Nymph   Adult

184

LESSON SUMMARY

▶ All insects lay eggs on or near a food supply.

▶ The changes in form and size during the stages of development of an insect are called metamorphosis.

▶ The three stages of incomplete metamorphosis in insects are egg, nymph, and adult.

▶ The four stages of complete metamorphosis in insects are egg, larva, pupa, and adult.

CHECK *Complete the following.*

1. In insects, the third stage in complete metamorphosis is the _____ . pupa

2. In insects, the first stage of metamorphosis is always an _____ . egg

3. A caterpillar is the _____ stage of a butterfly. larva

4. The stage of complete metamorphosis in which some insects look like a small adult is the _____ . nymph

5. The larva stage of a moth is a _____ . caterpillar

APPLY *Complete the following.*

6. **Compare:** In what way are the eggs of insects like the eggs of birds?

7. **Infer:** Why is the pupa called the resting stage?

8. **Sequence:** Place the stages in the development of the beetle shown below in the correct order.

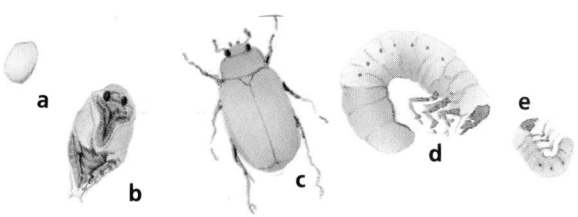

Skill Builder

Classifying When you classify, you group things based upon how they are alike. Find out whether each of the insects listed below undergoes complete or incomplete metamorphosis. If the insect undergoes complete metamorphosis, write the name of its larval stage.

a. locust I
b. cricket I
c. beetle C; grub
d. cockroach I
e. fly C; maggot
f. moth C; caterpillar
g. wasp C; grub

CAREER IN LIFE SCIENCE

EXTERMINATOR

Many insects, such as bees, are helpful to people. They supply honey and pollinate flowers. Other insects, such as termites, can destroy property. Still others, such as grasshoppers and locusts, can destroy crops. An exterminator (ik-STUR-muh-nayt-ur) gets rid of unwanted pests in buildings. Exterminators usually are called to get rid of termites and cockroaches. Some exterminators also rid buildings of mice and rats.

Exterminators work for city or county governments. Some work for private exterminating companies. Others have their own companies.

A high school diploma is needed to become an exterminator. You also need to take vocational courses in pest control methods. Courses in biology and chemistry should be taken in high school.

For more information, you may want to call your local board of health or write a letter to a private exterminating company.

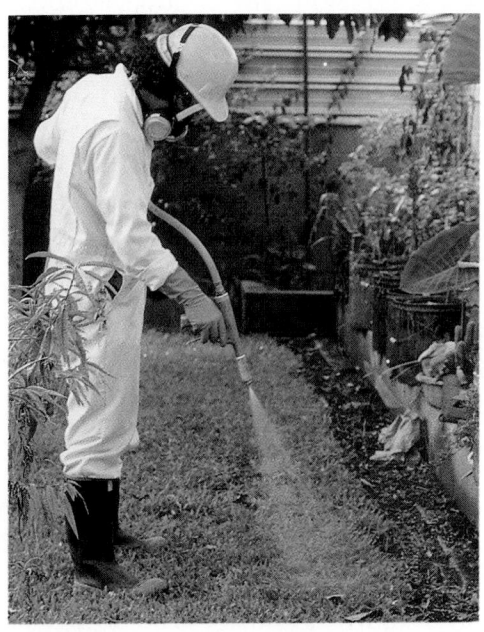

Objectives ▶ List the common characteristics of echinoderms. ▶ Name some echinoderms.

TechTerms

- ▶ **echinoderms** (ee-KY-noh-durms): spiny-skinned animals
- ▶ **endoskeleton** (en-doh-SKEL-un-tun): internal skeleton
- ▶ **tube feet:** small suckerlike structures of echinoderms

Echinoderms The **echinoderms** (i-KY-noh-durms) are the spiny-sinned animals. They are classified in the phylum *Echinodermata* (i-KY-noh-dur-muh-toh). They live on the ocean bottom. Sea stars are the best known echinoderms. Other echinoderms are sea urchins, sand dollars, brittle stars, and sea cucumbers. Some echinoderms move about slowly. Others attach themselves to rocks or other objects.

▦▶ *List:* **Name three echinoderms.** Answers will vary.

Anatomy of Echinoderms Echinoderms have an **endoskeleton** (en-doh-SKEL-un-tun), or internal skeleton. The endoskeleton is made up of spines. The most noticeable thing about echinoderms are their spiny skin.

In some echinoderms, such as the sea stars, the spines are hard, rounded lumps. In the sea urchins, the spines are like long needles. The skin of the sea cucumber is soft and leathery.

Echinoderms do not have a left side or a right side. Most have rays, or arms around a central point. Their body structures are arranged like the spokes of a wheel around a central body point. Echinoderms do not have circulatory, excretory, or respiratory systems. They have a nervous system, but echinoderms do not have a brain.

◉ *Observe:* **What is the most noticeable thing about the echinoderms in the photographs?** spines or spiny skin

Tube Feet Sea stars move using small, suckerlike structures called **tube feet.** The tube feet are part of a water-pumping system that works to pull the sea star forward. There are hundreds of tube feet. Each foot is like a suction cup. Using its tube feet, a sea star can move slowly across the ocean floor.

Tube feet also are used to get food. Sea stars eat mollusks. They use their tube feet to pull on mollusk shells, such as clams. The clam uses its muscles to keep its shell closed. Soon, the clam muscles tire and the shell opens a bit. The sea star then pushes its stomach out of its mouth into the clam. The clam is digested, and the sea star pulls its stomach back inside its body.

▦▶ *Name:* **What two things does a sea star use its tube feet for?** moving and food-getting

LESSON SUMMARY

▶ Echinoderms are the spiny-skinned animals.

▶ Echinoderms have an endoskeleton made up of spines.

▶ Echinoderms have body structures arranged like the spokes of a wheel around a central body point.

▶ Tube feet are part of a water-pumping system used to move and to get food.

CHECK *Answer the following.*

1. Name four echinoderms. Answers will vary.

2. What kind of skeleton do echinoderms have? endoskeleton

3. Which echinoderm has long needle-like spines? sea urchin

4. What are tube feet? small, suckerlike structures

Complete the following.

5. Sea stars eat oysters, mussels, and _____ . clams

6. Sea stars are classified in the phylum _____ . Echinodermata

APPLY *Complete the following.*

7. **Infer:** Why do you think a sea star would have trouble moving over sand or mud?

8. **Infer:** If all the sea stars in a clam bed were destroyed, what would happen?

Skill Builder

Building Vocabulary Animals have different kinds of symmetry. For example, sea stars have radial symmetry. Use a dictionary or library references to define bilateral symmetry, spherical symmetry, and radial symmetry. Then trace the outlines of the animals shown below. What kind of symmetry does each animal have? Draw a line or lines through each outline to show the animal's symmetry.

LEISURE ACTIVITY

SEASHORE COLLECTIONS

Making a seashore collection is a fun hobby. It also is an easy hobby to begin, especially if you live near an ocean. You can collect dried sea stars from the beach. Many different kinds of shells also can be collected. If you are very lucky, you may even find sand dollars on the beach. You should avoid collecting living animals.

If you do not live near a beach or if a trip to the ocean is not possible, you still can begin a seashore collection. Shells, sea stars, and sand dollars can be bought from shell dealers or other seashore collectors. There are mail-order catalogues, too. These catalogues offer many different seashore collectibles.

Once you begin gathering specimens for your seashore collection, you may want to buy a handbook or guide for collectors to help you identify your specimens. Most collectors label their collections. They mount their collections or keep them in small containers.

9-10 What is regeneration?

Objective ▶ Explain how some organisms can regrow lost parts.

TechTerm

▶ **regeneration** (ri-jen-uh-RAY-shun):   ability to regrow lost parts

Regeneration New plants can grow from a part of a plant by vegetative propagation (VEJ-uh-tayt-iv prahp-uh-GAY-shun). Does this kind of asexual reproduction also take place in animals? Can a new animal grow from part of an animal? Can parts of an animal that are broken off grow back? Some animals have the ability to regrow lost parts. The ability of an animal to regrow lost parts is called **regeneration** (ri-jen-uh-RAY-shun). In other animals, a whole new animal can develop from just a part of an animal. If an entire animal develops from a part, regeneration is a kind of asexual reproduction.

▶ *Define:* What is regeneration? ability of an animal to regrow lost parts

Regeneration in Animals All animals do not have the same abilities to regenerate, or regrow lost body parts. A few kinds of animals can regenerate large body parts. Most animals, however, can regrow only a small part. Lobsters and crabs can regenerate claws that have broken off. The glass-tailed lizard can regenerate its tail. If the lizard is attacked and grabbed by its tail, its tail breaks off. The lizard escapes. Gradually, its tail grows back. Most sea stars have five arms, or rays. If a ray is cut off, a new ray grows back.

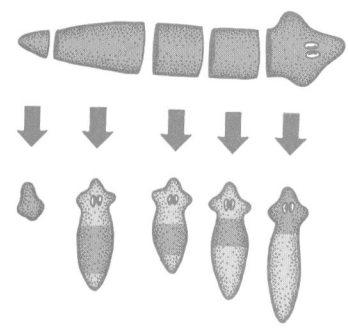

Some animals can reproduce asexually by regeneration. The flatworm planaria can be cut into several pieces. Each piece can regenerate a new planarian. Sea stars also can reproduce by regeneration. If a sea star is cut into pieces, each piece can develop into a new sea star. However, each piece must have part of the center of the sea star's body to regenerate a new sea star.

▶ *Name:* What are two organisms that can reproduce by regeneration? sea star; planarian

Regeneration in Humans The ability to regenerate body parts in humans is very small. The human body can regenerate some lost or damaged cells and tissues. If you cut yourself, new skin cells grow back to heal the cut. Broken bones grow back together again. The human body, however, cannot regenerate a whole organ, such as a kidney. The human body cannot regenerate large parts. A lost finger, for example, cannot grow back.

▶ *Describe:* What ability of regeneration does the human body have? very small—only some cells and tissues can regenerate

LESSON SUMMARY

▶ The ability of an animal to regrow lost parts is called regeneration.

▶ All animals do not have the same abilities to regenerate body parts.

▶ Some animals can reproduce asexually by regeneration.

▶ The human body only can regenerate some lost or damaged cells and tissues.

CHECK *Write true if the statement is true. If the statement is false, change the underlined term to make the statement true.*

1. Regeneration is a kind of <u>sexual</u> reproduction.
   asexual

2. Regeneration of lost parts takes place in <u>some</u> animals. true

3. The ability to regenerate in humans is very <u>small</u>. true

4. A <u>sea star</u> can regenerate lost rays. true

5. Crabs and lobsters can regenerate their <u>entire bodies</u>. claws

APPLY *Complete the following.*

6. How are vegetative propagation and regeneration similar?

▶ 7. **Infer:** Why is regeneration of a lobster's claw not a kind of asexual reproduction?

8. **Contrast:** How is regeneration in a crab different than regeneration in a sea star?

··
State the Problem...........................

Sea stars feed on clams, oysters, and mussels. People who gather clams, oysters, and mussels to sell as food used to catch sea stars. They would chop up the sea stars and throw the pieces back into the shellfish beds. What problem do you see with doing this?

⁝⁝⁝ TECHNOLOGY AND SOCIETY ⁝⁝⁝ ⦂⦂⦂ ⁝⁝⁝ ⦂⦂⦂ ⁝⁝⁝ ⦂⦂⦂ ⁝⁝⁝ ⦂⦂⦂ ⁝⁝⁝ ⦂⦂⦂ ⁝⁝⁝ ⦂⦂⦂ ⁝⁝⁝

ORGAN TRANSPLANTS

Humans can't regenerate lost or damaged organs. Doctors have found another way to help people who have lost certain organs or have damaged organs. Doctors have learned to transplant organs from one person to another. Today, many different organs are transplanted. The liver, kidneys, heart, pancreas, lungs, and skin are a few.

In the past, finding organs that were available for transplant could be difficult. To solve the problem, computer networks have been developed that keep records of available organs. Doctors can get the information they need quickly.

Before an organ can be transplanted, a person's tissue must be matched to the donor—the person who is giving the organ. This match is important so that the body of the person receiving the organ doesn't reject it. A new technique, called HLA matching, makes it possible to better match donors with those receiving the new organ. A drug called cyclosporine has been used since the 1970s to stop rejections of transplanted organs. Cyclosporine can have harmful side effects. New drugs that do not have these side effects are being tested.

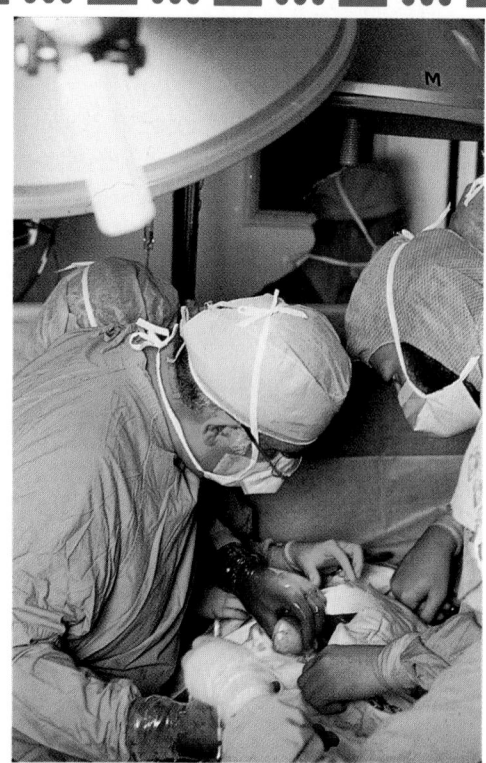

STUDY HINT Before you begin the Unit Challenges, review the TechTerms and Lesson Summary for each lesson in this unit.

TechTerms..

abdomen (182)
chitin (180)
closed circulatory system (176)
cnidocytes (172)
cocoon (184)
echinoderms (186)
ectoderm (174)
endoderm (174)
endoskeleton (186)
exoskeleton (180)

flagellum (170)
larva (184)
mantle (178)
medusa (172)
mesoderm (174)
metamorphosis (184)
molting (180)
nymph (184)
polyp (172)
pores (170)

pupa (184)
radula (178)
regeneration (188)
setae (176)
spicules (170)
spiracles (182)
tentacles (172)
thorax (182)
tube feet (186)
tympanum (182)

TechTerm Challenges...

Matching *Write the TechTerm that matches each description.*

1. whiplike structure on some cells flagellum
2. small, hard needle-like structures of a sponge spicules
3. long, thin armlike structures of a cnidarian tentacles
4. organ system where blood moves through the body in tubes closed circulatory system
5. thin membrane that covers the mollusk's body mantle
6. tough, lightweight material that makes up an arthropod's exoskeleton chitin
7. third section of an insect's body abdomen
8. section of insect where legs attach to thorax
9. protective covering of a pupa cocoon
10. resting stage of metamorphosis pupa
11. small, suckerlike structures that help echinoderms move tube feet

12. ability to regrow lost parts regeneration
13. spiny-skinned animals echinoderms
14. changes during the stages of development of an insect metamorphosis
15. hearing organ of grasshopper tympanum
16. openings to the air tubes of a grasshopper spiracles
17. shedding of an exoskeleton molting
18. tongue-like organ of snails and other mollusks radula
19. bristles on an earthworm that help it move setae
20. middle layer of cells mesoderm
21. stinging cells of a cnidarian cnidocytes
22. tiny openings pores

Applying Definitions *Explain the difference between the terms in each pair.* Answers will vary. Accept all logical responses.

1. ectoderm, endoderm
2. exoskeleton, endoskeleton

3. medusa, polyp
4. larva, nymph

Content Challenges...

Multiple Choice *Write the letter of the term that best completes each statement.*

1. Cnidarians can live either as a polyp or as a
   a. medusa. **b.** sponge. **c.** gemmule. **d.** echinoderm. a

2. Spicules are found in a sponge's
   a. jellylike substance. **b.** mesoderm. **c.** endoskeleton. **d.** ectoderm. a

3. All porifera and cnidarians have
   a. four cell layers. **b.** three cell layers. **c.** two cell layers. **d.** one cell layer. c

4. The simplest worms are the
   a. segmented worms. **b.** roundworms. **c.** flatworms. **d.** tapeworms. c

5. The worms that can live in the human body are
   a. planaria and flukes. **b.** flukes and tapeworms. **c.** tapeworms and segmented worms. **d.** planaria and hookworms. b

6. Roundworms belong to the phylum
   a. *Platyhelminthes.* **b.** *Porifera.* **c.** *Nematoda.* **d.** *Annelida.* c

7. Segmented worms include
   a. hookworms and trichina. **b.** hydra and tapeworms. **c.** roundworms and leeches. **d.** earthworms and leeches. d

8. The body of segmented worms is
   a. ringlike. **b.** smooth. **c.** threadlike. **d.** rough. a

9. Clams and oysters belong to the class of mollusks that have
   a. no shell. **b.** a one-part shell. **c.** a two-part shell. **d.** a three-part shell. c

True/False *Write true if the statement is true. If the statement is false, change the underlined term to make the statement true.*

1. The outer layer of cells of a cnidarian is called the endoderm. ectoderm

2. Invertebrates are animals with a backbone. without

3. The umbrellalike form of a cnidarian is called a polyp. medusa

4. An earthworm uses its setae and muscles to move. true

5. Snails, clams, and squids all are examples of echinoderms. mollusks

6. A sea star uses flagella to move. tube feet

7. All echinoderms have an endoskeleton. true

8. The development of a whole organism from one of its parts is called generation. regeneration

9. The largest group of animals on Earth is the mollusks. arthropods

10. Insects develop through a series of stages of development called mimicry. metamorphosis

Understanding the Features...

Reading Critically *Use the feature reading selections to answer the following. Page numbers for the features follow each question in parentheses.*

1. **Infer:** Why is it important to always snorkel with a buddy? (171)

2. **Name:** What are the three kinds of coral reef? (173)

3. **Hypothesize:** Do you think humans can get hookworms by walking in infected areas? (175)

4. How are leeches used in modern medicine? (177)

5. How is chitin used in surgery? (181)

6. **Explain:** How does the viceroy butterfly use mimicry? (183)

7. **Infer:** Why do you think biology and chemistry classes are important for an exterminator? (185)

8. Why should you avoid collecting live animals for your seashore collection? (187)

9. What are some organs that have been successfully transplanted? (189)

Concept Challenges

Interpreting a Diagram *Use the diagram of the grasshopper to answer the following.*

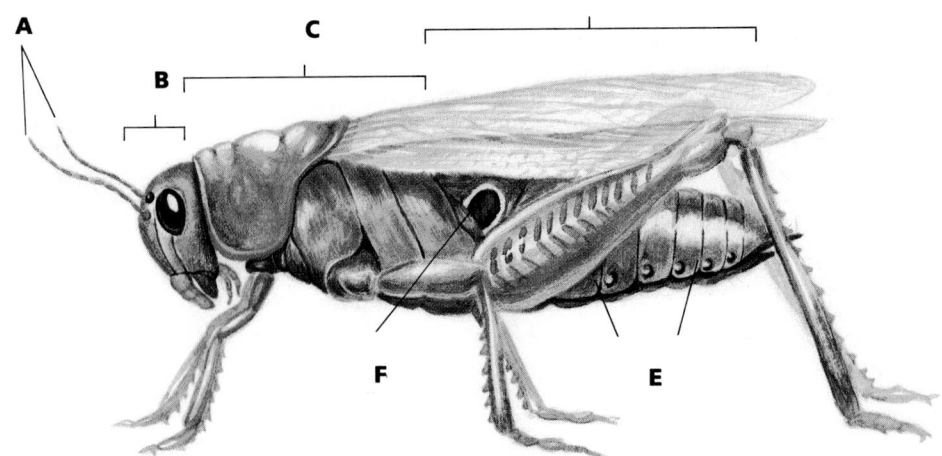

1. What letter represents a grasshopper's hearing organ?
2. What does letter B represent?
3. Which letter represents the openings to air tubes?
4. Which letter represents where an insect's legs attach to?
5. What does letter D represent?
6. Which letter represents the grasshopper's sense organs?

Critical Thinking *Answer each of the following in complete sentences.*

1. **Infer:** Until the mid-nineteenth century, most scientists thought that sponges were plants. Why might scientists have considered sponges to be part of the Plant kingdom?
2. **Infer:** Why do you think sponge farmers cut up sponges and throw them back in the water?
3. **Infer:** Why do you think earthworms avoid sunlight?
4. How does regeneration help some animal species survive?
5. **List:** What are some of the differences between insects and spiders? Why are spiders not classified as insects?

Finding Out More

1. Due to increasing technology, scientists are now able to build artificial reefs. Use library references to find information about the advantages and disadvantages of artificial reefs. Present your findings in a report.
2. Research some of the methods of insect control. Include one natural method of insect control as well as chemical methods. Write your findings in a report.
3. Use library references to find out how a pearl is formed in an oyster. Present your findings in a report to the class.
4. Soft-shell crabs only are available during certain months of the year. Visit a local fish market and find out when these crabs are available. Also, find out why soft-shell crabs are not always available.

ANIMALS WITH BACKBONES

CONTENTS

STUDY HINT Before beginning Unit 10, scan through the lessons in the unit looking for words that you do not know. On a sheet of paper, list these words. Work with a classmate to try to define each word on your list.

10-1 What are chordates?

Objective ▶ Identify the features of chordates.

TechTerms

- ▶ **endoskeleton** (en-duh-SKEL-uh-tun): skeleton inside the body
- ▶ **notochord** (NOHT-uh-kowrd): strong, rodlike structure in chordates that can bend
- ▶ **vertebrate** (VUR-tuh-brit): animal with a backbone

Phylum Chordata Fishes, frogs, snakes, birds, cats, and many other animals are classified in the phylum *Chordata* (KOWR-dayt-uh). All animals in this phylum have a notochord (NOHT-uh-kowrd) at some time during their development. A notochord is a strong, rodlike structure that can bend. It is used for support. The notochord is located just below the nerve cord.

▶ *Define:* What is a chordate? animal with a notochord at some time during its development

Other Chordate Features Besides a notochord, all chordates have two other features. All chordates have a hollow nerve cord. It runs down the back of the animal. Chordates also have paired gill slits at some time during their development. In fishes, the gill slits become gills. Gills are used to take in oxygen dissolved in water. In most other chordates, the gill slits disappear as the animal develops.

▶ *Name:* What are two chordate features besides a notochord? hollow nerve cord and gill slits

Vertebrates Animals with a backbone are called **vertebrates** (VUR-tuh-brits). There are five major groups of vertebrates. They are fishes, amphibians, reptiles, birds, and mammals. Vertebrates have an **endoskeleton** (en-duh-SKEL-uh-tun). An endoskeleton is a skeleton that is inside the body. The endoskeleton protects the inside organs. It also gives support.

▶ *Infer:* What organ is protected by the hard, bony skull of a vertebrate? brain

Lancelets In most adult chordates, the notochord is replaced by a backbone. Only a few kinds of simple chordates do not have a backbone. The best-known of these is the lancelet. Lancelets are small, fishlike animals. They live buried in the sand on the ocean floor. A lancelet keeps its notochord throughout its life. It is never replaced by a backbone.

▶ *Analyze:* Look at the lancelet. Why is it classified as a chordate? It has all three chordate features.

Body Plan of Chordates Chordates have a left side and a right side. They also have a head end and a tail end. During development there are three tissue layers. They are the endoderm, mesoderm, and ectoderm. Each tissue layer develops into different tissues and organs.

Chordates have many organ systems. One of these organ systems is a closed circulatory system. It is made up of a heart and many blood vessels. Chordates also have the most highly-developed nervous systems of all animals.

▶ *Infer:* Based upon the body plan of chordates, are you a chordate? yes

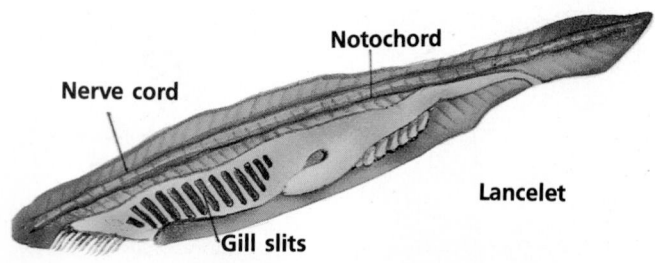

Notochord / Nerve cord / Gill slits / Lancelet

LESSON SUMMARY

▶ Chordates are animals that have a notochord at some time during their development.

▶ A hollow nerve cord and gill slits are other chordate features.

▶ Animals with a backbone are vertebrates.

▶ All chordates have a left and a right side, a head and tail end, and three tissue layers.

▶ Chordates have many organ systems.

CHECK *Complete the following.*

1. A notochord is a strong, flexible _____ structure that can bend. rodlike

2. The nerve cord of a chordate runs down the _____ of the animal. back

3. A skeleton that is inside the body is an _____ . endoskeleton

4. Animals with backbones are called _____ . vertebrates

5. An endoskeleton protects inside organs and gives the body _____ . support

6. The tissue layers of chordates are the endoderm, the _____, and the ectoderm. mesoderm

7. Chordates have a _____ circulatory system. closed

APPLY *Complete the following.*

8. **Identify:** What chordate characteristic makes a fish suited to life in the water?

9. **Infer:** All vertebrates are chordates. What structure do you think replaces the notochord in vertebrates?

10. **Contrast:** Identify two features of vertebrates that invertebrates do not have.

Skill Builder

Applying Definitions A prefix is a word part that is placed at the beginning of a word. Look up the meanings of the prefixes "endo-," "meso-," and "ecto-" in a dictionary. Write the definitions in your notebook. The diagram shows the endoderm, mesoderm, and ectoderm tissue layers.

Use the meanings of the prefixes to identify each of the lettered tissue layers in the diagram. Explain your choices.

CAREER IN LIFE SCIENCE

ANIMAL TECHNICIAN

Do you own a pet? Do you like to care for animals? If so, you may enjoy a career as an animal technician. Animal technicians help veterinarians treat sick animals. Animal technicians keep records for veterinarians. They do laboratory work, and dress wounds of animals. Animal technicians also help veterinarians with equipment. Technicians also may help animals during surgery.

Animal technicians need a high school diploma and must complete a two-year animal technology program. The program trains you in laboratory work and animal research. If you would like to become an animal technician, you should concentrate on doing very well in science courses. Summer or part-time job experience working with animals also is helpful.

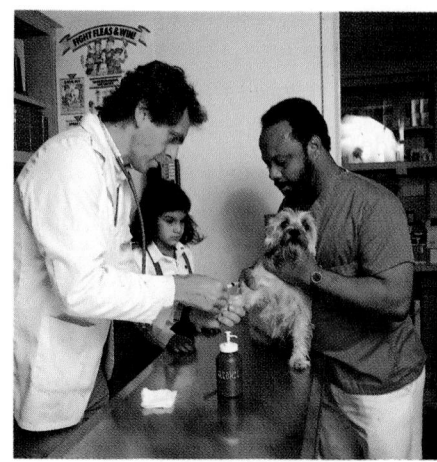

10-2 What are fishes?

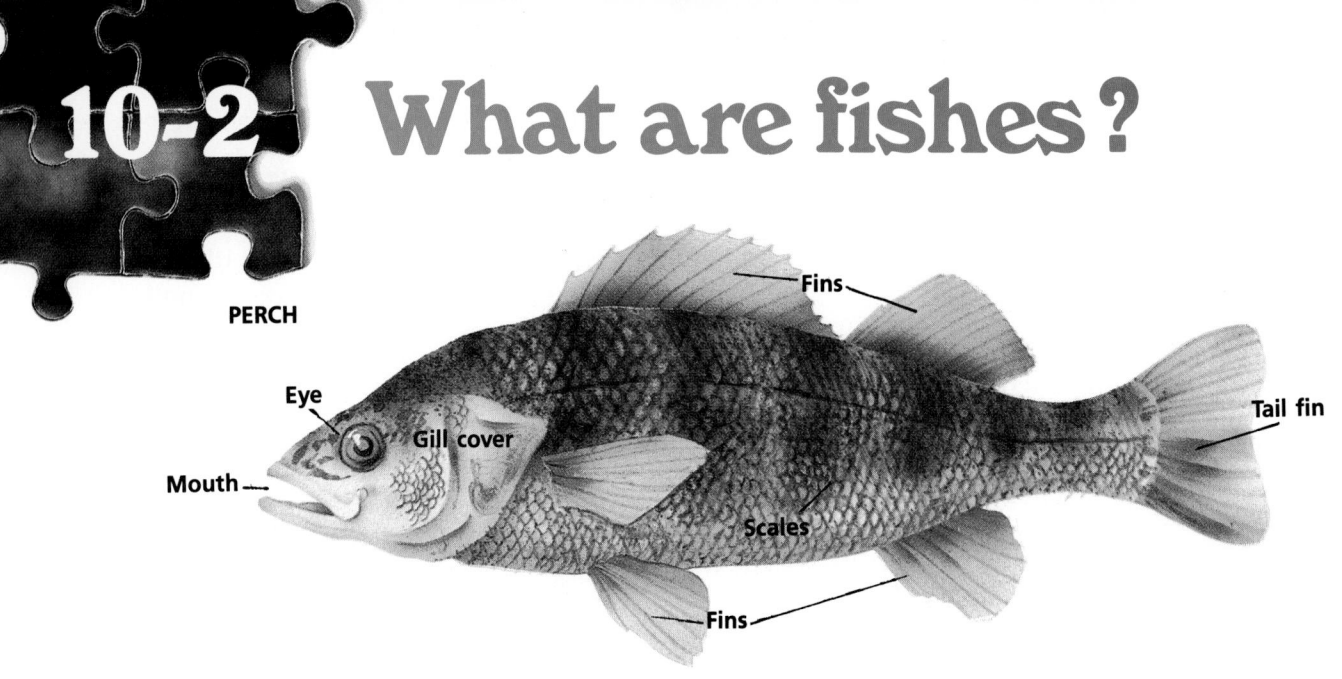

PERCH

Fins

Tail fin

Eye

Gill cover

Mouth

Scales

Fins

Objectives ▶ List three characteristics of fishes.
▶ Name examples of fishes in each class.

TechTerms

- **cartilage** (KART-ul-idj): kind of strong, flexible tissue
- **coldblooded:** having a body temperature that changes with the temperature of the surroundings
- **gills:** organs that absorb dissolved oxygen from water

Fishes Fishes are the simplest and oldest group of vertebrates. Fishes first appeared more than 500 million years ago. Today, fishes live in most of the earth's waters.

Fishes are **coldblooded** animals. The body temperature of a coldblooded animal changes with the temperature of its surroundings. For example, when the water temperature drops, the body temperature of a fish also drops.

▶ *Predict:* What would happen to the body temperature of a fish if the water temperature rose? Its body temperature would rise.

Gills Fish breathe through gills. Gills are feathery organs that have many blood vessels. Dissolved oxygen in the water is absorbed by the gills. The oxygen passes into the blood in the gills. Blood carries the oxygen to all the cells in the fish's body. Carbon dioxide passes out of the blood in

the gills, and then into the water.

▶ *Identify:* What organs do fish breathe through? gills

Three Classes The fishes are the largest group of vertebrates. Fishes have a two-chambered heart. The top chamber is the atrium (AY-tree-um). The bottom chamber is the ventricle (VEN-tri-kul). Fishes are classified in three classes. They are the jawless fishes, the cartilaginous (kahrt-ul-AJ-uh-nus) fishes, and the bony fishes.

Lampreys (LAM-prees) and hagfish are the only jawless fishes. They look very different from most fishes. These fishes are long and snakelike. They do not have scales. They have slimy skin.

The cartilaginous fishes include sharks, rays, and skates. These fish have skeletons made of **cartilage** (KART-ul-idj). Cartilage is a strong, flexible tissue. The tip of your nose and your ears are made of cartilage.

Bony fishes have skeletons made of bone. You probably are most familiar with these fish. Bony fishes include tuna, salmon, bass, and flounder.

Bony fishes are suited to many different environments. Most bony fishes have streamlined bodies for easy movement through the water. They also have different kinds of fins. The fins are used for steering and balance. The body of a bony fish is covered with tough, overlapping scales. The scales cover and protect the skin.

▶ *Classify:* What are the three classes of fish? jawless fish, cartilaginous fish, bony fish

LESSON SUMMARY

- ▶ Fishes are the simplest and oldest group of vertebrates.
- ▶ Fishes are coldblooded animals.
- ▶ Fishes breathe through gills.
- ▶ Fishes have a two-chambered heart.
- ▶ Lampreys and hagfish are jawless fishes.
- ▶ Sharks, skates, and rays are cartilaginous fishes.
- ▶ Bony fishes have skeletons made up of bone.
- ▶ Bony fishes have streamlined bodies, fins, and a body covered with scales.

CHECK *Find the sentence in the lesson that answers each question. Then, write the sentence.*

1. What is a coldblooded animal?
2. What are gills?
3. How many chambers does a fish's heart have?
4. What are the only two kinds of jawless fishes?
5. What is the main characteristic of a cartilaginous fish?
6. How do fishes use fins?

APPLY *Complete the following.*

7. **Observe:** Look at the picture of the perch on page 196. How many fins does a perch have?

8. **Classify:** Places each of the following fishes into its correct class:
   - **a.** sea horse
   - **b.** eel
   - **c.** hagfish
   - **d.** sea skate
   - **e.** lamprey
   - **f.** hammerhead shark
   - **g.** trout
   - **h.** whale shark

Skill Builder..

▶ *Inferring* When you infer, you form a conclusion based upon facts. A flounder is shown below. Both of a flounder's eyes are on the same side of its head. A flounder also is the color of sand or mud. Both of these features are adaptations. How do you think a sandy color and eyes on one side of the head made a flounder suited to life on the ocean floor?

SCIENCE CONNECTION ◆○◆○◆○◆○◆○◆○◆○◆○◆○◆○◆○◆○◆○◆○◆○◆

UNUSUAL FISHES

The fishes with unusual names and traits are the sea horse and the porcupine fish. Can you predict why a fish would be named after a horse or a porcupine?

The sea horse looks like a miniature horse. It is a bony fish, with an unusually shaped skeleton. It swims holding its horselike head in an upright position. Female sea horses lay their eggs in a pouch found only on the males. The males carry the eggs in the pouches until the eggs hatch.

The porcupine fish is another unusual bony fish. It is covered with spines. The spines protect the porcupine fish from other animals. When threatened, the porcupine fish makes its spines stick out by filling itself with water. As it takes in water, it becomes larger and rounder. It puffs up like a spiny balloon. Later, when it no longer needs to protect itself, it lets out the water. It becomes smaller and its spines lie flat. Its shape then looks more like that of other fishes.

10-3 What are amphibians?

Objective ▶ Identify the characteristics of amphibians.

TechTerm

▶ **amphibian** (am-FIB-ee-un): animal that lives part of its life in water and part on land

Amphibians An **amphibian** (am-FIB-ee-un) is an animal that lives part of its life in water and part on land. In fact the word "amphibian" comes from a Greek word meaning "double life." Most young amphibians live in water. As they grow, they undergo changes. Adult amphibians live mainly on land. Scientists think that the first amphibians developed from fish that could stay out of water for long periods of time. These fish had lungs and could breathe air.

Amphibians are coldblooded. Except for toads, amphibians have smooth, moist skin. Toads have bumpy skin. Amphibians also have webbed feet. Because they live part of their life in water and part on land, they use gills, lungs, and their skin to exchange oxygen and carbon dioxide. Amphibian eggs do not have shells and are laid in water.

▶ *Predict:* As the temperature of the mud that a salamander is in drops, what will happen to its body temperature? it will drop

Classifying Amphibians Scientists have classified about 2500 different kinds of amphibians. Scientists classify amphibians into three orders based upon their body structures. The best-known amphibians are frogs and toads. They are the tailless amphibians. Salamanders belong to a different order. They are the amphibians with tails. The third order of amphibians do not have legs. They are wormlike animals. These animals live in the forests of South America.

▶ *List:* What are the three orders of amphibians? tailed, tailless, without legs

More About Amphibians Amphibians have a closed circulatory system. They have a three-chambered heart. The heart has two atria and one ventricle. Almost all amphibians have gills during the early stages of development. As adults they have lungs. Some salamanders have gills throughout their lives. Many amphibians also breathe through their skin. Their skin must stay moist so that oxygen and carbon dioxide can be exchanged through the skin.

▶ *Infer:* If some kinds of salamanders have gills throughout their lives, in what kind of environment would they live? water

LESSON SUMMARY

▶ Amphibians are animals that live part of their lives in water and part on land.

▶ Amphibians are coldblooded animals with smooth skin and webbed feet.

▶ Amphibians are classified into three orders based upon their body structures.

▶ Amphibians have three-chambered hearts, gills when young, and lungs as adults.

CHECK *Find the sentence in the lesson that answers each question. Then, write the sentence.*

1. What does the word "amphibian" mean?

2. From what animals do most scientists think amphibians developed?

3. What kind of skin do toads have?

4. What kind of amphibians are frogs and toads?

5. Why must amphibians keep their skin moist?

APPLY *Complete the following.*

6. **Contrast:** How does the body structure of a frog differ from that of a salamander?

7. **Infer:** Why do you think most amphibians have webbed feet?

8. List six characteristics of amphibians.

InfoSearch

Read the passage. Ask two questions that you cannot answer from the information in the passage.

Caecilians Caecilians (see-SIL-ee-uns) are amphibians without legs. Caecilians look like long, colorful earthworms. In fact, a caecilian may be as much as 30-cm long. Like earthworms, caecilians live in soil. Some caecilians have very small eyes. Most caecilians, however, are considered blind.

SEARCH: Use library references to find answers to your questions.

TECHNOLOGY AND SOCIETY

COMPUTER DISSECTIONS

Computers have become useful tools in science. They can be used to store data and make calculations. They can be used to add color to photographs. In fact, many of the cell photographs in this book have had color added to them by computers. Computers also can make charts, tables, and graphs to keep track of research. They also can be used to run simulations (sim-yuh-LAY-shuns). A simulation is a moving model.

In many schools, animal dissections are no longer done on preserved specimens. Instead, computers are used to run a dissection simulation. A special computer program, such as a frog dissection, is on a computer disk. You can dissect the frog by using the dissection simulation disk. On the computer screen, you use laboratory equipment to open the frog. You can explore the different organs and organ systems of the frog on the computer screen.

Many people prefer using computer dissection. They do not think animals should be killed for dissections. Other people think that dissections on preserved specimens is important to the study of life science. What do you think?

10-4 How do frogs develop?

Objective ▶ Explain metamorphosis in frogs.

TechTerms

▶ **metamorphosis** (met-uh-MOWR-fuh-sis): changes during the stages of development of an organism

▶ **tadpole:** larval stage of a frog

Metamorphosis The changes during the stages of development of an organism are called **metamorphosis** (met-uh-MOWR-fuh-sis). Amphibians and insects change during their life cycles. During its life cycle, an amphibian changes the way it looks. During early stages, amphibians can live only in water. They breathe with gills. As an adult, amphibians live on land. They use lungs and their moist skin to breathe.

▶ *Name:* What are two groups of animals that change during their life cycle? amphibians and insects

Amphibian Eggs All amphibians lay eggs. The eggs do not have a shell. They usually are laid in water. For example, frogs and toads lay their eggs in freshwater lakes, ponds, and other bodies of water. They lay their eggs in the spring. Toads lay long strings of eggs. Frogs lay clumps of eggs. The eggs are surrounded by a jellylike substance. The eggs cling to water plants.

▶ *Observe:* Do frogs lay many eggs, a few eggs, or one egg? many

Tadpoles In about 12 days, frog eggs hatch into **tadpoles.** Tadpoles are the early stage of a frog. They are the larval stage. The larval stage does not look like a frog at all. Tadpoles look like very small fish. Their bodies are streamlined. They have a thin tail. They breathe with gills.

▶ *Name:* What is the early stage of a frog called? tadpole

Tadpole to Adult Frog As a tadpole grows, its body changes. Legs begin to develop. As the tadpole begins to develop into a young frog, its tail grows shorter. Gradually the tail disappears. In most amphibians, lungs develop and the gills disappear. At this point, the young frog leaves the water. It is adapted, or suited, to a life on land.

▶ *Infer:* What adaptation does the young frog have for breathing air? lungs

Adult frog · Young frog · Fertilized eggs · Tadpole with gills · Tadpole with limbs

LESSON SUMMARY

▶ The changes during the stages of development of an organism are called metamorphosis.

▶ Amphibians lay eggs without shells in water.

▶ A tadpole is the larval stage of a frog.

▶ As a tadpole develops into an adult frog, it develops legs, loses its tail, develops lungs, and loses its gills.

CHECK *Write true if the statement is true. If the statement is false, change the underlined term to make the statement true.*

1. During early stages in their development, amphibians breathe with <u>lungs</u>. gills

2. Amphibians and <u>insects</u> undergo metamorphosis. true

3. Most amphibians lay their eggs <u>on land</u>. in water

4. The larval stage in the development of a frog is a <u>toad</u>. tadpole

5. Frogs hatch into tadpoles in about 12 <u>weeks</u>. days

6. The eggs of frogs are surrounded by a <u>jellylike</u> substance. true

APPLY *Complete the following.*

7. **Sequence:** Place the events in the development of a frog in the correct order.
   a. Lungs develop and gills disappear. **b.** Eggs are laid in water. **c.** The tail begins to disappear. **d.** Tadpoles hatch from the eggs. **e.** Legs are almost fully developed and the tail is almost gone.

▲ 8. **Model:** Develop a flowchart that shows the stages in frog development.

▶ 9. **Infer:** Why do you think frogs lay so many eggs at one time?

🗐 10. **Hypothesize:** Why do you think amphibians lay their eggs in water?

Health & Safety Tip

A wart is a bumpy growth of the skin. People sometimes say that you can get warts by touching a toad. However, this is not true. Use library references to find out what causes warts. Also try to discover why many people associate warts with toads.

ACTIVITY

SEQUENCING TADPOLE DEVELOPMENT

You will need a pencil and a sheet of paper.

1. Study the photographs of different stages of development in a frog.

2. **Sequence:** Place the photos in the correct order to show frog metamorphosis. Write the correct order of the letters. C, D, A, B

Questions

1. **Analyze:** How does the frog change at each stage?

▰ 2. **Analyze:** Where does the tadpole live? How is it adapted to living there?

▰ 3. **Analyze:** Where does the frog live? How is it adapted to its environment?

A

B

C

D

10-5 What are reptiles?

Objectives ▶ Explain how reptiles are adapted to life on land. ▶ Describe the four orders of reptiles.

Life on Land Reptiles were the first true land animals. Unlike amphibians, reptiles do not need water for reproduction. Reptiles lay their eggs on land. The eggs are covered with a leathery shell. Young reptiles develop in the eggs.

Reptiles have lungs throughout their lives. They never have gills. They have hard, dry, skin covered with scales. The skin is waterproof. The waterproof skin cuts down on water loss from the body.

▶ *Explain:* How are reptiles adapted for life on land? They do not need to return to the water to reproduce or to keep their skin moist.

Reptiles Reptiles are coldblooded. Most have two pairs of legs with clawed feet. They have a three-chambered or four-chambered heart.

More than 100 million years ago the reptiles were the major group of animals on the earth. By about 65 million years ago, most of these reptiles including dinosaurs had died out. Today there are about 6500 different kinds of reptiles. They are classified into four orders.

▶ *Name:* What are some of the characteristics of reptiles? Answers will vary, but may include clawed feet, three- or four-chambered heart, scales

Orders of Reptiles The smallest order of reptiles are the tuataras (too-uh-TAY-ruhs). They are called "living fossils" because they have many features of ancient reptiles. These animals have changed very little since they first appeared about 200 million years ago.

The largest order of reptiles includes the snakes and lizards. The big difference between these two kinds of animals is that snakes do not have legs. There are about 4500 different kinds of snakes and lizards.

Turtles and tortoises make up another order of reptiles. Turtles live mostly in water. Tortoises live mostly on land. Turtles and tortoises have shells. Turtles have flat, streamlined shells. Tortoises have high, domed shells.

The fourth order of reptiles includes alligators (AL-uh-gayt-urs) and crocodiles. These animals spend much of their time in water. You can tell the difference between them by looking at their heads. Alligators have broad rounded heads. Crocodiles have more triangle-shaped heads.

▶ *Infer:* Why do you think a flat, streamlined shell is helpful to a turtle in water? It is better for swimming.

Crocodile

Alligator

LESSON SUMMARY

- ▶ Reptiles are land animals that lay eggs.
- ▶ Reptiles have lungs and scaly, waterproof skin.
- ▶ Reptiles are coldblooded, have a three- or four-chambered heart and most have two pairs of legs.
- ▶ Reptiles are classified into four orders.
- ▶ Tuataras are the smallest order of reptiles.
- ▶ Snakes and lizards make up the largest order of reptiles.
- ▶ Turtles and tortoises are reptiles with shells.
- ▶ Alligators and crocodiles make up an order of reptiles that spend much of their time in water.

CHECK *Complete the following.*

1. Where do young reptiles develop?
2. Why are tuataras called "living fossils?"
3. How do snakes differ from lizards?
4. Where do most tortoises live?
5. How could you tell an alligator from a crocodile?

APPLY *Complete the following.*

6. **Contrast:** How do snakes differ from all other reptiles?
7. Look at the dinosaurs in the feature. What characteristics of reptiles do these dinosaurs have?

InfoSearch

Read the passage. Ask two questions that you cannot answer from the information in the passage.

A Misunderstood Group Many people are afraid of snakes. They think that snakes are slimy and poisonous. Actually most snakes are not poisonous. Many snakes are helpful. They eat mice, rats, and other pests.

Poisonous snakes have long, curved hollow teeth called fangs. When a snake bites its victim, venom (VEN-um) in the fangs is injected into the wound. Venom is snake poison. Many venoms paralyze the muscles used for breathing, causing death.

SEARCH: Use library references to find answers to your questions.

▾▾ LOOKING BACK IN SCIENCE ▾▾▾▾▾▾▾▾▾▾▾▾▾▾▾▾▾▾▾

THE AGE OF DINOSAURS

The first dinosaurs appeared on the earth more than 200 million years ago. For nearly 140 million years dinosaurs were the dominant animals on the earth. Then about 65 million years ago, the dinosaurs died out. Scientists are not sure why dinosaurs became extinct.

Dinosaurs lived during a time in the history of the earth called the Mesozoic Era. Other reptiles lived at the same time as the dinosaurs. The Mesozoic Era is sometimes called the Age of Reptiles. Because dinosaurs were the dominant animals during this time, it also is called the Age of Dinosaurs.

You may think that all dinosaurs were large animals. In fact, some were quite large, but others were as small as hens. The largest known dinosaur is *Brachiosaurus.* It was 30 meters tall. *Tyrannosaurus rex* and triceratops are two other large dinosaurs. *Compsognathus* was one of the smallest dinosaurs. It was less than 1 meter tall.

10-6 What are birds?

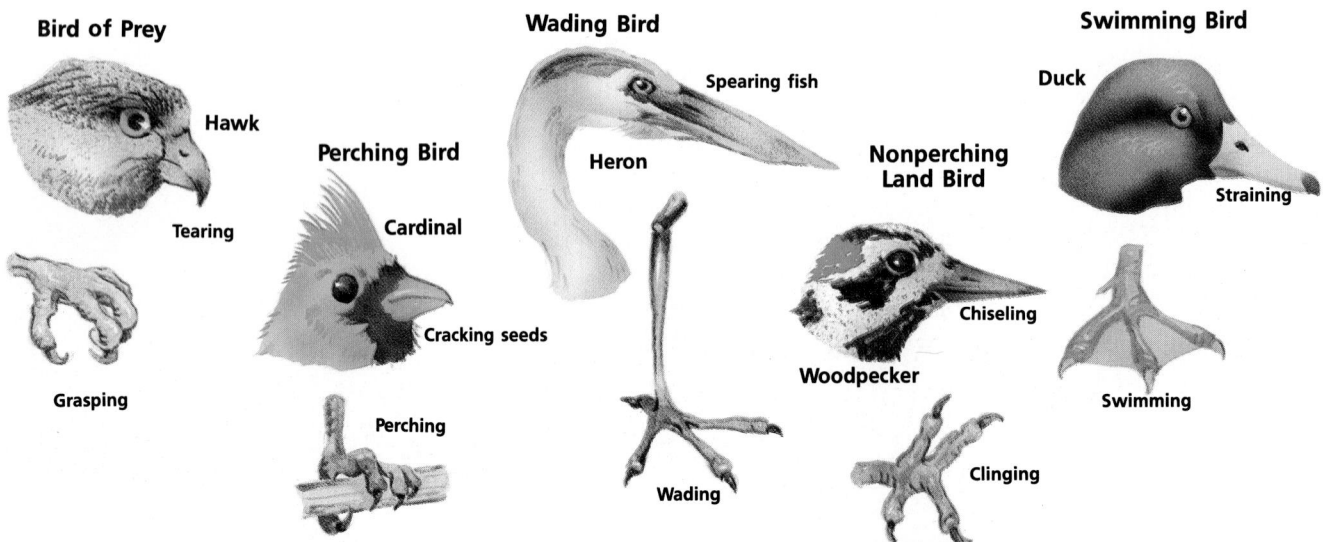
Contour feather   **Down feather**

Objectives ▶ Describe the characteristics of birds.
▶ Classify different kinds of birds.

TechTerm

▶ **warmblooded:** having a body temperature that remains about the same

Features of Birds Unlike fishes, amphibians, and reptiles, birds are **warmblooded.** The body temperature of a warmblooded animal remains about the same. It does not change when the temperature of the animal's surroundings changes. Birds maintain their body temperatures by using heat produced by the breakdown of food.

Birds are very easy to recognize. They are the only animals with feathers. Birds also have other features.

▶ Birds have two wings and two legs.

▶ Birds have lightweight bones.

▶ Birds have a beak without teeth.

▶ Birds lay hard-shelled eggs.

▷ **Compare:** What is the difference between coldblooded and warmblooded animals?

Coldblooded animals have body temperatures that change with the surrounding temperature; warmblooded animals have constant body temperatures.

Five Groups All birds are classified in the class *Aves.* They are classified into five groups based on their beaks and feet. Figure 1 shows the five groups of birds. Look at the swimming birds. All swimming birds, such as ducks, have webbed feet for paddling through water. Hawks and other meat-eating birds have long, sharp claws to capture animals.

Look at the structure of the bill, or beak in each group. The beak varies with eating habits. Birds that feed on seeds have short strong beaks. Hunting birds, such as owls and eagles, have curved beaks for tearing meat.

▶ **Infer:** Why do you think hunting birds need strong beaks? to capture their prey

Body Plan of Birds Most birds have a streamlined, cigar-shaped body. The feathers that cover the bird serve several functions. They give the bird its shape. Some feathers are important in flight. Other feathers, called down feathers, help to keep in body heat.

Birds have well-developed organ systems. Their respiratory system, in particular, works very well. It has to supply the muscles with large amounts of oxygen during flight. Birds have a four-chambered heart. The two upper chambers are the atria. The two lower chambers are the ventricles.

▷ **State:** How many chambers does a bird's heart have? 4

Figure 1 Five groups of birds

LESSON SUMMARY

▶ Birds are warmblooded animals.

▶ Birds are the only animals with feathers, have two wings and two legs, have lightweight bones, a beak, and lay eggs.

▶ Birds are classified into five groups based upon the shapes of their beaks and feet.

▶ Birds have a cigar-shaped body covered with feathers.

▶ Birds have well-developed organ systems.

CHECK *Write true if the statement is true. If the statement is false, change the underlined term to make the statement true.*

1. Birds are <u>coldblooded</u> animals. warmblooded

2. Birds are the only animals with <u>feathers</u>. true

3. Birds that eat <u>seeds</u> have strong, curved beaks for tearing. meat

4. All <u>perching</u> birds have webbed feet. swimming

5. Birds have <u>down</u> feathers to help keep in body heat. true

6. The upper chambers of a bird's heart are the <u>ventricles</u>. atria

APPLY *Complete the following.*

 7. **Classify:** Use the diagram of bird classification on page 204 to classify each of the birds listed.
   a. hawk   c. cardinal   e. heron
   b. duck   d. woodpecker   f. eagle

8. **Apply:** Sea gulls live near ocean waters. Describe what kind of feet and beaks you think sea gulls have.

9. **Infer:** People, like birds, have four-chambered hearts. What do you think the upper and lower chambers of the human heart are called?

10. What characteristic can you use to classify an animal as a bird?

Health & Safety Tip

The meat and eggs of poultry contain a bacteria called *Salmonella*. *Salmonella* causes food poisoning. Use library references to find out what the symptoms of *Salmonella* poisoning are. Also, find out two ways to help reduce your risk of poisoning from this bacterium.

ACTIVITY

OBSERVING A BIRD EGG

You will need a chicken egg and a small dish.

1. Obtain a raw chicken egg.

2. **Observe:** Describe the shell of the chicken egg.

3. Crack open the egg into the dish.

4. **Observe:** Look at the inside of the shell. Find the shell membrane and the air space. Draw a model of the inside of the egg shell. Label the parts.

5. **Model:** Look at the egg in the dish. Draw a model of the inside of the egg. Label the yolk and egg white.

Questions

1. a. **Observe:** What color is the egg shell? b. Is the shell smooth or slightly bumpy?

2. a. **Observe:** What color is the egg white? b. The yolk?

3. What two parts make up most of the bird egg?

4. a. **Infer:** What is the function of the shell? b. The yolk?

5. **Hypothesize:** Why do you think birds make nests for their eggs?

10-7 What are mammals?

Objective ▶ Describe the characteristics of mammals.

TechTerms

▶ **mammary** (MAM-ur-ee) **glands:** glands where milk is produced in female mammals

▶ **placenta** (pluh-SEN-tuh): organ through which materials are exchanged between the mother and developing embryo

Conquerors of the Earth More than 250 million years ago, animals called therapsids (THER-up-sidz) roamed the earth. Fossils show this animal had characteristics of reptiles and mammals. Biologists infer that all modern mammals came from the therapsids. When the dinosaurs died out, early mammals did not have to compete for food and living space. The mammals survived and reproduced. Today, mammals are one of the most successful groups of animals on the earth.

◢ *Analyze:* Why did mammals survive when the dinosaurs died out? They did not have to compete for food and shelter.

Characteristics of Mammals Mammals are a class of vertebrates that include humans and most of the best-known large animals. Mammals are warmblooded. Because they are warmblooded, mammals can live almost everywhere. They live on the plains, in forests, in deserts, and in swamps. They live in oceans, and a few can even fly.

Besides being warmblooded, mammals have these characteristics.

▶ Mammals have body hair.

▶ Mammals have a four-chambered heart.

▶ Most mammals have a highly-developed brain and nervous system.

▶ Female mammals nurse their young with milk. The milk is produced by **mammary** (MAM-ur-ee) **glands.**

▮▮▮▶ *List:* What are the characteristics of mammals? Students should restate the characteristics given.

Kinds of Mammals There are three basic mammal groups. One group is made up of egg-laying mammals. There are only two kinds of animals in this group. These are the duckbill platypus (PLAT-uh-pus) and the spiny anteater. In these animals, the young develop in an egg surrounded by a shell.

The second mammal group is the pouched mammals. In pouched mammals, the young are born at a very early stage of development. They then crawl into a pouch, or pocket, on the belly of the mother. They remain in the pouch until they are big enough to survive on their own. Kangaroos, opossums, and koala bears are pouched mammals.

The third and largest group of mammals is the placental (pluh-SEN-tul) mammals. In these animals a special structure called the **placenta** (pluh-SEN-tuh) develops in the female during pregnancy. The placenta connects the mother and developing organism. Dogs, cats, cattle, seals, whales, bats, apes, and humans are placental mammals.

▮▮▮▶ *List:* What are the three kinds of mammals? egg-laying mammals, pouched mammals, placental mammals

LESSON SUMMARY

▶ Scientists think that modern mammals came from the therapsids.

▶ Mammals include humans and most of the best-known large animals.

▶ Mammals are warmblooded, have body hair, a four-chambered heart, a highly-developed nervous system, and nurse their young with milk produced in mammary glands.

▶ The duckbilled platypus and the spiny anteater are mammals that lay eggs.

▶ The young of opossums, kangaroos, and koalas develop in the pouch of the mother.

▶ The young of most mammals develop attached to an organ called a placenta within the mother's body.

CHECK *Complete the following.*

1. There are _____ basic mammal groups. three

2. All mammals have _____ on their bodies. hair

3. Female mammals produce milk in _____ glands. mammary

4. Mammals have a _____ heart. four-chambered

5. The young of the largest group of mammals are connected to the mother by the _____ . placenta

6. The young of spiny anteaters develop inside a _____ . shell

7. Kangaroos and koalas are _____ mammals. pouched

APPLY *Complete the following.*

8. **Contrast:** How do spiny anteaters and duck-bill platypuses differ from reptiles?

9. **Compare:** What characteristic is used to classify mammals into each of their groups?

Skill Builder

📁 ***Classifying*** When you classify, you place things into groups based upon similarities. The placental mammals are classified into orders. These orders include the flying mammals, toothless mammals, insect-eating mammals, gnawing mammals, rodentlike mammals, aquatic mammals, trunk-nosed mammals, carnivorous mammals, hoofed mammals, and primates. Use library references to find the characteristics each of these mammal orders. Then, cut out pictures of twenty different mammals from newspapers or magazines. Use your pictures to make a poster that classifies each of your mammals into its order.

LEISURE ACTIVITY

PETS

People keep many different kinds of animals as pets. Small mammals, birds, and fish are common pets. Some people have unusual pets such as alligators and crickets. On farms, horses and baby pigs and ducks are sometimes pets. Dogs and cats are especially popular pets for the home.

Pets can be interesting and fun companions. Some pets are workers as well as companions. For example, dogs are trained to help guide blind people. Horses can be both companions and transportation for their owners.

By caring for a pet, you learn about responsibility. It is important to learn to care for your pet's special needs. Does your pet need exercise? What does it eat? How is grooming important to your pet's health?

Treat your pet fairly and you will have its respect and affection. Your pet's main role is to be your friend. As a pet owner, your role is to enjoy your pet while treating it fairly and taking care of it properly.

10-8 How do animal embryos develop?

Objective ▶ Recognize how the development of mammals differs from other animals.

TechTerms

- ▶ **egg:** female sex cell
- ▶ **fertilization** (fur-tul-i-ZAY-shun): union of a male sex cell and a female sex cell
- ▶ **sperm:** male sex cell

Water Animals Most fish and other animals that live in water lay their **eggs** in water. An egg is a female sex cell. The male deposits sperm on the eggs, as seen in the photo below. Sperm are male sex cells. The sperm join with the eggs. Only one sperm cell joins with each egg. The union of a sperm and an egg is called **fertilization** (fur-tul-i-ZAY-shun). In these animals, the eggs are fertilized outside the female's body. After fertilization, the embryo (EM-bree-oh) begins to develop. An embryo is a developing organism. The embryo develops inside the egg. Remember, the egg is outside the female's body. The embryo uses food stored in the egg.

▶ *Infer:* Where do the embryos of frogs develop? in an egg outside the body of the female

Land Animals The eggs of land animals and sea mammals are fertilized inside the body of the female. In some animals, such as snakes and birds,

the eggs develop in a hard shell after fertilization. The eggs are then laid. The embryos develop in the eggs outside the body of the female. The embryo uses the food stored in the egg. You know the food as the yolk.

▶ *State:* Where are the eggs of land animals fertilized? inside the female

Embryo Development in Mammals In all mammals, fertilization takes place inside the body of the female, or mother. Most mammals do not lay eggs. In these mammals, the embryo develops inside the mother's body. Most mammals give birth to living young.

▶ *State:* Where do the embryos of most mammals develop? inside the body of the mother

Embryo Nutrition The embryos of mammals get their food from the mother through the placenta. Digested food and oxygen from the mother's blood pass into the bloodstream of the embryo. The embryo uses this food and oxygen for growth and development. Waste substances produced by the embryo pass into the mother's blood. These wastes are then excreted from the mother's body along with her own waste products.

▶ *State:* Where do mammal embryos get their food supply? from the bloodstream of the mother

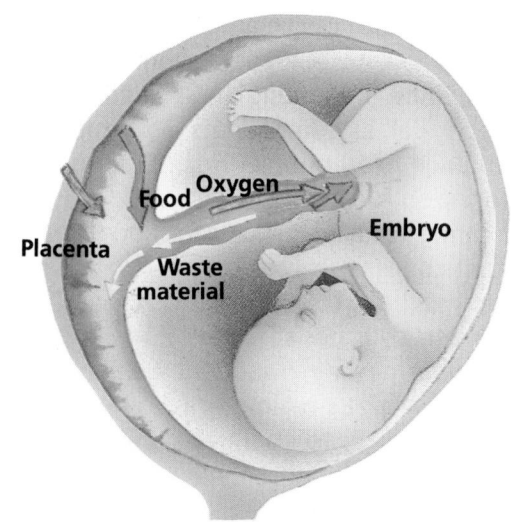

Food Oxygen
Placenta
Embryo
Waste material

LESSON SUMMARY

▶ The union of a sperm cell and an egg cell is called fertilization.

▶ The eggs of land and sea mammals are fertilized inside the body of the mother.

▶ In most mammals, the embryo develops inside the mother's body.

▶ The embryos of mammals get their food from the mother.

CHECK *Find the sentence in the lesson that answers each question. Then, write the sentence.*

1. What is an egg?
2. What is a sperm?
3. What is fertilization?
4. What is an embryo?
5. Where does an embryo that develops inside an egg get its food?
6. Where do the embryos of mammals get their food?
7. Where do the embryos of mammals develop?
8. Where do the embryos of animals such as birds and snakes develop?

APPLY *Complete the following.*

9. **Contrast:** How is the development of the embryos of most animals different from the development of a mammal embryo?

▶ 10. **Infer:** What structure in mammals is used to get food to a mammal embryo and to get rid of waste products?

Skill Builder

Researching When you do research, you gather information about a topic. The time it takes for an embryo to fully develop inside its mother's body is called the gestation (jes-TAY-shun) period. Gestation periods are different for different kinds of animals. Use library references to find out the gestation periods for the following mammals: elephant, mouse, dog, cat, human, guinea pig, horse, and cow. Present your findings in a graph.

Sperm cells

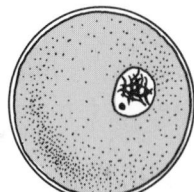

Egg cell

ACTIVITY

COMPARING GESTATION TIME AND ANIMAL SIZE

You will need a pencil and a sheet of graph paper.

1. Study the gestation times of the mammals in Table 1.
2. **Calculate:** Change all gestation times to days.
3. **Graph:** On a sheet of graph paper, make a bar graph showing the gestation times of the mammals. Show gestation time in number of days.

Questions

1. **Sequence:** Place the mammals in Table 1 in order from smallest to largest.

▲ 2. **Organize:** Use the sequence from smallest to largest, and make a table comparing relative size and gestation time in days.

3. Do larger or smaller mammals seem to need longer gestation times? Write one or two sentences to explain your answer.

Table 1 Mammal Gestation Times	
Dog	9 weeks
Elephant	20-22 months
Hamster	16 days
Humans	9 months
Gorilla	8-9 months
Cow	40 weeks
Rabbit	26-30 days
Sheep	about 2 months

UNIT 10 Challenges

STUDY HINT Before you begin the Unit Challenges, review the TechTerms and Lesson Summery for each lesson in this unit.

TechTerms

amphibians (198)
cartilage (196)
coldblooded (196)
egg (208)
endoskeleton (194)

fertilization (208)
gills (196)
mammary glands (206)
metamorphosis (200)
notochord (194)

placenta (206)
sperm (208)
tadpole (200)
vertebrate (194)
warmblooded (204)

TechTerm Challenges

Matching *Write the TechTerm that matches each description.*

1. union of sperm cell and an egg cell fertilization
2. organs used for obtaining oxygen dissolved in water gills
3. animal with a backbone vertebrate
4. organs in female mammals that produce milk mammary glands
5. organ through which materials are exchanged between the mother and developing embryo placenta
6. change during the development of an organism metamorphosis
7. larval stage of a frog tadpole

Applying Definitions *Explain the difference between the terms in each pair.* Answers will vary. Accept all logical responses.

1. sperm, egg
2. coldblooded, warmblooded
3. amphibians, reptiles
4. cartilage, bone
5. endoskeleton, exoskeleton
6. notochord, nerve cord
7. gills, lungs
8. vertebrate, invertebrate

Content Challenges

Multiple Choice *Write the letter of the term that best completes each statement.*

1. The three features common to all chordates are a hollow nerve cord, gill slits at some time during their development, and
   a. cartilage. **b.** a notochord. **c.** an endoskeleton. **d.** a placenta. b

2. In most adult chordates, the notochord is replaced by
   a. gills slits. **b.** lungs. **c.** a backbone. **d.** an endoskeleton. c

3. Fish are classified as either jawless, cartilaginous, or
   a. bony. **b.** tailless. **c.** tailed. **d.** venomous. a

4. Fish, amphibians, and reptiles all
   a. are cold blooded. **b.** are warmblooded. **c.** have a three chambered heart. **d.** have smooth, moist skin. a

5. In the larval stage, a frog is called a(n)
   a. toad.   **b.** egg.   **c.** adult.   **d.** tadpole. d

6. The largest order of reptiles is made up of
   a. tuataras.   **b.** snakes and lizards.   **c.** turtles and tortoises.   **d.** alligators and crocodiles. b

7. Both birds and mammals
   a. have lightweight bones.   **b.** have mammary glands.   **c.** are warmblooded.   **d.** are cold-blooded. c

8. Biologists believe that mammals come from a group of animals called
   a. dinosaurs.   **b.** therapsids.   **c.** carnivores.   **d.** marsupials. b

9. The duckbill platypus and the spiny anteater are
   a. placental mammals.   **b.** pouched mammals.   **c.** egg-laying mammals.   **d.** oceanic mammals. c

10. The developing organism that results from the union of an egg and a sperm cell is called a(n)
    a. embryo.   **b.** fetus.   **c.** baby.   **d.** mammal. a

True/False *Write true if the statement is true. If the statement is false, change the underlined term to make the statement true.*

1. Fishes, amphibians, reptiles, birds, and mammals are classified in the phylum *porifera*. chordata
2. All chordates have three tissue layers. true
3. Fish breathe through lungs. gills
4. In coldblooded animals, body temperature changes as the outside temperature changes. true
5. Amphibians usually lay their eggs on land. in water
6. Frog eggs have leathery shells. rough
7. Dinosaurs are an extinct group of mammals. reptiles
8. All birds belong to the class *Aves*. true
9. Birds are coldblooded animals. warmblooded
10. Birds have a two-chambered heart. four
11. Fish and other animals that live in water lay eggs that are fertilized outside the female's body. true
12. The embryo of an egg-laying land animal gets nutrition from the egg's yolk. true

Understanding the Features...

Reading Critically *Use the feature reading selections to answer the following. Page numbers for the features follow each question in parentheses.*

1. What are the two educational requirements for a career as an animal technician? (195)
2. What is the purpose of the spines on the porcupine fish? (198)
3. **Infer:** What might be some disadvantages of using computer dissection instead of dissection of preserved animals? (199)
4. During which era did the dinosaurs reign? (203)
5. Name three responsibilities of a pet owner. (207)

Concept Challenges..

Critical Thinking *Answer each of the following in complete sentences.*

1. How do coldblooded animals differ from warmblooded animals? Are humans coldblooded or warmblooded?
2. What are the major characteristics of an amphibian?
3. What are three differences between amphibians and reptiles?
4. **Infer:** Why do you think birds that feed on seeds have short strong beaks?
5. In what two ways are bird and mammals alike?

Interpreting a Diagram *Use the diagram to complete the following.*

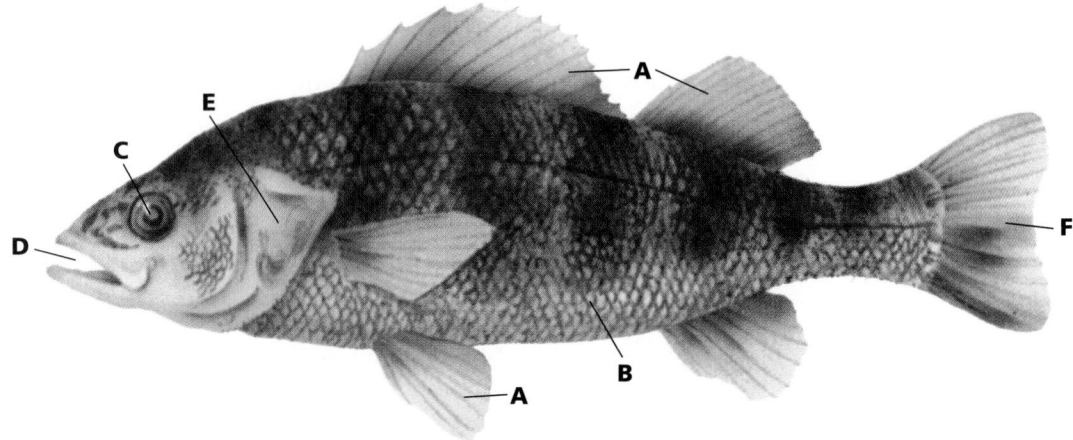

1. What is the part of the fish labeled C?
2. What is the part of the fish labeled E?
3. **Infer:** What does the part labeled E protect?
4. **Analyze:** Which parts help the fish swim through the water?
5. What is the part of the fish labelled D?
6. What does the fish use the part labeled D for?

Finding Out More..

1. **Research:** Scientists have come up with several different theories to explain why the dinosaurs became extinct. Using library reference books, research as many of these theories as you can. State which of the theories seems most logical to you and why.
2. Dianne Seale is a biologist who did research to find out how nutrients in a pond affect the development of a tadpole. Visit the library and find out about Dianne Seale's work. Report your findings to the class in the form of a scientific article.
3. **Classify:** With the assistance of your teacher or a field guide, find out the names of ten kinds of birds that live in your area. Then classify each bird you have identified into one of the five groups discussed in this unit.
4. **Classify:** Using old books or magazines, cut out five pictures of animals from each class of vertebrates: fishes, amphibians, reptiles, birds, and mammals. (You will have a total of 25 pictures.) Use your pictures to make a poster that indicates the class in which each animal belongs. Include the name of each class above each group of pictures.
5. Many animals today are currently in danger of becoming extinct. Use an encyclopedia to find out what some of these endangered species are. Also find out why they are becoming extinct and what you can do to prevent their total disappearance from the earth.

NUTRITION AND DIGESTION

CONTENTS

STUDY HINT As you read each lesson in Unit 11, write the topic sentence for each paragraph in the lesson on a sheet of paper. After you complete each lesson, compare your list of topic sentences to the Lesson Summary.

11-1 What are nutrients?

TechTerms

- **carbohydrate** (kar-buh-HY-drayt): nutrient that supplies energy
- **nutrient** (NOO-tree-unt): chemical substances in food needed by the body for growth, energy, and life processes
- **protein** (PRO-teen): nutrient needed to build and repair cells

Nutrients All foods contain **nutrients** (NOO-tree-unts). Nutrients are chemical substances in food that your body needs for growth and energy. Nutrients also are needed to carry out life processes. There are five kinds of nutrients. They are **carbohydrates** (kar-buh-HY-drayts), fats, **proteins** (PRO-teenz), vitamins, and minerals. Some foods are rich in one nutrient. Most foods contain more than one nutrient.

▐▐▐▶ *Define:* What are nutrients? materials needed by the body for growth, energy, and life processes

Carbohydrates Carbohydrates are nutrients that supply your body with energy. They are your main source of energy. Starches and sugars are carbohydrates.

There are two kinds of carbohydrates, simple and complex. Sugars are simple carbohydrates. They are used quickly by your body. Sugars give your body short, quick bursts of energy. Starches

are complex carbohydrates. They give your body energy over long periods of time. Breads and pasta contain starch.

▐▐▐▶ *Name:* What are the two kinds of carbohydrates? sugars (simple) and starches (complex)

Fats Fats are the energy-storage nutrients. The stored energy in fats can be used if energy from carbohydrates is used up. Fat that is stored in the body is used for insulation (in-suh-LAY-shun). It keeps your body warm. Fat also is used to protect your body organs.

Fats can be either solids or liquids. Solid fats come mostly from animals. Liquid fats are called oils. They usually come from vegetables, such as corn. Many oils are used in cooking.

▐▐▐▶ *List:* Identify ways the body uses fat. energy-storage, insulation and protection

Proteins Your body needs proteins for growth and repair. Proteins also are used to build tissues, such as muscles. You get some proteins from foods you eat. Other proteins are made in your body. When carbohydrates and fats have been used up, proteins also can be used for energy. Milk, fish, and cheese are good sources of protein. Peas, peanuts, and beans also are good sources of protein.

▐▐▐▶ *Explain:* Why are proteins needed by the body? growth, repair, and to build tissues

LESSON SUMMARY

▶ Nutrients are chemical substances in food that are needed by the body for growth, energy, and life processes.

▶ Carbohydrates are nutrients that supply the body's main source of energy.

▶ The two kinds of carbohydrates are simple and complex.

▶ Fats are the energy-storage nutrients.

▶ Fats can be either liquids or solids.

▶ Proteins are used to build and repair cells.

CHECK *Write true if the statement is true. If the statement is false, change the underlined term to make the statement true.*

1. Your body needs <u>nutrients</u> for growth, energy, and to perform life processes. true

2. <u>Simple</u> carbohydrates give your body energy over a <u>long</u> period of time. short

3. The energy-storage nutrients are <u>carbohydrates</u>. fats

4. Your body uses <u>fat</u> to build and repair cells. protein

5. Starches and grains are good sources of <u>complex carbohydrates</u>. true

APPLY *Answer the following.*

6. **Hypothesize:** Why do long distance runners eat foods rich in starch the evening before a race?

7. **Infer:** Why should you eat more complex carbohydrates than simple carbohydrates?

InfoSearch

Read the passage. Ask two questions that you cannot answer from the information in the passage.

Water Although it is not a nutrient, your body needs a constant supply of water. More than two-thirds of your body is made up of water. Water is needed to carry out your life processes. All of the chemical changes that take place in your body require water. Water also helps control your body temperature. You should try to drink at least six glasses of water each day.

SEARCH: Use library references to find answers to your questions.

ACTIVITY

TESTING FOR FATS

You will need a brown paper bag, scissors, and 5 small samples of different foods.

1. Cut the bag open so that you have a flat surface of brown paper.

2. Rub a piece of food on the bag. Write the name of the food near the spot.

3. Repeat Step 2 for each of your foods.

4. Let the spots dry. If the spots disappear, there is no fat in the food. If the spots remain, there is fat in the food.

5. Copy Table 1. Record your observations in the table by checking the correct box.

Questions

1. How do you test foods for the presence of fats?

2. **Observe:** Which foods left a spot on the paper?

3. **Summarize:** What can you conclude about the foods you tested?

4. Make a list of the foods you found contain fat.

Table 1			
FOOD	PREDICT	FAT	NO FAT
1.			
2.			
3.			
4.			
5.			

11-2 Why are proteins important?

Objective ▶ List five ways the body uses proteins.

TechTerms

- ▶ **amino acid:** building block of proteins
- ▶ **enzyme** (EN-zym): protein that controls chemical activities
- ▶ **molecule** (MAHL-uh-kyool): smallest part of a substance that has all the properties of that substance

Protein Molecules Proteins are giant **molecules** (MAHL-uh-kyoolz). A molecule is the smallest part of a substance that has all the properties of that substance. In fact, proteins are the largest molecules in living things. All proteins contain atoms of carbon, hydrogen, oxygen, and nitrogen.

Figure 1 Atoms in proteins

▶ *Name:* What atoms do protein molecules contain? carbon, hydrogen, oxygen, and nitrogen

Importance of Proteins Proteins are the building blocks of living material. Your body uses proteins in several ways. One important use of proteins is to build new cells. Another use of protein is to repair cells that are damaged. Proteins also are used to make **enzymes** (EN-zymz). Enzymes are substances that control many of the chemical activities in the body. Proteins also can be used as a source of energy for body cells.

▶ *Explain:* How are proteins used by the body? build new cells; repair damaged cells; make enzymes; source of energy; control chemical activities in cells

Protein Building Blocks The building blocks of proteins are **amino acids.** Proteins are formed when many smaller amino acid molecules join together. There are about 20 different amino acids. Twelve of these amino acids are made in the body. The other eight amino acids must be taken into the body. The foods you eat contain different amino acids. The amino acids are put together in many different ways to form thousands of different proteins. This is like making thousands of words from the 26 letters of the alphabet.

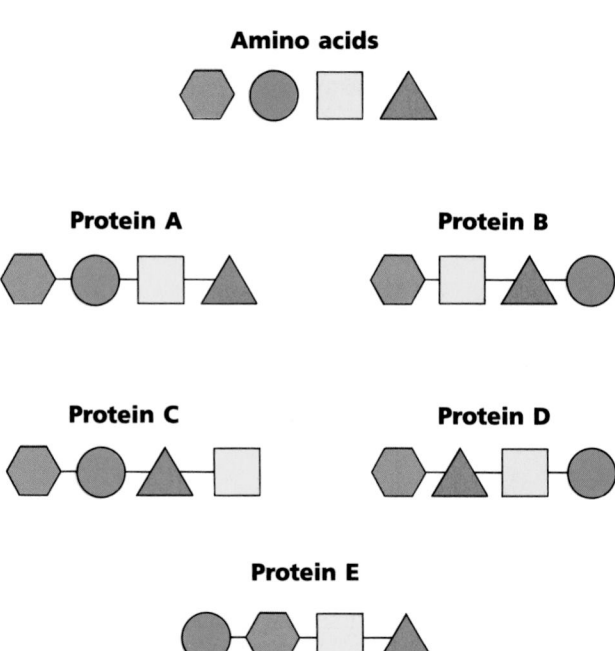

Figure 2 Protein building

▶ *Identify:* What are the building blocks of proteins? amino acids

Making Proteins The body uses proteins in foods to make the special proteins it needs. When proteins in food are digested, the amino acids are separated from one another. Cells in your body make their own proteins by putting these amino acids together again in their own special way.

▶ *Infer:* Why do you think the body can make so many proteins? There are infinite combinations of amino acids.

216

LESSON SUMMARY

- ▶ Proteins are the largest molecules in living things.
- ▶ Proteins are used to build new cells, repair damaged cells, make enzymes, control chemical activities, and as a source of energy.
- ▶ Amino acids are the building blocks of proteins.
- ▶ Cells in your body make their own proteins by combining amino acids.

CHECK *Complete the following.*

1. Substances that control chemical activities in cells are called _____ . enzymes

2. The building blocks of proteins are _____ . amino acids

3. There are about _____ different amino acids. 20

4. Proteins are the _____ molecules in living things. largest

5. All proteins contain atoms of carbon, oxygen, hydrogen, and _____ . nitrogen

APPLY *Complete the following.*

6. **Analyze:** Why is a diet low in protein not healthful?

7. **Infer:** Plant proteins are incomplete proteins because they do not contain all eight of the amino acids needed by the body. Why do you think it is important for people who do not eat animal proteins to eat a variety of plant proteins?

Use Figure 2 on page 216 to complete the following.

8. **Model:** Draw two proteins that could be formed by the amino acids shown. Do not copy any of the proteins shown.

Skill Builder

Researching Vegetarians (vej-uh-TER-ee-unz) are people who do not eat animal products. Therefore, they do not eat any complete proteins. Vegetarians must combine different incomplete vegetable proteins in order to make complete proteins. Some vegetarians include small amounts of milk and eggs in their diet to get complete proteins. Use library resources to find out the signs and symptoms of a low protein diet.

ACTIVITY

MODELING PROTEIN MOLECULES

You will need 1 sheet of red construction paper, 1 sheet of blue construction paper, and a scissors.

1. Cut various shapes from the red and blue construction paper. **Caution: Be careful when using sharp objects.**

2. Place the shapes side by side to form a chain modeling a protein molecule.

3. Repeat Step 2 making as many protein models as you are able. Do not repeat the same pattern twice.

Questions

1. **Model:** What do the pieces of paper represent?

2. **a.** How many amino acid molecules did you use? **b.** How many different protein models were you able to construct?

3. **a.** How many amino acids are there in your body? **b.** Why can your body make thousands of proteins from these amino acids?

4. What happens to the number of proteins as the number of amino acids increases?

11-3 Why are vitamins important?

Objective ▶ Explain why vitamins are important.

TechTerms

▶ **deficiency** (di-FISH-un-see) **disease:** disease caused by the lack of a certain nutrient

▶ **vitamin** (VYT-uh-min): nutrient made by living organisms

Vitamins Your body needs small amounts of **vitamins** (VYT-uh-minz) so it can function properly. Vitamins are nutrients that are made by living organisms. You get most of the vitamins you need from food. However, vitamins D and K and some B vitamins are made in your body.

▶ *Define:* What are vitamins? nutrients found naturally in many foods

Importance of Vitamins Vitamins are important for proper growth. They also are important for keeping bones and teeth strong and healthy. Your muscles and nerves are kept healthy by vitamins. Vitamins also help control many of the chemical activities that take place in your body.

Most vitamins work with other vitamins or nutrients. Some vitamins help change carbohydrates and fats to energy. Unlike carbohydrates and fats, vitamins do not give off energy.

▶ *Explain:* How are vitamins used in your body? Answers will vary, but should include those explained above.

Deficiency Disease Your body tissues need small amounts of vitamins every day. If your diet does not include enough of a certain vitamin, you can become sick. This kind of sickness is called a **deficiency** (di-FISH-un-see) **disease.** Rickets is a deficiency disease that causes soft bones and teeth. Rickets is caused by a lack of vitamin D. Look at Table 1 to see other deficiency diseases.

▶ *Define:* What is a deficiency disease? disease caused by a lack of a certain nutrient

Table 1	Vitamins and Deficiency Diseases		
VITAMIN	**USE IN BODY**	**SOURCES**	**DEFICIENCY DISEASE**
A	healthy skin, eyes, ability to see well at night, healthy bones and teeth	orange and dark green vegetables, eggs, fruit, liver milk	night blindness
B_1 thiamin	healthy nerves, skin, and eyes; helps body get energy from carbohydrates	liver, pork, whole grain foods	beriberi
B_2 riboflavin	healthy nerves, skin and eyes; helps body get energy from carbohydrates, fats, and proteins	eggs, green vegetables, milk	skin disorders
B_3 niacin	works with B vitamins to get energy from nutrients in cells	beans, chicken, eggs, tuna	pellagra
C	healthy bones, teeth, and blood vessels	citrus fruits, dark green vegetables	scurvy
D	healthy bones, teeth; helps body use calcium	eggs, milk, made by skin in sunlight	rickets
E	healthy blood and muscles	leafy vegetables, vegetable oil	none known
K	normal blood clotting	green vegetables, tomatoes	poor blood clotting

LESSON SUMMARY

▶ Vitamins are nutrients made by living organisms.

▶ Vitamins are important for growth and for proper body function.

▶ Most vitamins work with other vitamins or nutrients.

▶ A deficiency disease is caused by the lack of a certain nutrient.

CHECK *Complete the following.*

1. Nutrients that are found naturally in foods are _____ . vitamins

2. A _____ is caused by a diet that is missing a certain nutrient. deficiency disease

3. An example of a deficiency disease that causes soft bones is _____ . rickets

APPLY *Use Table 1 on page 218 to complete the following.*

4. **Analyze:** You have cut yourself and note that your blood is slow to clot. What vitamin are you lacking in your diet? Explain.

5. **Interpret:** What vitamins help the body get energy from carbohydrates?

6. **Analyze:** If you have scurvy, what vitamin are you missing in your diet?

7. **Interpret:** What is another name for vitamin B₂?

8. **Interpret:** What is the deficiency disease for vitamin A?

Skill Builder

▲ ***Organizing*** Using library references, look up the deficiency diseases listed in Table 1. Find out the signs and symptoms of each deficiency disease. Organize the information in a table.

Health & Safety Tip

The skins and peels of many fruits and vegetables are rich in vitamins and minerals. Fruits and vegetables often are sprayed with pesticides (PES-tuh-sydz). Pesticides are chemical substances used to kill pests such as insects. Pesticides can be harmful to people. Use library references to find out how to clean the skins and peels of fruits and vegetables so they are safe to eat.

LOOKING BACK IN SCIENCE

SCURVY

Until the 1700s, many sailors died at sea from a mysterious disease. The sailors would suffer from bleeding gums and loose teeth. Their skin would bruise easily. The disease the sailors suffered from is called scurvy (SKUR-vee). A few hundred years ago, the cause of scurvy was unknown. However, many sailors suffering from scurvy got better after their ships reached port. Therefore, people thought that scurvy was caused by "sea air."

In the 1700s, British doctors noticed that sailors ate mostly salted beef and biscuits. The doctors learned that the juice from citrus fruits, such as oranges, lemons, and limes, could prevent and cure scurvy. English ships started carrying a supply of lemons and limes. Citrus juice was given to the sailors daily. How did citrus juices prevent and cure scurvy? Scientists discovered that scurvy is a deficiency disease caused by a lack of vitamin C in the diet. Citrus fruits are an excellent source of vitamin C.

11-5 What is a balanced diet?

Objective ▶ Describe how to use the Food Guide Pyramid to plan a balanced diet.

TechTerm

▶ **malnutrition** (mal-noo-TRISH-un): poor nutrition caused by an unbalanced diet

A Balanced Diet Diets that contain the right amount of nutrients are called balanced diets. Eating a balanced diet will help you stay healthy. Many people think that eating a balanced diet is difficult. Eating a balanced diet is really quite simple.

▷ *Explain:* Why is a balanced diet important?
to get all the nutrients the body needs

The Food Guide Pyramid The U.S. Department of Agriculture has developed a simple way for people to know what to eat each day to maintain good health. The Food Guide Pyramid shows in pictures the kinds of foods and the number of servings a person should have each day. The pyramid does not tell exactly what foods to eat. Rather it shows you how to choose the right kinds of foods. The pyramid calls for eating a variety of foods to get the nutrients you need.

▷ *State:* What is the Food Guide Pyramid? a picture that shows the foods you should eat to stay healthy

Planning a Balanced Diet You can see in the pyramid below that foods are classified into six groups. The food group that should make up the largest proportion of your diet—breads, cereals, rice, and pasta—is on the bottom of the pyramid. The top of the pyramid shows foods that should make up the smallest amount of your diet—fats, oils, and sweets.

The pyramid also tells you how many servings you should eat from each food group. Be sure to eat at least the lowest number of servings from each of the major food groups.

▷ *Explain:* How can you use the Food Guide Pyramid to plan a balanced diet? eat the suggested number of servings from each food group

Malnutrition When your body is not properly nourished, it becomes weak. This disorder is called **malnutrition** (mal-noo-TRISH-un). Many people think malnutrition occurs only from a lack of food. However, anyone can be malnourished. If you eat too many foods from one group and not enough foods from another group, you can become malnourished.

▷ *State:* What might happen if you eat too much from one food group and not enough from another food group? malnutrition may occur

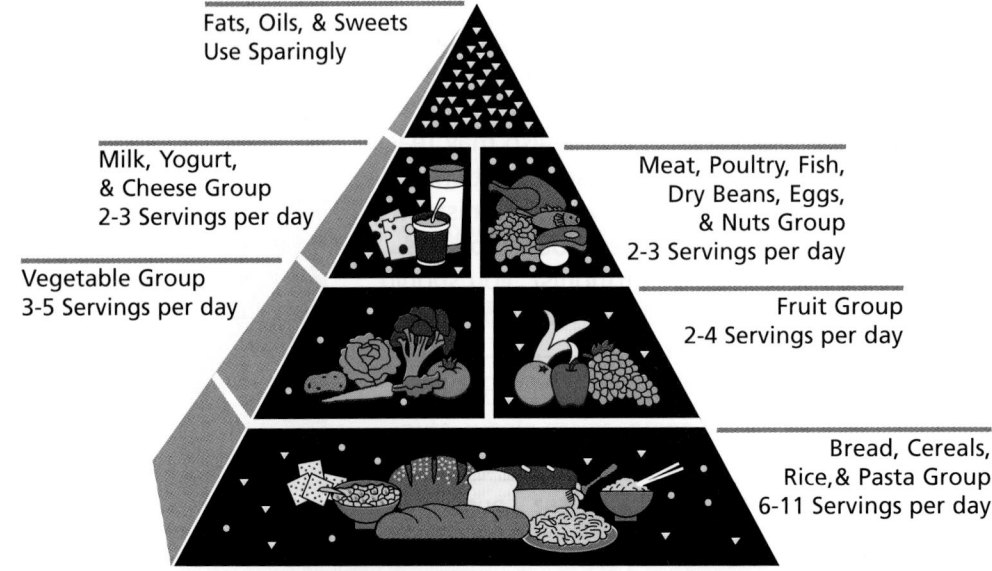

Fats, Oils, & Sweets
Use Sparingly

Milk, Yogurt,
& Cheese Group
2-3 Servings per day

Meat, Poultry, Fish,
Dry Beans, Eggs,
& Nuts Group
2-3 Servings per day

Vegetable Group
3-5 Servings per day

Fruit Group
2-4 Servings per day

Bread, Cereals,
Rice,& Pasta Group
6-11 Servings per day

LESSON SUMMARY

▶ Balanced diets contain the right amounts of nutrients to keep the body healthy.

▶ The Food Guide Pyramid shows in pictures the kinds of foods and the number of servings a person should have each day.

▶ The pyramid divides foods into six groups. Foods that you should eat the most of are at the bottom of the pyramid.

▶ Eat sparingly from the top group. Eat at least the lowest number of servings from other groups.

▶ Malnutrition occurs when you eat too much food from one group and not enough from another group.

CHECK *Complete the following.*

1. Balanced diets contain the proper amounts of _____ . nutrients

2. The _____ shows the kinds of foods and the number of servings you should eat each day.
   Food Guide Pyramid

3. The Food Guide Pyramid divides foods into _____ groups. six

4. You should eat at least the _____ number of servings in each food group of the pyramid.
   lowest

APPLY *Answer the following.*

5. **Identify:** Name two foods from each of the groups in the Food Guide Pyramid. Answers will vary. Accept all logical answers.

6. **Identify:** From which food group should you eat the most servings? bread, cereal, rice, and pasta group

7. **Hypothesize:** Can an overweight person be malnourished? Yes, if they do not eat a balanced diet.

InfoSearch

Read the passage. Ask two questions that you cannot answer from the information in the passage.

Eating Disorders Bulimia (buh-LEE-mee-uh) and anorexia (an-uh-REK-see-uh) are harmful eating disorders. Bulimia and anorexia threaten good health and even life. Bulimics are of normal weight. They eat large amounts of food at one time. Then they either throw up the food, or use laxatives. Anorexics are usually underweight. They refuse to eat food. There are many self-help groups that can help bulimics and anorexics.

SEARCH: Use library references to find answers to your questions.

ACTIVITY

PLANNING A BALANCED DIET

You will need paper and a pencil.

1. Divide a piece of paper into six columns. Label each column with the name of one of the food groups in the Food Guide Pyramid.

2. **Classify:** Classify each of the foods listed in the Data Table into the proper food group. Write the name of each food in the column.

3. Use the foods in the Data Table to plan a breakfast that contains foods from at least five food groups.

Questions

1. Which foods in the Data Table belong to the bread, cereal, rice, and pasta group?

2. Which foods belong to the fats, oils, and sweets group?

3. **Analyze:** From which group did you choose the most foods for the breakfast? Why?

4. **Analyze:** From which group did you choose the least foods? Why?

Data Table
FOOD
Apple
Banana
Bran flakes (1 cup)
Egg
Ham slice
Margarine (1 Tbs.)
Milk (2% fat)
Orange juice (6 oz.)
Slice of bread
Strawberry jam (1 tsp.)
Whole milk (8 oz.)

11-6 How do living things get energy?

Objective ▶ Explain how organisms "burn" food to get energy.

TechTerms

- ▶ **Calorie** (KAL-uh-ree): unit used to measure energy from foods
- ▶ **oxidation** (ahk-suh-DAY-shun): slow burning of foods in your body

Energy Your body needs energy to stay alive. Everything you do requires energy. You need energy to walk, to run, and even to sleep. Your heart needs energy to pump blood through the body. Right now, your body is growing. You need energy to grow.

▥▶ *State:* Why does your body need energy? Answers will vary, but should include the reasons listed above.

Oxidation You get the energy you need from food. As food gets broken down in the body, it produces energy. The slow burning of foods in your body is called **oxidation** (ahk-suh-DAY-shun). Oxidation produces the energy that your body needs. Living cells get most of their energy by the oxidation of sugar. Your body cells use energy to carry on their life activities. Some energy also is given off as heat.

▥▶ *Define:* What is oxidation? slow burning of foods in your body

Waste Products of Oxidation During oxidation, carbon dioxide and water are given off as waste products. To show that your body gives off water, breathe on a mirror. What do you see? Water collects on the mirror. The water is a waste product of oxidation going on in your body.

▥▶ *Identify:* What are the waste products of oxidation? carbon dioxide and water

Measuring Food Energy Different foods contain different amounts of energy. The amount of energy food gives off is measured in **Calories** (KAL-uh-reez). A Calorie is a unit used to measure food energy. Fat gives off the most energy. Each gram of fat gives off 9 Calories of energy. Proteins and carbohydrates each give off the same amount of energy. Each gram of protein or carbohydrate gives off 4 Calories of energy.

▥▶ *Define:* What is a Calorie? a unit used to measure food energy

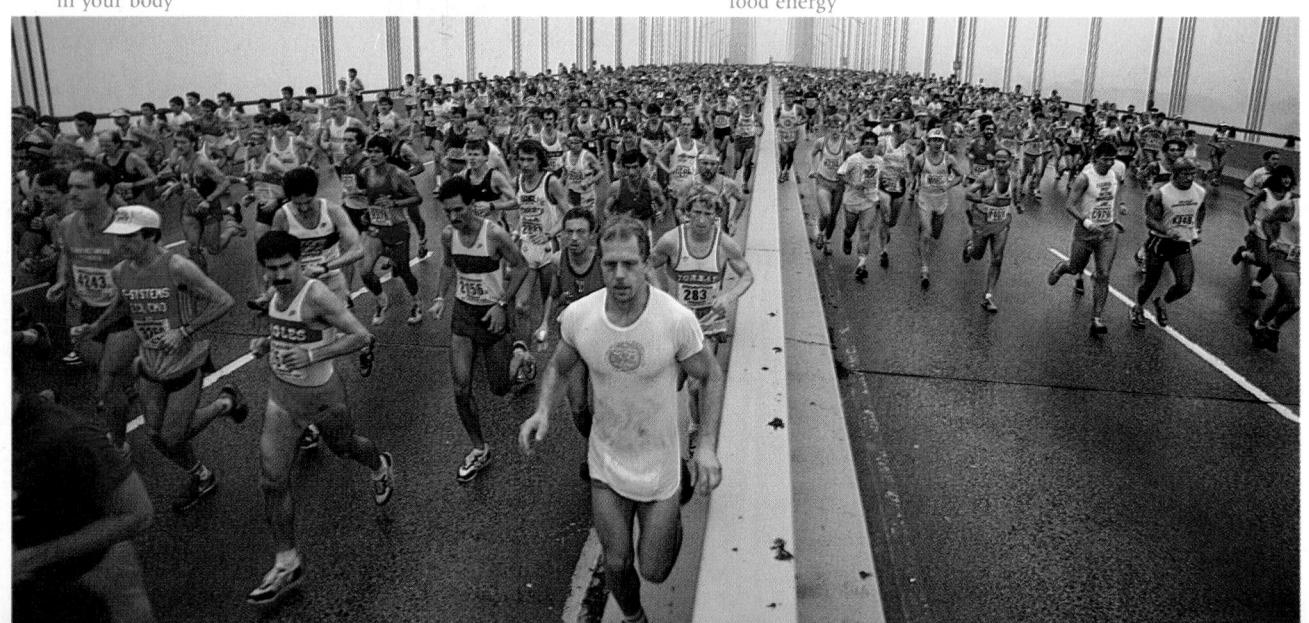

LESSON SUMMARY

▶ Your body needs energy to stay alive.

▶ Oxidation of foods produces the energy that your body needs.

▶ Carbon dioxide and water are waste products of oxidation.

▶ The amount of energy food gives off is measured in Calories.

CHECK *Find the sentence in the lesson that answers each question. Then, write the sentence.*

1. What process produces the energy your body needs?

2. What are the waste products of oxidation?

3. Do all foods give off the same amount of energy?

4. What unit is used to measure food energy?

5. Where do you get the energy you need?

6. What nutrient supplies the most energy?

APPLY *Complete the following.*

7. **Calculate:** If food contains 5 grams of fat, how many Calories of fat are in the food?

8. **Infer:** Why do foods with high amounts of fat have more Calories than foods that are high in carbohydrates?

9. **Hypothesize:** Boys ages 12 to 15 need about 2800 Calories each day. Girls the same age need about 2400 Calories each day. What do you think would happen if you ate more Calories than what you needed?

Skill Builder

Calculating Calculate how many Calories are in the following foods:
A: 8 g protein, 11 g carbohydrates, 1 g fat
B: 4 g protein, 10 g carbohydrates, 8 g fat
C: 0 g protein, 1 g carbohydrate, 5 g fat
D: 14 g protein, 4 g carbohydrates, 3 g fat
E: 5 g protein, 7 g carbohydrates, 6 g fat

Skill Builder

Comparing Keep a daily log of the foods you eat for one week. Also keep track of any physical activity you do. Use library references to calculate the number of Calories used up in activity. Also, calculate the number of Calories in the foods you ate. Compare the two totals. According to your records, did you take in more Calories, or burn up more Calories?

SCIENCE CONNECTION ◆○◆○◆○◆○◆○◆○◆○◆○◆○◆○◆○◆○◆○◆
CHEMOSYNTHESIS

Deep in the ocean, no sunlight can reach the ocean floor. Photosynthesis is not possible. However, bacteria that live on the bottom of the ocean floor have another way of making their own food. These bacteria live near vents, or openings in the ocean floor. The vents are formed by underwater volcanoes. Sulfur compounds shoot out of the vents. The bacteria change the compounds into food. The process of making food from chemicals is called chemosynthesis.

The temperature near the ocean vents is so great that most living things could not survive. However, tube worms and some clams and crabs live near the vents. They feed on the deep-sea bacteria. Because the bacteria are able to use chemicals to produce food, a chain of unusual life forms flourishes.

11-7 What is the digestive system?

Objective ▶ Identify the organs in the human digestive system.

TechTerms

- **digestion** (dy-JES-chun): process by which foods are changed into forms the body can use
- **epiglottis** (ep-uh-GLAT-is): flap of tissue that prevents food from entering the windpipe
- **esophagus** (i-SAF-uh-gus): tube that connects the mouth to the stomach
- **peristalsis** (per-uh-STAWL-sis): wavelike movement that moves food through the digestive tract

Digestion The foods that you eat are not in a form that your body can use. The foods you eat must be changed so that they can be used by the body. The process by which foods are changed into usable forms is called **digestion** (dy-JES-chun). During digestion, larger pieces of food are broken down into smaller pieces. Complex chemicals in food also are changed into simpler ones.

▶ *Define:* What is digestion? process by which foods are changed into forms that can be used by the body

The Digestive Tract The foods that you eat move through a coiled tube inside the body. This tube is called the digestive tract. It is about 10 meters long. Some parts are narrow. Other parts are wide. The digestive tract and other digestive organs make up your digestive system. Some digestive organs are the liver, pancreas (PAN-kree-us), and gall bladder. These organs are not part of the digestive tract. However, they do help with digestion.

▶ *Identify:* What organs help with digestion, but are not part of the digestive tract? liver, pancreas, and gall bladder

Parts of the Digestive System Figure 1 shows the digestive system. The mouth is the beginning of the digestive system. Once food is swallowed, it moves into a long tube called the **esophagus**

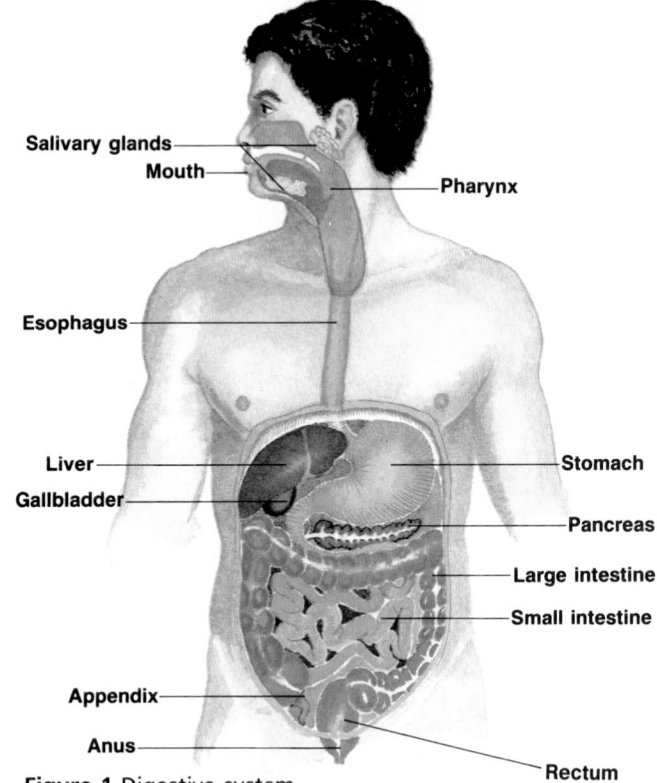

Figure 1 Digestive system

Labels: Salivary glands, Mouth, Pharynx, Esophagus, Liver, Gallbladder, Stomach, Pancreas, Large intestine, Small intestine, Appendix, Anus, Rectum

(i-SAF-uh-gus). The esophagus connects the mouth to the stomach. As you swallow, a thin flap of tissue keeps food from entering the windpipe. This flap of tissue is called the **epiglottis** (ep-uh-GLAT-is). From the stomach, food moves into another narrow tube called the small intestine. The small intestine leads to the large intestine. The end of the large intestine is called the rectum.

▶ *Name:* What are the organs of the digestive system? mouth, esophagus, stomach, small intestine, large intestine, rectum

Peristalsis Once food leaves the mouth, it enters the esophagus. The walls of the esophagus secrete mucus. The mucus helps the food move through the esophagus easily. Once food leaves the esophagus, it continues through the digestive system. Food is moved through the digestive system by wavelike movements of muscle. The wavelike movement that moves food through the digestive tract is called **peristalsis** (per-uh-STAWL-sis).

▶ *Define:* What is peristalsis? wavelike movement of muscle that moves food through the digestive tract

LESSON SUMMARY

- ▶ Digestion is the process by which foods are changed so that they can be used by the body.
- ▶ The digestive tract and other digestive organs make up your digestive system.
- ▶ The parts of the digestive system are the mouth, esophagus, small and large intestines, and rectum.
- ▶ Food is moved through the digestive system by mucus and peristalsis.

CHECK *Write true if the statement is true. IF the statement is false, changed the underlined term to make the statement true.*

1. The process by which foods are changed into usable forms is called <u>peristalsis</u>. digestion

2. The end of the large intestine is called the <u>pancreas</u>. rectum

3. Food is moved through the digestive tract by a wavelike movement called <u>digestion</u>. peristalsis

Answer the following.

4. What connects the mouth to the stomach? esophagus

5. What prevents food from entering the windpipe? epiglottis

APPLY *Complete the following.*

6. **Sequence:** Develop a flowchart to show the parts of the digestive tract through which food passes, in order, beginning with the mouth.

▶ 7. **Infer:** Why do you think food must be broken down into smaller pieces?

Health & Safety Tip

Sometimes a piece of food enters the windpipe. When this happens, choking occurs. To help prevent choking, you should chew your food carefully, eat slowly, and avoid talking or running with food in your mouth. Use library references to find out what to do if someone you are eating with begins to choke.

Figure 2 Universal sign of choking

SCIENCE CONNECTION ◆○◆○◆○◆○◆○◆○◆○◆○◆○◆○◆○◆○◆○◆○◆

VESTIGIAL ORGANS

Did you know that at the end of your spine is a small tailbone? The tailbone has no function in humans. It is a vestigial (ves-TIJ-ee-ul) organ. A vestigial organ is a small part of the body that seems to have no use.

Many animals have vestigial organs. For example, some snakes have small hip bones that have no function. Some scientists think that vestigial organs did have a function at one time. Scientists think the organs had a useful purpose in the ancestors of the animals that now have the vestigial organs. Snakes with vestigial hip bones probably evolved from animals with hips.

Humans have more than 100 vestigial structures, including the muscles used to move the ears, the third eyelid, and the appendix. You are probably most familiar with the appendix. It is a small fingerlike sac attached to the large intestine. It has no function. However, if food gets trapped in the appendix, it may become infected. An infected appendix must be removed surgically.

Tailbone

11-8 What is digestion?

▶ Compare mechanical and chemical digestion. ▶ Explain the function of enzymes.

TechTerms

▶ **chemical digestion:** process by which large food molecules are broken down into smaller food molecules

▶ **mechanical digestion:** process by which large pieces of food are cut and crushed into smaller pieces

▶ **saliva:** liquid in the mouth that helps in digestion

Digestion Digestion is the process of changing foods into usable forms. Food is changed two ways—physically and chemically. Changes in shape and size are examples of physical changes. A chemical change results in new substances. For example, a log burning is a chemical change. The wood is changed into ash and soot.

▶ **Identify:** What are two ways food is changed? chemically and physically

Mechanical Digestion You use your teeth to cut and crush foods. There are four different kinds of teeth. The four kinds of teeth and their jobs are shown in Figure 1. When food is crushed by the teeth, it is broken into small pieces. Your tongue moves the food around. This crushing of food is a physical change. The physical change of food is called **mechanical digestion.** Mechanical digestion breaks large pieces of food into smaller pieces.

▶ **State:** How is food broken down mechanically in the mouth? by the teeth

Chemical Digestion The process by which large food molecules are broken down into smaller molecules is called **chemical digestion.** Chemical digestion begins in the mouth with **saliva.** Saliva is a liquid found in the mouth. It mixes with foods and makes them soft and moist.

Incisors (cut and tear)

Premolars (grind and crush)

Canines (cut and tear)

Molars (grind and crush)

Saliva contains enzymes. Enzymes are chemicals that control chemical reactions in the body. Enzymes help digest food. They break down complex chemicals in food into simpler chemicals. Each enzyme can break down only one specific kind of food molecule. For example, the enzyme in saliva helps digest starch. It changes starch into sugar.

▶ **Define:** What is an enzyme? chemical that controls chemical reactions in the body

Process of Digestion Enzymes act only on the outside surface of food particles. The mechanical breakdown of food provides a larger surface area for the enzymes to work on. The digestion of food takes a number of steps. With each step, the food is broken down into smaller chemicals. The body can use only the smallest, simplest chemicals.

▶ **Infer:** Why is the mechanical breakdown of food important? it gives the enzymes a larger surface are to work on

LESSON SUMMARY

▶ Food is changed both physically and chemically.

▶ Large pieces of food are cut and crushed into smaller pieces of food during mechanical digestion.

▶ Large food molecules are broken down into smaller food molecules during chemical digestion.

▶ Enzymes are chemicals that control chemical reactions in the body.

▶ The body can only use the smallest, simplest chemicals in food.

CHECK *Write true if the statement is true. If the statement is false, change the underlined term to make the statement true.*

1. Shape and size are <u>chemical</u> properties. physical

2. The crushing of food by the teeth is a <u>mechanical</u> change. true

3. The liquid found in the mouth is called <u>enzymes</u>. saliva

4. Enzymes in saliva change <u>fat</u> into sugars. starch

5. The breakdown of large food molecules into small food molecules is <u>mechanical</u> digestion. chemical

APPLY *Answer the following.*

▶ 6. **Infer:** Why do you think it is important to chew your food into small pieces?

7. What nutrient begins to be digested in the mouth? starches and sugars

InfoSearch

Read the passage. Ask two questions that you cannot answer from the information in the passage.

Tooth Decay Tooth decay is a problem of the digestive system. Tooth decay causes cavities. A cavity is a hole in the tooth. Saliva, food, and bacteria in the mouth mix to form a film called plaque (PLAK). Plaque breaks down the hard, outer covering of the tooth. If plaque is allowed to build up, it spreads to the soft parts of the tooth. Brushing your teeth and flossing daily can help prevent the buildup of plaque.

SEARCH: Use library references to find answers to your questions.

CAREER IN LIFE SCIENCE ◆◆◆◆◆◆◆◆◆◆◆◆◆◆◆◆◆◆◆◆◆◆◆◆◆◆

DENTAL HYGIENIST

A trip to the dentist often includes a session with a dental hygienist. Dental hygienists clean and polish patients' teeth and remove plaque from under the gums. They also look for signs of tooth decay or gum disease and report these problems to the dentist. Dental hygienists also may take X-rays or assist a dentist with procedures such as pulling teeth. They also teach people the best way to brush their teeth and to remove plaque on a daily basis.

To be a dental hygienist, a person needs to complete a two-year course at a college or professional school. Some students take additional training to earn a bachelor's or master's degree. Dental hygienists need to be skillful in working with their hands. They also need to be skillful in working with worried patients.

11-9 What happens to food in the stomach?

Objective ▶ Describe what happens to food once it enters the stomach.

TechTerms

- **chyme** (KYM): thick liquid form of food
- **gastric juice:** juice produced in the stomach that contains mucus, pepsin, and hydrochloric acid
- **pepsin** (PEP-sin): enzyme that digests proteins

The Stomach Once food leaves the esophagus, it enters the stomach. The stomach is a J-shaped, baglike organ that stores food. The stomach also breaks down food. In fact, mechanical digestion takes place in the stomach as well as in the mouth. The walls of the stomach are made up of layers of strong muscles. These muscles tighten and squeeze the food. The food is broken into small pieces.

▶ **Describe:** How does the stomach aid in mechanical digestion? muscles in the stomach wall tighten and squeeze the food breaking it into small pieces

Gastric Juice The small pieces of food in the stomach are mixed with stomach juice. This juice makes the food soft. The juice the stomach produces is called **gastric juice.** Gastric juice contains mucus, **pepsin** (PEP-sin), and hydrochloric (hy-druh-KLAWR-ik) acid.

▶ **Identify:** What is gastric juice made up of? mucus, pepsin, and hydrochloric acid

Chemical Digestion in the Stomach One of the enzymes in gastric juice is pepsin. Pepsin is an enzyme. It begins the digestion of proteins. Hydrochloric acid is a very strong acid. It is needed to make the stomach acidic. Pepsin can work only in an acidic environment. Hydrochloric acid kills bacteria in the stomach. It also helps to break down food. The mucus in gastric juice protects the stomach lining from the hydrochloric acid and pepsin. Figure 1 shows how chemical digestion takes place.

Food enters the stomach as a solid.

Pepsin and hydrochloric acid break down the food.

Food leaves the stomach as a liquid.

Figure 1

▶ **Define:** What is pepsin? enzyme that digests proteins

Chyme Once food has been crushed by the stomach and mixed with gastric juice, it is ready to leave the stomach. Food that leaves the stomach is in the form of a thick liquid. This liquid is called **chyme** (KYM). Chyme is released slowly from the stomach into the small intestine.

▶ **Define:** What is chyme? thick liquid form of food

► The stomach is a baglike organ that stores food.

► Gastric juice contains mucus, pepsin, and hydrochloric acid and is produced by the stomach.

► Hydrochloric acid makes the stomach acidic so that pepsin can digest proteins. Mucus protects the stomach from the hydrochloric acid and pepsin.

► Chyme is a thick liquid form of food that leaves the stomach.

CHECK *Find the sentence in the lesson that answers each question. Then, write the sentence.*

1. What does mucus in the gastric juice do?

2. How is food mechanically digested in the stomach?

3. What enzyme digests proteins?

4. In what form is food that leaves the stomach?

5. What does the stomach look like?

APPLY *Answer the following.*

6. Why is the stomach an important part of the digestive system?

7. **Infer:** What would happen if the stomach did not produce hydrochloric acid?

8. **Analyze:** How can you tell that digestion has taken place in test tube 3?

9. **Sequence:** Describe the change that food undergoes from the time it enters the mouth to the time it enters the small intestine.

Skill Builder

Researching An ulcer occurs when the stomach acids digest the lining of the stomach. The hole that occurs in the stomach lining is called an ulcer. Ulcers also can occur in the small intestine. Use library references to find out the causes of ulcers, the signs and symptoms of ulcers, and the treatment of ulcers. Present your findings in a table.

LOOKING BACK IN SCIENCE

WILLIAM BEAUMONT (1785-1853)

William Beaumont was an American army doctor in the early 1800s. On June 6, 1822, an 18-year-old named Alexis St. Martin was accidentally shot in the stomach. Dr. Beaumont saved the young man's life and eventually the wound healed. However, the wound never completely closed. For the rest of his life, St. Martin had a two and a half inch opening in his left side.

William Beaumont discovered that he could view the workings of the stomach through the opening. For the next nine years, with St. Martin's cooperation, Beaumont studied the stomach. At the time, most information about human digestion was obtained by examining the remains of the deceased. The use of X-rays had not been discovered yet. Therefore, the ability to view a functioning body system was extraordinary. Beaumont published his findings in 1833, providing other doctors with valuable information about human digestion. Much of what people know today about the functions of the stomach is based on the observations of Dr. Beaumont.

11-10 What happens to food in the small intestine?

Objective ▶ Describe what happens to foods in the small intestine.

TechTerms

- **bile:** green liquid that breaks down fats and oils
- **emulsification** (i-mul-suh-fi-KAY-shun): process of breaking down large droplets of fat into small droplets of fat
- **lipase** (LY-pays): enzyme that digests fats and oils

The Small Intestine The small intestine is a long coiled tube. It is about 6.5 m long and 2.5 cm wide. Like the stomach, the walls of the small intestine are muscular. Food moves through the small intestine by peristalsis. Most of the chemical digestion of food takes place in the small intestine.

▶ *Explain:* What happens in the small intestine? most of the chemical digestion of food takes place

Digestion in the Small Intestine Digestive juices in the small intestine contain many enzymes. These enzymes complete digestion. One of these enzymes is **lipase** (LY-pays). Lipase digests fats and oils. Unlike starch and proteins, fats are not digested in the mouth or stomach. Fats are digested only in the small intestine. Table 1 reviews the digestion of the three main nutrients. Notice that all digestion is completed in the small intestine.

Table 1	Summary of Digestion	
NUTRIENT	DIGESTION BEGINS	DIGESTION COMPLETED
proteins	stomach	small intestine
carbohydrates	mouth	small intestine
fats	small intestine	small intestine

▶ *Define:* What is lipase? enzyme that digests fats and oils

The Pancreas The pancreas is a small organ that lies below the stomach. When food first enters the small intestine, the pancreas releases digestive juices. These digestive juices travel to the small intestine through a small tube. Pancreatic digestive juices contain enzymes. These enzymes change starches, proteins, and fats into simpler forms.

▶ *Identify:* How does the pancreas aid in chemical digestion? The pancreas releases enzymes into the small intestine that change starch, protein, and fats into simpler forms.

The Liver The liver is the largest organ in the human body. One job of the liver is to produce **bile.** Bile is a green liquid that breaks down large droplets of fat into smaller droplets of fat. The breaking down of large fat droplets into smaller fat droplets is called **emulsification** (i-mul-suh-fi-KAY-shun).

Bile does not move directly from the liver to the small intestine. Bile is stored in a small sac under the liver. This sac is called the gall bladder. Bile moves from the gall bladder into the small intestine through a small tube.

▶ *Define:* What is emulsification? breaking of large droplets of fat into smaller droplets of fat

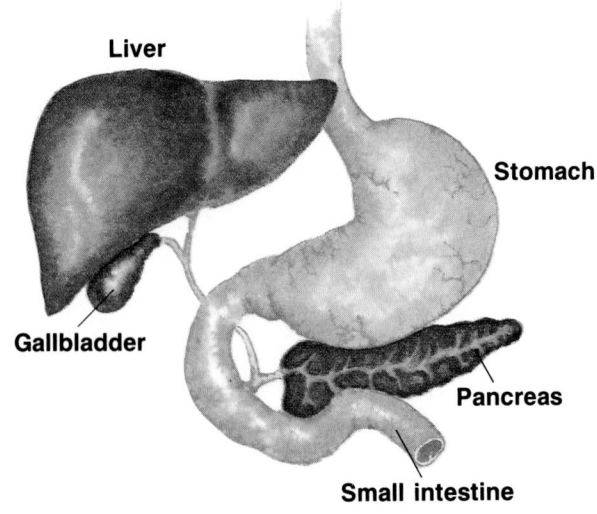

Figure 1 Organs that aid in the digestion of fat

- Most of the chemical digestion of food takes place in the small intestine.
- Lipase is an enzyme that digests fats and oils.
- The pancreas releases digestive juices into the small intestine to break up starch, protein, and fat.
- The liver produces bile which emulsifies fats and oils.
- Bile is stored in the gall bladder.

CHECK *Write true if the statement is true. If the statement is false, change the underlined term to make the statement true.*

1. Most <u>mechanical</u> digestion takes place in the small intestine. chemical
2. Lipase is an enzyme that digests <u>fats</u>. true
3. The gall bladder stores <u>digestive juices</u>. bile
4. The <u>pancreas</u> produces bile. liver
5. Bile is responsible for the <u>emulsification</u> of fat. true
6. Food moves through the small intestine by <u>peristalsis</u>. true

APPLY *Use table 1 on page 232 to answer the following.*

7. Where does the digestion of carbohydrates begin?
8. Where does the digestion of protein begin?
9. What is the only nutrient that begins its digestion in the small intestine?

InfoSearch

Read the passage. Ask two questions that you cannot answer from the information in the passage.

Digestive System Problems There are many different problems of the digestive system. One problem of the digestive system is indigestion. Indigestion is caused by eating too much, too little, or too fast. Another problem of the digestive system is heartburn. Heartburn occurs when stomach acids go up into the esophagus. This causes a burning sensation in the esophagus. The esophagus is located behind the heart, so the burning feels like it is coming from the heart.

SEARCH: Use library references to find answers to your questions.

ACTIVITY

INVESTIGATING FAT DIGESTION

You will need 2 test tubes with stoppers, cooking oil, baking soda, a medicine dropper, a measuring spoon, and water.

1. Fill each test tube halfway with water.
2. Using the medicine dropper, put 4 drops of cooking oil in each test tube.
3. Use the measuring spoon to add ¼ teaspoon of baking soda to one of the test tubes.
4. Stopper each test tube and shake the test tubes well.

Questions

1. **Observe:** What happened in the test tube containing only oil and water?
2. What happened in the test tube containing oil, water, and baking soda?
3. Which test tube contains fats that are not broken down?
4. Which test tube contains fats that are partly broken down?
5. **Compare:** How is the action of the baking soda similar to that of enzymes?

11-11 How is food absorbed by the body?

Objectives ▶ Describe absorption. ▶ Describe what happens to food after it leaves the small intestine.

TechTerms

- ▶ **absorption** (ab-SAWRP-shun): movement of food from the digestive system to the blood
- ▶ **colon:** large intestine
- ▶ **villi:** fingerlike projection on the lining of the small intestine

Absorption in the Small intestine After food has been changed in usable forms, it is ready to be absorbed (ub-ZOWRBD), or taken into the bloodstream. **Absorption** (ab-SAWRP-shun) is the movement of food from the digestive system to the blood. Absorption of fats, proteins, carbohydrates, vitamins, and water takes place through the walls of the small intestine. Once inside the blood, digested food is carried to all of your body cells.

The inner lining of the small intestine is folded. The folds have millions of tiny fingerlike projections called **villi** (VIL-y). Villus is the singular form of villi. The folds and villi make the surface area of the small intestine bigger. Digested food passes through the absorptive layer of the villus and into the blood vessels.

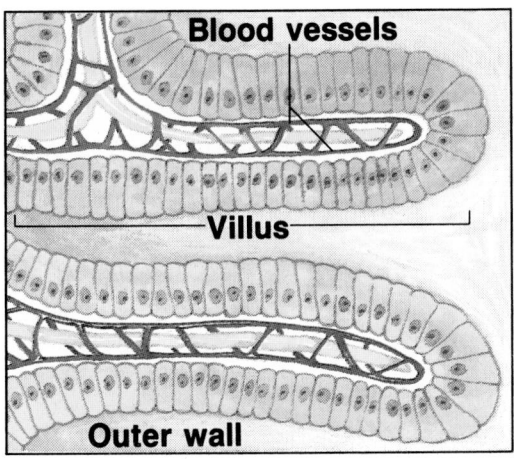

Explain: What happens to food in the small intestine? it is absorbed into the bloodstream

The Large Intestine The large intestine is the last part of the digestive system. It also is called the **colon.** Some undigested food, minerals, and water are not absorbed in the small intestine. They form a watery mixture. This mixture enters the large intestine. Water and minerals are absorbed into the blood in the large intestine. The remaining solid wastes are stored temporarily in the rectum. Then they are eliminated from the body.

Describe: What happens to food in the large intestine? water and minerals are absorbed into the bloodstream

The Appendix There is a small, thin sac located where the small intestine and large intestine meet. This sac is called the appendix (uh-PEN-diks). Scientists do not know what the appendix does in humans.

Sometimes food gets trapped in the appendix. The appendix becomes infected with bacteria. This infection of the appendix is called appendicitis (uh-PEN-duh-SY-tis). An infected appendix must be removed.

State: What is the job of the appendix? Scientists are unsure of the function.

LESSON SUMMARY

▶ Absorption is the movement of food from the digestion system to the blood.

▶ Villi on the walls of the small intestine make the surface area of the small intestine bigger.

▶ The large intestine, or colon, is the large part of the digestive system where the absorption of minerals and water takes place.

▶ The appendix is a small sac located where the small intestine and large intestine meet, that has no known purpose.

▶ An infected appendix is called appendicitis.

CHECK *Answer the following.*

1. **Explain:** How does food get to all the body cells? by the bloodstream

2. **What are villi?** small fingerlike projections on the walls of the small intestine

3. **What happens to undigested food?** it is stored in the rectum and then eliminated

4. **Where is the appendix located?** where the small and large intestine meet

Complete the following.

5. The process by which food moves from the digestive system to the bloodstream is called _____ . absorption

6. Solid wastes are stored in the _____ . rectum

APPLY *Answer the following.*

7. **Infer:** Why must food be absorbed?

8. **Hypothesize:** How do folds increase the surface area of the small intestine?

9. **Infer:** Why do you think it is important to have an infected appendix removed?

Ideas in Action

IDEA: Whole wheat and other whole grains are more healthful than processed grains, such as white flour.

ACTION: List five ways that you can substitute whole grains for processed grains in your diet.

Health & Safety Tip

A healthful diet includes fiber. Fiber is the part of a plant that cannot be digested by humans. There are different kinds of fiber. Some kinds of fiber are effective in decreasing fat absorption. Other kinds of fiber help lower cholesterol levels. Scientific studies have shown that diets high in fiber also offer some protection against colon cancer. Use library references to write a report about foods that are high in fiber. Include ways to substitute these foods into your everyday diet.

ACTIVITY

CALCULATING SURFACE AREA

You will need string, scissors, tape, and a ruler.

1. Cut a piece of string to extend across the top of your desk. Tape the ends of the string to opposite sides of the desk.

2. Tape the end of another piece of string to one side of the desk. Form a series of "S" curves across the desk with the string similar to line AB. Tape the other end of the string to the desk.

3. Use a ruler to measure the distance between the taped ends of each piece of string.

4. Place the curved string in a straight line along the floor. Measure the distance between the string's ends.

Questions

1. What was the distance between the taped ends of each piece of string?

2. What was the distance between the ends of the curved string when it was straightened on the floor?

3. Which piece of string had more surface area?

4. **Analyze:** How do folds in the inner lining of the small intestine aid in digestion?

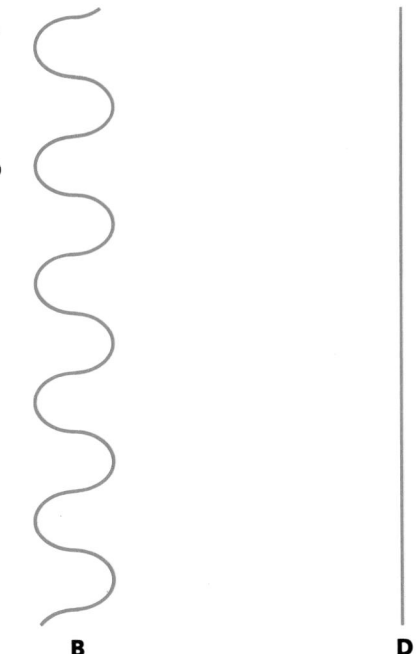

STUDY HINT Before you begin the Unit Challenges, review the TechTerms and Lesson Summary for each lesson in this unit.

TechTerms

absorption (234)
amino acid (216)
bile (232)
Calorie (224)
carbohydrates (214)
chemical digestion (228)
chyme (230)
colon (234)
deficiency disease (218)

digestion (226)
emulsification (232)
enzyme (216)
epiglottis (226)
esophagus (226)
gastric juice (230)
lipase (232)
malnutrition (222)
mechanical digestion (228)
mineral (220)

molecule (216)
nutrient (214)
oxidation (224)
pepsin (230)
peristalsis (226)
protein (214)
saliva (228)
villi (234)
vitamin (218)

TechTerm Challenges

Matching *Write the TechTerm that matches each description.*

1. fingerlike projections on the lining of the small intestine villi
2. enzyme that digests fats and oils lipase
3. enzyme that begins the digestion of protein pepsin
4. breaking down of large food molecules into small food molecules chemical digestion
5. long tube that connects the mouth to the stomach esophagus
6. process by which foods are changed into forms the body can use digestion
7. slow burning of foods in the body oxidation
8. nutrient made by living organisms vitamin
9. smallest part of a substance that has all the properties of that substance molecule
10. chemical substances in food needed by the body for growth, energy, and life processes nutrient

11. protein that controls chemical activities enzyme
12. disease caused by the lack of a certain nutrient deficiency disease
13. nutrient needed by the body to develop properly mineral
14. amount of energy given off by food Calorie
15. thin flap of tissue that keeps food from entering the windpipe epiglottis
16. wavelike motion that moves food through the digestive tract peristalsis
17. thick liquid form of food chyme
18. breakdown of fat into smaller pieces emulsification
19. large intestine colon

Identifying Word Relationships *Explain how the words in each pair are related. Write your answers in complete sentences.* Answers will vary. Accept all logical responses.

1. amino acid, protein
2. saliva, carbohydrates

3. bile, fat
4. gastric juice, stomach

Content Challenges

Multiple Choice *Write the letter of the term that best completes each statement.*

1. The wavelike movement that moves food through the digestive system is called
   a. chyme.   **b.** mechanical digestion.   **c.** peristalsis.   **d.** chemical digestion. c

2. The largest organ inside the body is the
   a. stomach.   **b.** gallbladder.   **c.** liver.   **d.** pancreas. c

3. The largest amount of food energy comes from
   a. fats.   **b.** carbohydrates.   **c.** vitamins.   **d.** proteins. a

4. Anemia is caused by a diet that lacks
   a. zinc.   **b.** protein.   **c.** iron.   **d.** vitamin A. c

5. Starches are
   a. proteins.   **b.** simple carbohydrates.   **c.** fats.   **d.** complex carbohydrates. d

6. Mechanical digestion begins in the
   a. esophagus.   **b.** pharynx.   **c.** mouth.   **d.** stomach. c

7. Undigested food from the small intestine moves into the
   a. pancreas.   **b.** appendix.   **c.** stomach.   **d.** large intestine. d

8. Saliva begins the chemical digestion of
   a. protein.   **b.** starches.   **c.** fats.   **d.** nutrients. b

9. Amino acids make up
   a. proteins.   **b.** fats.   **c.** water.   **d.** carbohydrates. a

10. More than two-thirds of the human body is made up of
    a. protein.   **b.** fat.   **c.** water.   **d.** carbohydrates. c

Completion *Write the term that best completes each statement.*

1. Chemical reactions that take place in the body are controlled by _____ . enzymes
2. Gastric juice contains pepsin, _____, and mucus. hydrochloric acid
3. Bile is produced in the _____ . liver
4. The _____ releases digestive juices into the small intestine. pancreas
5. The _____ stores and breaks down food. stomach
6. When food is swallowed, it enters the _____ . esophagus
7. Liquid fats usually are called _____ . oils
8. Nutrients made up of amino acids are _____ . proteins
9. A weakened condition that results from a lack of a certain nutrient is called a _____ . deficiency disease

Understanding the Features

Reading Critically *Use the feature reading selections to answer the following. Page numbers for the features follow each question in parentheses.*

1. **Identify:** What are some of the signs and symptoms of scurvy? (219)
2. **Name:** Where are three places where a nutritionist may work? (221)
3. **Define:** What is chemosynthesis? (225)
4. **Name:** What are four vestigial organs in humans? (227)
5. **Infer:** Why do dental hygienists need good hand control and coordination? (229)
6. What is William Beaumont most known for? (231)
7. **Infer:** Why should a person studying to be a nutritionist take science and math classes? (221)

Concept Challenges

Critical Thinking *Answer each of the following in complete sentences.*

1. **Explain:** Is the action of bile on fat part of mechanical digestion or chemical digestion? Explain your answer.
2. **Infer:** What role does the large surface area of the small intestine play in absorption?
3. Why is absorption important?

4. **Hypothesize:** Why do you think low-carbohydrate 'liquid diets' are unhealthy?
5. What would you eat before an athletic competition, a bowl of spaghetti or a steak? Explain your answer.

Interpreting a Diagram *Use the diagram of the human digestive system to answer the following.*

1. What is the function of the part labeled B?
2. What letter indicates a vestigial organ?
3. What letter indicates where gastric juice is produced?
4. What is the function of the part labeled H?
5. What letter indicates where bile is produced?
6. What does letter F represent?

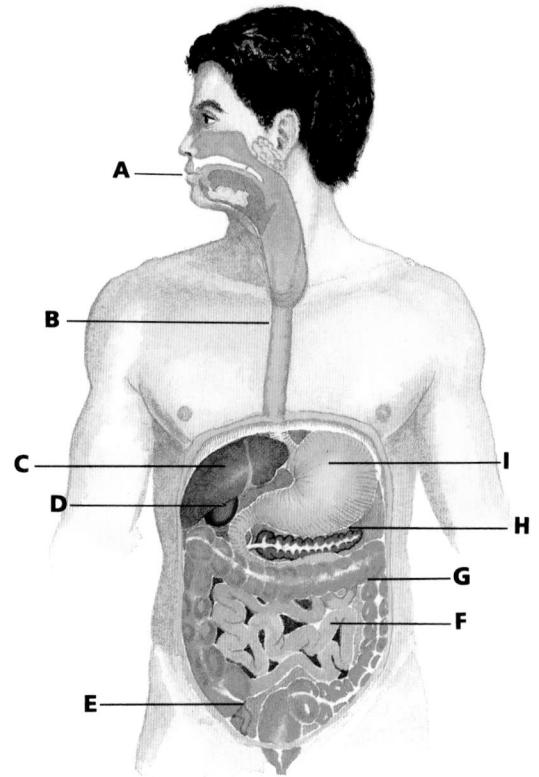

Finding Out More

1. Most nutritionists believe that fiber plays an important role in the prevention of cancer. Use library references to find out the role of fiber in the diet and how it helps to prevent cancer.
2. Two problems of the digestive system are diarrhea and constipation. Use library references to find out what causes each of the these two problems. Find out what can be done to treat each of these digestive system problems.
3. Studies have shown that people who eat a lot of fish have less heart disease than people who eat a lot of red meat. Use library references to find out about Omega 3, an oil found in fish. Find out the benefits of Omega 3, as well as information on fish oil capsules found in many health food stores.
4. Sodium is an important part of the diet. However, most people consume too much salt. An excess of salt can cause many health problems. Develop a chart that lists the effects of too much salt on the different body systems.
5. Some people drink "sports drinks" after they have exercised. Visit your local food store and find a "sports drink." Write down the ingredients of the drink, as well as the claims the drink makes. Using this book as a reference, decide whether the claims that are made are true. Present your findings to the class.

SUPPORT AND MOVEMENT

CONTENTS

STUDY HINT After you read each lesson in Unit 12, write a brief summary on a sheet of paper explaining how the information in each lesson applies to your everyday life.

12-1 What is the skeletal system?

Objective ▶ Describe the functions of the skeletal system and its parts.

TechTerms

- **cartilage** (KART-ul-idj): tough, flexible connective tissue
- **endoskeleton** (en-duh-SKEL-uh-tun): internal skeleton
- **exoskeleton** (ek-soh-SKEL-uh-tun): external skeleton

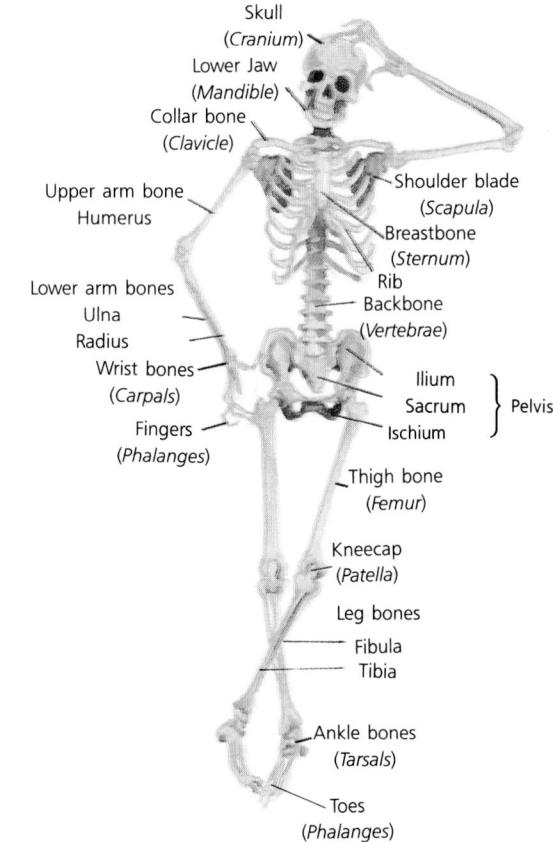

Skull (*Cranium*)
Lower Jaw (*Mandible*)
Collar bone (*Clavicle*)
Upper arm bone Humerus
Shoulder blade (*Scapula*)
Breastbone (*Sternum*)
Rib
Backbone (*Vertebrae*)
Lower arm bones Ulna Radius
Wrist bones (*Carpals*)
Ilium
Sacrum
Ischium } Pelvis
Fingers (*Phalanges*)
Thigh bone (*Femur*)
Kneecap (*Patella*)
Leg bones
Fibula
Tibia
Ankle bones (*Tarsals*)
Toes (*Phalanges*)

The Skeletal System Have you ever seen a house being built? If you have, you have probably seen the wooden framework that makes up a house. The framework of a house is important. It gives a house its shape. The framework also supports a house. You also have a frame that supports your body. This frame is your skeleton. Most of your skeletal system is made up of bone. Bone is a very hard tissue.

▸ *Compare:* How is a skeleton similar to the frame of a house? Both a frame and a skeleton offer support and give the object its shape.

Kinds of Skeletons Some living things do not have a skeleton. Their bodies are entirely soft. Other organisms, such as lobsters and insects, have a skeleton outside their bodies. An external skeleton is called an **exoskeleton** (ek-soh-SKEL-uh-tun). An exoskeleton is tough and hard. It protects the animal. Human beings and many other animals have a skeleton inside their bodies. An internal skeleton is called an **endoskeleton** (en-duh-SKEL-uh-tun).

▸ *Infer:* List three organisms with an exoskeleton and three with an endoskeleton. Answers will vary.

Cartilage Feel your knee. The bones of your knee are very hard. Some parts of your skeleton are not as hard. Move the tip of your nose. Bend one of your ears with your hand. These two parts of your body are not made of bone. They are made up of **cartilage** (KART-ul-idj). Cartilage is a tough, but flexible connective tissue. When you were a baby, most of your skeleton was made up of cartilage. However, during the second and third months of development, bone slowly replaced the cartilage in your skeleton.

▸ *Define:* What is cartilage? tough, flexible connective tissue

Jobs of the Skeleton Besides giving support and shape to your body, your skeletal system has many important jobs. One of the these jobs is to move the body. The bones work together with muscles to move the body. Another job of the skeleton is to protect organs. For example, the ribs protect the heart and lungs. Some bones have a very special job. Blood cells are made inside some bones. Bones also store minerals that the body needs.

▸ *Infer:* What do you think the skull protects? the brain

LESSON SUMMARY

▶ The skeleton supports the body and gives it its shape.

▶ Most organisms have either an exoskeleton or an endoskeleton.

▶ Cartilage is a tough, flexible connective tissue that makes up parts of the skeletal system.

▶ The skeletal system has many important jobs and functions, including protecting organs and making red blood cells.

CHECK *Complete the following.*

1. A very hard tissue that makes up the skeletal system is _____ tissue. bone

2. As a developing baby, most of your skeleton was made up of _____ . cartilage

3. The skeletal system works with _____ to move the body. muscles

Answer the following.

4. What kind of skeleton do humans have? endoskeleton

APPLY *Complete the following.*

5. **Classify:** Which animal, a grasshopper or a fish, has an endoskeleton? Which has an exoskeleton?

Use the diagram of the skeletal system on page 240 to answer the following.

6. **Analyze:** How many bones make up the lower arm? 2

7. **Analyze:** What is another name for the breastbone? sternum

Skill Builder

Relating Roots and Word Parts Many words that begin with "oss" and "oste" refer in some way to bones. "Os" is the Latin word for bone. "Osteon" is the Greek word for bone. Use a dictionary to find five words that begin with "oss" and "oste" and refer to bone. Write definitions for each of the five words. Circle the part of the word that relates to bone.

TECHNOLOGY AND SOCIETY

ARTHROSCOPIC SURGERY

Can you imagine having surgery done through a small tool inserted into your body? Due to advances in both medicine and technology, operations are now being performed in this way. This kind of operation is called arthroscopic (ahr-thruh-SKAHP-ik) surgery. Most often arthroscopic surgery is done on the knee. A small cut is made on the body. A small instrument, called an arthroscope, is put into the cut. A special light also is inserted into the cut. The arthroscope, working with the light, projects an image on the screen. By looking at the screen, doctors can see what they are doing.

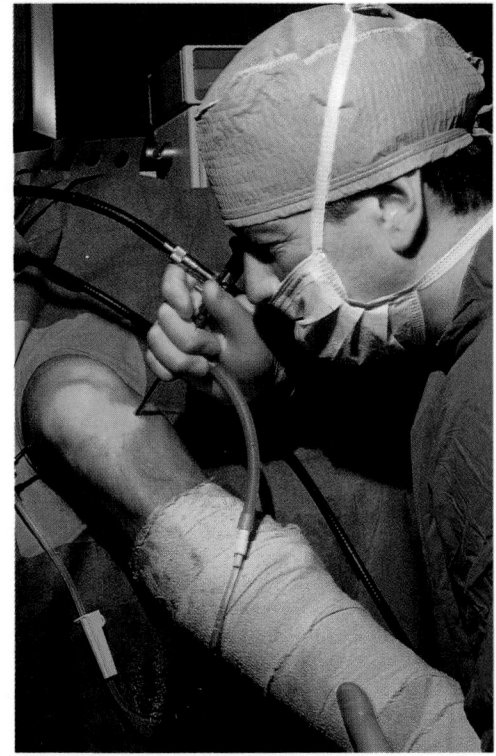

One of the advantages of arthroscopic surgery is that instead of being put to sleep, the person stays awake during surgery. Doctors have discovered that when people are awake during surgery, they recover faster. People who have arthroscopic surgery recover faster than people who have regular surgery. Because the cut is so small, less tissue is damaged. The body does not need to repair itself as much. The other advantage of arthroscopic surgery is only a very small scar is left.

12-2 What are bones?

Figure 2 Bone Cells

Objective ▶ Describe the parts of a bone.

TechTerms

▶ **compact bone:** hardest part of bones

▶ **periosteum** (per-i-AS-tee-um): thin membrane that covers a bone

▶ **spongy bone:** bone cells that make up the soft and spongy ends of bones

Bones The human skeleton is made up of about 206 bones. Bones come in all shapes and sizes. Some bones are very small. There are three small bones in your ear that help you hear. They are the smallest bones in your body. Other bones are quite large. The bone in your thigh is the largest bone in the body. Some bones are tubelike. Others are flat. Although bones are different in size and shape, they all have a similar structure.

Stirrup (Stapes)

Anvil (Incus)

Hammer (Malleus)

Figure 1 Ear Bones

▶ *Infer:* Name some places in your body where there are small bones. Answers will vary, but may include ears, fingers, toes, vertebrae.

Structure of Bones Bones are made up of both living and nonliving material. Each bone is covered by the **periosteum** (per-i-AS-tee-um). It is a thin membrane. The periosteum has many blood vessels in it. These blood vessels bring food and oxygen to the living bone cells.

The hardest part of a bone is called **compact bone.** Compact bone is made up of living bone cells, protein fibers, and nonliving minerals. The mineral calcium makes compact bone hard. Calcium in your diet helps keep your bones hard and strong. Dairy products are rich in calcium.

Bones are not entirely hard, however. The ends of bones are soft and spongy. The soft part of bones is called **spongy bone.** Spongy bone looks like a sponge. It has many holes in it. Spongy bone is lightweight and gives the bone its strength.

▷ *Describe:* What is the function of the periosteum? supply the bone with oxygen and food

Marrow The spaces in spongy bone are filled with bone marrow. Bone marrow is a soft tissue. It is red or yellow in color. Spongy bone contains red bone marrow. New blood cells are made in the red bone marrow. Long bones contain yellow marrow. Yellow marrow is mostly fat.

▷ *Name:* In which kind of bone marrow are red blood cells made? red blood marrow

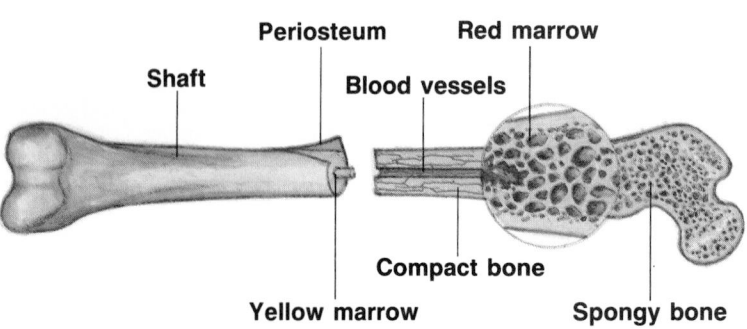

Periosteum   Red marrow

Shaft   Blood vessels

Compact bone   Spongy bone

Yellow marrow

Figure 3 Structure of a Bone

▶ Bones are different in size and shape, but they have similar structures.

▶ Bones have both living and nonliving materials in them.

▶ The hardest part of a bone is called compact bone.

▶ The soft and spongy ends of bones are called spongy bone.

▶ The spaces in spongy bone are filled with red or yellow bone marrow.

CHECK *Write true if the statement is true. If the statement is false, change the underlined term to make the statement true.*

1. New <u>bone</u> cells are made in spongy bone. blood

2. The mineral <u>calcium</u> keeps bones strong and hard. true

3. Blood vessels in <u>spongy bone</u> supply the bones with food and oxygen. the periosteum

4. Most bones have <u>the same</u> sizes and shapes.
different

5. Bone cells and protein fibers make up <u>compact bone</u>. true

APPLY *Complete the following.*

▶ 6. **Infer:** Is the periosteum living or nonliving? Explain your answer. living; Answers will vary.

▶ 7. **Infer:** What would happen if you did not eat foods containing calcium? Answers will vary, but may include that bones will get soft and weak.

InfoSearch...................................

Read the passage. Ask two questions about the topic that you cannot answer from the information in the passage.

Vitamin D Sunshine and the right foods are important for proper bone growth. Bones are made up of the minerals calcium and phosphorus. To make sure your bones are healthy, you should eat foods containing these minerals each day. Vitamin D is also needed for healthy bones. Vitamin D is found in many foods. Your body can also produce vitamin D, by being exposed to sunlight. This is why vitamin D is also called the sunshine vitamin.

SEARCH: Use library references to find answers to your questions.

TECHNOLOGY AND SOCIETY

BONE MARROW TRANSPLANTS

Bone marrow transplants are used to treat many different bone disorders. Certain kinds of anemia and leukemia may be treated with bone marrow transplants. A bone marrow transplant is needed when bone marrow produces abnormal blood cells, instead of normal cells.

A healthy donor is needed for a bone marrow transplant. Radiation treatments are given to the person with the abnormal bone marrow cells. The radiation kills the abnormal marrow cells in the body. Healthy bone marrow is then taken from the donor's hip. The healthy marrow is inserted into the patient's bones.

The success of a bone marrow transplant depends on whether the healthy bone marrow produces more healthy bone marrow. Another factor in the success of a bone marrow transplant is if the patient's body accepts or rejects the new bone marrow. Rejection of the new bone marrow is one of the major drawbacks of bone marrow transplants. Another drawback is infection.

12-3 How do joints work?

Objective ▶ Identify the motions and locations of the four kinds of movable joints.

TechTerms

▶ **joint:** place where two or more bones meet
▶ **ligaments** (LIG-uh-ments): tissue that connects bone to bone

Joints The place where two or more bones meet is called a **joint.** Some bones are connected to other bones at the joint. However, most bones are connected at joints by **ligaments** (LIG-uh-ments). A ligament is a tough band of tissue that connects one bone to another bone.

▶ **Define:** What is a joint? place where two or more bones meet

Kinds of Joints There are three main kinds of joints in the body. They are fixed joints, partly-movable joints, and movable joints. Fixed joints do not allow any movement. The joints in your skull are fixed. Partly movable joints allow a little bit of movement. The joints between your ribs and breastbone move a little bit. However, most of the joints in the body are movable. Your arms and legs have several movable joints.

▶ **State:** What are the three kinds of joints in the body? fixed, partly movable, and movable

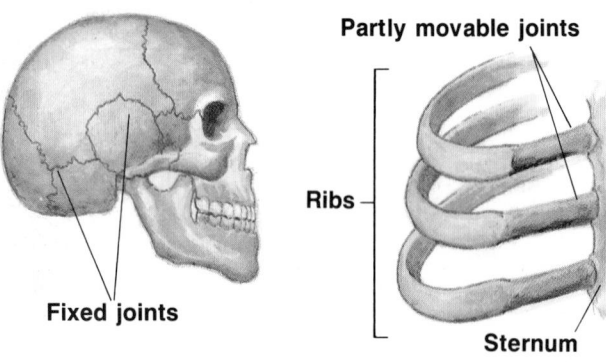

Partly movable joints

Ribs

Fixed joints

Sternum

Movable Joints There are four kinds of movable joints. These joints are ball-and-socket joints, gliding joints, hinge joints, and pivotal joints.

Pivotal joint

Ball-and-socket joint

Gliding joint

Hinge joint

▶ **Ball-and-socket Joints** Ball-and-socket joints allow bones to move in all directions. The joint between your upper arm and shoulder is a ball-and-socket joint. Your arm can move up and down, side to side, front to back, and around in a circle.

▶ **Gliding Joints** Gliding joints allow some movement in all directions. In a gliding joint, the bones slide along each other. Your wrist has gliding joints.

▶ **Hinge Joints** Hinge joints allow bones to move forward and backward in only one direction. This movement is similar to a door opening and closing. Hinge joints are located in your elbows and knees.

▶ **Pivotal Joints** Pivotal joints allow bones to move side to side and up and down. The joint between your skull and neck is a pivotal joint.

▶ **List:** List the four kinds of movable joints and give examples of where they are found in the body. Answers will vary. Accept all logical responses.

LESSON SUMMARY

▶ A joint is where two bones meet.

▶ The three kinds of joints are fixed joints, partly-movable joints, and movable joints.

▶ The four kinds of movable joints are ball-and-socket joints, gliding joints, hinge joints, and pivotal joints.

CHECK *Complete the following.*

1. Joints can be either fixed, partially movable, or _____ . movable

2. The joints between your breastbone and ribs are ____ . partly movable

3. A _____ is a band of tissue that connects one bone to another bone. ligament

4. The joint in your elbow is a ____ joint. hinge

APPLY *Complete the following.*

5. Hypothesize: What would happen if the joint between your arm and shoulder was not a ball-and-socket joint?

6. Infer: Why do you think the joints between your rib cage and sternum are partly-movable?

Read the passage. Ask two questions about the topic that you cannot answer from the information in the passage.

Arthritis Do you know anyone that has arthritis? Arthritis affects people who are both young and old. Arthritis is a term that describes many different joint problems. The most common form of arthritis occurs when the cartilage between the bones is replaced with bone deposits. A person with arthritis has swollen joints. Movement in these joints is limited and can be very painful.

SEARCH: Use library references to find answers to your questions.

⠂⠦⠂ ACTIVITY ⠂⠢⠒⠶⠶⠶⠒⠶⠶⠒⠶⠶⠒⠶⠶⠒⠶⠶⠒⠶⠒⠶⠶⠒⠶⠶⠒⠶⠶

OBSERVING JOINT MOVEMENTS

You will need a paper and pencil.

1. Move your ankle in as many different ways as possible. Write down all the movements your ankle can make.

2. Move your fingers in as many different ways as possible. **CAUTION:** Do not force movements at the joint. Write down all the movements your fingers can make.

3. Move your head in as many different ways as possible. Write down all the movements your head can make.

4. Move your leg and hip joint in as many different ways as possible. Write down all the movements your leg can make at the hip.

Questions

1. a. What kind of joint was used in each step? **b.** How can you tell? gliding; limited range of motion in all directions

2. Observe: Look at the X-ray of the hand. **a.** How many joints can you count? **b.** What kind of joints are shown? a. about 25; b. gliding, hinge

12-4 What is the muscular system?

Objective ▶ Describe how muscles work.

TechTerms

▶ **extensor** (ik-STEN-sur): muscle that straightens a joint

▶ **flexor** (FLEK-sur): muscle that bends a joint

▶ **tendons** (TEN-duns): tissue that connects muscle to bone

Muscles More than 600 muscles make up the muscular system. Muscles are tissues that can shorten along their length. Without muscles, the bones of the skeletal system could not move the body. Muscles are attached to bones by **tendons** (TEN-duns). A tendon is a strong elastic band of tissue. Tendons make movement possible. When a muscle contracts, or shortens, it pulls on the tendon, which makes the muscle move.

▶ *Contrast:* What is the difference between a tendon and a ligament? tendons connect bone to muscle; ligaments connect bone to bone

Muscle Actions Muscles only move bones when they contract. For this reason, muscles can only pull bones. They cannot push bones. For example, there are muscles that bend, or flex your knee joint. These muscles are called **flexors** (FLEK-surs). There are other muscles that straighten, or extend your knee joint. These muscles are **extensors** (ik-STEN-surs).

▶ *Define:* What does a flexor muscle do? flexes, or bends a joint

Teamwork In order to move your body, most muscles must work in teams of two. The muscles that bend and straighten the arm are good examples of flexors and extensors working together. These muscles are called the biceps (BY-seps) and triceps (TRY-seps). The biceps are the flexors. They bend the arm at the elbow. The triceps are the extensors. They straighten the arm at the elbow. As you bend your arm, the biceps contract, and the triceps relax. As you straighten your arm, the opposite takes place. The biceps relax, while the triceps contract and pull the arm straight.

▶ *State:* Which muscle in the arm is the flexor? The extensor? biceps, triceps

Triceps relaxed
Biceps contracted

Figure 1

Triceps contracted
Biceps relaxed

Figure 2

LESSON SUMMARY

▶ Muscles are tissues that can shorten along their length.

▶ Muscles can only pull bones.

▶ Muscles usually work in pairs to move the body.

CHECK *Find the sentence or sentences that answers the question. Then write the sentence.*

1. What is a tendon?

2. Are muscles relaxed or contracted when they move bones?

Answer the following.

3. What is the main function of the muscular system? to move the body

4. What do extensor muscles do? extend, or straighten a joint

5. Why must muscles work together? because muscles can only pull bones

APPLY *Use Figures 1 and 2 one page 246 to answer the following.*

6. **a.** In Figure 1, which muscle is contracted? **b.** Which muscle is relaxed?
   a. biceps; b. triceps

7. **a.** In Figure 2, which muscle is contracted? **b.** Which muscle is relaxed? a. triceps; b. biceps

Skill Builder

Researching A good way to make muscles strong is to exercise. Design your own individual exercise program. Keep in mind the following important parts of a good workout: warm up, exercise time, and cool down. Other factors to include are mode, duration, intensity, and frequency. Use library references to find out what mode, duration, intensity, and frequency mean in regard to exercise. Then in a report, write up an individualized exercise program for yourself.

Skill Builder

Researching Find out what each of the following muscle and skeletal problems are: sprains, strains, charley horses, muscle cramps, and tendonitis. Circle the word or words in each definition that is part of the muscular system. Draw a square around the word or words that are part of the skeletal system. What can cause each of these problems.

SCIENCE CONNECTION

ANABOLIC STEROIDS

You have probably read about athletes being disqualified from sporting events for taking steroids (STIR-oyds). These athletes have taken anabolic (an-uh-BAHL-ik) steroids. Anabolic steroids are synthetic, or made in a lab. Steroids are male hormones. Hormones are chemicals that regulate body functions. Steroids were developed to help people with muscle diseases. However, athletes began taking steroids to increase their muscle strength and muscle mass.

Humans are born with a fixed number of muscle fibers. The size of muscle fibers can increase, but the number will never change. People take steroids because they believe that steroids will increase the number of muscle fibers. The only way to increase muscle mass and strength is through weight-training exercise.

Steroids are considered illegal unless taken under a doctor's care. There are many harmful side effects of steroids. Some of the side effects include high blood pressure, liver damage, kidney damage, and damage to reproductive organs.

12-5 What are the kinds of muscles?

Objective ▶ Name the three kinds of muscle and identify where they are located in the body.

TechTerms

- ▶ **cardiac** (KAHR-dee-ak) **muscle:** type of muscle found only in the heart
- ▶ **smooth muscle:** muscle that causes movements that you cannot control
- ▶ **striated** (STRY-ayt-ed) **muscle:** muscle attached to the skeleton, making movement possible

Striated Muscle There are three different kinds of muscle tissue in the human body. Each kind of muscle tissue has a different job. One kind of muscle tissue is **striated** (STRY-ayt-ed) **muscle.** Striated means striped. If you look at Figure 1, you can see how striated muscle gets its name.

Figure 1 Striated muscle

Striated muscle also is called skeletal muscle because it is attached directly to the skeleton. Striated muscles are what makes the body move. Move your foot. Open and close your fingers. These are movements you can control. Striated muscles are usually voluntary (VAHL-un-ter-ee) muscles. They are voluntary muscles because you can control their movements.

▐▐▶ **Name:** Give three places on your body where striated muscle is found. Answers will vary. Accept all logical responses.

Smooth muscle Muscle tissue that is found in

the walls of blood vessels, the stomach, and other internal organs is called **smooth muscle.** Smooth muscle causes movements that you cannot control. For this reason, smooth muscle is sometimes called involuntary muscle. For example, after you eat, you cannot stop the muscles lining your stomach from digesting the food.

Figure 2 Smooth muscle

▶ **Infer:** Why do you think smooth muscle is often called involuntary muscle? Because you have no control over smooth muscle.

Cardiac Muscle The third kind of muscle is called **cardiac** (KAHR-dee-ak) **muscle.** The word 'cardiac' means 'heart.' Cardiac muscle is found only in the heart. Cardiac muscle is very strong. The heart must be strong to pump blood throughout the body. Cardiac muscle is striated. Unlike most striated muscle, cardiac muscle is involuntary. You have no control over your heart beating.

Figure 3 Cardiac muscle

▐▐▶ **Identify:** Where is the only place cardiac muscle is found? in the heart

248

LESSON SUMMARY

▶ There are three different kinds of muscle tissue in the body, each with a different job.

▶ Striated muscles are muscles that you control for movement.

▶ Smooth muscle causes movements that you cannot control.

▶ Cardiac muscle is involuntary muscle found only in the heart.

CHECK *Write true if the statement is true. If the statement is false, change the underlined term to make the statement true.*

1. The word "cardiac" means "heart." true

2. Smooth muscles are <u>voluntary</u> muscles. involuntary muscles

3. Blinking your eyes is caused by <u>involuntary</u> muscles. true

4. Striated muscle is usually <u>voluntary</u>. true

5. The heart is made of <u>smooth</u> muscle. cardiac

APPLY *Complete the following.*

6. Which kind of muscle tissue is responsible for walking? striated

7. **Infer:** What kind of muscle tissue is responsible for breathing? smooth

8. **Observe:** Look at Figures 1 and 3 on page 248. What is similar in striated and cardiac muscle? They both are striped, or striated.

Skill Builder

Classifying When you classify, you group things together based upon similarities. Using reference materials, classify the following muscles as being voluntary or involuntary:

a. muscles in the eye that move your eye back and forth

b. cardiac muscle

c. muscles in your stomach that you use to do sit-ups

d. muscles in the stomach that digest your food

e. muscles in your blood vessels

f. muscles in your jaw

g. muscles in your legs

CAREER IN LIFE SCIENCE

EXERCISE SPECIALIST

Do you like to exercise? Do you enjoy working with people? If you do, you may enjoy a career as an exercise specialist. Exercise specialists work for corporations, health clubs, and even hospitals. Exercise specialists perform many different jobs. Exercise specialists may teach classes or give lectures. They may teach people how to use exercise equipment. Exercise specialists also help people start exercising. They set up individualized exercise programs. Hospitals often use exercise specialists. They develop exercise programs for patients who have had heart attacks or who are overweight.

If a career as an exercise specialist interests you, you should take science and health classes. A four year college degree is needed for an exercise specialist. Many community colleges, and organizations, such as the YMCA, offer certification programs in exercise.

12-6 What is skin?

Objective ▶ Identify the layers and some of the structures of skin.

TechTerms

▶ **dermis:** inner layer of skin

▶ **epidermis** (ep-uh-DUR-mis): outer layer of skin

▶ **pores:** tiny openings on the skin's surface

The Largest Organ The skin is the largest organ of the human body. It covers the entire outside of your body. The main function of skin is to cover and protect the body. The skin is made up of two layers. There is an outer layer and an inner layer. Skin also contains blood vessels, nerves, and other tissues.

◉ *Observe:* Look at the picture. Which is thicker: the outer layer or the inner layer of skin? the inner layer

Epidermis The outer layer of skin is called the **epidermis** (ep-uh-DUR-mis). The epidermis covers and protects the body. It is made up of living and dead skin cells. The dead skin cells are replaced constantly by the living skin cells beneath them. Each time you scrape your knee, or even wash your hands, thousands of dead skin cells are worn away.

▶ *Infer:* Why do you think skin cells are constantly being replaced? Answers will vary, but should include that dead skin cells are constantly being wiped away.

Dermis The inner layer of the skin is called the **dermis.** The dermis is the living layer of skin. The dermis is much thicker than the epidermis.

The dermis has many different structures in it. One of these structures is sweat glands. Sweat glands remove liquid wastes from the body in the form of sweat, or perspiration (pur-spuh-RAY-shun). Perspiration leaves the body through tiny openings in the skin called **pores.**

Hair follicles (FAHL-ih-kuls) also are in the dermis. Each hair on your body grows from a hair follicle. Oil glands are located near the hair follicles. Oil glands produce oil. The oil softens and moistens the skin. Nerve endings and many tiny blood vessels also are located in the dermis.

▶ *Name:* What are three structures found in the dermis? Answers will vary, but should include sweat glands, hair follicles, oil glands, nerve endings and blood vessels.

Sense Receptors in the Skin The nerve endings in the skin receive many messages. These nerve endings are called sense receptors (ri-SEP-turs). When you think of the skin, you probably think of the sense of touch. The skin also is sensitive to heat, cold, pain and pressure. There are special nerve endings for each of these. The skin does not have the same number of each kind of receptor. For example, touch receptors are far apart on the back. They are close together at the tip of your nose.

▶ *Name:* To what five things is the skin sensitive? touch, heat, cold, pain, and pressure

► The main function of skin is to support and protect the body.

► The outer layer of skin, the epidermis, covers and protects the body.

► The dermis is the living inner layer of the skin.

► Sweat glands, located in the dermis, remove liquid wastes from the body through pores.

► Hair follicles, oil glands, nerve endings, and blood vessels, are all found in the dermis.

► The skin has sense receptors for touch, heat, cold, pain, and pressure.

CHECK *Answer the following.*

1. Where is skin found? covering the entire body as well as covering most of the organs.

2. Is the outer layer of skin alive or dead? dead

3. What is the function of oil glands? waterproof skin; keeping it soft

4. What are pores? tiny openings on the skin's surface

5. What are the nerve endings in the skin called? sense receptors

Explain the difference between the words in each pair.

6. dermis; epidermis

7. oil gland; sweat gland

APPLY *Complete the following.*

► 8. **Infer:** Why are organs covered with skin?

9. **Hypothesize:** Why do skin cells reproduce so rapidly?

10. If you cut yourself and it bleeds, which layer of skin have you cut into? How do you know?

► 11. **Infer:** Do you think there are more touch receptors on the tip of your tongue or your wrist? Explain.

Health & Safety Tip

Getting a "healthy" tan can be damaging to your skin. You should always wear a sunscreen to protect your skin from the ultraviolet rays of the sun. Long-term abuse of the sun can cause skin cancer. Using library references, make a chart that lists signs and symptoms of skin cancer, as well as ways to prevent skin cancer.

ACTIVITY

TOUCH RECEPTORS

You will need a pencil and a paper clip.

1. Work with a partner.

2. Straighten the paper clip. Bend the paper clip until its ends are about 2 cm apart.

3. Have your partner close their eyes. Touch the ends of the paper clip to your partner's arm.

4. Ask your partner how many points touched their arm.

5. Repeat this three times touching different parts of your partner's arm, hand, and fingers. Record responses.

6. Repeat Steps 3-5 with your partner recording your responses.

Questions

► 1. **Infer:** Were your responses always correct? Explain your answer.

2. **a.** Which part of your arm, hand, or fingers was most sensitive? ►**b. Infer:** Why do you think this part of your body is so sensitive?

STUDY HINT Before you begin the Unit Challenges, review the TechTerms and Lesson Summary for each lesson in this unit.

TechTerms

cardiac muscle (248)
cartilage (240)
compact bone (242)
dermis (250)
endoskeleton (240)
epidermis (250)

exoskeleton (240)
extensor (246)
flexor (246)
joint (244)
ligament (244)
periosteum (242)

pores (250)
smooth muscle (248)
spongy bone (242)
striated muscle (248)
tendons (246)

TechTerm Challenges

Matching *Write the TechTerm that matches each description.*

1. outer covering of a bone periosteum
2. striated, involuntary muscle found in the heart cardiac muscle
3. place where two or more bones meet joint
4. connective tissue that connects bone to bone ligament
5. bone made up of bone cells, protein fibers, and nonliving minerals compact bone
6. connective tissue that connects muscle to bone tendons
7. strong, lightweight bone with many holes in it spongy bone
8. tiny openings on the skin's surface pores
9. involuntary muscle smooth muscle
10. dead, outer layer of skin epidermis

Identifying Word Relationships *Explain how the terms in each pair are related. Write your answers in complete sentences.* Answers will vary. Accept all logical responses.

1. extensor, flexor
2. bone, cartilage
3. striated muscle, smooth muscle
4. dermis, epidermis
5. endoskeleton, exoskeleton

Content Challenges

Multiple Choice *Write the letter of the term that best completes each statement.*

1. The human skeletal system is made up of 206
   a. bones. **b.** muscles. **c.** tendons. **d.** ligaments. a
2. Blood cells are made in the
   a. periosteum. **b.** compact bone. **c.** spongy bone. **d.** red bone marrow. d
3. The kind of muscle found in the walls of the blood vessels is
   a. cardiac muscle. **b.** skeletal muscle. **c.** smooth muscle. **d.** striated muscle. c
4. Joints that allow movement in only one direction are
   a. hinge joints. **b.** ball-and-socket joints. **c.** fixed joints. **d.** gliding joints. a

5. The joints that are found in the shoulder are
   a. gliding joints.   **b.** pivotal joints.   **c.** hinge joints.   **d.** ball-and-socket joints. d

6. As an embryo develops, the cartilage in the skeleton is replaced by
   a. bone.   **b.** tendon.   **c.** ligaments.   **d.** muscle. a

7. The connective tissue that connects a muscle to a bone is a
   a. ligament.   **b.** tendon.   **c.** skeletal muscle.   **d.** bone marrow. b

8. The main job of the skin is to
   a. make blood cells.   **b.** move muscles.   **c.** cover and protect the body.   **d.** store minerals. c

9. The inner layer of the skin is the
   a. epidermis.   **b.** pore.   **c.** sweat gland.   **d.** dermis. d

10. Skeletal muscle is
    a. found in the heart.   **b.** found in the stomach.   **c.** involuntary.   **d.** voluntary. d

11. Sweat leaves the body through
    a. hair follicles.   **b.** sweat glands.   **c.** pores.   **d.** oil glands. c

12. Skin is sensitive to all of the following EXCEPT
    a. touch.   **b.** temperature.   **c.** pain.   **d.** atmosphere. d

13. Spongy bone is strong and
    a. flexible.   **b.** lightweight.   **c.** fat.   **d.** heavy. b

True/False *Write true if the statement is true. If the statement is false, change the underlined term to make the statement true.*

1. The hardest part of bone is <u>compact</u> bone. true

2. Spongy bone is filled with <u>cartilage</u>. bone marrow

3. Fixed joints are found in the <u>neck</u>. skull

4. You have over 600 <u>muscles</u>. true

5. The tip of your nose is <u>bone</u>. cartilage

6. Muscles only can <u>push</u> bones. pull

7. Your skin is made up of <u>two</u> layers. true

8. Human beings have an <u>exoskeleton</u>. endoskeleton

9. Muscles that <u>bend</u> a joint are called extensors. straighten

10. Smooth muscle is <u>voluntary</u> muscle. involuntary

11. Striated muscle also is called <u>skeletal</u> muscle. true

12. The epidermis is the <u>inner</u> layer of skin. outer

13. Touch receptors on the skin of the back are <u>far apart</u>. true

Understanding the Features

Reading Critically *Use the feature reading selections to answer the following. Page numbers for the features follow each question in parentheses.*

1. **Infer:** Why do people recover quicker from arthroscopic surgery than from regular surgery? (241)

2. **Name:** What are two problems that affect the success of bone marrow transplants? (243)

3. **Hypothesize:** What benefits do athletes think they can get by taking steroids (247)

4. **Infer:** Why should you take science classes if you are interested in becoming an exercise specialist? (249)

Concept Challenges...

Critical Thinking *Answer each of the following in complete sentences.*

1. **Explain:** How do muscles work to move bones?
2. **Infer:** Discs of cartilage are found between the vertebrae. What function do you think these discs serve?
3. **Infer:** What happens to the cartilage between your ribs and breastbone when you breathe?
4. **Hypothesize:** What might happen to you if your skin was not sensitive to pain or pressure?
5. **Locate:** Name three places on the human skeleton that are cartilage rather than bone.

Interpreting a Diagram *Use the diagram of the human skeletal system to answer the following.*

1. **Observe:** What three bones make up the pelvis?
2. How many bones are there in the lower leg?
3. What is the scientific name for the skull?
4. **Observe:** Where is your patella located?
5. **Analyze:** What bones are important for holding a pen or pencil?
6. What is the common name for clavicle?

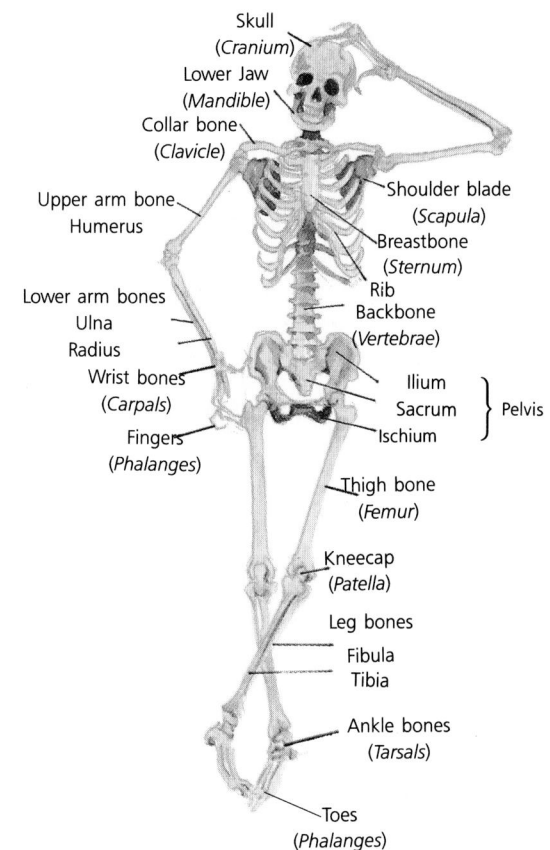

Skull (*Cranium*)
Lower Jaw (*Mandible*)
Collar bone (*Clavicle*)
Upper arm bone Humerus
Lower arm bones Ulna Radius
Wrist bones (*Carpals*)
Fingers (*Phalanges*)
Shoulder blade (*Scapula*)
Breastbone (*Sternum*)
Rib
Backbone (*Vertebrae*)
Ilium
Sacrum
Ischium
} Pelvis
Thigh bone (*Femur*)
Kneecap (*Patella*)
Leg bones
Fibula
Tibia
Ankle bones (*Tarsals*)
Toes (*Phalanges*)

Finding Out More...

1. Use a first-aid manual to prepare a table on sports injuries. List whether bones, muscles, or both are involved, symptoms, and the first aid treatment for each injury. Include: sprains, strains, dislocations, tendonitis, muscle cramps, and fractures.
2. Scoliosis is an abnormal curvature of the spine. Use library references to find out how people get scoliosis and the different methods of treating people with scoliosis.
3. Muscular dystrophy is a muscular system disease. Using library references, find out the causes of muscular dystrophy, its effect on the body, and treatments that are being tested.
4. Acne is a combination of skin diseases. Prepare a chart that lists some of the causes of acne as well as the ways of controlling acne. Present your chart to the class.
5. Using library references, develop a chart that lists five careers that involve muscles, bones, and skin. Write the name of the career, the job description, and the educational requirements of each career.

254

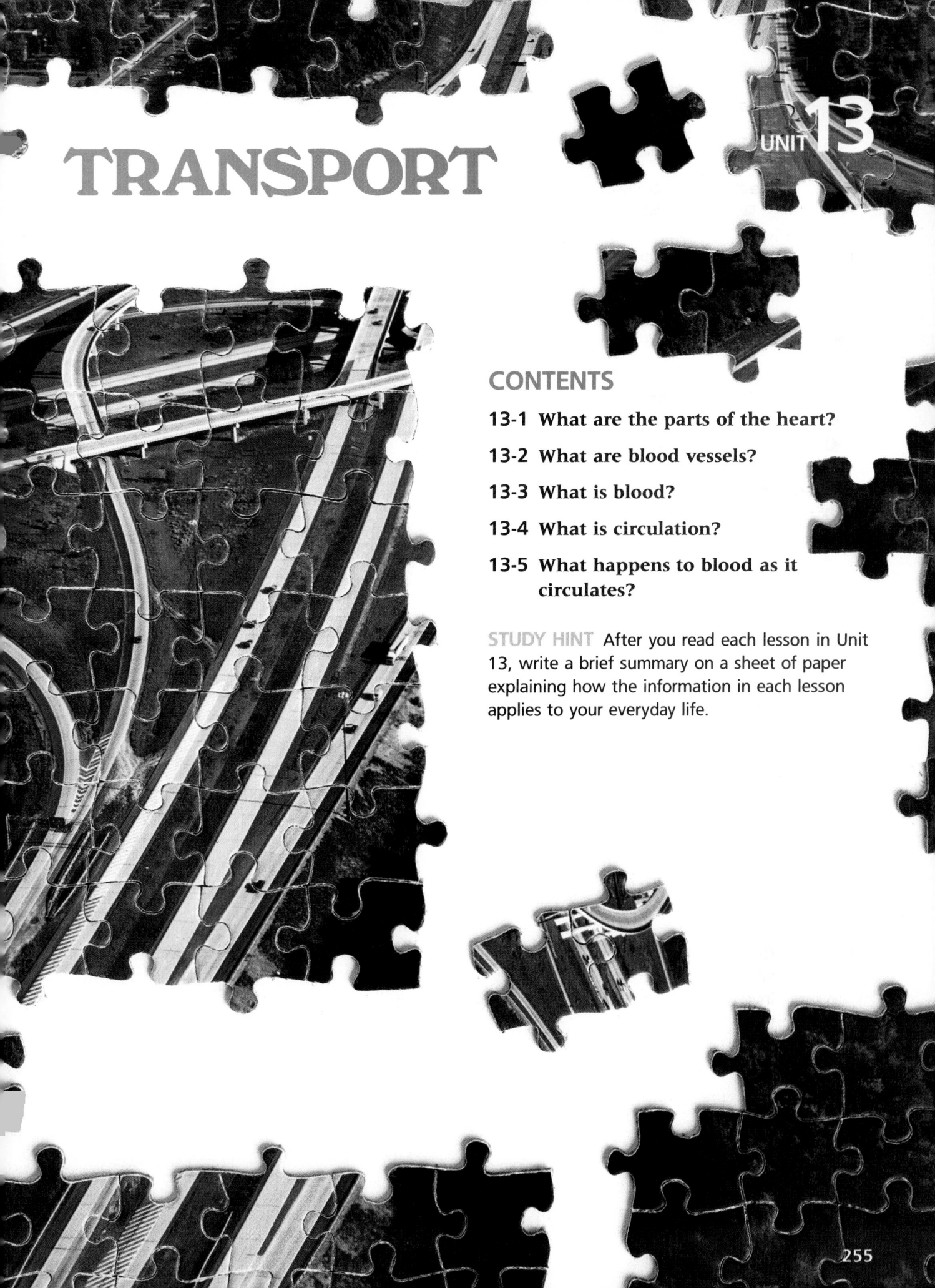

TRANSPORT

CONTENTS

13-1 What are the parts of the heart?

13-2 What are blood vessels?

13-3 What is blood?

13-4 What is circulation?

13-5 What happens to blood as it circulates?

STUDY HINT After you read each lesson in Unit 13, write a brief summary on a sheet of paper explaining how the information in each lesson applies to your everyday life.

13-1 What are the parts of the heart?

Objectives ▶ Describe the heart. ▶ Explain how blood moves through the heart.

TechTerms

- **atrium** (AY-tree-um): upper chamber of the heart
- **septum:** thick tissue wall that separates the left and right sides of the heart
- **valve:** thin flap of tissue that acts like a one-way door
- **ventricle** (VEN-tri-kul): lower chamber of the heart

A Muscular Organ The heart is a muscular organ. Its job is to pump blood. The heart is divided into four parts, or chambers. There are upper and lower chambers. Each upper chamber of the heart is called an **atrium** (AY-tree-um). The plural of atrium is atria. The atria receive blood. The lower chambers are called **ventricles** (VEN-tri-kuls). The ventricles pump blood out of the heart.

▶ *Identify:* How many chambers does the heart have? 4

Blood Flow in the Heart Look at Figure 1. You can see that the heart is divided into two sides—a left side and a right side. A thick tissue wall separates the two sides of the heart. This tissue wall is called the **septum.**

Blood flows into the atria of the heart. When the atria are full of blood, they contract. This motion pumps the blood into the ventricles. Once the ventricles are full of blood, they contract. This motion pushes the blood out of the heart.

▶ *Sequence:* List the flow of blood from when it enters the heart to when it leaves the heart. Blood flows from the atria to the ventricles, from the ventricles to the body.

Heart Valves Inside the heart, there are four **valves.** A valve is a thin flap of tissue. It acts like a one-way door. The valves keep the blood moving

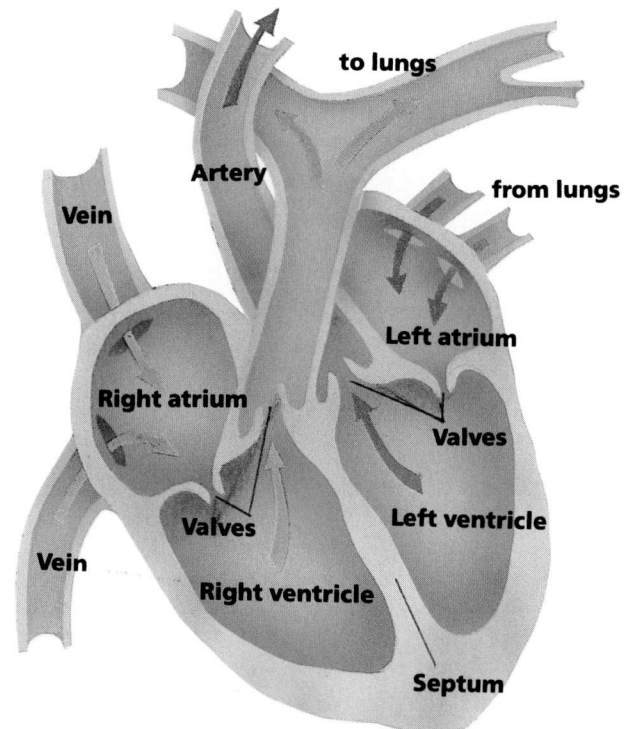

Figure 1 The human heart

in only one direction. Blood can flow only from the atria to the ventricles. Blood cannot flow backwards. Between the atria and ventricles there are valves. If the blood tries to go backwards, the valve shuts. There also are valves between the ventricles and the blood vessels. As blood leaves the ventricles, it goes through the valves.

▶ *Identify:* What keeps blood from flowing backwards in the heart? valves

Heartbeat Your heartbeat is the rhythm of your heart pumping blood. A stethoscope (STETH-uh-skohp) is an instrument doctors use to listen to heartbeat. If you were to listen to your heartbeat, you would hear a lub-dub sound. The lub-dub sound is made by your valves opening and closing. When the valves between the atria and ventricles snap shut, they make a ''lub'' sound. When the valves between the ventricles and blood vessels snap shut, they make a ''dub'' sound.

▶ *Define:* What is a stethoscope? instrument used to listen to heart beat

256

LESSON SUMMARY

▶ The heart is divided into atria, or upper chambers, and ventricles, or lower chambers.

▶ The septum is a thick tissue wall that separates the left and right sides of the heart.

▶ Blood flows from the atria to the ventricles then out into the body.

▶ Heart valves prevent blood from flowing backwards.

▶ Heartbeat is the rhythm of your heart pumping blood.

CHECK *Complete the following.*

1. The _____ divides the heart into left and right sides. septum

2. The upper chambers of the heart are called _____ . atria

3. There are _____ chambers in the heart. 4

4. The _____ pumps blood into the body. left ventricle

Answer the following.

5. Where are valves found? between atria and ventricles and between ventricles and blood vessels

6. What causes the sound of the heartbeat? valves opening and closing

APPLY *Answer the following.*

7. **Infer:** What do you think would happen if a valve was damaged? blood might flow backward

8. **Hypothesize:** What might cause your heartbeat to increase? Answers will vary, but may include any activity, exercise, or stress.

Ideas in Action..............................

IDEA: Cholesterol is a fatlike substance found in the body. Too much cholesterol can clog your arteries. A buildup of cholesterol may be the cause of high blood pressure, heart attack, or stroke.

ACTION: Look at different food products that contain nutrition labels. Find the section of the label that lists the amount of cholesterol in the product. Which foods have a high level of cholesterol? Which foods have a low level of cholesterol? Present your findings in a table.

Artery with cholesterol   **Normal artery**

ACTIVITY

COMPARING ANIMAL HEART RATES

You will need a pencil and paper.

1. Study Table 1.
2. **Sequence:** List the animals according to their heart rates from fastest to slowest.
3. **Sequence:** List the animals according to their relative sizes from smallest to largest.

Questions

1. **a. Analyze:** Which animal has the fastest heart rate? **b.** Is the animal large or small?

2. **a. Analyze:** Which animal has the slowest heart rate? **b.** Is the animal large or small?

3. **Infer:** Do you think there is a relationship between animal size and heart rate? Explain.

4. **a. Hypothesize:** Do you think heart rates vary among humans according to body size? **b.** How could you find out?

Table 1	Heartbeat Rates
ANIMAL	HEART RATE/MINUTE
elephant	25
mouse	1000
human	72
cat	120
cow	65
bird	570

13-2 What are blood vessels?

Objective ▶ Name and describe the three kinds of blood vessels.

TechTerms

- ▶ **aorta** (ay-OWR-tuh): largest artery in the body
- ▶ **arteries** (ART-ur-ees): blood vessels that carry blood away from the heart
- ▶ **capillaries** (KAP-uh-ler-ees): tiny blood vessels that connect arteries to veins
- ▶ **veins** (VANES): blood vessels that carry blood to the heart

Blood Vessels Blood moves in the body through a closed system of tubes. These tubes are called blood vessels. The human body has three kinds of blood vessels. The **arteries** (ART-ur-ees) are blood vessels that carry blood away from the heart. Blood vessels that carry blood back to the heart are **veins** (VANES). Veins and arteries are connected by **capillaries** (KAP-uh-ler-ees). Capillaries are tiny blood vessels.

▶ **Name:** What are the three kinds of blood vessels? arteries, veins, and capillaries

Arteries Arteries have thick muscular walls. As the heart beats, it pumps blood through the arteries at high pressure. The arteries must be strong to be able to handle this pressure. The strong walls prevent the arteries from bursting. The largest artery in the body is the **aorta** (ay-OWR-tuh).

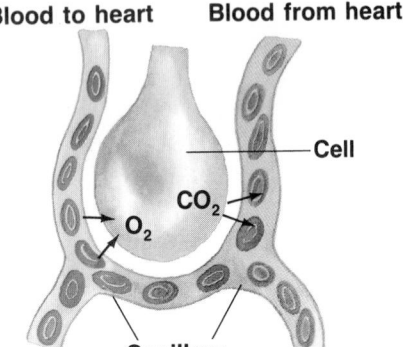

Blood to heart   **Blood from heart**

Cell

CO_2

O_2

Capillary

▶ **List:** What are some characteristics of arteries? thick muscular walls, strong, elastic

Pulse As your heart beats, it pushes blood through the arteries in spurts. With each spurt of blood, a beat can be felt. The beat you feel is your pulse. You can feel a pulse wherever an artery is close to the skin's surface. Your pulse rate and heartbeat rate are the same.

▶ **Identify:** Can you feel your pulse in a vein, artery, or capillary? artery

Veins Veins have thinner walls than do arteries. Blood pumps through the veins at less pressure than it does in arteries. Blood does not flow as easily through veins as it does through arteries. The contraction of muscles keeps the blood flowing. Some veins also have valves that keep the blood from flowing backwards.

▶ **Explain:** Why are the walls of veins thinner than the walls of arteries? Blood in veins is under less pressure than blood in arteries.

Capillaries Capillaries have walls that are only one cell thick. Blood cells travel through capillaries in a single file. The capillaries are where blood and body cells exchange nutrients and waste. For example, carbon dioxide and waste products move from body cells into the blood through capillaries. Food and oxygen in the blood move through the capillaries into the body cells.

▶ **Describe:** What happens in capillaries? substances are exchanged between the blood and body cells

LESSON SUMMARY

▶ The three kinds of blood vessels are arteries, veins, and capillaries.

▶ Arteries have thick muscular walls and are strong and elastic.

▶ A pulse is felt in an artery each time the heart beats.

▶ Veins have thin walls and have valves to keep blood flowing towards the heart.

▶ Capillaries are where the exchange of oxygen, carbon dioxide, food, and wastes take place between the blood and body cells.

CHECK *Write true if the statement is true. If the statement is false, change the underlined term to make the statement true.*

1. Arteries, veins, and <u>valves</u> are the three kinds of blood vessels. capillaries

2. Blood is pumped through the arteries at a <u>low</u> pressure. high

3. You can feel your pulse only in an <u>artery</u>. true

4. Blood is prevented from flowing backward in veins by <u>capillaries</u>. valves

5. Because blood is pumped through them at low pressure <u>arteries</u> have thin walls. Veins

6. The aorta is the largest <u>vein</u> in the body. artery

APPLY *Answer the following.*

7. **Compare:** What are the differences between arteries and veins?

8. **Infer:** Why do you think you cannot feel a pulse in a vein?

InfoSearch

Read the passage. Ask two questions that you cannot answer from the information in the passage.

High Blood Pressure Blood pressure is a measure of the force of blood on the arteries. An average blood pressure is 120/80. The top number, 120, is the pressure on the arteries when the ventricles are contracting. The bottom number, 80, is the pressure on the arteries when the ventricles are at rest. High blood pressure causes the heart to overwork. Some people inherit high blood pressure. Other people get it from stress. Still other people get high blood pressure from their diets. Over time, high blood pressure causes the arteries to weaken.

SEARCH: Use library references to find answers to your questions.

ACTIVITY

MEASURING PULSE RATE

You will need a clock or watch with a second hand.

1. Sit quietly for two minutes. Place your middle and index finger over the inside of your wrist. Find your pulse.

2. **Measure:** Take your pulse for 30 seconds. Multiply this number by 2. Record your answer.

3. Stand up for two minutes. Take your pulse for 30 seconds. Multiply this number by 2. Record your answer

4. Jog in place for two minutes. Take your pulse for 30 seconds. Multiply this number by 2. Record your answer.

5. Rest for two minutes. Take your pulse for 30 seconds. Multiple this number by 2. Record your answer.

Questions

1. **Analyze:** How did your pulse change when you stood up?

2. **Analyze:** How did your pulse change when you stopped jogging?

3. **Analyze:** What affect did exercise have on your heart rate?

13-3 What is blood?

Objective ▶ Describe the different parts of blood.

TechTerms

- ▶ **hemoglobin** (HEE-moh-gloh-bin): iron compound in red blood cells
- ▶ **plasma** (PLAZ-muh): liquid part of blood
- ▶ **platelets** (PLAYT-lits): tiny colorless pieces of cells

Blood Blood is a liquid tissue. You have about 5 liters of blood in your body. Blood makes up about 9 percent of your body weight.

Blood is a mixture. It has a liquid part and a solid part. Scientists use a centrifuge (SEN-truh-fyooj) to separate blood into its two parts. The blood is spun around in the centrifuge. The solid part of the blood is forced to the bottom of a test tube. The liquid part of blood remains on top.

▐▐▐▶ *Define:* What is a centrifuge? tool used by scientists to separate blood

Plasma The liquid part of blood is called **plasma** (PLAZ-muh). Plasma is a straw-colored liquid. It is made up mostly of water. Digested nutrients, dissolved vitamins, and minerals are found in plasma. Carbon dioxide also is dissolved in plasma.

▐▐▐▶ *List:* What are some things found in plasma? water, dissolved vitamins, nutrients, minerals and carbon dioxide

Red Blood Cells The red blood cell is different from any other cell in the body. It has no nucleus. The job of red blood cells is to carry oxygen. Red blood cells contain **hemoglobin** (HEE-moh-gloh-bin). Oxygen attaches to hemoglobin molecules. Hemoglobin is an iron compound. Hemoglobin gives red blood cells their color.

▐▐▐▶ *Define:* What is hemoglobin? iron compound found in the blood

White Blood Cells White blood cells are larger than red blood cells. White blood cells have a nucleus, but they do not contain hemoglobin. White blood cells destroy germs that are harmful to the body. By destroying germs, white blood cells help fight disease. There are many more red blood cells than white blood cells. For every white blood cell there are about 1000 red blood cells.

▐▐▐▶ *Describe:* What does a white blood cell do? destroys germs that are harmful to the body

Platelets Have you ever cut yourself? What happens to the wound? Soon after you cut yourself, a clot forms. Clotting is controlled by **platelets** (PLAYT-lits). Platelets are tiny, colorless pieces of cells. When tissues are injured, chemicals are given off by the blood. These chemicals form tiny, sticky threads. The threads stick together and form a clot. The clot prevents the body from losing blood.

▐▐▐▶ *Name:* What controls blood clotting? platelets

LESSON SUMMARY

- ▶ Blood is a liquid tissue.
- ▶ Scientists use a centrifuge to separate blood into its liquid and solid parts.
- ▶ Plasma is the liquid part of blood.
- ▶ Red blood cells transport oxygen and give blood its color.
- ▶ White blood cells destroy germs and help fight disease.
- ▶ Platelets form clots, which prevent the body from losing blood.

Plasma 55%

White blood cells 2%

Red blood cells 43%

CHECK *Complete the following.*

1. Red blood cells do not have a _____ . nucleus
2. Your body contains about _____ liters of blood. 5
3. The liquid part of blood is called _____ . plasma
4. Blood gets its red color from _____ . hemoglobin
5. Platelets help the body to form _____ . clots

APPLY *Answer the following.*

6. **Infer:** When a person is sick, the number of white blood cells increases. Why do you think this happens? The number of white blood cells increases to fight the disease.
7. **Predict:** What would happen is there were no platelets in the blood? If a person was cut or injured, they would bleed to death.

Health & Safety Tip

The four major blood types are A, B, AB, and O. You should know what your blood type is in case of an emergency. If you do not know your blood type, ask your doctor. Record your blood type on a piece of identification and always it with you.

▶■◀ PEOPLE IN SCIENCE ▶■◀◆▶■◀◆▶■◀◆▶■◀◆▶■◀◆▶■◀◆▶■◀◆▶■◀◆▶■◀◆▶■◀◆▶■◀◆▶■◀◆

CHARLES DREW (1904–1950)

Charles Drew was an American doctor, medical teacher, and hospital administrator. He also was the first director of the Red Cross. Drew was born in Washington, DC. In 1933, he graduated from McGill University Medical School. Drew is best known for his research on blood plasma, and setting up blood banks to collect blood plasma. He did most of his research in New York City at Columbia University between 1938 and 1940. From his research, Drew concluded that plasma could be used in blood transfusions, instead of whole blood. Using plasma in blood transfusions had two advantages. Whole blood stays fresh only about one week. Plasma can last for a longer period of time. Plasma also can be used in a transfusion for any blood type.

Drew's research findings were timely. During World War II, Drew set up blood banks in the United States to collect plasma. The blood plasma was then sent to the armed forces. The blood plasma that was collected saved many lives.

13-4 What is circulation?

TechTerms

- **circulation** (sur-kyuh-LAY-shun): movement of blood through the body
- **closed circulatory** (SUR-kyuh-luh-towr-ee) **system:** system in which blood is carried through the body in tubes

Circulation Your body has a transport system. It is your circulatory (SUR-kyuh-luh-towr-ee) system. The circulatory system transports, or moves, blood throughout the body. The movement of blood through the body is called **circulation** (sur-kyuh-LAY-shun).

▶ *Define:* **What is circulation?** transport of blood through the body

The Circulatory System Your circulatory system is made up of your heart, blood vessels, and blood. The blood vessels form a **closed circulatory system.** In a closed circulatory system, the blood moves through the blood vessels. The arteries are connected to veins by capillaries. The arteries, veins, and capillaries form a large network of tubes that form a continuous closed system.

▶ *List:* **What makes up your circulatory system?** heart, blood vessels, and blood

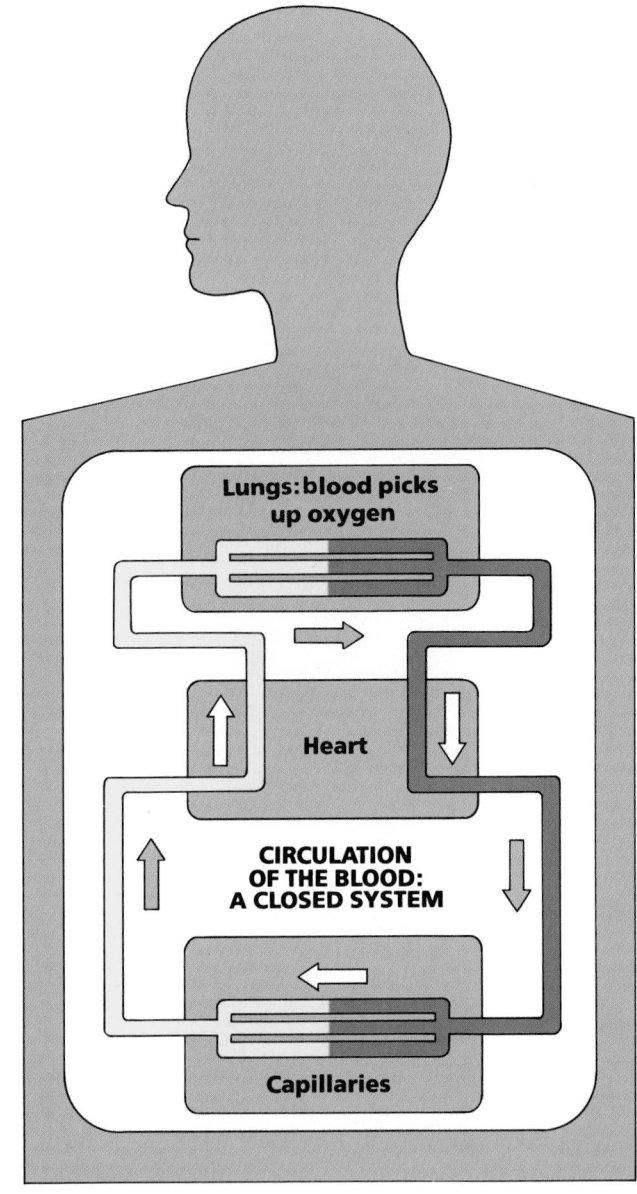

Lungs: blood picks up oxygen

Heart

CIRCULATION OF THE BLOOD: A CLOSED SYSTEM

Capillaries

Jobs of the Circulatory System The main job of the circulatory system is transport. However, the circulatory system has many other jobs as well. Some of these jobs are as follows.

- **Transport of Food and Oxygen** The circulatory system transports food and oxygen to the cells of your body. Hemoglobin in red blood cells carries the oxygen.
- **Transport of Wastes** The circulatory system carries away wastes produced by the cells. One important waste is carbon dioxide.

- **Protection** Another job of the circulatory system is protection. White blood cells in your blood fight disease and harmful chemicals.
- **Transport of Hormones** The circulatory system carries chemicals called hormones (HAWR-mohns). Hormones carry "messages" from one part of your body to another part of the body.
- **Regulation** The circulatory system helps regulate your body temperature.

▶ *List:* **What are some jobs of the circulatory system?** Students should restate the jobs listed.

LESSON SUMMARY

- ► Circulation is the movement of blood through the body.

- ► In a closed circulatory system, blood travels within a system of blood vessels.

- ► The circulatory system transports food and oxygen, and carries away wastes such as carbon dioxide.

- ► The circulatory system protects your body from disease, carries hormones, and regulates body temperature.

CHECK *Complete the following.*

1. The circulatory system _____ blood and oxygen to all parts of the body. transports, or carries

2. Arteries, veins, and capillaries form a _____ circulatory system. closed

3. Carbon dioxide is a _____ that is removed from the body by blood. waste

4. Chemical "messengers" that are carried in the blood are called _____ . hormones

5. The job of _____ blood cells is to fight disease. white

APPLY *Answer the following.*

► 6. **Infer:** Why do you think blood is sometimes called "the river of life"?

InfoSearch

Read the passage. Ask two questions that you cannot answer from the information in the passage.

Sickle-Cell Anemia Anemia (uh-NEE-mee-uh) is a disease of the blood. There are many different kinds of anemia. One kind is called sickle-cell anemia. The red blood cells are sickle-shaped. The sickle shape of the red blood cells may cause them to clog blood vessels. Their shape also causes them to break apart easily. Sickle-cells do not have as much hemoglobin as normal red blood cells. Therefore, they cannot carry enough oxygen. Sickle-cell anemia is a disease that you are born with. Sickle-cell anemia is most common among African Americans.

SEARCH: Use library references to find answers to your questions.

PEOPLE IN SCIENCE

WILLIAM HARVEY (1578–1657)

William Harvey was an English physician. He was born on April 1, 1578 in Kent, England. Harvey attended a 2 1/2 year medical training course at the University of Padua, Italy. The university was considered the best medical school in Europe during the 16th century.

In the beginning of the 17th century, Harvey studied circulation in humans. Harvey also studied the circulation of blood in living animals. He thought that he could apply what he learned about circulation in snakes to circulation in humans. From his research, Harvey concluded that blood moved in a circular path through the human body. He also hypothesized that the heart acted like a pump, and helped to move blood through the body. Harvey used his knowledge about the structure of the heart and its valves to form his conclusions. Harvey's conclusions were based on careful observations and experiments.

What happens to blood as it circulates?

Objective ▶ Describe what happens to blood as it circulates.

TechTerm

▶ **pulmonary** (PUL-muh-ner-ee) **artery:** artery that carries blood from the heart to the lungs

Exchange of Substances The flow of blood throughout the body is quite simple. Blood is pumped from the left ventricle into the aorta. The aorta is the largest artery in the body. Blood that enters the aorta carries food and oxygen to the body cells.

Once the aorta leaves the heart, it branches into many smaller arteries. These arteries divide again and again until they form capillaries in all the body tissues. Substances are exchanged through the walls of the capillaries. Food and oxygen pass out of the blood in the capillaries and into the body cells. At the same time, carbon dioxide and other wastes pass from the body cells into the blood in the capillaries.

▶ *Identify:* Where are materials exchanged between the blood and the body cells? at the capillaries

Return to the Heart Once the exchange of substances has taken place, the blood must be returned to the heart. The capillaries in the body tissues join to form small veins. These, in turn, join to form larger veins. Blood containing carbon dioxide and other wastes is carried in the veins to the right atrium of the heart. Before it can be sent out to the body tissues again, the blood must get a fresh supply of oxygen. It also must give up its carbon dioxide. To do this the blood must be sent to the lungs.

▶ *Name:* What part of the heart does blood containing wastes return to? right atrium

Heart and Lung Circulation Once the blood is received in the right atrium, it passes into the

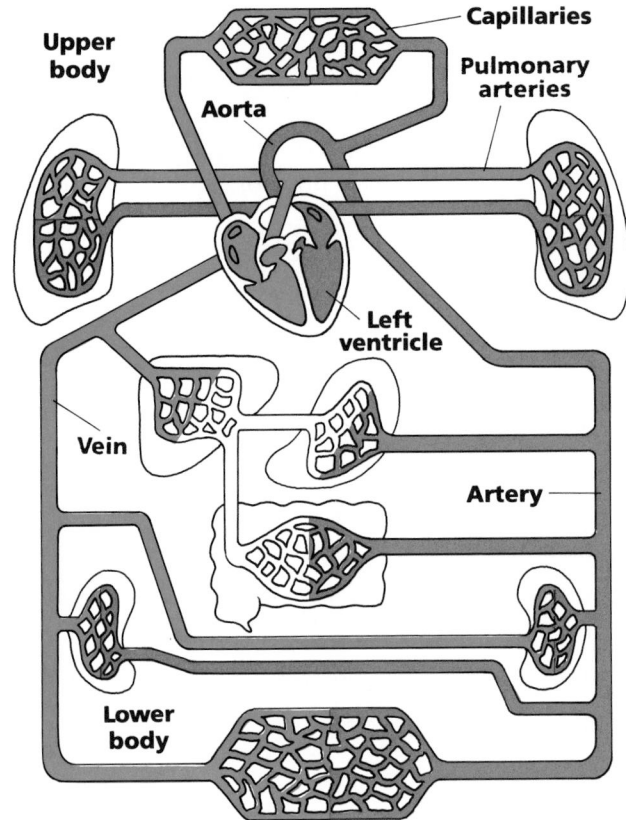

right ventricle. The right ventricle pumps blood into the **pulmonary** (PUL-muh-ner-ee) **artery.** The pulmonary artery is the artery that carries blood from the heart to the lungs. The pulmonary artery has two branches. One branch goes to each lung. In the lungs, the pulmonary arteries divide many times, until they form capillaries. As blood passes through these lung capillaries, it picks up oxygen and gives up carbon dioxide. The carbon dioxide is then exhaled from the body.

Once the blood has picked up a fresh supply of oxygen, it is ready to be circulated through the body again. The capillaries in the lungs join together to form veins. The pulmonary veins carry the blood from the lungs to the left atrium of the heart. The left atrium pumps blood into the left ventricle. The left ventricle pumps the blood throughout the body.

▶ *Identify:* Where does the blood pick up oxygen and get rid of carbon dioxide? lungs

LESSON SUMMARY

- Blood containing food and oxygen is pumped through the aorta to the body cells.

- As the blood goes through the capillaries, the exchange of food, oxygen, and carbon dioxide takes place.

- Blood containing carbon dioxide is returned to the heart through veins.

- In the lung capillaries, blood gives off carbon dioxide and picks up oxygen.

- Blood containing oxygen is returned to the heart to be circulated to the body again.

CHECK *Write true if the statement is true. If the statement is false, change the underlined word to make the statement true.*

1. Blood is pumped through the aorta to the <u>lungs</u>. body

2. Arteries divide many times until they form <u>capillaries</u>. true

3. Blood picks up oxygen in the <u>heart</u>. lungs

4. Blood is returned to the heart through <u>arteries</u>. veins

Complete the following.

5. Materials are exchanged between the blood and the body cells through the walls of _____ . capillaries

6. Blood is carried to the lungs by the _____ . pulmonary arteries

7. Blood leaving the right atrium passes into the _____ . right ventricle

APPLY *Complete the following.*

8. **Sequence:** Develop a flow chart that illustrates the flow of blood through the body and lungs.

9. What changes take place in the blood as it circulates?

Skill Builder

Building Vocabulary You can sometimes infer where an artery carries blood to, just by knowing its name. Some of the major arteries of the body include: carotid artery, femoral artery, bronchial artery, brachial artery, renal artery and coronary artery. Use library references to find out where each of these arteries carries blood in the body.

LEISURE ACTIVITY

AEROBIC EXERCISE

Aerobic (er-OH-bik) exercise is any activity that increases your heart rate and makes you breathe faster. There are many different kinds of aerobic exercise. Jogging, swimming, dancing, and walking briskly all are forms of aerobic exercise.

Aerobic exercise has many benefits. If you do aerobic exercise regularly, you will feel better. Other benefits include better physical shape, and a stronger heart. As your heart gets stronger, it pumps more blood with each beat. The heart does not have to beat as often because more blood is being pumped with each beat. This helps to keep the heart from overworking.

Aerobic exercise also can lower the risk of heart disease. Doctors believe that regular exercise lowers the amount of fatty materials in the blood. Removing fatty material from the blood helps keep them from building up on the walls of the blood vessels.

To get the most benefits from aerobic exercise, you should try to exercise at least three times a week. You should try to exercise for 30 minutes at a time. The important thing to remember is to pick an activity you enjoy.

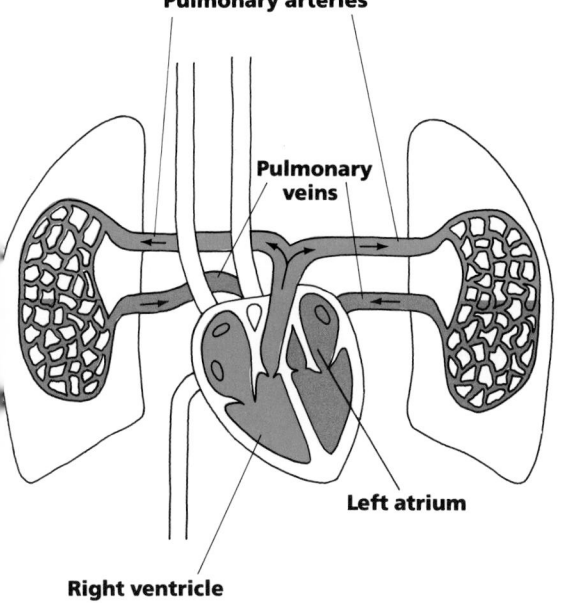

Pulmonary arteries

Pulmonary veins

Left atrium

Right ventricle

UNIT 13 Challenges

STUDY HINT Before you begin the Unit Challenges, review the TechTerms and Lesson Summary for each lesson in this unit.

TechTerms

aorta (258)
arteries (258)
atrium (256)
capillaries (258)
circulation (262)

closed circulatory system (262)
hemoglobin (260)
plasma (260)
platelets (260)
pulmonary artery (264)

septum (256)
valve (256)
veins (258)
ventricle (256)

TechTerm Challenges

Matching *Write the TechTerm that best matches each description.*

1. cell parts that control clotting platelets
2. iron compound in red blood cells that carries oxygen hemoglobin
3. liquid part of blood plasma
4. movement of blood through the body circulation
5. circulation of blood within blood vessels closed circulatory system
6. thick wall of tissue that separates the left and right sides of the heart septum
7. flap of tissue that prevents blood from flowing backwards valve

Fill in *Write the TechTerm that completes each statement.*

1. When it reaches the lungs, the _____ divides into two branches. pulmonary artery
2. Blood is pumped out of the heart by the _____ . ventricles
3. Blood vessels with thick muscular walls are _____ . arteries
4. The upper chambers of the heart are the _____ . atria
5. The blood vessels that carry blood back to the heart are the _____ . veins
6. The largest artery in the body is the _____ . aorta
7. The exchange of food, oxygen and wastes takes place through the _____ . capillaries

Content Challenges

Multiple Choice *Write the letter of the term that best completes each statement.*

1. The heart is divided into four
   a. valves. **b.** chambers. **c.** atria. **d.** ventricles. b

2. The instrument doctors use to listen to your heartbeat is a
   a. stethoscope. **b.** telescope. **c.** thermometer. **d.** centrifuge. a

3. When blood is pushed through the arteries, the resulting beat felt at the skin's surface is your
   a. blood pressure. **b.** heartbeat. **c.** pulse. **d.** contraction. c

4. The blood vessels through which blood flows at high pressure are
   a. arteries. **b.** veins. **c.** capillaries. **d.** valves. a

5. The tiniest blood vessels are
   a. arteries. **b.** veins. **c.** capillaries. **d.** valves. c

6. Disease-causing germs within the body are destroyed by
   a. red blood cells. **b.** hemoglobin. **c.** platelets. **d.** white blood cells. d

266

7. The substance that gives red blood cells their color is
   a. plasma. **b.** hemoglobin. **c.** iron. **d.** platelets. c

8. The circulatory system is made up of the heart, the blood vessels, and
   a. oxygen. **b.** hormones. **c.** blood. **d.** enzymes. c

9. The main job of the circulatory system is
   a. regulation of temperature. **b.** transport of blood. **c.** protection against disease.
   d. exchange of substances. b

10. In the lungs, blood picks up oxygen and gives off
    a. hormones. **b.** food. **c.** oxygen. **d.** carbon dioxide. d

True/False *Write true if the statement is true. If the statement is false, change the underlined term to make the statement true.*

1. The structures that prevent blood from flowing backwards in the heart are called <u>values</u>. true
2. Blood flows from the atria to the <u>ventricles</u>, then back into the body. true
3. The walls of arteries are <u>thinner</u> than the walls of veins. thicker
4. With each heartbeat, a pulse can be felt in a <u>capillary</u>. artery
5. Scientists use a <u>stethoscope</u> to separate blood into liquid and solid parts. centrifuge
6. Blood plasma is primarily made up of <u>digested nutrients</u>. water
7. Platelets help prevent the loss of blood by forming <u>clots</u>. true
8. The job of red blood cells is to carry <u>oxygen</u> throughout the body. true
9. A waste product carried away by the circulatory system is <u>carbon dioxide</u>. true
10. Blood is pumped into the pulmonary artery from the right <u>atrium</u>. ventricle
11. Inside the lungs, the blood picks up a fresh supply of <u>nutrients</u>. oxygen

Understanding the Features

Reading Critically *Use the feature reading selections to answer the following. Page numbers for the features follow each question in parentheses.*

1. What are two advantages of using blood plasma in a transfusion instead of whole blood? (261)
2. Name two of Charles Drew's contributions to the field of medicine. (261)
3. From his study of snakes, what conclusions did William Harvey reach concerning human circulation? (263)
4. **Infer:** Why might studying an animal such as a snake be useful in learning about humans? (263)
5. **List:** Identify three ways that regular aerobic exercise benefits the body. (265)

Concept Challenges

Critical Thinking *Answer each of the following in complete sentences.*

1. Trace the complete flow of blood from where it leaves the heart to where it enters the heart.
2. **Describe:** Describe the process of blood clotting.
3. **Predict:** What happens to the number of white blood cells in your body when you become sick? Why?
4. Explain how the circulatory system provides protection for the body.

Interpreting a Diagram *Use the diagram to answer each of the following.*

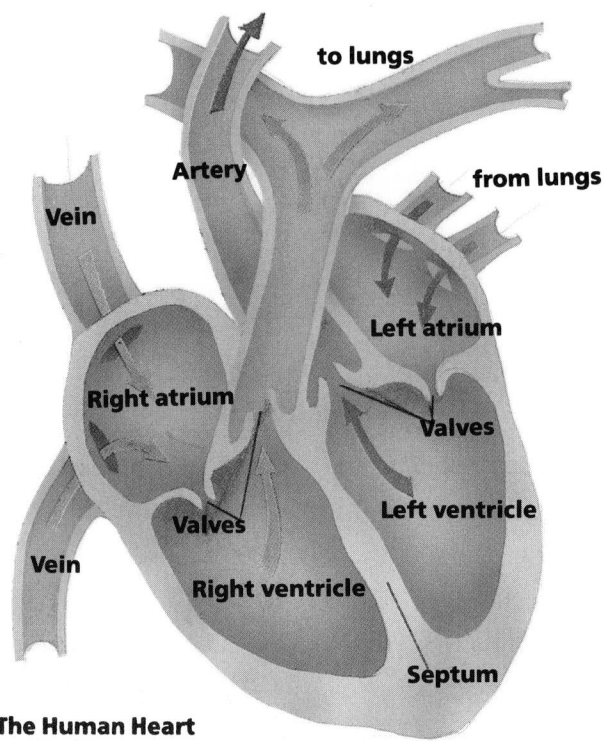

The Human Heart

1. What are the upper chambers of the heart called?
2. What are the lower chambers of the heart called?
3. **Describe:** Where is the septum located?
4. **Locate:** Where is the aorta located?
5. What is the job of the aorta?
6. Which chamber of the heart receives blood from the lungs?
7. In which direction does blood flow in the heart?
8. What blood vessels carry blood to the left atrium?
9. Is blood leaving the right ventricle carrying more oxygen or more carbon dioxide?
10. Is blood carried from the heart to the lungs by a vein or an artery?

Finding Out More

1. Two problems that could arise from circulatory system disorders are high blood pressure and heart attack. Using a first aid manual or other health book, do a report on one of these problems. Find out what causes the problem, what its symptoms and warning signs are, and how the problem can be prevented.

2. It is important to be aware of your blood pressure. Visit your doctor to find out what your blood pressure is. Be sure to ask the doctor to explain what both the top and bottom numbers mean in relationship to your heart activity and your health.

3. A stethoscope is one instrument doctors use to gather information about your circulatory system. What other instruments or tools are available to the medical profession to gather information on the circulatory system? Using a health book or other library reference book, find out about at least three of these instruments. List the three, giving a brief explanation of how each is used in the field of medicine.

4. The following words each have Latin origins: "pulmonary," "circulation," "vein," and "septum." Use a dictionary to find out the Latin word from which each of these words is derived. Then write the word and the meaning of the term from which each originated. Example: capillary—L. *capillus*—hair.

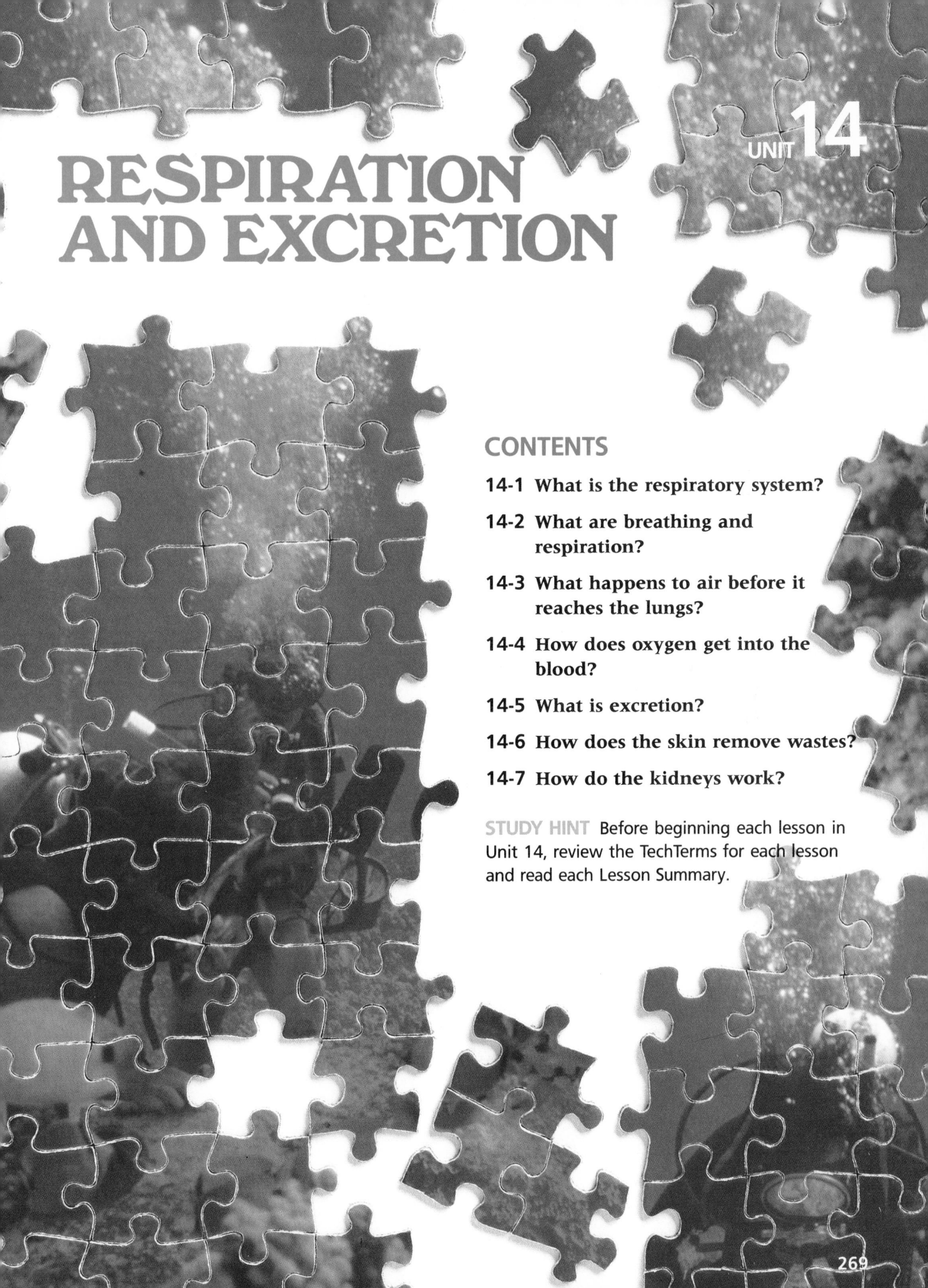

RESPIRATION AND EXCRETION

CONTENTS

STUDY HINT Before beginning each lesson in Unit 14, review the TechTerms for each lesson and read each Lesson Summary.

14-1 What is the respiratory system?

Objective ▶ Describe the parts of the respiratory system.

TechTerms

- ▶ **alveoli** (al-VEE-uh-ly): microscopic air sacs in the lungs
- ▶ **bronchi** (BRAHN-kee): tubes leading to the lungs

The Respiratory System Each time you breathe in your lungs fill with air. The lungs, tubes, and passageways through which air moves in your body make up the respiratory (RES-pur-uh-towr-ee) system. The job of this system is to take oxygen into the lungs and to get rid of carbon dioxide and water.

▰ *Analyze:* What are the waste products of respiration? water and carbon dioxide

Passages to the Lungs Air enters your body through your nose and mouth. Then air moves into your throat and enters the windpipe. The windpipe is a tube about 10 cm long. The end of the windpipe divides into two smaller tubes. These tubes are the **bronchi** (BRAHN-kee). Each bronchus extends into a lung.

👁 *Observe:* How many bronchi are there? 2

Lungs The lungs are the main organs of the respiratory system. In the lungs, the bronchi divide many times. The tubes become smaller and smaller. At the ends of the smallest tubes are microscopic air sacs. These air sacs are called **alveoli** (al-VEE-uh-ly). Each lung contains millions of alveoli.

▷ *Name:* What are the main organs of the respiratory system? lungs

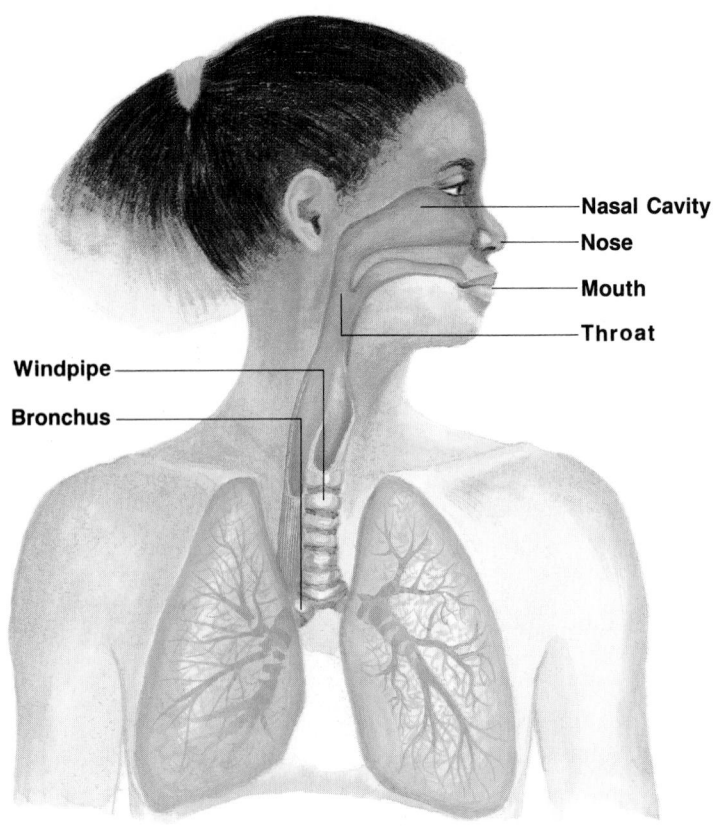

Nasal Cavity
Nose
Mouth
Throat
Windpipe
Bronchus

Right Lung   **Left Lung**

LESSON SUMMARY

▶ The respiratory system is made up of the lungs, tubes, and passageways through which air moves in the body.

▶ Air enters the body through the nose and mouth, and passes into the windpipe and bronchi.

▶ The lungs are the main respiratory organs.

CHECK *Complete the following.*

1. The organ system that helps you breathe is the _____ . respiratory system

2. Microscopic air sacs in the lungs are called _____ . alveoli

3. The windpipe branches into two tubes called _____ . bronchi

4. The main organs of the respiratory system are the _____ . lungs

5. Air enters the body through your mouth and _____ . nose

APPLY *Answer the following.*

6. **Sequence:** Place the following words in order to show how air moves in the body.

a. windpipe **b.** nose **c.** bronchi **d.** throat **e.** lungs **f.** alveoli

7. **Compare:** The windpipe, bronchi, and branches of the bronchi are sometimes called the bronchial tree. How is the arrangement of these structures similar to the arrangement of a tree? (Hint: Turn your textbook upside-down and carefully study the diagram of the respirator system.)

InfoSearch

Read the passage. Ask two questions that you cannot answer from the information in the passage.

Asthma Many people suffer from asthma (AZ-muh). Asthma usually is caused by something that irritates the smallest tubes in the lungs. The muscles in these tubes cause the tubes to get narrower. Air cannot pass easily into and out of the alveoli. Breathing becomes very difficult. Drugs often are used to help relax the muscles in the air tubes.

SEARCH: Use library references to find answers to your questions.

CAREER IN LIFE SCIENCE

RESPIRATORY THERAPIST

Few sensations are more frightening than not being able to get enough air into the lungs. A respiratory therapist works with doctors and other health care workers to help patients with breathing problems. Breathing problems can arise from diseases such as asthma or pneumonia. Accident victims or people recovering from surgery also may need help in breathing.

A respiratory therapist helps patients in different ways. A therapist may teach patients exercises that will help them to breathe more easily. A respiratory therapist also sets up and checks the various devices that are used to help treat patients with breathing disorders.

A respiratory therapist must be certified as a registered respiratory therapist, or RRT. Certification requires completion of a one- or two-year training program and then passing an examination. A respiratory therapist also should be able to work with others.

14-2 What are breathing and respiration?

Objectives ▶ Compare breathing and respiration. ▶ Explain the process of breathing.

TechTerms

▶ **diaphragm** (DY-uh-fram): sheet of muscle below the lungs

▶ **exhale:** to breathe out

▶ **inhale:** to breathe in

▶ **respiration** (res-puh-RAY-shun): the process of carrying oxygen to cells, getting rid of carbon dioxide, and releasing energy

Comparing Breathing and Respiration Breathing is the process by which air is taken into the body. It is a mechanical (muh-KAN-i-kul) process. When you breathe, oxygen is not carried to your cells. Breathing does not release energy for your body to use. Carrying oxygen to your cells, getting rid of carbon dioxide, and releasing energy is called **respiration** (res-puh-RAY-shun).

Respiration is a chemical process. It has three parts.

▶ **External Respiration** During external respiration, oxygen and carbon dioxide are exchanged between the lungs and the blood.

▶ **Internal Respiration** During internal respiration, oxygen and carbon dioxide are exchanged between the blood and the cells of the body.

▶ **Cellular Respiration** Cellular (SEL-yoo-lur) respiration is the chemical process by which energy is released by cells. The cells change food into energy. Carbon dioxide and water are given off as waste products.

👉 *Classify:* Is breathing a chemical or mechanical process? mechanical

The Diaphragm Below the lungs, there is a sheet of muscle. It is the **diaphragm** (DY-uh-fram). The diaphragm helps you breathe. It works

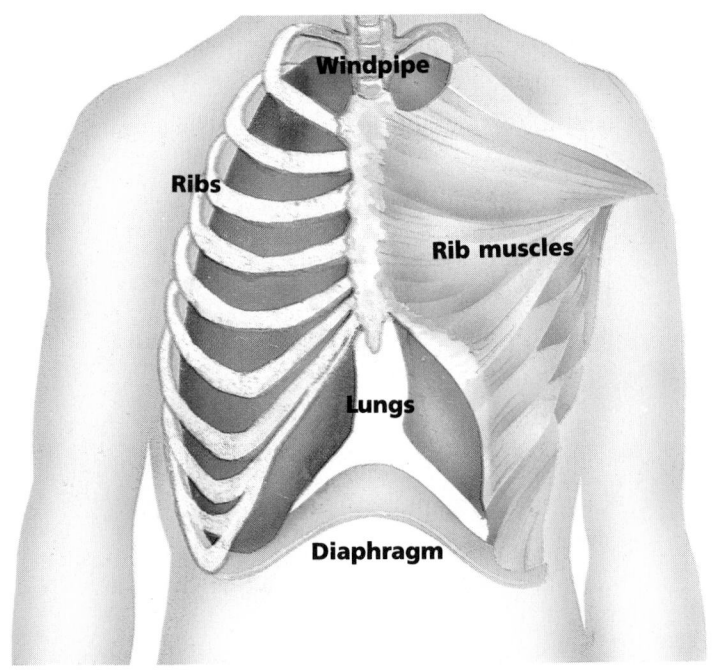

with the ribs and rib muscles. Many organs work together to help you breathe.

▶ *List:* What parts of the body work together to help you breathe? diaphragm, ribs, rib muscles

Breathing In When you **inhale,** or breathe in, your ribs move up and out. The diaphragm moves downward, away from the lungs. The space inside the chest becomes larger. Because of this, there is less air pressure in the lungs than outside the body. The outside air pressure causes air to rush into the lungs. The lungs fill with air and expand.

▶ *Define:* What does the word "inhale" mean? to breathe in

Breathing Out When you **exhale,** or breathe out, the ribs move down and in. The diaphragm moves upward, toward the lungs. The space inside the chest becomes smaller. Because of this, the air pressure in the lungs is greater than the air pressure outside the body. Air moves out of the lungs. The lungs contract and take up less space in the chest.

▶ *Describe:* What happens to the size of the space in the chest when you exhale? It gets smaller.

LESSON SUMMARY

► Breathing is the process by which air enters and leaves the body. Respiration is the process of carrying oxygen to cells, getting rid of carbon dioxide, and releasing energy.

► The diaphragm, ribs, and rib muscles work together to help you breathe.

► When you inhale, the lower air pressure in the lungs causes air to rush into the lungs.

► When you exhale, the air pressure in the lungs is higher than the air pressure outside the body, causing air to move out of the lungs.

CHECK *Find the sentence in the lesson that answers each question. Then, write the sentence.*

1. How does the diaphragm move when you exhale?

2. What is breathing?

3. Does breathing release energy?

4. What are the waste products of cellular respiration?

5. What happens to the space inside your chest when you inhale?

6. What does "inhale" mean?

7. What does "exhale" mean?

APPLY *Use the model to answer the questions.*

8. **a.** Which model shows inhaling? **b.** Which model shows exhaling?

9. What do the balloons represent?

10. What does the rubber sheet represent?

11. What does the jar represent?

Ideas in Action

IDEA: Breathing is a mechanical process. A mechanical process is one that involves only physical changes.

ACTION: List three examples of things that you do that involve only mechanical processes.

ACTIVITY

EXERCISE AND BREATHING RATE

You will need a watch or clock with a second hand.

1. **Measure:** Breathe in and out normally. Have a partner time the number of breaths you take in one minute. Record the number of breaths.

2. Jog in place for 20 seconds. Then stop. Have a partner time the number of breaths you take in one minute. Record this number.

3. Jog in place for 40 seconds. Then stop. Have a partner time the number of breaths you take in one minute. Record.

4. Change places with your partner and repeat the activity.

Questions

1. **a.** What was your breathing rate at rest? **b.** After 20 seconds of jogging? **c.** After 40 seconds of jogging?

2. **Compare:** How did your breathing rates compare to your partner's breathing rates?

3. **Analyze:** What effect does exercise have on breathing rate?

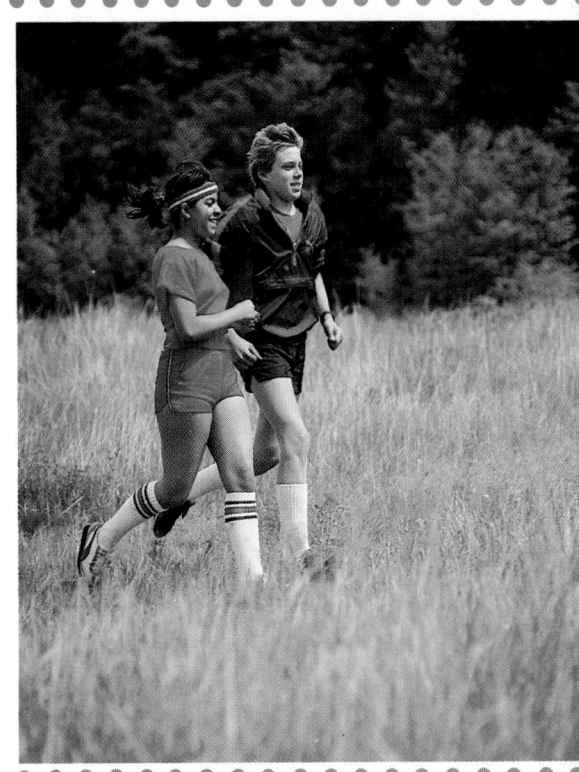

14-3 What happens to air before it reaches the lungs?

Objective ► Explain how air is cleaned, warmed, and moistened as it moves through the respiratory system.

TechTerms

- ► **cilia** (SIL-ee-uh): microscopic hairs
- ► **mucus** (MYOO-kus): sticky liquid

Filtering Air You normally breathe through your nose. The air that you breathe in contains dirt and dust particles. These particles may be harmful to the lungs. Inside your nose, there are many hairs. These hairs filter out and trap many dust and dirt particles.

► *Infer:* Why do you think that it is better to breathe through your nose than through your mouth? Nose hairs clean the air; there is nothing in the mouth to do this.

Mucus The cells inside the nose and windpipe form a sticky liquid called **mucus** (MYOO-kus). Mucus covers the inside of the nose and windpipe. Dust, dirt, bacteria, and other harmful particles stick to the mucus. Mucus stops many particles from reaching the lungs. Mucus also keeps the tissues of the respiratory system from drying out.

▐▐▶ *Explain:* What are the two jobs of mucus? cleans the air entering the body and keeps respiratory tissues moist

Cilia Many single-celled living things have **cilia** (SIL-ee-uh). Cilia are microscopic hairs on cells. Your windpipe is lined with millions of cilia. The cilia move back and forth, pushing mucus toward the nose. Trapped particles are pushed into the nose with the mucus. Some mucus with its trapped particles is swallowed.

Sometimes mucus can irritate your nose. When this happens, you respond by sneezing. A sneeze is a burst of air. Sneezing blows harmful particles out of the nose.

▐▐▶ *Name:* Where are cilia located in the respiratory system? windpipe

Warm, Moist Air Sometimes the air you inhale is cold and dry. When the air enters your body, it is warmed by heat from the body. Remember you are warmblooded. Your body works to keep your body temperature at about 37 °C, except when you have a fever. Air that enters the lungs has been warmed in your nose and throat. The body also

Dust filtered from air by nasal hairs

Cool, dry air

Cilia and mucus filter and moisten air

Warm, moist air

adds water vapor to the air you inhale. The air is made moist as it moves through the nose and windpipe. Air reaching the lungs is warm and moist. Warm, moist air prevents damage to the lungs.

► *Infer:* What happens to dry, warm air before it reaches the lungs? It is moistened.

LESSON SUMMARY

▶ Hairs in the nose filter dust particles from the air.

▶ Mucus in the nose and windpipe helps trap harmful particles contained in air.

▶ Cilia in the windpipe push mucus and trapped particles toward the nose.

▶ A sneeze is a burst of air that blows harmful particles out of the nose.

▶ Air that enters the body is warmed and moistened before it reaches the lungs.

CHECK *Complete the following.*

1. A burst of air that blows harmful particles out of the nose is a _____ . sneeze

2. The windpipe is lined with tiny hairs called _____ . cilia

3. Air that enters the lungs is warm and _____ . moist

4. The sticky liquid that traps harmful particles in the respiratory tubes is _____ . mucus

5. You normally breathe through your _____ . nose

APPLY *Complete the following.*

6. How is the air you breathe in changed before it reaches the lungs? It is warmed, moistened, and cleaned.

7. Which of the following have cilia?
   a. the human windpipe **b.** *Paramecium*
   c. sponges **d.** *Amoeba*

8. **Diagram:** Develop a flowchart that traces the pathway of air from the nose to the lungs. List each organ the air passes through. Beneath each organ, identify how air passing through the organ is changed.

Health & Safety Tip

Smoking is harmful to the lungs. Smoking can cause the cilia in the windpipe to stop moving. When this happens, dust, dirt, and germs are not removed. These substances are now able to get into the lungs. They may cause disease. Some diseases of the lungs can cause death. The choice you make about smoking can affect your health for years to come. Cigarette packages have warnings about the dangers of smoking. Make a list of the different warnings written on cigarette packs or in cigarette advertisements.

SCIENCE CONNECTION

RESPIRATORY DISEASES

Air taken into the body contains the oxygen needed for life. Air also can contain substances that may be harmful. Sometimes these substances cause respiratory diseases.

Asbestos (eh-SPEH-stahs) is a material that was used in the past to insulate buildings. Inhaling asbestos fibers can cause lung disease. Today, asbestos is being removed from buildings to eliminate the danger.

Tobacco smoking releases chemicals that can cause respiratory problems, too. You do not need to smoke the tobacco yourself. Just inhaling secondhand smoke—the smoke from another person's cigarette—can cause serious respiratory problems.

A study in 1992 by the Environmental Protection Agency showed that secondhand smoke causes asthma, especially in children. The study also showed that secondhand smoke causes lung cancer deaths in nonsmokers. Secondhand smoke has been linked to other health problems as well. These include brain tumors, birth defects, and sudden infant death syndrome. To protect nonsmokers, some states and many communities have passed laws to restrict smoking in public places.

14-4 How does oxygen get into the blood?

Objectives ▶ Explain gas exchange in the lungs and between the blood and body cells. ▶ Compare the gas makeup of inhaled air and exhaled air.

Oxygen in the Air Air is a mixture of gases. It is made up mostly of nitrogen and oxygen. Your body cells need oxygen to carry out respiration. Oxygen enters the lungs in the air you inhale. One of the jobs of the lungs is to take in oxygen from the air.

◢ *Analyze:* What percentage of air is made up of oxygen? 21%

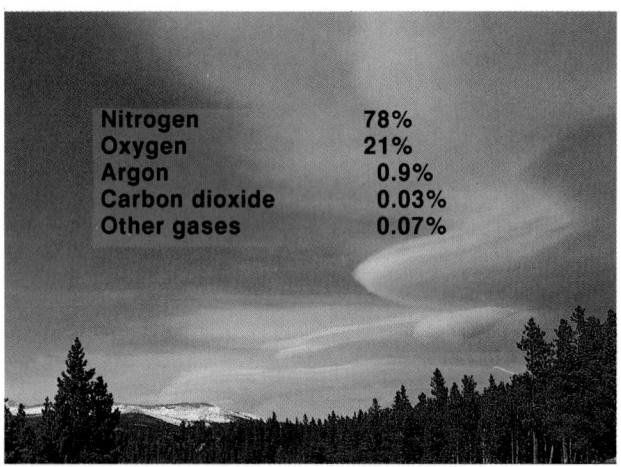

Nitrogen	78%
Oxygen	21%
Argon	0.9%
Carbon dioxide	0.03%
Other gases	0.07%

Alveoli The alveoli are where gases are exchanged in the lungs. Alveoli look like a bunch of grapes. The alveoli have very thin walls. They are surrounded by many capillaries. Capillaries are very tiny blood vessels. Red blood cells move through the capillaries in single file.

In the lungs, oxygen and carbon dioxide are exchanged between the alveoli and the blood. Oxygen molecules pass through the walls of the alveoli into the capillaries. The oxygen molecules attach to red blood cells. The red blood cells carry the oxygen to cells of the body. Carbon dioxide molecules pass from the red blood cells

through the capillary walls into the alveoli. The carbon dioxide is removed from your body when you exhale.

▶ *Describe:* What happens to oxygen molecules in the lungs? They pass into the blood in the capillaries.

Gas Exchange in Cells Oxygen and carbon dioxide are exchanged between the body cells and red blood cells. Oxygen moves from the red blood cells into the body cells. Carbon dioxide moves from the body cells into the capillaries. The carbon dioxide is carried back to the lungs.

▶ *Describe:* What happens to carbon dioxide molecules in the body cells? They pass into the blood in the capillaries.

Air In and Air Out The gas makeup of the air you breathe in is different from the gas makeup of the air you breathe out. Inhaled air contains more oxygen than does exhaled air. Exhaled air contains more carbon dioxide than does inhaled air. Some oxygen from the air you breathe in is removed by the lungs. Your body cells add carbon dioxide to the air you breathe out. Water also is added to the air you exhale.

◢ *Analyze:* Why is there more carbon dioxide in exhaled air than inhaled air? Carbon dioxide is produced as a waste product during cellular respiration.

Bronchiole

Alveoli   Air sac

▶ Air is a mixture of gases including nitrogen, oxygen, and carbon dioxide.

▶ The alveoli are the places where gases are exchanged in the lungs.

▶ In the lungs, oxygen and carbon dioxide are exchanged between the alveoli and the blood.

▶ Oxygen and carbon dioxide are exchanged between body cells and red blood cells at the capillaries.

▶ The air that you inhale has more oxygen and less carbon dioxide in it than the air that you exhale.

CHECK *Find the sentence in the lesson that answers each question. Then, write the sentence.*

1. What is air?

2. Where are gases exchanged in the lungs?

3. What are capillaries?

4. How is carbon dioxide removed from the body?

5. Does inhaled air contain more oxygen or more carbon dioxide than exhaled air?

6. Does exhaled air contain more oxygen or more carbon dioxide than inhaled air?

APPLY *Complete the following.*

7. How much of the air is made up of nitrogen?

▶ 8. **Infer:** Which percentages would most likely be inhaled air?
   a. 78% nitrogen; 21% oxygen
   b. 78% nitrogen; 17% oxygen

▶ 9. **Infer:** Which percentage would most likely be air you exhaled? How do you know?
   a. 21% oxygen; 0.03% carbon dioxide
   b. 17% oxygen; 4% carbon dioxide

Skill Builder....................................

Graphing A graph is a good way to organize information. Use the percentages of the gases contained in air shown on page 276 to make a graph of this data. Use either a bar graph or a pie graph.

ACTIVITY

ANALYZING EXHALED AIR

You will need a flat piece of glass, such as a window pane, 25 mL of limewater, a drinking glass, and a drinking straw.

1. Breathe out onto the flat piece of glass.

2. Add the 25 mL of limewater to the drinking glass. Limewater is used to test for carbon dioxide. If carbon dioxide is present, the limewater becomes cloudy.

3. Put the straw into the limewater. Gently blow through the straw into the glass of limewater. **Caution: Do not inhale while the straw is in the limewater.**

Questions

👁 1. **a. Observe:** What forms on the pane of glass? **b.** Where did it come from?

▶ 2. **Infer:** What happens to the limewater when you bubble exhaled air into it? Explain your answer.

▶ 3. **Infer:** What does this tell you about the air you exhale?

14-5 What is excretion?

Objective ▶ Understand how waste products are formed and removed by the body.

TechTerm

▶ **excretion** (ik-SKREE-shun): process of removing waste products from the body

Forming Waste Products Foods are combined with oxygen in your cells. Heat and other kinds of energy are produced. The energy is used by the body to carry out its life processes. When the foods are used to produce energy, waste products are formed.

Many waste products are formed by the cells of your body. Carbon dioxide and water are waste products of cellular respiration. Other waste products made by the cells are salts and nitrogen compounds. Heat also is a waste product.

▸ **List:** What are some waste products formed by your body? Answers will vary.

Excretion The many waste products formed by your body must be removed from your body. If these waste products build up in your body, they can be harmful to you. The process of removing waste products from the body is called **excretion** (ik-SKREE-shun).

▸ **Define:** What is excretion? process of removing waste products from the body

The Excretory System Removing waste products from the body is the job of the excretory system. It is made up of many different organs. The lungs are part of the excretory system. You know that the lungs get rid of carbon dioxide and water. The kidneys also are organs of the excretory system. They get rid of liquid wastes. The largest organ of the excretory system is your skin. It gets rid of liquid wastes and helps you get rid of extra heat.

▸ **List:** What are the three main organs of excretion? lungs, kidney, skin

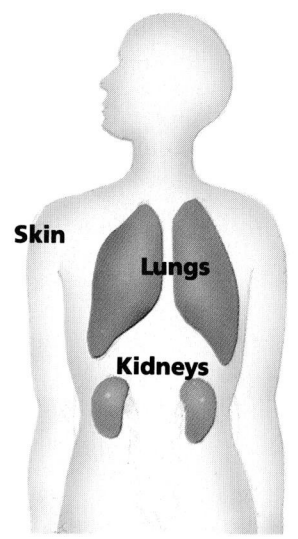

Solid Wastes Some parts of the foods that you eat cannot be digested. They cannot pass through the villi. Undigested foods form wastes. These wastes move along in the small intestine. They enter the large intestine. Water is removed from the wastes in the large intestine. As water is removed, the wastes become solid. The solid wastes move along in the large intestine and into the rectum. From there, the solid wastes are excreted through the anus (AY-nus).

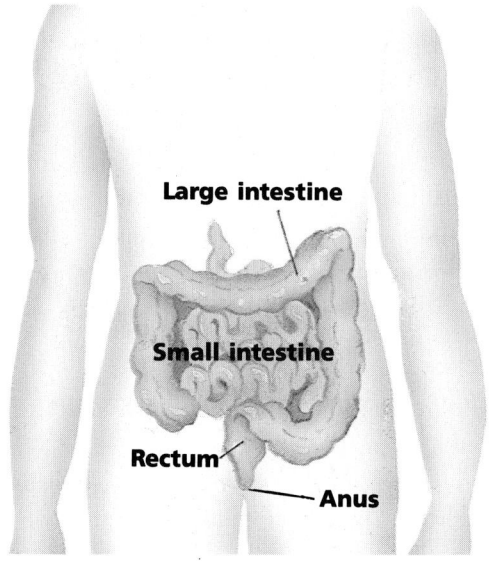

▸ **Describe:** What is the job of the large intestine? to remove water from undigested wastes

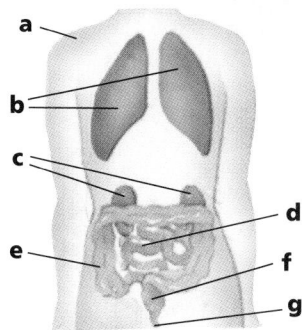

LESSON SUMMARY

▶ Waste products are formed as the body uses food to produce energy.

▶ Carbon dioxide, water, salts, nitrogen compounds, and heat are waste products formed by the body.

▶ Waste products are removed from the body in a process called excretion.

▶ The lungs, kidneys, and skin are the main organs of the excretory system.

▶ Solid wastes leave the body through the anus.

CHECK *Find the sentence in the lesson that answers each question. Then, write the sentence.*

1. What are the waste products of cellular respiration?

2. What is excretion?

3. What does the excretory system do?

4. What does skin do?

5. What is the job of the large intestine?

6. How do solid wastes leave the body?

APPLY *Use the letters in the diagram to answer the following questions.*

7. Which organs in the diagram excrete liquid wastes?

8. Which organ in the diagram is used to rid the body of excess heat?

9. Through which organ is solid waste excreted?

10. To what two organ systems do the lungs belong?

Ideas in Action

IDEA: Many of the things you use every day are thrown away as wastes.

ACTION: List five examples of products you dispose of as wastes. What happens to these products after you dispose of them?

TECHNOLOGY AND SOCIETY

USING SOUND TO BREAK APART KIDNEY STONES

Mineral compounds that are not excreted by the body can build up and form kidney stones. Kidney stones form inside the kidneys. Large kidney stones can completely block the passage of liquid wastes from the kidneys. Urine then backs up into the kidneys. Waste products can quickly destroy kidney cells.

Large kidney stones must be removed to prevent kidney damage. Medications are sometimes used to dissolve or break apart the stones. Unfortunately, these medications do not always work. Until recently, the only other way of eliminating kidney stones was to remove them surgically. However, doctors now have another way of removing kidney stones. Doctors carefully aim sound waves at the kidney stone. The sound waves cause particles in the stone to vibrate. The motion of the particles makes the stone break apart. The small parts of the kidney stone can then be passed from the body along with liquid wastes.

Kidney stones

14-6 How does the skin remove wastes?

Objective ▶ Explain why the skin is an organ of excretion.

TechTerms

- **evaporation** (i-VAP-uh-ray-shun): changing of a liquid to a gas
- **perspiration** (pur-spuh-RAY-shun): waste water and salts that leave the body through the skin
- **pore:** tiny opening in the skin

Perspiration Some waste water leaves your body through your skin. This waste water is called **perspiration** (pur-spuh-RAY-shun), or sweat. Perspiration is mostly water. It also contains salts.

▌▶ *Define:* What is perspiration? waste water and salts that leave the body through the skin

Sweat Glands Your skin contains many sweat glands. A sweat gland is a coiled tube surrounded by capillaries. Water molecules in the blood pass through the walls of the capillaries into the sweat gland. Each sweat gland extends to a tiny opening in the skin called a **pore.** Waste water leaves the sweat gland through the pore.

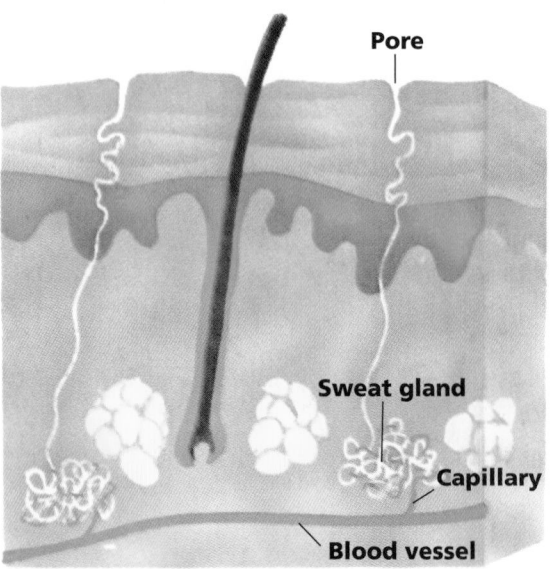

Pore

Sweat gland

Capillary

Blood vessel

▌▶ *Describe:* What is a sweat gland? coiled tube surrounded by capillaries

An Air Conditioning System Your body has a built in cooling system. When it is very hot, do you feel warm? Do you sweat after you exercise or do heavy work? Perspiration, or sweating, helps your body "cool off". The **evaporation** (i-VAP-uh-ray-shun) of perspiration from your skin cools the body. Evaporation is the changing of a liquid to a gas. As perspiration evaporates, it removes heat from your body.

❯ *Predict:* Are you likely to perspire if your body temperature drops below 37°C?

Explain. No; perspiration helps to cool the body. If the body temperature drops below 37°C, shivering helps to warm the body.

LESSON SUMMARY

- ▶ Perspiration is a waste excreted by the skin.
- ▶ Perspiration is formed by sweat glands and is excreted through pores in the skin.
- ▶ Evaporation of perspiration helps to cool the body.

CHECK *Complete the following.*

1. Perspiration, or sweat, is made up mostly of _____ . water

2. A sweat gland is a coiled tube surrounded by _____ . capillaries

3. Perspiration leaves the body through _____ in the skin. pores

4. The changing of a liquid to a gas is called _____ . evaporation

5. Evaporation of perspiration helps to _____ the body. cool

APPLY *Answer the following.*

6. **Infer:** When you are cold, you shiver. What do you think shivering does for the body?

7. **Hypothesize:** Why do you think it is important to take in more salts when the weather is hot?

Designing an Experiment

Design an experiment to solve the problem.

PROBLEM: Does your body perspire more heavily when you exercise?

You experiment should:

1. List the materials you would need.
2. Identify safety precautions that should be followed.
3. List a step-by-step procedure.
4. Describe how you would record your data.

Skill Builder

Building Vocabulary Use a dictionary to find the meanings of the terms "deodorant" and "antiperspirant." Write the definitions in your notebook. Use the definitions to explain how a deodorant differs from an antiperspirant.

ACTIVITY

EVAPORATION AND COOLING

You will need water, isopropyl alcohol and a cotton ball.

1. Hold two fingers in front of your mouth. Blow on them. Record which finger feels cooler.

2. Dip one finger in water. Blow on the wet finger and a dry finger. Record which finger feels cooler.

3. Wet the cotton ball with isopropyl alcohol. Wet one finger. Blow on the wet finger and a dry finger. Record which finger feels cooler.

4. Wet one finger with water and one finger with isopropyl alcohol. Blow on them. Record which finger feels cooler.

Questions

1. Did the finger wet with water or the dry finger feel cooler? Explain your answer.

2. Did the finger wet with water or the finger wet with isopropyl alcohol feel cooler? Explain your answer.

3. **a.** Which step is your control?   **b.** Why is it a control?

14-7 How do the kidneys work?

Objective ▶ Describe how the kidneys act as a filtering system for the blood.

TechTerms

- ▶ **urea** (yoo-REE-uh): nitrogen compound formed as a waste product
- ▶ **urine** (YOOR-in): liquid waste formed in the kidneys

The Kidneys You have two kidneys. Each kidney is about 10 cm long. The kidneys are located just above your waist. One kidney is behind your liver. The other is behind the stomach. The main job of the kidneys is to filter out wastes from the blood.

�III▶ *Identify:* What is the main job of the kidneys? to filter out wastes from the blood

Waste Liquid Like the skin, the kidneys help the body get rid of liquid wastes. The liquid waste formed in the kidneys is **urine** (YOOR-in). Urine is mostly water, but it also contains other materials. Urine contains many salts. Some of these salts give urine its yellow color. Urine also contains **urea** (yoo-REE-uh). Urea is a waste product formed when proteins are used by the body. It is a nitrogen compound.

▏III▶ *Name:* What is the liquid waste formed in the kidneys called? urine

Kidney Tubes The inside of each kidney is made up of millions of tiny tubes. Each tube has a small cup at one end. Many coiled capillaries are found inside each cup. Blood flows through the capillaries. Water and other materials are filtered out of the blood here. These materials move through the walls of the cup and into the tube.

▏III▶ *Sequence:* How do materials get into the kidney tubes? They move from the capillaries into the cup of the tubes.

Formation of Urine Water and other materials move through the kidney tube. The kidney tube is surrounded by capillaries. Some of the materials in the kidney tube are still needed by the body. These materials move out through the walls of the tube, back into the capillaries. These materials enter the blood again. Water, salts, and urea remain in the tube. This is urine. The urine forms in the kidney tube. Then it moves into the hollow, middle part of the kidney. Urine passes out of the kidneys through the ureters (yoo-REET-urz). Urine collects in the bladder. Urine passes out of the body through the urethra (yoo-REE-thruh).

▶ *Infer:* What happens to materials that pass from the kidney tube into the capillaries? They are carried to parts of the body where they are needed by the blood.

Coiled capillaries **Cup**

Vein **Artery** **Collecting tube**

Kidneys

Ureters

Urinary bladder

Urethra

LESSON SUMMARY

▶ The main job of the kidneys is to filter wastes from the blood.

▶ Urine is made up of water, salts, and a nitrogen compound called urea.

▶ Wastes are filtered out of the blood in tubes inside the kidneys.

▶ Urine formed in the kidneys leaves the body through the urethra.

CHECK *Choose the term that makes each statement true.*

1. Urea is a (nitrogen/protein) compound.
   nitrogen
2. You have (two/ten) kidneys. two
3. The kidneys help to get rid of (solid/liquid) wastes. liquid
4. The liquid waste formed in the kidneys is (urea/urine). urine
5. Urine leaves the body through the (urethra/ureters). urethra

6. Urine leaves the kidneys through the (urethra/ureters). ureters

APPLY *Complete the following.*

7. **Identify:** The urinary system excretes liquid wastes. What organs make up the urinary system?

▲ 8. **Model:** Develop a flowchart that traces the path of urine from the kidneys out of the body.

▶ 9. **Infer:** What element do you think is present in all proteins?

10. **Apply:** What happens to nutrients that are removed from the blood in the kidneys?

Ideas in Action

IDEA: Many things that you use every day have filters or use filters.

ACTION: List several objects that have filters. Explain what the filter does in each object.

TECHNOLOGY AND SOCIETY

DIALYSIS

A field of study that uses engineering ideas to help design machines that help or replace diseased organs is called biomedical engineering. Biomedical engineers have developed a machine that acts like a kidney. The machine is called a dialysis (dy-AL-uh-sis) machine. People who have lost their kidneys or have kidney damage are kept alive by using a dialysis machine.

A patient is connected to the machine by a tube. The tube is connected to an artery in the patient's arm. Blood from the artery flows into the tube to the dialysis machine. The machine filters the patient's blood, removing waste materials. The blood then flows out of the machine through a tube connected to a vein in the patient's arm.

Many people use a dialysis machine twice a week. However, some people need to use the machine more often. Depending on how serious kidney damage is, some patients need to use the machine every two days.

STUDY HINT Before beginning the Unit Challenges, review the TechTerms and Lesson Summary for each lesson in this unit.

TechTerms

alveoli (270)	excretion (276)	pores (276)
bronchi (270)	exhale (272)	respiration (272)
cilia (274)	inhale (272)	urea (278)
diaphragm (278)	mucus (274)	urine (278)
evaporation (276)	perspiration (276)	

TechTerm Challenges

Matching *Write the TechTerm that matches each description.*

1. microscopic air sacs in the lungs alveoli
2. breathe out exhale
3. tubes leading into the lungs bronchi
4. liquid waste excreted by the skin perspiration
5. sticky liquid mucus
6. liquid waste excreted by the kidneys urine
7. process of carrying oxygen to cells, getting rid of carbon dioxide, and releasing energy respiration
8. sheet of muscle below the lungs diaphragm

Fill-in *Write the TechTerm that best completes each statement.*

1. When you breathe in, you _____ . inhale
2. Tiny hair-like structures called _____ filter particles from air as the air passes through the windpipe. cilia
3. The removal of wastes from the body is called _____ . excretion
4. The changing of a liquid to a gas is called _____ . evaporation.
5. Perspiration leaves the body through openings in the skin called _____ . pores
6. A nitrogen waste that is found in urine is _____ . urea

Content Challenges

Multiple Choice *Write the letter of the term that best completes each statement.*

1. The waste products of cellular respiration are
   a. water and carbon dioxide.   **b.** water and oxygen.   **c.** salts.   **d.** nitrogen compounds. a

2. A sweat gland is a coiled tube surrounded by
   a. alveoli.   **b.** mucus.   **c.** capillaries.   **d.** cilia. c

3. Urine passes out of the body through the
   a. ureters.   **b.** urethra.   **c.** kidneys.   **d.** urea. b

4. Cilia are found in the
   a. lungs.   **b.** nose.   **c.** mouth.   **d.** windpipe. d

5. When you inhale, the
   a. ribs move up and out.   **b.** ribs move down and in.   **c.** diaphragm moves upward.   **d.** chest cavity becomes smaller. d

6. The largest organ of the excretory system is the
   a. large intestine.   **b.** kidney.   **c.** small intestine.   **d.** skin. d

7. Oxygen is carried to the cells of the body by
   a. white blood cells.   **b.** red blood cells.   **c.** alveoli.   **d.** cilia. b

8. Air enters the body through the
   a. lungs.   **b.** skin.   **c.** nose and mouth.   **d.** windpipe. c

9. The windpipe divides into two smaller tubes called
   a. alveoli.   **b.** capillaries.   **c.** bronchi.   **d.** ureters. c

10. Air reaching the lungs is
    a. cold and dry.   **b.** warm and moist.   **c.** cold and moist.   **d.** warm and dry. b

11. Oxygen and carbon dioxide are exchanged between the lungs and the blood during
    a. external respiration.   **b.** internal respiration.   **c.** cellular respiration.   **d.** breathing. a

12. Air is 21%
    a. oxygen.   **b.** carbon dioxide.   **c.** nitrogen.   **d.** helium. a

13. Air rushes into the lungs during
    a. inhalation.   **b.** exhalation.   **c.** cellular respiration.   **d.** evaporation. d

14. Alveoli are found in the
    a. bronchi.   **b.** lungs.   **c.** windpipe.   **d.** kidneys. b

15. The process of removing waste products from the body is called
    a. respiration.   **b.** digestion.   **c.** evaporation.   **d.** excretion. d

True/False *Write true if the statement is true. If the statement is false, change the underlined term to make the statement true.*

1. Breathing is a <u>chemical</u> process. mechanical
2. Inhaled air contains more <u>oxygen</u> than exhaled air. true
3. Water is removed from wastes in the <u>small</u> intestine. large
4. Perspiration is made up mostly of <u>salts</u>. water
5. The <u>lungs</u> are the main organs of the respiratory system. true
6. The chemical process by which energy is released by cells is called <u>cellular respiration</u>. true
7. Waste water leaves sweat glands through <u>capillaries</u>. pores
8. When particles irritate your nose, you respond by <u>sneezing</u>. true
9. Urea is a <u>protein</u> compound. nitrogen
10. When you <u>inhale</u>, the diaphragm moves upward. exhale
11. Urine collects in the <u>bladder</u> after passing out of the kidneys. true
12. The job of the respiratory system is to take <u>carbon dioxide</u> into the lungs. oxygen

Understanding the Features..

Reading Critically *Use the feature reading selections to answer the following. Page numbers for the features follow each question in parentheses.*

1. Why is asbestos being removed from buildings? (275)
2. **Define:** What is biomedical engineering? (283)
3. What are three ways to treat kidney stones? (279)
4. **List:** What are two diseases that can cause breathing problems? (271)

Concept Challenges

Critical Thinking *Answer each of the following in complete sentences.*

1. **Sequence:** Through what tubes and passageways does air pass from the outside of the body to the lungs?
2. How do mucus and cilia help you fight infection?
3. **Contrast:** What is the difference between breathing and respiration?
4. **Relate:** How do the respiratory system and circulatory system work together?
5. **Compare:** How is the skin like an air-conditioning system?

Interpreting a Diagram *Use the diagram to answer each of the following questions.*

1. Once air leaves the throat, where does it enter next?
2. What are the tubes that enter the lungs called?
3. **Locate:** Where are two places that air enters the body?
4. How does the nose help in purifying air?
5. Where are cilia found in the respiratory system?

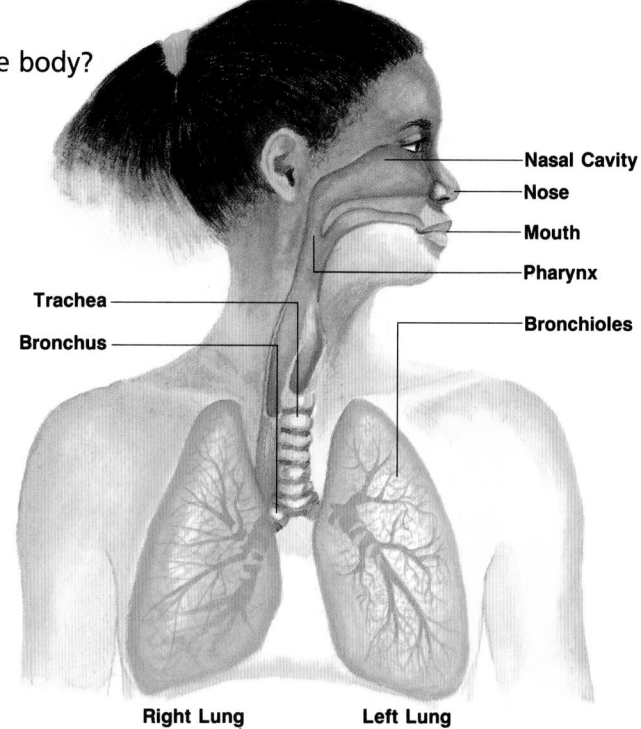

Nasal Cavity
Nose
Mouth
Pharynx
Bronchioles
Trachea
Bronchus
Right Lung   Left Lung

Finding Out More

1. If a person stops breathing, artificial respiration is necessary to save the person's life. Contact your local Red Cross Chapter to find out information about mouth-to-mouth resuscitation and other lifesaving techniques.
2. **Organize:** Pneumonia, bronchitis, emphysema, and tuberculosis are four respiratory diseases. Find out the symptoms, causes, and treatments for each of these diseases.
3. **Research:** At the top of the windpipe is an organ called the larynx. Using library references, find out why the larynx is important. Write your findings in a report.
4. **Model:** Using the diagrams in this unit as guides, make models of the respiratory system and the urinary system. Label each structure on your models.

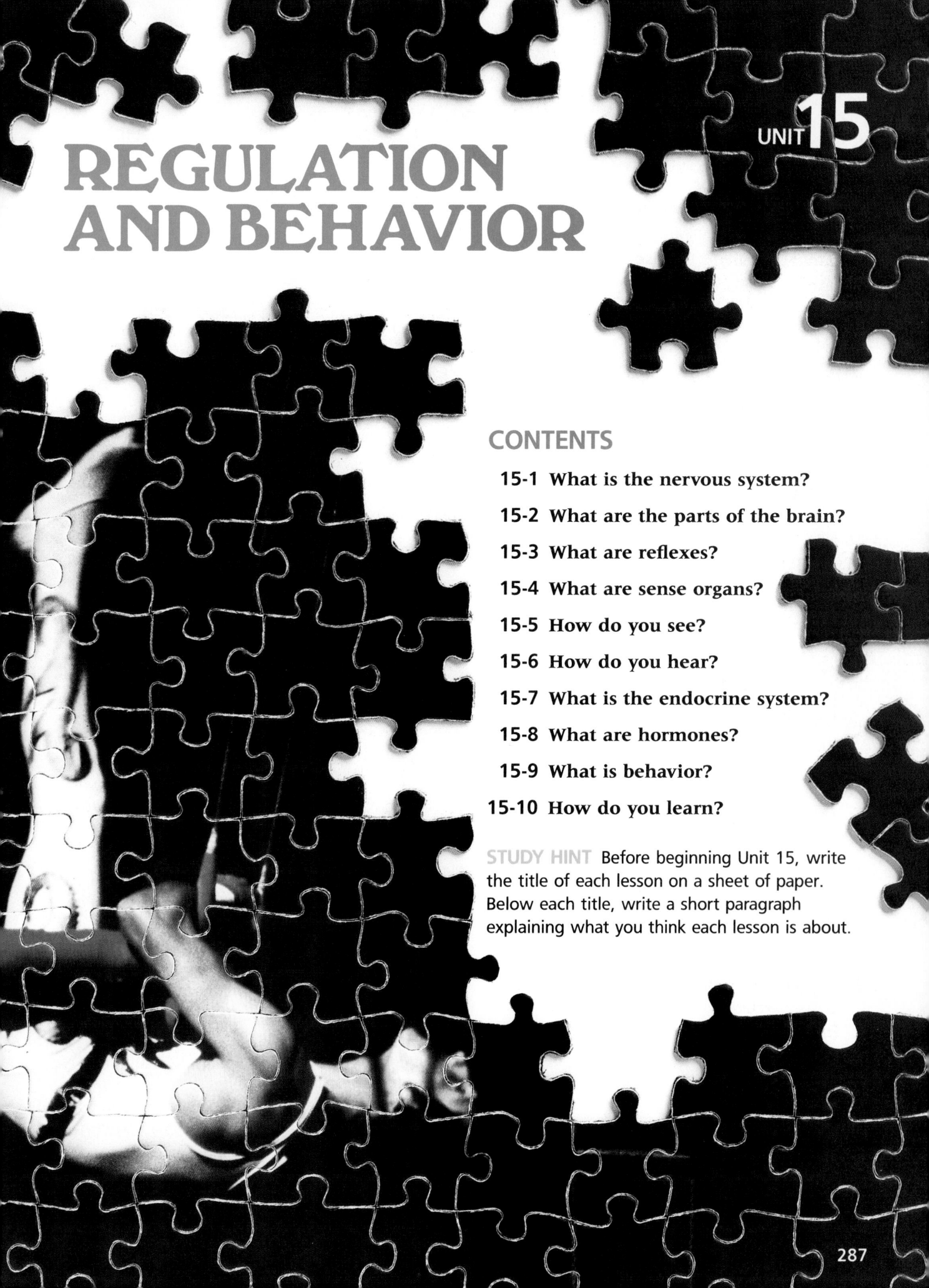

REGULATION AND BEHAVIOR

CONTENTS

STUDY HINT Before beginning Unit 15, write the title of each lesson on a sheet of paper. Below each title, write a short paragraph explaining what you think each lesson is about.

15-1 What is the nervous system?

Objectives ▶ Identify the function of the nervous system. ▶ Name the parts that make up the nervous system.

TechTerms

- ▶ **axon:** fiber that carries messages away from a nerve cell
- ▶ **dendrite** (DEN-dryt): fiber that carries messages from other neurons to the nerve cell body
- ▶ **neuron** (NOOR-ahn): nerve cell

The Nervous System Do you belong to an athletic team? Does your team have a captain? Most teams do. The captain gets information and makes important decisions. The team carries out the captain's orders. Your body works in a similar way. The nervous system is the captain of your body. The nervous system controls all of your body's activities.

The nervous system is shown in Figure 1. The nervous system is made up of the brain, the spinal cord, and nerves. Nerves carry information to the spinal cord and brain. Other nerves then carry messages from the brain and spinal cord to the muscles and glands in your body. The muscles and glands carry out the orders of the brain and spinal cord.

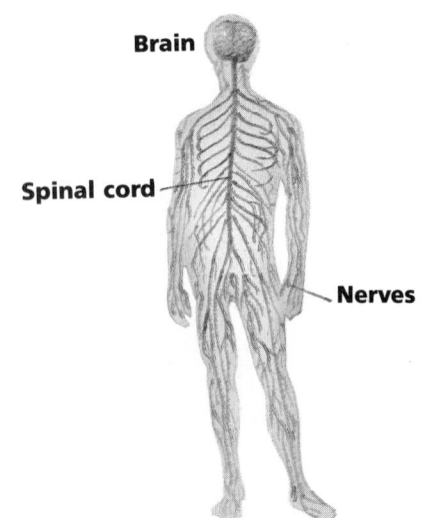

Figure 1 The nervous system

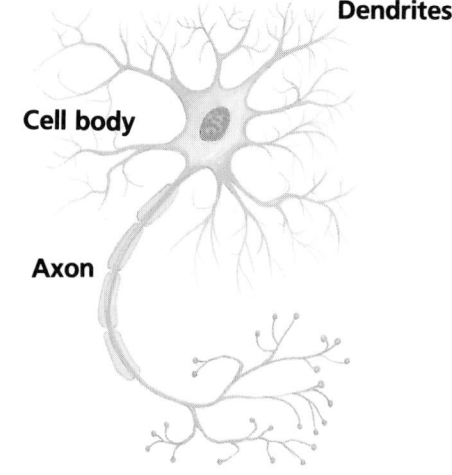

Figure 2 Structure of a neuron

▶ **Identify:** Name the parts of the nervous system. brain, spinal cord, and nerves

The Central Nervous System Your brain is the control center of your body. The brain is made up of a mass of nervous tissue. The brain is protected by your skull. The spinal cord is made up of many nerves that extend down your back. The spinal cord is protected by the backbone. The brain and spinal cord make up the central nervous system.

▶ **Name:** What structure protects the spinal cord? backbone

Nerve Cells Thirty one pairs of nerves branch out from your spinal cord. These nerves branch many times and extend to all parts of your body. Each of the nerves in your body is made up of nerve cells called **neurons** (NOOR-ahns). Neurons are the largest cells in your body. In fact, one neuron in your leg may be as long as 1 meter.

The job of a neuron is to carry messages. Messages travel through a neuron in only one direction. You can see the structure of a neuron in Figure 2. The **dendrites** (DEN-dryts) carry messages toward the nerve cell body, or center of the neuron. The **axon** carries messages away from the cell body. The cell body contains the nucleus of the neuron. It also contains most of the cytoplasm.

▶ **Describe:** Describe the structure of a neuron. Neurons are large cells made of a cell body, an axon, and dendrites.

LESSON SUMMARY

▶ The nervous system controls all of the body's activities.

▶ The nervous system is made up of the brain, the spinal cord, and nerves.

▶ The brain and spinal cord make up the central nervous system.

▶ A neuron is a nerve cell.

▶ Neurons are made up three parts: a cell body, an axon, and dendrites.

CHECK *Answer the following questions.*

1. What is the job of the nervous system? to control the body's activities

2. What are the parts of the nervous system? brain, spinal cord, nerves

3. What parts make up the central nervous system? brain and spinal cord

4. What is a neuron? nerve cell

5. How many pairs of nerves branch out from the spinal cord? 31

6. What are the parts of a neuron? cell body, axon, dendrites

Axon **Synapse** **Dendrites**

APPLY *Complete the following.*

7. **Infer:** What is the job of nerve tissue? to carry messages throughout the body

8. **Model:** Draw and label a neuron. Draw arrows on the diagram to show the direction a message travels through the neuron. Check students' drawings.

9. **Predict:** Unlike other body cells, nerve cells cannot reproduce themselves. What might happen if all of the nerve cells in your hand were destroyed? Answers may vary, but should include that control of the affected hand would be impossible.

InfoSearch

Read the passage. Ask two questions that you cannot answer from the information in the passage.

Synapses The axon of one nerve cell normally does not touch the dendrites of the next nerve cell. Usually, there is a small gap between the two cells. This gap is called a synapse (SIN-aps). Chemicals released by the axon help to carry messages across the synapse.

SEARCH: Use library references to find answers to your questions.

⁞⁞⁞ TECHNOLOGY AND SOCIETY ⁞⁞⁞ ⁞⁞⁞ ⁞⁞⁞ ⁞⁞⁞ ⁞⁞⁞ ⁞⁞⁞ ⁞⁞⁞ ⁞⁞⁞ ⁞⁞⁞ ⁞⁞⁞ ⁞⁞⁞

SEEING SOFT TISSUES

X-rays can take clear pictures of the bones, but soft tissues, such as the brain, do not show up as well. To see images of soft tissues, doctors use a technique known as magnetic resonance imaging, or MRI. This technique involves the use of magnets and radio waves to form pictures of organs. Using MRI, doctors can pinpoint the exact location of tumors in soft tissues. The picture shows an MRI image.

Another technique, called positron emission tomography or PET, is also used to study body organs, especially the brain. The patient is injected with glucose, a form of sugar. A computer records information about the movement of the glucose in the brain. The computer uses this information to make an image showing brain structure and activity. PET is used to diagnose brain tumors and strokes.

15-2 What are the parts of the brain?

Objective ▶ Identify and describe the functions of the three parts of the brain.

TechTerms

- ▶ **cerebellum** (ser-uh-BELL-um): part of the brain that controls balance and body motion
- ▶ **cerebrum** (suh-REE-brum): large part of the brain that controls the senses and thinking
- ▶ **medulla** (muh-DULL-uh): part of the brain that controls heartbeat and breathing rate

The Brain The main job of the brain is to receive and interpret messages. These messages may come from inside or outside your body. Your brain responds to the messages and then controls all of your body's activities. For example, movement, thinking, breathing, and sleeping all are controlled by your brain.

The brain often is called the control center of the body. The brain is made up of three main parts. These parts are the cerebrum (suh-REE-brum), the cerebellum (ser-uh-BELL-um), and the medulla (muh-DULL-uh). Each part of the brain performs a different function.

▦▶ **Identify:** What is the main job of the brain? to receive and interpret messages

The Cerebrum The largest part of the brain is the **cerebrum.** You can see in the diagram that the cerebrum makes up more than two-thirds of the brain. The cerebrum has two main jobs. One job of the cerebrum is to interpret information from the sense organs. Your sense organs are your eyes, ears, nose, tongue, and skin. A second job of the cerebrum is to control thinking. Your cerebrum helps you learn, remember, and make decisions.

▦▶ **Identify:** What are two jobs of the cerebrum? to interpret information from the senses and to control thinking

The Cerebellum The part of the brain located at the back of the brain is the **cerebellum.** The cerebellum controls all body movements. The cerebellum also helps to maintain balance. As your body changes position, the cerebellum receives messages. Then the cerebellum sends messages out to your muscles. The muscles work to help you keep your balance.

▦▶ **Locate:** Where is the cerebellum located? at the back of the brain

The Medulla The smallest part of the brain is the **medulla.** It is made up of nerves from the cerebrum and cerebellum. These nerves form a thick stalk at the base of the skull.

The medulla connects the brain to the spinal cord. The medulla controls digestion, breathing, and heartbeat rate. It also controls the activities of many glands and muscles.

▦▶ **Classify:** Does the medulla control voluntary or involuntary body activities? involuntary

Cerebrum

Cerebellum

Medulla

LESSON SUMMARY

▶ The main job of the brain is to receive and interpret messages from inside and outside the body.

▶ The brain is the control center of the body.

▶ The cerebrum is the large part of the brain that controls the senses and thinking.

▶ The cerebellum is the part of the brain that controls body motion and balance.

▶ The medulla is the small part of the brain that connects the brain and spinal cord and controls heartbeat rate, digestion, and breathing.

CHECK *Find the sentence in the lesson that answers each question. Then, write the sentence.*

1. What are the three parts of the brain?
2. What is the largest part of the brain?
3. Where is the cerebellum located?
4. Where is the medulla located?
5. What is the main job of the brain?
6. What are the sense organs?

APPLY *Identify the part of the brain that controls each of the actions described.*

7. You memorize someone's telephone number. cerebrum
8. You walk to the store. cerebellum
9. You breathe faster when you run. medulla
10. You smell smoke. cerebrum
11. You taste butter in your food. cerebrum
12. Your heart rate increases as you ride your bicycle. medulla
13. You begin to fall, but then regain your balance. cerebellum

Skill Builder

▶ *Inferring* When you infer, you form a conclusion based upon fact. Think about the functions of the brain. Then, identify how your body might be affected if the cells making up the medulla of your brain were damaged. Describe how a loss of function of the medulla would affect you.

ACTIVITY

MODELING THE BRAIN

You will need a piece of cardboard, clay of three colors, toothpicks, tape, paper, and a pencil.

▲ 1. **Model:** Using the drawing on page 290 as a guide, draw an outline of the brain on the cardboard. Be sure to include the cerebrum, medulla, and cerebellum in your drawing.

2. Place a piece of clay on top of your cardboard outline. Use the outline to mold the clay into the shape of one part of the brain.

3. Repeat Step 2 for each of the other parts of the brain. Use a different color clay for each part.

4. Cut three rectangles from the paper. Label these cerebrum, medulla, and cerebellum. Use tape to attach each rectangle to a toothpick. Label the parts of your model by placing each toothpick in the clay.

Questions

👁 1. **a. Observe:** Which part of the model is the largest? **b.** Why?

2. **Relate:** If you were to add to your model, what part of the nervous system would come next?

3. To which part of the nervous system does the medulla connect?

15-3 What are reflexes?

Objectives ▶ Define reflex. ▶ Relate reflexes to the stimuli that cause them.

TechTerms

- ▶ **reflex:** automatic response to a stimulus
- ▶ **reflex arc:** path of a message in a reflex
- ▶ **response:** action caused by a stimulus
- ▶ **stimulus** (STIM-yuh-lus): any action that causes a response

Stimuli and Responses Do you jump at a sudden loud noise? Does your mouth water when you smell food? Do you pull your hand away quickly if you touch something hot? Loud sounds, the smell of food, and heat all are examples of stimuli (STIM-yu-ly). A **stimulus** is any action that causes you to react in some way. The reaction to a stimulus is called a **response**.

▶ *Relate:* How are stimuli and responses related? Stimuli cause responses.

Reflexes Some responses are simple. You cannot control them. They happen without you thinking about what you are doing. An automatic response to a stimulus is called a **reflex.**

A reflex usually is a response that protects you in some way. For example, when dust gets into your nose, you sneeze. Dust is a stimulus. Sneezing is the response. Sneezing helps to prevent harmful substances from entering your lungs.

Figure 1 Tearing is a reflex

When dirt gets into your eyes, you blink. Your eyes may also water, or form tears. Blinking your eyes and forming tears are your body's way of protecting your eyes from harmful substances. Sneezing, blinking, and tearing are examples of reflexes.

▶ *Apply:* Is answering a ringing telephone an example of a reflex? Explain. No; answering a telephone involves thinking.

A Reflex Arc Reflexes usually occur very quickly. One reason reflexes occur so quickly is that they do not involve the brain. Reflexes are controlled by the spinal cord. You can trace the path of a reflex in Figure 2.

4. Response: Hand pulled back

3. Message carried to muscle

2. Message carried to spinal cord

Spinal cord

1. Stimulus received by receptor

Figure 2 A reflex arc

When a reflex takes place, nerves and muscles work together. The stimulus is received by special nerve cells called receptors (ree-SEP-tors). Other nerve cells carry a message to the spinal cord. Another nerve carries a message from the spinal cord to a muscle or a gland. A muscle causes you to move some part of your body. A gland may make your mouth or eyes water. The message travels along a path formed by nerve cells. This path is called a **reflex arc.**

◉ *Observe:* What is the stimulus in Figure 2? What is the response? touching the hot pan; pulling the hand away

LESSON SUMMARY

- ▶ Any action that causes a response is a stimulus.
- ▶ An automatic response to a stimulus is called a reflex.
- ▶ Most reflexes help to protect the body from harm.
- ▶ Reflexes are controlled by the spinal cord.
- ▶ The path of a message in a reflex is called a reflex arc.

CHECK *Write true if the statement is true. If the statement is false, change the underlined term to make the statement true.*

1. A reflex is a <u>voluntary</u> response. automatic
2. Reflexes usually work to <u>protect</u> you. true
3. The path of a message in a reflex action is called a <u>reflex arc</u>. true
4. Any reaction to a stimulus is a <u>reflex</u>. response
5. Any change that causes a response is a <u>reflex</u>. stimulus
6. Stimuli are received by special nerve cells called <u>receptors</u>. true

APPLY *Complete the following.*

7. **Relating Cause and Effect:** Identify the stimulus and the response in each statement.
   a. You step on a tack and pull your foot away.
   b. You open the door after hearing a knock.
   c. You blink when a bright light is shined in your eyes.
   d. Food in your windpipe causes you to cough.

Designing an Experiment

The pupil of your eye controls how much light enters your eye. The pupil changes size in response to different amounts of light.

Design an experiment to solve the problem.

PROBLEM: How does the size of the pupil change as the amount of light in a room changes?

Your experiment should:

1. List the materials you would need.
2. Identify safety precautions that should be followed.
3. List a step-by-step procedure.
4. Describe how you would record your data.

┅ TECHNOLOGY AND SOCIETY

TREATING SPINAL INJURIES WITH BIONICS

A broken or damaged spinal cord can leave a person paralyzed, or unable to move. The nerve signals needed to move muscles can no longer get through the spinal cord to the brain. The degree of paralysis depends on where in the spinal cord the damage occurs. A person might be paralyzed from the neck down or from the waist down.

The science of bionics, or computerized replacements for injured body parts, has given some paralyzed patients new hope. For a patient unable to walk, doctors connect wires to muscles needed for walking. These wires are connected to a small computer attached to the chest. Instead of passing through the spinal cord on the way to the brain, nerve signals pass through the computer. The computer sends signals back to the muscles, making them move.

Researchers continue to improve the use of bionics. Two treatments showing promise are transplanting nerve cells from other parts of the body and using transplanted fetal cells to grow new nerve cells. These treatments have been tried only on laboratory animals. These and other treatments offer hope to those with spinal cord injuries.

15-4 What are sense organs?

Objective ▶ Name the five sense organs and their jobs.

TechTerm

▶ **receptor** (ree-SEP-tor): organ that receives stimuli from the environment

Sense organs Sound, light, and temperature are examples of stimuli. Stimuli are messages. You have special organs that receive stimuli from your environment. These organs are the sense organs. The sense organs are the eyes, nose, skin, ears and tongue.

▶ *Name:* What are the sense organs? eyes, ears, skin, nose, and tongue

Jobs of the Sense Organs Sense organs work to help you respond to your environment. Sense organs are called **receptors** (ree-SEP-tors) because they receive things. Each sense organ receives certain kinds of messages. The eyes receive pictures of things you look at. These pictures are formed by changes in light. The nose is used for smell. Your skin responds to changes in temperature and pressure. Your skin also responds to pain and touch. Your ears receive sounds from the environment. Your tongue helps you identify different tastes.

▶ *Describe:* What do sense organs do? receive stimuli from the environment

Senses Work Together Your senses do not work alone. What do you do when you walk into a darkened room? Your hands reach out to touch things that might be in front of you. Your ears listen for the slightest sound. Your eyes search the dark for some sign of light. Your senses work together to help you.

Your senses help you gather many different kinds of information about your surroundings. In this way, your senses help you to learn. Much that you see, hear, taste, smell, and feel is stored in your mind. This information becomes part of your memory. You remember things when you need to use them. Using information gathered by the senses is important for your safety and for all the things you do.

▶ *Explain:* How do your senses help you to learn? Accept all logical responses.

LESSON SUMMARY

▶ The sense organs are the eyes, nose, skin, ears, and tongue.

▶ Sense organs are used to receive stimuli from the environment.

▶ Your senses work together to help you.

▶ Your senses help you to learn.

CHECK *Match each sense organ to the kind of message it receives.*

1. pain, temperature, pressure, and touch e
2. smell d
3. sounds b
4. tastes a
5. changes in light c

   a. tongue
   b. ears
   c. eyes
   d. nose
   e. skin

Complete the following.

6. Sense organs receive stimuli from the _____ . environment

7. Sense organs are examples of _____ . receptors

8. Your sense organs work _____ to help you. together

APPLY *Complete the following.*

9. How do you think the senses work together? Accept all logical responses.

10. What four senses does the skin detect? pain, pressure, touch, and temperature

11. How does your skin cause your body to respond to cold temperatures? you shiver

InfoSearch

Read the passage. Ask two questions that you cannot answer from the information in the passage.

Taste Buds Your tongue is covered with receptors called taste buds. Your taste buds can detect only four tastes: sweet, sour, bitter, and salty. The taste buds that detect each taste are located at different parts of your tongue. Your taste buds cannot taste dry foods. They can only taste foods that are moist. Dry foods do not have a taste. For this reason, foods must be dissolved in water before your taste buds will recognize the food.

SEARCH: Use library references to find answers to your questions.

ACTIVITY

LOCATING TASTE RECEPTORS

You will need colored pencils or markers in four colors, a glass, water, 4 cotton swabs, sugar, lemon juice, table salt, and tonic water.

▲ 1. **Model:** Make a drawing representing your tongue.

2. Wet a cotton swab in the water. Place the cotton swab in the sugar. Touch your tongue with the cotton swab. Observe what part of your tongue detects the sweetness of the sugar. Shade in this part of the tongue in your drawing.

3. Rinse your mouth with water.

4. Repeat Steps 2 and 3 for the table salt.

5. Dip a cotton swab in the lemon juice. Touch the swab to your tongue as you did in Step 2. Rinse your mouth.

6. Repeat Step 5 using the tonic water.

Questions

👁 1. **Observe:** Describe the taste of each substance using the terms salty, bitter, sweet, and sour.

2. **a. Compare:** Look at the models made by two of your classmates. How are your models the same?   **b.** How are your models different?

15-5 How do you see?

Objective ► Name and describe the functions of the parts of the eye.

TechTerms

- **cornea** (KOR-nee-uh): clear covering at the front of the eye
- **iris** (Y-ris): part of the eye that controls the amount of light entering the eye
- **lens:** part of the eye that forms an image on the retina
- **pupil** (PYOO-pil): opening in the center of the iris
- **retina** (RET-in-uh): part of the eye on which images form.

The Eyes The eyes are the organs of sight. The eyes work by responding to light. In order to see an object, your eyes must respond to light from that object. Different parts of the eye work together to form an image, or a picture from this light. Your brain then receives messages from your eye and interprets what you are looking at.

▦▶ *Identify:* What are the eyes? organs of sight

Parts of the Eye Different parts of the eye work together to help you see. Figure 1 shows the parts of the eye. As you read about each part of the eye, locate that part on Figure 1.

- **Cornea** The **cornea** (KOR-nee-uh) is a clear covering at the front of the eye.
- **Iris** Behind the cornea is a round, colored disk called the **iris** (Y-ris). The iris controls the amount of light entering the eye.
- **Pupil** At the center of the cornea is a hole called the **pupil** (PYOO-pil). Light must pass through the pupil to get to the inside of your eye.
- **Lens** After light passes through the pupil it passes through the **lens** of the eye. The lens forms an image from the light entering the eye.

- **Retina** At the back of the eye is the **retina** (RET-in-uh). The lens of the eye forms images on the retina. The retina responds to the light by generating nerve signals.
- **Optic Nerve** Nerve signals formed by the retina are carried to the brain by the optic nerve. The brain then interprets the signals it receives from the optic nerve and tells you what you are seeing.

▦▶ *Sequence:* List, in the correct order, the parts of the eye through which light passes. cornea, iris, pupil, lens

Protecting the Eyes The eyes are protected in many ways. The bones of the face extend in front of the eyes. These bones keep large objects from hitting and damaging the eyes. Eyelids and eyelashes help keep small pieces of matter from entering the eyes. Any particles that do reach the eyes usually are washed away by tears. Tears also keep the eyes from becoming too dry.

▦▶ *Identify:* How do the bones of the face protect the eyes? They extend in front of the face to keep large objects from entering the eyes.

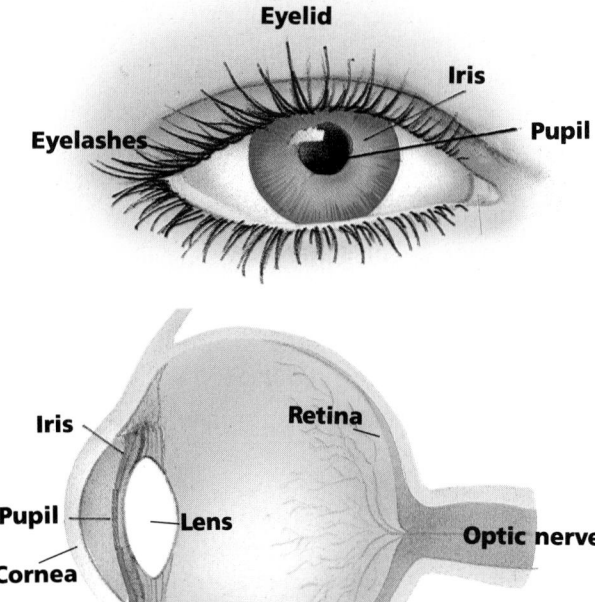

Figure 1 Parts of the eye

LESSON SUMMARY

▶ The eyes are the organs of sight.

▶ Different parts of the eye work together to help you see. The main parts of the eye are the cornea, iris, pupil, lens, retina, and optic nerve.

▶ The eyes are protected by the eyelids, eyelashes, tears, and the bones of the face.

CHECK *Complete the following.*

1. The eyes work by responding to _____ . light

2. The clear covering at the front of the eye is the _____ . cornea

3. The size of the pupil is controlled by the _____ . iris.

4. Images are formed on the part of the eye called the _____ . retina

5. Nerve signals from the eye are carried to the brain by the _____ . optic nerve

APPLY *Answer the following.*

👁 6. **Observe:** What color are the pupils of your eyes? black

👁 7. **Observe:** What color are your irises? Answers will vary.

8. What structure of the eye forms images on the retina? lens

Skill Builder ....

Applying Definitions Look up the word "lens" in the dictionary. Write the definition in your notebook. How does the function of the lens of your eye compare to the function of lenses made of glass?

Skill Builder ....

Applying Concepts Many people wear eyeglasses to correct vision problems. Two problems often corrected with eyeglasses are myopia and astigmatism. Use a dictionary or library references to find out what these terms mean. Then, try to find out what features eyeglasses must have to correct these problems.

ACTIVITY

ANALYSING OPTICAL ILLUSIONS

You will need a metric ruler and a pencil.

👁 1. **Observe:** Look at Figure 1. Which line appears longer?

2. Look at Figure 2. Which are longer?

3. Look at Figure 3. Which post is tallest?

4. Measure and record the length of each line in Figure 1.

5. Trace the top arc in Figure 2 on a piece of tracing paper. Place the top arc over the bottom arc. Describe your observation.

Questions

1. **a.** Which line looked longer than the other? **b.** How long is each line?

2. Are the arches the same size?

3. **a.** Which post looked shortest? **b.** Which looked tallest? **c.** How tall was each post?

4. Explain why your eye was fooled by the optical illusion in each figure.

Figure 1   Figure 2

Figure 3

15-6 How do you hear?

Objective ▶ Describe the jobs of the main parts of the ear.

TechTerms

▶ **cochlea** (KOK-lee-uh): part of the ear that changes vibrations into nerve signals

▶ **eardrum:** sheet of tissue that vibrates when sounds strike it

The Ears The ears are the organs of hearing. The three sections of the ear are the outer ear, the middle ear, and the inner ear. Locate each of these sections on Figure 1.

Each part of the ear has a different job. As you read about the jobs of the parts of the ear, locate each part on Figure 1.

The **outer ear** gathers sounds. The larger the outer ear, the more sound it can gather. Rabbits have larger outer ears than humans. This is one reason why rabbits have better hearing than humans. Between the outer ear and the middle ear is a thin sheet of tissue called the **eardrum.** The eardrum vibrates when sound waves hit it. The ear bones are three small bones in the middle ear. When the eardrum vibrates, it makes the ear bones vibrate also.

A coiled structure called the **cochlea** (KOK-lee-uh) is located in the inner ear. The cochlea receives the vibrations of the ear bones. The cochlea changes vibrations to nerve signals. The nerve signals are sent to the brain. The brain interprets the signals so you can understand what the signals mean.

▶ **State:** What makes the ear bones vibrate?
sound waves

Sound Waves When someone speaks to you, sound waves are formed. The sound waves are different for each word. These sound waves travel in the air and are gathered by your outer ear. They make your eardrum vibrate. Your ear bones also vibrate. The vibrations are different for each word. The cochlea changes these vibrations into nerve signals. The signals are sent to the brain. The brain figures out what the signals mean.

▶ **Identify:** What happens when signals are sent to the brain? The brain figures out what the signals mean.

What You Hear Some sounds are too soft to hear. Their vibrations are not strong enough to make your eardrums vibrate. No signal is sent to the brain. You hear nothing. Other sounds are too high-pitched to hear. The cochlea cannot change these sounds into nerve signals. You do not hear anything.

▶ **Explain:** Why are soft sounds not detected by the ear? Soft sounds are not strong enough to make the eardrum vibrate.

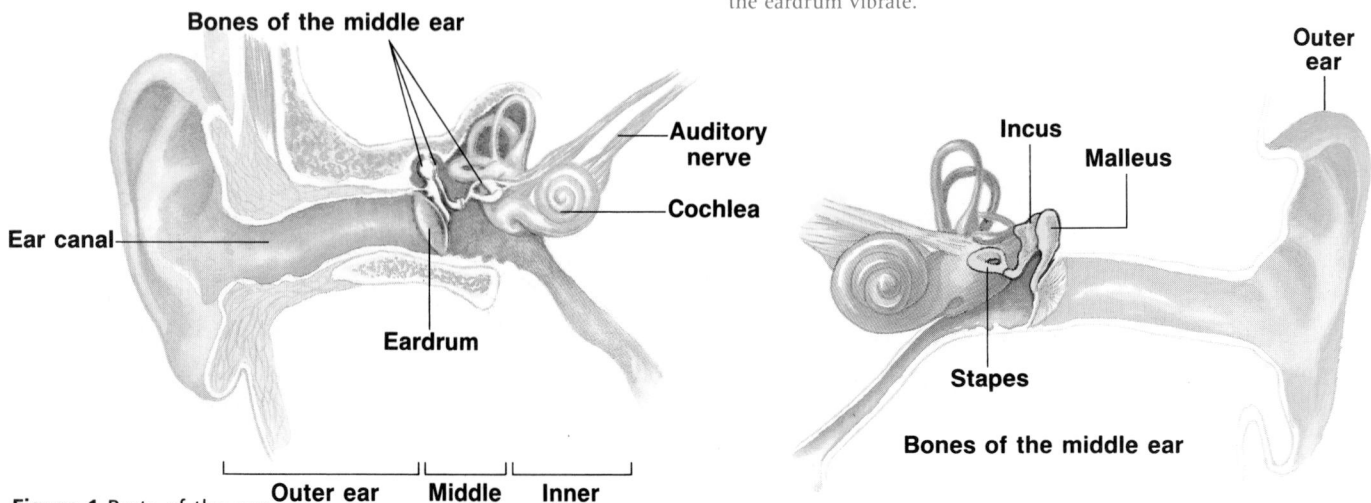

Figure 1 Parts of the ear

LESSON SUMMARY

▶ The ears are the sense organs of hearing.

▶ Each part of the ear has a different job.

▶ The outer ear gathers sounds.

▶ The ear bones and cochlea are parts of the middle ear.

▶ Some sound waves are too soft or too high-pitched to hear.

CHECK *Complete the following.*

1. The sense organs of hearing are _____ . the ears

2. The three main parts of the ear are _____ . the outer ear, the middle ear, and the inner ear

3. The cochlea receives the vibrations of the ear bones and changes them to _____ . nerve signals

4. Ear vibrations changed to nerve signals are sent to the _____ . brain

APPLY *Complete the following.*

5. How do a rabbit's large ears help it to hear?

6. Why can't we hear certain kinds of sounds?

7. What is the brain's role in hearing?

InfoSearch

Read the passage. Ask two questions that you cannot answer from the information in the passage.

Hearing in Animals Many animals have ears that are different from the human ear. Many animals can hear higher-pitched sounds than can humans. Many animals also can hear softer sounds than can humans.

SEARCH: Use library references to find answers to your questions.

Health & Safety Tip

Loud sounds can be damaging to the ears. Many people who work in noisy environments must wear devices to protect their ears. Use library references to find out at what level sounds may damage the ears. Also, find out how you can protect your ears from damage by loud noises.

TECHNOLOGY AND SOCIETY

HEARING AIDS

Anything that stops part of the ear from working can cause deafness. Each part of the ear is needed for good hearing. Sometimes the ear can be damaged but still work a little bit. This is partial deafness. Sometimes deafness is caused by an infection of the ear bones. After the infection, the bones may no longer be able to vibrate.

Deafness sometimes can be corrected by surgery. Damaged parts of the ear often can be repaired or replaced. Materials have been made to replace damaged parts of the ears. Sometimes replacement parts are made from plastic.

Partial deafness can often be corrected by using hearing aids. Hearing aids are like small radios that fit near or into the ear. They make sounds louder, so that even damaged parts of the ear may vibrate.

15-7 What is the endocrine system?

Objective ▶ Describe the function of the endocrine system.

TechTerms

▶ **endocrine** (EN-duh-krin) **gland:** gland that does not have ducts

▶ **gland:** organ that makes chemical substances used or released by the body

Glands with Ducts A **gland** is an organ that makes substances used or released by the body. Some glands have ducts, or tubes. Substances made by these glands leave the gland through the ducts. Your skin has many sweat glands. Perspiration, or sweat, is made by these glands. Sweat moves from the sweat gland to the surface of the skin by passing through a duct. Salivary (SAL-uh-ver-ee) glands also have ducts. Saliva passes from the salivary glands into the mouth through these ducts.

▶ *Name:* What are two glands that have ducts? Answers may vary, but probably will include the sweat and salivary glands.

Endocrine Glands Some glands do not have ducts. Glands that do not have ducts are called **endocrine** (EN-duh-krin) **glands.** Substances made by endocrine glands pass from the glands directly into the bloodstream. The blood vessels

then carry the substances to the parts of the body where they are needed.

▶ *Identify:* How do substances made by endocrine glands get to other parts of the body? they pass directly into the blood, which carries substances to other parts of the body

The Endocrine System There are only about ten endocrine glands in the human body. Together, these glands make up the endocrine system. Most of the glands that make up the endocrine system are shown in Figure 1.

▶ *Observe:* Where are the adrenal glands located? in the abdominal region

Control for Body Functions The job of the endocrine system is to help control bodily functions. Each gland in the endocrine system has a different job. The way each gland works is similar to the way a thermostat and a furnace work. If the temperature of a room goes down, the thermostat signals the furnace to turn up the heat. The "thermostat" of the body is the hypothalamus (hy-puh-THAL-uh-mus). If the hypothalamus senses a need for a certain chemical substance in the body, it stimulates an endocrine gland to produce that chemical.

▶ *State:* What is the function of the endocrine system? to help control body functions

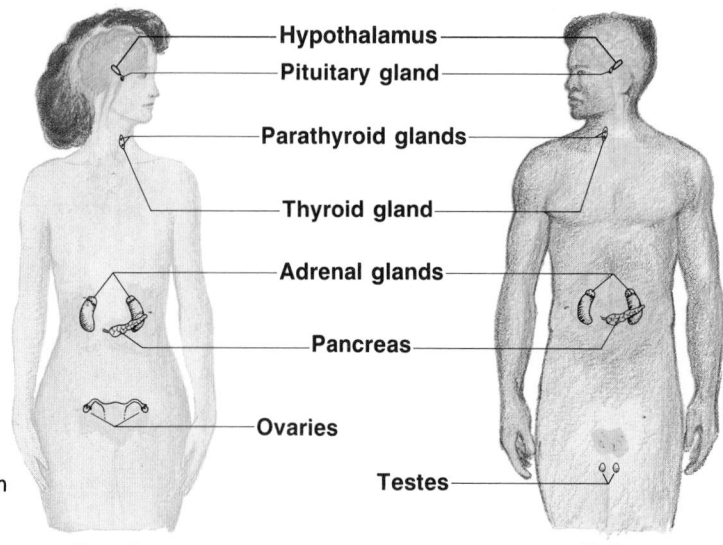

Figure 1 The endocrine system

Female

Male

LESSON SUMMARY

▶ A gland is an organ that makes substances used or released by the body.

▶ Substances formed by endocrine glands pass directly into the blood.

▶ About ten glands make up the human endocrine system.

▶ The job of the endocrine system is to help control body functions.

CHECK *Write true if the statement is true. If the statement is false, change the underlined term to make the statement true.*

1. An organ that makes substances used or released by the body is called a <u>gland</u>. true

2. Glands that do not have ducts are called <u>exocrine</u> glands. endocrine

3. The substances made by endocrine glands are carried by <u>ducts</u> to other parts of the body.
blood vessels

4. <u>Sweat</u> glands are endocrine glands. any gland shown on p. 300

5. There are about <u>ten</u> endocrine glands in the body. true

APPLY *Use the diagram of the endocrine system on page 300 to answer the questions.*

6. **Observe:** What endocrine glands are found only in males?

7. **Observe:** Where is the pituitary gland located?

8. **Identify:** Which glands are found in pairs in the body?

9. The prefix "para-" means "by the side of." Based on this information, where do you think the parathyroid gland is located? beside the thyroid

Skill Builder..

Using Prefixes A prefix is a word part placed at the beginning of a word. Knowing what the prefix means provides a clue to the meaning of the entire word. Look up the prefixes "endo-" and "exo-" in the dictionary. Write the meanings of these prefixes in your notebook. Next, review what you have learned about endocrine glands and about glands with ducts. Glands with ducts are called exocrine glands. How will knowing the meanings of "endo-" and "exo-" help you remember the two types of glands?

⠿ TECHNOLOGY AND SOCIETY ⠿ ⠿ ⠿ ⠿ ⠿ ⠿ ⠿ ⠿ ⠿ ⠿ ⠿ ⠿ ⠿

HUMAN GROWTH HORMONE

One hormone produced by the pituitary gland is human growth hormone, or HGH. During childhood, the pituitary gland releases HGH. The amount of HGH released determines how tall a child will grow.

In some children, the pituitary gland does not release enough HGH. As a result, the children's bones and tissues grow very slowly. Without treatment, the children would not grow to normal heights. For many years, children who lacked HGH were treated with injections of the hormone. Unfortunately, there was not enough HGH available to treat all the children suffering from an HGH deficiency.

In 1982, scientists were able to produce HGH in laboratories by genetic engineering. Using genetic techniques, scientists got bacteria to produce large amounts of HGH. As a result, supplies of this hormone greatly increased. Today, a child whose pituitary gland does not produce enough HGH has a good chance of reaching normal height.

15-8 What are hormones?

Objectives ▶ Define hormones. ▶ Explain some of the jobs of hormones.

TechTerm

▶ **hormone** (HAWR-mohn): chemical substance that regulates body functions

Hormones The chemical substances made by the endocrine glands are called **hormones** (HAWR-mohns). Hormones affect many of your body's functions. For example, growth hormone, which is made by the pituitary (pi-TOO-uh-ter-ee) gland, controls how fast and how much you grow.

▶ *Define:* What is a hormone? chemical substance made by an endocrine gland

Jobs of Hormones Growth hormone is only one of many hormones made by your body. Hormones may speed up a body function or slow it down. Other hormones do other jobs. Insulin (IN-suh-lin) is a hormone made by the pancreas. Insulin is

needed to keep a balanced amount of sugar in the blood. Still other hormones regulate other glands. Table 1 shows some of the different hormones of the body and what each hormone does.

▶ *Infer:* What do you think would happen if a person had too much growth hormone? person would grow very tall

Table 1 Hormones and What They Do		
GLAND	HORMONE	JOB OF HORMONE
Pineal	Melatonin	Helps regulate pituitary gland
Pituitary	Growth hormone	Controls the growth of bones
	ATCH	Controls the release of hormones from the adrenal glands
Thyroid	Thyroxin	Controls rate of body growth
Parathyroid	Parathyroid hormone	Controls the amount of calcium and phosphorus in the blood
Thymus	Thymosin	Controls growth of certain white blood cells
Adrenal	Adrenalin	Controls muscle reaction, blood clotting, and blood pressure
Pancreas	Insulin	Controls blood sugar levels

Reproductive Hormones Some hormones control the development of reproductive organs. The glands that control reproductive organs are different in men and women. Men have glands called testes (TES-teez). The testes produce a hormone called testosterone (tes-TAWS-tur-ohn). Females have glands called ovaries (OH-vuhr-eez). Ovaries produce hormones called estrogen (ES-truh-jun) and progesterone (proh-JES-tur-ohn).

▶ *State:* What hormone does the testes produce? testosterone

LESSON SUMMARY

▶ Hormones, produced in endocrine glands, control many of the body's activities.

▶ Each hormone has a specific job.

▶ Ovaries and testes produce hormones that control the development of reproductive organs.

CHECK *Complete the following.*

1. A chemical substance that regulates body functions is called a _____ . hormone

2. Insulin is made by the _____ . pancreas

3. The two endocrine glands that produce substances that develop reproductive organs are testes and _____ . ovaries

4. Testes are glands found only in _____ . males

5. Ovaries are glands found only in _____ . females

Answer the following.

6. How are insulin and blood sugar level related?

7. What is the job of growth hormone?

APPLY *Use the table of hormones on page 302 to answer the questions.*

8. **Classify:** Which hormones are found in both males and females and which are found in only one sex or the other?

9. **Infer:** What health problems might someone have if the pituitary gland produced too much or too little growth hormone?

10. **Analyze:** What hormone is needed to release adrenal hormones?

11. **Analyze:** What gland produces thymosin?

InfoSearch

Read the passage. Ask two questions that you cannot answer from the information in the passage.

Thyroxine Thyroxine is the hormone made in the thyroid gland. Thyroxine regulates growth and metabolism. Metabolism refers to the rate at which your body cells use and produce energy. If too little thyroxine is produced, the body metabolism slows down.

SEARCH: Use library references to find answers to your questions.

TECHNOLOGY AND SOCIETY

INSULIN PUMPS AND PENS

The pancreas releases a hormone called insulin. Insulin helps your body use sugar properly. If the pancreas does not produce enough insulin, sugar stays in the blood instead of passing to the body's cells. When the cells do not get enough sugar, a person may become weak, lose weight, and be very hungry and thirsty. A person suffering from this illness has diabetes (dy-ah-BEET-eez).

Diabetes is serious, but it can be treated. One kind of diabetes must be treated with a carefully balanced diet, regular exercise, and daily insulin injections.

Some diabetics use an insulin pump in place of injections. Insulin pumps are computerized pumps about the size of a call-beeper. They can be worn on a belt or in a pocket. The pump is connected to a small needle that is placed in the skin and taped in place. Insulin pumps release very small amounts of insulin continuously as the body needs it. Another way of getting insulin is through an insulin pen. The pen resembles a cartridge pen, but instead of a writing point, the insulin pen has a needle to inject the insulin. Instead of an ink cartridge, it has an insulin cartridge.

15-9 What is behavior?

Objective ▶ Describe the two main kinds of behaviors.

TechTerms

- **conditioned** (kun-DISH-und) **response:** learned behavior in which a new stimulus causes the same response that an old one did
- **innate behavior:** behavior you are born with
- **learned behavior:** behavior you practice and learn

Reflexes Everything you do is part of your behavior. There are two main kinds of behavior. One kind of behavior is called inborn, or **innate behavior.** An innate behavior is a behavior you are born with. Reflexes are innate behaviors. Reflexes are automatic responses. You do not learn to make these responses. You cannot control the response. A reflex does not involve any learning or thought. Crying, coughing, swallowing, sneezing, and blinking all are innate behaviors.

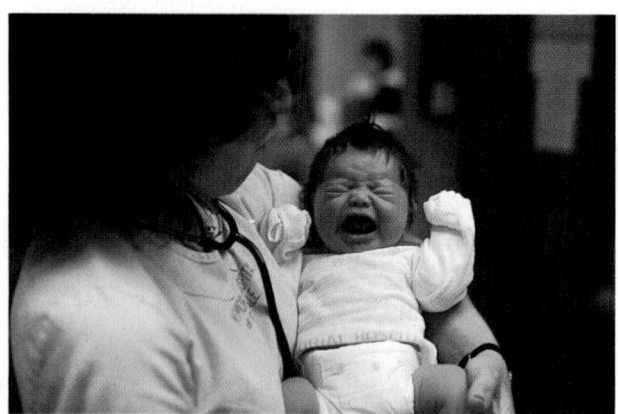

▶ **Identify:** What kind of behavior is a reflex? innate

Learned Behavior Many of your responses are not automatic. You must learn to make these responses. These responses are called **learned behavior.** You are learning new responses all the time. Learned behavior must be practiced. You also can change learned behavior. Throwing a ball, reading a book, and playing games are examples of learned behaviors.

▶ **Describe:** What are learned behaviors? behavior you practice and learn

Conditioned Responses A **conditioned** (kun-DISH-und) **response** is one kind of learned behavior. In a conditioned response, one stimulus takes the place of another. Ivan Pavlov, a Russian scientist, experimented with this kind of behavior. Pavlov observed that when a dog smells food, its mouth waters. Pavlov decided to ring a bell before he fed the dog. Pavlov repeated this pattern many times. After a while, Pavlov observed something new in the dog's behavior. Whenever the dog heard the bell, its mouth watered, even if there was no food. The dog soon learned that the sound of the bell meant it would be fed. The dog was responding to a new stimulus. The bell took the place of the food. This was a conditioned response.

▶ **Explain:** In Pavlov's experiment, why did the ringing bell cause the dog's mouth to water? the dog expected to be fed

LESSON SUMMARY

▶ A reflex is an innate, or inborn, behavior.

▶ Learned behavior must be practiced.

▶ A conditioned response is a kind of learned behavior.

CHECK *Write true if the statement is true. If the statement is false, change the underlined term to make the statement true.*

1. The two main kinds of behavior are innate behavior and <u>reflexes</u>. learned behavior

2. A new stimulus causes the same response that an old one did in a <u>conditioned response</u>. true

3. Ivan Pavlov studied <u>innate behavior</u> in dogs. conditioned responses

4. A conditioned response is an example of the kind of behavior called <u>learned behavior</u>. true

5. Behavior that can be changed is <u>innate</u>. learned

APPLY *Complete the following.*

6. Which type of behavior, innate or learned, would follow most quickly an accident like stepping on a sharp object?

▶ 7. **Predict:** How would your classmates learn to behave if each time a student was late the teacher awarded that student an "A" for the day?

Ideas in Action

IDEA: Learning to read is a learned behavior.
ACTION: List ten other activities that you have mastered using learned behavior.

PEOPLE IN SCIENCE

B. F. SKINNER (1904-1990)

B. F. Skinner was an American psychologist. He spent many years studying the way animals learn and demonstrated that the behavior of animals is greatly influenced by learning. During the 1930s, Skinner performed important experiments with rats. One of the experiments involved placing a hungry rat in a special box known as a Skinner box. Inside the box was a lever. Behind the lever was food. When the rat was first put in the box, it ran around nervously. While moving, the rat accidentally touched the lever and food dropped into the box. The rat soon learned that pressing the lever caused food to appear.

During the 1950s, Skinner studied how humans learn. He concluded that people learn difficult tasks in a manner similar to that of the rats. Skinner concluded that the easiest way for a person to learn a complex task is to receive rewards after completing each step of the task. He supported the use of teaching machines in the classroom. A teaching machine presents difficult material in a series of small steps. After each step, a student must respond to questions. A teaching machine rewards correct answers.

15-10 How do you learn?

Trial and Error Have you ever borrowed a bunch of keys and then forgotten which one to use? What did you do? You take any key and try it. If it does not open the lock, you try another key. You keep trying the keys until you find the right one. In this way you learn which key to use without being told. This is called trial and error learning. Each time you make an error, you try something else.

▶ **Describe:** What is trial and error learning?
Kind of learning in which each time you make an error, you try something else.

Memory Do you memorize (MEM-uh-rize) things easily? How long does it take you to memorize something? How many of your friends' telephone numbers do you know without looking them up? You memorize things by studying them carefully or by repeating them many times. Memorizing is another way of learning.

▶ **Explain:** How do you memorize things?
Answers will vary. Accept all logical responses.

Reasoning Reasoning is not the same as trial and error learning or memorizing. Reasoning means solving a problem by thinking about it. You solve the problem by putting together things you have learned in the past. Reasoning can be used to save time in solving problems. Suppose you are given ten keys and asked to open a lock. How can reasoning help you? Look at the shapes of the keys. Look at the shape of the keyhole. You will be able to see that certain keys will not go into the keyhole. You can put them aside. Now you have fewer keys to try. Time is saved.

▶ **Define:** What does reasoning mean? using past information to help solve a problem

Reward and Punishment Reward and punishment are often used in learning. This is especially true in training animals. You can teach a dog to stand up by holding food above its head and repeating the words "stand up." When the dog stands up, it is rewarded. It gets the food. After you do this many times, the dog learns to stand up on command, even if there is no food. Other types of behavior can be conditioned by punishment. How can a dog be taught to stop barking a people? What rewards and punishments affect your own behavior?

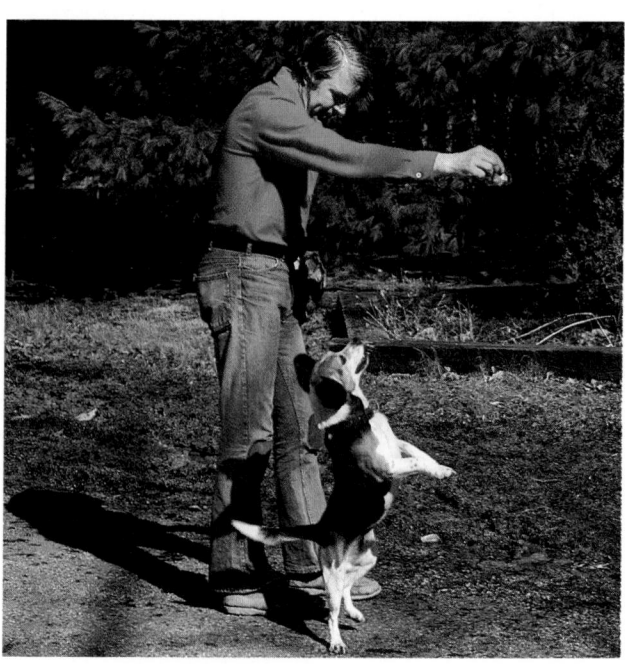

▶ **Describe:** How can a reward or punishment be a stimulus for a learned behavior? Accept all logical responses.

LESSON SUMMARY

► One type of learning is trial and error learning, or trying something new each time you make an error.

► You memorize things by studying them carefully or repeating them many times.

► Reasoning is a way to solve problems by thinking about past experiences.

► Behavior can be conditioned by rewards and punishment.

CHECK *Find the sentence in the lesson that answers each question. Then, write the sentence.*

1. What is trial and error learning?

2. How do you memorize things?

3. What kind of learning helps you save time?

Answer the following.

4. If you can remember your friend's telephone number, what kind of learning have you used? memorizing

APPLY *Read each description. Then decide what kind of learning was used.*

5. Dialing each number in the phone book before getting the person you want. trial and error

6. Looking up the person's name in the phone book in order to find his or her phone number. reasoning

7. Calling the number you have memorized memorizing

Answer the following.

8. Explain how you could use reward to change a behavior of your pet.

► 9. **Infer:** Why are good study habits important for learning?

Ideas in Action

IDEA: Most human behavior is learned behavior.
ACTION: Make a list of 10 learned behaviors. Identify each type of behavior as a result of trial and error, memorization, or reasoning.

ACTIVITY

REMEMBERING INFORMATION

You will need 7 index cards, a clock or watch with a second hand, paper, and a pencil.

1. Write a different letter of the alphabet on each of seven index cards.

2. Shuffle the cards and place them face down on a desk.

3. Turn over all 7 index cards. Underneath each letter, write a word that begins with the letter. Try to use words that form a sentence or complete thought.

4. Memorize the sentence. Turn the cards face down.

5. Wait 2 minutes. Then write the sentence on a piece of paper. Underneath the sentence, write the letters that appear on the index cards. Check your answers.

Questions

1. What was the sentence or thought you created from the 7 letters?

2. After waiting 2 minutes, did you correctly identify all 7 letters?

3. What other sentences have you used to help memorize a list of items?

UNIT 15 Challenges

STUDY HINT Before you begin the Unit Challenges, review the TechTerms and Lesson Summary for each lesson in this unit.

TechTerms

axon (288)	endocrine gland (300)	neuron (288)
cerebellum (290)	gland (300)	pupil (296)
cerebrum (290)	hormone (302)	receptor (294)
cochlea (298)	innate behavior (304)	reflex (292)
conditioned response (304)	iris (296)	reflex arc (292)
cornea (296)	learned behavior (304)	response (292)
dendrite (288)	lens (296)	retina (296)
eardrum (298)	medulla (290)	stimulus (292)

TechTerm Challenges

Matching *Write the TechTerm that matches each description.*

1. clear covering at the front of the eye cornea
2. part of the ear that changes vibrations into nerve signals cochlea
3. organ that receives stimuli from the environment receptor
4. sheet of tissue that vibrates when sounds strike it eardrum
5. part of the brain that controls heartbeat and breathing rate medulla
6. nerve cell neuron
7. organ that makes chemical substances used or released by the body gland
8. learned behavior in which a new stimulus causes the same response that an old one did conditioned response
9. part of the brain that controls the senses and thinking cerebrum
10. fiber that carries messages away from a nerve cell axon

Identifying Word Relationships *Explain how the words in each pair are related. Write your answers in complete sentences.* Answers will vary. Accept all logical responses.

1. endocrine gland, hormone
2. axon, dendrite
3. cerebellum, cerebrum
4. pupil, iris
5. reflex, reflex arc
6. response, stimulus
7. lens, retina
8. innate behavior, learned behavior

Content Challenges

Multiple Choice *Write the letter of the term that best completes each statement.*

1. Coughing is
   a. a learned behavior.   **b.** a conditioned response.   **c.** an innate behavior.   **d.** a stimulus. c

2. The lens of the eye forms images on the
   a. cornea.   **b.** pupil.   **c.** iris.   **d.** retina. d

3. Insulin is made by the
   a. pituitary gland. **b.** pancreas. **c.** ovaries. **d.** thyroid. b
4. The smallest part of the brain is the
   a. medulla. **b.** cerebrum. **c.** cerebellum. **d.** skull. a
5. Adrenalin controls
   a. muscle reaction. **b.** growth. **c.** the amount of calcium in the blood. **d.** blood sugar levels. a
6. The cochlea is found in the
   a. outer ear. **b.** middle ear. **c.** inner ear. **d.** eardrum. c
7. The 'thermostat' of the body is the
   a. cerebrum. **b.** hypothalamus. **c.** pituitary gland. **d.** cerebellum. b
8. The nervous system is made up of the brain, the spinal cord, and
   a. muscles. **b.** glands. **c.** nerves. **d.** the skull. c
9. The clear covering at the front of the eye is the
   a. retina. **b.** iris. **c.** pupil. **d.** cornea. d
10. The largest cells in the body are
    a. axons. **b.** dendrites. **c.** hormones. **d.** neurons. d
11. Sneezing and blinking are
    a. receptors. **b.** reflexes. **c.** stimuli. **d.** reflex arc. b

True/False *Write true if the statement is true. If the statement is false, change the underlined term to make the statement true.*

1. Estrogen and progesterone are produced by the <u>ovaries</u>. true
2. When you solve a problem by thinking about it, you are <u>reasoning</u>. true
3. The amount of light entering the eye is controlled by the <u>cornea</u>. iris
4. The ear responds to <u>light</u> waves. sound
5. The brain is connected to the spinal cord by the <u>medulla</u>. true
6. The path of a message in a reflex is called a <u>conditioned response</u>. reflex arc
7. Reflexes are controlled by the <u>brain</u>. spinal cord
8. The brain and spinal cord make up the <u>central nervous</u> system. true
9. Growth hormone is made by the <u>pituitary</u> gland. true
10. Messages are carried toward the nerve cell body by <u>axons</u>. dendrites
11. You are born with <u>learned</u> behaviors. innate
12. Glands that do not have ducts are called <u>endocrine</u> glands. true

Understanding the Features

Reading Critically *Use the feature reading selections to answer the following. Page numbers for the features follow each question in parentheses.*

1. What does human growth hormone control? (301)
2. **Define:** What is bionics? (299)
3. In what field did B. F. Skinner specialize? (305)
4. **Explain:** Why is MRI valuable in detecting tumors? (289)
5. **Identify:** What are plant hormones called? (303)
6. **Analyze:** Why must a physical therapy assistant be patient and understanding? (293)

Concept Challenges

Interpreting a Table *Use the table to answer the following.*

1. What does thyroxine control?
2. **Classify:** What are two pituitary hormones?
3. **Analyze:** What hormone is needed to regulate the pituitary gland?
4. What gland produces insulin?
5. What minerals are affected by parathyroid hormone?
6. **Hypothesize:** What health problems might a person have if their thymus gland produced too little thymosin?
7. **List:** What three things does adrenalin control?

Table 1 Hormones and What They Do		
GLAND	HORMONE	JOB OF HORMONE
Pineal	Melatonin	Helps regulate pituitary gland
Pituitary	Growth hormone	Controls the growth of bones
	ATCH	Controls the release of hormones from the adrenal glands
Thyroid	Thyroxin	Controls rate of body growth
Parathyroid	Parathyroid hormone	Controls the amount of calcium and phosphorus in the blood
Thymus	Thymosin	Controls growth of certain white blood cells
Adrenal	Adrenalin	Controls muscle reaction, blood clotting, and blood pressure
Pancreas	Insulin	Controls blood sugar levels

Critical Thinking *Answer each of the following in complete sentences.*

1. How do reflexes help an organism survive?
2. **Compare:** How is the eye like a camera?
3. **Contrast:** How is reasoning different from trial and error learning?
4. How is the spinal cord like a tree trunk?
5. How do the nervous system and the endocrine system work together?

Finding Out More

1. Injury to the central nervous system often results from automobile accidents, serious falls, and sports injuries. Make a poster showing some of the ways that people can protect their nervous systems from injury.
2. **Research:** Other parts of the brain are the thalamus, the pons, and the midbrain. Using library references, find out what each of these parts of the brain controls. Organize your findings in a table.
3. Sound intensity is measured in decibels. Find out the safe decibel range for the human ear in an encyclopedia. Then find out the decibel range of ten common noises. Identify any noises that are above the safe range and can damage your ears.
4. Meningitis is a serious disease. Using library references, find out more about meningitis. Write your findings in a report.

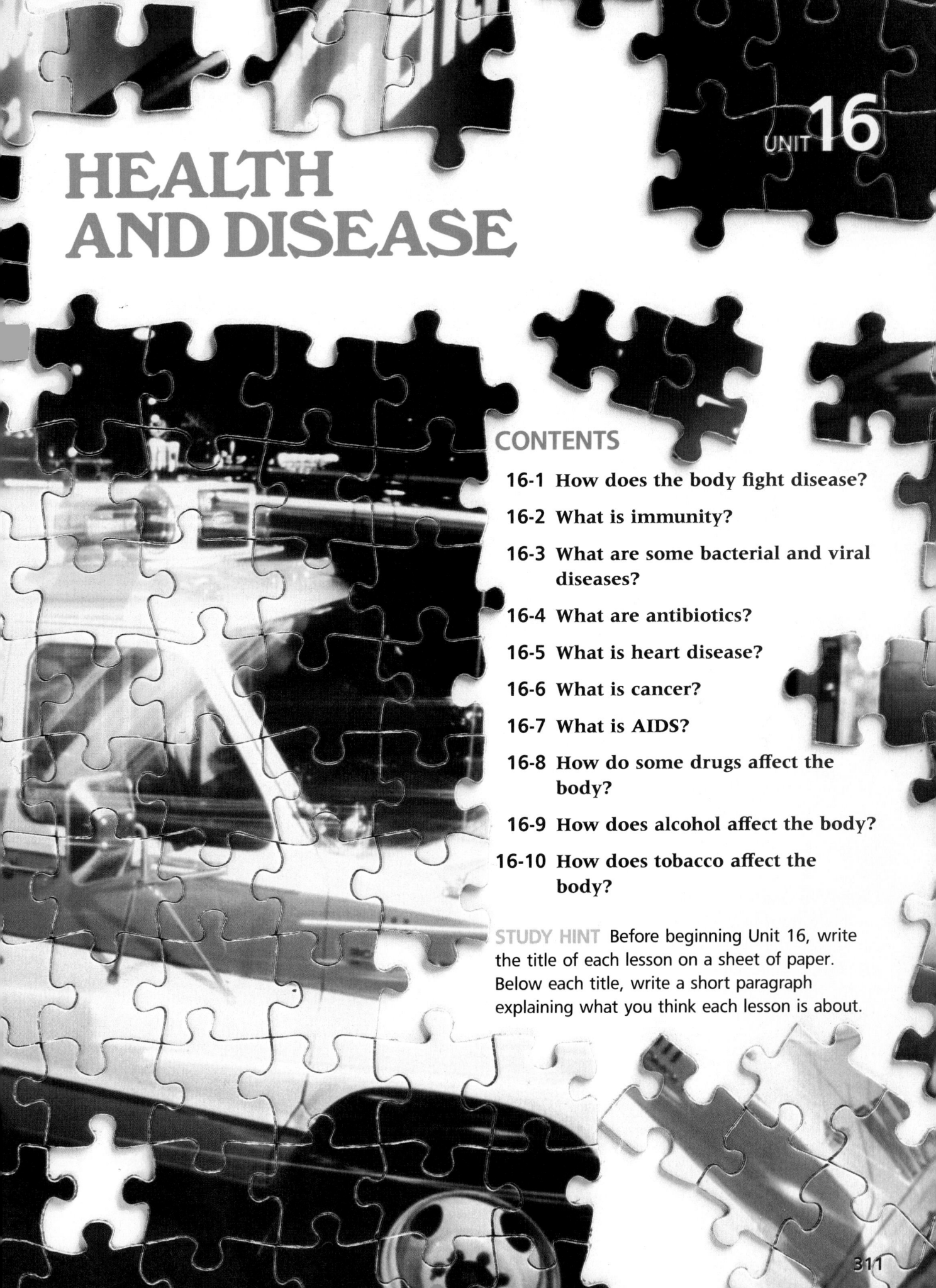

HEALTH AND DISEASE

CONTENTS

STUDY HINT Before beginning Unit 16, write the title of each lesson on a sheet of paper. Below each title, write a short paragraph explaining what you think each lesson is about.

16-1 How does the body fight disease?

Objective ▶ Identify the ways your body fights disease.

TechTerms

▶ **antibodies** (AN-ti-bahd-eez): substances the body makes to protect itself from disease

▶ **white blood cells:** cells that protect the body against disease

Defense Systems Your body is under constant attack by bacteria, viruses, and other harmful substances. However, your body usually can protect itself from illness. Your body has defenses against disease. These defenses include your skin, and the respiratory, digestive, and circulatory systems.

▐▶ *Identify:* What parts of the body defend it from bacteria and viruses? skin, and the respiratory, digestive, and circulatory systems

Skin The skin is a waterproof, germ-proof barrier that covers your body. It is made up of several layers of cells. Working together, the layers of the skin act like a wall to prevent disease-causing substances from entering the body.

▐▶ *Describe:* How does the skin protect the body? It acts like a wall to stop tiny particles from entering the body.

Digestive System Although the skin protects the body from most germs, bacteria and viruses can enter the body through the mouth. The digestive system helps to destroy these substances. Hydrochloric acid in the stomach helps to destroy bacteria and viruses that enter the stomach.

▐▶ *Explain:* How does the digestive system help to protect the body from disease-causing substances? Hydrochloric acid found in the digestive system destroys the harmful organisms.

Respiratory System Bacteria and viruses also can enter the body through the nose. Hairs in the nose filter the air and trap many small particles. Cilia and mucus in the respiratory system also trap germs before they can enter the lungs. The body gets rid of the trapped particles by sneezing and coughing. Sneezing and coughing force mucus and trapped particles out of the body.

▐▶ *Explain:* How does mucus in the nose and windpipe protect the body? Disease-causing substances get stuck in the mucus.

White Blood Cells When germs get past the defenses of the skin, digestive, and respiratory systems, the body's second line of defense goes to work. The **white blood cells** are the body's second line of defense. White blood cells are part of the circulatory system. They travel through the blood in search of bacteria. When white blood cells find bacteria, they surround them. The white blood cells destroy the bacteria by digesting them.

▐▶ *Describe:* How do white blood cells help protect the body? They seek out bacteria and then surround and destroy them.

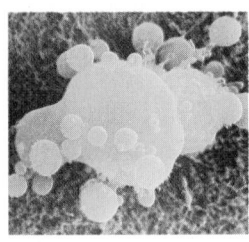

Final Line of Defense If bacteria get through the skin and past the white blood cells, the body still has another line of defense. The body is able to make substances that can destroy the bacteria. These substances are called **antibodies** (AN-ti-bahd-eez). Some antibodies cause bacteria to break up or clump together. Other antibodies make bacterial poisons harmless. Still other antibodies destroy virus particles.

▐▶ *Identify:* What are antibodies? substances the body makes to protect itself from disease

LESSON SUMMARY

- ▶ The defense systems of the body include the skin, and the respiratory, digestive, and circulatory systems.
- ▶ The skin acts like a wall to stop tiny particles from entering the body.
- ▶ Hydrochloric acid in the digestive system destroys disease-causing organisms.
- ▶ The hairs in the nose, cilia, and mucus trap small particles, preventing them from entering the body.
- ▶ White blood cells, produced in the circulatory system, surround and destroy bacteria in the body.
- ▶ The body produces antibodies that can destroy foreign substances.

CHECK *Write true if the statement is true. If the statement is false, change the underlined term to make the statement true.*

1. Bacteria and <u>viruses</u> can cause disease. true
2. The <u>skin</u> allows germs to enter the body. mouth or nose
3. Acid in your <u>blood</u> kills disease-causing organisms. stomach
4. Particles trapped in mucus are removed from the body by <u>sneezing</u> and coughing. true

5. White blood cells travel through the body in search of <u>antibodies</u>. bacteria
6. The body's first line of defense is <u>antibodies</u>. skin

APPLY *Complete the following.*

▶ 7. **Infer:** Why is it important to cover your nose with a tissue when you sneeze?

▶ 8. **Infer:** How does putting a bandage over a cut help defend the body against disease?

▶ 9. **Hypothesize:** What do you think would happen if germs could enter the skin easily?

Health & Safety Tip

You should always wash a cut thoroughly and apply an antiseptic. An antiseptic is a substance that helps prevent infection. Use a first aid handbook or other references to find out the names of three antiseptics. Describe how each of these antiseptics should be used. Present your findings in a report.

SCIENCE CONNECTION

PREVENTIVE MEDICINE

One way of keeping healthy is to practice preventive medicine. Preventive medicine means taking steps to prevent sickness. When you keep your body strong and healthy, you are practicing preventive medicine. This means eating a balanced diet and getting the proper amount of rest. Regular exercise also is necessary for a healthy body. Keeping your body clean and free of dirt and germs is another way of preventing disease.

Your doctor and dentist can help you practice preventive medicine. Regular yearly checkups by these professionals can help detect health problems early. The earlier a health problem is caught, the easier it is to treat. This is especially important as you get older.

Good health is not an accident. You must work hard to keep healthy. The way you take care of your body today determines how healthy it will be in the future.

16-2 What is immunity?

Objectives ▶ Define immunity. ▶ Explain the difference between natural immunity and acquired immunity.

TechTerm

▶ **immunity** (im-MYOON-i-tee): resistance to a specific disease

Resisting Disease Antibodies protect the body against foreign substances. After these foreign substances are destroyed, many of the antibodies remain. If the same kind of foreign substances enter the body once again, the remaining antibodies will destroy the substances before they can do any harm. The body has become resistant to these diseases. This resistance to a specific disease is called **immunity** (im-MYOON-i-tee).

▶ **Identify:** What is immunity? resistance to a specific disease

Types of Immunity There are two kinds of immunity. One kind is called natural immunity. The other is called acquired (uh-KWY-urd) immunity. Natural immunity is an immunity that people are born with. In fact, some people have certain kinds of antibodies already in their bodies at birth. Natural immunity is your body's natural defense against certain diseases. Acquired immunity is an immunity that people develop, or acquire, at some time during their lives.

▶ **Compare:** What is the difference between natural and acquired immunity? People are born with natural immunity. They develop an acquired immunity during their lives.

Active Acquired Immunity There are two kinds of acquired immunity. One kind is called active acquired immunity. With this kind of immunity, the body resists a certain disease because it has already developed antibodies against the disease. Once you have been exposed to some diseases, your body continues to make the antibodies for that disease. For example, if you have already had chicken pox, you will not get it again.

Your body has developed permanent immunity against chicken pox.

▶ **Explain:** How do you develop active acquired immunity? by having a disease and making antibodies against it

Passive Acquired Immunity The second kind of acquired immunity is passive acquired immunity. In this kind of immunity, antibodies are not produced by your body. The antibodies are obtained from somewhere else. You may be injected with antibodies against a certain disease. The person then has a passive acquired immunity against that disease. However, this kind of immunity does not last long. Antibodies that are not made by the body usually are destroyed after a short time.

▶ **Compare:** Which type of acquired immunity lasts the longest? active acquired immunity

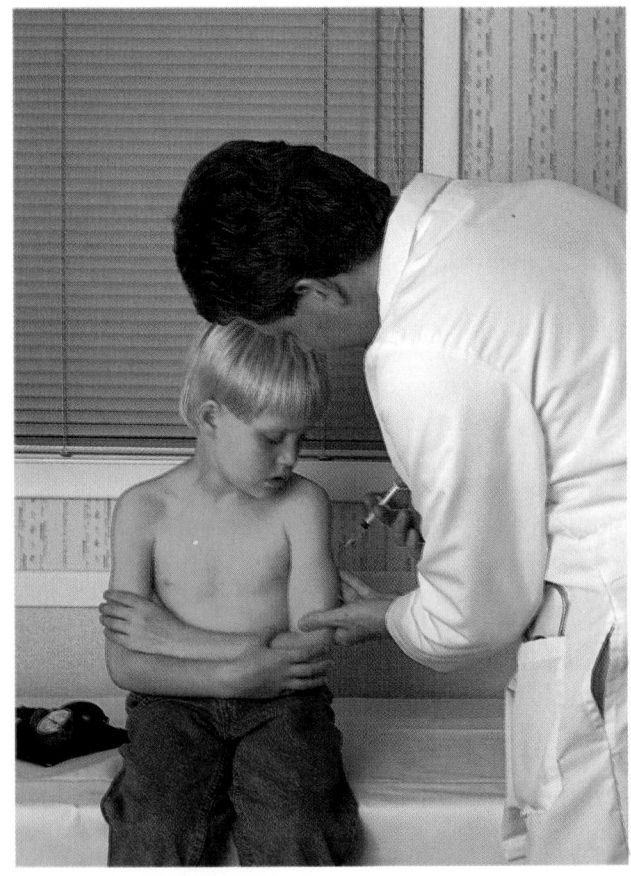

▶ Immunity is a resistance to a specific disease.

▶ There are two kinds of immunity—natural immunity and acquired immunity.

▶ Active acquired immunity develops after the body has developed antibodies against a certain disease.

▶ Passive acquired immunity develops when antibodies are injected into the body.

CHECK *Write true if the statement is true. If the statement is false, change the underlined term to make the statement true.*

1. A resistance to disease is called <u>immunity</u>. true

2. Immunity a person is born with is called <u>acquired</u> immunity. natural

3. Immunity a person develops is called <u>natural</u> immunity. acquired

4. Antibodies made by a body remain a <u>short</u> time after the disease it fights is gone. long

5. The immunity that results when a body makes antibodies against a disease is an <u>active acquired immunity</u>. true

6. Passive acquired immunity <u>is permanent</u>. lasts a short time

APPLY *Complete the following.*

7. **Compare:** How are natural immunity, active acquired immunity, and passive acquired immunity similar?

8. **Relate:** Sometimes a developing baby receives antibodies from its mother. Is this immunity a natural or an acquired immunity? Explain.

InfoSearch

Read the passage. Ask two questions that you cannot answer from the information in the passage.

Vaccines One way of getting active acquired immunity is through a vaccine. A vaccine is a serum made from a dead or a weakened form of bacteria or viruses. The serum is injected into the body. Vaccines do not cause you to get the disease. The body responds to the vaccine by making antibodies against the disease-causing substance. The antibodies remain in the body and protect it from the disease.

SEARCH: Use library references to find answers to your questions.

▼ LOOKING BACK IN SCIENCE ▼

EDWARD JENNER'S DISCOVERY OF VACCINATIONS

Modern medicine has become more successful in treating different diseases since the discovery of vaccines. The first vaccine was developed and used in 1796 by Edward Jenner, an English doctor. Jenner noticed that many people who worked near cattle got a mild disease called cowpox. He also noticed that these same people did not get the fatal disease smallpox. To find out why, Jenner tried injecting material from cowpox sores into people. Antibodies against cowpox were produced in these people. Jenner found that these same antibodies were able to destroy the smallpox virus. The people did not get smallpox because the cowpox antibodies protected them against smallpox too.

The vaccine Edward Jenner developed was made directly from a disease-causing substance. Today many vaccines are made from chemicals that resemble bacteria and viruses. The human body responds to these artificial vaccines by making antibodies. Diseases that were once widespread, such as polio, have been almost eliminated due to the creation of vaccines.

16-3 What are some bacterial and viral diseases?

Objective ▶ Describe the causes of different types of disease.

Germ Theory Years ago, people believed that a person became ill when evil spirits entered the body. They tried to drive the evil spirits away with magic. About 100 years ago, Louis Pasteur showed that some diseases are caused by bacteria and other microscopic organisms. The idea that diseases are caused by microscopic organisms, or germs, is called the germ theory of disease.

▐▐▐▶ *Explain:* What does the germ theory of disease state? Diseases are caused by microscopic organisms.

Identifying Germs Pasteur showed that bacteria could cause certain diseases. To fight a disease, it is important to identify the kind of bacteria that causes the disease. Robert Koch studied many of the bacteria that cause diseases in animals and people. He discovered how to grow bacteria outside a living body. This made it possible to study and find ways of destroying the bacteria. Table 1 lists the symptoms of some common diseases caused by bacteria.

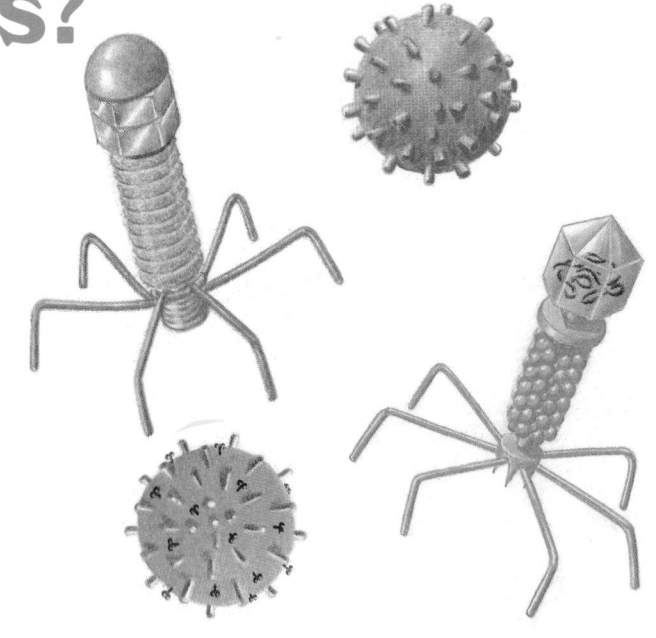

Viruses and Disease Some kinds of disease are caused by viruses. The invention of the electron microscope has helped scientists learn about viruses and disease. Scientists have discovered that different kinds of viruses attack different parts of the body. Each virus usually attacks only a certain kind of cell or tissue. For example, the viruses that cause smallpox, measles, and warts seem to attack cells only in the skin. Viruses that cause yellow fever attack cells in the liver. Information about how viruses attack the body helps in the fight against the disease the virus causes. Table 2 lists some common viral diseases and their symptoms.

Table 1 Common Bacterial Diseases	
DISEASE	SYMPTOMS
Diphtheria	Sore throat, fever
Meningitis	fever, headache
Strep throat	sore throat, fever
Tetanus	tightening of body muscles
Toxic Shock Syndrome	fever, low blood pressure

Table 2 Common Viral Diseases	
DISEASE	SYMPTOMS
Chicken pox	skin rash, fever
Hepatitis	jaundice, loss of appetite
Influenza	muscle aches, fever, chills
Measles	pink rash over the body
Mumps	swollen glands, fever

▐▐▐▶ *Describe:* Why is it important to find the germ that causes a disease? Once the germ is identified, ways of destroying the germ can be determined.

▐▐▐▶ *Describe:* In what way are viruses particular? A virus attacks only a certain part of the body.

LESSON SUMMARY

▶ The germ theory of disease states that diseases are caused by microscopic organisms.

▶ Robert Koch discovered how to grow single kinds of bacteria outside a living organism.

▶ The invention of the electron microscope greatly aided the study of viruses and the diseases they cause.

CHECK *Complete the following.*

1. The work of _____ showed that diseases are caused by microscopic organisms. Pasteur

2. The invention of the _____ helped scientists study viruses. electron microscope

3. Many kinds of bacteria that cause disease were identified and studied by _____ . Robert Koch

4. The idea that diseases are caused by microscopic organisms is called the _____ . germ theory of disease

5. Particular kinds of _____ usually attack only certain types of cells and tissues. viruses

APPLY *Answer the following.*

6. **Infer:** Why do you think the invention of the electron microscope helped in the study of viruses?

Use Tables 1 and 2 on page 316 to answer the following.

7. **Analyze:** If you had a sore throat and fever, what two diseases might you have?

8. **Analyze:** You have swollen glands and a fever. What disease might you have?

9. **Identify:** What are the symptoms of Toxic Shock Syndrome?

InfoSearch

Read the passage. Ask two questions that you cannot answer from the information in the passage.

Food Preservation There are several ways to package and preserve food to prevent spoilage. When foods are canned, they are cooked at high temperatures to kill any bacteria. The foods are then stored in airtight cans or jars. Other foods are preserved by drying. Most of the water is removed from the food. This decreases the chance of spoilage. Raisins are an example of food that has been dried. Another method of food preservation is curing. Food is cooked or dried. Then chemical preservatives such as salt, vinegar, or sugar are added to the food.

SEARCH: Use library references to find answers to your questions.

LOOKING BACK IN SCIENCE

KOCH'S POSTULATES

Bacteriologists are scientists who study bacteria. Many bacteriologists study disease-causing bacteria. They study these organisms to identify the diseases each kind of bacteria causes.

Robert Koch was the first bacteriologist to show that a certain kind of bacterium causes a certain kind of disease. In the late 1800s, he developed a way to determine the

relationship between a particular bacterium and a particular disease. This procedure, called Koch's postulates, includes a series of four steps.

The first step is to remove disease-causing bacteria from a diseased animal. The bacteria are then isolated and grown in a laboratory. Next, the laboratory-grown bacteria are injected into a healthy animal.

When the healthy animal becomes sick with the disease, the bacteria are removed from the animal. These bacteria are compared with the original bacteria. If the two bacteria match, bacteriologists assume that the particular bacterium causes the same disease in similar organisms. Modern bacteriologists still follow this same set of steps in their study of bacteria and diseases.

16-4 What are antibiotics?

Objective ▶ Explain how antibiotics are used to fight disease.

TechTerm

▶ **antibiotic** (an-ti-by-AHT-ik): chemical made by a living organism that kills bacteria

Treating Disease Sometimes your body needs help in fighting off disease. Your doctor may prescribe medicine, or you may get an injection. If you are suffering from a disease caused by bacteria, you may be treated with an **antibiotic** (an-ti-by-AHT-ik). An antibiotic is a chemical substance that kills harmful bacteria.

▨▶ *Identify:* What is an antibiotic? substance that kills harmful bacteria

Discovery of Antibiotics The use of antibiotics to treat disease is a fairly recent discovery. In 1929, Alexander Fleming, an English bacteriologist (bak-tir-ee-AHL-uh-jist), was the first person to observe the action of an antibiotic. Fleming was growing bacteria in a dish. He noticed that the bacteria did not grow in a part of the dish where some mold had formed. Fleming guessed that the mold produced a substance that was harmful to bacteria. Thirteen years later, scientists were able to separate this substance from the same kind of

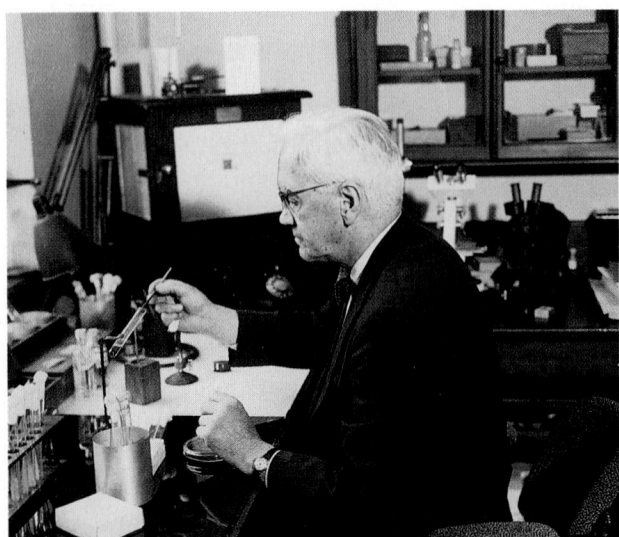

Figure 1 Alexander Fleming

mold. The scientists called this substance penicillin (pen-uh-SIL-in). Penicillin was the first antibiotic.

Since the discovery of penicillin, many other antibiotics have been discovered. Most antibiotics are produced from molds. Other antibiotics are made from fungi and bacteria. Certain kinds of plants and animals also produce some types of antibiotics.

Figure 2 Growing Mold

▨▶ *Explain:* Where does penicillin come from? a mold

How Antibiotics Work Antibiotics are not all the same. Different antibiotics have different effects on a particular disease. This means that each antibiotic can be used to fight only certain kinds of organisms. For example, penicillin works only against certain bacteria. The penicillin destroys the bacteria and stops it from reproducing. Penicillin does not work against viruses. No antibiotic can destroy all types of bacteria.

A problem with antibiotics is that they may make some people sick. Antibiotics also can cause an allergic reaction. For example, some people are allergic to penicillin. If they take this antibiotic, a fever or rash may develop. In severe reactions, the person may not be able to breathe. For this reason, it is important that you tell your doctor if you are allergic to any medications.

▨▶ *Apply:* Why is it important to inform your doctor of any drug allergies you might have? so that a different medication can be prescribed

- ▶ Antibiotics are chemical substances that kill harmful bacteria.
- ▶ Alexander Fleming was the first person to discover the use of antibiotics to treat disease.
- ▶ Antibiotics are produced from molds, fungi, and bacteria.
- ▶ Each antibiotic can be used to fight specific bacteria.
- ▶ Antibiotics may make some people sick or cause an allergic reaction.

CHECK *Find the sentence in the lesson that answers each question. Then, write the sentence.*

1. In Fleming's experiment, where did the bacteria not grow?
2. What was the first antibiotic discovered?
3. What are antibiotics?
4. Do antibiotics work against viruses?
5. What kind of reaction do antibiotics have on some people?
6. What are most antibiotics made from?
7. Who was the first person to observe an antibiotic?

APPLY *Complete the following.*

8. **Hypothesize:** Is it possible for a person taking penicillin for a bacterial disease to get sick with a different type of disease? Explain.
9. **Infer:** Would penicillin be an effective treatment for a person suffering with the measles?

Skill Builder

Building Vocabulary The prefix ''anti-'' means ''against''. Use this information to write a definition of the word ''antibiotic.'' Then look up the word in a dictionary to check your definition. Write definitions for the terms ''antibodies'' and ''antiseptic.'' Use a dictionary to check your definitions.

Health & Safety Tip

If you are allergic to any antibiotic, such as penicillin, you should have some kind of identification on you at all times. Visit a pharmacy to get information about bracelets or charms that contain medical information. It is important to have this kind of information on you in case of an emergency.

PEOPLE IN SCIENCE

JOSEPH LISTER (1827–1912)

Joseph Lister was an English doctor who practiced medicine during the middle of the 19th century. He read about the discoveries of Louis Pasteur regarding bacteria. Lister guessed that there was a connection between bacteria and infections.

During the time that Lister practiced medicine, most people who underwent surgery developed some kind of infection after the surgery. Many of the patients died from these infections. Joseph Lister hypothesized that these infections were caused by bacteria. He thought that if the tools the doctor used during surgery were cleaned, bacteria on the tools would be removed, and infections would decrease. Lister introduced sterilization (ster-uh-li-ZAY-shun) as a means of cleaning surgical instruments. In this method, surgical instruments are placed in boiling water. The heat destroys bacteria. Lister also insisted that doctors carefully wash their hands in antiseptic solutions before operating on patients. When doctors began following Lister's suggestions, the number of post-operative infections declined. The work of Lister saved many lives.

What is heart disease?

Objective ▶ Identify types of heart disease and their causes.

TechTerms

- ▶ **atherosclerosis** (ath-ur-oh-skluh-ROH-sis): buildup of fat deposits on artery walls
- ▶ **coronary** (KOWR-uh-ner-ee) **arteries**: arteries that carry blood and oxygen to the tissues of the heart
- ▶ **heart attack**: lack of blood and oxygen to a part of the heart

Heart Disease More than half of all deaths in the United States are caused by heart disease. Heart disease affects both the heart and the blood vessels. Some kinds of heart disease are genetic (juh-NET-ik), or passed from parent to offspring. If someone in your family has heart disease, there is a chance that you also may develop heart disease. Other kinds of heart disease are the result of the person's lifestyle and environment. Table 1 lists some of the factors that contribute to heart disease.

Table 1 Factors Contributing to Heart Disease	
▶ age	▶ high blood pressure
▶ family history	▶ obesity
▶ gender	▶ physical inactivity
▶ smoking	▶ high cholesterol levels

▶ *Infer:* What are some ways you can prevent heart disease? Answers will vary. Accept all logical responses.

Atherosclerosis In one kind of heart disease, fatty substances coat the inside walls of the arteries. One of these fatty substances is cholesterol (kuh-LES-tuh-rohl). Cholesterol is a fatty substance found in animal products. As fat builds up in an artery, the artery becomes more narrow. This condition is known as **atherosclerosis** (ath-ur-oh-skluh-ROH-sis). The heart must work harder to pump blood through the narrow arteries.

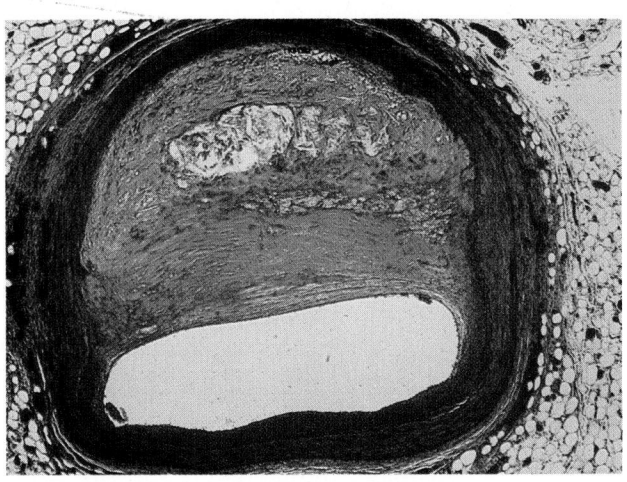

▶ *Explain:* What is atherosclerosis? a buildup of fat deposits on the walls of arteries

Heart Attack Like other body cells, the cells of the heart need food and oxygen. Heart cells also need to get rid of waste materials. The heart has its own system of blood vessels to take care of these needs. This system is called the coronary (KOWR-uh-ner-ee) system. **Coronary arteries** carry oxygen and blood to the heart.

Atherosclerosis may make the coronary arteries narrower. Sometimes a clot forms and completely blocks a coronary artery. This blockage stops blood and oxygen from reaching a part of the heart. The affected part of the heart cannot do its work. This condition is called a **heart attack.** A person having a heart attack usually feels a sharp pain in the chest. Heart attacks often are fatal.

▶ *Describe:* What is a heart attack? a blockage in a coronary artery

LESSON SUMMARY

- ▶ Heart disease affects both the heart and the blood vessels.
- ▶ Atherosclerosis is a condition in which fat deposits build up on the walls of arteries.
- ▶ Coronary arteries carry blood to the heart.
- ▶ A heart attack occurs when part of the heart does not receive blood and oxygen.

CHECK *Complete the following.*

1. More than half of all deaths in the United States are caused by _____ . heart disease
2. The _____ arteries carry blood and oxygen to all parts of the heart. coronary
3. A blockage in a coronary artery can cause a person to suffer a _____ . heart attack
4. A fatty substance that can coat the inside walls of arteries is _____ . cholesterol
5. A buildup of cholesterol on the artery walls causes the heart to work _____ . harder

APPLY *Complete the following.*

6. **Hypothesize:** Does the width of an artery increase or decrease as a person ages?

7. **Hypothesize:** What do you think you can do to reduce the chance that you will be affected by atherosclerosis later in life?

8. **Analyze:** Which of the factors listed in Table 1 can be controlled?

9. Pick three factors in Table 1. Explain how you can lower your risk of getting heart disease for each of the three factors chosen.

InfoSearch

Read the passage. Ask two questions that you cannot answer from the information in the passage.

Strokes Atherosclerosis affects all the arteries in the body, not only the coronary arteries. Atherosclerosis also makes the arteries leading to the brain narrower. These narrow arteries may become blocked by a blood clot. The blocked artery prevents blood and oxygen from reaching the brain. A lack of oxygen to the brain is called a stroke. A stroke may cause paralysis. A serious stroke may even cause death.

SEARCH: Use library references to find answers to your questions.

SCIENCE CONNECTION ◆○◆○◆○◆○◆○◆○◆○◆○◆○◆○◆○◆○◆○◆○◆○◆○

CHOLESTEROL

Cholesterol is a fatty substance found in meats and other animal products. Cholesterol also is made by the cells of the body. Cholesterol is needed by the body for most chemical reactions to take place. However, many people eat foods that contain a high amount of cholesterol. This increases the level of cholesterol in the blood. This in turn increases the chance that cholesterol will build up on artery walls.

Research suggests that you can reduce your risk of developing heart disease by eating foods that are low in cholesterol. To cut back on cholesterol, limit the amount of red meat, eggs, and whole milk dairy products you eat. However, since these foods contain many valuable vitamins and minerals, they should not be totally eliminated from your diet. Low-cholesterol foods, such as chicken and fish, can be substituted for red meat. Studies have shown that people who eat more fish than red meat have less heart disease than people who eat red meat more often. By developing healthful eating habits now, you can help avoid serious health problems.

16-6 What is cancer?

Objectives ▶ Describe the effect of cancer on the body. ▶ Identify some possible causes of cancer.

TechTerms

▶ **benign** (bi-NYN) **tumor:** mass of cells that is usually harmless

▶ **malignant** (muh-LIG-nunt) **tumor:** harmful mass of cells that can spread throughout the body

▶ **tumor** (TOO-mur): mass or lump of cells

Growing Wild Most cells in the body divide and produce new cells. Sometimes the growth of cells goes wild. New cells grow where they are not needed. Their growth becomes rapid and uncontrolled. The new cells crowd nearby cells and rob these cells of their nutrients. They prevent the nearby cells from working in a normal way. The new cells form a mass, or lump, called a **tumor** (TOO-mur).

▶ *Identify:* What is a tumor? mass or lump of cells

Kinds of Tumors There are two kinds of tumors. One kind grows in one place in the body. It does not spread to other places. This type of tumor often stops growing once it gets to a certain size. Tumors of this kind are called **benign** (bi-NYN) **tumors.** Benign tumors usually are not a serious health problem.

The other kind of tumor spreads to other places in the body. As it spreads, it causes harm to the body. If the growth of the tumor is not stopped, the person eventually may die. This kind of tumor is called a **malignant** (muh-LIG-nunt) **tumor.** The condition the body is in after the spread of malignant tumors is called cancer.

▶ *Describe:* What is a cancer? a condition of the body characterized by the spread of malignant tumors

How Cancer Spreads Cancer spreads from one part of the body to another part of the body in different ways. In one way, cancer cells break away from the tumor. The cancer cells enter the bloodstream. They travel with the blood to other parts of the body. A new tumor will then begin to grow at the place where the cancer cells come to rest.

▶ *Explain:* How can cancer cells spread through the body? Cells break away from the tumor and travel to a new location through the bloodstream.

Possible Causes Scientists are not sure what causes a cancer to start growing. They do know that certain chemicals increase the chance of getting cancer. Studies have shown that exposure to too much sunlight and X rays can cause cancer. Scientists believe that certain viruses and hormones also may cause cancer. Research also has shown that people who smoke cigarettes are more likely to get lung cancer than nonsmokers.

▶ *List:* What are three possible causes of cancer? chemicals, exposure to sunlight and X rays, certain viruses and hormones, and smoking cigarettes

Early Signs The earlier cancer is detected, the more likely a person is to survive the disease. Table 1 lists the seven warning signs of cancer. If you ever have any of these warning signs, you should see a doctor immediately.

Table 1   Seven Warning Signs of Cancer
1. A sore that does not heal
2. Unusual bleeding
3. A lump in the breast or other area beneath the skin
4. Constant indigestion or trouble swallowing
5. A nagging cough
6. A change in the size, shape, or color of a wart or mole
7. A change in bowel or bladder habits

▶ *Explain:* Why is it important to detect cancer early? The person has a better chance of survival if the cancer is detected early.

LESSON SUMMARY

▶ A tumor is a mass or lump of cells.

▶ Benign tumors are harmless growths of cells.

▶ The spread of harmful malignant tumors is called cancer.

▶ Overexposure to sunlight and X rays, and cigarettes contribute to developing cancer.

▶ The chances of curing cancer are best when treatment starts early.

CHECK *Complete the following.*

1. A tumor that does not spread to other parts of the body is a _____ tumor. benign

2. A cancer is the spread of _____ tumors. malignant

3. Cells from a tumor sometimes travel through the _____ to new places in the body. bloodstream

4. Nonsmokers are less likely to get cancer than _____ . smokers

5. The earlier cancer is detected, the better a person's chance of _____ . survival

APPLY *Complete the following.*

▶ 6. **Infer:** Why do X-ray technicians wear lead aprons when taking X rays? to protect their bodies from the X rays

7. Why is it important to wear a sunscreen when out in the sun? to protect your skin from too much sunlight

8. **Hypothesize:** The incidence of lung cancer in women has increased greatly in the past ten years. Why do you think this is so?

Skill Builder

Building Vocabulary Look up the words "benign" and "malignant" in a dictionary. Determine whether these words are antonyms or synonyms. Write two sentences for each term that describe different kinds of tumors.

Health & Safety Tip

One way to prevent cancer is to detect it early. You should look over your entire body for abnormalities, such as growths or sores. Use library references or first-aid books to find out about self-examination. Practice self-examination every month. The more familiar you are with these practices, the better chance you have of finding an abnormality and getting it treated early.

☷ TECHNOLOGY AND SOCIETY ☷ ☷ ☷ ☷ ☷ ☷ ☷ ☷ ☷ ☷ ☷ ☷

CANCER DETECTION AND TREATMENT

Different forms of cancer are detected in different ways. Noting a change in a mole or skin mark is a common method of detecting skin cancer. Breast cancer can sometimes be detected by examining the breast for a lump or by breast X-ray, called mammogram. Different methods are used for other types of cancer.

Cancer treatment also varies with different forms of cancer. Sometimes a tumor is surgically removed from the body. This treatment often works when the tumor is found early, before it has spread. Sometimes the tumor cannot be removed without damaging the organ in which it is growing. Doctors then use radiation to kill the cancer cells. Certain drugs have also been found to slow down the growth of tumors. The problem with these drugs is that they harm normal cells as well as cancerous ones.

Some new methods of cancer detection and treatment include using information that scientists gather from studying genes. Gene study has helped doctors diagnose certain cancers, such as colon cancer, more quickly. Treatment can begin earlier, when it is more effective.

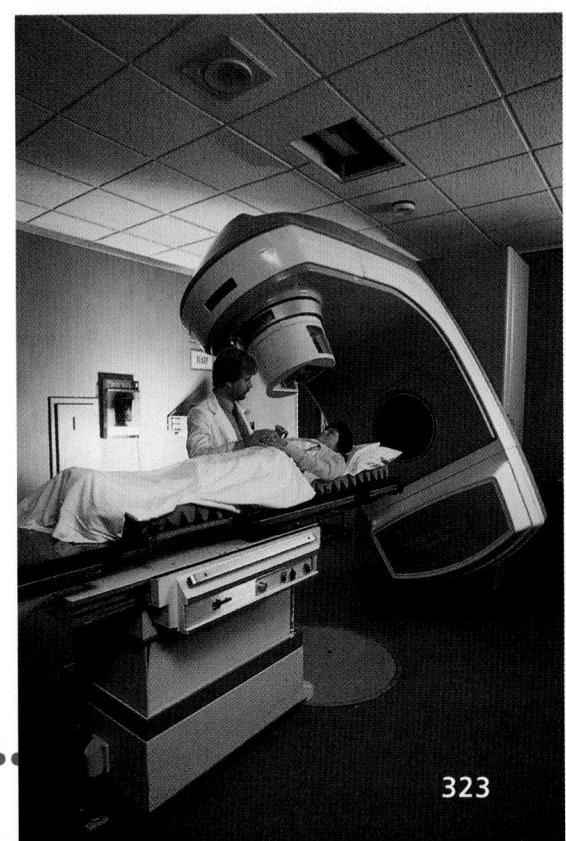

16-7 What is AIDS?

TechTerms

- **AIDS:** viral disease that attacks a person's immune system
- **immune system:** body system made up of cells and tissues that help a person fight disease

Immune System Your body is constantly fighting off germs and disease-causing organisms. The first line of defense against bacteria and viruses are structures located at body openings. For example, hairs in your nose work to filter particles from air taken in through the nose. However, some disease-causing substances manage to get past these hairs. Your body's second line of defense must then work to destroy the foreign substances. This second line of defense is called the **immune system.** The immune system is made up of cells and tissues that fight disease.

� *Identify:* What is the immune system? body system made up of cells and tissues that fight disease

HIV Viruses cause disease. They are selective in the cells or tissues that they attack. A particular virus, called HIV, attacks a person's immune system. The illness caused by HIV is called Acquired Immune Deficiency Syndrome, or **AIDS.** AIDS is a viral disease that kills white blood cells in a person's immune system. The person loses the ability to fight disease. For this reason, people with AIDS easily get diseases that most healthy people can fight off. These diseases often are fatal for a person with AIDS.

▶ *Describe:* What effect does HIV have on the body? attacks the immune system; causes AIDS

Transmission of AIDS AIDS cannot be transmitted by casual contact. It cannot travel through air, food, or water. People with AIDS have HIV in their blood and body fluids. In order to contract AIDS, you must exchange bodily fluids with an infected person. The virus can enter the bloodstream by sexual contact with someone who has HIV. The virus also can enter the bloodstream of intravenous drug users who use contaminated needles. Another way HIV enters the bloodstream is through blood transfusion of infected blood.

▶ *Explain:* How is HIV transmitted? sexual contact, contaminated needles, transfusion of infected blood, or exchange of bodily fluids

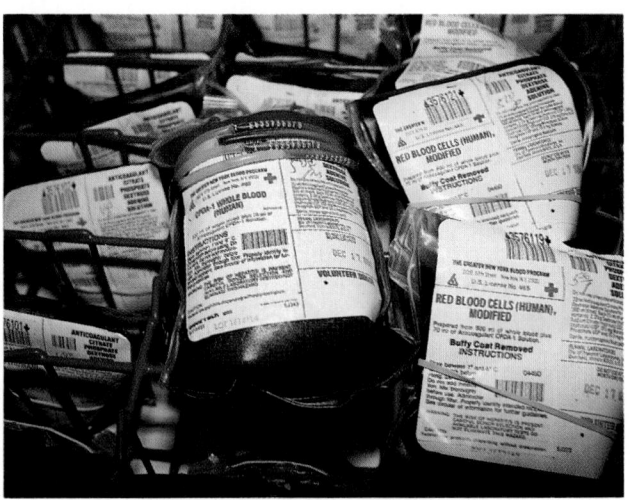

AIDS Treatment There is no known cure for AIDS at this time. However, scientists are working on ways to treat AIDS patients. Doctors have developed ways to strengthen the immune systems of people with AIDS. Scientists have been able to prolong the life of a person with AIDS, but there is no long-term cure.

▶ *Infer:* Why do you think AIDS research is so important? Answers will vary. Accept all logical responses.

LESSON SUMMARY

▶ The immune system is made up of cells and tissues that help the body fight disease.

▶ AIDS is a viral disease that kills white blood cells in a person's immune system.

▶ AIDS cannot be transmitted by casual contact.

▶ At present, there is no long-term treatment or cure for AIDS.

CHECK *Complete the following.*

1. The body's first line of defense against disease are structures located at _____ . body openings

2. The immune system is made up of cells and _____ that fight disease. tissues

3. HIV attacks the body's _____ . immune system

4. People with AIDS have HIV in their _____ and body fluids. bloodstream

5. HIV can enter the bloodstream through

_____ . sexual contact, contaminated needles, transfusion of infected blood, or exchange of bodily fluids

APPLY *Complete the following.*

▶ 7. **Infer:** The leading cause of death among AIDS patients is an infection of the lungs. How is HIV responsible for such infections?

HIV attacks a person's immune system, making that person more prone to the lung infection.

8. Could a person with AIDS transmit the virus to another person sitting on the opposite side of the room? No, because HIV cannot travel through the air.

▶ 9. **Infer:** Some large cities distribute clean needles to drug users. Why do you think they do this?

▶ 10. **Infer:** How does making the immune system stronger lengthen the life of a person infected with AIDS?

InfoSearch

Read the passage. Ask two questions that you cannot answer from the information in the passage.

Blood Screening Blood transfusions often are necessary to save lives. During a transfusion, the person is given blood that was previously taken from a blood donor. In 1985, hospitals began testing donor blood for HIV. This test looks for certain antibodies in the blood, indicating that it is contaminated with HIV. The test works only on the blood of a person who has been infected with HIV at least 10 weeks before the test. In 1996, a test became available that screens for antigens of HIV. This test gives results more quickly.

SEARCH: Use library references to find answers to your questions.

ACTIVITY

INVESTIGATING THE SPREAD OF AIDS

You will need paper, pencil, and a calculator (optional).

1. Study Table 1.
2. Rank the states in order from the state with the most reported AIDS cases to the fewest reported AIDS cases.

Questions

1. **a.** Which state has the most reported AIDS cases?
   b. Which state has the fewest reported AIDS cases?

2. **Calculate:** What is the total number of reported AIDS cases in Table 1?

▶ 3. **Analyze:** Do you think AIDS is a nationwide problem?

Table 1 Reported AIDS Cases in 10 States Through June 1996*

STATE	TOTAL CASES
California	93,749
Florida	55,690
Georgia	15,866
Illinois	17,584
Maryland	14,082
Massachusetts	11,287
New Jersey	31,124
New York	101,049
Pennsylvania	16,270
Texas	37,320

*Source: CDC

16-8 How do some drugs affect the body?

Objective ▶ Describe the effects of some drugs on the body.

TechTerms

- **addiction** (uh-DIK-shun): uncontrollable dependence on a drug
- **depressant** (di-PRES-unt): drug that slows down the central nervous system
- **hallucinogen** (hul-LOO-suh-nuh-jen): drug that causes a person to see, hear, smell, and taste things in a strange way
- **stimulant** (STIM-yuh-lent): drug that speeds up the central nervous system

Drugs A drug is a chemical substance that causes a change in the body. Aspirin and antacids are drugs that can be bought in a store. You do not need a doctor's prescription for these drugs. Other drugs, such as antibiotics, can be bought only with a doctor's prescription.

▶ *Define:* **What is a drug?** chemical substance that causes a change in the body

Depressants Drugs are grouped according to the effects they have on the body. **Depressants** (di-PRES-unts) are drugs that slow down the central nervous system. They slow down the heartbeat and breathing rate. Large amounts of depressants can cause a person to go into a coma, or even die.

The most widely abused depressant is alcohol. Barbiturates (bar-BICH-uhr-its) are depressants commonly used in sleeping pills and sedatives.

Narcotics (nar-KOT-iks) are depressants used as pain killers. If barbiturates or narcotics are used over a period of time, the user may develop an **addiction** (uh-DIK-shun) to the drug. An addiction is an uncontrollable dependence on a drug. People can develop both physical and mental addictions to drugs. The addicted person cannot stop using the drug without going through a period of sickness.

▶ *Describe:* **What effect do barbiturates have on the body?** They slow down the central nervous system.

Stimulants Some drugs speed up the action of the central nervous system. These drugs are called **stimulants** (STIM-yuh-lents). In many ways, the effects of stimulants are opposite those of depressants. Stimulants speed up a person's heartbeat and rate of breathing. Cocaine is a commonly abused stimulant. Crack is a purified form of cocaine that is extremely dangerous. You may be surprised to learn that caffeine also is a stimulant. Caffeine is found in coffee, tea, cola, and chocolate.

▶ *Contrast:* **How does the effect of a stimulant differ from the effect of a depressant?** Stimulants speed up the central nervous system while depressants slow it down.

Hallucinogens Some drugs change the way a person receives information through the senses. For example, they cause a person to see, hear, smell, and taste things in a strange way. These drugs are called **hallucinogens** (hul-LOO-suh-nuh-jenz). Hallucinogens often make a person feel panicked or threatened. For this reason, people who take hallucinogens often are dangerous to themselves and others. LSD and marijuana are two commonly abused hallucinogens.

▶ *Explain:* **What effect do hallucinogens have on the body?** They change the way a person receives information through the senses.

LESSON SUMMARY

▶ A drug is a chemical substance that causes a change in the body.

▶ Depressants slow down the action of the central nervous system.

▶ People who use drugs, such as depressants, can become addicted to the drug.

▶ Stimulants speed up the action of the central nervous system.

▶ Hallucinogens change the way a person receives information through the senses.

CHECK *Answer the following.*

1. What are two drugs that you can buy without a doctor's prescription? Answers will vary. Accept all logical responses.
2. What effect do depressants have on the body? slow down the action of the central nervous system
3. What group of depressants often are used as pain killers? narcotics
4. What effect do stimulants have on the body? speed up the action of the central nervous system
5. What kind of drug is marijuana? hallucinogen
6. What is the most abused depressant drug? alcohol

APPLY *Complete the following.*

7. What effect does coffee have on the central nervous system?

8. **Relate:** Which drug, a barbiturate or cocaine, would most likely make a person feel wide awake? Explain your answer. Cocaine; because it is a stimulant.

Health & Safety Tip

The vapors from certain common household products can have a harmful effect on the body when inhaled. Sniffing large amounts of airplane cement, cleaning fluids, and paint thinners can cause damage to the tissues of the heart, liver, and kidneys. Sniffing such substances may cause unconsciousness, drowsiness, and even death. You should be sure to work with these products only in well-ventilated areas.

Skill Builder

📁 **Classifying** Use library references to find out information about the following drugs: amphetamines, heroin, morphine, tranquilizers, PCP, and nicotine. Then classify each drug as either a stimulant, a depressant, or a hallucinogen. Present your findings in a report.

ACTIVITY

READING DRUG LABELS

You will need 3 different over-the-counter drug or medication labels or packaging, paper and a pencil.

1. Examine one of your drug or medication labels. Write the name of the drug or medication and its use.
2. Find the dosage instructions and record the dosage.
3. Find the expiration date and record it.
4. Record any special warnings or precautions.
5. Repeat Steps 1–4 for each drug or medication.

Questions

1. What does the expiration date tell you about the drug?
2. What information is given in the dosage directions?
3. **Hypothesize:** Why is the recommended dosage of a drug for an adult different from that for a child?
4. **Observe:** What warning statement is found on all labels?

16-9 How does alcohol affect the body?

Objective ▶ Describe the effects alcohol has on the body.

TechTerms

▶ **alcoholic** (al-kuh-HOWL-ik): person who is dependent on alcohol

▶ **cirrhosis** (suh-ROH-sis): liver disorder caused by damaged liver cells

Ethyl Alcohol You have learned that a drug is a substance that causes a change in the body. One of the most commonly abused drugs is ethyl (ETH-ul) alcohol. Ethyl alcohol is the alcohol that is in drinks, such as beer, wine, and whiskey. Alcohol is a drug because it causes a change in the body. Most people think that alcohol is a stimulant. However, alcohol is a depressant. It slows down the action of the central nervous system.

▶ *Explain:* What effect does alcohol have on the body? slows down the central nervous system

Alcohol and the Brain The amount of alcohol present in the bloodstream is called Blood Alcohol Concentration (BAC). The effect of alcohol on the body increases as the Blood Alcohol Concentration increases. When people drink alcohol, their body systems slow down. They think and react more slowly. Their movements become clumsy.

▶ *Infer:* Why do you think it is dangerous for a person who has been drinking to drive a car? Answers will vary, but should include mention that alcohol slows down the actions of their body systems.

Alcohol and the Body Alcohol affects many organs of the body. If a person does not drink very much, or very often, the effects of alcohol wear off after a period of time. However, if the drinking continues over a period of time, the body can be harmed. The liver can be greatly affected by alcohol. Large amounts of alcohol taken over a long period of time slowly destroy the liver tissues. The liver then loses its ability to carry out its functions. This condition is called **cirrhosis** (suh-ROH-sis). Cirrhosis of the liver often leads to death.

▶ *Identify:* What is cirrhosis of the liver? destruction of liver tissue by drinking large amounts of alcohol

Alcoholics Alcohol is addictive for some people. These people drink more and more alcohol as time goes by. They become dependent on alcohol. A person who cannot control his or her drinking of alcohol is called an alcoholic (al-kuh-HOWL-ik). Alcoholism is a disease because it causes harmful changes in body organs. Many alcoholics get help from groups such as Alcoholics Anonymous or AL-ATEEN.

▶ *Describe:* What is an alcoholic? person who is dependent upon alcohol

LESSON SUMMARY

▶ Ethyl alcohol is a depressant drug.

▶ Alcohol slows down the working of the body systems.

▶ Cirrhosis is a liver disorder caused by destroyed liver cells.

▶ An alcoholic is a person who is dependent upon alcohol.

CHECK *Find the sentence in the lesson that answers each question. Then, write the sentence.*

1. What kind of alcohol is in alcoholic drinks?

2. What effect does alcohol have on body systems?

3. How does a person act after drinking alcohol?

4. What effect does drinking over a long period of time have on the body?

5. What is a person who is dependent on alcohol called?

APPLY *Answer the following.*

6. **Relate:** A person drinks a glass of wine every night before dinner. Is this person an alcoholic? Explain your answer.

Health & Safety Tip

When two different drugs are taken together, their effects can be increased greatly. Therefore, even a single alcoholic drink should not be taken with any other kind of drug. Even a harmless drug, such as an aspirin, can change the way alcohol affects a person. To be safe, alcohol should never be mixed with other drugs.

Skill Builder

Researching Pregnant woman who drink have a high risk of giving birth to babies with fetal alcohol syndrome. Fetal alcohol syndrome can cause low birth weight, and both physical and mental disabilities. Use library resources to find out more about fetal alcohol syndrome. Present your findings in a report.

ACTIVITY

COMPARING BLOOD ALCOHOL CONCENTRATION

You will need graph paper and a pencil.

1. Carefully read the table.

2. Use the information in the table to make a bar graph.

Questions

👁 1. **Observe:** At what blood alcohol concentration does the drinker have difficulty thinking?

👁 2. **Observe:** About how much alcohol is present in the bloodstream of a person who has had 4 drinks in two hours?

✏ 3. **Analyze:** Is it possible to "drink yourself to death"? Explain your answer.

Table 1 Blood Alcohol Concentration (BAC) and its Effects		
*DRINKS PER HOUR	BAC (PERCENT)	EFFECTS
1	0.02–0.03	Feeling of relaxation
2	0.05–0.06	Slight loss of coordination
3	0.08–0.09	Loss of coordination, trouble talking and thinking, legal intoxication
4	0.11–0.12	Slowed reaction time; lack of judgement
7	0.20	Difficulty thinking; loss of motor skills
14	0.40	Unconsciousness; vomiting may occur
17	0.50	Deep coma; if breathing ceases, death
* 1 drink equals 12 oz beer, 4 oz wine, or 1 oz whisky		

16-10 How does tobacco affect the body?

Objective ▶ Explain the effects of tobacco on the body.

TechTerm

▶ **nicotine** (NIK-uh-teen): stimulant found in tobacco

Tobacco Tobacco contains more than 100 chemical substances. When tobacco burns, many new substances are formed. All of these substances are taken into the body with the tobacco smoke. One of the harmful substances in tobacco smoke is **nicotine** (NIK-uh-teen). Nicotine is a stimulant drug. Tars and carbon monoxide are other harmful substances found in tobacco smoke. When inhaled, tar coats the lining of the lungs. Carbon monoxide is a poisonous gas that may cause dizziness and headaches.

▬▶ *Identify:* What are three harmful substances found in tobacco smoke? nicotine, tar, and carbon monoxide

Effect on Breathing The air tubes in the lungs are lined with cells. These cells have tiny hairs called cilia. The cilia beat back and forth to push mucus from the lungs toward the throat. Foreign substances trapped in the mucus get pushed out of the lungs. Smoking causes the cilia to stop working. Without the action of the cilia, mucus collects in and blocks the air tubes. This trapped air causes the air sacs in the air tubes to break. With fewer air sacs at work, less oxygen flows into the lungs with each breath. Less carbon dioxide is released from the body with each exhalation. The smoker must breathe harder and more often to get enough oxygen.

▬▶ *Explain:* What effect does smoking have on the cilia in the air tubes of the lungs? It causes them to stop beating.

Illnesses When the cilia stop beating, foreign substances remain trapped in the lungs. There, these substances may cause infection and disease. Smokers are more likely to get heart disease, cancer, and emphysema (em-fuh-SEE-muh) than nonsmokers. Smokers have a higher death rate from these diseases than do nonsmokers. Compare the healthy lung on the left in the picture with the smoker's lung on the right.

Smoking also places a great strain on the heart. With fewer air sacs in the lungs, the blood gets less oxygen. The heart must work harder to supply enough fresh oxygen for body cells. Nicotine also makes the blood vessels become narrower. The heart must work harder to pump the blood through the smaller openings. This puts an even greater strain on the heart.

▬▶ *Describe:* What effect does nicotine have on blood vessels? It causes them to become narrower.

LESSON SUMMARY

▶ Tobacco smoke contains many different kinds of harmful chemicals, including nicotine, tar, and carbon monoxide.

▶ Smoking causes the cilia lining the air tubes in the lungs to stop working.

▶ Smoking increases the chance of getting certain serious illnesses.

▶ Smoking puts a strain on the heart and blood vessels.

CHECK *Complete the following.*

1. Nicotine, carbon monoxide, and _____ are examples of harmful substances found in tobacco smoke.   tar

2. When cilia in the air tubes stop beating, _____ collects and blocks the tubes.   mucus

3. Nicotine makes blood vessels become _____ .   narrower

4. Smoking puts a great strain on the _____ .
heart

APPLY *Complete the following.*

5. **Infer:** What effect would cigarette smoking have on a person's ability to exercise?

6. **Hypothesize:** Nicotine is an addictive drug. Why do you think it may be difficult for a person to quit smoking?

InfoSearch

Read the passage. Ask two questions that you cannot answer from the information in the passage.

Secondhand Smoke Research has shown that cigarette smoke has a harmful effect on nonsmokers as well as smokers. For example, children of smokers are twice as likely to have respiratory problems as children of nonsmokers. This is caused by the exposure to secondhand smoke from a burning cigarette. In recent years, smoking has been banned from many public places. For example, smoking is restricted or banned from many restaurants, offices, airplanes, and trains. This was done in an attempt to protect nonsmokers from secondhand smoke.

SEARCH: Use library references to find answers to your questions.

ACTIVITY

CLASSIFYING CIGARETTE ADVERTISEMENTS

You will need magazines, newspapers, paper and pencil.

1. Find several advertisements for cigarettes.
2. Find several advertisements against smoking.
3. Read the advertisements carefully.
4. List the warnings contained in the advertisements.
5. **a.** Make a list of the pictures found in the cigarette advertisements.   **b.** Make another list of the pictures which discourage people from smoking.

Questions

1. Did you find more advertisements for or against smoking?
2. How many different warning statements were in the advertisements?
3. **a. Analyze:** Which companies or organizations sponsor the pro-smoking advertisements?   **b.** Which organizations sponsor the anti-smoking advertisements?

STUDY HINT Before you begin the Unit Challenges, review the TechTerms and Lesson Summary for each lesson in this unit.

TechTerms

addiction (326)
AIDS (324)
alcoholic (328)
antibiotic (318)
antibodies (312)
atherosclerosis (320)
benign tumor (322)

cirrhosis (328)
coronary arteries (320)
depressant (326)
hallucinogen (326)
heart attack (320)
immune system (324)

immunity (314)
malignant tumor (322)
nicotine (330)
stimulant (326)
tumor (322)
white blood cells (312)

TechTerm Challenges

Matching *Write the TechTerm that best matches each description.*

1. cells that protect the body against disease
   white blood cells
2. stimulant drug found in tobacco nicotine
3. resistance to a certain disease immunity
4. liver disorder caused by damaged liver cells cirrhosis
5. buildup of fat deposits on artery walls atherosclerosis
6. person who is dependent on alcohol alcoholic
7. arteries that carry blood and oxygen to the tissues of the heart coronary arteries
8. kind of drug that causes a person to see, hear, mell, and taste things in a strange way hallucinogen
9. lack of blood and oxygen to a part of the heart heart attack
10. uncontrollable dependence on a drug addiction
11. mass or lump of cells tumor
12. body system made up of cells and tissues that help a person fight disease immune system
13. viral disease that attacks a person's immune system AIDS

Identifying Word Relationships *Explain how the terms in each pair are related. Write your answers in complete sentences.* Answers will vary. Accept all logical responses.

1. benign tumor, malignant tumor
2. depressant, stimulant
3. antibiotic, antibodies
4. coronary arteries, atherosclerosis
5. alcohol, cirrhosis
6. immunity, immune system

Content Challenges

Multiple Choice *Write the letter of the term that best completes each statement.*

1. All of the following are stimulants EXCEPT
   a. nicotine. **b.** tar. **c.** caffeine. **d.** cocaine. b

2. Drugs that slow down the central nervous system are
   a. hallucinogens. **b.** depressants. **c.** barbiturates. **d.** stimulants. b

3. The immunity a person is born with is called
   a. active immunity. **b.** acquired immunity. **c.** passive immunity. **d.** natural immunity. d

4. AIDS is a disease of the
   a. circulatory system. **b.** immune system. **c.** digestive system. **d.** respiratory system. b

5. All of the following body systems help prevent infection EXCEPT the
   a. respiratory system.   b. digestive system.   c. circulatory system.   d. nervous system. d

6. AIDS is a disease that is NOT transmitted by
   a. infected blood.   b. casual contact.   c. contaminated needles.   d. sexual contact. b

7. Hepatitis usually is caused by a
   a. virus.   b. bacterium.   c. fungus.   d. protozoan. a

8. Drugs that cause people to see things that do not exist are
   a. sleeping pills.   b. barbiturates.   c. depressants.   d. hallucinogens. d

9. The stimulant drug found in tobacco is
   a. tar.   b. nicotine.   c. carbon monoxide.   d. carbon dioxide. b

10. The risk factor for heart disease that you can control is
    a. age.   b. gender.   c. physical inactivity.   d. family history. c

11. Cirrhosis of the liver is a disease caused by
    a. hepatitis.   b. alcohol.   c. tobacco.   d. depressants. b

12. The body's first line of defense against disease is the
    a. mouth.   b. white blood cells.   c. skin.   d. nose. c

13. All of the following are caused by viruses EXCEPT
    a. strep throat.   b. chicken pox.   c. measles.   d. mumps. a

14. All of the following are caused by bacteria EXCEPT
    a. influenza.   b. meningitis.   c. tetanus.   d. toxic shock syndrome. b

15. Crack is a form of
    a. heroin.   b. cocaine.   c. LSD.   d. opium. b

Completion *Write the term that best completes each statement.*

1. Alcohol is classified as a _____ drug. depressant

2. Nicotine is classified as a _____ drug. stimulant

3. When the body has developed an uncontrollable dependance on the drug, it has become _____ . addicted

4. Vaccines are used to acquire _____ immunity. passive

5. Active acquired immunity lasts a _____ time. long

6. The germ theory was first stated by _____ . Pasteur

7. Substances produced by the body to fight disease are called _____ . antibodies

8. Most antibiotics are produced from _____ . molds

9. The kind of tumor that may be harmless is a _____ tumor. benign

10. When there is a blood clot in the brain, it is called a _____ . stroke

Understanding the Features

Reading Critically *Use the feature reading selections to answer the following. Page numbers for the features are shown in parentheses.*

1. **Identify:** What are some ways you can practice preventive medicine? (313)

2. How has the discovery of vaccines helped in the prevention of disease? (315)

3. **List:** What are the four steps in Koch's Postulates? (317)

4. How has the work of Joseph Lister saved lives? (319)

5. **List:** What are some low-cholesterol foods that can be substituted for red meat? (321)

6. **Identify:** What are some of the ways cancers are treated? (323)

Concept Challenges ....

Interpreting a Table *Use the following table to answer the questions.*

Table 1	Blood Alcohol Concentration (BAC) and its Effects	
*DRINKS PER HOUR	BAC (PERCENT)	EFFECTS
1	0.02–0.03	Feeling of relaxation
2	0.05–0.06	Slight loss of coordination
3	0.08–0.09	Loss of coordination, trouble talking and thinking, legal intoxication
4	0.11–0.12	Slowed reaction time; lack of judgement
7	0.20	Difficulty thinking; loss of motor skills
14	0.40	Unconsciousness; vomiting may occur
17	0.50	Deep coma; if breathing ceases, death

* 1 drink equals 12 oz. beer, 4 oz. wine, or 1 oz whisky

1. What is the percent of alcohol in the bloodstream when you are considered legally intoxicated?
2. What is the effect of one drink in one hour on the body?
3. What is the percent of alcohol in the body when the body goes into a coma?
4. **Calculate:** How many ounces of wine is there in 7 'drinks'?
▶ 5. **Infer:** Why do you think it is dangerous to drive after 4 drinks?
6. **Calculate:** If a person had a drink that contained two ounces of whisky, what effect would it have on the body?
7. What is the BAC percent when vomiting or unconsciousness may occur?
8. What does BAC stand for?

Critical Thinking *Answer each of the following in complete sentences.*

1. Why is it dangerous for drug users to share hypodermic needles?
▶ 2. **Infer:** A person has smoked cigarettes for over ten years. Do you think it is too late for this person to quit smoking? Explain your answer.
3. The surgeon general has issued a warning statement that must appear on all containers of alcoholic beverages. Do you agree or disagree with this labeling?
▶ 4. **Infer:** Why do you think dentists often wear face masks and rubber gloves when examining patients?
▶ 5. **Infer:** How do you think a drug addiction affects a person's life? Explain your answer.

Finding Out More ....

1. Caffeine is an addictive drug that may be associated with heart disease and certain kinds of cancers. Use library references to find out some of the common food or drink items that contain caffeine. Research the dangers of caffeine addiction, as well as the symptoms of caffeine withdrawal.
2. Many schools now have chapters of SADD (Students Against Drunk Drivers). Investigate the process of setting up a chapter at your school. Then as a class, set up a chapter at your school.
3. Immunization against disease is important to good health. Use library references to find out the different immunizations that are recommended. Visit or call your doctor and find out if your immunizations are up to date.
4. Obtain information about cancer prevention from the local chapter of the American Cancer Society. Create a classroom display of the pamphlets and other information your receive.

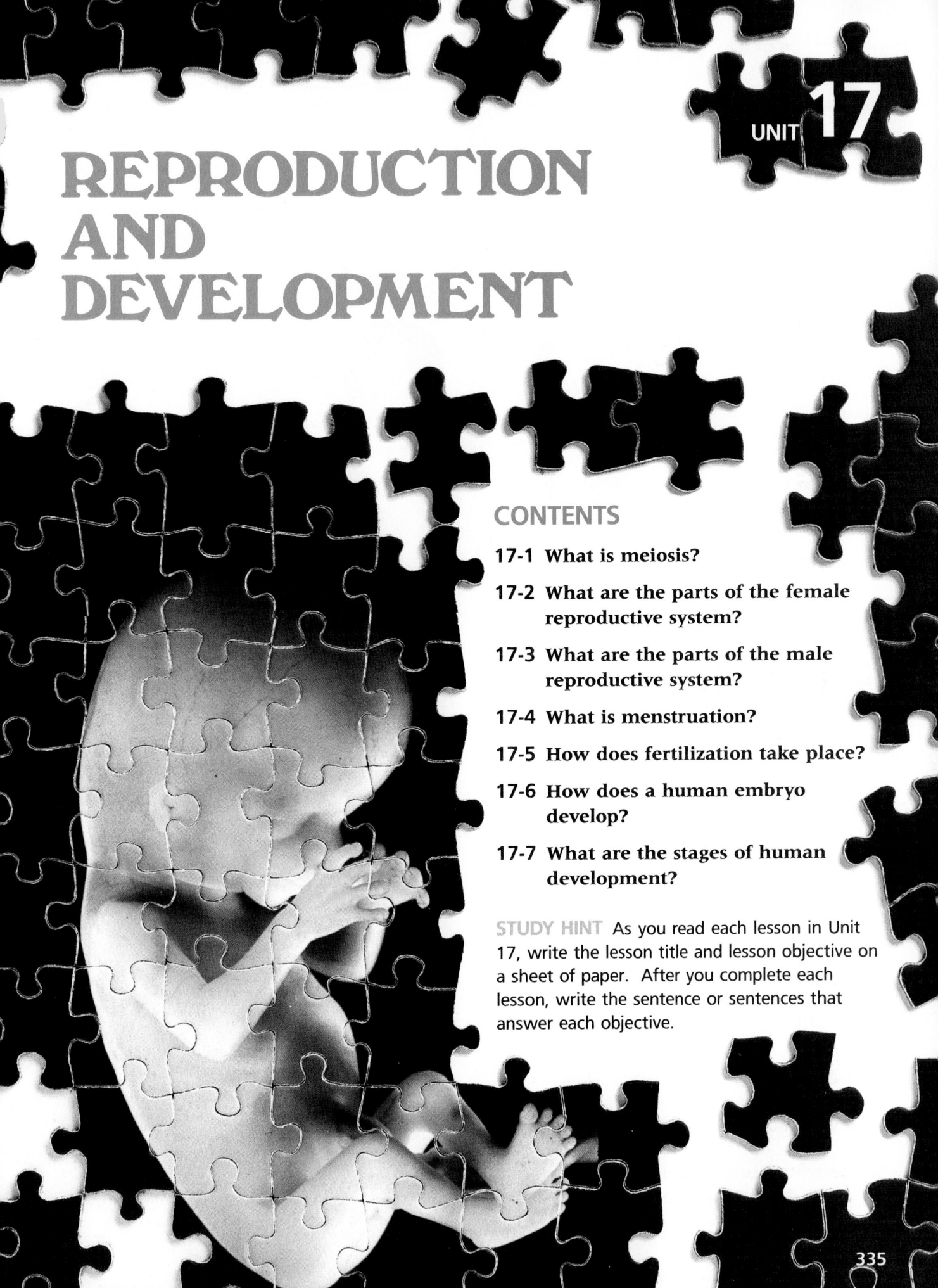

REPRODUCTION AND DEVELOPMENT

CONTENTS

STUDY HINT As you read each lesson in Unit 17, write the lesson title and lesson objective on a sheet of paper. After you complete each lesson, write the sentence or sentences that answer each objective.

What is meiosis?

TechTerms

> ► **gamete** (GAM-eet): reproductive cell
> ► **meiosis** (my-OH-sis): cell division that produces gametes

Body Cells Each body cell of an animal contains the same number of chromosomes. For example, each body cell in a bullfrog contain 26 chromosomes. Fruit flies have 8 chromosomes in each body cell. The body cells of humans contain 46 chromosomes.

▐▐▶ *Identify:* How many chromosomes are in each human body cell? 46

Gametes Sperm cells and egg cells are reproductive cells. Reproductive cells also are called **gametes** (GAM-eets). Gametes develop from special cells in the body. During the formation of gametes, the number of chromosomes changes. It is cut in half. Each gamete contains only half as many chromosomes as a body cell. The process by which gametes form is called **meiosis** (my-OH-sis). The cells formed by meiosis have half the number of chromosomes as body cells.

Nucleus of fruit fly body cell

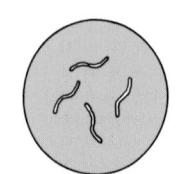

Nucleus of fruit fly gamete

▐▐▶ *Compare:* What is the relationship between the number of chromosomes in body cells and gametes? Gametes contain half the number of chromosomes of body cells.

Meiosis Meiosis begins when the nucleus of a cell breaks down. The pairs of chromosomes in the cell split apart and move to opposite ends of the

cell. The cell divides into two daughter cells. Each daughter cell is a gamete. Each gamete contains half the number of chromosomes of the original cell.

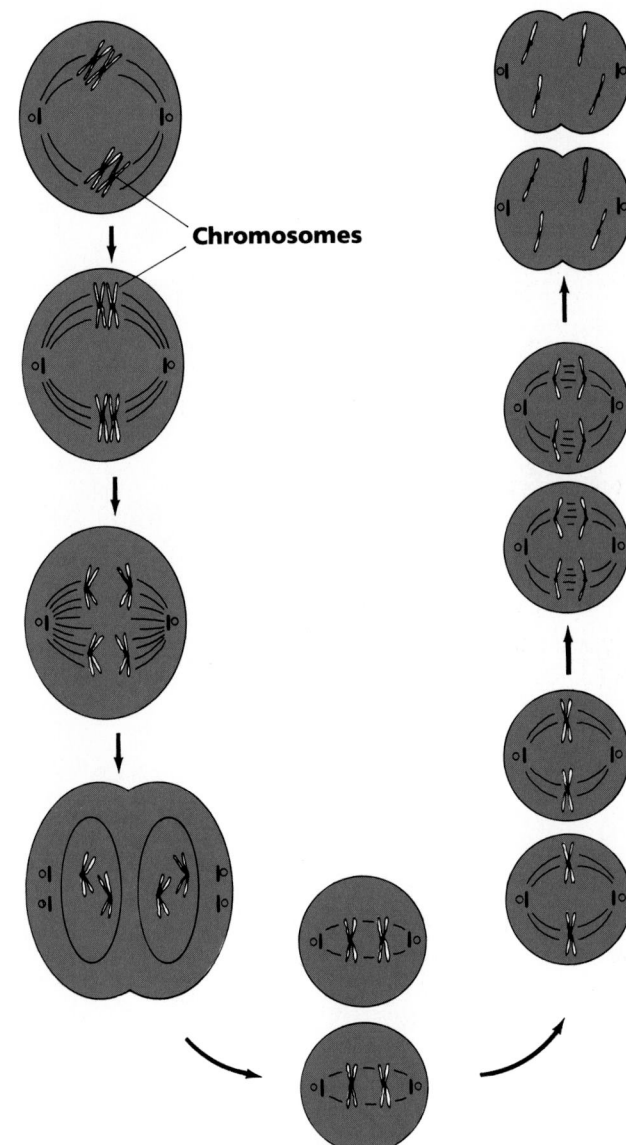

Chromosomes

The body cell of a fruit fly contains 8 chromosomes. After meiosis, there are only 4 chromosomes in each gamete. Your body cells contain 46 chromosomes. After meiosis, there are only 23 chromosomes in each gamete that forms.

▐▐▶ *Explain:* Why do gametes contain half the number of chromosomes as body cells? When the cell divides in half, each gamete receives half the chromosomes found in the parent cell.

LESSON SUMMARY

▶ Each body cell of an animal contains the same number of chromosomes.

▶ Reproductive cells are called gametes.

▶ Gametes are produced by meiosis.

▶ A gamete contains half the number of chromosomes of a body cell.

CHECK *Complete the following.*

1. All human body cells contain _____ chromosomes. 46

2. Sperm cells and egg cells are _____ cells. reproductive

3. The process that reduces the number of chromosomes in a cell by one-half is _____ . meiosis

4. Meiosis occurs only in the formation of _____ . gametes

APPLY *Complete the following.*

5. How many chromosomes does a human egg cell contain? Why? 23

6. **Relate:** What would happen if the chromosomes did not move to opposite sides of the nucleus before the cell divided? Daughter cells could contain uneven numbers of chromosomes.

7. **Compare:** How are mitosis and meiosis similar? Hint: review the process of mitosis discussed in Lesson 4-6. Both processes produce daughter cells.

8. **Analyze:** Which of the gametes shown would be produced by an organism with 14 chromosomes in its body cells? b

 a. b. 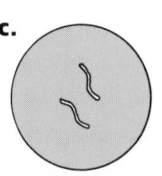 c.

State the Problem

Study the illustrations. Then, state the problem.

 Human body cell

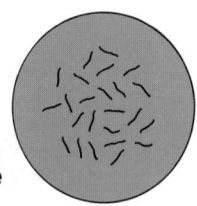 Human gamete

Skill Builder

▲ ***Organizing Information*** When you organize information, you put the information in some kind of order. Divide a sheet of paper into two columns labeled "Mitosis" and "Meiosis." Beneath each heading, list all the facts you have learned about each process.

SCIENCE CONNECTION ◆○◆○◆○◆○◆○◆○◆○◆○◆○◆○◆○◆○◆○◆○◆○◆

NONDISJUNCTION

During meiosis, chromosome pairs separate to form gametes. Usually, a gamete receives one chromosome from each pair. Sometimes, however, the chromosome pairs do not separate correctly. This condition is called nondisjunction (nahn-dis-JUNK-shun).

When nondisjunction occurs, both chromosomes in a pair go to the same gamete. As a result, one gamete has too many chromosomes and the other gamete has too few. If either of these gametes unites with a normal gamete during fertilization, the organism does not develop properly.

There are several conditions that result from nondisjunction. One of these conditions is Down syndrome. The body cells of a person with Down syndome contain 47 chromosomes instead of 46. People with Down syndrome can lead productive lives, but they usually have some degree of mental retardation.

17-2 What are the parts of the female reproductive system?

Objective ▶ Describe the organs of the female reproductive system.

TechTerms

- ▶ **cervix** (SUR-viks): narrow end of the uterus
- ▶ **ovaries** (OH-vuhr-eez): main organs of the female reproductive system
- ▶ **oviduct** (OH-vuh-dukt): long tube between the ovary and the uterus
- ▶ **uterus** (YOOT-ur-us): organ in which an embryo develops
- ▶ **vagina** (vuh-JY-nuh): birth canal

Reproductive Systems Most systems of the body are the same in males and females. This is not true of reproductive systems. The male and female reproductive systems are quite different. All the organs of the female reproductive system are located inside a female's body. In the male reproductive system, some organs are inside the body, while other organs are located outside the body. The main job of both the male and female reproductive systems is to produce offspring.

▶ **Compare:** How is the reproductive system different from other body systems? It is different in males and females.

Ovaries The **ovaries** (OH-vuhr-eez) are the main organs of the female reproductive system. Ovaries are egg-shaped structures. One ovary lies on each side of the female's body.

The ovaries contain two different kinds of cells. One kind of cell produces hormones. The other kind of cell produces eggs. Eggs are female sex cells.

▶ **Describe:** What do the ovaries produce? hormones and eggs

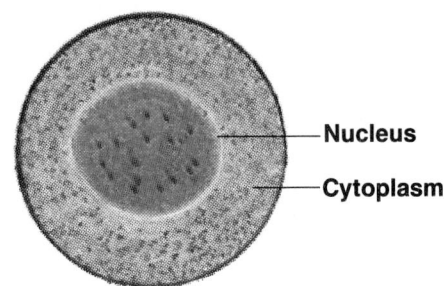

Figure 1 An egg cell

Pathway of Eggs Study the female reproductive system shown in Figure 2. A long tube called an **oviduct** (OH-vuh-dukt) lies near each ovary. The oviduct carries eggs to the **uterus** (YOOT-ur-us). The uterus is a hollow organ with thick, muscular walls. This is where an embryo develops.

As the uterus extends downward, it becomes narrower. The narrow end of the uterus is called the **cervix** (SUR-viks). The cervix connects the uterus to the **vagina** (vuh-JY-nuh). The vagina is the opening through which a baby passes during birth. The vagina is also called the birth canal.

▶ **Explain:** Why is the vagina called the birth canal? It is the opening through which a baby passes during birth.

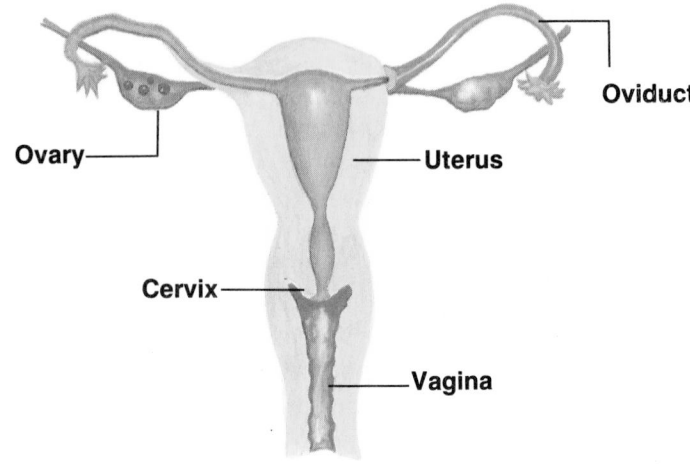

Figure 2 The female reproductive system

LESSON SUMMARY

▶ All the parts of the female reproductive system are located inside the female's body.

▶ The main organs of the female reproductive system are the ovaries.

▶ The ovaries produce hormones and eggs.

▶ An embryo develops inside the uterus.

▶ The vagina is the passageway through which a baby moves during birth.

CHECK *Answer the following.*

1. What are the main organs of the female reproductive system? ovaries

2. What are female sex cells called? eggs

3. What is the long tube that carries an egg from the ovary to the uterus? oviduct

4. What is the narrow end of the uterus? cervix

5. What is another name for the vagina? birth canal

APPLY *Answer the following.*

6. **Relate:** Through which structures of the female reproductive system does a baby pass? uterus, cervix, and vagina

7. **Describe:** Where are the female reproductive organs located? inside the body cavity

8. **Infer:** The walls of the uterus are flexible, and can expand and contract. How does this help a developing embryo? As the embryo grows in size, the uterus can become larger.

9. **Relate:** What happens to the size of the uterus as the embryo becomes larger? The uterus also becomes larger.

10. **Infer:** Why is the vagina also called the birth canal? The baby passes through the vagina during birth.

11. **Applying definitions:** The term "ova" means "egg." A duct is a tube. Relate these definitions to the function of the oviduct. The oviduct is the tube through which the egg passes.

Skill Builder

Making a Diagram A diagram is a way to organize information. Diagrams also illustrate relationships between the parts of a group. Make a diagram that shows how the parts of the female reproductive system are related. Label the parts of your diagram.

SCIENCE CONNECTION

ECTOPIC PREGNANCY

The joining together of a sperm cell and an egg cell is called fertilization (fur-tul-ih-ZAY-shun). Fertilization usually occurs in the oviducts. The fertilized egg then travels through the oviduct to the uterus. Once inside the uterus, the egg attaches to the wall of the uterus. Here the fertilized egg develops into an embryo.

Sometimes, a fertilized egg attaches to a structure outside the uterus. This condition is called an ectopic (ek-TAHP-ik) pregnancy. Ectopic pregnancies can occur in the oviducts, in the abdomen, or in the ovaries.

An ectopic pregnancy in the oviducts is called a tubal ectopic pregnancy. A tubal ectopic pregnancy is the most common ectopic pregnancy. This kind of ectopic pregnancy can be caused by a swelling of the oviducts. It also can be caused by scar tissue. As the embryo develops in the oviducts, it blocks the blood supply. This blockage causes severe pain in the pregnant woman.

What are the parts of the male reproductive system?

Objective ▶ Describe the structures of the male reproductive system.

TechTerms

▶ **scrotum** (SKROH-tum): pocket of skin that protects and holds the testes

▶ **testes** (TES-teez): main organs of the male reproductive system

▶ **testosterone** (tes-TAWS-tuhr-ohn): hormone produced in the testes

▶ **urethra** (yoo-REETH-ruh): tube that carries sperm to the outside of the male's body

The Testes The main organs of the male reproductive system are the **testes** (TES-teez). The testes are egg-shaped structures located outside the body. The testes rest in a pocket of skin called the **scrotum** (SKROH-tum). The organs of the male reproductive system are shown in Figure 1.

▶ *Identify:* What are the main organs of the male reproductive system? testes

Figure 2 Sperm cells

Testosterone Two kinds of cells are located in the testes. One type of cell produces **testosterone** (tes-TAWS-tuhr-ohn). Testosterone is a hormone that controls the development of secondary sex characteristics. In a male, these characteristics include a deeper voice and the growth of body hair. Testosterone also causes male sex cells to develop inside the testes. Male sex cells are called sperm.

▶ *Describe:* What substances are produced inside the testes? testosterone and sperm

The Urethra The **urethra** (yoo-REETH-ruh) is part of the excretory system. Urine made in the kidneys travels from the bladder to the outside of the body through the urethra.

In males, the urethra performs another job. It is the passageway through which sperm leaves a male's body. For this reason, the urethra is considered to be a part of the male reproductive system.

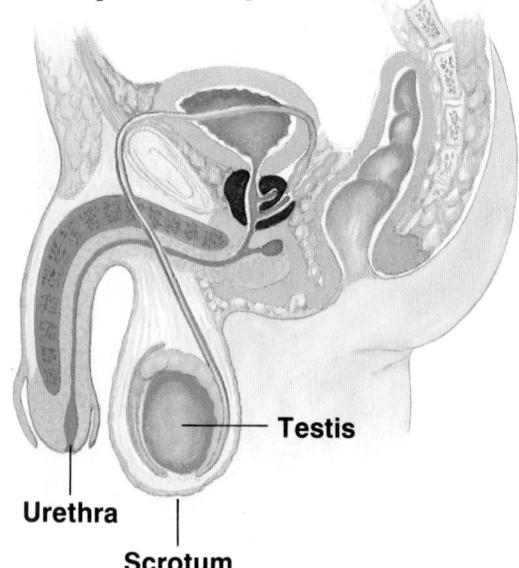

Urethra

Scrotum

Testis

Figure 1 The male reproductive system

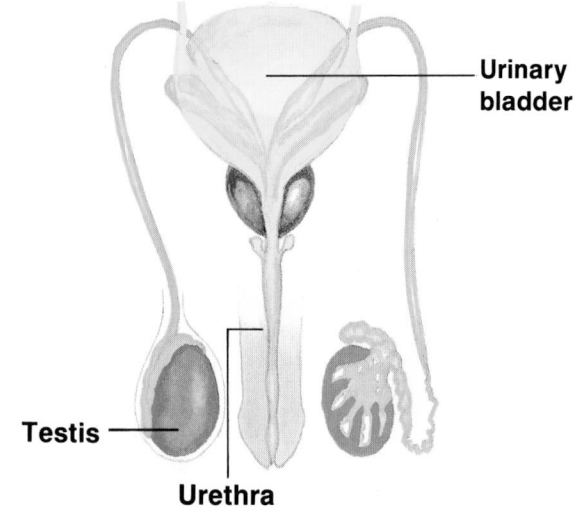

Urinary bladder

Testis

Urethra

▶ *Explain:* Why is the urethra part of two different body systems in males? Both urine and sperm leave the body through this passageway.

LESSON SUMMARY

▶ The testes are the main organs of the male reproductive system.

▶ Testosterone is a male hormone that triggers the development of secondary sex characteristics.

▶ The urethra is part of the excretory system.

▶ In males, both urine and sperm leave the body through the urethra.

CHECK *Complete the following.*

1. The main organs of the male reproductive system are the _____ . testes

2. The testes are suspended within a pocket of skin called the _____ . scrotum

3. One kind of cell in the testes produces the hormone _____ . testosterone

4. Male sex cells are called _____ . sperm

5. In males, both sperm and urine leave the body through the _____ . urethra

6. Two secondary sex characteristics in males are a deeper _____ and the growth of body hair. voice

7. The testes produce both testosterone and _____ . sperm or male sex cells

APPLY *Complete the following analogies.*

8. **Relate:** Ovaries are to females as _____ are to males. testes

9. Eggs are to females as _____ are to males. sperm

Answer the following.

10. **Compare:** How is the shape of the testes similar to the shape of the ovaries? Both are egg-shaped.

11. **Name:** To what two body systems does the urethra belong? excretory, reproductive

12. **Define:** What is a hormone? Use the glossary of this text for help if necessary. chemical substance produced by the body

13. **Define:** What is the scrotum? pocket of skin that protects and supports the testes

Skill Builder

▲ *Organizing Information* When you organize information, you put the information in some kind of order. A table is one way to organize information. Make a table that describes the parts of the male reproductive system. Include a description of each part in the table.

SCIENCE CONNECTION

SEXUALLY TRANSMITTED DISEASES

A disease that can be passed from one person to another is called a contagious (kun-TAY-jus) disease. Some contagious diseases are spread by pathogens (PATH-uh-junz), or germs, in the air. Other contagious diseases are spread by pathogens contained in food or water.

A few contagious diseases are spread through sexual contact with an infected person. These diseases are called sexually transmitted (trans-MIT-ed) diseases. The pathogens that cause sexually transmitted diseases can live only inside a human body. When outside the body, these pathogens die. Sexually transmitted diseases are not spread by casual contact.

Gonorrhea (gahn-uh-REE-uh) and syphilis (SIHF-uh-lihs) are two sexually transmitted diseases. These diseases usually are treated with penicillin or other antibiotics. Many cases of gonorrhea and syphilis are cured through early diagnosis and treatment.

AIDS is also a sexually transmitted disease. HIV, the virus that causes AIDS, attacks an infected person's immune system. The person cannot fight disease. There is no known cure for AIDS.

Microscopic view of pathogens

17-4 What is menstruation?

Objective ▶ Describe the menstrual cycle.

TechTerms

▶ **menstrual** (MEHN-struhl) **cycle:** monthly cycle of change that occurs in the female reproductive system

▶ **menstruation** (men-stroo-WAY-shun): process by which blood and tissue from the lining of the uterus break apart and leave the body

▶ **ovulation** (oh-vyuh-LAY-shun): release of a mature egg from the ovary

Menstrual Cycle When a female is born, her body contains all the egg cells she will ever have. However, the eggs are not mature, or fully developed. The eggs do not begin to mature until the female reaches puberty (PYOO-bur-tee). Puberty generally begins between the ages of 10 and 14. In females, puberty is marked by the beginning of the **menstrual** (MEHN-struhl) **cycle.** The menstrual cycle is a monthly cycle of change that occurs in the female reproductive system.

▶ *Identify:* What is the menstrual cycle?
monthly cycle of change in the female reproductive system

Ovulation The menstrual cycle occurs every 28 to 32 days. It is triggered by the release of hormones in the female reproductive system. One hormone causes an egg to mature in an ovary. Another hormone causes the walls of the uterus to thicken and the supply of blood to the uterus to increase. Yet another hormone triggers **ovulation** (oh-vyuh-LAY-shun). Ovulation occurs when a mature egg leaves an ovary and travels into an oviduct.

▶ *Explain:* What causes ovulation? hormones

Menstruation After an egg is released from the ovary, it travels through an oviduct. If the egg does not meet sperm in the oviduct, it begins to break apart. The amount of hormones in the reproductive system decreases. This causes the thickened walls of the uterus to also break apart. About 14 days after ovulation, **menstruation** (men-stroo-WAY-shun) occurs. Menstruation is the process by which blood and tissue from the uterus break apart and leave the body.

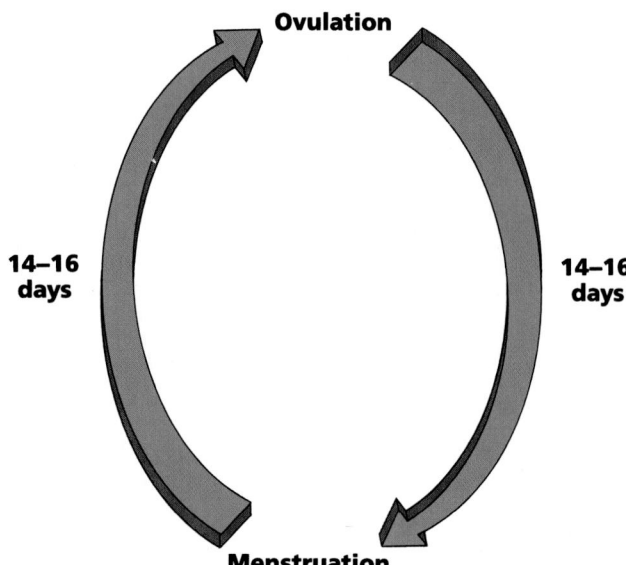

Soon after menstruation, a new egg begins to mature in the ovary. The menstrual cycle is repeated. The cycle is continuously repeated well into adulthood. For most females, the menstrual cycle continues until around age 50.

▶ *Identify:* At about what age does the menstrual cycle stop occurring? about 50

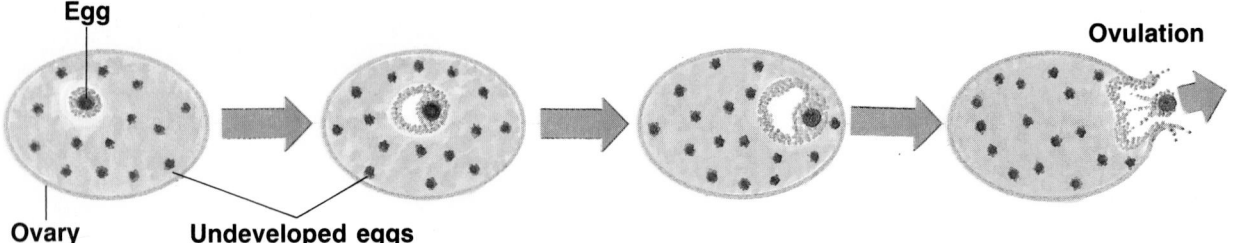

Egg

Ovary   Undeveloped eggs

Ovulation

LESSON SUMMARY

▶ The menstrual cycle is a series of changes in the female reproductive system that occur about once a month.

▶ During ovulation, a mature egg leaves an ovary and travels to the oviduct.

▶ The process by which blood and tissue lining leave the uterus is called menstruation.

CHECK *Complete the following.*

1. A female is born with all the _____ cells she will have in her lifetime. egg

2. The series of monthly changes in a female's reproductive system is called the _____ . menstrual cycle

3. Ovulation is triggered by the release of _____ into parts of the reproductive system. hormones

4. During _____, blood and tissue from the uterus are released from the body. menstruation

5. A mature egg moves from an ovary into an oviduct during _____ . ovulation

APPLY *Complete the following.*

6. **Hypothesize:** Could a female over age 50 continue to have a menstrual cycle? Explain.

7. **Compare:** What effect do hormones have on the development of sex cells in the male and female reproductive systems?

8. **Sequence:** The pictures below show how an egg changes before ovulation. Place the pictures of the changing egg into the correct order.

a. b.

c. 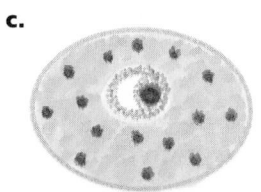 d.

Skill Builder

Diagraming When you organize information, you put the information in some type of order. A diagram is one way to organize information. Draw a diagram of the female reproductive system. Indicate the path a mature egg takes through the system during menstruation.

SCIENCE CONNECTION

HORMONE THERAPY

In order to work properly, the body needs a certain amount of hormones. Sometimes, a person's body does not produce enough of one or more hormones. This is called a hormone deficiency. Certain diseases, such as diabetes, are caused by a hormone deficiency.

Hormone therapy is a way of treating people suffering from a hormone deficiency disease. In hormone therapy, patients are given doses of hormones that their bodies lack. As hormone levels become normal, the symptoms of the disease lessen. The patient's body works properly. However, hormone therapy does not cure the disease.

Addison's disease is a hormone deficiency disease. A person with Addison's disease does not have a proper amount of hormones made by the adrenal glands. As a result, the person may experience a loss of body fluids and muscle weakness. If left untreated, the disease can be fatal. However, through hormone therapy, the person can live a normal life.

17-5 How does fertilization take place?

TechTerms

▶ **fertilization** (fur-tul-i-ZAY-shun): joining of one sperm cell and one egg cell

▶ **zygote** (ZY-gote): fertilized egg produced by fertilization

Sperm Cells Sperm cells are microscopic. The largest part of a sperm cell is a round part called the head. The head contains the cell nucleus. A sperm cell also has a long tail. The motion of the tail helps the sperm cell move. This helps the sperm cell reach the egg.

Figure 1 Parts of a sperm cell

▦▶ **Describe:** How does a sperm cell move? by the motion of its long tail

Mature Egg During ovulation, a mature egg is released from an ovary. The egg passes into the oviduct. Tiny hairs line the walls of the oviduct. The motion of these hairs move the egg through the oviduct.

▦▶ **Explain:** What causes an egg to move through the oviduct? motion of hairs that line the oviduct walls

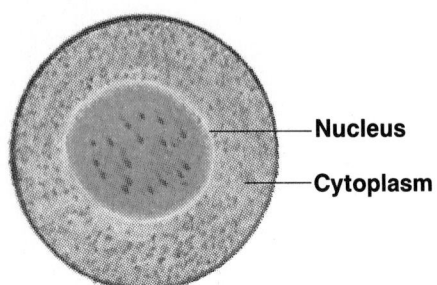

Fertilization Sperm cells enter the female reproductive system through the uterus. The sperm cells move across the uterus and into the oviduct. Of the millions of sperm cells that enter the uterus, only a few may reach the oviduct.

During ovulation, an egg leaves an ovary and enters the oviduct. If a sperm cell meets an egg cell in the oviduct, **fertilization** (fur-tul-i-ZAY-shun) can occur. Fertilization is the joining of one sperm and one egg. An egg can be fertilized only during ovulation.

▦▶ **Identify:** What is fertilization? joining of a sperm cell and an egg cell

Zygote During fertilization, the nuclei of a sperm cell and an egg cell join together. The new cell that results from fertilization is called a **zygote** (ZY-gote). A zygote is a fertilized egg. The zygote travels down the oviduct and enters the uterus.

▦▶ **Explain:** What causes a zygote to form? the joining of nuclei from a sperm cell and an egg cell

344

LESSON SUMMARY

▶ Sperm cells have a head that contains the cell nucleus, and a tail that helps the sperm cell move.

▶ A mature egg is released from the ovary, and passes through the oviduct.

▶ Only a few sperm cells reach the oviduct.

▶ Fertilization can occur only during ovulation.

▶ The new cell produced by fertilization is called a zygote.

CHECK *Complete the following.*

1. A sperm cell moves due to the motion of its ———— . tail

2. During ————, a mature egg leaves an ovary and travels into the oviduct. ovulation

3. The joining of a sperm cell and an egg cell is called ———— . fertilization

4. The new cell produced by fertilization is called a ———— . zygote

5. Fertilization occurs in the ———— of a female. oviduct

APPLY *Complete the following.*

6. Relate: During which stage of a female's menstrual cycle can fertilization occur? Why?

7. Contrast: How is the motion of sperm cells and egg cells different?

Answer the questions about the diagram.

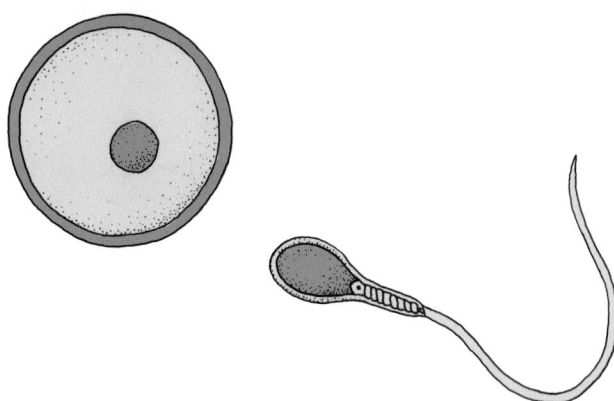

8. Analyze: The sperm cell shown is a human gamete. How many chromosomes does the sperm cell contain?

9. How many chromosomes does the human egg cell contain? Explain your answer.

Health & Safety Tip..........................

The length of a woman's menstrual cycle can be affected by outside factors such as illness, stress, weight loss, or weight gain. Use a health book to find out two other factors that affect the length of a woman's menstrual cycle.

TECHNOLOGY AND SOCIETY

REPRODUCTIVE TECHNOLOGIES

In order for fertilization to occur, a mature egg first must be released into the oviduct. Certain disorders of the female reproductive system make fertilization by natural means impossible. These disorders might include blocked or missing oviducts, or ovaries that cannot release eggs.

One technique to help fertilization is called *in vitro* fertilization. In this procedure, eggs are removed from the ovaries. These eggs are put into a laboratory dish and mixed with sperm. Fertilization occurs in the dish. The fertilized eggs are placed inside the woman's uterus. Chances are that one of the fertilized eggs will develop into a fetus.

Two newer techniques also are used to aid fertilization. In one technique, sperm and eggs are collected and inserted into the oviduct near the ovary. Fertilization occurs in the oviduct. In the other technique, eggs are removed from the ovary and placed into the oviduct near the opening to the uterus. This is helpful to women with blocked oviducts.

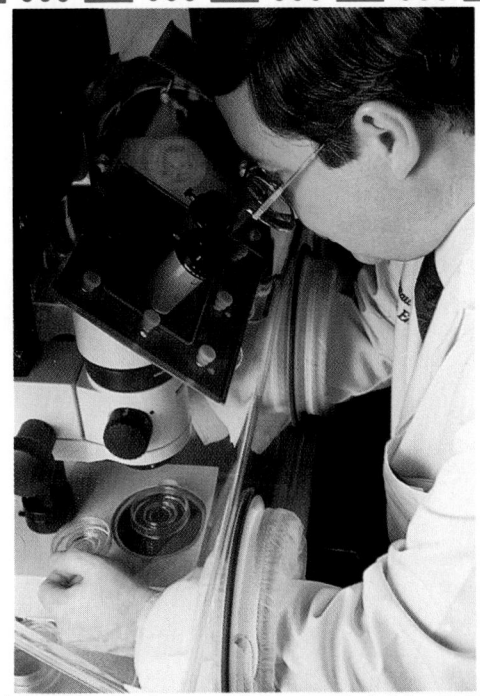

17-6 How does a human embryo develop?

Objective ▶ Describe the process by which an embryo develops into a fetus.

TechTerms

- **amnion** (AM-nee-on): fluid-filled membrane that surrounds an embryo
- **embryo** (EM-bree-oh): hollow ball of cells formed by cell division of the zygote
- **fetus** (FEET-us): developing baby
- **placenta** (pluh-SEN-tuh): organ through which an embryo receives nourishment and gets rid of wastes
- **umbilical** (um-BIL-ih-kul) **cord:** connects the embryo to the placenta

Early Changes After fertilization, the zygote divides by mitosis. Two cells are formed. These cells are attached to one another. Both of these cells divide to form four attached cells. This cell division continues until a hollow ball of cells is formed. The hollow ball of cells attaches itself to a wall of the uterus. This mass of cells is now called an **embryo** (EM-bree-oh). All of the tissues and organs of the body form from the cells in the embryo.

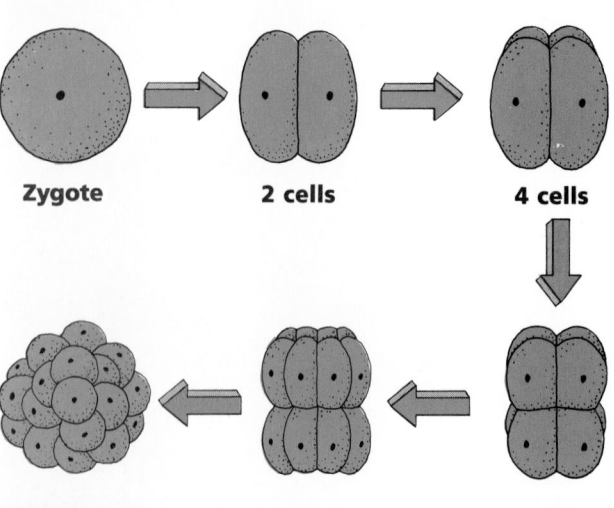

Zygote **2 cells** **4 cells**

Hollow ball **16 cells** **8 cells**

▶ **Identify:** What is an embryo? hollow ball of cells attached to a wall of the uterus

Needs of the Embryo Tissues that surround the embryo develop into a thick flat structure called the **placenta** (pluh-SEN-tuh). The placenta is an organ through which the embryo receives nourishment. The embryo also gets rid of wastes through the placenta.

The embryo is attached to the placenta by the **umbilical** (um-BIL-ih-kul) **cord.** The umbilical cord is a thick, ropelike structure. One kind of blood vessel in the umbilical cord carries nourishment from the placenta to the embryo. A different kind of blood vessel carries wastes from the embryo to the placenta.

▶ **Describe:** How does an embryo receive nourishment? Nutrient-rich blood is carried from the placenta through the umbilical cord to the embryo.

Protection The embryo is surrounded by a clear, fluid-filled sac. This sac is called the **amnion** (AM-nee-on). The fluid inside the sac cushions and protects the developing embryo.

▶ **Explain:** How does the amnion help the developing embryo? It cushions and supports the embryo.

Fetus After about eight weeks, the embryo begins developing a heart, brain, and nerve cord. Eyes and ears also begin to form. When bone forms in the organism's skeleton, it is called a **fetus** (FEET-us). The fetus continues to grow and develop inside the uterus. Finally, about nine months after fertilization, a baby is born.

▶ **Describe:** When is a developing organism called a fetus? After about eight weeks when bone forms in the skeleton of the organism.

LESSON SUMMARY

▶ An embryo is a hollow ball of cells attached to a wall of the uterus.

▶ An embryo receives nourishment and rids itself of wastes through the placenta.

▶ The umbilical cord connects an embryo to the placenta.

▶ The amnion cushions and protects the developing embryo.

CHECK *Complete the following.*

1. After fertilization, a zygote divides by _____ . mitosis

2. All the tissues and organs of the body form from the cells of the _____ . embryo

3. The umbilical cord connects the embryo to the _____ . placenta

4. When the skeleton of an embryo is filled with bone, the embryo is called a _____ . fetus

5. The embryo receives nourishment and gets rid of wastes through the _____ . placenta

APPLY *Complete the following.*

6. **Relate:** Identify the stages of development that occur after an egg is fertilized. zygote, embryo, fetus, baby

7. Why does one type of blood vessel bring nutrients to the embryo while another removes its waste products? Blood flows in one direction through the vessels.

Ideas in Action.................................

IDEA: Parts of a chicken egg contain structures for a developing embryo much like the structures that surround a human embryo.

ACTION: Study the parts of an uncooked egg. Identify structures of the egg that resemble structures that surround a developing embryo.

ACTIVITY

GRAPHING CHANGES IN FETAL DEVELOPMENT

You will need graph paper and a pencil.

1. Study the information in the Data Table.

2. Make a bar graph that shows how the length of a baby changes as it develops.

3. Find the difference between the shortest and longest lengths in the Data Table. The difference is the total length that needs to be represented on the vertical axis. Use this information to determine the length one box on the axis represents.

4. Label each column along the horizontal axis with the time it represents.

5. Fill in the column above each time label with a bar whose top ends at the appropriate length line.

5 weeks   **9 weeks**   **14 weeks**

Questions

1. How long is the embryo at the end of 9 weeks of development? 5 cm

2. Between which weeks does the developing baby have the greatest increase in length? between weeks 14 and 26

3. **Analyze:** Does the length of a developing baby increase in a set pattern? Explain. It continually grows longer. However, the rate of growth is uneven throughout its development.

Data Table:	Growth of a Developing Baby	
TIME (WEEKS)	MASS (g)	LENGTH (cm)
5	0.5	1.3
9	10	5
14	113	18
26	907	38
38	3180	51

17-7 What are the stages of human development?

Objective ▶ Identify the stages of the human life cycle.

Life Cycle A developing baby goes through a series of stages before birth. After birth, a human also goes through a series of stages. The stages of development are called a life cycle. There are five stages in the human life cycle.

▷ *Identify:* What is a life cycle? stages of development an organism goes through during its lifetime

Early Years The earliest stage of human life is called infancy. Infancy begins at birth and ends at age 2. This stage of life is marked by a rapid increase in size. The muscles and nerves of the infant also develop quickly. Mental skills develop and the infant begins to interact with its surroundings. By age 2, most infants are able to walk and speak a few words.

Childhood usually is defined as between ages 2 and 12. During childhood, muscle development allows more complex activities. Children become more independent and are able to feed and dress themselves. Mental abilities also increase. Most children learn to read and write during this stage of development.

▷ *Describe:* What are some of the changes a person goes through during childhood? greater muscle development, becomes more independent, mental abilities increase

Adolescence Between the ages of 11 and 14, most young people go through a period of rapid physical change. This stage is called adolescence (ad-ul-ES-uns). The beginning of adolescence is called puberty (PYOO-bur-tee). During puberty, the sex organs develop. These organs release hormones that cause growth spurts. Adolescents of both sexes develop the ability to reproduce.

▷ *Explain:* What causes rapid growth spurts during puberty? hormones released by sex organs

Later Years Adulthood is the stage at which the physical growth of the human body is complete. Muscle development and coordination reach their peak during early adulthood. Between the ages of 30 and 50, muscle tone often decreases.

Old age, or the beginning of the aging process, occurs at different times in different people. People who have exercised regularly and eaten a balanced diet all of their lives may not show signs of aging until their late 70s or early 80s. Old age usually is marked by a decline in muscle strength. Sense organs such as the eyes and ears may not work as well. The bones of older adults often become brittle and can break more easily.

▷ *Describe:* What effect do diet and exercise have on the aging process? The effects of aging are lessened by eating properly and exercising throughout one's lifetime.

LESSON SUMMARY

▶ The stages of development in humans is called the human life cycle.

▶ The earliest stage of human life is called infancy.

▶ The second stage in the human life cycle is childhood.

▶ During adolescence, a person goes through a period of rapid physical change.

▶ Adulthood is the stage at which the physical growth of the body is complete.

▶ Old age is the last stage of the human life cycle.

CHECK *Complete the following.*

1. The human life cycle consists of _____ stages. 5

2. The earliest stage of human development is called _____ . infancy

3. The period between ages 2 and 12 is generally called _____ . childhood

4. A person develops the ability to reproduce during the stage called _____ . adolescence

5. The stage during which the physical growth of the human body is complete is _____ . adulthood

APPLY *Complete the following.*

6. **Relate:** Usually, a very young infant does not cry in the presence of a stranger, but a 9-month old will scream for a parent. What does this behavior indicate about the development of the infant?

7. **Compare:** What is a general statement that compares muscle development during infancy with that of old age?

8. **Relate:** At what stage in the life cycle is a person most likely to first put together a jigsaw puzzle?

Skill Builder

▲ *Organizing Information* When you organize information, you put the information in some kind of order. A table is one way of organizing information. Make a table with five columns. Label the columns with the stages of the human life cycle. Then list the traits of each stage under the appropriate heading.

CAREER IN LIFE SCIENCE

DAY CARE WORKER

Day care workers supervise groups of infants or young children. They carry out educational plans under the supervision of a certified teacher. With a group of infants, this means feeding and changing the babies on schedule. It also means creating an environment that is stimulating to the infants. In groups of young children, the plan may call for reading a book, instructing a craft, or supervising free play.

Day care workers generally work in a center for young children. A day care worker must be familiar with the general stages of emotional, social, physical, and intellectual skills that a child goes through. Day care workers also should be patient and understanding. To be a day care worker you need a high school diploma. Many day care workers also have a two-year degree in Early Childhood education.

STUDY HINT Before you begin the Unit Challenges, review the TechTerms and Lesson Summary for each lesson in this unit.

TechTerms......

amnion (346)
cervix (338)
embryo (346)
fertilization (344)
fetus (346)
gamete (336)
meiosis (336)

menstrual cycle (342)
menstruation (342)
ovaries (338)
oviduct (338)
ovulation (342)
placenta (346)
scrotum (340)

testes (340)
testosterone (340)
umbilical cord (346)
urethra (340)
uterus (338)
vagina (338)
zygote (344)

TechTerm Challenges......

Matching *Write the TechTerm that matches each description.*
1. process by which gametes form meiosis
2. hollow organ in which an embryo develops uterus
3. process by which blood and tissue from the uterine lining breaks apart and leaves the body menstruation
4. clear, fluid-filled sac that protects the developing embryo amnion
5. developing baby fetus
6. organ through which an embryo receives nourishment and gets rid of waste placenta
7. hollow ball of cells formed by cell division of the zygote embryo
8. fertilized egg zygote
9. main organs of the male reproductive system testes
10. long tube between an ovary and the uterus oviduct
11. thick, ropelike structure umbilical cord

Fill in *Write the TechTerm that best completes each statement.*
1. Reproductive cells also are called _____ . gametes
2. The main organs of the female reproductive system are the _____ . ovaries
3. The pocket of skin that surrounds and protects the testes is called the _____ . scrotum
4. Sperm is carried to the outside of the body through the _____ . urethra
5. The release of a mature egg from the ovary is called _____ . ovulation
6. The joining of one sperm cell and one egg cell is called _____ . fertilization
7. The start of the _____ marks the beginning of puberty in females. menstrual cycle
8. The hormone that controls the development of male characteristics is _____ . testosterone
9. The _____ often is called the birth canal. vagina
10. The _____ connects the uterus to the vagina. cervix

Content Challenges......

Multiple Choice *Write the letter of the term that best completes each statement.*
1. In females, puberty begins with the start of
   a. diffusion.   b. fertilization.   c. menstruation.   d. pregnancy. c

2. Muscular strength begins to decrease during
   a. infancy.   b. adolescence.   c. adulthood.   d. old age. d

3. The release of an egg is called
   a. fertilization. **b.** ovulation. **c.** menstruation. **d.** pregnancy. b

4. The structure that performs the jobs of excretion, respiration, and circulation for the developing fetus is called the
   a. amnion. **b.** uterus. **c.** birth canal. **d.** placenta. d

5. Fertilization in humans takes place in the
   a. vagina. **b.** uterus. **c.** ovary. **d.** oviduct. d

6. Sperm are stored in the
   a. urethra. **b.** vas deferens. **c.** epidymis. **d.** testes. c

7. Sperm and testosterone are produced in the
   a. epidymis. **b.** scrotum. **c.** testes. **d.** urethra. c

8. The ovaries produce all of the following EXCEPT
   a. eggs. **b.** progesterone. **c.** estrogen. **d.** testosterone. d

9. The most rapid physical changes take place in humans during
   a. infancy. **b.** adolescence. **c.** adulthood. **d.** old age. b

10. The narrow end of the uterus is called the
    a. vagina. **b.** cervix. **c.** oviduct. **d.** ovary. b

True/False *Write true if the statement is true. If the statement is false, change the underlined term to make the statement true.*

1. Once bone replacement is complete, the embryo is called a <u>fetus</u>. true
2. The <u>urethra</u> carries material between the embryo and the placenta. umbilical cord
3. The process by which blood and tissue leave the uterus is called <u>fertilization</u>. menstruation
4. Reproductive cells are sometimes called <u>gametes</u>. true
5. Gametes are formed by <u>mitosis</u>. meiosis
6. The growth process in humans ends at <u>adolescence</u>. adulthood
7. Eggs are <u>female</u> sex cells. true
8. An egg can be fertilized by <u>many</u> sperm. one
9. The clear fluid-filled membrane surrounding the embryo is called the <u>placenta</u>. amnion
10. A <u>zygote</u> undergoes cell division until a hollow ball of cells forms. true
11. People develop the ability to reproduce during <u>adulthood</u>. adolescence
12. Humans reproduce by <u>asexual</u> reproduction. sexual

Understanding the Features..

Reading Critically *Use the feature reading selections to answer the following. Page numbers for the features follow each question in parentheses.*

1. **Define:** What is nondisjunction? (337)
2. **Infer:** Why is an ectopic pregnancy dangerous? (339)
3. **Name:** What are three sexually transmitted diseases? (341)
4. How is hormone therapy useful in treating Addison's disease? (343)
5. **Analyze:** Why is fertilization by natural means impossible for some women? (345)
6. **Infer:** Why do day care workers need to be patient and understanding? (349)

Interpreting a Diagram *Use the following diagram of meiosis to complete the following.*

Chromosomes

1. **Observe:** How many cells are formed when meiosis is complete?
2. **Observe:** How many chromosomes are in each cell when meiosis is complete?
3. In what stage does the nucleus break down?
4. **Describe:** What is happening in Step 7?

Critical Thinking *Answer each of the following in complete sentences.*

1. **Compare:** How are the functions of the testes and ovaries similar?
2. **Infer:** Why do you think it is important for a pregnant woman to avoid alcohol, tobacco, and drugs?
3. **Identify:** How do you think you can slow down the effects of aging?
4. **Hypothesize:** What would happen if the placenta became detached from the fetus?
5. **Infer:** Why do you think the regular monthly changes in females is called a cycle?
6. **Contrast:** What is the difference between meiosis and mitosis?

Finding Out More...

1. Find out some of the dangers that are associated with teenage pregnancy. Use library references to find out any complications for the mother as well as for the child. Present your findings in a report.
2. During the 1950s, doctors prescribed a drug called thalidomide for morning sickness. Research what effect thalidomide had on the developing fetus. Report your findings to the class.
3. Use library references to research some of the ways technology is being used to help couples who have trouble conceiving. Write a report on one of these techniques. Include a description of the technique, the costs involved, and the success rate of the technique. Present your findings in an oral report.
4. Use library references to make a time line showing the different stages in a developing fetus. Break the time line into trimesters. Include when organs are formed, when the arms and legs form, when the heart and brain form, and when the fetus begins to rapidly gain weight.

HEREDITY AND GENETICS

CONTENTS

STUDY HINT As you read each lesson in Unit 18, write the topic sentence of each paragraph in the lesson on a sheet of paper. After you complete each lesson, compare your list of topic sentences to the Lesson Summary.

18-1 What is heredity?

Objective ► Explain why offspring have some of the traits of their parents.

TechTerms

- **genetics** (juh-NET-iks): study of heredity
- **heredity** (huh-RED-uh-tee): passing of traits from parents to offspring
- **inherited** (in-HER-uh-ted) **traits:** traits that are passed from parents to their offspring
- **traits:** characteristics

Traits Suppose you were asked to make a list of ten characteristics that describe your appearance. Your list might include: brown eyes, black hair, 5 feet tall. It is unlikely that another student would list the same exact characteristics. This is because each person is unique. The characteristics you might include on your list are called **traits.** Traits are characteristics of an organism.

▌▌▶ *Define:* What are traits? characteristics of an organism

Identifying Traits Do you look like your mother, your father, or a mixture of both your parents? Children often look like their parents or grandparents in some way.

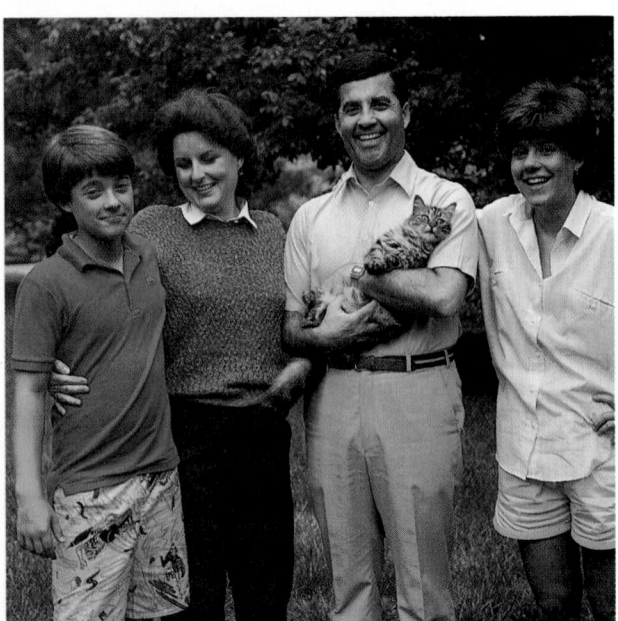

There is a reason for this. During fertilization, male and female sex cells join together. Each of these sex cells contains material that affects the development of the offspring. Traits that are passed from parents to their offspring are called **inherited** (in-HER-uh-ted) **traits.** Eye color is an example of an inherited trait.

▶ *Infer:* How was your eye color determined? by traits inherited from parents

Heredity The passing of traits from parents to their offspring is called **heredity** (huh-RED-uh-tee). The first person to study heredity was Gregor Mendel, an Austrian monk. Mendel studied how traits are passed from one generation to the next. The field of biology that studies heredity is called **genetics** (juh-NET-iks). Gregor Mendel often is called the "father of genetics."

▌▌▶ *Describe:* What is the relationship between traits and genetics? Genetics is the study of inherited traits.

LESSON SUMMARY

▶ Traits are the characteristics of an organism.

▶ Traits that are passed from parents to their offspring are called inherited traits.

▶ The passing of traits from parents to offspring is called heredity.

CHECK *Complete the following.*

1. Characteristics of an organism are called _____ . traits.

2. An example of an inherited trait is _____ . eye color

3. Inherited traits are passed from _____ to their offspring. parents

4. The first scientist to study inherited traits was _____ . Gregor Mendel

5. The modern science of heredity is called _____ . genetics.

APPLY *Answer the following.*

▶ 6. **Infer:** Why do brothers and sisters often have similar traits?

▶ 7. **Analyze:** Two children have the same last name, the same birthdate, and the same inherited traits. How are the children related?

▶ 8. **Infer:** Why do you think the study of genetics is important?

InfoSearch

Read the passage. Ask two questions that you cannot answer from the information in the passage.

Human Genetics Human genetics is a difficult field to study. One difficulty is that the life span of humans is long compared with the life span of other animals. As a result, a scientist could not study all of the offspring produced in many generations of one family. Another difficulty is that humans produce fewer offspring than other animals. It is hard to compare traits with fewer offspring to observe. Scientists often study the genetics of plants and animals to learn more about human genetics.

SEARCH: Use library references to find answers to your questions.

▶■◀ PEOPLE IN SCIENCE ▶■◀◆▶■◀◆▶■◀◆▶■◀◆▶■◀◆▶■◀◆▶■◀◆▶■◀◆▶■◀◆▶■◀◆

GREGOR MENDEL (1822–1884)

In the mid-1800s, a young monk named Gregor Mendel took care of a monastery garden in Czechoslovakia. Mendel noticed that the pea plants growing in the garden had a variety of characteristics. Some plants had tall stems. Other plants had short stems. The seeds of some plants were round; others were wrinkled. Mendel wondered what caused the plants to have these different characteristics.

Mendel began to experiment with the pea plants. Because pea plants grow and reproduce quickly, Mendel was able to observe many generations of the pea plants. From his experiments, Mendel concluded that traits were passed from the parent plants to their offspring. The results of Mendel's experiments were published in 1866. However, it was not until 1900 that scientists began to analyze Mendel's research. Since that time, many new discoveries have been made about heredity. However, Mendel's original hypothesis still forms the basis of modern genetics.

◀ ▶■◀ ▶■◀ ▶■◀ ▶■◀ ▶■◀ ▶■◀ ▶■◀ ▶■◀ ▶■◀ ▶■◀ ▶■◀ ▶■◀

18-2 What are genes and chromosomes?

Objective ▶ Describe how genes and chromosomes are involved in heredity.

TechTerms

- ▶ **chromosomes** (KROH-muh-sohms): threadlike structures in the nucleus of a cell that control heredity
- ▶ **genes** (JEENS): parts of a chromosome that control inherited traits

Threads of Life Fine, threadlike structures are located in the nucleus of a cell. These threadlike structures are called **chromosomes** (KROH-muh-sohms). Chromosomes control heredity. Chromosomes sometimes are called the "threads of life" because they control heredity during cell division. During cell division, each chromosome makes a copy of itself. A pair of identical chromosomes is formed. Each new daughter cell receives one chromosome from each of the pairs.

▐▐▐▶ *Define:* What are chromosomes? threadlike structures in the nucleus of a cell

Chromosomes and Reproduction In both asexual and sexual reproduction, chromosomes are passed from parent to offspring. During asexual reproduction, each daughter cell receives its chromosomes from the single parent. During sexual reproduction, the daughter cell receives chromosomes from each parent cell. All new organisms contain chromosomes from both of its parents.

▐▐▐▶ *Explain:* How does an organism produced by sexual reproduction get its chromosomes? Each parent gives a set of chromosomes to the offspring.

Chromosomes and Genes Along each chromosome, there are many dark bands. Each band is a small part of the chromosome called a **gene.** A gene is a part of the chromosome that controls inherited traits. Each gene affects a different trait. Genes determine your height, eye color, hair color, and many other characteristics. Each gene is located at a certain place on the chromosome. Genes also control the life processes of your cells.

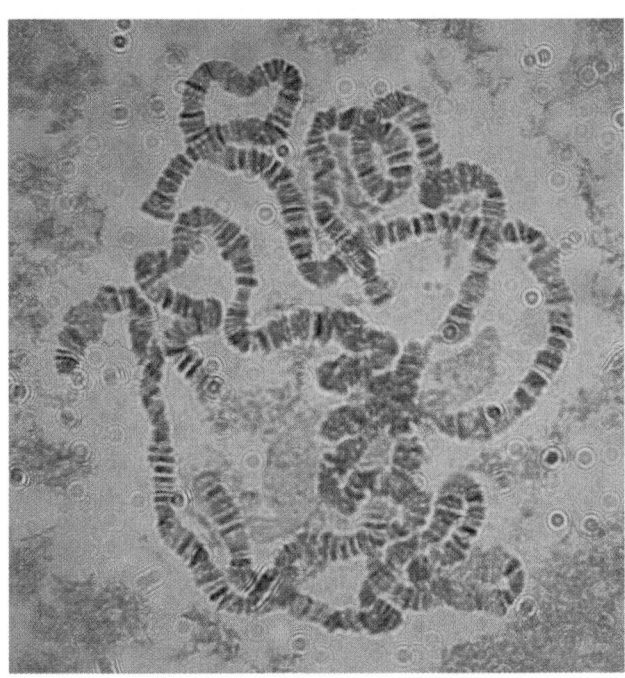

▐▐▐▶ *Identify:* What do genes control? inherited characteristics

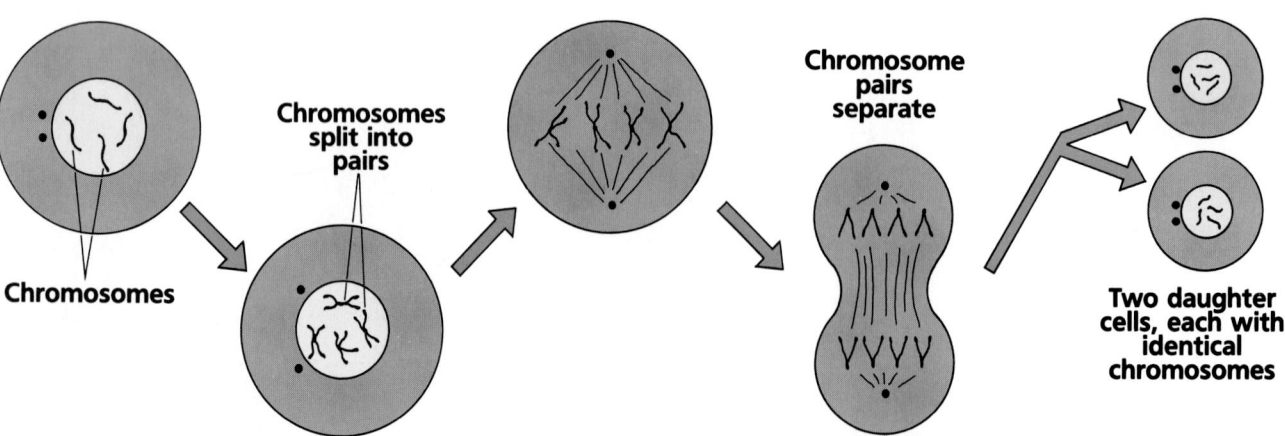

Chromosomes

Chromosomes split into pairs

Chromosome pairs separate

Two daughter cells, each with identical chromosomes

LESSON SUMMARY

▶ Chromosomes are threadlike structures in the nucleus of a cell that control heredity.

▶ An organism receives chromosomes from its parent or parents.

▶ Genes control inherited traits.

CHECK *Answer the following.*

1. Where are chromosomes located?

2. Where does an organism produced by sexual reproduction receive its chromosomes from?

3. Where are genes located?

4. What are the life processes of cells controlled by?

5. What kind of traits are controlled by genes?

APPLY *Answer the following.*

▶ 6. **Infer:** Which organism would more closely resemble its parent or parents, one produced by asexual reproduction or one produced by sexual reproduction? Why?

▶ 7. **Analyze:** Suppose the chromosomes in a cell did not double to form pairs of identical chromosomes during cell division. What effect would this have on the daughter cells?

Ideas in Action

IDEA: Your inherited traits are controlled by the genes that you received from your parents. Eye color, eye shape, hair color, nose shape, and skin color all are inherited traits.

ACTION: Divide a piece of paper into four columns. Label the first column "Traits." In the first column, list ten inherited traits. Label the second column "Me," the third column "Mother," and the fourth column "Father." Then in each of the columns, describe the traits for each individual. Circle the traits that you share with one or both of your parents. Analyze your findings to see which parent you most closely resemble.

PEOPLE IN SCIENCE

BARBARA MCCLINTOCK (1902-1992)

Barbara McClintock was an American plant geneticist (juh-NET-uh-sist). For more than 60 years, she studied the inherited traits of corn. Dr. McClintock was especially interested in the color of corn kernels. By careful experimentation, she identified the genes that control this trait.

In 1931, Dr. McClintock made a startling discovery. She found that some genes "jump," or change position on a chromosome. The "jumping" gene caused changes in the traits controlled by the genes next to the place where it landed. For example, when a "jumping" gene landed next to the gene that controlled kernel color, the kernels were speckled.

Dr. McClintock announced her results in 1951. Most scientists at this time did not take her work seriously. They thought genes always remained in a definite position on a chromosome. It was not until the 1970s that other scientists began to take note of her conclusions. In 1983, more than 50 years after she made her discoveries, Dr. McClintock received the Nobel Prize.

18-3 How do chromosomes carry traits?

Objective ▶ Describe the chemical makeup of chromosomes.

TechTerms

▶ **DNA:** chemical contained in chromosomes

▶ **replication** (rep-luh-KAY-shun): process by which DNA is duplicated

Composition of Chromosomes Many years of research were needed before scientists learned that chromosomes contained genes. Scientists then wondered what chemical makes up chromosomes. Their question was answered with the discovery of **DNA.** DNA stands for deoxyribonucleic (dee-oks-ee-ry-boh-noo-KLEE-ik) acid. DNA is the chemical that makes up chromosomes.

�no▶ *Define:* What is DNA? chemical contained in chromosomes

Structure of DNA A molecule of DNA looks like a twisted ladder. The sides of the DNA ladder are made up of sugars and phosphates. The steps of the DNA ladder are made up of four kinds of nitrogen bases.

The four nitrogen bases that make up a DNA molecule are adenine (AD-uh-neen), guanine (GWAH-neen), thymine (THY-meen), and cytosine (SYT-oh-seen). Scientists use the capital letters A, G, T, and C to represent each of the four nitrogen bases. For example, A stands for adenine. Each step on the DNA ladder is made up of two bases. The bases always join together in certain pairs. Base A always pairs with base T. Base G always pairs with base C.

▶ *Describe:* How are nitrogen bases arranged in a DNA molecule? Two bases form a step on the DNA ladder.

Genetic Code A single DNA molecule, or ladder, can have thousands of steps. The number and arrangement of these steps form a genetic "code."

This code determines the kind of gene that forms. Different genes determine different kinds of inherited traits of an organism.

▶ *Explain:* What determines the inherited traits of an organism? genetic codes, formed by a DNA ladder

Replication During cell division, each chromosome doubles to form a pair of identical chromosomes. Molecules of DNA in the parent chromosome also double. The process by which DNA is duplicated is called **replication** (rep-luh-KAY-shun). The DNA ladder breaks between the nitrogen bases in the steps. This is similar to the process of unzipping a zipper. Then other nitrogen bases attach to each half of the ladder. The result is two new DNA ladders that are exact copies of the original DNA molecule. Replication produces two daughter DNA molecules that carry the same genetic code as the parent molecule.

▶ *Define:* What is replication? process by which DNA is duplicated

- ▶ Chromosomes are made up of DNA.
- ▶ A molecule of DNA contains sugars, phosphates, and four nitrogen bases.
- ▶ The four nitrogen bases always join together in certain pairs.
- ▶ The genetic code controls inherited traits.
- ▶ DNA duplicates itself in a process called replication.

CHECK *Find the sentence in the lesson that answers each question. Then, write the sentence.*

1. What is the main substance in chromosomes?
2. What are the steps of a DNA ladder made up of?
3. What base does base G always pair with?
4. What does the genetic code determine?
5. How does DNA duplicate itself?

APPLY *Answer the following.*

▶ 6. **Predict:** Suppose DNA in the chromosomes of a cell did not replicate. What effect would this have on the daughter cells?

7. **Hypothesize:** Two developing human embryos contain the same genetic code. How will these offspring resemble one another?

Use the art showing replication on page 358 to answer the following.

8. **Observe:** What are the sides of the DNA ladder made up of?

9. **Observe:** Can base C ever pair with base T? Explain your answer.

InfoSearch...

Read the passage. Ask two questions that you cannot answer from the information in the passage.

Mutations Sometimes a DNA molecule does not replicate itself exactly. The chromosomes do not pair correctly. Such changes in genes and chromosomes are called mutations (myoo-TAY-shuns). Most mutations are harmful to organisms. However, some mutations make an organism more suited to its environment. The mutation can help the organism survive. Many scientists think that helpful mutations lead to the development of new kinds of organisms.

SEARCH: Use library references to find answers to your questions.

LOOKING BACK IN SCIENCE

DISCOVERING THE STRUCTURE OF DNA

The structure of DNA was discovered in 1953 by an American biologist, James Watson, and a British scientist, Francis Crick. Watson and Crick built a model of a DNA molecule. Their model showed how the atoms in a DNA molecule resemble a twisted ladder. Watson and Crick also discovered that the order of nitrogen bases in the steps of the DNA molecule determine the particular traits controlled by the genes.

The discovery of Watson and Crick is considered one of the greatest scientific breakthroughs of the twentieth century. However, Watson and Crick were not the only scientists working with DNA. Watson and Crick based their discovery on the work of another British scientist, Rosalind Franklin. Franklin had taken many X-ray photographs of DNA crystals. Based on these photographs, Franklin predicted the shape and composition of a DNA molecule.

18-4 Why can offspring differ from their parents?

Objective ► Explain the difference between dominant and recessive traits.

TechTerms

- **dominant** (DOM-uh-nuhnt) **gene:** gene that always shows itself
- **hybrid** (HY-brid): having two unlike genes
- **pure:** having two like genes
- **recessive** (ri-SES-iv) **gene:** gene that is hidden when the dominant gene is present

Genes and Traits Gregor Mendel hypothesized that inherited factors produced certain traits. These factors are now called genes. Mendel based his hypothesis on the pea plants he was studying. Some of the plants were tall. Others were short. Mendel decided there must be a gene for tallness and another gene for shortness. The trait of height for a pea plant is determined by two genes, one from each parent. Each trait of an organism is determined by at least one gene from each parent.

▎▶ **Describe:** How are traits determined? by two genes for the trait

Pure Plants Mendel found that one kind of tall pea plant always had tall offspring. These plants have two tall genes, one from each parent. Mendel called these plants, **pure** tall. An organism is pure if it has two like genes for a given trait. Mendel found that some short pea plants always have short offspring. These plants have two short genes, one from each parent. Mendel called these plants pure short.

Short   Short   Short

▎▶ **Identify:** What genes does a short pea plant always have? A short pea plant will always have two short genes.

Hybrids Mendel wondered what the offspring of one pure tall parent and one pure short parent would look like. He cross-pollinated a pure tall pea plant and pure short pea plant. All of the offspring were tall. They had received a tall gene from the tall parent and a short gene from the short parent. They had one tall gene and one short gene and grew up tall. Mendel called these plants hybrids (HY-bridz). Organisms that have two unlike genes for a trait are **hybrid** for that trait.

▎▶ **Contrast:** What is the difference between a pure tall plant and a hybrid tall plant? A pure tall plant has two tall genes, a hybrid tall plant has one tall and one short gene.

Tall   Short   Tall

Dominant Genes Mendel found that in a hybrid, one gene always shows itself. The other gene is hidden. Mendel called the gene that shows itself the **dominant** (DOM-uh-nuhnt) **gene.** He called the hidden gene a **recessive** (ri-SES-iv) **gene.** The tall gene is dominant in pea plants. The short gene is recessive. That is why plants with one tall gene and one short gene are always tall.

▎▶ **Compare:** What is the difference between a dominant and a recessive gene? The dominant gene always shows itself. The recessive gene remains hidden.

▶ Each trait is determined by at least one gene from each parent.

▶ An organism with two like genes for a trait is called pure for that trait.

▶ An organism with two unlike genes for a trait is called hybrid for that trait.

▶ A dominant gene always shows itself over a recessive gene.

CHECK *Complete the following.*

1. A pea plant with two tall genes is called _____ . pure tall

2. A hybrid tall pea plant has one tall gene and one _____ gene. short

3. The gene that always shows itself is called the _____ gene. dominant

4. The recessive gene for height in pea plants is _____ . short

5. All short pea plants have two _____ genes. short

APPLY *Answer the following.*

6. **Relate:** What combinations of genes could a tall pea plant have?

▶ 7. **Predict:** Could a short pea plant be hybrid? Explain your answer.

8. One parent is pure for brown hair. The other parent is pure for blond hair. Brown hair is the dominant trait. What color hair will the offspring have?

▶ 9. **Infer:** Why do you think scientists use symbols to represent dominant and recessive genes?

Skill Builder...

Researching Gregor Mendel often is called the "Father of Genetics." Use library references to find information about Gregor Mendel's life. Make a poster that illustrates Mendel's work. Diagram and illustrate his experiments and the results. Present your poster to the class.

Skill Builder...

Defining There are three basic principles of genetics that are based on Mendel's studies. The three principles are: The Principle of Dominance, The Principle of Segregation, and the Principle of Independent Assortment. Use library references to define each of these terms.

ACTIVITY

MODELING THE STRUCTURE OF DNA

You will need a pair of scissors, tracing paper, and construction paper in white, black, green, red, blue, and yellow.

1. Trace the DNA parts shown on tracing paper.

2. Trace and cut out 12 white sugar molecules and 21 black phosphate molecules. Label the molecules.

3. Trace and cut out 3 green T's, 3 red A's, 3 yellow G's, and 3 blue C's. Label the bases.

4. Construct the sides of the DNA molecule with the sugars and phosphates.

5. Complete the DNA molecule by fitting the base pairs along the sides of the molecule.

Questions

1. **a.** Which nitrogen base always pairs with C? **b.** Which base always pairs with T?

2. **a.** What chemicals make up the sides of the DNA molecule? **b.** Which chemicals make up the rungs?

▶ 3. **Infer:** Do all DNA models look exactly the same? Explain.

18-5 How do genes combine in offspring?

Objective ▶ Identify what causes differences in the traits of parents and their offspring.

TechTerm

▶ **Punnett square:** chart that shows possible gene combinations

Gene Symbols Organisms have at least two genes for every trait. They receive at least one gene from each parent. Symbols are used to represent the combinations of genes. A capital letter represents a dominant trait. A lower case letter represents a recessive trait. In humans, the gene for brown eyes is dominant. The symbol for this gene is B. The gene for blue eyes is recessive. The symbol for this gene is b.

▶ *Explain:* What does a capital letter show about a gene? It is a dominant trait.

Predicting Traits Suppose a father has pure brown eyes. His genes are BB. Suppose a mother has pure blue eyes. Her genes are bb. What color eyes will the offspring have? One way to predict the eye color trait is to use a **Punnett square.** A Punnett square is a chart used to show possible gene combinations.

You can use a Punnett square to predict the eye color of the offspring in the above example. Draw a box with four squares in it, as shown in Figure 1. Write the genes for brown eyes (BB) from the father across the top. Write the genes for blue eyes (bb) from the mother down the side. Now fill in each square with a gene from the father, and a gene from the mother. As you can see, all the offspring will be hybrid dominant.

▶ *Observe:* What color eyes will all the offspring shown in Figure 1 have? brown

Combining Hybrids What happens when both parents are hybrid for a trait? A Punnett square also can be used to predict the genetic makeup of their offspring. Figure 2 shows that one-fourth of the offspring will be BB, or pure dominant. One-half will be Bb, or hybrid dominant. One-fourth will be bb, or pure recessive. This means that three-fourths of the offspring will have brown eyes. Only one-fourth will have blue eyes.

Figure 1

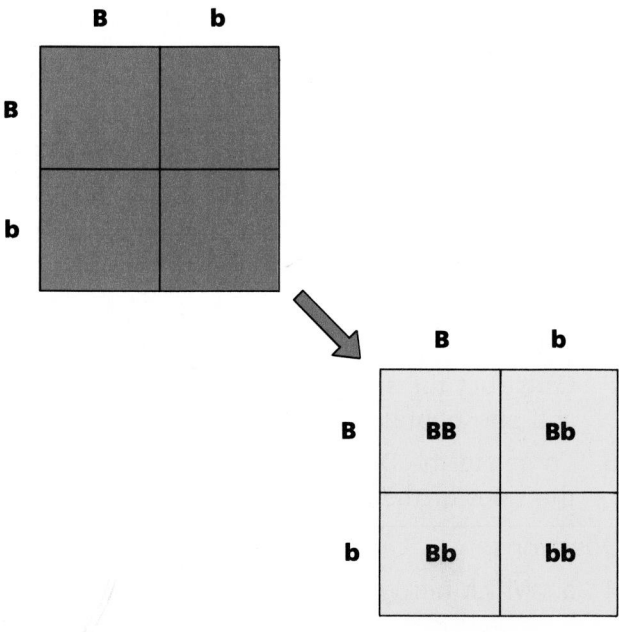

Figure 2

▶ *List:* What are the three kinds of traits that the offspring of hybrid parents can have? pure dominant, pure recessive, hybrid dominant

LESSON SUMMARY

▶ A capital letter represents a dominant gene, and a lower case letter represents a recessive gene.

▶ A Punnett square is a chart used to show possible gene combinations.

▶ When one parent is pure dominant and the other is pure recessive, the offspring are all hybrid dominant.

▶ When both parents are hybrid for a trait, one-fourth of the offspring are pure dominant, one-half are hybrid dominant, and one-fourth are pure recessive.

CHECK *Complete the following.*

1. A capital letter always represents a _____ gene. dominant

2. The recessive gene for blue eye color in humans is shown by the symbol _____ . b

3. When one parent is pure dominant and the other parent is pure recessive, their offspring are all hybrid _____ . dominant

4. If both parents are hybrid then one-half of their offspring will have _____ genes. hybrid dominant

5. A person with blue eyes always has the gene combination _____ . bb

APPLY *Use the Punnett square and information to answer the following. A pure white (bb) guinea pig is crossed with a hybrid black (Bb) guinea pig. There are four offspring.*

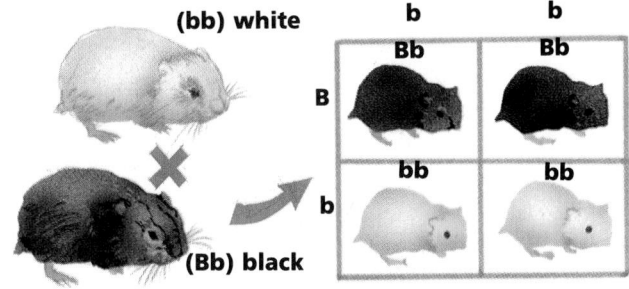

6. How many of the offspring will be black?

7. How many of the offspring will be white?

8. Are any of the offspring hybrid?

InfoSearch...

Read the passage. Then ask two questions that cannot be answered from the information in the passage.

Height In humans, height is affected by many genes. None of these genes is dominant. Therefore, the height of a person depends upon the total effect of all the genes for height. This results in a wide range of heights among humans.

SEARCH: Use library references to find answers to your questions.

ACTIVITY

INVESTIGATING THE EFFECT OF CHANCE ON HEREDITY

You will need a penny, a nickel, masking tape, a marker, paper, and a pencil.

1. Place a piece of tape on both sides of each coin.

2. Label one side of each coin with an F to represent the gene for unattached ear lobes. Label the other side of each coin with an f to represent the gene for attached ear lobes.

3. Copy the Data Table on a sheet of paper.

4. Flip the two coins 50 times each. Record the gene combination that results from each flip by placing a dash in the appropriate column on your paper.

5. After 50 flips, total the number of dashes in each column.

Data Table: Gene Pairs		
FF	Ff	ff
1.		
2.		
3.		
4.		
5.		

Questions

1. **a.** Which trait is dominant?   **b.** Which trait is recessive?

2. What were the results of the coin flips for each pair of genes?

18-6 How are traits blended?

Objective ▶ Describe what occurs when a dominant gene is not present in a gene pair.

TechTerm

▶ **blending:** combination of genes in which a mixture of both traits shows

Eye Color In humans, the gene for brown eyes is dominant. The gene for blue eyes is recessive. Yet some people have eyes that are not brown or blue. They have hazel or green eyes. This is caused by genes for eye color that are neither dominant nor recessive. When these genes combine, a mixture of both traits shows. This kind of gene combination is called **blending.** A person's skin color and hair color also can result from the blending of genes.

Blue   **Brown**   **Green**

▶ *Define:* What is blending? combination of genes that shows a mixture of traits

Melanin Scientists have learned that four pairs of genes control skin color. None of these genes is dominant and each affects skin color equally. These genes control the amount of melanin found in the skin. Melanin is a chemical substance that gives skin its color. The more melanin found in the skin, the darker the color.

▶ *Hypothesize:* Why are no two skin colors exactly alike? because skin color depends upon the amount of melanin that is found in the skin

Blending in Chickens There is a kind of chicken that has a gene for black feathers and a gene for white feathers. Neither of these genes is dominant over the other. The capital letter B stands for black feathers. The capital letter W stands for white feathers. A chicken that is BB, or pure black, has black feathers. A chicken that is WW, or pure

white, has white feathers. When a pure black chicken and a pure white chicken are mated, all of the offspring have the gene combination BW. These hybrids are neither black nor white. They are grey. Blending has taken place.

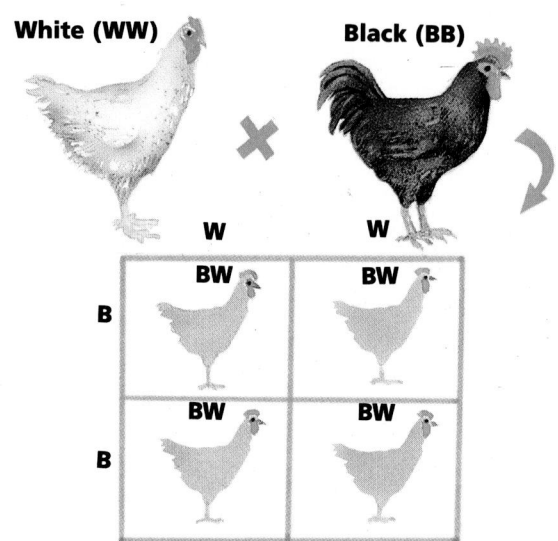

White (WW)   **Black (BB)**

	W	W
B	BW	BW
B	BW	BW

▶ *Describe:* What causes a chicken to have grey feathers? blending of a black and a white gene

Blended Genes Blended genes do not disappear. They show up again when hybrids are mated. If two hybrid grey chickens are mated, one-fourth of the offspring are BB, or pure black. One-half of the offspring are BW, or hybrid grey. One-fourth of the offspring are WW, or pure white.

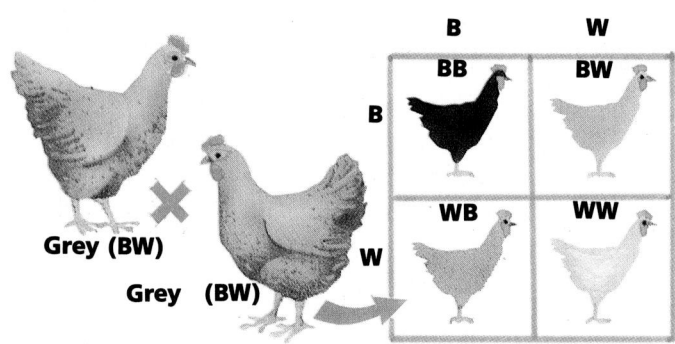

Grey (BW)

Grey (BW)

	B	W
B	BB	BW
W	WB	WW

▶ *Relate:* What kinds of gene combinations can the offspring of two hybrid grey chickens have? BB, BW, and WW

LESSON SUMMARY

▶ Blending is a gene combination in which a mixture of traits shows.

▶ Four different pairs of genes control skin color.

▶ There is no dominant gene in blending.

▶ When hybrids with blended traits are mated, the pure traits show again in some of the offspring.

CHECK *Answer the following.*

1. What are green eyes in humans caused by? blending

2. What color feathers will a chicken with the gene combination WW have? white

3. What is the gene combination for a chicken with grey feathers? BW

Complete the following.

4. A person who is very fair-skinned has a _____ amount of melanin. small

5. If two hybrid grey chickens are mated, one-half of their offspring will have the gene combination _____ . BW

6. Chickens with a gene combination of BW will be _____ in color. grey

7. The offspring of two hybrid grey chickens can have feathers that are colored black, _____, or grey. white

APPLY *Answer the following.*

8. **Infer:** Why are capital letters used to represent all the genes for feather color in certain types of chickens?

9. **Hypothesize:** Why does blending occur only in hybrids?

Skill Builder

▶ *Predicting* Some traits in animals are determined by blending. For example, neither of the genes for tail length in cats is dominant. Use a Punnett square to predict the tail length in the kittens if two short-tailed cats (LN) are crossed. Let L represent the gene for long tail and N represent the gene for no tail.

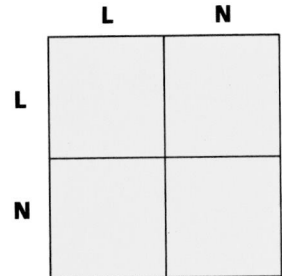

TECHNOLOGY AND SOCIETY

HUMAN GENOME PROJECT

Scientists around the world are inventing and using new technologies to map the human genome. The goal of the project is to identify the nearly 100,000 genes that are in human chromosomes. Another goal is to find the sequence of the 3 billion base pairs that make up the genes.

The Human Genome Map will provide detailed DNA information to biologists, genetic counselors, researchers, and doctors. Researchers may find the causes and cures of genetic diseases, such as cancer and diabetes. Doctors will be able to use these findings to diagnose and treat genetic disorders.

When it's finished, the human DNA sequence may take up the space of 200 telephone books of 1,000 pages each. A computer database has been developed to keep track of the project as scientists piece together this giant genome puzzle.

18-7 How is sex determined?

Objective ▶ Explain how chromosomes in a sperm cell determine the sex of offspring.

X and Y All human traits are determined by 23 pairs of chromosomes. Look at the 23 pairs of chromosomes below.

Do you see the difference between the two chromosomes in pair 23? In the male, the chromosomes of this pair are not alike. These different chromosomes are called X and Y. Male cells have one X chromosome and one Y chromosome. Female cells have two X chromosomes. The X and Y chromosomes determine the sex of an organism.

�iIiⅡ▶ *Identify:* Which chromosomes determine sex? X and Y

Sperm Cells Male cells have an XY pair of chromosomes. During meiosis, each sperm cell receives only one chromosome from each pair. One-half of the sperm cells receive an X chromosome. The other half receive a Y chromosome. Every sperm contains either an X or a Y chromosome.

▣iⅡ▶ *Explain:* Why do some sperm cells have an X chromosome while other sperm cells have a Y chromosome? Each sperm cell receives only one chromosome from the XY pair of chromosomes in the male parent cell.

Egg Cells Female cells have an XX pair of chromosomes. During meiosis, each egg cell receives one chromosome from each pair of chromosomes. Therefore, each egg cell receives one X chromosome. All egg cells contain X chromosomes.

▣iⅡ▶ *Relate:* Why do egg cells contain only one X chromosome? Due to meiosis, each egg cell receives only one X chromosome from the pair of X chromosomes in the female parent cell.

Sex of Offspring The sex of offspring is controlled by chromosomes in male sperm cells. As a result, all children inherit their sex from their fathers. During fertilization, if the egg cell is fertilized by a sperm cell carrying an X chromosome, the fertilized egg will have two X chromosomes (XX). It will develop into a female. If the sperm is carrying a Y chromosome, the zygote will have one X chromosome and one Y chromosome (XY). It will develop into a male. Half the sperm cells carry the X chromosome. The other half carry the Y chromosome. Therefore, over a large number of births, half will be female and half will be male.

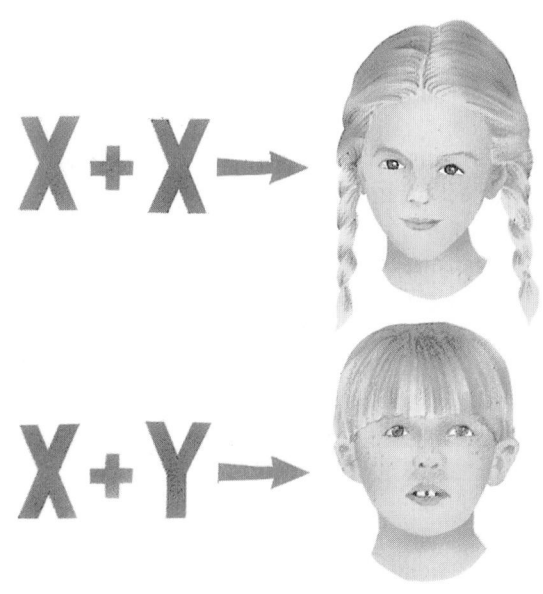

▣iⅡ▶ *Identify:* Which parent is responsible for the sex of the offspring? male

366

▶ Male cells are XY, while female cells are XX.

▶ Each sperm cell has either an X or a Y chromosome.

▶ Each egg cell always has one X chromosome.

▶ When a sperm cell fertilizes an egg cell, the zygote becomes a female if it is XX or a male if it is XY.

CHECK *Write true if the statement is true. If the statement is false, change the underlined term to make the statement true.*

1. The sex of offspring is controlled by chromosomes in the <u>female</u>. male

2. A <u>female</u> cell contains two X chromosomes. true

3. An <u>egg</u> cell can contain either an X or a Y chromosome. A sperm

4. A zygote that has two X chromosomes will develop into a <u>male</u>. female

5. A zygote that has an X and a Y chromosome will develop into a <u>male</u>. true

APPLY *Answer the following.*

6. **Hypothesize:** Which are more alike, sperm cells or egg cells?

7. **Calculate:** Last year, 250 babies were born at a certain hospital. Estimate the number of males born there during the year. Explain your answer.

InfoSearch

Read the passage. Ask two questions that you cannot answer from the information in the passage.

Sex Chromosomes In birds, moths, butterflies, and some fish, the sex chromosomes are the reverse of human sex chromosomes. In these animals, the male has two identical (XX) chromosomes, and the female has two different ones (XY). In these animals, it is the egg cell, not the sperm cell, that determines the sex of the offspring.

SEARCH: Use library references to find answers to your questions.

TECHNOLOGY AND SOCIETY

AMNIOCENTESIS

Amniocentesis (am-nee-oh-sen-TEE-sis) is a test performed during a woman's pregnancy. The test involves inserting a needle through the woman's abdomen and into her uterus. Some of the fluid that surrounds the fetus is removed through the needle. The fluid contains cells that have been shed by the fetus. Doctors can learn about fetal chromosomes and enzymes by studying cell structures.

More than 175 different genetic disorders can be identified by amniocentesis. The test also reveals the sex of the fetus. This is important when looking for sex-linked disorders. Hemophilia and Duchenne's muscular dystrophy are two sex-linked disorders that can be detected by amniocentesis.

An advantage of determining if a developing fetus has an inherited disease is that treatment can begin early—sometimes before that baby is born. Doctors are developing techniques for replacing faulty genes with normal genes before birth.

18-8 What are sex-linked traits?

Objective ▶ Describe how certain traits are inherited along with sex.

TechTerm

▶ **sex-linked traits:** traits that are controlled by the sex chromosomes

Inherited Traits Some traits are inherited along with sex. These traits are controlled by the X and Y sex chromosomes. Traits that are inherited along with sex are called **sex-linked traits.**

Like all other chromosomes, the sex chromosomes carry genes. The X chromosome carries many genes, but the Y chromosome carries few genes. Most of the genes for sex-linked traits are found on the X chromosome.

� **Define:** What are sex-linked traits? traits that are controlled by the sex chromosomes

Sex-linked Disorders Some hereditary disorders are controlled by the sex chromosomes. Two sex-linked disorders are hemophilia (hee-moh-FIL-ee-uh) and colorblindness. Hemophilia is a disorder in which the blood does not clot properly. People with hemophilia can easily bleed to death. Even a small cut can prove to be life-threatening. Colorblindness is a disorder in which a person cannot see the difference between certain colors.

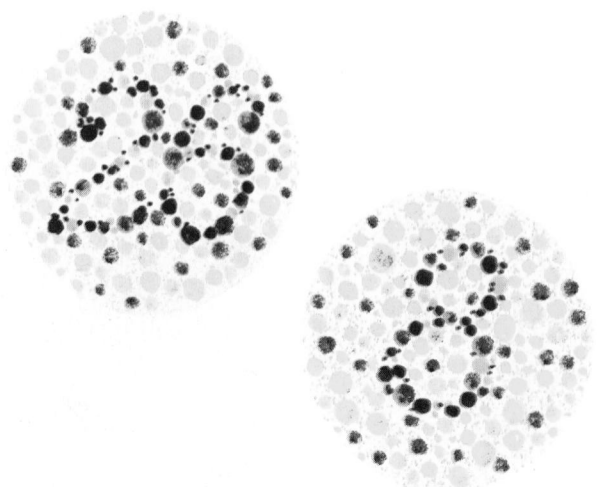

Sex-linked disorders are found more often in men than in women. This occurs because the genes for most sex-linked disorders are recessive. In women there are two X chromosomes. Both X chromosomes contain genes for these traits. While one of these chromosomes may have the gene for the disorder, the other X chromosome usually has a normal gene. Since the gene for the disorder is recessive, a female with each type of gene still appears normal.

	X	X⁻
X	Normal XX	Carrier XX⁻
Y	Normal XY	Color blind X⁻Y

▶ **Explain:** Why does a female with a gene for a sex-linked disorder appear normal? The female also has a normal gene that is dominant.

Carriers Woman who have one normal gene and one gene for a sex-linked disorder are said to be carriers of the disorder. Although they do not show the disorder, they can pass the gene for it to their children. Men who have a sex-linked disorder also are called carriers, because they can pass the disorder to their offspring.

When the sex chromosomes of a female carrier separate during meiosis, half the eggs get the normal chromosome and half get the chromosome for the disorder. If an egg cell containing the X chromosome for the disorder is fertilized by a sperm containing the normal X chromosome, the daughter will be normal. If an egg containing the X chromosome for the disorder is fertilized by a sperm with a Y chromosome, the son will have the disorder.

▶ **Explain:** Why do more men have sex-linked disorders? because males do not have two X chromosomes

LESSON SUMMARY

▶ Traits that are inherited with the sex chromosomes are called sex-linked traits.

▶ Most of the genes for sex-linked traits are carried on the X chromosome.

▶ Hemophilia and colorblindness are two sex-linked disorders.

▶ Most of the genes for sex-linked traits are recessive.

▶ Females can be carriers of genes for sex-linked disorders without actually having the disorder.

▶ Half the eggs of a female carrier of a sex-linked disorder get a normal chromosome and half get a chromosome for the disorder.

CHECK *Write true if the statement is true. If the statement is false, change the underlined term to make the statement true.*

1. Most of the genes for sex-linked traits are found on the <u>X</u> chromosome. true

2. The genes for most sex-linked disorders are <u>dominant</u>. recessive

3. Traits that are inherited along with sex are called <u>sex chromosomes</u>. sex-linked traits

4. A female who has a gene for a sex-linked disorder but does not show the disorder is a <u>carrier</u>. true

5. A male who has a normal Y chromosome and an X chromosome for a disorder <u>will not</u> have the disorder. will

APPLY *Answer the following.*

▶ 6. **Infer:** How can a female have the sex-linked disorder of hemophilia?

7. **Describe:** What kind of gene pair is found in the female carrier of a sex-linked disorder?

State the Problem

State the problem for this experiment.

A person once tried to develop a breed of mice without tails. He cut off the tails of mice before letting them mate. He repeated this for many generations. The results were always the same. All the offspring were born with normal tails.

LOOKING BACK IN SCIENCE

HEMOPHILIA IN THE ROYAL FAMILY

Hemophilia is a sex-linked disorder. Since it is a recessive trait, males generally have the disease. Females generally are carriers who do not show the disease. A famous carrier of hemophilia was Queen Victoria of England. Three out of her four offspring inherited the gene for hemophilia. Two of Queen Victoria's daughters were carriers of hemophilia. One of her sons was a hemophiliac. These offspring passed the trait along to each of their own children. Four of Queen Victoria's granddaughters were carriers. Three of her grandsons were hemophiliacs. As her grandchildren married members of other royal families, the disorder continued to spread. As a result, hemophilia was quite common among European royalty during the nineteenth century.

18-9 What are some inherited diseases?

Objective ▶ Identify some inherited diseases.

TechTerm

▶ **inherited disease:** disease caused by an inherited gene

Inherited Diseases Sometimes a gene is defective or abnormal. The abnormal gene stops the body from working properly. An abnormal gene can be passed from the parents to their offspring. The gene can cause disease in the offspring. A disease that is caused by an inherited abnormal gene is called an **inherited disease.**

▶ *Define:* What is an inherited disease? disease caused by an inherited abnormal gene

Sickle-Cell Anemia Sickle-cell anemia is an inherited disease that mainly affects people of African descent. The red blood cells of a person with sickle-cell anemia are not shaped normally. Rather than being rounded, these red blood cells are shaped like a sickle or crescent. Because of their abnormal shape, sickle cells are easily trapped in blood vessels. They clog the blood vessels and block the flow of blood. The clogged blood vessels may cause severe pain and, in some cases, an early death.

The gene for sickle-cell anemia is recessive (s). The gene for normal red blood cells is dominant (S). People who inherit two recessive genes (ss) for the trait have the disease. People who inherit one dominant and one recessive gene (Ss) for the trait are carriers of the disease.

▶ *Explain:* People with one recessive gene for the sickle-cell anemia trait do not show the disease. Why? The dominant gene for normal red blood cells hides the recessive gene.

Tay-Sachs Disease Tay-Sachs is a disease that affects mainly Jewish children with Eastern European ancestry. An abnormal gene stops the child's body from producing an enzyme that breaks down fat. As a result, the fat gathers in the brain cells. This can cause brain damage and death.

The gene for Tay-Sachs disease also is recessive. A person who inherits two recessive genes for this trait will have the disease. A person who inherits one recessive gene and one dominant gene is a carrier.

▶ *Relate:* What body function does the recessive gene for Tay-Sachs disease affect? production of an enzyme that breaks down fat

PKU PKU, or phenylketonuria (fen-il-keet-uh-NYOOR-ee-uh), is another kind of inherited disease. People with PKU are missing an important enzyme that is made in the liver. As a result, they cannot break down certain chemicals in food. The chemicals build up in the body and may cause brain damage and mental retardation.

▶ *Describe:* What effect does the disease PKU have on the body? Certain chemicals in food cannot be broken down because a certain enzyme is missing.

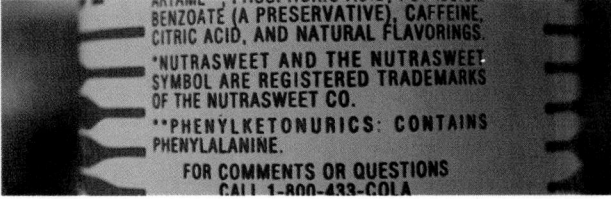

LESSON SUMMARY

▶ An inherited disease is caused by an abnormal gene that is inherited.

▶ Sickle-cell anemia is an inherited disease in which red blood cells are irregularly shaped.

▶ The gene for sickle-cell anemia is recessive.

▶ Tay-Sachs disease is an inherited disease that stops the body from producing an enzyme that breaks down fat.

▶ The gene for Tay-Sachs disease is recessive.

▶ PKU is an inherited disease that prevents the body from breaking down certain chemicals found in foods.

CHECK *Find the sentence in the lesson that answers each question. Then, write the sentence.*

1. What are inherited diseases caused by?

2. How do sickle cells differ from normal red blood cells?

3. Who is considered a carrier of Tay-Sachs disease?

4. What is PKU?

Complete the following.

5. A person with Tay-Sachs disease lacks an enzyme that breaks down _____ . fat

6. A person with PKU cannot break down _____ found in foods. certain chemicals

7. Sickle cells clog the blood vessels and block the flow of _____ . blood

8. A defective gene can be passed from _____ to their offspring. parents

APPLY *Answer the following.*

9. **Compare:** How are the effects of PKU and Tay-Sachs disease similar?

10. **Hypothesize:** Are the offspring of parents who are both pure dominant for normal red blood cells in danger of getting sickle-cell anemia? Why?

InfoSearch

Read the passage. Ask two questions that you cannot answer from the information in the passage.

Treating PKU PKU is not a curable disease. However, if the disease is detected early enough, it can be treated. All newborn babies are given a simple blood test that checks for the presence of PKU. A child who has PKU is put on a special diet. Foods high in protein must be avoided. By following the special diet, the child can grow and live a normal life.

SEARCH: Use library references to find answers to your questions.

ACTIVITY

PREDICTING TAY-SACHS DISEASE

You will need paper and a pencil.

1. Copy the chart shown on a piece of paper.

2. Predict the gene combinations each child will inherit from its parents. Fill in the gene combinations on the chart.

Questions

1. Are the parents pure dominant, pure recessive, or hybrid dominant for the trait?

2. What gene combination is found in a carrier for the trait?

3. How many of the offspring have Tay-Sachs disease?

4. What is the gene combination found in normal offspring?

5. **Analyze:** What is the chance that parents who are both carriers of the Tay-Sachs trait will produce a child who has the disease?

18-10 Can the environment affect inherited traits?

Objective ▶ Understand how the living conditions of an organism affect the way it develops.

Genes and Traits Genes control many of your traits. This is true for all living things. Your hair color and skin color are determined by genes. So is your sex. The size and color of flowers also are determined by genes. However, other factors can affect traits. The environment affects the traits of living things in many ways.

▷ *Identify:* What affects the traits of living things besides genes? environment

Conditions in the Environment The right environment is important for the development of certain traits. Food, air, water, and sunlight all are parts of the environment. Organisms need all of these things to grow and survive. Green plants need sunlight to develop and grow properly. Plants that do not get enough sunlight will be smaller and weaker than normal. When the environment is not right for an organism, certain traits many not develop at all.

Living things are affected by a shortage of food. A young organism may not develop properly if it does not get the right food. If the food supply increases, development may become normal again. Living things can develop normally only when conditions in the environment are normal.

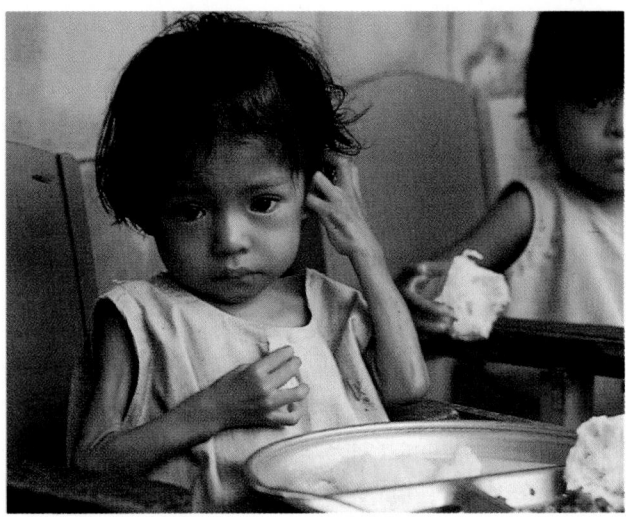

Malnourished children

▶ *Infer:* What might happen to a green plant if its environment is not right? The plant will not grow and develop properly.

Environment and Genes Plants that are grown in poor soil are small in size. They produce only a few fruits. Adding nutrients to the soil changes the environment. The plants grow larger and produce more fruit. The size of a plant and the amount of fruit it produces are traits. The genes for these traits are not affected by the environment. Only the development of the trait is affected by the environment. A change in the environment does not change the genes. A change in the environment can help the gene to do its work. A change in the environment also can prevent the gene from doing its work.

▷ *Describe:* What effect does the environment have on the genes in a plant? The environment cannot change the genes.

LESSON SUMMARY

▶ The environment affects the traits of certain things.

▶ The right environment is important for the development of living things.

▶ Living things develop normally when the conditions in the environment are normal.

▶ A change in the environment does not change the genes.

CHECK *Complete the following.*

1. The traits of all living things are controlled by _____ . genes

2. Food, air, _____, and sunlight are all parts of the environment. water

3. The environment affects the development of _____ . traits

4. A change in the environment of an organism has no effect on the _____ of the organism. genes

5. A young organism does not develop normally if its environment does not supply enough of the right _____ . food

6. Living things develop normally when conditions in the _____ are normal. environment

APPLY *Answer the following.*

7. **Infer:** A green plant was stored in a school closet during the summer vacation. When students returned to the school in the fall, they found the plant had died. What probably caused the plant to die?

8. Gardeners often add fertilizer to soil. Does the fertilizer affect the genes of plants growing in the soil?

9. **Hypothesize:** Sunlight helps the body to synthesize vitamin D. What would happen to a person if they were never exposed to sunlight?

Designing an Experiment.................

Design an experiment to solve the problem.

PROBLEM: How does the amount of water affect the growth and development of a plant?

Your experiment should:

1. List the materials you would need.

2. Identify safety precautions that should be followed.

3. List a step-by-step procedure.

4. Describe how you would record your data.

SCIENCE CONNECTION ◆○◆○◆○◆○◆○◆○◆

PLANT FERTILIZERS

Have you ever "fed" your plants? Although plants can make their own food, they need nutrients from the soil to carry on their food-making processes. For example, plants need phosphorus, potassium, nitrogen, sulfur, and magnesium. Sometimes soil does not have enough of these substances. This results in a need for plant food to be added to the soil. Plant food contains the nutrients a plant needs to grow.

The scientific name for plant food is fertilizer (fur-TUL-i-zur). Some fertilizers come directly from living things. Other fertilizers are mixtures of chemicals. Chemical fertilizers are produced in factories. The most widely used chemical fertilizers contain nitrogen, phosphorus, and potassium. These are the three plant nutrients in which soil is most frequently deficient. The amount of these nutrients needed by a plant varies according to the kind of plant and the type of soil in which the plant is growing.

18-11 How is genetics used to improve living things?

Objective ► Explain the different methods of controlled breeding.

TechTerms

- ► **controlled breeding:** mating organisms to produce offspring with certain traits
- ► **hybridization** (hy-brid-ih-ZAY-shun): mating two different kinds of organisms
- ► **inbreeding:** mating closely related organisms
- ► **mass selection:** crossing plants with desirable traits

Controlled Breeding People have raised animals and planted crops for thousands of years. Over time, they have learned that some plants produce better crops than others. They saw that some animals had more desirable traits than others. People learned to mate animals with desirable traits. Mating organisms to produce offspring with certain traits is called **controlled breeding.** The offspring produced usually had the same desirable traits as their parents.

▐▐▐► **Define:** What is controlled breeding? mating organisms to produce offspring with certain favorable traits

Mass Selection Plant growers use a process called **mass selection** to produce plants with certain traits. In mass selection, plants with desirable traits are crossed. Seeds produced by these plants are collected and planted. New plants develop from these seeds. If the new plants have the same desirable traits, their seeds are collected and planted. The process goes on for many generations of the plants. The result of mass selection is a new kind of plant with certain desirable traits.

▐▐▐► **Describe:** What is the purpose of mass selection? to develop a new kind of plant with certain desirable traits

Inbreeding Another way of producing organisms with favorable traits is by **inbreeding.** In-breeding is the mating of closely related organisms. Offspring produced by inbreeding have genes that are very similar to their parents' genes. For example, inbreeding is used to breed racehorses, whose desirable trait is speed.

▐▐▐► **Compare:** How do the genes of offspring produced by inbreeding compare with the parents' genes? They are very similar.

Hybridization Sometimes two organisms with different kinds of genes are crossed. The offspring show traits of both parents. The mating of two different kinds of organisms is called **hybridization** (hy-brid-ih-ZAY-shun). A mule is the result of hybridization. Its father is a donkey and its mother is a horse.

When two different organisms are crossed, the offspring usually shows the best traits of both parent organisms. For example, when a rye plant and a wheat plant are crossed, they produce triticale (trit-i-KAY-lee). Triticale is more nutritious than either wheat or rye.

▐▐▐► **Explain:** How is a mule produced? by the hybridization of a donkey and a horse

LESSON SUMMARY

Mating organisms with certain traits to produce offspring with those same traits is called controlled breeding.

In mass selection, plants with desirable traits are crossed until a new variety of plant is developed.

Inbreeding is the mating of organisms with similar genes.

In hybridization, two different kinds of organisms are mated.

A hybrid organism usually shows the best traits of both parents.

CHECK *Find the sentence in the lesson that answers each question. Then, write the sentence.*

1. What is the purpose of controlled breeding?
2. How are new plants with desirable traits produced?
3. What is the mating of closely related organisms called?
4. What is hybridization?
5. How are the genes of offspring produced by inbreeding related to their parents' genes?

APPLY *Complete the following.*

6. **Compare:** How are mass selection, inbreeding, and hybridization alike?
7. **Relate:** Could inbreeding and hybridization be considered opposite processes? Why?
8. **Infer:** Why is inbreeding dangerous to the organism?
9. Would you rather have an inbred dog as a pet or a hybrid dog as a pet? Explain your answer.

InfoSearch

Read the passage. Ask two questions that you cannot answer from the information in the passage.

Problems with Inbreeding When inbreeding is allowed to continue for a number of generations, undesirable traits may begin to show. For example, inbreeding of plants may cause the crop yield to become smaller and smaller. The plants themselves may become smaller and weaker. Hereditary diseases in animals usually are very rare. However, inbreeding of animals may cause these diseases to appear much more often.

SEARCH: Use library references to find answers to your questions.

CAREER IN LIFE SCIENCE

ANIMAL BREEDER

Animal breeders study the genes that control certain traits in animals. They use this information to breed animals and produce offspring with desirable traits. Animal breeders also identify the traits that are desirable in different kinds of animals. For example, a thoroughbred racehorse is bred for speed. A workhorse is bred for strength. A cow may be bred to produce more milk.

Most animal breeders work directly with animals outdoors. Other animal breeders do research in a laboratory. In order to become an animal breeder, you need a high-school diploma. You should take courses in agriculture and biology. A four-year degree in animal science often is necessary. For more information, write to your county or state department of agriculture.

18-12 What is genetic engineering?

Objective ▶ Describe one method used to produce new DNA.

TechTerms

- **genetic engineering** (juh-NET-ik en-juh-NEER-ing): methods used to produce new forms of DNA
- **gene splicing** (SPLYS-ing): moving a section of DNA from the genes of one organism to the genes of another organism

Changing DNA Until recently, new forms of life could only be invented in books and movies. Today, however, advances in modern genetics have made it possible for new forms of bacteria and other simple organisms to be made in the laboratory. This is the result of a new technology called **genetic engineering** (juh-NET-ik en-juh-NEER-ing). Genetic engineering is a process by which new forms of DNA are produced.

▶ **Define:** What is genetic engineering? process by which new forms of DNA are produced

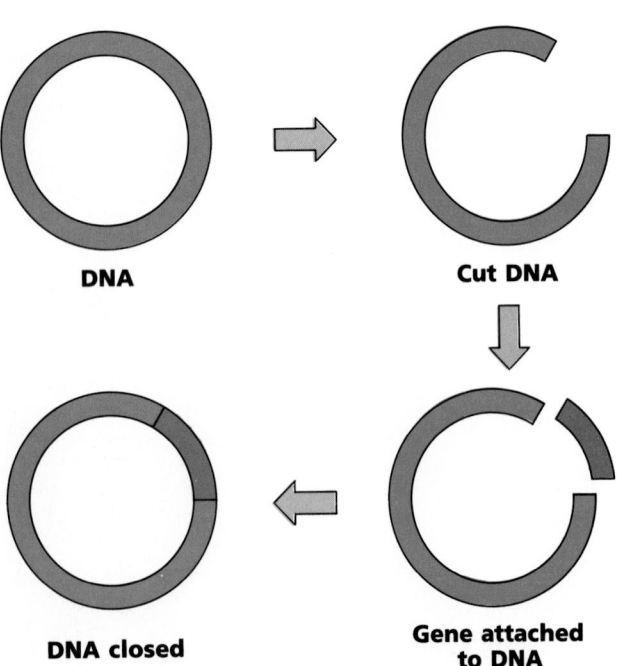

DNA

Cut DNA

Gene attached to DNA

DNA closed

Gene Splicing One method of genetic engineering is called **gene splicing** (SPLY-sing). Gene splicing is a process in which a section of DNA from one organism is transferred to another organism.

The diagram shows the three steps in gene splicing. First, a DNA ring is temporarily opened up. This is done with certain enzymes. New genes from another organism are then added, or spliced, into the DNA. Finally, the DNA ring is closed.

▶ **Describe:** What occurs during gene splicing? Genes from the DNA strand of one organism are added to the DNA strand of another organism.

Benefits Genetic engineering has many benefits. New genes have been added to the DNA of certain bacteria. These bacteria can then produce substances that otherwise could only be made by the human body. Human insulin needed by diabetics is an example of such a substance. Bacteria can produce insulin after human genes are spliced into the DNA of bacteria.

Scientists hope that someday genetic engineering can be used to correct genetic disorders. This may involve adding normal genes to cells that are missing these genes. Another use of genetic engineering could be to improve certain traits in plants and animals used for food.

▶ **Explain:** How can bacteria produce human insulin? Splicing human genes into the DNA of the bacteria enables the bacteria to produce human insulin.

Disadvantages Some scientists are concerned about possible dangers in working with new forms of DNA. There is some concern that experiments with the DNA of bacteria might produce an organism that causes a disease for which there is no cure. To help prevent this from happening, the federal government has set up special rules that must be followed in experiments using genetic engineering.

▶ **Identify:** What is a possible danger in working with new forms of DNA? producing a disease-causing organism for which there is no defense

▶ Genetic engineering is a process used to produce new forms of DNA.

▶ Gene splicing is a form of genetic engineering in which part of a DNA ring from one organism is added to a DNA ring from a different organism.

▶ Genetic engineering can produce substances normally made only by the human body.

▶ Scientists hope genetic engineering may be used to correct genetic disorders in the future.

▶ There are possible dangers involved in working with new forms of DNA.

CHECK *Complete the following.*

1. Methods used to produce new forms of DNA are called _____ . genetic engineering

2. A process in which DNA from one organism is added to the DNA of another organism is called _____ . gene splicing

3. Certain kinds of genetically engineered bacteria can produce _____ , which is needed by diabetics. insulin

4. Scientists hope that someday genetic engineering can be used to correct _____ . genetic disorders.

5. A danger with genetic engineering is the possibility of producing a _____ organism for which there is no known cure. disease-causing

APPLY *Answer the following.*

6. **Relate:** PKU is a genetic disorder that causes the lack of a certain enzyme. How might genetic engineering someday be used to correct this disorder?

▶ 7. **Infer:** Through genetic engineering, scientists have been able to place a gene from a firefly into the DNA of a plant. What effect do you suppose this gene has on the plant?

Skill Builder ....

▲ *Modeling* When you model, you use a copy or an imitation of an object to help explain or understand something. Make a model showing the three stages in gene splicing. Use one colored piece of construction paper to represent the original gene. Use another colored piece of construction paper to represent the new section. Make one model for each step in the process. Write an explanation of what is happening under each step.

TECHNOLOGY AND SOCIETY

GENETIC ENGINEERING

Many farmers are now raising genetically engineered plants and animals. One problem food growers have is that food ripened on the vine becomes too soft to ship. For example, tomatoes are often picked green and then refrigerated while they are shipped. When they reach their destination, the tomatoes are sprayed with ethylene gas to make them turn red. These tomatoes usually do not have a good flavor. Using genetic engineering, scientists have produced a tomato that can ripen on the vine without becoming soft. Food stores get a better tasting tomato.

Scientists can now get an enzyme from genetically engineered sheep that helps fight a lung disease called emphysema. An enzyme that dissolves blood clots has been obtained from the milk of genetically engineered goats. A protein called lactoferrin which fights bacteria can be produced in the milk of genetically engineered cows. These genetically altered animals are saving the lives of many people.

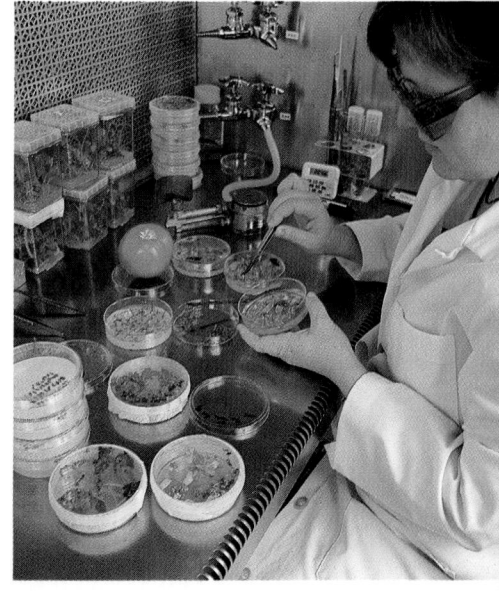

STUDY HINT Before you begin the Unit Challenges, review the TechTerms and Lesson Summary for each lesson in this unit.

TechTerms

blending (364)
chromosomes (356)
controlled breeding (374)
DNA (358)
dominant gene (360)
gene splicing (376)
genes (356)
genetic engineering (376)

genetics (354)
heredity (354)
hybrid (360)
hybridization (374)
inbreeding (374)
inherited disease (370)
inherited traits (354)

mass selection (374)
Punnett square (362)
pure (360)
recessive gene (360)
replication (358)
sex-linked traits (368)
trait (354)

TechTerm Challenges

Matching *Write the TechTerm that matches each description.*

1. moving a section of DNA from the genes of one organism to the genes of another organism gene splicing
2. field of biology that studies heredity genetics
3. mating of closely related organisms inbreeding
4. traits that are passed from parents to their offspring inherited traits
5. mating organisms to produce offspring with certain traits controlled breeding
6. threadlike structures that control heredity chromosomes
7. traits that are inherited along with sex sex-linked traits
8. chemical that makes up chromosomes DNA
9. combination of genes in which a mixture of both traits shows blending
10. gene that always shows itself dominant gene
11. chart that shows possible gene combinations Punnett square

Fill-in *Write the TechTerm that best completes each statement.*

1. The characteristics of an organism are called _____ . traits
2. The process by which DNA is duplicated is called _____ . replication
3. An organism is _____ if it has two like genes for a given trait. pure
4. A disease caused by an inherited abnormal gene is called a(n) _____ . inherited disease
5. Crossing plants with desirable traits over many generations is called _____ . mass selection
6. The process by which new forms of DNA are produced is called _____ . genetic engineering
7. The mating of two different kinds of organisms is called _____ . hybridization
8. The gene that is hidden when a dominant gene is present is a(n) _____ . recessive gene
9. Organisms that have two unlike genes for a trait are _____ for that trait. hybrid

Content Challenges

Multiple Choice *Write the letter of the term that best completes each statement.*

1. Mendel found that when he crossed pure tall pea plants with pure short pea plants, the offspring were all
   a. short. b. tall. c. medium height. d. both tall and short. b
2. Male organisms have
   a. two X chromosomes. b. two Y chromosomes. c. three Y chromosomes. d. one X and one Y chromosome. d

3. The nitrogen base adenine always pairs with the nitrogen base
   a. cytosine.   **b.** guanine.   **c.** thymine.   **d.** chromosomes. c

4. Two sex-linked traits that are carried on the X chromosome are
   a. hemophilia and skin color.   **b.** hemophilia and color blindness.   **c.** color blindness and sickle-cell anemia.   **d.** sickle-cell anemia and PKU. b

5. Humans have
   a. 46 pairs of chromosomes.   **b.** 23 chromosomes.   **c.** 21 chromosomes.   **d.** 23 pairs of chromosomes. d

6. Triticale, produced by crossing wheat plants and rye plants, is an example of
   a. hybridization.   **b.** mass selection.   **c.** inbreeding.   **d.** self-pollination. a

7. The field of biology that studies the inheritance of traits is
   a. heredity.   **b.** embryology.   **c.** genetics.   **d.** ecology. c

8. When Mendel crossed pure short plants with pure tall plants, the result was tall plants. He concluded that the tall trait is
   a. dominant.   **b.** pure.   **c.** hidden.   **d.** recessive. a

9. A special diet can be prescribed for a child with
   a. hemophilia.   **b.** Down's syndrome.   **c.** sickle-cell anemia.   **d.** PKU. d

10. The sides of a DNA ladder are made up of
    a. nitrogen bases.   **b.** sugars and phosphates.   **c.** proteins.   **d.** melanin. b

True/False *Write true if the statement is true. If the statement is false, change the underlined term to make the statement true.*

1. Sex-linked traits are found more often in <u>females</u>. males
2. Organisms with two of the same genes for a particular trait are <u>hybrids</u>. pure
3. Inbreeding is the crossing of organisms that are from <u>different</u> species. true
4. The process of transferring genes from the DNA of one organism to the DNA of another organism is called <u>gene splicing</u>. true
5. In the labeling of traits, a capital letter represents a <u>recessive</u> trait. dominant
6. The parent who determines the sex of the offspring is the <u>female</u>. male
7. A change in a gene or chromosome is called a <u>mutation</u>. true
8. When two hybrids are crossed, the offspring will be one-fourth pure dominant, one-fourth pure recessive, and one-half <u>hybrid dominant</u>. true
9. During reproduction, one <u>chromosome</u> from each pair goes to each offspring. true
10. The trait of skin color is determined by <u>dominant genes</u>. blending
11. The gene that carries sex-linked diseases is <u>dominant</u>. recessive

Understanding the Features...

Reading Critically *Use the feature reading selections to answer the following. Page numbers for the features follow each question in parentheses.*

1. **Infer:** Why do you think Mendel often is referred to as the 'father of genetics?' (355)
2. What contributions has Barbara McClintock made to the field of genetics? (357)
3. **Name:** Who were James Watson and Francis Crick? (359)
4. What is one of the goals of the Human Genome Project? (365)

5. Why is amniocentesis performed? (367)
6. How did hemophilia spread during the 19th century? (369)
7. What is the scientific term for plant food? (373)

8. **Infer:** How do courses in biology and agriculture help an animal breeder? (375)
9. How can genetic engineering be used to make better foods? (377)

Concept Challenges...

Critical Thinking *Answer each of the following in complete sentences.*

1. **Infer:** Why do you think some people are against genetic engineering?
2. If a genetic disorder was present in your family, would you go to a genetic counselor before having children? Why or why not?
3. **Explain:** How does the genetic code control an organism's traits?

4. How do Punnett squares help in the prediction of the inheritance of traits?
5. If you were a geneticist, what animals or plants would you study? Why?

Interpreting a Diagram *Use the diagram of DNA replication to answer the following.*

1. What does the letter A stand for?
2. What does the letter C stand for?
3. What does the letter T stand for?
4. What does the letter G stand for?
5. How do the nitrogen bases pair up during DNA replication?
6. What happens during the process of replication?

Finding Out More...

1. Some law enforcement agencies use DNA in addition to fingerprints as a method of identifying criminals. Use library references to find out more about DNA testing. Write your findings in a report.
2. Cloning is the production of organisms with identical genes. Seedless grapes and seedless oranges are two types of fruit that are produced by cloning. Find out two cloning techniques. Describe the techniques in a written report.

3. Blood type is controlled by different genes. Research the four major blood groups and which genes are dominant. Write the different gene combinations each blood type may have.
4. Use library references to research the work of Walter Sutton. Compare his findings to the findings of Mendel.

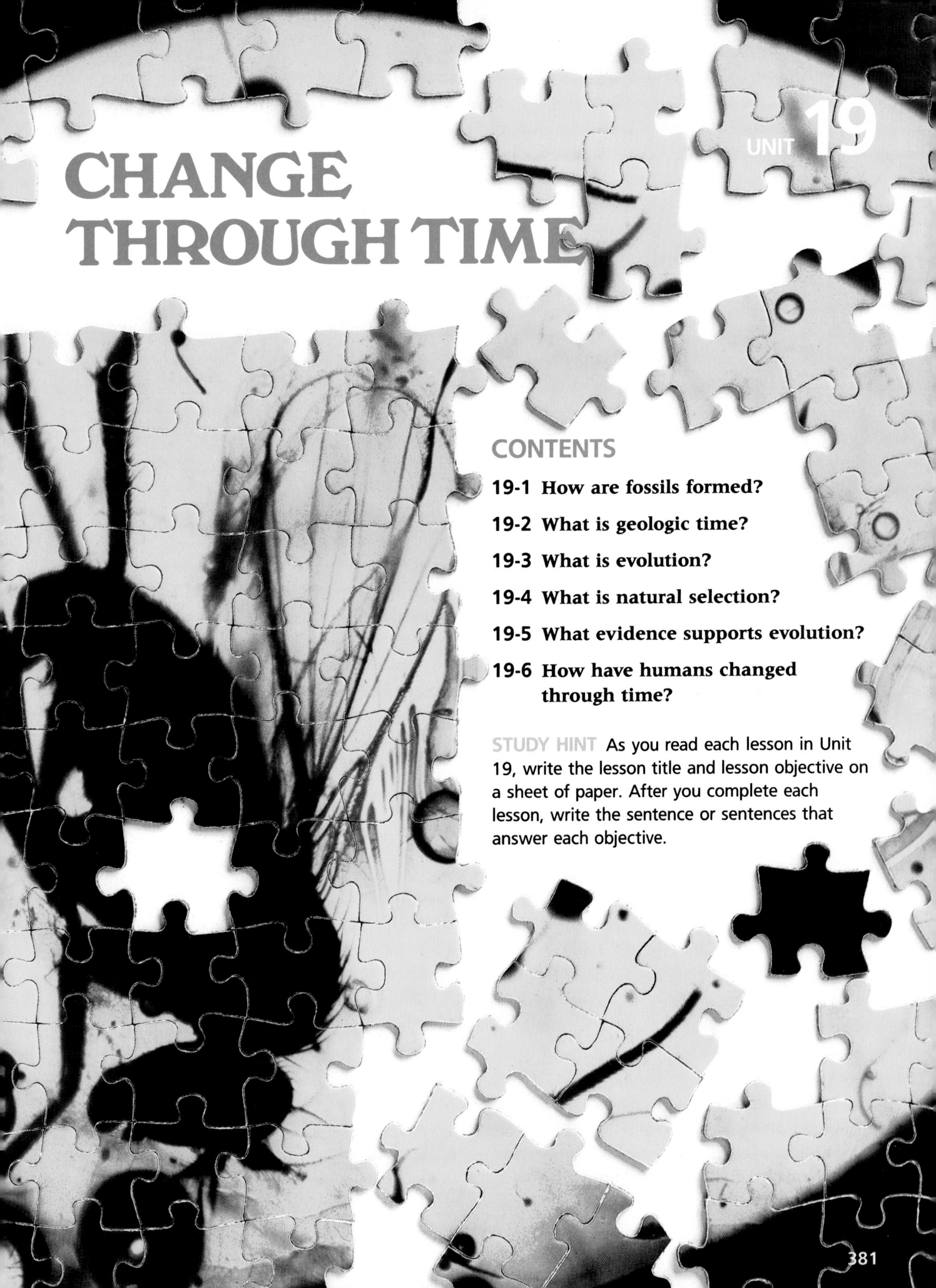

CHANGE THROUGH TIME

CONTENTS

STUDY HINT As you read each lesson in Unit 19, write the lesson title and lesson objective on a sheet of paper. After you complete each lesson, write the sentence or sentences that answer each objective.

19-1 How are fossils formed?

Objective ▶ Explain how different kinds of fossils are formed.

TechTerms

- **amber:** hardened tree sap
- **extinct** (ik-STINKT): species that is no longer found alive
- **fossil** (FAHS-ul): remains or traces of a once-living organism

Figure 1 Fingerprints

Fossils At the scene of a crime, detectives look for fingerprints. The criminals are gone, but they may have left behind clues. Many kinds of organisms are now **extinct** (ik-STINKT), or no longer found as a living species. However, some of these organisms left behind clues that they existed. These clues are **fossils** (FAHS-uls). Fossils are the remains or traces of once-living organisms.

Figure 2 Fossil in mud

Define: What are fossils? remains or traces of a once-living organism

Kinds of Fossils There are many kinds of fossils. Some fossils are footprints in mud that later changed to rock. Sometimes, an entire organism is found. In March, 1990, a whole mammoth was discovered in Siberia. It had been frozen in ice. A mammoth was an elephantlike animal. Insects have been trapped and preserved in **amber.** Amber is hardened tree sap. Most fossils, however, are the remains of hard parts of organisms, such as bones, teeth, and shells.

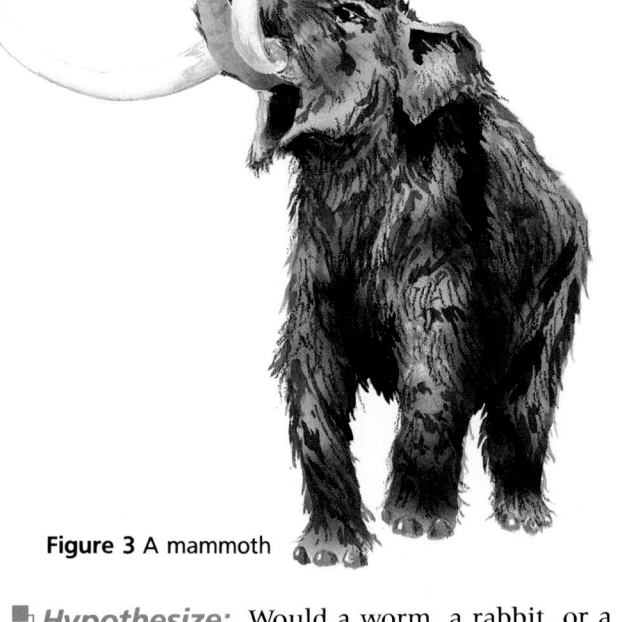

Figure 3 A mammoth

Hypothesize: Would a worm, a rabbit, or a butterfly most likely leave fossil remains? **Explain.** a rabbit, because it contains hard parts such as bones and teeth.

Fossils in Rocks Most fossils are found in sedimentary (sed-uh-MEN-tar-ee) rocks. Sedimentary rock is made up of layers of sediments. Sediments are bits of clay, soil, sand, and other earth materials.

Sedimentary rocks usually form in water. When an animal living in the water dies, its body may sink to the bottom. The soft parts decay quickly. The bones or shells may remain and become covered by sediments. The sediments build up, layer by layer. Great pressure and weight press the sediments together. Slowly, the sediments change to rock. The fossil bones or shells are preserved in the rock.

Figure 4 Fossils in rock layers

Name: In what kind of rock are most fossils found? sedimentary rock

LESSON SUMMARY

▶ Any remains or traces of a once-living organism is a fossil.

▶ Most fossils are the remains of hard parts of organisms, such as bones, teeth, and shells.

▶ Most fossils are formed in sedimentary rock.

▶ Fossils form in sedimentary rock when organisms were buried quickly beneath layers of sediment.

CHECK *Write true if the statement is true. If the statement is false, change the underlined term to make the statement true.*

1. A mammoth is an example of <u>a living</u> species. an extinct

2. Insect fossils often are found preserved in <u>tar</u>. amber

3. Sand and mud that are carried and deposited by a river are <u>sediments</u>. true

4. Most fossils form in <u>sedimentary</u> rock. true

APPLY *Complete the following.*

5. Most fossils in sedimentary rock cannot be seen unless the rock has been cut across from top to bottom. Explain why.

6. Analyze: Study the diagram. Explain how the bones of the animals could have been trapped in the tar.

InfoSearch

Read the passage. Ask two questions that you cannot answer from the information in the passage.

Petrified Wood The remains of an organism may decay very slowly. Minerals dissolved in water take the place of the original materials. The minerals form an exact stone copy of the remains. The fossil that forms is called petrified (PET-ruh-fyd). Many trees are petrified. You can see petrified trees in the Petrified Forest of Arizona.

SEARCH: Use library references to find answers to your questions.

ACTIVITY

MAKING FOSSILS

You will need 3 large paper cups, clay, a small object such as a shell, a key, or a coin, plaster of Paris, petroleum jelly.

1. Press some clay into each of two paper cups so that the clay is 2-3 cm high in each cup.

2. Push a small object down into the clay of one cup. Then carefully remove the object.

3. Coat the object with petroleum jelly. Very lightly press the object into the clay of the second cup.

4. Prepare the plaster of Paris according to the directions.

5. Pour some of the plaster into each cup. Let the cups stand overnight. After the plaster hardens, tear away the cups. Remove the clay from the plaster.

Questions

1. **Observe:** Describe the two fossils.

2. **Analyze:** Which fossil is the mold? Which is the cast?

What is geologic time?

Objectives ▶ Explain how the layering of rocks forms a record of life on the earth. ▶ Describe how scientists use the geologic time scale.

TechTerms

▶ **geologic** (jee-oh-LAHJ-ik) **time scale:** record of the earth's history based upon types of organisms that lived at different times

▶ **era:** largest division of geologic time

▶ **relative age:** age of something compared with the age of something else

Relative Age By comparing the positions of the layers of sedimentary rocks in which fossils are found, scientists can find the **relative ages** of different fossils. Relative age is the age of something compared with the age of something else. As a general rule, the lower the layer of rock in which a fossil is found, the older the fossil. Thus, a fossil found in the bottom layer of rock usually is older than a fossil found in a higher layer.

▨▶ **Define:** What is relative age? the age of something compared with the age of something else

The Fossil Record Scientists have studied fossils from rocks all over the world. They have arranged the fossils in order, from oldest to youngest. Scientists use this information to construct a **geologic** (jee-oh-LAHJ-ik) **time scale.** A geologic time scale is a record of the earth's history based upon the types of organisms that lived at different times.

Look at the geologic time scale. An **era** is the largest time division on the scale. Eras are divided into periods. The periods of the most recent era, the Cenozoic era, are further divided into epochs (EP-uks).

Fossil evidence shows that life first appeared on the earth about 4.5 billion years ago. This date marks the beginning of the geologic time scale. Fossils also show that life on the earth started out simple and became more and more complex.

▨▶ **Sequence:** Name the three time divisions in the geologic time scale, from largest to smallest. era, period, epoch

Table 1 Geologic Time Scale				
ERA	**PERIOD**	**EPOCH**	**START DATE (MILLIONS OF YEARS AGO)**	**ORGANISMS**
Cenozoic	Quaternary	Recent	0.025	Modern Humans
		Pleistocene	1.75	Mammoths
	Tertiary	Pliocene	14	Large carnivores
		Miocene	26	Many land mammals
		Oligocene	40	Primitive apes
		Eocene	55	Early horses
		Paleocene	65	Primates
Mesozoic	Cretaceous		130	Flowering plants
	Jurassic		180	Dinosaurs, birds
	Triassic		225	Conifers
Paleozoic	Permian		275	Seed Plants
	Carboniferous		345	Reptiles
	Devonian		405	Insects, amphibians
	Silurian		435	Fishes
	Ordovician		480	Algae, fungi
	Cambrian		600	Invertebrates
Precambrian			**over 600** billion	Bacteria, blue-green algae

LESSON SUMMARY

▶ The relative age of a fossil can be found by comparing it with the age of another fossil.

▶ The geologic time scale arranges fossils in order from oldest to youngest.

▶ The geologic time scale is divided into eras, periods, and epochs.

CHECK *Answer the following.*

1. What are the largest time divisions in the geologic time scale? eras

2. Is a fossil older or younger than another fossil found in a higher layer? older

3. How would the age of a fossil shell compare with the age of a fossil leaf found in the same layer of rock? It would be the same age.

4. About how long ago did life first appear on the earth? about 4.5 billion years ago.

5. In what era did modern humans first appear? Cenozoic

APPLY *Complete the following.*

6. **Analyze:** Why are the oldest layers of a sedimentary rock found at the bottom?

Use the Geologic Time Scale to answer the following.

7. During what era did the dinosaurs live?

8. **Analyze:** During what era of geologic time are you living?

Skill Builder

Sequencing When you sequence, you place things in order. The diagram shows layers of sedimentary rocks. Use the diagram to place the fossils in the rock layers in order from oldest to youngest. How does the age of fossil B compare with the age of fossil D?

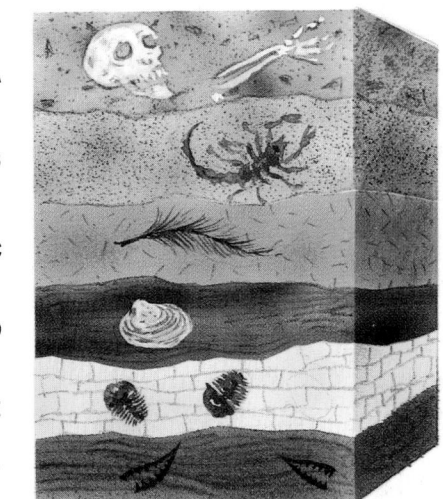

A
B
C
D
E
F

SCIENCE CONNECTION ◆○◆○◆○◆○◆○◆○◇○◇○◆○◆○◆○◆○◆○◆○◆○◆○◆○◆○◆○◆○◆○

RADIOACTIVE DATING

Scientists can measure the actual age of a fossil or a rock by a method called radioactive (ray-dee-oh-AK-tiv) dating. Radioactive dating involves the use of radioactive elements. The atoms of radioactive elements decay, or break down, into atoms of other elements. The unit used to measure the rate of decay of a radioactive element is called a half-life. A half-life is the time it takes for one-half of the atoms in a sample of a radioactive element to decay.

Carbon-14, or C-14, is the radioactive form of carbon. The half-life of C-14 is 5730 years. If you had a 10-gram sample of C-14 today, in 5730 years, only half of the C-14 atoms, or 5 grams, would remain. The other 5 grams would have broken down into nitrogen. At the end of two half-lives (11,460 years), only one fourth of the C-14 atoms, or 2.5 grams, would be present.

Carbon-14 is present in all living things. When an organism dies, the C-14 continues to decay. By measuring the amount of C-14 in a fossil, a scientist can tell how old the fossil is.

19-3 What is evolution?

Objectives ▶ Define evolution. ▶ Explain how organisms change due to adaptations and mutations.

TechTerms

- ▶ **adaptation** (ad-up-TAY-shun): trait that helps an organism survive in its environment
- ▶ **evolution** (ev-uh-LOO-shun): process by which organisms change over time
- ▶ **mutation** (myoo-TAY-shun): change in a gene

Evolution Fossil evidence shows that the earliest living things on the earth were very simple organisms. In the billions of years that have passed, living things have become more and more complex. The study of fossils also shows that old species became extinct and new species took their place. Most scientists believe that new species develop from old species as a result of gradual change, or **evolution** (ev-uh-LOO-shun). Evolution is the process by which organisms change over time.

�▶ *Define:* **What is evolution?** process by which organisms change over time

Adaptations Living things are found everywhere on the earth, from the highest mountain tops to the deep oceans, and from hot, dry deserts to polar ice caps. How do different organisms survive such a wide variety of conditions? They often have **adaptations** (ad-up-TAY-shuns). An

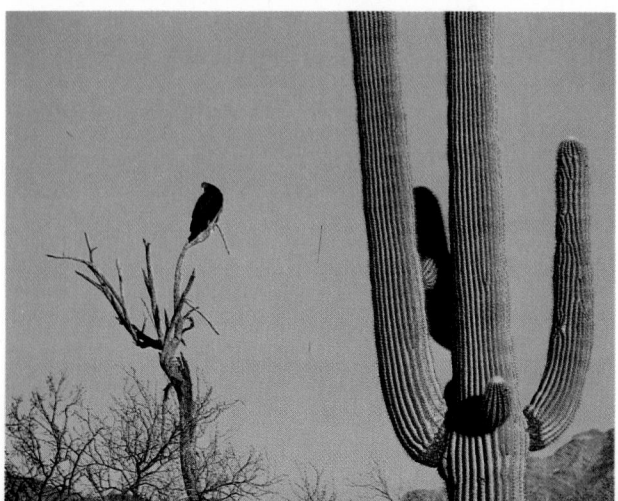

adaptation is a feature, or trait, that helps an organism to live in a certain environment.

The plants in the picture at the bottom of the page have needlelike leaves. They also have a thick, tough covering on their stems. These adaptations make it possible for these plants to live in the dry conditions of a desert environment.

▶ *Hypothesize:* **What adaptations help birds to live in trees?** Birds have wings and can fly.

Mutations Species change, or evolve, over time. Generally, a change in a species is caused by new combinations of genes that occur with each new generation. Such changes take place over a very long period of time. Sometimes, however, something may cause a gene to change suddenly. A sudden change in a gene is called a **mutation** (myoo-TAY-shun). A mutation can produce a change in an organism. If the change is helpful to the organism, it will be kept and passed on to future generations. This may eventually result in a new species. If the variation is harmful, the species will die out.

▶ *Define:* **What is a mutation?** sudden change in a gene

LESSON SUMMARY

▶ Evolution is the process by which organisms change over time.

▶ Adaptations are special traits that help organisms to survive in their environments.

▶ A mutation is a sudden change in a gene.

▶ Mutations can produce a change in an organism that can be passed on to future generations and may eventually result in a new species.

CHECK *Write true if the statement is true. If the statement is false, change the underlined term to make the statement true.*

1. Organisms change over time by the process of <u>evolution</u>. true

2. The needlelike leaves of a cactus is an example of a <u>mutation</u>. an adaptation

3. A sudden change in a gene is an <u>adaptation</u>. a mutation

APPLY *Answer the following.*

4. What do you call a trait that helps an organism to survive in its environment? an adaptation

5. From what do new species develop? old species

6. Not all mutations are passed on to future offspring. Explain why.

Skill Builder...

Designing an Experiment Desert plants, such as the cactus, have certain adaptations that help them to survive in a hot, dry environment. Design an experiment to show what would happen to a cactus if its environment suddenly changed to a cool, wet environment. Include a control in your experiment.

▼.▼. LOOKING BACK IN SCIENCE ▼▼▼▼▼▼▼▼▼▼▼

THE VOYAGE OF THE *BEAGLE*

In 1831, a young biologist named Charles Darwin set sail on a British ship called the HMS *Beagle.* The ship left port on a five-year journey to the South Pacific and South America. The purpose of the trip was to prepare maps and to observe and collect specimens of various plants and animals. As the ship's naturalist (NACH-ur-ul-ist), Darwin made many observations. He kept careful records of his observations. He collected many different kinds of plants and animals. He also collected tiny fossils of different organisms.

Of all the places he visited, Darwin was most excited by the Galapagos (guh-LAH-puh-gos) Islands. The Galapagos Islands are located off the coast of South America. On these islands, Darwin discovered 13 species of finches. Darwin observed that the beak of each species of finch had a different shape. Each beak was adapted for eating a certain kind of food. Most other traits of the finches were very similar. Darwin inferred that all the finches had evolved from a common ancestor. Darwin used his observations of the finches as the basis for his ideas about natural selection.

▲ ▲

19-4 What is natural selection?

Objective ▶ Explain Darwin's theory of natural selection.

TechTerms

▶ **natural selection:** survival of offspring that have favorable traits

▶ **variation** (ver-ee-AY-shun): differences in traits among individuals of a species

Explaining Evolution The fossil record shows that living things have evolved throughout the earth's history. However, knowing this fact does not explain how the changes happened. Offspring are supposed to be the same species as their parents. How then, can a new species develop from an old one? Over 100 years ago, the English biologist Charles Darwin suggested a theory of evolution as an answer to this question. Darwin's theory is accepted by most scientists today.

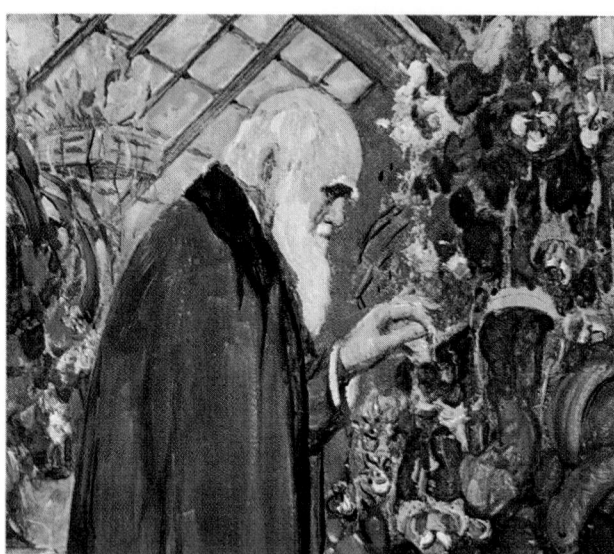

�▶ *State:* What evidence shows that organisms have changed throughout the earth's history? fossil record

Natural Selection Darwin used the term **natural selection** to describe his theory of evolution. Natural selection is the survival of organisms that have favorable traits. The theory of natural selection includes the following ideas:

▶ **Overproduction** Each species produces more offspring than can survive. There is not enough food or living space for all of the offspring.

▶ **Struggle for Existence** The young of each generation compete for those things they need to live. Only a few will live long enough to reproduce. The others will die.

▶ **Variation** The young of each generation are not exactly alike. For example, some individuals are bigger or stronger than others. Differences in traits among individuals of a species are called **variations** (ver-ee-AY-shuns).

▶ **Survival of the Fittest** Some variations make individuals better suited for survival in their environments. These individuals are more likely to survive and reproduce than others.

▶ **Evolution of New Species** Individuals with favorable variations survive and reproduce. They pass their favorable traits to their offspring. Therefore, their offspring are more likely to survive and reproduce in the next generation. Unfavorable variations die out. In this way, favorable variations stay in the species. Over many generations, these changes can result in the appearance of a new species.

▶ *List:* List the main ideas of the theory of natural selection. Students should list the five ideas stated.

388

LESSON SUMMARY

▶ A new species can develop from an old one by the process of evolution.

▶ Natural selection describes how evolution may occur.

▶ Differences among individuals in a species are called variations.

CHECK *Write true if the statement is true. If the statement is false, change the underlined term to make the statement true.*

1. The idea which states that a species produces more offspring than can survive is called <u>competition</u>. overproduction

2. Individuals with favorable <u>variations</u> survive and reproduce. true

3. Natural selection is a theory of <u>evolution</u>. true

APPLY *Use the pictures of the giraffes to complete the following.*

4. **Sequence:** Each picture of the giraffes shows one idea of natural selection. Identify the three ideas in the order in which they are shown.

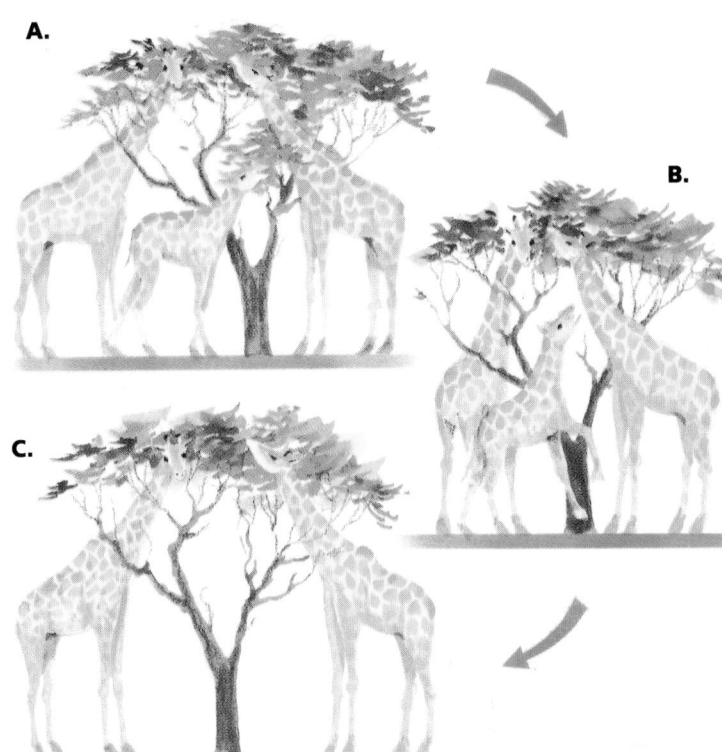

A.

B.

C.

Skill Builder...................................

Researching Use library references to find out how Jean Baptiste Lamarck's ideas of evolution differ from Darwin's. Present your findings in a report.

ACTIVITY

MODELING NATURAL SELECTION

You will need 3 sheets of brown construction paper, 11" × 17", 1 sheet of green construction paper, 11" × 17", and scissors.

1. Work with a partner.

2. Copy the Data Table shown.

3. Cut out 15 brown squares and 15 green squares, 3 cm × 3 cm. **Caution: Be very careful when working with sharp objects.** These squares represent brown and green insects.

4. Have your partner place 2 sheets of brown construction paper on the floor to represent the environment.

5. While you turn your head, have your partner scatter the 30 insects on the brown paper.

6. At the signal ''Ready,'' pick up 15 insects as fast as you can.

7. Count the number of insects of each color that you picked up. Record the results in the Data Table.

8. Repeat Steps 5 through 7 two more times.

9. Find the total number of brown insects and the total number of green insects in the three trials.

Data Table: Insect Trials		
TRIAL	NUMBER OF INSECTS	
	Brown Insects	Green Insects
1.		
2.		
3.		
Total		

Questions

1. Which color insect is most visible in a brown environment? green

2. **Hypothesize:** Which insects would more likely be picked from a green leaf by a bird? Why? brown; they are easier to see

19-5 What evidence supports evolution?

Objective ▶ Understand how fossils are used to support the theory of evolution.

A Record of Change The fossil record clearly shows that changes have taken place throughout the earth's history. There is evidence that the earth's climate has changed many times. There are fossils of many species of organisms that no longer exist. Perhaps the best-known group of extinct organisms is the dinosaurs. Fossils of about 400 different species of dinosaurs have been found. Some of these species roamed the earth for more than 100 million years. Yet, dinosaurs died out and have been extinct for more than 65 million years. Many possible theories have been suggested to explain why such a large and successful group of organisms died out. However, nobody knows for sure.

▶ **Describe:** What does the fossil record indicate about the earth's past? The kinds of organisms that have lived on the earth have changed.

The Changing Horse Evolution deals with changes within a species. The most complete fossil record of evolutionary change is that of the horse. Through fossils, scientists have traced animals related to the modern horse as far back as 60 million years. The earliest member of this family was a four-toed animal about the size of a small dog. Later fossils show how this animal changed through time. There were changes in the animal's teeth, its legs, its toes, and its size.

👁 **Observe:** In what ways have horses changed through time? Accept all logical responses.

Eohippus Mesohippus Merychippus Equus

38 cm   52 cm   100 cm   135 cm

Eohippus	Mesohippus	Merychippus	Equus
Skull			
Tooth			
Lower legs			
Front Hind	Front Hind	Front Hind	Front Hind

LESSON SUMMARY

▶ The fossil record clearly shows that living things have changed throughout the earth's history.

▶ The most complete fossil record of evolutionary change is that of the horse.

CHECK *Find the sentence in the lesson that answers each question. Then write the sentence.*

1. Why is the horse used to support the history of evolution?

2. In addition to changes in living things, what other changes are shown in the fossil record?

3. What caused the dinosaurs to die out?

4. How many species of dinosaurs have been identified?

5. About how big was the earliest horse?

APPLY *Complete the following.*

▶ 6. **Infer:** How can the fossil record show changes in climate?

👁 7. **Observe:** How has the size of the horse's jaw changed through time?

Skill Builder

Measuring and Calculating Measure the height of each horse in the scale drawings of the evolutionary stages of the horse. Using the heights given in each drawing, find out what scale was used for the drawings.

Mesohippus

Merychippus

Equus

LOOKING BACK IN SCIENCE

THE MOTHS OF MANCHESTER

A species of moth known as the British peppered moth lived during the early 1800s. This moth can be used to support the idea that natural selection can help an organism to survive in its environment. In 1800, most of the peppered moths in England were light gray in color. A few of the moths were black. The moths spent a good deal of time on the tree trunks in the area. The trunks were the same color as the light gray peppered moths. Birds could not easily see these moths. The black moths were easily seen. As a result, many black moths were eaten by the birds. Few survived to reproduce.

Many large coal-burning factories were built near where the moths lived. The soot given off by these factories soon changed the color of the tree trunks in the area from gray to black. Now the gray moths were easily seen and eaten by the birds. The black moths blended in with the color of the tree trunks. Many black moths survived and reproduced. In a short period of time, most British peppered moths were black.

19-6 How have humans changed through time?

▶ Describe some of the ways that humans have changed through time.

TechTerm

▶ **anthropology** (an-thruh-PAHL-uh-jee): science that deals with the study of human beings

Early Humanlike Species The fossil record of human evolution is not complete. It is still being pieced together by scientists who work in the field of **anthropology** (an-thruh-PAHL-uh-jee) Anthropology is the science that deals with the study of human beings.

The oldest humanlike fossil that has been found is thought to be about 3.5 million years old. The skeleton indicates that the individual was a little more than 1 m tall and walked upright. Later humanlike fossils of different species of humans also have been found. The ages of these fossils range from about 3 million years to as late as 0.5 million years. Fossils of each species show more humanlike traits and behaviors than the species that lived before them. These changes include increased body size and larger skulls. Evidence also indicates that some of the later species lived in caves, used fire, and made tools.

Figure 1 Early human

◗◗▶ *Interpret:* What does fossil evidence show about the evolution of humanlike species?
Each species had more humanlike traits and behaviors than earlier species.

Modern Humans All modern humans belong to the species *Homo sapiens* (say-PEE-uns), which means "wise human." Fossils of two early types of *Homo sapiens* have been found. The two types are the Neanderthals (nee-AN-dur-thals) and Cro-Magnons (kroh-MAG-nunz). Neanderthals lived from 130,000 to 35,000 years ago. They were shorter than modern humans and they had much larger skulls than did earlier humanlike species. The skulls had sloping foreheads and heavy brow ridges.

Figure 2 Cro-Magnon skull

Figure 3 Neanderthal skull

Cro-Magnons replaced Neanderthals when they died out. Cro-Magnons looked like modern humans. They were tall and had large brain cases and rounded skulls. Fossil evidence shows that Cro-Magnons lived together in large groups. They were skilled hunters and toolmakers.

◗◗▶ *Contrast:* How are the fossils of Neanderthals different from fossils of earlier humanlike species? They were shorter and had larger skulls.

▶ Anthropology is the science that deals with the study of human beings.

▶ The oldest humanlike fossil found to date is thought to be about 3.5 billion years old.

▶ Modern humans belong to the species *Homo sapiens*. Two early examples of this species are Neanderthals and Cro-Magnons.

CHECK *Write true if the statement is true. If the statement is false, change the underlined term to make the statement true.*

1. The science that deals with the study of human beings is <u>biology</u>. anthropology

2. The oldest humanlike fossil found to date is about <u>3.5 billion</u> years old. true

3. <u>Neanderthals</u> looked like modern humans. Cro-Magnons

Answer the following.

4. What evidence tells anthropologists about early humanlike activities? tools, use of fire

5. Which *Homo sapiens* skulls had sloped foreheads and heavy brow ridges? Neanderthal

6. **Infer:** Why do you think modern humans were named *Homo sapiens?*

APPLY *Complete the following.*

7. **Hypothesize:** A fossil skeleton is found in a layer of sedimentary rock. The skull has a sloped forehead and heavy brow ridges. Several years earlier, a Cro-Magnon skeleton was found several layers deeper in the same sedimentary rock. Why might an anthropologist be puzzled by the arrangement of the two fossil skeletons? How might this situation be explained?

Skill Builder

Building Vocabulary Anthropology is the science that deals with the study of human beings. Find out where the word "anthropology" comes from. In the dictionary, look up the prefix "anthropo-" and the suffix "-logy". Write the meanings on a piece of paper along with their origins.

Ideas in Action

IDEA: Anthropologists have discovered that Cro-Magnons were skilled tool makers. People today also use many tools.

ACTION: List three kinds of tools that you use often. Explain how you use each tool.

PEOPLE IN SCIENCE

THE LEAKEYS

In the field of anthropology, no name is more familiar than that of the Leakey family. For more than 50 years, Mary and Louis Leakey searched for and studied fossil remains of early ancestors of humans. Like most anthropologists, the goal of the Leakeys was to trace the evolutionary development of humans.

In 1959, Mary Leakey found a humanlike skull that was more than 1.75 million years old. In 1972, Richard Leakey, son of Mary and Louis, discovered a skull similar to the one found by his mother. This second skull was determined to be about 2 million years old. Crude stone tools found with fossils led the Leakeys to call their discovery "Handy Man."

In 1984, Richard Leakey and his co-workers made a very significant discovery in Kenya, Africa. They found a skull and almost complete skeleton of a 12 year old male. The skeleton, which was about 1 million years old, was of a species known as "Upright Human." This species is the closest known ancestor to modern humans. The skeleton is one of the most complete specimens discovered to date.

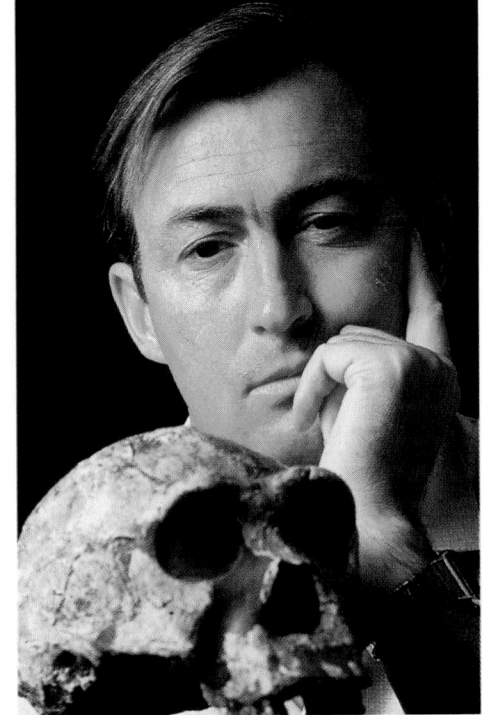

STUDY HINT Before you begin the Unit Challenges, review the TechTerms and Lesson summary for each lesson in this unit.

TechTerms

adaptation (386)
amber (382)
anthropology (392)
era (384)

evolution (386)
extinct (382)
fossil (382)
geologic time scale (384)

mutation (386)
natural selection (388)
relative age (384)
variation (388)

TechTerm Challenges

Matching *Write the TechTerm that matches each description.*
1. largest division of the geologic time scale era
2. change in organisms over time evolution
3. sudden change in a gene mutation
4. remain of a once-living organism fossil
5. survival of offspring that have favorable traits natural selection
6. differences in traits among individuals of a species variation
7. no longer found as a living species extinct
8. hardened tree sap amber
9. science that deals with the study of human beings anthropology
10. special trait that helps an organism survive in its environment adaptation

Fill in *Write the TechTerm that best completes each statement.*
1. A record of the earth's history based on the kinds of organisms that lived at different times is a _____ . geologic time scale
2. The age of a fossil compared with that of a different fossil is _____ . relative age
3. The changes shown in the fossil record of the horse illustrate _____ . evolution
4. Dinosaurs are an example of a group of organisms that are _____ . extinct

Content Challenges

Multiple Choice *Write the letter of the term that best completes each statement.*
1. An insect in amber is an example of
   a. a mutation. **b.** a fossil. **c.** variation. **d.** evolution. b
2. Organisms that are no longer found as living species are
   a. mammals. **b.** fossils. **c.** extinct. **d.** endangered. c
3. The shortest time division on a geologic time scale is
   a. an epoch. **b.** a century. **c.** an era. **d.** a period. a
4. A sudden change in a gene is called
   a. an adaptation. **b.** a variation. **c.** evolution. **d.** a mutation. d
5. Most fossils are found
   a. frozen in ice. **b.** in igneous rocks. **c.** in sedimentary rocks. **d.** in tar. c

6. The long neck of a giraffe is an example of
   a. an adaptation.   **b.** a mutation.   **c.** a variation.   **d.** extinction. a
7. The animal with the most complete fossil record is the
   a. elephant.   **b.** finch.   **c.** human.   **d.** horse. d
8. Fossil evidence indicates that the first living things appeared on the earth about
   a. 10 million years ago.   **b.** 4.5 billion years ago.   **c.** 10 thousand years ago.   **d.** 1 billion years ago. b
9. The science that deals with the study of humans is
   a. geology.   **b.** genetics.   **c.** anthropology.   **d.** biology. c
10. Of the organisms listed, the one least likely to be found as a fossil is a
    a. dinosaur.   **b.** horse.   **c.** jellyfish.   **d.** finch. c

True/False *Write true if the statement is true. If the statement is false, change the underlined term to make the statement true.*
1. Rocks that usually form in water are <u>metamorphic</u>. sedimentary
2. In a geologic time scale, eras are divided into <u>periods</u>. true
3. The change in a species over time is called <u>variation</u>. evolution
4. Survival of the fittest also is known as <u>natural selection</u>. true
5. All modern humans belong to the species <u>*Homo sapiens*</u>. true
6. Dinosaurs are examples of a <u>living</u> species. an extinct
7. The smallest time division in a geologic time scale is an <u>era</u>. epoch
8. The age of something compared to the age of something else is <u>absolute</u> age. relative
9. In a sedimentary rock, the bottom layer usually is the <u>oldest</u> layer. true
10. Differences in traits among organisms of the same species is called <u>variation</u>. true

Understanding the Features

Reading Critically *Use the feature reading selections to answer the following. Page numbers for the features follow each question in parentheses.*
1. What was the purpose of the voyage of the HMS *Beagle?* (387)
2. **Infer:** How might the story of the British peppered moths have been different if the factories burned natural gas? (391)
3. Why is carbon-14 an important tool of anthropologists? (385)
4. What discoveries have been made by members of the Leakey family in the field of anthropology? (393)

Critical Thinking *Answer each of the following in complete sentences.*
1. Explain why carbon-14 cannot be used to find the ages of fossils of the earliest living things.
2. Explain the difference between variation and mutation.
3. At one time there were as many short-necked giraffes as there were long-necked giraffes. Using the theory of natural selection, explain why the long-necked giraffes survived , while the short-necked giraffes died out.
4. Why are few fossils found in metamorphic and igneous rocks?
5. Artifacts (AHR-tuh-fakts) are items made by humans. Explain why the study of artifacts is an important part of an anthropologist's work.

Concept Challenges

Interpreting a Table *Use the geologic time scale to answer the following questions.*

Table 1 Geologic Time Scale				
ERA	PERIOD	EPOCH	START DATE (MILLIONS OF YEARS AGO)	ORGANISMS
Cenozoic	Quaternary Tertiary	Recent Pleistocene Pliocene Miocene Oligocene Eocene Paleocene	0.025 1.75 14 26 40 55 65	Modern Humans Mammoths Large carnivores Many land mammals Primitive apes Early horses Primates
Mesozoic	Cretaceous Jurassic Triassic		130 180 225	Flowering plants Dinosaurs, birds Conifers
Paleozoic	Permian Carboniferous Devonian Silurian Ordovician Cambrian		275 345 405 435 480 600	Seed Plants Reptiles Insects, amphibians Fishes Algae, fungi Invertebrates
Precambrian			over 600 billion	Bacteria, blue-green algae

1. What are the three divisions of geologic time?
2. **Analyze:** What is the name of the most recent era in geologic time?
3. How long ago did dinosaurs roam the Earth?
4. **Explain:** What is the geologic time scale?
5. **Analyze:** During which epoch did reptiles first appear?
6. **Analyze:** During which period did flowering plants first appear?
7. **Analyze:** What organisms are found in the Oligocene epoch?
8. What are the four eras?
9. **Analyze:** When did modern humans first appear?

Finding Out More

1. Visit a zoo and observe the behavior of some primates, such as monkeys, apes, and gorillas. List several kinds of behavior, and compare that behavior in each of the primates you observe.
2. Use library references to find out more about Charles Darwin and his voyage on the *Beagle*. Include a discussion on his theory of evolution. Present your findings in a report.
3. Write a report on one of the following scientists: Charles Lyell, Thomas Huxley, or Joseph Hooker. Include in your report how the scientist you chose influenced Charles Darwin.
4. Write to your state wildlife agency and get a list of organisms that are endangered and threatened. Pick five endangered animals and five threatened animals and find out what is being done to protect these animals. Compare your findings with those of your classmates.
5. Use library references to find out about Donald Johanson and his theory of evolution. Develop a chart illustrating your findings.

Appendix A

THE METRIC SYSTEM AND SI UNITS

The metric system is an international system of measurement based on units of 10. More than 90 percent of the nations of the world use the metric system. In the United States, both the English or Imperial Measurement System and the metric system are used.

Systeme International, or SI, has been used as the international measurement system since 1960. SI is a modernized version of the metric system. Like the metric system, SI is a decimal system based on units of 10.

In both SI and the metric system, prefixes are added to base units to form larger or smaller units. Each unit is 10 times larger than the next smaller unit, and 10 times smaller than the next larger unit. For example, the meter is the basic unit of length. The next larger unit is a dekameter. A dekameter is 10 times larger than a meter. The next smaller unit is a decimeter. A decimeter is 10 times smaller than a meter. Ten decimeters is equal to one meter. How many meters equal one dekameter? 10

When you want to change from one unit in the metric system to another unit, you multiply or divide by a multiple of 10.

• When you change from a smaller unit to a larger unit, you divide.

• When you change from a larger unit to a smaller unit, you multiply.

SI UNITS

The basic unit is printed in capital letters.

Length	Symbol
kilometer	km
METER	m
centimeter	cm
millimeter	mm

Area	Symbol
square kilometer	km²
SQUARE METER	m²
square millimeter	mm²

Volume	Symbol
CUBIC METER	m³
cubic millimeter	mm³
liter	L
milliliter	mL

Mass	Symbol
KILOGRAM	kg
gram	g
tonne	t

Temperature	Symbol
KELVIN	K
degree Celsius	°C

SOME COMMON METRIC PREFIXES

Prefix		Meaning
micro-	=	0.000001, or 1/1,000,000
milli-	=	0.001, or 1/1000
centi-	=	0.01, or 1/100
deci-	=	0.1, or 1/10
deka-	=	10
hecto-	=	100
kilo-	=	1000
mega-	=	1,000,000

SOME METRIC RELATIONSHIPS

Unit	Relationship
kilometer	1 km = 1000 m
meter	1 m = 100 cm
centimeter	1 cm = 10 mm
millimeter	1 mm = 0.1 cm
liter	1 L = 1000 mL
milliliter	1 mL = 0.001 L
tonne	1t = 1000 kg
kilogram	1 kg = 1000 g
gram	1 g = 1000 mg
centigram	1 cg = 10 mg
milligram	1 mg = 0.001 g

SI-ENGLISH EQUIVALENTS

	SI to English	English to SI
Length	1 kilometer = 0.621 mile (mi)	1 mi = 1.61 km
	1 meter = 0.914 yards (yd)	1 yd = 1.09 m
	1 meter = 3.28 feet (ft)	1 ft = 0.305 m
	1 centimeter = 0.394 inch (in)	1 in = 2.54 cm
	1 millimeter = 0.039 inch	1 in = 25.4 mm
Area	1 square kilometer = 0.3861 square mile	$1 \text{ mi}^2 = 2.590 \text{ km}^2$
	1 square meter = 1.1960 square yards	$1 \text{ yd}^2 = 0.8361 \text{ m}^2$
	1 square meter = 10.763 square feet	$1 \text{ ft}^2 = 0.0929 \text{ m}^2$
	1 square centimeter = 0.155 square inch	$1 \text{ in}^2 = 6.452 \text{ cm}^2$
Volume	1 cubic meter = 1.3080 cubic yards	$1 \text{ yd}^3 = 0.7646 \text{ m}^3$
	1 cubic meter = 35.315 cubic feet	$1 \text{ ft}^3 = 0.0283 \text{ m}^3$
	1 cubic centimeter = 0.0610 cubic inches	$1 \text{ in}^3 = 16.39 \text{ cm}^3$
	1 liter = .2642 gallon (gal)	1 gal = 3.79 L
	1 liter = 1.06 quart (qt)	1 qt = 0.94 L
	1 liter = 2.11 pint (pt)	1 pt = 0.47 L
	1 milliliter = 0.034 fluid ounce (fl oz)	1 fl oz = 29.57 mL
Mass	1 tonn = .984 ton	1 ton = 1.016 t
	1 kilogram = 2.205 pound (lb)	1 lb = 0.4536 kg
	1 gram = 0.0353 ounce (oz)	1 oz = 28.35 g
Temperature	Celsius = 5/9 (°F −32)	Fahrenheit = 9/5°C + 32
	0°C = 32°F (Freezing point of water)	72°F = 22°C (Room temperature)
	100°C = 212°F (Boiling point of water)	98.6=F = 37°C
		(Human body temperature)

Appendix B

SAFETY IN THE SCIENCE CLASSROOM

Safety is very important in the science classroom. Science classrooms and laboratories have equipment and chemicals that can be dangerous if not handled properly. To avoid accidents in the science laboratory, always follow proper safety rules. Listen carefully when your teacher explains precautions and safety rules that must be followed. You should never perform an activity without your teacher's direction. By following safety rules you can help insure the safety of yourself and your classmates. Safety rules that should be followed are listed below. Read over these safety rules carefully. Always look for caution statements before you perform an activity.

Clothing Protection • Wear your laboratory apron. • Confine loose clothing.

Eye Safety • Wear safety goggles in the laboratory. • If anything gets in your eyes, flush them with plenty of water. • Be sure you know how to use the emergency wash system in the laboratory.

Heat and Fire Safety • Be careful when handling hot objects. • Use proper procedures when lighting Bunsen burners. • Turn off all heat sources when they are not in use. • Tie back long hair when working near an open flame. • Confine loose clothing. • Turn off gas valves when not in use.

Electrical Safety • Keep all work areas clean and dry. • Never handle electrical equipment with wet hands. • Do not overload an electric circuit. • Do not use wires that are frayed.

Glassware Safety • Never use chipped or cracked glassware. • Never pick up broken glass with your bare hands. • Allow heated glass to cool before touching it. • Never force glassware into a rubber stopper.

Chemical Safety • Never taste chemicals as a means of identification. • Never transfer liquids with a mouth pipette. Use a suction bulb. • Be very careful when working with acids or bases. Both can cause serious burns. • Never pour water into an acid or base. Always pour an acid or base into water. • Inform your teacher immediately if you spill chemicals or get any chemicals on your skin. • Use a waving motion of your hand to observe the odor of a chemical. • Never put your nose near a chemical. • Never eat or drink in the laboratory.

Sharp Objects • Use knives, scissors, and other sharp instruments with care. • Cut in the direction away from your body.

Cleanup • Clean up your work area before leaving the laboratory. • Follow your teacher's instructions for disposal of materials. • Wash your hands after an activity.

Appendix C   *The Microscope*

One of the most important tools in biology is the microscope. A microscope enables scientists to view and study objects or structures not visible to the unaided eye. The compound microscope is used most often in biology classes.

A compound microscope has two or more lenses. One lens, called the ocular lens, is located in the eyepiece. The ocular lens usually has a magnification of 10X. An object viewed through this lens would appear 10 times larger than it would look with the unaided eye.

The second lens is called the objective lens. Compound microscopes may have many objective lenses. Most compound microscopes, however, have two objective lenses. Each objective lens has a different magnification. The magnification is printed on each objective lens.

To find the total magnification of a microscope, multiply the magnification of the ocular lens by the magnification of the objective lens that you are using. For example, the ocular lens magnification of 10X multiplied by the objective lens magnification of 10X equals 100X. The total magnification of the microscope is 100X. Looking at an object under this total magnification, you would be seeing the object 100 times larger than the object would look with the unaided eye.

A microscope is a delicate, but relatively uncomplicated, easy-to-use tool. Before you try to use a microscope, however, you should know the parts of a microscope and what each part does. Study the parts of the microscope and their functions.

Parts of the Microscope

1. Eyepiece: holds the ocular lens
2. Body tube: keeps the ocular and objective lenses the proper distance apart
3. Arm: supports the body tube
4. Stage: platform that supports the slide
5. Stage clips: hold slide in position
6. Diaphragm: adjusts the amount of light entering the stage opening
7. Base: supports the microscope
8. Illuminator: mirror or electric light that is the light source of the microscope
9. Revolving nosepiece: holds the objectives and can be turned to change objectives
10. Low-power objective: shorter objective that contains a lens with a magnification of 10X
11. High-power objective: longer objective that contains a lens with a magnification of 40X
12. Coarse adjustment knob: moves the body tube up and down for bringing the object into view
13. Fine adjustment knob: moves the body tube up and down for focusing clearly

Appendix D

PREFIXES AND SUFFIXES

Prefixes and suffixes are word parts that can be helpful in determining the meaning of an unfamiliar term. Prefixes are found at the beginning of word. Suffixes are found at the end of words. Both prefixes and suffixes have meanings that mainly come from Latin and Greek words. Some meanings of prefixes and suffixes commonly used in life science words are listed below.

PREFIX	MEANING	EXAMPLE	SUFFIX	MEANING	EXAMPLE
a-	not; without	abiotic	-derm	skin, covering	echinoderm
aero-	air	aerobic	-itis	disease of	appendicitis
anti-	against	antibodies	-logy	study of; science of	biology
bi-	two	biceps	-ose	carbohydrate	glucose
bio-	life	biotechnology	-phyte	a plant; to grow in a certain way or place	bryophyte
centi-	hundred	centimeters			
chemo-	of, with, or by chemicals	chemosynthesis	-vore	to eat	carnivore
chloro-	green	chloroplasts			
cyto-	cell	cytoplasm			
deca-	ten	decameter			
deci-	one tenth	deciliter			
di-	twice; double	dicot			
eco-	environment; habitat	ecosystem			
ecto-	outer	ectoderm			
endo-	inside	endospore			
epi-	on; on the outside	epidermis			
exo-	outside	exocrine			
geo-	earth	geologic			
hemo-	blood	hemoglobin			
hydro-	water	hydroponics			
kilo-	thousand	kilometer			
leuco-	white	leucocyte			
mono-	one	monocot			
photo-	light	photosynthesis			
syn-	together with; by means of	synthetic			
thigmo-	touch	thigmotropism			
tri-	three	triceps			
trop-	turn; respond to	tropism			
uni-	one	univalve			
zoo-	animal	zoology			

Glossary

Pronunciation and syllabication have been derived from *Webster's New World Dictionary,* Second College Edition, Revised School Printing (Prentice Hall, 1985). Syllables printed in capital letters are given primary stress (Numbers in parentheses indicate the page number, or page numbers, on which the term is defined.)

PRONUNCIATION KEY

Symbol	Example	Respelling	Symbol	Example	Respelling
ah	molecule	(MAHL-uh-kyool)	k	Calorie	(KAL-uh-ree)
aw	absorption	(ab-SAWRP-shun)	ks	thorax	(THOR-aks)
ay	adaptation	(ad-up-TAY-shun)	oh	embryo	(EM-bree-oh)
ee	ecology	(ee-KAHL-uh-jee)	oo	asexual	(ay-SEK-shoo-wul
ew	nucleus	(NEW-klee-us)	sh	circulation	(sur-kyuh-LAY-shun)
f	phloem	(FLOH-em)	uh	data	(DAY-tuh)
g	gamete	(GAM-eet)	y	migration	(my-GRAY-shun)
ih	specialization	(SPESH-uh-lih-zay-shun)	yoo	cellulose	(SEL-yoo-lohs)
j	genes	(JEENS)	z	organism	(AWR-guh-niz-um)

A

abdomen (AB-duh-mun): third section of an insect's body (182)

absorption (ab-SAWRP-shun): movement of food from the digestive system to the blood (234)

adaptation (ad-up-TAY-shun): trait of a living thing that helps it live in its environment (36, 386)

addiction (uh-DIK-shun): uncontrollable dependence on a drug (326)

AIDS: viral disease that attacks a person's immune system (324)

alcoholic (al-kuh-HOWL-ik): person who is dependent on alcohol (328)

alveoli (al-VEE-uh-ly): microscopic air sacs in the lungs (270)

amber: hardened tree sap (382)

amino acid: building block of proteins (216)

amnion (AM-nee-on): fluid-filled membrane that surrounds an embryo (346)

amphibian (am-FIB-ee-un): animal that lives part of its life in water and part on land (198)

angiosperms (AN-jee-uh-spurms): flowering plants (140)

anther: part of the stamen that produces pollen (156)

anthropology (an-thruh-PAHL-uh-jee): science that deals with the study of human beings (392)

antibiotic (an-ti-by-AHT-ik): chemical made by a living organism that kills bacteria (318)

antibodies (AN-ti-bahd-eez): substances the body makes to protect itself from disease (312)

aorta (ay-OWR-tuh): largest artery in the body (258)

arteries (ART-ur-ees): blood vessels that carry blood away from the heart (258)

asexual reproduction (ay-SEK-shoo-wul ree-pruh-DUK-shun): reproduction needing only one parent (42, 126, 162)

atherosclerosis (ath-ur-oh-skluh-ROH-sis): buildup of fat deposits on artery walls (320)

atrium (AY-tree-um): upper chamber of the heart (256)

axon: fiber that carries messages away from a nerve cell (288)

B

bacilli (buh-SIL-y): rod-shaped bacteria (116)

bacteriology (bak-tir-ee-AHL-uh-jee): study of bacteria (118)

bacteriophage (bak-TIR-ee-uh-fayj): virus that infects bacteria (106)

behavior (bi-HAYV-yur): ways in which living things respond to stimuli (38)

benign (bi-NYN) **tumor:** mass of cells that is usually harmless (322)

bile: green liquid that breaks down fats and oils (232)

biome (BY-ohm): large region of the earth with particular plant and animal communities (68)

blade: wide, flat part of a leaf (150)

blending: combination of genes in which a mixture of both traits shows (364)

bronchi (BRAHN-kee): tubes leading to the lungs (270)

bryophytes (BRY-uh-fyts): plants that reproduce by spores and have no transport tubes (108, 134)

budding: kind of asexual reproduction in which a new organism forms from a bud on a parent (126)

bulb: underground stem covered with fleshy leaves (162)

C

Calorie (KAL-uh-ree): unit used to measure energy from foods (224)

cap: umbrella-shaped top of a mushroom (124)

capillaries (KAP-uh-ler-ees): tiny blood vessels that connect arteries to veins (258)

capsid (KAP-sid): protein covering of a virus (106)

carbohydrate (kar-buh-HY-drayt): nutrient that supplies energy (214)

cardiac (KAHR-dee-ak) **muscle:** type of muscle found only in the heart (248)

carrying capacity: largest amount of a population that can be supported by an area (58)

cartilage (KART-ul-idj): tough, flexible connective tissue (196, 240)

cell: basic unit of structure and function in living things (34, 78)

cell division: process by which cells reproduce (88)

cell membrane (MEM-brayn): thin structure that surrounds a cell (80)

cell wall: outer, nonliving part of a plant cell (84)

cellulose (SEL-yoo-lohs): hard, nonliving material that makes up the cell wall of a plant cell (84)

cerebellum (ser-uh-BELL-um): part of the brain that controls balance and body motion (290)

cerebrum (suh-REE-brum): large part of the brain that controls the senses and thinking (290)

cervix (SUR-viks): narrow end of the uterus (338)

chemical digestion: process by which large food molecules are broken down into smaller food molecules (228)

chitin (KYT-in): hard material that makes up the exoskeleton of arthropods (180)

chlorophyll (KLOR-uh-fil): green material in chloroplasts that is needed for plants to make food using photosynthesis (84, 122, 152)

chloroplast: organelle of green plant cells where photosynthesis takes place (84, 152)

chromosomes (KROH-muh-sohms): cell parts that determine what traits a living thing will have (88); threadlike structures in the nucleus of a cell that control heredity (356)

chyme (KYM): thick liquid form of food (230)

cilia (SIL-ee-uh): microscopic hairlike structures (120, 274)

circulation (sur-kyuh-LAY-shun): movement of blood through the body (262)

cirrhosis (suh-ROH-sis): liver disorder caused by damaged liver cells (328)

classification (klas-uh-fi-KAY-shun): grouping things according to similarities (100)

climate: overall weather in an area over a long period of time (68)

climax (KLY-maks) **community:** last community in a succession (66)

closed circulatory (SUR-kyuh-luh-towr-ee) **system:** organ system in which blood moves through blood vessels (176, 262)

cnidocytes (NY-duh-syts): stinging cells (172)

cocci (KAK-sy): spherical bacteria (116)

cochlea (KOK-lee-uh): part of the ear that changes vibrations into nerve signals (298)

cocoon (kuh-KOON): protective covering around the pupa (184)

coldblooded: having a body temperature that changes with the temperature of the surroundings (196)

colon: large intestine (234)

community: all the populations that live in a certain place (54)

compact bone: bone cells that make up the hardest part of bones (242)

conditioned (kun-DISH-und) **response:** learned behavior in which a new stimulus causes the same response that an old one did (304)

conifer (KAHN-uh-fur): tree that produces cones and has needlelike leaves (138)

connective tissue: tissue that holds parts of the body together (92)

conservation (kon-sur-VAY-shun): wise use of natural resources (70)

consumer (kun-SOO-mur): organism that obtains food by eating other organisms (62)

control: part of the experiment in which no change is made (20)

controlled breeding: mating organisms to produce offspring with certain traits (374)

controlled experiment: two experiments exactly alike except for one change in one of them (20)

cornea (KOR-nee-uh): clear covering at the front of the eye (296)

coronary (KOWR-uh-ner-ee) **arteries:** arteries that carry blood and oxygen to the tissues of the heart (320)

cotyledon (kaht-LEED-on): seed structure that contains food for the developing plant (140)

cycle (SY-kul): something that happens over and over in the same way (60)

cytoplasm (SYT-uh-plaz-um): all the living material inside a cell except the nucleus (80)

D

data (DAY-tuh): information (18)

daughter cells: new cells produced by cell division (88)

decomposer (dee-kum-POHZ-er): organism that breaks down the wastes or remains of other organisms (62)

deficiency (di-FISH-un-see) **disease:** disease caused by the lack of a certain nutrient (218)

degree Celsius: metric unit of temperature (24)

dendrite (DEN-dryt): fiber that carries messages from other neurons to the nerve cell body (288)

depressant (di-PRES-unt): drug that slows down the central nervous system (326)

dermis: inner layer of skin (250)

diaphragm (DY-uh-fram): sheet of muscle below the lungs (278)

dicots: seed plants with two cotyledons (140)

diffusion (dih-FYOO-shun): movement of material from an area where molecules are crowded to an area where they are less crowded (86)

digestion (di-JES-chun): process of breaking down food into forms that can be used by living things (44, 226)

DNA: chemical contained in chromosomes (358)

dominant (DOM-uh-nuhnt) **gene:** gene that always shows itself (360)

E

eardrum: sheet of tissue that vibrates when sounds strike it (298)

echinoderms (ee-KY-noh-durms): spiny-skinned animals (186)

ecology (ee-KAHL-uh-jee): study of living things and their environments (52)

ecosystem (EE-koh-sis-tum): living and nonliving things in an environment, together with their interactions (54)

ectoderm (EK-tuh-durm): outer tissue layer (174)

egg: female sex cell (208)

embryo (EM-bree-oh): undeveloped plant or animal (156); hollow ball of cells formed by cell division of the zygote (346)

emulsification (i-mul-suh-fi-KAY-shun): process of breaking down large droplets of fat into small droplets of fat (232)

endangered species (in-DAYN-jurd SPEE-sheez): living things that are in danger of dying out (72)

endocrine (EN-duh-krin) **gland:** gland that does not have ducts (300)

endoderm (EN-duh-durm): inner tissue layer (174)

endoskeleton (en-doh-SKEL-uh-tun): internal skeleton (110, 186, 194, 240)

endospore: inactive cell surrounded by a thick wall (116)

energy pyramid (PIR-uh-mid): way of showing how energy moves through a food chain (64)

environment (in-VY-run-munt): everything that surrounds a living thing (36, 52)

enzyme (EN-zym): protein that controls chemical activities (216)

epidermis (ep-uh-DUR-mis): outer, protective layer of the leaf (150); outer layer of skin (250)

epiglottis (ep-uh-GLAT-is): flap of tissue that prevents food from entering the windpipe (226)

epithelial (ep-uh-THEEL-ee-uhl) **tissue:** tissue that covers and protects parts of the body (92)

era: largest division of geologic time (384)

esophagus (i-SAF-uh-gus): tube that connects the mouth to the stomach (226)

evaporation (i-VAP-uh-ray-shun): changing of a liquid to a gas (276)

evolution (ev-uh-LOO-shun): process by which organisms change over time (386)

excretion (ik-SKREE-shun): process of removing waste products from the body (44, 276)

exhale: to breathe out (272)

exoskeleton (ek-so-SKEL-uh-tun): external skeleton (110, 180, 240)

experiment (ik-SPER-uh-munt): something that is done to test a hypothesis or prediction (20)

extensor (ik-STEN-sur): muscle that straightens a joint (246)

extinct (ik-STINKT): species that is no longer found alive (382)

F

fertilization (fur-tul-i-ZAY-shun): union of nuclei of a male sex cell and a female sex cell (156, 208, 344)

fetus (FEET-us): developing baby (346)

fibrous (FY-brus) **root system:** root system made up of many thin, branched roots (146)

filament: stalk of the anther (156)

flagella (fluh-JEL-uh): whiplike structures on a cell (116, 170)

flexor (FLEK-sur): muscle that bends a joint (246)

food chain: way of showing the food relationships among a group of organisms (64)

food web: way of showing how food chains are related (64)

fossil (FAHS-ul): remains or traces of a once-living organism (382)

frond: featherlike leaf of a fern (136)

fungi (FUN-gy): plantlike organisms that lack chlorophyll (104)

G

gamete (GAM-eet): reproductive cell (336)

gastric juice: juice produced in the stomach that contains mucus, pepsin, and hydrochloric acid (230)

gene splicing (SPLYS-ing): moving a section of DNA from the genes of one organism to the genes of another organism (376)

genes (JEENS): parts of a chromosome that control inherited traits (356)

genetic engineering (juh-NET-ik en-juh-NEER-ing): methods used to produce new forms of DNA (375)

genetics (juh-NET-iks): study of heredity (354)

genus (JEE-nus): classification group made up of related species (102)

geologic (jee-oh-LAHJ-ik) **time scale:** record of the earth's history based upon types of organisms that lived at different times (384)

gills: structures that produce mushroom spores (124); organs that absorb dissolved oxygen from water (196)

gland: organ that makes chemical substances used or released by the body (300)

gram: basic metric unit of mass (22)

guard cell: cell in a plant that helps control the passage of materials into and out of the stomates (90)

gymnosperms (JIM-nuh-spurms): group of land plants with uncovered seeds (138)

H

habitat (HAB-i-tat): place where an organism lives (56)

hallucinogen (hul-LOO-suh-nuh-jen): drug that causes a person to see, hear, smell, and taste things in a strange way (326)

heart attack: lack of blood and oxygen to a part of the heart (320)

hemoglobin (HEE-moh-gloh-bin): iron compound in red blood cells (260)

herbaceous (hur-BAY-shus) **stem:** stem that is soft and green (148)

heredity (huh-RED-uh-tee): passing of traits from parents to offspring (354)

hibernation (HY-bur-nay-shun): inactive state of some animals during winter months (38)

hilum (HY-lum): mark on the seed coat where the seed was attached to the ovary (160)

homeostasis (hoh-mee-oh-STAY-sis): ability of a living thing to keep conditions inside its body constant (46)

hormone (HAWR-mohn): chemical substance that regulates body functions (302)

hybrid (HY-brid): having two unlike genes (360)

hybridization (hy-brid-ih-ZAY-shun): mating two different kinds of organisms (374)

hypothesis (hy-PAHTH-uh-sis): suggested answer to a problem (16)

I

immune system: body system made up of cells and tissues that help a person fight disease (324)

immunity (im-MYOON-i-tee): resistance to a specific disease (314)

inbreeding: mating closely related organisms (374)

ingestion (in-JEST-shun): process of taking in food (44)

inhale: to breathe in (272)

inherited disease: disease caused by an inherited gene (370)

inherited (in-HER-uh-ted) **traits:** traits that are passed from parents to their offspring (354)

innate behavior: behavior you are born with (304)

interact: to act upon each other (52)

invertebrates (in-VUR-tuh-brayts): animals without backbones (110)

iris (Y-ris): part of the eye that controls the amount of light entering the eye (296)

J

joint: place where two or more bones meet (244)

K

kingdom: classification group made up of related phyla (102)

L

larva (LAHR-vuh): wormlike stage of insect development (184)

learned behavior: behavior you practice and learn (304)

legumes (LEG-yooms): group of plants that includes beans and peas (132)

lens (LENZ): piece of curved glass that causes light rays to come together or spread apart as they pass through (26); part of the eye that forms an image on the retina (296)

ligaments (LIG-uh-ments): tissue that connects bone to bone (244)

limiting factors: conditions in the environment that put limits on where an organism can live (58)

lipase (LY-pays): enzyme that digests fats and oils (232)

liter: basic metric unit of volume (22)

M

magnify: to make something look larger than it is (26)

malignant (muh-LIG-nunt) **tumor:** harmful mass of cells that can spread throughout the body (322)

malnutrition (mal-noo-TRISH-un): poor nutrition caused by an unbalanced diet (222)

mammary (MAM-ur-ee) **glands:** glands where milk is produced in female mammals (206)

mantle: thin membrane that covers a mollusk's organs (178)

mass: amount of matter in an object (22)

mass selection: crossing plants with desirable traits (374)

mechanical digestion: process by which large pieces of food are cut and crushed into smaller pieces (228)

medulla (muh-DULL-uh): part of the brain that controls heartbeat and breathing rate (290)

medusa (muh-DOO-suh): umbrellalike form of a cnidarian (172)

meiosis (my-OH-sis): cell division that produces gametes (336)

menstrual (MEHN-struhl) **cycle:** monthly cycle of change that occurs in the female reproductive system (342)

menstruation (men-stroo-WAY-shun): process by which blood and tissue from the lining of the uterus break apart and leave the body (342)

mesoderm (MES-uh-durm): middle tissue layer (174)

mesophyll (MES-uh-fil): middle layer of leaf tissue in which food-making occurs (150)

metamorphosis (met-uh-MOWR-fuh-sis): changes during the stages of development of an organism (184, 200)

meter (MEE-tur): basic metric unit of length (22)

microscope (MIKE-roh-scope): tool that makes things look larger than they really are (26)

migration (my-GRAY-shun): movement of animals from one living place to another (38)

mineral: nutrient needed by the body to develop properly (220)

mitochondria (myt-uh-KAHN-dree-uh): rice-shaped structures that produce energy for a cell (82)

mitosis (my-TOH-sis): division of the nucleus (88)

molecule (MAHL-uh-kyool): smallest part of a substance that has all the properties of that substance (216)

molting: process by which an animal sheds its outer covering (180)

monerans (muh-NER-uns): single-celled organisms that do not have a nucleus (104)

monocots: seed plants with only one cotyledon (140)

mucus (MYOO-kus): sticky liquid (274)

mutation (myoo-TAY-shun): change in a gene (386)

N

natural resources (REE-sowrs-ez): materials found in nature that are used by living things (70)

natural selection: survival of offspring that have favorable traits (388)

neuron (NOOR-ahn): nerve cell (288)

niche (NICH): organism's role, or job, in its habitat (56)

nicotine (NIK-uh-teen): stimulant found in tobacco (330)

nitrogen-fixing bacteria: bacteria that can use nitrogen in soil to make nitrogen compounds (60)

nonrenewable resources: natural resources that cannot be renewed or replaced (70)

notochord (NOHT-uh-kowrd): strong, rodlike structure in chordates that can bend (194)

nucleus (NEW-klee-us): control center of a cell (80)

nutrient (NOO-tree-unt): chemical substances in food needed by the body for growth, energy, and life processes (214)

nymph (NIMF): young insect that looks like the adult (184)

O

offspring: new organisms produced by a living thing (42)

organ (OWR-gun): group of tissues that work together to do a special job (94)

organ system: group of organs that work together (94)

organelles (or-guh-NELS): small structures in the cytoplasm that do special jobs (82)

organism (AWR-guh-niz-um): any living thing (34)

osmosis (ahs-MOH-sis): movement of water through a membrane (86)

ovaries (OH-vuhr-eez): main organs of the female reproductive system (338)

ovary (OH-vuhr-ee): bottom part of the pistil (158)

oviduct (OH-vuh-dukt): long tube between the ovary and the uterus (338)

ovulation (oh-vyuh-LAY-shun): release of a mature egg from the ovary (342)

ovule (OH-vyool): part of the ovary that develops into a seed after fertilization (158)

oxidation (ahk-suh-DAY-shun): slow burning of foods in your body (224)

P

pepsin (PEP-sin): enzyme that digests proteins (230)

periosteum (per-i-AS-tee-um): thin membrane that covers a bone (242)

peristalsis (per-uh-STAWL-sis): wavelike movement that moves food through the digestive tract (226)

perspiration (pur-spuh-RAY-shun): waste water and salts that leave the body through the skin (276)

petal: kind of leaf that is often brightly colored (152)

phloem (FLOH-em): tissue that carries food from the leaves throughout the plant (148)

photosynthesis (foht-uh-SIN-thuh-sis): food-making process in leaves that uses sunlight (108, 152)

phylum (FY-luhm): classification group made up of related classes (102)

pistil: female reproductive organ in a flower (152)

placenta (pluh-SEN-tuh): organ through which materials are exchanged between the mother and developing embryo (206, 346)

plankton (PLANK-tun): organisms that float at the water's surface (122)

plasma (PLAZ-muh): liquid part of blood (92, 260)

platelets (PLAYT-lits): tiny, colorless pieces of cells (260)

pollen grains: male plant reproductive cells (156)

pollination (pahl-uh-NAY-shun): movement of pollen from a stamen to a pistil (156)

pollution: release of harmful materials into the environment (72)

polyp (PAL-ip): cuplike form of a cnidarian (172)

population: group of the same kind of organism living in a certain place (54)

pore: tiny opening (170, 250, 276)

producer (pruh-DOOS-ur): organism that makes its own food (62)

protein (PRO-teen): nutrient needed to build and repair cells (214)

protists (PROHT-ists): single-celled organisms that have a nucleus (104)

protozoans (proh-tuh-ZOH-uns): one-celled, animallike protists (120)

pseudopod (SOO-duh-pod): fingerlike projections of cytoplasm used for movement and food-getting (120)

pulmonary (PUL-muh-ner-ee) **artery:** artery that brings blood from the heart to the lungs (264)

Punnett square: chart that shows possible gene combinations (362)

pupa (PYOU-puh): resting stage during complete metamorphosis (184)

pupil (PYOO-pil): opening in the center of the iris (296)

pure: having two like genes (360)

R

radula (RAJ-oo-luh): rough, tonguelike organ of a snail (178)

range (RAYNJ): area where a type of animal or plant population is found (58)

receptor (ree-SEP-tor): organ that receives stimuli from the environment (294)

recessive (ri-SES-iv) **gene:** gene that is hidden when the dominant gene is present (360)

red blood cell: blood cell that carries oxygen (90)

reflex: automatic response to a stimulus (292)

reflex arc: path of a message in a reflex (292)

regeneration (ri-jen-uh-RAY-shun): ability to regrow lost parts (188)

relative age: age of something compared with the age of something else (384)

renewable resources: natural resources that can be renewed or replaced (70)

replication (rep-luh-KAY-shun): process by which DNA is duplicated (358)

reproduction: process by which living things produce new organisms like themselves (42)

respiration (res-puh-RAY-shun): process of carrying oxygen to cells, getting rid of carbon dioxide, and releasing energy (44, 272)

response (ri-SPAHNS): reaction to a change, or stimulus (34, 292)

retina (RET-in-uh): part of the eye on which images form (296)

rhizoids (RY-zoidz): rootlike structures that anchor fungi (124); fine, hairlike structures that act as roots (134)

rhizome (RY-zohm): underground stem (136)

ribosomes (RY-buh-sohms): small, round structures that make proteins (82)

root cap: cup-shaped mass of cells that covers and protects a root tip (146)

root hair: thin, hairlike structure on the outer layer of the root tip (146)

S

saliva: liquid in the mouth that helps in digestion (228)

scavenger (SKAV-in-jur): animal that eats only dead organisms (62)

scientific method: model, or guide, used to solve problems and to get information (18)

scrotum (SKROH-tum): pocket of skin that protects and holds the testes (340)

seed: structure that contains a tiny living plant and food for its growth (138)

seed coat: outside covering of a seed (160)

sepal (SEE-pul): special kind of leaf that protects the flower bud (152)

septum: thick tissue wall that separates the left and right sides of the heart (256)

setae (SEET-ee): tiny, hairlike bristles (176)

sex-linked traits: traits that are controlled by the sex chromosomes (368)

sexual (SEK-shoo-wul) **reproduction:** reproduction needing two parents (42)

smooth muscle: muscle that causes movements that you cannot control (248)

specialization (SPESH-uh-lih-zay-shun): studying or working in only one part of a subject (14)

species (SPEE-sheez): group of organisms that look alike and can reproduce among themselves (102)

sperm: male sex cell (208)

spicules (SPIK-yools): small, hard, needlelike structures of a sponge (170)

spiracles (SPIH-ruh-kuls): openings to air tubes of a grasshopper (182)

spirilla (spy-RIL-uh): spiral-shaped bacteria (116)

spongy bone: bone cells that make up the soft and spongy ends of bones (242)

spontaneous generation (spahn-TAY-nee-us jen-uh-RAY-shun): idea that living things come from nonliving things (40)

spore: reproductive cell of bryophytes (134)

spore cases: structures that contains spores (126)

sporulation (spowr-yoo-LAY-shun): kind of asexual reproduction in which a new organism forms from spores released from a parent (126)

stamen (STAY-mun): male reproductive organ in a flower (152)

stigma (STIG-muh): top part of the pistil (158)

stimulant (STIM-yuh-lent): drug that speeds up the central nervous system (326)

stimulus (STIM-yuh-lus): something that causes a reaction to take place (38, 162, 292)

stomata (STOH-muh-tuh): tiny openings in the upper and lower epidermis of the leaf (150)

striated (STRY-ayt-ed) **muscle:** muscle attached to the skeleton, making movement possible (248)

succession (suk-SESH-un): gradual change in organisms that occurs when the environment changes (66)

T

tadpole: larval stage of a frog (200)

taproot system: root system made up of one large root and many small, thin roots (146)

taxonomy (tak-SAHN-uh-mee): science of classifying living things (100)

temperature: measure of how hot or cold something is (24)

tendons (TEN-duns): tissue that connects muscle to bone (246)

tentacles: long, armlike structures (172)

testes (TES-teez): main organs of the male reproductive system (340)

testosterone (tes-TAWS-tuhr-ohn): hormone produced in the testes (340)

theory (THEE-uh-ree): idea that explains something and is supported by data (78)

thorax (THOR-aks): middle section of an insect's body (182)

tissue: group of cells that look alike and work together (92)

tracheophytes (TRAY-kee-uh-fyts): division of plants that have conducting tubes (108)

trait: characteristic (354)

transport: process of moving nutrients and wastes in a living thing (44)

tropism: growth of a plant in response to something in the environment (162)

tube feet: small, suckerlike structures of echinoderms (186)

tuber: underground stem (162)

tumor (TOO-mur): mass or lump of cells (322)

tympanum (TIM-puh-num): hearing organ in a grasshopper (182)

U

umbilical (um-BIL-ih-kul) **cord:** structure that connects the embryo to the placenta (346)

urea (yoo-REE-uh): nitrogen compound formed as a waste product (278)

urethra (yoo-REETH-ruh): tube that carries sperm to the outside of the male's body (340)

urine (YOOR-in): liquid waste formed in the kidneys (278)

uterus (YOOT-ur-us): organ in which an embryo develops (338)

V

vacuoles (VAK-yoo-wohls): liquid-filled spaces in the cytoplasm (82)

vagina (vuh-JY-nuh): birth canal (338)

valve: thin flap of tissue that acts like a one-way door (256)

variable: anything that can be changed in an experiment (20)

variation (ver-ee-AY-shun): differences in traits among individuals of a species (388)

vegetative propagation (VEJ-uh-tayt-iv prahp-uh-GAY-shun): kind of asexual reproduction that uses parts of plants to grow new plants (162)

veins (VANES): bundles of tubes that contain the xylem and phloem in a leaf (150); blood vessels that carry blood to the heart (258)

ventricle (VEN-tri-kul): lower chamber of the heart (256)

vertebrate (VUR-tuh-brit): animal with a backbone (110, 194)

villi: fingerlike projections on the lining of the small intestine (234)

virus (VY-rus): piece of nucleic acid covered with a protein (106)

vitamin (VYT-uh-min): nutrient made by living organisms (218)

W

warmblooded: having a body temperature that remains about the same (204)

white blood cells: blood cells that protect the body against disease (90, 312)

woody stem: stem that contains wood and is thick and hard (148)

X

xylem (ZY-lum): tissue that carries water and dissolved minerals upward from the roots (148)

Z

zygote (ZY-gote): fertilized egg produced by fertilization (344)

Index

chlorophyll, 84, 108, 116, 117, 120, 122, 124, 152
chloroplast, 84, 152
cholesterol, 235, 257, 320, 321
chordate, 194
chromosomes, 88, 336, 337, 356, 367
chyme, 230
cigarette, 275, 322, 330, 331
cilia, 120, 274, 275, 312, 330
circulation, 262
circulatory system, 94, 312
cirrhosis, 328
classes, 102
classification, 100
classifying, 16
climate, 68
cloning, 43
closed circulatory system, 176, 198, 262
clotting, 260
cnidarian, 172
cnidocyte, 172
coal, 70, 136, 137
cocci, 116
cochlea, 298
cocoon, 184
coldblooded, 196, 198, 202
collar cell, 170
colon, 234, 235
colorblindness, 368
commensalism, 55
common cold, 107
communicating, 16
community, 54
compact bone, 242
complete metamorphosis, 184
complete proteins, 217
complex carbohydrates, 214
compound, 35
compound leaves, 150, 151
compound microscope, 26, 27, 78
computer, 199, 293
cones, 138
conifer, 138
connective tissue, 92, 240
conservation, 70
consumer, 62, 63, 64
contagious disease, 341
control, 20, 40
controlled breeding, 374
controlled experiment, 20
cooking, 47
coral, 172, 173
coral reefs, 173
cork, 78
cornea, 93, 296
coronary arteries, 320
cotyledon, 140, 160
cough, 312
cowpox, 315
Crick, Francis, 359
crocodile, 202
Cro-Magnon, 392, 393
crop, 176
cross-pollination, 156

crustaceans, 180
cuttings, 163
cycad, 138
cycles, 60
cytology lab technician, 91
cytoplasm, 80, 116, 120, 288
cytosine, 358

D

Darwin, Charles, 387, 388
data, 17, 18
daughter cells, 88, 336
day care worker, 349
deafness, 299
deca-, 22
decay, 62, 116
deci-, 22
deciduous forest, 68, 69
decomposer, 62
defense system, 312
deficiency disease, 218, 220
degree Celsius, 24
dendrite, 288, 289
deodorant, 281
depressant, 326, 328
dermis, 250
desert, 68
diabetes, 303, 343
dialysis, 283
diaphragm, 272
dicot, 140, 148
diffusion, 86, 87
digestion, 44, 165, 226, 228, 290
digestive system, 44, 94, 226, 312
digestive tract, 226
dinosaur, 202, 203, 206, 390
diphtheria, 316
disease, 43, 312, 314, 318, 324
disperal, 58
dissection, 199
DNA, 358, 376
dominant gene, 360
Down syndrome, 337
Drew, Charles, 261
drugs, 326, 327
drug allergies, 318, 319
Duchenne's muscular dystrophy, 367
duckbill platypus, 206

E

eardrum, 298
ears, 290, 294, 298
earthworm, 176, 177
echinoderm, 186
ecologist, 37, 52
ecology, 14, 52
ecosystem, 54, 56, 58, 59, 64, 72
ectoderm, 174, 194
ectopic pregnancy, 339
egg, 184, 200, 202, 204, 206, 208, 336, 338, 339, 344, 366
electron, 26, 83
electron microscope, 26, 27, 82, 83, 117, 316

elements, 35
embryo, 158, 160, 208, 338, 346
embryology, 111
emphysema, 330, 377
emulsification, 232
endangered species, 72
endo-, 111
endocrine gland, 30, 302
endocrine system, 94, 300
endoderm, 174, 194
endoskeleton, 110, 186, 194, 240
endospore, 116
energy, 34, 46, 52, 54, 64, 70, 71, 214, 216, 224, 272, 278
energy pyramid, 64
enriched foods, 221
environment, 36, 37, 38, 52, 54, 55, 58, 64, 66, 72
enzyme, 216, 228, 230, 232, 377
epidermis, 95, 150, 250,
epiglottis, 226
epithelial tissue, 92
epoch, 384
era, 384
esophagus, 226, 230, 233
estrogen, 302
ethyl alcohol, 328
Euglena, 122
evaporation, 60, 280, 281
evergreen, 138
evolution, 386, 388, 390
excretion, 44, 278
excretory system, 94
exercise, 247, 249
exhale, 272, 276
exo-, 111
exocrine glands, 301
exoskeleton, 110, 180, 240
experiment, 18, 20
extensor, 246
exterminator, 185
external respiration, 272
extinct, 382
eyeglasses, 297
eyes, 290, 294, 296
eyespot, 122

F

Fahrenheit scale, 24
family, 102
fats, 214, 215, 232, 234
FDA, 45
feathers, 204
fern, 136, 137
fertilization, 156, 158, 208, 339, 344, 345, 354, 366
fertilizers, plant, 373
fetal alcohol syndrome, 329
fetus, 346
fiber, 235
fibrous root system, 146
field study, 20, 21
filament, 156
filter, 282, 283
fins, 196

pollen, 156, 157, 158
pollen tube, 158, 160
pollination, 156, 157
pollutants, 53
pollution, 53, 72, 73
polyp, 172
population, 54, 56, 58, 59, 64, 72
pore, 170, 250, 280
Porifera, 170
positron emission tomography (PET), 289
pouched mammals, 206
predator, 53
predicting, 16
preservatives, 317
preventive medicine, 313
prey, 53
primary consumers, 62, 64
Principle of Dominance, 361
Principle of Independent Assortment, 361
Principle of Segregation, 361
problem-solving, 18
producer, 62, 64
progesterone, 302
prop roots, 147
protein, 35, 82, 91, 214, 216, 217, 234
Protista, 104, 117, 120
protists, 104, 120
protozoans, 120
pseudopod, 120
pulmonary artery, 264
pulmonary vein, 264
pulse, 258, 259
Punnett square, 362, 365
pupa, 184
pupil, 296
pure, 360
pure science, 19

Q

quinine, 132

R

radial symmetry, 187
radiation, 323
radioactive, 71
radioactive dating, 385
radioactive elements, 385
radula, 178
rainfall, 68
range, 58
Ray, John, 103
rays, 196
reasoning, 306
receptors, 292, 294, 295
recessive gene, 360
rectum, 226, 278
recycling, 54
red algae, 122
red blood cells, 90, 220, 260, 263, 276
red bone marrow, 242
Redi, Francesco, 40
reflex, 292, 304

reflex arc, 292
regeneration, 188
regulation, 262
relative age, 384
renewable resources, 70, 71
replication, 358
reproduction, 42, 88
reproductive system, 338, 340, 342
reptiles, 193, 202
research, 18
respiration, 44, 45, 272
respiratory system, 94, 270, 274, 312
response, 34, 38, 164, 165, 292, 304
retina, 296
reward and punishment, 306
rhizoid, 124, 134
rhizome, 136
ribosomes, 82
ribs, 272
rickets, 218
rock cycle, 60, 61
root cap, 146
root hair, 146
roots, 94, 146, 152, 159, 162
rot, 118
roundworm, 174, 175

S

salamander, 198
saliva, 228
salivary glands, 300
Salmonella, 205
sand dollar, 186
scales, 196
scanning electron microscope, 83
scavenger, 62
Schleiden, Matthias, 79
Schwann cells, 79
Schwann, Theodor, 79
science, 14
science skills, 16, 53
scientific method, 18
scientific research, 14, 19
scouring rushes, 135
scrotum, 340
scurvy, 218
sea stars, 186, 188
sea urchin, 186
seaweed, 62
secondary consumers, 62, 64
sediment, 382
sedimentary rock, 61, 382, 384
seed, 138, 140, 158, 159, 160
seed coat, 160
seed dispersal, 67
segmented worms, 176
self-pollination, 156
sense organs, 290, 294
sense receptors, 250
senses, 16
sepal, 154
septum, 256
sequoias, 138
serum, 315
setae, 176

sex chromosomes, 367
sex-linked traits, 368
sexual reproduction, 42, 154, 156, 356
sexually transmitted disease, 341
SI, 22, 24
sickle-cell anemia, 263, 370
sidestream smoke, 330
simple carbohydrates, 214
simple leaves, 150, 151
simple microscope, 26, 27
skate, 196
skeletal muscle, 248
skeletal system, 94, 240
skeleton, 170, 240
skin, 250, 278, 280, 290, 294, 312, 316
skin cancer, 250, 323
Skinner, B. F., 305
skull, 288
slime molds, 120, 121
small intestine, 226, 230, 232, 234, 278
smallpox, 315, 316
smoking, 275
smooth muscle, 248
snail, 178
snake, 202, 203
sneeze, 274, 292, 312
snorkeling, 171
social insects, 182
sound, 298, 299
specialization, 14
species, 72, 102, 382, 386, 388, 390, 391, 392
sperm, 208, 336, 339, 344, 366
spherical symmetry, 187
spicule, 170
spider, 180
spinal cord, 92, 93, 288, 292, 293
spinal injuries, 293
spiracles, 182
spirilla, 116
sponge, 170
spongin, 170
spongy bone, 242
spontaneous generation, 40, 41
spore, 124, 134, 136
spore cases, 126, 136
sporulation, 126
sprain, 247
squid, 178, 179
stalk, 124
stamen, 154, 156
staminate flowers, 155
starches, 214
stem, 94, 148, 159, 162
sterilization, 319
steroids, 247
stethoscope, 256
stigma, 158
stimulant, 326, 328, 330
stimulus, 38, 164, 165, 292, 294
stomach, 226, 230, 232, 312
stomate, 90, 150
strep throat, 316
streptobacillus, 117

striated muscle, 248
stroke, 321
style, 158
succession, 66
sugars, 214
sulfa drugs, 125
sunlight, 34, 322
sunscreen, 250
support, 240
sweat gland, 250, 280, 300
symmetry, 187
synapse, 289
synthetic, 247
syphilis, 341
Systeme International, 22

T

tadpole, 200, 201
taiga, 59
tapeworm, 174
taproot system, 146
tar, 330
taste buds, 295
taxonomists, 100
taxonomy, 100
Tay-Sachs disease, 370
technology, 19, 119
teeth, 228
temperature, 24, 46, 58, 68
tendon, 92, 246
tendonitis, 247
tentacle, 172
territories, 59
tertiary consumers, 62, 64
testes, 300, 302, 340
testosterone, 302, 338, 340
tetanus, 316
Theophrastus, 103
theory, 55, 78
therapsid, 206
thermometer, 24, 25
thorax, 182
thrush, 125
thymine, 358
thyroid gland, 300
thyroxine, 303
ticks, 180, 181
tissue, 91, 92, 94

tobacco, 330
tongue, 290, 294, 295
tooth decay, 229
tortoise, 202
touch, 250
touch receptor, 251
toxic shock syndrome, 316
tracheophytes, 108
traits, 354, 374
transmission electron microscope, 83
transplants, 93
transport, 44, 45, 148, 262
transport system, 146
trial and error, 306
trichinosis, 175
triticale, 374
tropical rain forest, 68
tropism, 164, 165
trypanosome, 120
tuataras, 202
tube feet, 186
tuber, 162
tumor, 322
tundra, 68
turtle, 202
tympanum, 182

U

ulcer, 231
umbilical cord, 346
unit, 22
urea, 282
ureters, 282
urethra, 282, 340
urine, 282
U.S. RDA, 45
uterus, 338, 341

V

vaccine, 315
vacuoles, 82, 84
vagina, 328
valve, 256, 263
variable, 20
variation, 388

vascular tissue, 95
vegetable, 159
vegetarian, 217
vegetative propagation, 162, 188
vein, 150, 152, 258, 259
ventricle, 196, 198, 204, 206, 256, 264
Venus' flytrap, 164
vertebrates, 110, 194, 196
veterinarian, 195
villi, 234, 278
viruses, 106, 312, 315, 316, 324
Visible Human project, 95
vitamin D, 243
vitamins, 214, 218, 219, 220, 234
volume, 22, 24, 25

W

warmblooded, 204, 206, 274
wart, 201, 316
waste products, 278, 279
water, 215, 234
water cycle, 60
Watson, James, 359
white blood cell, 90, 91, 260, 312
Whittaker, Robert, 105
wildlife biologist, 15
windpipe, 227, 270, 274, 275
woody stem, 148

X

X rays, 289, 322, 323
XX, 366
XY, 366
xylem, 148, 149, 150

Y

yeast, 104, 124, 126
yellow bone marrow, 242
yolk, 184, 208

Z

zoology, 14
zygote, 344, 346

Photo Credits